MACROECONOMIC ACTIVITY

MACROECONOMIC ACTIVITY
Theory, Forecasting, and Control

AN ECONOMETRIC APPROACH

MICHAEL K. EVANS

Wharton School of Finance and Commerce
University of Pennsylvania

Foreword by L. R. KLEIN

HARPER & ROW, PUBLISHERS

New York, Evanston, and London

TO ELLEN

MACROECONOMIC ACTIVITY:
Theory, Forecasting, and Control

Copyright © 1969 by Michael K. Evans

Library of Congress Catalog Card Number: 69-11111

CONTENTS

LIST OF TABLES

FOREWORD

The quantitative approach to macroeconomics is surely the wave of the future. It becomes essentially applied econometrics when pursued by Michael Evans to fashion a complete, self-contained book on macroeconomics. His work goes far beyond the pedagogy of diagrams or the manipulation of simple deterministic equation systems; it presents the whole of macroeconomics in the process of constructing a large, sophisticated, and realistic statistical model of the American economy. Dr. Evans then continues the effort by making applications of the complete system to problems of multiplier evaluation, forecasting, business cycle analysis, and quantitative guidance of economic policy.

There is one distinct flavor that permeates every page of this book. It is written by a worker in the field, who is active on the very frontiers of the subject, and who has intimate knowledge of the quantitative characteristics of the American and other national economies. It is sometimes claimed that there are two camps—the teachers and the researchers—and that an accomplished researcher is not necessarily a good pedagogue. I have a fundamental distrust of the pure teacher. He cannot really know his subject the way a creative researcher does, and he will always be teaching yesterday's ideas. The ideal combination is found in Michael Evans' book. He knows the details of his subject matter as well as anyone in the field, and he is in the vanguard of those finding new results. At the same time, he has written a clear exposition that takes the student over the whole course of the subject, step-by-step, as the quantitative findings have laid it out into a complete system.

The course (in American universities) for which this book is intended as a text is one that has been transformed and renamed from "Business Cycles" to "Macroeconomics" or the "Theory of Income and Employment." It is noteworthy that Michael Evans has not overlooked the ancestry of present teachings and includes a good deal of material on business cycles and their statistical analysis. When cyclical problems arise again, as they undoubtedly shall, it will be welcome to find a modern text that combines cycle analysis with today's macroeconomics.

This book serves in part as a detailed theoretical and informational background for what is known as the Wharton Econometric Forecasting Unit (EFU) model, a model on which I have collaborated with Michael Evans in building and applying. There is no other comparable explanation in detail for the system as a whole. This fact does not, however, mean that I must endorse every aspect of the present book. I think that it is too partial to the permanent income hypothesis of consumption or too unfavorable on the Brookings Econometric Model Project. In spite of these specific differences, I can look at the entire book and feel that here is a freshness and boldness of approach that is rarely found in a textbook. In trial uses of the manuscript, at both graduate and undergraduate levels, I have found this book to be eminently successful in opening new pathways for the teaching of macroeconomics.

L. R. KLEIN

PREFACE

This book has evolved from lectures given for the past several years in a course in business cycles and forecasting at the Wharton School of Finance and Commerce of the University of Pennsylvania, and from estimation of and prediction with the Wharton Econometric Forecasting Unit (EFU) model. The lectures are given as a one-semester course to junior and senior undergraduates, with the more difficult material omitted. This text can be used either at that level or, with a more complete treatment, for graduate students. Depending on the emphasis of the course, the sections on technical econometric material, pre-Keynesian theories of the cycle, or comparison of forecasting records could be excluded with little loss of continuity.

The tone of the book is designed to be primarily empirical. While a good theoretical base should include quantitative research, the main purpose of this text is to present empirical estimates that not only are based on sound theoretical structure but also have worked well in actual predictions. In this respect, the Wharton EFU model is the heart of the book. Since early 1963, the author and Lawrence R. Klein have used this model (or earlier versions of it) to generate forecasts at least one year ahead which have been publicly released. These forecasts have by no means been perfect—the failures as well as the successes are recorded in the text. Nevertheless, we feel that these forecasts have proved more accurate than other forecasts which have continuously been placed on record a year or more in advance. The Econometric Forecasting Unit is currently supported by more than 60 corporations which subscribe to its forecasting service, and the latest results are released quarterly through national news media. In this way we feel that the results which form an integral part of this book have been tested and have been found useful in actual *ex ante* decision making.

This book would never have been started, nor would it have been completed, without the inspiration and guidance of Professor Klein. The Wharton EFU model itself, an outgrowth of his older models, has been described separately in a joint publication.[1] Though I take sole responsibility for the sections of this text that deal with other topics, the book as a whole has benefited from numerous discussions with and suggestions by Dr. Klein, which have played a major role in shaping it.

The computer work connected with both the estimating of various equations and the solution of the model itself has sometimes assumed heroic proportions, and I have been fortunate in having superior assistance. Morris Norman wrote the multiple regression programs, George Schink wrote the program for solution of the Wharton EFU model, and Nancy Blossom was responsible for the actual solution of the forecasts, often on very short notice. Without the assistance of these and other dedicated research helpers, the empirical work in this book would never have been finished.

I also wish to thank Professor F. Gerard Adams, director of the Econometric Forecasting Unit, Paul Davidson, Phoebus Dhrymes, Irwin Friend, Michael Hamburger, Paul Taubman, and Sidney Weintraub for their help in clarifying various issues. Finally, I wish to thank my wife, who besides acting as typist, style editor, and proofreader at various stages of preparation of the book, showed unusual understanding and patience as I "disappeared" for many evenings and weekends. To all who helped so generously, I express my appreciation. They deserve any credit this book might earn.

MICHAEL K. EVANS

Philadelphia

---

[1] M. K. Evans and L. R. Klein, *The Wharton Econometric Forecasting Model* (Philadelphia: University of Pennsylvania, 1967).

MACROECONOMIC
ACTIVITY

CHAPTER 1

INTRODUCTION

1.1 PLAN OF THE BOOK

There is little question that the emphasis on business cycle theory has shifted in recent years. Whereas older treatises centered on the inevitability of the cycle and its causes, 1965 was widely hailed as the year the business cycle was "conquered." Less has been heard about the eight- to ten-year cycle dominated by fixed investment which formed the backbone of older cycle theory, and more emphasis has been placed on the three- or four-year inventory cycle. In other respects, the field of business cycles has often been relegated to a position secondary to a static theory of macroeconomics. The empirical, policy-oriented approach to business cycle problems was curtailed in the classroom, while at the same time it was being expanded in the actual worlds of government and business.

Clearly, a restructuring of this area is in order. Although the basic tools of macroeconomic theory are essential for all economists, they cannot be used alone to select the degree and type of policy action necessary to control the economy under various alternative situations. Two essential ingredients are missing: numerical magnitudes of the parameters suggested by theory and a specific lag structure. One of the major purposes of this book is to provide empirical estimates of the equations for the various sectors of the economy and then to combine these equations into an empirical model that can be used for forecasting and policy simulation.

Unlike the results of pure theory, which can be derived with mathematical

1

rigor, the empirical estimates of theoretical coefficients and lag structures cannot be determined with certainty. Lack of controlled experiments, small samples, and many other statistical problems virtually assure the research worker that his degree of precision will be much smaller than desired, and even then will almost certainly be overstated by the standard statistical tests. Thus it is not surprising to find alternative theories presenting conflicting empirical evidence or the same theory tested over different sample periods giving significantly different results for each period. Worse still, the same equation estimated over the same sample period sometimes gives inconsistent results with pre-revised and post revised data. Such results hamper efforts to determine "best" estimates of these coefficients and give skeptics a large arsenal of weapons with which to attack empirical methods in general.

These problems must be faced, however, if an attempt is to be made to estimate the structure of the economy by empirical methods. Rejecting all empirical results out of hand because of visible disagreement among different studies will not help bring about a solution to these problems. Furthermore, closer inspection often reveals that some of the existing differences can be reconciled by making the assumptions correspond more closely and by using the same statistical techniques; in other cases, no agreement seems possible, and one or more sets of results must be rejected.

Another major task of this book is thus to try to determine basic areas of agreement and disagreement among some of the empirical macroeconomic studies that have been undertaken. Certainly not all empirical estimates that have become available will be reviewed. There are many empirical studies that can be rejected out of hand because of poor econometric method, obsolete theory, inappropriate sample data, or other errors. For example, there is very little reason for cataloguing the numerous estimates of the consumption function of the form $C = a + bY$, for this simple function was shown to be erroneous as early as 1945, when it was used to predict a postwar unemployment figure of 8 million. There are many varying forms of the consumption function that might be considered acceptable on an a priori basis; all of them rely on the fact that consumer spending decisions are planned over a longer horizon than the current period. Another class of results that can quickly be dismissed is investment functions which depend only on unlagged values of the interest rate and possibly on output. These functions are directly contradictory both to the evidence that movements in investment lag the business cycle and to the common-sense notions that investment decisions take time to make and capital goods take time to produce. To confound the problem, this type of function has sometimes been estimated entirely during the period when interest rates remained virtually unchanged, from which the conclusion has been drawn that interest rates and investment are uncorrelated. Yet these very oversimplified consumption and investment functions often pass for an explanation of aggregate demand in many expositions of macroeconomic theory. Certainly this structure should be expanded and modified so that it is realistic enough to be applied to present problems.

Restructuring of business cycle theory is also needed in another area. There has been a tendency to denigrate older existing theories because they do not seem to explain the much milder nature of all the postwar recessions and, more recently, the longest peacetime expansion on record. Much of this criticism is justified because a large part of older business cycle theory has become obsolete, although not quite so much as is commonly supposed. It would indeed be inappropriate not to accept recent developments and discard outmoded theories. However, it is sometimes forgotten that recent changes in cyclical behavior are due at least as much to postwar automatic stabilizers and countercyclical monetary and fiscal policies as to underlying changes in the endogenous functional relationships of the economy. Many of the same relationships that led to cyclical instability and served as the basis for earlier business cycle theories still influence the economy today. Another purpose of this book is to identify these relationships and demonstrate their present-day importance and applicability.

Cyclical disturbances in the economy are currently multiplied by a much smaller factor than previously, and effective monetary and fiscal policy controls are now available to offset them. The tax cut of 1964 should have convinced the last remaining skeptics that discretionary fiscal policy can be effective. But the very fact that a variety of policy activities is now available and has been used successfully makes it even more important than before to measure the effects of each of these policies so that they may be used *more* effectively. The fact that the cycle can in large part be controlled, far from making its study obsolete, should result in a more intensive investigation of the empirical relationships governing cyclical behavior.

With these overall objectives in mind, the scope of this book can be divided into three parts.

1. A discussion on both a theoretical and empirical level of the individual equations of the macroeconomic system, with a comparison and determination of parameter estimates and lag structures.

2. A combination of these functions into a complete theory of the cycle which combines strands of both older and more modern theories with the empirical results obtained in the first part.

3. Expression of this theory and these results in the form of an econometric model that can be used both to forecast aggregate economic activity and to guide policy decisions used for control of the business cycle.

The purpose of this book is thus to provide a unified approach to the problem of how the cycle can best be explained and controlled by combining theory, empirical results, and multiplier analysis and calculations.

1.2   THE NATURE OF POSTWAR BUSINESS CYCLES: AN OVERVIEW

In this book we shall be concerned primarily with the postwar business cycle in the U.S. economy. Theories expounded and empirical estimates gathered for other time periods or other countries may be of considerable interest in other contexts. However, we are interested in formulating a working model of the U.S. economy which can be used for forecasting and control of the cycle; it is thus appropriate to confine our analysis primarily to the postwar U.S. situation. The interwar period is not examined in detail because of substantial institutional shifts since then and also for a more prosaic reason—lack of adequate data.

Before examining the components of aggregate demand and supply in detail, it may be useful to inspect the general nature of the cycle itself. We concentrate exclusively on the short cycle which has historically averaged about 44 months and has been dominated by inventory investment. The record of behavior of these cyclical fluctuations has been tabulated since 1854 by the National Bureau of Economic Research. A firm record of cyclical behavior exists from that date, and cycles are generally agreed to have taken place in earlier decades and centuries. Although we concentrate on the postwar business cycle, it should be remembered that similar cycles have existed throughout much of the history of this country.

The cycles of the postwar period have enough repetitive elements in common to enable one to form a theory of the cycle. On the other hand, these cycles are certainly not identical in all respects, nor were they caused by the same phenomena. In fact, the seeming variety of causes of the cycle has given rise to the question of whether business cycles are endogenously generated or are caused primarily by exogenous or random shocks. This controversy was due in part to a famous article by Slutzky,[1] who showed that the summation of random shocks would generate a sine curve, generally accepted to be the approximate pattern of economic activity over the cycle. Later, Adelman and Adelman[2] showed that the Klein–Goldberger model[3] did not generate cycles by itself, but gave patterns very similar to observed business cycles when shocked by random elements.

The Slutzky argument is instructive but fails to take into account the existence of certain repetitive elements common to virtually all cycles. To give just a few examples, inventory investment almost always fluctuates more than any other component of aggregate demand, consumption of nondurables and services are relatively unaffected by mild recessions, and the pattern of the

---

[1] E. Slutzky, "The Summation of Random Causes as the Source of Cyclic Process," *Econometrica*, Vol. 5, No. 2 (April, 1937), pp. 105–146.

[2] I. Adelman and F. L. Adelman, "The Dynamic Properties of the Klein–Goldberger Model," *Econometrica*, Vol. 27, No. 4 (October, 1959), pp. 596–625.

[3] L. R. Klein and A. S. Goldberger, *An Econometric Model of the United States Economy, 1929–1952* (Amsterdam: North-Holland, 1955).

ratio of disposable income to gross national product always has a counter-cyclical movement. If cycles were true random fluctuations, these repetitive patterns would not occur.

The Adelman and Adelman experiment suggests that endogenous cyclical patterns, if they do exist, are quite heavily damped, so that exogenous factors play an important role in causing cycles.[4] It also suggests that if there were no fluctuations in any of the exogenous variables and if the economy were originally at equilibrium, it would undoubtedly continue to grow smoothly; any cycles that developed would be very slight and heavily damped. But these equilibrium conditions are the exception rather than the rule. Erratic fluctuations in exogenous variables occur for a number of reasons. Defense expenditures and other government obligations change, situations in foreign markets are apt to fluctuate, and strikes may disrupt economic activity. Prolonged periods of full employment are often accompanied by inflation, which causes redistribution of income, relative increases in investment and decreases in consumption, deterioration of the net foreign balance, and stringent monetary and fiscal policies. Existing social legislation changes and transfer payments are increased. These are only a few of the ways in which equilibrium conditions can be disturbed.

Even more important, the economy is usually not in a position of equilibrium at any given time. At the beginning of expansionary periods, excess capacity in fixed business investment invariably exists, and stocks of consumer durables and inventories are almost always below equilibrium levels. Adjustments in these components of aggregate demand will set in motion forces that are quite likely to overshoot equilibrium levels, necessitating an adjustment in the other direction, which will lead to a recession. On the other hand, such cyclical forces are likely to be mild if not reinforced by changes in exogenous variables and are unlikely to continue to generate more than one or two cycles.

These considerations suggest that it is possible to have continued growth without cyclical fluctuations. If proper steps are taken to guide the economy and offset unfavorable movements in exogenous variables, this may well be a likely occurrence. If, on the other hand, stringent monetary and fiscal policies are applied to reduce increases in output and prices at the same time that an expansion would be likely to end of its own accord, three- to four-year cycles dominated by changes in inventory investment are almost sure to occur. It is this overall view of the business cycle that is represented in this text. Before the complete cycle can be intelligently discussed, however, it is necessary to examine each of the components of the economy in detail. This task is attempted in Part I, which immediately follows a brief outline of the general nature of macroeconomic systems.

---

[4] It should be pointed out that variables such as monetary policy which are traditionally counter-cyclical are considered to be exogenous in the Klein–Goldberger and similar models. An endogenous interpretation of these variables would undoubtedly increase the likelihood that these models would generate endogenous cyclical fluctuations.

1.3   A GENERAL OUTLINE
OF THE MACROECONOMIC SYSTEM

In its broadest sense, aggregate economic activity is determined by the intersection of the aggregate demand and the aggregate supply function. The first part of this book contains a detailed disaggregation and examination of the various components of these functions. This section presents an overview of the particular pattern of disaggregation that will be followed.

The aggregate demand schedule is traditionally disaggregated into consumption, investment, exports and imports, and government purchases. Our treatment follows this general classification with considerable additional subdivision of the consumption and investment sectors. A common method of disaggregating aggregate supply is not so well defined. Although it would be possible to estimate supply functions that were directly paired with the components of aggregate demand, this method is seldom used and is not applied here. Instead we assume that supply restrictions are manifested in pressure on factor and product *prices*. Equations are estimated for maximum output and the labor force; as the demand for goods and services and for labor approaches these limits, prices and wages start to rise more rapidly. The distribution of income is also treated in the aggregate supply sector. As output and price change, different proportions of aggregate output go to labor income, rentier income, profits, taxes, and depreciation. Separate functions for each of these are needed to explain income distribution, which in turn affects aggregate demand.

We turn now to the individual components of aggregate demand, beginning with consumption. All types of consumption depend on present and past levels of personal disposable income. The price of the particular good relative to the overall consumer price index is usually an important determinant also. In this book consumption of nondurables and services are treated together because of the basic similarities in the functions explaining individual items in this overall category. For virtually all these goods and services, changes in the income elasticity will be smaller in the short run than in the long run. Consumer durables follow the opposite pattern of behavior with respect to income; the short-run income elasticity is greater than the long-run value. For this reason purchases of consumer durables are treated separately. Because these items are purchased for the services they yield instead of for their own use, the existing amount of stocks has a negative effect on current purchases. Strategic factors particular to the automobile market also have a marked influence on car purchases, so they are treated separately within the broader framework of consumer durable purchases.

Gross private domestic investment is divided into three distinctly separate categories: fixed business investment, residential construction, and inventory investment. Each of these is not only determined by quite different factors but exhibits different cyclical patterns. Even within these finer categories, fixed business investment and inventory investment are subdivided further because of fundamental differences in explanatory variables and lag structure.

Fixed business investment in each sector is positively related to output originating in that sector, negatively related to capital stock, and also depends on various financial variables. In the manufacturing sector both corporate cash flow (retained earnings plus depreciation) and the long-term interest rate are important. In the regulated sector cash flow is no longer significant but the importance of the interest rate is increased. In the commercial and other sectors, the spread between the long-term and the short-term interest rates, representing availability rather than cost of credit, is the relevant financial variable. In all these functions, the proper lag structure is very important. For each sector there is a lag of two to three quarters from the time economic variables change to the beginning of investment appropriations; the actual purchases or construction associated with these appropriations is spread over the next two years, with the peak activity occurring after about one year. Meanwhile, changes in sales may result in modifications in these investment plans; in all cases these sales variables are quite important.

Residential construction behaves in a generally countercyclical fashion because it receives residual factors of production not used by the fixed business investment sector. Here the availability of credit, again measured by the spread between the long-term and short-term interest rate, and the cost of construction relative to the price of rent are both important. Modifications in original plans depend on recent movements in personal disposable income.

Inventory investment can be expressed as a fraction of the difference between desired inventory stocks and actual stocks of the previous period. Desired stocks in turn depend primarily on sales but are also influenced by unfilled orders. There is also an interrelationship between the manufacturing sector and the trade sector, because changes in manufacturing production often cause changes in holding of inventories at the trade level. For these and other reasons, separate functions are necessary for these two sectors.

In the equations explaining demand in the foreign sector, exports depend on an index of world trade and the prices of U.S. exports relative to a price index of world trade. Imports are divided into food, raw materials and semi-manufactured goods, and all other goods and services on current account. In all cases domestic income or sales and relative prices are the important independent variables. Government purchases of goods and services are treated exogenously; thus behavioral equations are not estimated for them.

We now consider the various aspects of the aggregate supply sector. First, a production function, which explains maximum output, is estimated; although this type of equation could be estimated for both the manufacturing and nonmanufacturing sectors of the model, the empirical estimation that is made here is confined to the manufacturing sector. Maximum output is a function of the available labor force, capital stock, and a productivity trend. Actual output originating in the manufacturing sector depends in turn on the various components of aggregate demand. An index of capacity utilization can then be defined as the ratio of actual output to maximum output.

We also need to measure the demand and supply for labor. The number of man-hours demanded depends on the demand for output, utilized capital stock, and the same productivity trend used in the production function. A separate function is estimated for hours, which depend on output and capacity utilization. Employment is then determined as the ratio of man-hours to hours worked. A labor-force-participation equation is estimated which depends upon unemployment, which is defined as the labor force less employment. Thus the size of the labor force and unemployment are determined simultaneously. As the demand for labor increases, more hours will be worked by the existing labor force, and more people will enter the labor force.

We have established the constraints on output and labor; it is assumed that capital stock is fixed in the short run because investment is affected by changes in output only with a lag, and productivity trend is assumed to be exogenous. Thus actual and maximum output of the economy are now determined, and wage and price equations can now be formulated. The wage rate depends in a nonlinear fashion on the rate of unemployment and also on previous changes in the price level. The price level in turn depends on unit labor costs and the degree of capacity utilization. The closer the economy comes to maximum output and full utilization of factor resources, the faster wages and prices will rise.

We now consider the problem of income distribution. The total wage bill is identically equal to the triple product of employment, hours worked, and the wage rate, all of which have already been determined. Income of unincorporated businesses and rental and interest income depend on movements of various prices and output in the economy. Depreciation depends on capital stock and changes in the relevant tax laws, while indirect business taxes depend on national income and changes in the tax laws. If all these income shares are known, corporate profits is then determined as the residual factor of production. Personal disposable income can be calculated if separate functions are added for dividends (which depend on corporate profits), transfer payments, and personal income taxes. Corporate cash flow is found by subtracting dividends and corporate taxes from corporate profits and adding depreciation allowances. All these factor shares are used in simultaneous solution for the components of aggregate demand.

The solution of the aggregate economic system is not complete, however, until individual component prices have been determined. Since all the aggregate demand equations are formulated in constant dollars, appropriate deflators must be used to link constant-dollar purchases (quantities) with current-dollar income flows (wages, profits, and others). The price deflators for each component of aggregate demand are estimated as a function of the price of output originating in the manufacturing sector and strategic factors particular to each market. Finally, because interest rates are important determinants of fixed business investment and residential construction, the equations for short-term and long-term interest rates are estimated. In a more detailed model these interest rates would be tied directly to financial constraints of the economy, but in this exposition they are taken to depend on monetary policy variables that are controlled by the Federal Reserve System.

The overall macroeconomic system is highly simultaneous, because aggregate demand depends on various incomes and prices, which in turn depend on the level of demand. Thus no one part of the system can be solved in isolation.[5] Both demand and supply variables are dependent on the exogenous variables of the system, such as government expenditures, monetary policy variables, tax laws, foreign income and prices, and other variables of less importance. In Parts II and III the behavior of the complete system is analyzed and various multiplier and simulation calculations are discussed. In contrast, the first part of the book is devoted to a discussion and exploration of each of the individual functions that determine the aggregate economic system; the order of analysis followed is consistent with the outline given in this section. Our discussion of the individual equations will begin with consumption and pass to investment, the foreign sector, aggregate supply, and price determination.

---

[5] Although some of the equations depend only on lagged variables and can thus be solved separately for one period, the dynamic solution for the variables requires input values from all the equations in the system.

P A R T 1

COMPONENTS OF AGGREGATE DEMAND AND SUPPLY

CHAPTER 2

THE CONSUMPTION FUNCTION

2.1 INTRODUCTORY ELEMENTS OF THE CONSUMPTION FUNCTION

We begin the explanation of the components of aggregate demand with an analysis of consumption. At the outset we must distinguish clearly between purchases of consumer durables and other consumption. Purchases of durables depend on prior stocks and can be postponed or accumulated much more easily than other consumer purchases. It is thus not surprising to find that purchasing patterns for durables are different from those for other consumption. Any set of national income accounting definitions designed to separate these categories of consumption must be somewhat arbitrary. It is not immediately obvious whether a man's overcoat or an automobile is more durable. Although there is little hesitation about characterizing an automobile as a consumer durable, all clothing is treated as a nondurable in the U.S. national income accounts. However, such "borderline" items as overcoats account for a very small percentage of consumption, so that their effect on empirical findings should be negligible. Unless specifically stated otherwise, in this chapter "consumption" will refer to consumption of nondurables and services plus the use value of the services rendered by durables. Empirical calculations performed in this chapter and in Chapter 3 exclude purchases of consumer durables in all cases. Consumption of durables themselves are examined separately in Chapter 6.

The consumption function as it exists today stems from the "fundamental psychological law" stated by Keynes that "men are disposed, as a rule and on the average, to increase their consumption as their income increases, but not by as much as the increase in their income."[1] Keynes listed a number of "principal objective factors" and modifications of this function, the most important of which, in terms of future economic investigation, can be summarized here:

1. The correct income variable should be personal disposable income, not national income (although Keynes did not use these exact terms).[2]

2. [For] "the wealth-owning class ... changes in the money-value of wealth ... should be classified amongst the major factors capable of causing short-period changes in the propensity to consume."[3]

3. The short-run marginal propensity to consume (mpc) is less than the long-run mpc because "A man's habitual standard of life usually has the first claim on his income, and he is apt to save the difference which discovers itself between his actual income and the expense of his habitual standard,"[4] while over a longer period of time, his standard of living will become more flexible.

4. Even in the long run, "as a rule, a greater proportion of income [will be] saved as real income increases."[5]

Statement 1 has been generally accepted by economists analyzing the consumption function. Statements 2, 3, and 4 have been the basis for most of the empirical investigation of the last 30 years centering on consumer behavior. In this chapter we shall outline the major advances in the theory of the consumption function during this period and show how these statements have been modified, verified, or disproved. Statement 3 is now generally accepted; virtually all current consumption functions distinguish between the short-run and long-run mpc. No definite consensus has been reached on statement 2; however, evidence presented in this chapter tends to cast some doubt on this hypothesis. Statement 4 is false from the aggregate viewpoint; the constancy of the overall consumption disposable income (C/Y) ratio over the past hundred years has been shown by several empirical studies.[6] However, it is still an open question whether relatively wealthy individuals save a greater proportion of their income than do relatively poor individuals.

In the interwar period economists who estimated consumption functions for the U.S. economy accepted statements 1 and 4 but ignored the other

---

[1] J. M. Keynes, *The General Theory of Employment, Interest, and Money* (New York: Harcourt, Brace, 1936), p. 96.

[2] *Ibid.*, pp. 92, 94; Keynes's paragraphs (2) and (5).

[3] *Ibid.*, p. 93.

[4] *Ibid.*, p. 97.

[5] *Ibid.*, p. 97.

[6] Klein and Kosobud argue that the C/Y ratio has actually increased slightly over the long run. Their long-run estimate of the upward trend in the C/Y ratio is given by $C/Y = 0.9134 \, (1.00129)^t$; that is, this ratio has increased by 0.129 percent each year. See L. R. Klein and R. F. Klein and R. F. Kosobud, "Some Econometrics of Growth: Great Ratios of Economics," *Quarterly Journal of Economics*, Vol. 75, No. 2 (May, 1961), p. 177.

modifications. Such a simplified consumption function can be represented as $C = a + bY$, where $a > 0, b < 1$. Note in particular that b is "the" marginal propensity to consume; no allowance is made for differences between the short-run and long-run mpc's. Several functions that were estimated during the period showed results that clearly fitted this pattern and appeared to explain the data very well.[7] This type of function was used to try to predict postwar demand for the U.S. economy.[8] In this first attempt to predict gross national product with an aggregate consumption function, different levels of government expenditures and investment were assumed. These values were combined with various empirical consumption functions of the above sort to predict postwar gross national product. Typical of the predictions was the one that investment would have to be $2\frac{1}{4}$ to 3 times its 1941 peak in constant dollars if the economy were to remain at full employment.[9] All predictions were expressed in constant dollars, as inflation was not considered an immediate threat. In fact, both 1946 and 1947 investment were only 1.1 times 1941 levels, and early postwar government expenditures were below 1941 levels (all comparisons in constant dollars). However, total aggregate demand was large enough not only to ensure full employment but to cause substantial inflation, because the level of consumption was far above that predicted by the simplified consumption function. Partially because of errors of this sort, it was felt that the "Keynesian" consumption function (as then interpreted) was not very useful for explaining consumer behavior.

There were additional reasons for discarding this simplified function. This form of the consumption function implies that the percentage of income consumed decreases as income increases, as was mentioned above. Yet data made available by Kuznets showed that during the period 1869–1929 the ratio of consumption to national income had remained constant while income had quadrupled.[10] This finding was later verified by Goldsmith for consumption and personal income. He stated that a "main enduring characteristic" of saving was "long-term stability of aggregate personal saving at approximately one-eighth of income."[11] These data, representing values of aggregate consumption and income over many different years, are an example of *time-series data*.

Although the C/Y ratio has been constant over long periods of time, data made available in the form of budget studies for the years 1935–1936 and 1941–1942 show that for any given period of time, an individual's C/Y ratio

[7] See, for example, T. Haavelmo, "Measuring the Marginal Propensity to Consume," reprinted in W. C. Hood and T. C. Koopmans, eds., *Studies in Econometric Method* (New York: Wiley, 1953).

[8] A. Smithies, S. M. Livingston, and J. L. Mosak, "Forecasting Postwar Demand," *Econometrica*, Vol. 13, No. 1 (January, 1945), pp. 1–37.

[9] *Ibid.* The range of investment needed depended on the particular consumption function chosen.

[10] S. Kuznets, *Uses of National Income in Peace and War* (New York: National Bureau of Economic Research, 1942), p. 30.

[11] R. Goldsmith, *A Study of Saving in the United States*, Vol. 1 (Princeton, N.J.: Princeton University Press for NBER, 1955), p. 22.

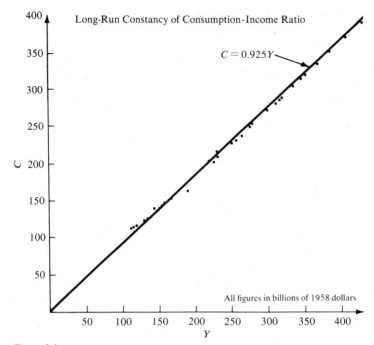

Figure 2.1

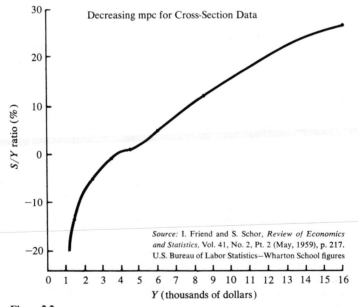

Figure 2.2

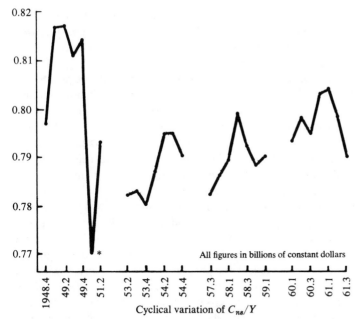

Figure 2.3

*Income temporarily raised by veterans' dividend payment.

decreases as his income increases.[12] These results were also verified by other studies, such as the one by Friend and Schor quoted below.[13] Such data, representing values of consumption and income for many different individuals during a given year, are an example of *cross-section data*. Furthermore, the C/Y ratio fluctuates cyclically; it is not constant over short periods of time. Consumption falls much less than proportionately during minor recessions and sometimes continues to rise when income is decreasing. Clearly modifications of the existing theory were needed to explain these diverse facts pertaining to consumption (which are represented graphically in Figures 2.1, 2.2, and 2.3).

2.2   THE RELATIVE INCOME HYPOTHESIS

The first attempt to reconcile these apparently contradictory facts was provided by Duesenberry in his *Income, Saving, and the Theory of Consumer Behavior.*[14] Duesenberry's theory, known as the *relative income*

---

[12] U.S. Bureau of Labor Statistics, *Bulletins 642–649, 723, 724.*
[13] I. Friend and S. Schor, "Who Saves?" *Review of Economics and Statistics,* Vol. 41, No. 2, Pt. 2 (May, 1959), pp. 213–248.
[14] J. S. Duesenberry, *Income, Saving, and the Theory of Consumer Behavior* (Cambridge, Mass.: Harvard University Press, 1949).

hypothesis, is based on a reversal of two assumptions previously thought to be fundamental to aggregate demand theory. He states that (1) the consumption behavior of individuals is interdependent (rather than independent), and (2) consumption relations are irreversible over time.[15]

Duesenberry uses statement 1 to develop the proposition that the percentage of income consumed by any individual does not depend on his absolute income but rather on his "percentile position in the income distribution," or his relative income. In any given year, an individual will consume a smaller percentage of his income the higher his percentile position. This is in agreement with evidence from the cross-section data. However, if an individual remains in the same percentile position over time, he will continue to consume the same percentage of his income as his absolute income increases. For all individuals remaining in the same percentile position, the secular growth of personal disposable income will result in an equal percentage growth of consumption. Although some consumers will find their relative income position changing over time, these changes will balance in the aggregate, so that the aggregate C/Y ratio will remain unchanged. This part of the theory agrees with the findings from time-series data. The relative income hypothesis thus explains the apparent paradox between the cross-section and time-series evidence.

The second key assumption of the relative income hypothesis is used to explain cyclical fluctuations in the aggregate C/Y ratio. It was previously stated that a rise in disposable income would leave the C/Y ratio unchanged. However, we now proceed to argue that a fall in disposable income will raise the C/Y ratio. If consumer standards are irreversible, a decrease in income will have a smaller than proportional effect on consumption. Individuals will continue to base their consumption patterns partially on higher previous levels of income, which can be represented by peak previous income. The fact that consumption does not fall proportionally with income during recessions accounts for the cyclical behavior of the C/Y ratio.

The relative income hypothesis can be represented functionally as

(2.1)
$$\frac{C}{Y} = a + b\left(\frac{Y}{Y^0}\right) \qquad b < 0$$

where Y^0 is peak previous income. Clearly the value of C/Y predicted by this function is higher in recessions, when $Y < Y^0$, than in expansions, when $Y > Y^0$. If only long-run patterns are considered, so that in general $Y^0 = Y_{t-1}$ (income of the previous period), Y/Y^0 equals some constant value $1 + \gamma$, where γ is the growth rate of income per unit time. In the long run the C/Y ratio itself is equal to a constant value, as required by the theory.

---

[15] Duesenberry's original statements refer to the savings/income ratio rather than the consumption/income ratio. However, his later modifications refer to the latter ratio, and we shall do the same here.

Duesenberry's theory is ingenious in many ways and represents significant advances over previous consumption functions. However, there are occasional circumstances for which the theory gives somewhat less than satisfactory results. First, given the estimated parameters of the regression equation, this hypothesis states that consumption and income always change in the same direction.[16] Yet mild declines in income often occur concomitantly with increases in consumption. Second, the function states that increases in consumption are proportional to any size increase in income, no matter how large or small. It seem reasonable to suggest that unexpectedly large increases in income result, at least initially, in less than proportional increases in consumption. Third, one might argue that consumer behavior is slowly reversible over time, instead of being truly irreversible. Then previous peak income would have less effect on current consumption the greater the elapsed time from the last peak. Advances in the theory of the consumption function have been able to resolve these difficulties.

A theory resulting in virtually same form of the consumption function was developed at approximately the same time by Modigliani,[17] and the consumption function discussed above is sometimes known as the Duesenberry–Modigliani hypothesis. However, Modigliani's underlying reasoning is somewhat different from Duesenberry's and has been substantially modified since it first appeared. The contributions of Modigliani will be discussed later.

2.3   THE PERMANENT INCOME HYPOTHESIS

We now turn to the question of habit persistence and lags in consumer behavior. This aspect of consumption was first explored by Brown,[18] who states that "the full reaction of consumers to change in income does not occur immediately but instead takes place gradually."[19] He develops a theory to explain this gradual adjustment in terms of psychological characteristics of consumers (as was also done by Duesenberry). Brown stresses that the habits and customs that people have previously enjoyed become "impressed" on their minds, which produces "inertia" in their behavior. Thus consumers are rather slow to react to changes in income. As Brown points out, "This theory assumes

---

[16] We can see this by rewriting the function as $C = aY + bY^2/Y^0$. At any given time Y^0 is a constant, because it represents previous peak income. Thus $C = aY + (b/Y^0) \cdot Y^2$. Consumption can increase when income decreases only if $\Delta C/\Delta Y < 0$, that is, $a + (2b/Y^0) \cdot Y < 0$. Since $Y \cong Y^0$, this would imply that $a < 2b \, (b < 0)$. However, Duesenberry's actual estimates are $a = 1.2$, $b = -0.25$. Thus it is virtually impossible for $a < -2b$, even if there are large sampling errors attached to a and b.

[17] F. Modigliani, "Fluctuations in the Saving-Income Ratio: A Problem in Economic Forecasting," in *Studies in Income and Wealth*, Vol. 11 (New York: National Bureau of Economic Research, 1949).

[18] T. M. Brown, "Habit Persistence and Lags in Consumer Behavior," *Econometrica*, Vol. 20, No. 3 (July, 1952), pp. 355–371.

[19] *Ibid.*, p. 355.

that the decline of the effect of past habits is *continuous* over time, rather than discontinuous as the Modigliani–Duesenberry hypothesis suggests."[20] The most suitable form for testing this hypothesis, Brown argues, is to include previous consumption as the relevant lagged variable rather than previous income. This function can be represented as $C_t = a + bY_t + dC_{t-1}$, where the subscript t represents time periods. We shall examine the implications of this function after discussing the work of Friedman.

The question of lags in consumer behavior was investigated from a more rigorous point of view by Friedman in his *Theory of the Consumption Function.* Friedman approaches the problem by making a sharp distinction between income actually received, which he calls *measured income,* and the income on which consumers actually base their behavior, which he calls *permanent income.* A similar distinction is drawn between measured and permanent consumption.[21] These concepts are easy to state in general terms but hard to define precisely. However, following Friedman, we can define permanent income as "the amount a consumer unit could consume (or believes that it could) while maintaining its wealth intact." Similarly, permanent consumption is "the value of the services that it is planned to consume during the period in question."[22]

The principal hypothesis of the permanent income theory states that the ratio of permanent consumption to permanent income is independent of the level of permanent income. Since permanent consumption is also taken to be proportional to permanent income, the long-run mpc for each consumer is equal to his average propensity to consume (apc), and thus the aggregate long-run mpc is equal to the aggregate apc. The apc's need not be the same for all individuals or for all time periods. In particular, they may depend on the interest rate, the ratio of nonhuman wealth to permanent income, the dispersion of measured income around its mean value, or the age and composition of the consumer unit. However, the value of the apc is independent of the level of permanent income. Wealthy people do not save a higher proportion of their permanent income than poor people.

These ideas can be incorporated into a formal statement of the permanent income hypothesis, which is given by the following:

(2.2) $$C_p = k(i, w, u)Y_p$$

(2.3) $$Y = Y_p + Y_{tr} \qquad \rho(Y_p Y_{tr}) = 0 \qquad \bar{Y}_{tr} = 0$$

(2.4) $$C = C_p + C_{tr} \qquad \rho(C_p C_{tr}) = 0 \qquad \bar{C}_{tr} = 0$$

(2.5) $$\rho(Y_{tr} C_{tr}) = 0$$

---

[20] *Ibid.,* p. 370.

[21] M. Friedman, *A Theory of the Consumption Function* (Princeton, N.J.: Princeton University Press for NBER, 1957), p. 221.

[22] *Ibid.,* pp. 10–11.

where Y = personal disposable income

   Y_p = permanent income

   Y_{tr} = transitory income

   C = consumption of nondurables and services plus use value of consumer durables

   C_p = permanent consumption

   C_{tr} = transitory consumption

   k = proportionality constant between permanent consumption and permanent income

   i = interest rate

   w = ratio of nonhuman wealth to permanent income

   u = other economic and demographic factors affecting k

In addition, ρ is the correlation coefficient and the barred variables represent mean values.

   Equation (2.2) explains that C_p is proportional to Y_p, with the proportionality factor depending on various economic and demographic factors. Equations (2.3) and (2.4) state that measured income and consumption can each be divided into a permanent and a transitory component, that these components are independent, and that the mean value of the transitory component is zero. Equation (2.5) states that the transitory components of income and consumption are independent. Thus a windfall gain (for example) will be completely saved; none of it will be spent. However, this last stringent conclusion can be relaxed and a small positive correlation between Y_{tr} and C_{tr} permitted if the consumer's horizon is assumed to be of less than infinite length.[23]

   We first consider the implications and tests of this theory for time-series analysis. If i, w, and u remain constant over time, then the ratio of C_p/Y_p will maintain the same value over time. If short-run fluctuations in C and Y are averaged over time (for example, by taking business cycle averages so that $\bar{C}_{tr} \cong \bar{Y}_{tr} \cong 0$), then the long-run C/Y ratio will remain constant and will not exhibit any trend. This conclusion agrees with the evidence shown in Figure 2.1. Furthermore, the long-run constancy of the C/Y ratio implies that consumption and income are proportional in the long run and that the long-run mpc is equal

---

[23] It is sometimes stated that an unexpected windfall gain will add to permanent income and thus consumption. The transitory income connected with the windfall will then be the excess over the permanent income component. However, such an assumption violates equation (2.3), which states that the transitory and permanent components of income are uncorrelated. This explanation cannot be used to justify the permanent income hypothesis.

to the apc.[24] Some regression equations presented in Chapter 3 suggest that these results are quite consistent with empirical studies.

To test this theory empirically and to determine whether the regression estimate of k is equal to the observed apc, it is necessary to derive empirical approximations for C_p and Y_p. The former is handled simply by substituting C for C_p; differences in the two are relatively small, because purchases of consumer durables are already excluded from consumption. In any case, Friedman argues that on the average C equals C_p for any given value of measured income. Such a simple expedient cannot be used for the income term. Permanent income is approximated by a weighted average of present and past measured income with the weights declining exponentially. The actual formula given by Friedman is[25]

$$(2.6) \qquad (Y_p)_T = \beta \int_{-\infty}^{T} e^{(\beta - \alpha)(t - T)} Y_T \, dt$$

where β = an adjustment coefficient between measured and expected income

α = average annual growth rate

T = present time period

t = index of time periods; $t = T$ back to $-\infty$

In reality, continuous figures of income do not exist; they only appear yearly (or quarterly), and the series terminate after a finite number of years. In performing his empirical tests, Friedman uses a decreasing weighted average[26] of yearly income figures for the past 17 years:

$$(2.7) \qquad (Y_p)_t = \beta[Y_t + e^{(\beta - \alpha)} Y_{t-1} + e^{2(\beta - \alpha)} Y_{t-2} + \cdots + e^{17(\beta - \alpha)} Y_{t-17}]$$

The function estimated to test the permanent income hypothesis is

$$C_t = k(\beta[Y_t + e^{(\beta - \alpha)} Y_{t-1} + e^{2(\beta - \alpha)} Y_{t-2} + \cdots + e^{17(\beta - \alpha)} Y_{t-17}]) + \gamma$$

The constant term γ is very close to zero (only 0.24 times its standard error)

---

[24] This can be easily shown as follows. Consider the consumption function

$$C^L = a + bY^L$$

(where the superscripts L represent long-run values) at two points in time t_0 and t_1, and let income be α units larger at t_1. Then

$$C_0^L = a + bY_0^L \qquad \text{and} \qquad C_1^L = a + b(Y_0^L + \alpha) = a + bY_1^L$$

If the C^L/Y^L ratios are to be equal at both points of time, then

$$\frac{a + bY_0^L}{Y_0^L} \qquad \frac{a + bY_0^L + \alpha b}{Y_0^L + \alpha}$$

This equality can hold only if $a = 0$, so C^L and Y^L are proportional. Furthermore, the consumption function $C^L = bY^L$ implies that b is both the long-run mpc and the apc.

[25] Friedman, op. cit., pp. 143–144.

[26] We are following accepted usage that such weights are *exponentially* distributed for the continuous case and *geometrically* distributed for the discrete case. Future comments for such distributed lags will be confined to the latter case.

and the estimate of k is 0.88, very close indeed to the observed apc of 0.877 over the sample period. The estimates also provide some information on the length of the consumer's horizon. If his horizon were infinite, each term in the expression for permanent income would receive equal weight. The particular weighting scheme used shows that consumption plans are influenced more by present than past income. The mpc of the current year's income is equal to $k\beta$, or 0.33. This suggests that the consumer's horizon is approximately three years, since an individual will spend one third of his windfall gain (for example) on consumption in the current year. This estimate of three years is corroborated by evidence from other sources. The estimation of the permanent income hypothesis thus yields a value for the yearly mpc as well as verifying that the long-run mpc equals the apc.

Although this empirical implementation of Friedman's hypothesis gives satisfactory results, the long string of terms for permanent income is extremely unwieldy for more detailed econometric analysis. However, since the weights for the measured income terms decline geometrically, the equation can be transformed into a much simpler relationship. This manipulation was first proposed by Koyck with respect to investment functions and is often called the *Koyck transformation*.[27] It is designed for expressions with an infinite number of terms, although the modification for a finite number of terms is very slight. If

(2.8) $$C_t = k(Y_p)_t$$

or

(2.9) $$C_t = k(Y_t + \lambda Y_{t-1} + \cdots + \lambda^{17} Y_{t-17})$$

or, in general,

$$C_t = k \sum_{i=0}^{\infty} \lambda^i Y_{t-i}$$

then

(2.10) $$\lambda C_{t-1} = k(\lambda Y_{t-1} + \cdots + \lambda^{17} Y_{t-17} + \lambda^{18} Y_{t-18})$$

or, in general,

$$\lambda C_{t-1} = k \sum_{i=0}^{\infty} \lambda^{i+1} Y_{t-i-1}$$

Subtracting (2.10) from (2.9) gives[28]

(2.11) $$C_t - \lambda C_{t-1} = kY_t \quad \text{or} \quad C_t = kY_t + \lambda C_{t-1}$$

(t represents time periods, not transitory components).

---

[27] L. M. Koyck, *Distributed Lags and Investment Analysis* (Amsterdam: North-Holland, 1954).
[28] In the finite case, the term $\lambda^{18} Y_{t-18}$ is left, but we have assumed this is very close to zero.

This form of the consumption function is almost identical to the one proposed by Brown. This was pointed out by Klein, who stated that "In this form ($C_t = kY_t + \lambda C_{t-1}$) we recognize a consumption function that has been used to good advantage in previous Keynesian models.... Brown's work on lags in consumer behavior is truly a complete anticipation of Friedman." In his reply, Friedman admits that "This procedure was equivalent to Brown's use of consumption of the preceding year, and Klein is quite right in criticizing me for this error of omission."[29]

However, there is one difference in the two equations. The form suggested by Friedman does not contain a constant term. Although this may at first appear to be a minor adjustment, it is in fact of primary importance. Consider the two functions

$$(2.12) \qquad\qquad C_t = a + bY_t + dC_{t-1}$$

$$(2.13) \qquad\qquad C_t = b'Y_t + d'C_{t-1}$$

Both functions explain short-term fluctuations in the C/Y ratio and are compatible with situations in which consumption may rise when income is falling. *However, this type of function is consistent with the long-run stability of the C/Y ratio only if the constant term is zero.*

Consider a long-run situation with consumption growing at γ per time period (we again neglect short-term fluctuations). Then $C_t = (1 + \gamma)C_{t-1}$ and in equilibrium the functions become

$$(2.14) \qquad\qquad C = a + bY + \frac{d}{1 + \gamma} C$$

$$(2.15) \qquad\qquad C = b'Y + \frac{d'}{1 + \gamma} C$$

Collecting terms, we have

$$(2.16) \qquad\qquad C = \frac{a(1 + \gamma)}{1 + \gamma - d} + \frac{b(1 + \gamma)}{1 + \gamma - d} Y$$

$$(2.17) \qquad\qquad C = \frac{b'(1 + \gamma)}{1 + \gamma - d'} Y$$

Only in the second case is consumption proportional to income in the long run. The permanent income hypothesis as stated by Friedman assumes that the long-run consumption function passes through the origin, whereas the function proposed by Brown makes no such assumption. We can identify b and b'

[29] L. R. Klein, "The Friedman-Becker Illusion," *Journal of Political Economy*, Vol. 66, No. 6 (December, 1958), p. 541, and M. Friedman, "Supplementary Comment," *ibid.*, p. 549.

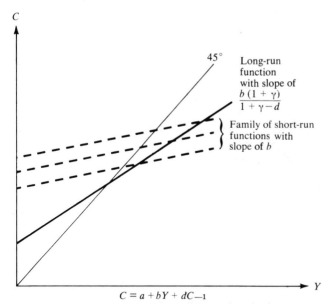

Figure 2.4

in the above functions as short-run mpc's and

$$\frac{b(1 + \gamma)}{1 + \gamma - d} \quad \text{and} \quad \frac{b'(1 + \gamma)}{1 + \gamma - d'}$$

as long-run mpc's. Properties of these two consumption functions are graphed in Figures 2.4 and 2.5.

It should be noted here that sometimes the long-run mpc calculated from the function $C_t = a + bY_t + dC_{t-1}$ is found merely by setting $C_t = C_{t-1}$ and thus obtaining

(2.18) $\qquad C = a + bY + dC \qquad \text{or} \qquad C = \dfrac{a}{1 - d} + \dfrac{b}{1 - d} Y.$

In this case the "long-run mpc" is $b/(1 - d)$. However, as Ball and Drake mention,[30] this is really a stationary situation in which there is no growth, rather than a truly long-run situation. The latter should take account of growth of income, as is done here.

We can think of the short-run consumption function approaching the long-run function in at least two ways. If income is growing over time, each short-run function (with the same slope) will have a higher intercept as last period's consumption increases. If we consider the relevant levels of income at each time

[30] R. J. Ball and P. S. Drake, "The Relationship Between Aggregate Consumption and Wealth," *International Economic Review*, Vol. 5, No. 1 (January, 1964), p. 68.

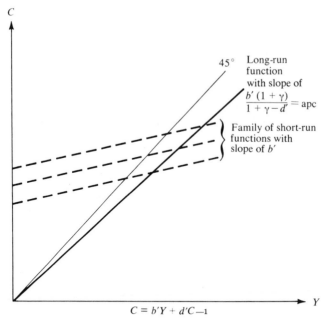

Figure 2.5

period, the points on the short-run functions trace out a long-run function that goes through the origin and has a slope equal to the apc. This process is illustrated in Figure 2.6. If income remains constant over time, we can think of the slope of the short-run consumption function as increasing continuously as time progresses until it finally merges with the long-run function. This process is shown in Figure 2.7.

Figures 2.6 and 2.7 illustrate how the mpc approaches the apc over time. In the long run, after the consumer has become fully accustomed to receiving a given amount of additional income, he will spend the same proportion of this income as of all his other income. There is little reason for an individual to spend a different percentage of one part of his income if he has fully adjusted to receiving this income. At a minimum the burden of proof is on those who wish to show that a function which utilizes a different assumption about long-run consumer behavior agrees with the empirical evidence.

We now consider the implications and tests of the permanent income hypothesis for the cross-section (budget study) evidence. Unlike the time-series analysis, it would not be realistic to pretend that the presently available evidence is conclusive. It should be possible, however, to examine some of the empirical studies that have been performed and reach some qualified judgment on the relevance of the theory for cross-section analysis.

If i, w, and u are constant for different individuals, the ratio of C_p/Y_p should be invariant with the level of Y_p. In particular, individuals with higher permanent

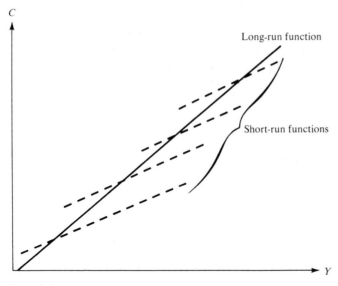

Figure 2.6

incomes would not have a higher saving rate. At first this conclusion seems to be contradictory to the cross-section evidence, such as that shown in Figure 2.2. There, a strong positive correlation between income and the savings/income ratio can be observed. However, the permanent income hypothesis alleges that measured income is a poor measure of permanent income. Relatively

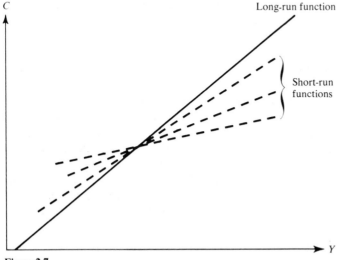

Figure 2.7

higher incomes are quite likely to contain a large positive transitory component. Since (almost) all transitory income is saved, these empirical results do not necessarily contradict the permanent income hypothesis. Instead, many individuals in the highest income brackets for any given year do not usually have such high incomes. Their measured income happened to be higher than usual in the year in which the budget study was taken, and thus a larger than average proportion was saved.

The discrepancy between measured and permanent income can be made even more explicit by examining the lower end of the income scale. In the cross-section study cited, and in cross-section studies generally, individuals in lower income groups spend more than their measured income. Yet it is virtually impossible for an individual to continue to consume more income than he receives.[31] Individuals who do so during any given year must be receiving less income than usual. Their transitory income in the year of the budget study is clearly negative, which accounts for their negative saving.

Not quite as strong a case for the permanent income hypothesis can be stated for the upper end of the income scale. The idea that an individual with a permanent annual income of $50,000 has a higher savings rate than an otherwise identical individual with a permanent annual income of $10,000 is an intuitively appealing one. However, let us examine the implications of the assumption that permanent income and the savings rate are positively correlated. This would mean that the rich would save proportionately more and their wealth would increase proportionately. Since the rate of return of wealth and the aggregate wealth/income ratio have remained approximately constant over the long run (as shown in Table 2.3) this would lead to an increase in income inequality over time. Yet the degree of income inequality is less in the postwar period than earlier in the century. Although part of this may be due to increased progressiveness in the personal income tax schedule, much of wealth income is received in the form of interest from tax-free bonds or lightly taxed capital gains. The noticeable absence of the rich to get richer, coupled with the near-constancy of the aggregate wealth/income ratio, implies that over their lifetimes the rich have not been saving proportionately more than any other income group.

Even if the C_p/Y_p ratio is independent of the level of Y_p, it need not be the same for all individuals. Differences in this ratio may occur because of variations in the parameters affecting the proportionality constant k. From theoretical considerations it would be expected that a rise in the interest rate would lower k and a rise in the wealth/income ratio would raise k. However, at any given time most individuals are able to lend their funds at the same rate, so that differences in i are unlikely to explain differences in k among individuals. The wealth/income ratio is quite likely to vary among individuals, but it is positively

---

[31] This could be true only if an individual had a stock of assets very large relative to this income, continually depleted this stock, and earned virtually no income from these assets.

correlated with permanent income. If W/Y_p is positively correlated with Y_p, and W/Y_p is assumed to be positively correlated with C_p/Y_p, the C_p/Y_p would be positively correlated with Y_p, cet. par. This does not agree with the tendency for C_p/Y_p to be negatively correlated with Y_p, if indeed there is any correlation. The dependence of k on the wealth/income ratio cannot be used to explain the negative correlation between the observed C/Y ratio and measured income.

Variations in measured income around its mean are a primary cause of differences in individual C_p/Y_p ratios. Self-employed individuals generally have a proportionately greater transitory component of their income than do wage and salary workers. For this reason one would expect the apc of the former group to be smaller. Since the self-employed usually have higher than average permanent incomes, this explains some of the results showing that higher income groups have a higher savings rate—within a framework consistent with the permanent income hypothesis.

Demographic factors may also have an effect on k. The apc will increase somewhat as the size of the family increases, although this relationship clearly becomes less important as the size of the family continues to increase. Even very large families do not continually consume more than their total income. Young and old families will generally save somewhat less than middle-aged families. These points are discussed in more detail in Section 2.6. Here we merely wish to point out that there are several possible explanations for differing apc's among individuals.

To test the validity of the permanent income hypothesis for cross-section data, two major empirical considerations must be met. First, it is necessary to obtain some measure of permanent income that does not require a large number

TABLE 2.1 RELATION BETWEEN CONSUMPTION
AND INCOME IN SELECTED COMMUNITIES

	White			Negro		
Community	Mean Income, $	apc	$(C/Y)_{\bar{Y}}{}^a$	Mean Income, $	apc	$(C/Y)_{\bar{Y}}{}^a$
Southeast villages	1674	0.92	0.96	500	1.00	1.02
Southeast small cities	1683	0.95	0.97	620	0.99	0.98
Southeast medium cities	2086	n.a.	0.94	686	n.a.	0.98
Atlanta, Ga.	2158	0.93	0.96	888	0.96	0.98
Columbus, Ohio	2058	n.a.	0.94	1130	n.a.	0.96
New York, N.Y.	2645	0.98	1.00	1500	0.99	1.01

[a] Ratio of consumption to income at mean income of group.

of previous values of measured income. Second, data must be obtained for values of i, w, and u for individual consumers, or groups must be chosen for which differences in these variables are negligible. We discuss some of the principal methods used which resolve most of these difficulties.

One method used is the comparison of the apc's for several different communities with widely varying average incomes. Although incomes of many individuals in a given community will include transitory components, the average measured income for the total community is likely to be close to its average permanent income. Furthermore, the average W/Y_p ratio, percentage of self-employed, and age and composition of the population can be very similar for properly chosen units.[32]

Some results are shown in Table 2.1 for a study presented by Friedman based on an extensive 1935–1936 cross-section survey.[33] The white and Negro sections of the population were separated because (1) a much smaller percentage of Negroes employed are self-employed or independent professionals, (2) the W/Y_p ratio is lower for Negroes at any given income, and (3) the family size of Negroes is somewhat larger than for whites. It is seen that the apc and $(C/Y)_{\bar{Y}}$ are higher for Negroes than for whites in every community.

If the absolute income hypothesis is correct, there should be a negative correlation between $(C/Y)_{\bar{Y}}$ and Y; if the permanent income hypothesis is correct there should be no correlation. If each community observation is weighted equally, there is a slight *positive* correlation for the white group ($r = 0.48$) and an even smaller negative correlation ($r = -0.15$) for the Negro group.[34] In both cases the value of r at the 5 percent level of significance is 0.82.[35]

A similar test is performed by Modigliani and Ando using the 1950 U.S. Bureau of Labor Statistics data.[36] They consider small cities, large cities, and suburbs in the North, South, and West, respectively. Again they find no correlation between Y and C/Y.

A second method of measuring permanent income is to choose some particular expenditure that represents permanent income better than measured

---

[32] It is, of course, easy enough to think of situations that do not meet these standards. The choice of Pittsburgh during the year of a major steel strike or Detroit during the year of a major auto slump would clearly be inappropriate. Similarly, a suburb containing a high percentage of professional people or a town built for retired people would not satisfy these conditions. But it should be easy to exclude such cases from a properly designed sample.

[33] Friedman, *op. cit.*, p. 82. Unfortunately the apc's were not available for all classifications, so Friedman computes the C/Y ratio at the mean income ($\bar{Y}$). Since the ranking of this statistic and the apc are the same in all cases where the data exist, this should not significantly affect the results.

[34] All tests are reported only for the $(C/Y)_{\bar{Y}}$ statistics. Using the values of the apc where available did not alter the results.

[35] This test somewhat inadvertently illustrates the fallacy involved in testing the permanent income hypothesis without adjusting for *nonincome* differences in k. If the 12 values of $(C/Y)_{\bar{Y}}$ are correlated with income without any distinguishing feature, there is a much stronger negative correlation than appears for either the white or Negro group separately.

[36] F. Modigliani and A. Ando, "The 'Permanent Income' and the 'Life Cycle' Hypothesis of Savings Behavior: Comparisons and Tests," in I. Friend and R. Jones, eds., *Consumption and Saving*, Vol. II (Philadelphia: University of Pennsylvania Press, 1960), p. 126.

income does. A very good variable for this purpose is housing expenditure: either the value of the house or the yearly rental. Individuals change residences very seldom and choose their living quarters based on their permanent income. It is desirable to calculate the relationship between C/Y and housing separately for homeowners and renters for several reasons. Homeowners usually have larger families than those who rent. They generally have higher W/Y_p ratios because the purchase of a house usually requires a substantial down payment. Homeowners are more likely to be middle-aged (in broadly defined terms); heads of households who are particularly young or old are more likely to rent. It is still necessary to consider self-employed and wage and salary workers separately, because the former group has a lower apc. Such a test was performed by Modigliani and Ando.[37] Their results for non-self-employed homeowners are reproduced in Table 2.2. Similar results are obtained for non-self-employed who rent their housing. In fact, for that group the C/Y ratio is slightly higher for higher rentals. However, these results are partially due to the extremely small number of observations available for the higher rental groups.

The results in Table 2.2 represent a striking verification of the permanent income hypothesis for a sample where permanent income is correctly measured and other factors affecting the proportionality constant k are taken into account. For comparison we have listed the C/Y ratios *for the same individuals* classified by measured income groups. For this tabulation a very strong negative correlation can be observed between the C/Y ratio and the level of measured income.

If similar statistics are examined for the self-employed, it is found that not only is the apc lower than for other employed workers, but it definitely

TABLE 2.2 RELATIONSHIP BETWEEN CONSUMPTION AND INCOME FOR GROUPS CLASSIFIED BY VALUE OF HOUSING EXPENDITURE

Value of House, $	Average Income, $	C/Y	Income Class, $	C/Y
1– 4,999	3,606	0.98	0– 999	4.79
5,000– 7,499	4,274	0.98	1,000–1,999	1.19
7,500– 9,999	4,649	0.99	2,000–2,999	1.03
10,000–12,499	5,191	0.99	3,000–3,999	0.98
12,500–14,999	5,729	0.98	4,000–4,999	0.96
15,000–17,499	5,948	1.00	5,000–5,999	0.96
17,500–19,999	7,547	0.95	6,000–7,499	0.95
20,000–24,999	9,607	0.99	7,500–9,999	0.87
25,000–above	11,267	0.99	10,000–above	0.82

[37] *Ibid.*, pp. 153–154.

decreases as income increases. However, this should not be very surprising. The income variability (in percentage terms) of self-employed earning a high income is certainly greater than those earning a low income. This will be true as long as profit is considered to be partially a return to risk and uncertainty. It is not necessary to argue that these results are inconsistent with the permanent income hypothesis.

Another method used to test the permanent income hypothesis is to compare the apc's of low-income and high-income occupations. While an individual worker is likely to receive transitory components of income in any given year, the permanent income of an unskilled worker is clearly lower than that of an executive. If occupations can be stratified by incomes, the apc's of various occupations can then be correlated with permanent income. The self-employed should be excluded from any such comparison because, as has already been noted, they have lower apc's for any given income level.

One such thorough study has recently been undertaken by Mayer.[38] He compares low-income and high-income occupations for a variety of countries, time periods, and groups of occupations. In 29 of 34 cases he finds that the lower-income occupations have higher apc's than do the higher-income occupations. Furthermore, the studies for which the findings are reversed are among the smallest and least reliable in his entire sample. It would be hard to find reasons that would disprove Mayer's claim that traditionally higher-income occupations (mainly white collar) save proportionally more than lower-income occupations (mainly blue collar).[39]

It is *not* clear, however, whether this result can be attributed to differences in income. It might be due to differences in savings patterns engendered by different occupational distinctions or the fact that different sociological groups have traditionally held blue-collar jobs. The crucial question is not whether a blue-collar worker saves proportionately less than a white-collar worker; it is whether he does so *at the same level of permanent income*. It is not unreasonable to argue as follows. Most college professors have higher permanent incomes than most steelworkers. Most college professors save a greater percentage of their income than most steelworkers. A college professor whose permanent income is identical to a steelworker's still saves more than the steelworker. If this is in fact the case, differential savings rates between high- and low-income occupations would not necessarily be related to the level of permanent income. It is this last piece of information for which data are needed. Unfortunately, it is also the hardest to get because data on permanent income are not

---

[38] T. Mayer, "The Propensity to Consume Permanent Income," *American Economic Review,* Vol. 56, No. 5 (December, 1966), pp. 1158–1177.

[39] Two possibilities come to mind readily. First, employers' contributions to social security might be inadvertently excluded. Since these are proportionately much more important for lower-paid workers, this would understate their savings ratio. Second, higher-income groups might save more while they are employed because they dissave more before employment (owing partially to the high cost of education) and after retirement. However, I doubt whether inclusion of these points would reverse Mayer's findings.

usually available for individuals. Additional testing is needed and undoubtedly will continue in this area.

One more test should be mentioned at this point, because it has received a fair amount of attention and at first glance seems to contradict the permanent income hypothesis. In early 1950 a number of war veterans received a national life insurance dividend. This can clearly be treated as transitory income, because it was unexpected and was also not expected to be repeated. Bodkin compared the mpc from this windfall gain with the mpc from other income and with the mpc of similar veterans who did not receive this dividend.[40] He found that the mpc of transitory income was significantly *greater* than the mpc of other income. At face value Bodkin would have seemed to disprove not only the permanent income hypothesis but the absolute income hypothesis as well.

The apparent paradox is in this case easily resolved. The data used for Bodkin's experiment included purchases of consumer durables, which are treated as savings by Friedman and others. In an ordinary year this might not make too much difference, but 1950 marked the beginning of the Korean War, which was accompanied by panic buying of consumer durables. The veterans did not necessarily spend their dividends on current consumption, but they did invest heavily in consumer durables. A proper definition of consumption, which was unfortunately not available from the existing data, would have remedied this problem.

There are many other tests of the permanent income hypothesis which have been calculated with cross-section data. It is not our intention to list all these tests or even the major ones but rather to suggest the kinds of tests that are possible and the general outline of results that have emerged. Some other important tests of this hypothesis are given below.[41]

At this point it is appropriate to compare the major implications of the relative and permanent income hypotheses. Both theories agree that the aggregate long-run mpc is equal to the apc, which is itself constant in the long run. However, they reach different conclusions about the cross-section evidence. Duesenberry suggests that the rich save proportionately more of their (permanent) income, within a given socioeconomic unit, but Friedman claims that this is not the case. The evidence presented for different communities in Table 2.1 is consistent with both theories. Those inhabitants of higher-income communities who have higher absolute incomes may not be in a higher relative percentile position. The evidence presented by the occupations study, however, cannot agree with both theories. If people with higher incomes do save

---

[40] R. G. Bodkin, "Windfall Income and Consumption," *American Economic Review*, Vol. 49, No. 4 (September, 1959), pp. 602–614.

[41] M. R. Fisher, "Exploration in Savings Behaviour," *Bulletin of the Oxford Institute of Statistics*, Vol. 18, No. 3 (August, 1956), pp. 201–277. A symposium based on Fisher's results is found in *Bulletin of the Oxford Institute of Statistics*, Vol. 19, No. 2 (May, 1957). H. W. Watts, "Long Run Income Expectations and Consumer Savings," in *Studies in Household Economic Behavior*, Yale Studies in Economics, Vol. 9 (New Haven: Yale University Press, 1958), pp. 103–144. Friend and Jones, *op. cit.*, contains several tests and discussions of the permanent income hypothesis.

proportionately more and people with the same incomes save the same amount, this provides verification of the relative income hypothesis. If people have different savings patterns which are independent of their income level, this provides verification of the permanent income hypothesis. Of course, the possibility exists that elements of both these theories enter into the explanation of the observed data.

Without making a final judgment on whether the strict terms of the permanent income hypothesis all hold, it can be fairly said that the weight of the evidence supports this theory. Even if parts of the hypothesis are ultimately shown to be incorrect, Friedman's formulation has reshaped and redirected much of the research on the consumption function. It is indeed unusual to discuss the consumption function today without referring to Friedman's terms of reference.

2.4   THE ROLE OF WEALTH IN THE CONSUMPTION FUNCTION

Except for income itself, wealth has been analyzed most thoroughly and tested most extensively as a possible determinant of consumption. This is due to two reasons. First, disposable income consists of returns from both human and nonhuman wealth. Second, wealth can be stored and the income derived from it used to offset both planned and unexpected changes in labor income. The fundamental distinction between labor and property income is stressed by Friedman[42]:

> All forms of nonhuman wealth are not equally satisfactory as a reserve for emergencies; this is the reason why certain kinds of nonhuman wealth, such as so-called "liquid assets," have been singled out for special attention in some empirical studies. But none of the other distinctions among forms of wealth seems as pervasive and fundamental as the distinction between human and nonhuman wealth.

As we have seen, the empirical form employed by Friedman to test the permanent income hypothesis did not include this distinction. Income from both labor and nonhuman wealth was included in a single term. However, a consumption function with just this distinction has been proposed by Modigliani and others. Since wealth may be used to balance income streams over long periods of time, they consider the *lifetime* resources available to the consumer. Such a formulation of consumer behavior is usually known as the *"life-cycle"* hypothesis.[43]

---

[42] Friedman, *op. cit.*, p. 17.

[43] A. Ando and F. Modigliani, "The 'Life Cycle' Hypothesis of Saving: Aggregate Implications and Tests," *American Economic Review*, Vol. 53, No. 1 (March, 1963), pp. 55–84.

Ando and Modigliani posit a consumption function in which individual consumption[44] depends on the resources available to the individual, the rate of return on capital, and the age of the consumer unit. Available resources are defined as existing net worth (wealth) plus the present value of all current and future nonproperty (that is, labor) earnings. According to this theory, the rational consumer considers all his existing resources when planning his consumption. He allocates his income so that utility is maximized over his lifetime. An increase in income will add to an increase in consumption only inasmuch as it adds to total lifetime resources. Thus for any given age classification, consumption is proportional to those resources, both labor and property, instead of current income. As Modigliani states, "The cornerstone of the ... model is the notion that the purpose of saving is to enable the household to redistribute the resources it gets (and expects to get) over its life cycle in order to secure the most desirable pattern of consumption over life."[45] Such a consumption function for the individual can be represented as[46]

$$(2.19) \qquad c_t^T = k_t^T [(y_L)_t^T + (N - T)(y_L^e)_t^T + w_{t-1}^T]^6$$

where t = time period

T = present age of individual

N = earning span of individual

k = proportionality factor

y_L = current labor income of individual

y_L^e = expected future labor income of individual

w = net worth of individual

This function can be aggregated to the form

$$(2.20) \qquad C_t = \alpha_1 (Y_L)_t + \alpha_2 (Y_L^E)_t + \alpha_3 W_{t-1}$$

where the capital letters represent aggregates of the individual variables. Note the clear distinction that occurs between labor income and wealth.

Changes in income derived from wealth may occur both because the rate of return changes and because the value of the stock of wealth appreciates. If the rate of return on net worth is given by ρ, and if net worth grows at an average rate γ, then the mpc out of wealth, or α_3 in the above formulation, will be equal to (long-run mpc) $(\rho + \gamma)$, or about 0.08.[47] In the case where individuals decrease their stock of wealth over their lifetime, α_3 would also depend on $1/N - T$ and would thus be higher than 0.08. However, given the way in which

---

[44] Consumption here is defined in the same way as it is by Friedman: excluding purchases of durables but including the use value of their services. However, all terms are now defined in current prices rather than the constant prices used in previous studies.

[45] F. Modigliani, "Savings Behavior: A Symposium" *Bulletin of the Oxford Institute of Statistics*, Vol. 19 (May, 1957), p. 105.

[46] Ando and Modigliani, *op. cit.*, p. 58.

[47] Approximate values are $\rho = 0.05$, $\gamma = 0.04$, lr mpc = 0.93.

individuals actually do behave, this is an unlikely assumption. Thus 0.08 should set an approximate upper limit to the empirical estimates of d_3.

Ando and Modigliani have chosen to analyze and estimate this function in ratio form:

$$(2.21) \qquad \left(\frac{C}{Y_L}\right)_t = \alpha_1 + \alpha_2 \left(\frac{Y_L^E}{Y_L}\right)_t + \alpha_3 \frac{W_{t-1}}{(Y_L)_t}$$

Although this is done partially for statistical reasons, some of which are discussed in Chapter 3, this form also presents the long-run implications of the function more clearly. If short-run fluctuations are ignored, the C/Y_L ratio is equal to some constant times a multiple of the W/Y_L ratio. Since the W/Y_L ratio has been approximately constant over long periods of time (see Table 2.3), this implies that the C/Y_L ratio is also constant in the long run. Thus their theory also stresses the long-run constancy of the consumption/income ratio, but, unlike the previous theories discussed, posits that it is due to the constancy of the wealth/income ratio.

We now examine additional implications of this function. Although it may well be appropriate for explaining observed cross-section phenomena, the above function was formulated explicitly for analyzing aggregate data. Therefore the following discussion will concentrate on the time-series aspects of this equation.

Empirically it is true that year to year percentage fluctuations in wealth are much smaller than those in income. In a period of general prosperity, such as the postwar U.S. economy, wealth has increased fairly steadily each year. During minor recessions, the W/Y_L ratio increases; thus C/Y_L rises. Short-run cyclical fluctuations in the C/Y_L ratio are compatible with this function. Furthermore, household net worth continues to rise in recessions as long as personal saving is positive and the value of equities does not decrease; thus consumption may also increase in absolute terms. These figures are presented in Table 2.3.

To assess the long-run properties of this function it is necessary to examine the W/Y ratio in terms of the parameters of the equation. Previous functions discussed have not explicitly contained terms other than consumption and income. The necessary transformations express wealth as a function of income alone and thus express W/Y as a constant. We use the identities (1) $S = Y - C$, and (2) $S = \Delta W$. Then $C/Y = a + b(W_{-1}/Y)$ becomes

$$(2.22) \qquad \frac{Y - S}{Y} = a + b\frac{W_{-1}}{Y} \qquad \text{or} \qquad \frac{Y - \Delta W}{Y} = a + b\frac{W_{-1}}{Y}$$

Therefore,

$$(2.23) \quad 1 - \frac{W}{Y} + \frac{W_{-1}}{Y} = a + b\frac{W_{-1}}{Y} \qquad \text{and} \qquad (1 - b)\frac{W_{-1}}{Y} = a - 1 + \frac{W}{Y}$$

TABLE 2.3 YEARLY NET WORTH OF THE
HOUSEHOLD SECTOR 1929–1964
(*net worth figures are in billions of current dollars*)

Year	Net Worth $(W)^a$	W/Y^b
1929	466.8	6.27
1930	444.3	5.96
1931	383.7	6.00
1932	319.4	6.56
1933	305.0	6.70
1934	324.3	6.19
1935	336.9	5.76
1936	362.9	5.47
1937	376.9	5.29
1938	357.2	5.45
1939	368.0	5.23
1940	397.0	5.24
1941	426.0	4.60
⋮		
1946	696.4	4.35
1947	767.5	4.52
1948	845.0	4.47
1949	884.6	4.69
1950	933.2	4.51
1951	1025.6	4.53
1952	1089.2	4.57
1953	1106.6	4.38
1954	1181.2	4.59
1955	1268.4	4.61
1956	1372.0	4.68
1957	1453.5	4.71
1958	1508.1	4.73
1959	1640.8	4.86
1960	1674.5	4.78
1961	1714.7	4.71
1962	1821.9	4.73
1963	1919.9	4.75
1964	2041.8	4.69

^{a} Net worth figures kindly supplied by Albert Ando.
^{b} Income figures are from *Survey of Current Business*.

Assume now that W grows at a constant long-run rate γ. Then

$$(2.24) \qquad W = (1 + \gamma)W_{-1} \qquad \text{and} \qquad \left(\frac{1 - b}{1 + \gamma}\right)\frac{W}{Y} = a - 1 + \frac{W}{Y}$$

Therefore,

$$(2.25) \qquad \frac{W}{Y} = \frac{(1 - a)(1 + \gamma)}{\gamma + b}$$

This function has some interesting implications. If it is assumed that wealth is not growing (that is, $\gamma = 0$), $W_{-1} = W$ and $W/Y = W_{-1}/Y = (1 - a)/b$. Substituting this in the original consumption function, $C/Y = a + bW/Y$, we have

$$(2.26) \qquad \frac{C}{Y} = a + \frac{b(1 - a)}{b} = a + (1 - a) = 1$$

Thus by postulating a function in which consumption depends on income and wealth, we obtain the result that the long-run marginal propensity to consume, which is equal to the average propensity to consume, is unity for conditions of no growth. Under such conditions consumers would not save any of their income in the long run but would consume it all. Although the no-growth condition does not in itself describe a realistic situation for the postwar U.S. economy, it does focus attention on various aspects of the consumption–savings relationship. Specifically it suggests that personal savings occur only when the economy is growing and that the savings rate depends on the growth rate of the economy.

It has been shown by Spiro[48] and Ball and Drake[49] that if consumption is proportional to wealth, the long-run mpc will be unity under conditions of no growth even if wealth is not explicitly included in the consumption function. For, using the identities above and the proportionality of consumption to wealth, we have: (1) $S = Y - C$, (2) $S = \Delta W$, and (3) $C = k \cdot W$. Therefore,

$$(2.27) \qquad C = Y - S = Y - W + W_{-1} = Y - \frac{1}{k}C + \frac{1}{k}C_{-1}$$

Therefore,

$$(2.28) \qquad C\left(1 + \frac{1}{k}\right) = Y + \frac{1}{k}C_{-1} \qquad \text{and} \qquad C = \frac{k}{k+1}Y + \frac{1}{k+1}C_{-1}$$

The long-run mpc for no growth (that is, $C = C_{-1}$) is

$$(2.29) \qquad \frac{k/k + 1}{1 - (1/[k + 1])} = \frac{k}{k} = 1$$

It should also be noted that the coefficients of Y and C_{-1}, $(k/k + 1) + (1/k + 1)$, sum to unity. This provides a test of the hypothesis that $C = k \cdot W$ and that

---

[48] A. Spiro, "Wealth and the Consumption Function," *Journal of Political Economy*, Vol. 70, No. 4 (August, 1962), pp. 339–354.
[49] Ball and Drake, *op. cit.*

the long-run mpc equals unity for periods of no growth. This is done by estimating $C = aY + bC_{-1}$ and determining whether $a + b$ sum to a value that is not significantly different from unity.[50] The results are discussed in Chapter 3.

Parenthetically, it might be added that although a value of unity for the mpc during periods of no growth (such as the 1930s) may not seem likely, it would not result in the explosive situation deduced from the elementary multiplier $1/(1 - \text{mpc})$. Even if people did eventually spend all the extra disposable personal income they received, the extra disposable income would be less than the total addition to the national product. Part of the extra national product would go to other factor shares, such as taxes, profits, and rents. The correctly stated elementary multiplier, assuming no endogenous effects of investment or net foreign balance, is $1/[1 - \text{mpc} \cdot (\Delta Y/\Delta X)]$, where $\Delta Y/\Delta X$ represents the proportion of additional disposable personal income received per unit of additional gross national product.

To assess the validity of wealth in the consumption function it is useful to investigate the more realistic case of growth in the economy. Under the Spiro–Ball–Drake hypothesis, the long-run equilibrium situation becomes

$$(2.30)\quad C\left(1 + \frac{1}{k}\right) = Y + \frac{1}{k(1 + \gamma)}C \quad \text{or} \quad C = \frac{k}{k + 1}Y + \frac{1}{(k + 1)(1 + \gamma)}C$$

The long-run mpc would then be

$$(2.31)\qquad \frac{k/(k + 1)}{1 - [1/(k + 1)(1 + \gamma)]} = \frac{k}{k + [\gamma/(1 + \gamma)]}$$

The parameter k is interpreted here to be the C/W ratio, or about 0.18[51] Then the value of the yearly mpc, $k/(k + 1)$, is only 0.15. This value is quite unrealistically low compared to estimates obtained from a wide variety of other consumption functions.[52] Furthermore, the long-run mpc $k/[k + (\gamma/[1 + \gamma])]$ $= 0.86$, less than the apc of 0.93 for total consumption, for a value of $\gamma = 0.03$, the average postwar growth rate. This finding is also contrary to all the other consumption functions examined.

The analysis becomes more complicated when the Ando–Modigliani function is considered. In the long run, their hypothesis states that

$$(2.32)\qquad \frac{C}{Y_L} = a + b\frac{W_{-1}}{Y_L}$$

---

[50] It is not necessary to specify strict proportionality between consumption and wealth to obtain this result. For this result will apply for any linear relationship, such as $C = a + bW$. Then $Y = C + W - W_{-1}$,

$$Y = C + \frac{C - a}{b} - \frac{C_1 - a}{b} \quad \text{and} \quad C\left(1 + \frac{1}{b}\right) = Y + \frac{1}{b}(C_{-1})$$

which is the same form as above.

[51] It is possible that the function could have been written $C = a + kW$, in which case k would be the marginal consumption/wealth ratio. This would have made its value even smaller.

[52] Some of these results are presented in Tables 3.5 and 3.6.

Furthermore, if the Y_L/Y ratio is constant in the long run, then we can write

(2.33)
$$\frac{C}{Y} = a' + b' \frac{W_{-1}}{Y}$$

Using a previous result (equation [2.25]), that

(2.34)
$$\frac{W_{-1}}{Y} = \frac{1}{1+\gamma} \frac{W}{Y} = \frac{1-a}{\gamma+b}$$

gives

(2.35)
$$\frac{C}{Y} = a' + \frac{b'(1-a)}{\gamma+b}$$

The terms a', b', and b are estimated empirically (γ is the growth rate of wealth) in Chapter 3. At this point we say only that these results do not on an a priori basis lead to unreasonable estimates of the short-run or long-run mpc's.

Thus the Ball–Drake–Spiro and Ando–Modigliani formulations, although giving the same result for no growth, will in general give quite different results when wealth is increasing. This is due to the strict dependence of consumption on wealth in one case, compared to the joint dependence of consumption on wealth and income in the other case. We reject the strict formulation of wealth alone because it leads to unreasonable results regarding both short-run and long-run behavior of consumers. On the other hand, the functional relationship that consumption depends on income and wealth gives results that may well be compatible with established patterns of consumer behavior.

It is still necessary to examine whether the inclusion of wealth significantly improves the explanation of consumer behavior on an empirical basis. This will be done in Chapter 3. Moreover, there is some question whether the "cornerstone" of the life-cycle hypothesis—that householders plan their consumption over their entire lifetimes—is entirely valid. This seems to be quite a rigorous constraint and ignores the propensity of individuals to concentrate more heavily on the present, which was found in previous formulations. As Ball and Drake point out, "individuals on average are 'short-sighted' in the face of considerable uncertainty ... the principal motive for accumulating assets is not related to some lifetime plan in any very precise sense, but is more satisfactorily thought of in terms of a broad precautionary motive."[53]

Another possibility is that individuals may curtail consumption to increase their wealth, owing to uncertainty about future income and inability to borrow if income does decrease. Two individuals with the same income and same initial assets might have widely differing consumption wealth ratios; one with a very steady income might well consume much more than one with a widely fluctuating income. Short-run movements in consumption and wealth will not be in the same direction if wealth is increased for precautionary motives rather than for future increased expenditures.

[53] Ball and Drake, op. cit., p. 65.

2.5   THE EFFECT OF LIQUID ASSETS ON CONSUMPTION

Another possible determinant of consumption, which is often considered in connection with wealth, is liquid assets. It is usually argued either that liquid assets are a good proxy variable for wealth or that they are a strategic component of wealth for influencing consumption. The first claim is easily checked. It is true that both liquid assets (L) and wealth (W) have increased over time as the economy has continued to expand. However, the relevant question is whether movements in L and W are correlated after the common trend has been removed. For the postwar period, the correlation coefficient between both L/Y and W/Y and ΔL and ΔW (annual changes) is only 0.23, far below standard levels of significance.[54] The postwar period has been characterized by a shift from liquid assets to other forms of wealth. Most other assets have appreciated in price, whereas liquid assets, almost by definition, have not.[55] For these reasons there is very little justification for using liquid assets as a proxy variable for wealth.

The claim that liquid assets have a greater influence on consumption than do other forms of wealth deserves more attention. This hypothesis received great attention shortly after World War II (1946–1948), when it was claimed that both the C/Y ratio and the L/Y ratio were quite high by historical standards. For this reason it was assumed that the former was due to the latter. Although this explanation will undoubtedly remain a favorite of many economists, considerable doubt can be cast on the veracity of this hypothesis. To do this, one would show in general that (1) this hypothesis does not hold for the total postwar period, (2) the L/Y ratio was not particularly high in 1946–1948 relative to current levels, and (3) alternative hypotheses can adequately explain the high C/Y ratio during 1946–1948 without the aid of a liquid assets term.

The question of whether liquid assets are significant in a postwar consumption function is open to some interpretation. Although several workers have found that liquid assets are not significant in consumption functions that are part of econometric models, other econometricians have estimated consumption functions that do contain significant liquid-assets terms. There is no particular reason for this because the same national income accounts data are being used in both cases.[56] The distinction must then be made on other

---

[54] The value of r at the 5 percent level of significance for 19 observations is 0.45.

[55] Liquid assets are usually defined as those assets (including money) that have a fixed monetary value and can easily be converted into money at that value.

[56] In L. R. Klein, "A Quarterly Model of the American Economy, 1948–1961," mimeographed release, 1963, the consumption function for nondurables contains a nonsignificant liquid-assets term while the functions for durables and services contain no liquid-assets term. More recent models by Klein and others have no liquid assets term in any of the consumption functions. In J. S. Duesenberry, G. Fromm, L. R. Klein, and E. Kuh, eds., *The Brookings Quarterly Model of the United States* (Chicago: Rand McNally, 1965), only the consumer services function contains a liquid-assets term. However, this term is significant in studies by Arnold Zellner, "The Short-Run Consumption Function," *Econometrica*, Vol. 25, No. 4 (October, 1957), pp. 552–567, and Z. Griliches, G. S.

levels. First, cross-section studies have generally failed to reveal any significant effect of liquid assets on consumption.[57] Second, functions designed to omit the common trend, such as ratio functions, also show no significant effect of liquid assets.[58] This holds true even for functions estimated during the first part of the postwar period. Third, since 1961 the L/Y ratio has risen considerably, whereas the C/Y ratio has remained constant. This fact would undoubtedly make liquid assets less important in more recently estimated levels functions. Since the more stringent tests (removal of common trend) show no effect of liquid assets on consumption, we believe that the weight of the evidence would argue against their inclusion in consumption functions.

Statement 2 can be verified with the use of Table 2.4. It can be seen that the most recent ratios of L/Y are actually higher than they were immediately following World War II. Also note the almost steady rise of the L/Y ratio since 1953 compared with the stability of the C/Y ratios.

In support of statement 3 it is claimed that the high early postwar C/Y ratios can be explained either by the relative income hypothesis or the permanent income hypothesis (but not by the wealth–income hypothesis). Personal disposable income *fell* considerably in real terms from 1945 to 1948. There are two reasons for this:

1. The economy was at overfull employment and capacity during the war. When hostilities ceased, gross national product dropped substantially in constant dollars and did not regain its former level until 1950.

2. Prices rose substantially during 1946–1948. When prices rise, income is redistributed toward profits and away from wage earners and rentiers. At full employment, this means that personal disposable income fell absolutely as well as relatively, because total income in constant dollars did not increase. This was especially true during this particular period (before automatic escalator clauses in wage contracts), when wages lagged prices more than they do now.

When real personal disposable income fell, individuals based present consumption standards on previous peak income (relative income hypothesis) or, since actual income was less than the income to which people had been accustomed during the war, they spent a greater percentage of their income than usual (permanent income hypothesis). In either case, real personal income in 1947–1948 was well below wartime levels. This accounted for the unusually high level of the C/Y ratio in the early postwar years.

Maddala, R. Lucas, and N. Wallace, "Notes on Estimated Aggregate Quarterly Consumption Functions," *Econometrica*, Vol. 30, No. 3 (July, 1962), pp. 491–500. For a fuller list of consumption functions with liquid-assets terms, see Don Patinkin, *Money, Interest and Prices*, 2nd ed. (New York: Harper & Row, 1965), appendix M.

[57] In particular, see I. Friend and Jean Crockett, "A Complete Set of Consumer Demand Relationships," in Friend and Jones, eds., *op. cit.*

[58] See J. S. Duesenberry, O. Eckstein, and G. Fromm, "A Simulation of the United States Economy in Recession," *Econometrica*, Vol. 28, No. 4 (October, 1960), pp. 749–809.

TABLE 2.4 COMPARISON OF L/Y AND C/Y RATIOS

Year	L/Y	Total C^a $\overline{Y}$	C_{ns}/Y^b
1946	0.68	0.916	0.817
1947	0.71	0.972	0.851
1948	0.68	0.942	0.862
1949	0.62	0.955	0.833
1950	0.62	0.939	0.800
1951	0.59	0.922	0.799
1952	0.58	0.921	0.803
1953	0.58	0.921	0.792
1954	0.62	0.926	0.800
1955	0.61	0.936	0.792
1956	0.61	0.921	0.789
1957	0.61	0.924	0.792
1958	0.65	0.922	0.803
1959	0.65	0.930	0.798
1960	0.66	0.938	0.805
1961	0.69	0.925	0.798
1962	0.72	0.928	0.792
1963	0.75	0.931	0.790
1964	0.76	0.925	0.793

^{a} Consumption including purchases of consumer durables.
^{b} Consumption excluding purchases of consumer durables.
Source: Liquid-assets figures from the *Flow of Funds Accounts*, Federal Reserve System; other figures from the *Survey of Current Business*.

An alternative explanation sometimes given for the high C/Y ratios is simply that consumers were ordering extra amounts of goods that had been rationed during wartime. This argument applies much more forcefully to purchases of consumer durables, which are excluded from most of the present analysis. Although there may have been some extra buying of semidurables such as clothing, most nondurables and services are used almost immediately. It is quite unlikely that the rationing of food or transportation during the war caused postwar buying splurges of these or similar items.

One other minor point needs to be cleared up. During the war years the S/Y ratio for individuals reached an unprecedented 25 percent. With this massive accumulation of savings, it is often surprising at first to find that the L/Y ratio in 1946 was not particularly high by postwar standards and that the W/Y ratio in 1946 was at a postwar low, having fallen considerably from 1941. Most wartime savings was done in the form of liquid assets, partially because other types of assets were not readily available. The real value of these assets was appreciably diminished by the severe postwar inflation. This did not prevent individuals from raising their C/Y ratios, but it did keep the L/Y and W/Y ratios from increasing as much as they otherwise would have.

The great majority of the evidence presented above suggests that there is very little justification for using liquid assets as a strategic component of wealth in the consumption function. Instead it is more realistic to say that for a given level of wealth, substitution between liquid and other assets is due to the respective rates of return, expectations of changes in the respective prices of the assets, and possibly the unavailability of durable assets during wartime. Some additional empirical tests presented in Chapter 6 bolster this conclusion by showing that liquid and durable assets are substitutes.

2.6   OTHER DETERMINANTS OF THE CONSUMPTION FUNCTION

Other factors besides those already discussed may influence consumption. One of these is the division of personal disposable income between wage income and property income. In general, an individual's short-run mpc is smaller the more variable his income is. We have shown in Section 2.3 that an individual whose transitory income is proportionately larger than average will consume less in both the short run and the long run than an individual with the same permanent income but less income variability. The macroeconomic implications of this relationship are now considered.

We note that empirically the wage share of personal disposable income falls during booms and rises during recessions.[59] This tends to add stability to the cycle. During a boom, nonwage income becomes a larger percentage of disposable income. Since this income is more variable than wage income, its recipients have lower mpc's. Thus proportionately less is spent, mitigating the boom. During a recession, the opposite shift takes place. The drop in consumption due to the relative loss of nonwage income is much less than the increase in consumption due to the relative shift toward wage income. This is another possible explanation why the C/Y ratio rises during recessions and falls during booms. This process is illustrated in Table 2.5.

The effect of income distribution on aggregate consumption has been measured at least two ways by Klein, who has used these variables in some of his consumption functions. The most straightforward way to measure this effect would be to estimate the function $C_t = aW_t + bP_t + dC_{t-1}$. However, W and P not only have similar trends but also similar turning points. This makes it very difficult to distinguish statistically between their effects and to measure a and b accurately. This particular problem can be avoided by rewriting the function as $C_t = a(W_t + b/aP_t) + dC_{t-1}$ and estimating b/a independently from cross-section data. This was done in the Klein–Goldberger

---

[59] This phenomenon is discussed in much greater detail in Chapter 11.

TABLE 2.5   EFFECTS OF SHIFTS IN INCOME DISTRIBUTION ON CONSUMPTION

	Level of			
C	Y	W	P	
350	400	300	100	Equilibrium conditions
335	360	290	70	Decrease in income: relative shift toward W^a
329	360	270	90	Decrease in income: consumption falls further if factor shares remain constant
365	440	310	130	Increase in income: relative shift toward P^b
371	440	330	110	Increase in income: consumption rises further if factor shares remain constant

[a] W, wage income (short-run mpc assumed to be 0.6 for this example).

[b] P, property income (short-run mpc assumed to be 0.3 for this example).

model,[60] where it was found that $b/a = 0.74$. Although this method is interesting and informative, it does not tell us whether the cyclical redistribution of income makes a significant net addition to the explanation of the consumption function, because b/a is already predetermined by other data. This problem can also be avoided by introducing the ratio of wage to property income as a separate variable in the consumption function and writing it as $C_t = aY_t + b(W/P)_t + dC_{t-1}$. This has been done by Klein in one of his quarterly models,[61] in which he disaggregates consumption into durables, nondurables, and services. However, the parameter estimate of the W/P term is significantly positive in one equation, significantly negative in another, and not significantly different from zero in the third. This does not appear to be a satisfactory result. It is rather doubtful whether the cyclical redistribution of disposable income affects aggregate consumption significantly for the degree of income inequality in the postwar U.S. economy.[62]

These results should not be taken to negate the cross-section findings that both the short-run and long-run mpc's of the self-employed are lower than for employees. A substantial income distribution (much larger than that which occurs cyclically) would undoubtedly change the aggregate mpc and apc. It

[60] L. R. Klein and A. S. Goldberger, *An Econometric Model of the United States, 1929–1952* (Amsterdam: North-Holland, 1955). This function also contained a separate category for farm income.

[61] L. R. Klein, "A Quarterly Model . . . ," *op. cit.* An earlier version of this model appeared in L. R. Klein, "A Postwar Quarterly Model: Descriptions and Applications," in *Models of Income Determination, Studies in Income and Wealth*, Vol. 28 (Princeton, N.J.: Princeton University Press for NBER, 1964).

[62] It is possible that the distribution of disposable income does influence aggregate consumption patterns significantly in countries with greater income inequality. A significant effect of the W/P term for the Japanese economy is found in L. R. Klein and Y. Shinkai, "An Econometric Model of Japan, 1930–1959," *International Economic Review*, Vol. 4, No. 1 (January, 1963), pp. 1–28.

has often been suggested that economies faced with chronic unemployment could raise aggregate demand by redistributing disposable income in favor of employees. The reverse proposal—that inflation could be cured by redistributing disposable income in favor of the self-employed—is seldom mentioned, even though the two suggestions are logically equivalent.

Finally, we consider the effects of family composition (size and age) on consumption. These variables have been used mainly in cross-section analysis and are usually considered to be more important in influencing purchases of consumer durables than other consumption. For total consumption it has been found that for a given income, consumption is proportional to the sixth root of the number of members of the family.[63] The high order of nonlinearity arises from the fact that the C/Y ratio must remain less than unity in the long run even as the size of the family grows very large. Since larger family units have larger short-run and long-run mpc's, redistribution of income toward these families would raise aggregate consumption. As a policy matter this is presently accomplished by the use of tax deductions for each member of a family, and a rise in consumption could easily be obtained by increasing these deductions. Of course, here again the reverse argument applies—that inflation could be curtailed by reducing the deductions.

The age of the head of the household is also thought to have some effect on consumption, although again this effect is stronger on the purchase of consumer durables. However, the direction of this effect has not yet been definitely verified. The typical income stream of an individual during his earning period has approximately the shape shown in Figure 2.8. According to the permanent income and life-cycle hypotheses, the C/Y ratio would be high during the earlier years, low during the years of peak earning power, and higher again in years of retirement or reduced earnings.[64] Although this seems reasonable, M. R. Fisher and Modigliani got opposite results using overlapping data, which Modigliani calls "meagre" and "confusing".[65] In another study, Janet A. Fisher found a low savings ratio for the earlier years but a high savings ratio for retired people.[66] More cross-section analysis is needed before the role of the age of the head of a spending unit can be pinpointed. In the aggregate, a population with a younger average age would probably have a higher mpc, but this cannot be definitely established from the existing results.

In this chapter we have examined the major theories of consumer behavior that have been advanced. We have found that it is logical to expect consumption

[63] Friedman, *op. cit.*, p. 122.

[64] The reader is reminded that according to both of these hypotheses, consumption excludes purchases less use value of consumer durables.

[65] M. R. Fisher, *op. cit.*; Franco Modigliani, "Savings Behavior: A Symposium," *Bulletin of the Oxford Institute of Statistics*, Vol. 19, No. 2 (May, 1957), pp. 107, 123.

[66] Janet A. Fisher, "Income, Spending, and Saving Patterns of Consumer Units in Different Age Groups," *Studies in Income and Wealth*, Vol. 15 (New York: National Bureau of Economic Research, 1952), pp. 77–102.

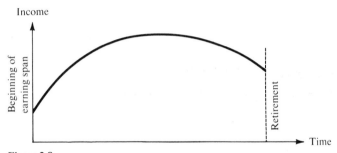

Figure 2.8

to depend on income and past patterns of consumer behavior, and possibly on wealth. Other variables that have been used in various consumption functions explain significant differences in cross-section analysis but do not appear to have major effects on aggregate consumer behavior. The theoretical properties of the short-run and long-run marginal propensities to consume have been described, and the relationship that the long-run mpc equals the apc has been stressed. However, few actual values have yet been assigned to these concepts. It is the purpose of Chapter 3 to examine in some detail the values that have been estimated. For purposes of forecasting and control of business cycles and policy applications there is probably no parameter that is more important than the mpc. We shall discuss briefly the statistical problems inherent in estimating the mpc and examine the estimates for different types of consumption functions.

EMPIRICAL ESTIMATES OF
THE CONSUMPTION FUNCTION

3.1   PROBLEMS IN MEASURING
THE MARGINAL PROPENSITY TO CONSUME

In this chapter we shall present and examine actual time-series estimates of the various forms of the consumption function discussed earlier. First, however, it should be helpful to discuss some of the statistical biases that are found in many estimates. The same general type of function estimated with the same national income accounts data for similar time periods often gives remarkably different estimates of the mpc. Many of these differences can be reconciled by adjusting for various biases and distortions in the parameter estimates. We do not intend to use statistically rigorous methods in examining the source of these biases, and in general the explanations presented are only approximations of more complicated proofs. It is hoped, however, that this discussion will allow the reader to evaluate different consumption function estimates more clearly.

One of the most commonly estimated forms of the consumption function, and one that is often estimated by biased methods, is the function $C_t = a + bY_t + dC_{t-1} + u_t$, where u_t represents a random error term. This term occurs in all stochastic equations because it is not possible to explain all the variance of the dependent variable.[1] The size of $(1/[T-1]) \sum_{t=1}^{T} u_t^2$

---

[1] The variance of a random variable X is defined as $(1/[T-1]) \sum_{t=1}^{T} (X_t - \bar{X})^2$, where $\bar{X}$ is the mean value and T is the number of observations.

is generally less than $\frac{1}{2}$ percent of the variance of consumption, so this is not likely to be a serious problem. Instead, the assumptions that u_t is random and that it is uncorrelated with any of the independent variables in the equations are the ones most likely to cause biased parameter estimates.

The most common method of estimation used in empirical analysis is the method of least squares.[2] This method minimizes the sum of the squares of the error term over the sample period; that is, it minimizes $\sum_{t=1}^{T} u_t^2$. One of the fundamental assumptions of the method of least squares is that u_t is uncorrelated with any of the independent variables in the estimated equation. The parameter estimates obtained by least squares are always based on the premise that this assumption holds. If it does not, the estimates will be biased. In the strictest sense this condition is met by stating that the independent variables are known numbers at time t; they contain no random components. Exogenous variables, such as time trends, dummy variables, government defense expenditures, or foreign trade prices, meet this criterion.[3] Lagged variables, which are also known at time t, do not always meet this condition, which often leads to an additional source of bias. Assume for the present, however, that exogenous and lagged variables are known at time t in the sense that they contain no random elements and thus cannot be correlated with the random error term u_t.

It is quite straightforward to show that all the variables in the consumption function given above cannot meet this criterion. We know that

(3.1) $C_t = a + bY_t + dC_{t-1} + u_t$ and $C_t + I_t + G_t = Y_t$

Therefore,

(3.2) $Y_t = a + bY_t + dC_{t-1} + u_t + I_t + G_t$

It is seen that Y_t is a function of u_t instead of being independent of it. The assumption necessary for unbiased least-squares estimates no longer holds, and the parameter estimates are biased. In particular, the estimate of b is biased upward.[4]

A verbal example may strengthen the intuitive understanding of this point. Suppose that consumption increases because of a change in the factors affecting the random error term. Such an occurrence might be the "scare buying" that occurred at the outset of the Korean War. Then consumption

[2] A discussion of the method of least squares may be found in many standard statistics and econometrics textbooks. One useful source is J. Johnston, *Econometric Methods* (New York: McGraw-Hill, 1963).

[3] A variable is *exogenous* to a given system if it is used to determine the value of other variables in the system but is not itself determined within the system.

[4] This problem was originally discussed by T. Haavelmo, "Measuring the Marginal Propensity to Consume," in W. C. Hood and T. C. Koopmans, eds., *Studies in Econometric Method* (New York: Wiley, 1953). The general problem is more fully discussed in "The Estimation of Simultaneous Linear Economic Relationships" by Koopmans and Hood in the same volume. A later reference, including recent developments, is found in Johnston, *op. cit.*

would rise considerably even if income remained unchanged. However, income would be almost certain to increase in the absence of unusual offsetting factors,[5] because consumption is one of the determinants of income. The direction of causality here is that income rose because consumption rose. However, it would appear from a statistical point of view that just the opposite had happened. In the form in which the consumption function is being estimated, the rise in consumption would be due to the corresponding increase in income. This would bias the parameter estimate of the income term upward. This problem would not arise if consumption and income were independent, but this is definitely not the case. This problem is generally known as *simultaneity bias* or *least-squares bias*.

Two general methods have been advanced for treating this problem. Although these elements have the same objective, which is to find independent variables that are uncorrelated with u, the results are quite different. In the first case, use is made of the identity $Y = C + S$ (S is savings), which is then substituted into the consumption function. This gives

$$(3.3) \qquad C_t = a + b(C_t + S_t) + dC_{t-1} + u_t$$

Solving for like terms reduces this to

$$(3.4) \qquad C_t = \frac{1}{1 - b}(a + bS_t + dC_{t-1} + u_t)$$

Since personal savings are not one of the components of aggregate demand or income, the least-squares assumption is fulfilled. However, an even more serious bias, which is due to errors of measurement, arises in the other direction. Savings in the national income accounts are calculated as a residual between income and consumption. Thus any errors of measurement that tend to increase the reported value of consumption relative to its true value will understate the amount of savings. This introduces a spurious negative relationship between consumption and savings. Ando and Modigliani have shown that this bias may be severe enough to explain otherwise nonsensical results in which the estimate of mpc is less than zero.[6] Since the bias this method introduces is worse than the one it eliminates, it can hardly be recommended.

An alternative method used is to calculate a regression of income on all the exogenous and lagged variables in the system; for the simple case given above, this would be

$$(3.5) \qquad Y_t = \alpha C_{t-1} + \beta I_t + \gamma G_t + \varepsilon_t$$

Designate the values of Y_t calculated from this regression as $\hat{Y}_t$; they are independent of u_t because they depend only on known numbers at time t and

[5] National product need not rise if the fall in investment and government spending offsets the rise in consumption. This was certainly not the case at the beginning of the Korean War, however, nor is it usually the case.

[6] A. Ando and F. Modigliani, "The 'Life-Cycle' Hypothesis of Saving: Aggregate Implications and Tests," *American Economic Review*, Vol. 53, No. 1 (March, 1963), pp. 55–84.

thus satisfy this least-squares assumption. Then the regression equation for consumption is calculated substituting the $\hat{Y}_t$ values for the original Y_t. The resulting parameter estimates obtained from the equation

(3.6) $$C_t = a + b\hat{Y}_t + dC_{t-1} + u_t$$

will then be unbiased, at least in large samples. This method of calculation is known as *two-stage least squares*. Asymptotically it gives the same estimates as other more complicated single-equation methods of estimation. It is also preferred because it is not as sensitive to multicollinearity, a point discussed next.

Multicollinearity in time-series analysis often occurs when several of the variables in a given function have very similar trends or other movements throughout the entire sample period.[7] In this case it is not possible in a statistical sense to determine which of the independent variables is actually causing the dependent variable to change. In the case of the consumption function, both income and lagged consumption follow smooth upward patterns. Either variable could be used to explain a large part of the movements in consumption, and it is often not possible to sort out the independent contributions of each variable. When this is the case, the sum of the coefficients is likely to remain approximately the same when different estimates are calculated, but the magnitudes of the individual coefficients for income and lagged consumption are likely to vary appreciably. Then it will not be possible to determine the short-run mpc and the time pattern of adjustment to a change in income. Although these estimates are distorted, there is no particular direction in which the error is most likely to occur. The estimate of the income coefficient may be low one time and high the next. In general, it has been the case that multicollinearity is more likely to distort these estimates calculated by more complex methods of estimation. As an example of this, consider different values obtained by Klein for the same consumption function estimated by different methods.[8] One would expect that the parameter estimate of income would be biased upward in the first equation, which is estimated by ordinary least squares; the other three equations are obtained by consistent estimates and should be free of bias.[9] However, the results, shown in Table 3.1, present a rather different picture.[10] Note that although the sum of

---

[7] This problem is discussed briefly in Johnston, *op. cit.*, chap. VIII, and is also examined in detail by L. R. Klein and M. Nakamura, "Singularity in the Equation Systems of Econometrics: Some Aspects of the Problem of Multicollinearity," *International Economic Review*, Vol. 5, No. 3 (September, 1962), pp. 274–295.

[8] L. R. Klein, "Problems in the Estimation of Interdependent Systems," in H. Wold, ed., *Model Building in the Human Sciences* (Monaco: Union Européenne d'Editions, 1967).

[9] The other three methods in the order of the equations presented are two-stage least squares, limited information, and full information. For a discussion of these see Johnston, *op. cit.*, chap. IX. Consistent estimates are those with no asymptotic (large-sample) biases.

[10] The numbers in parentheses are standard-error estimates. In general, a coefficient is said to be significantly different from zero if it is at least twice as large as its standard error. This form of listing standard errors and definition of significance will be used throughout the book unless otherwise stated.

TABLE 3.1   RESULTS OF USING DIFFERENT METHODS FOR ESTIMATING THE CONSUMPTION FUNCTION[a]

(1) $C^b = -4.93 + 0.559Y^c + 0.445C_{-1}$
          (0.065) (0.070)

(2) $C = -4.94 + 0.560Y + 0.444C_{-1}$
          (0.066) (0.071)

(3) $C = -5.33 + 0.634Y + 0.364C_{-1}$
          (0.069) (0.074)

(4) $C = -3.41 + 0.352Y + 0.663C_{-1}$
          (0.074) (0.088)

[a] All equations are estimated for the period 1929–1962, omitting 1942–1945.
[b] C, total purchases of consumer goods and services, billions of constant dollars.
[c] Y, personal disposals income, billions of constant dollars.

the income and lagged consumption coefficients all total to almost exactly unity, there are great differences among the estimates of the individual terms. This is largely due to the presence of extreme multicollinearity and illustrates the difficulty of using highly complex methods of estimating parameters where strong common trends are in evidence.

We now return to the problems caused by the inclusion of the lagged consumption term. It was convenient to assume earlier that this term was independent of the random error term, but in general this will not be the case. Since consumption generally describes a smooth upward trend with relatively minor fluctuations, consumption of this period and the previous period will be very highly correlated. If this is the case, and C_t and u_t are correlated, it is highly probable that C_{t-1} and u_t will also be correlated. Formally this problem is known as the "distributed lag" bias or "serial correlation" bias[11] and can easily be shown to exist as follows. Assume that the consumption function under consideration was originally transformed from an equation in which consumption depended on an infinite distributed lag of income, so that

(3.7) $$C_t = a \sum_{i=0}^{\infty} \lambda^i Y_{t-i} + e_t$$

where e_t is another random variable. In performing the Koyck transformation

---

[11] For a discussion of this see Z. Griliches, "A Note on Serial Correlation Bias in Estimates of Distributed Lags," *Econometrica*, Vol. 29, No. 1 (January, 1961), pp. 65–73.

previously, the error term was neglected. We should have written

(3.8) $$\lambda C_{t-1} = \lambda a \sum_{i=0}^{\infty} \lambda^{i+1} Y_{t-i-1} + \lambda e_{t-1}$$

with the result that

(3.9) $$C_t = aY_t + \lambda C_{t-1} + (e_t - \lambda e_{t-1})$$

The error term previously designated as u_t is really a composite error term of the form $e_t - \lambda e_{t-1}$. Since C_t and e_t are correlated, C_{t-1} and e_{t-1}, and thus C_{t-1} and u_t, are also correlated. This again invalidates this fundamental assumption of least-squares estimates, and the resulting parameter estimates will again be biased. This bias is in practice even more serious than the simultaneity bias, because no straightforward methods are available to correct the error. Furthermore, standard statistical tests designed to measure and correct this bias are themselves biased and thus of little use. The only way in which this problem has been successfully met in practice is to reformulate the function so that C_t and C_{t-1}, and thus e_t and e_{t-1}, are not so highly correlated. One method that has been widely used for quarterly data is to form a four-quarter moving average for the lagged consumption term of the form $\frac{1}{4} \sum_{i=1}^{4} C_{t-i}$. Another method, discussed below, is to use ratios. Since there is virtually no trend in the consumption/income ratio, other statistical problems are also reduced.

It should be pointed out that in the consumption function the biases due to simultaneity and to the distributed lag will counteract each other. The simultaneity bias will raise the parameter estimate of income; in doing so, it will lower the parameter estimate of lagged consumption. The distributed lag bias will act in the opposite direction. Under some happy but presently undefined set of circumstances these two biases would exactly cancel each other, and unbiased estimates of the consumption function would result. Unfortunately, this is an improbable result. However, the relative magnitudes of these biases can be assessed for different situations, and an estimate of the net bias for each term can be described.

Two general situations can be assessed with some accuracy. First, the simultaneity bias will be stronger and the distributed lag bias will be weaker for total consumption than for consumption excluding durables. This occurs because durable consumption fluctuates much more than other consumption and thus there is not as high a correlation between present and lagged values. Furthermore, there are likely to be more times when purchases of durables are influenced by forces other than income, reversing the direction of causality and increasing the simultaneity bias. Second, the distributed lag bias will be weaker the longer the time period is. For quarterly observations this bias is probably quite strong; for yearly observations it is less important. Thus in a quarterly function for nondurable consumption, the upward bias in the lagged consumption term would considerably outweigh the upward bias in the income term, leading to a net understatement of the short-run mpc. In an annual function for total consumption, the reverse would be more likely to be true and the short-run mpc would probably be overstated. These biases are quite difficult to isolate and measure correctly, so that the above conditions should be taken only to indicate the direction of bias and not any precise magnitude. However, these general guidelines should be useful in interpreting various estimates of the consumption function.

It would seem highly desirable to find some method of eliminating these biases and distortions from the estimates of the parameters of the consumption function without introducing any new biases. In most cases the method of ratios will accomplish this. This form of the function is also preferred for theoretical considerations, since all the theories presented earlier stress the long-run constancy of the C/Y ratio. The use of ratios will reduce the magnitude of all three problems discussed above. First, most of the simultaneity bias is eliminated by making the C/Y ratio primarily a function of lagged variables. A simultaneous upward or downward movement in both consumption and income will tend to keep the C/Y ratio constant rather than move both consumption and income in the same direction, which was the main cause of this bias. It is also clear that ratios remove the common trends of all the variables. The movements of each independent variable are now dissimilar enough to estimate the relative importance of each term much more clearly. The distributed lag bias is also much smaller in ratio form, because the C/Y ratio does not follow as smooth a pattern as does the level of consumption. Although present and lagged C/Y terms may still be correlated, more of this will probably be due to economic reasons and less to spurious statistical correlation.[12]

Consumption functions estimated in ratio form may not be entirely free of bias. The distributed lag bias may still remain, especially for consumption excluding durables. For this reason it has been found advisable to use a four-quarter average of the lagged C/Y ratio rather than the value of the previous quarter. Furthermore, under certain circumstances an additional bias may be introduced into the equation by dividing all the independent variables by income. This will not occur as long as all the variables in the equation are homogeneous,[13] that is, if all the independent variables are proportional to income. This bias will not occur in the case of lagged consumption or wealth, but it may be present in the cases where the percentage change in income is

---

[12] Since the use of ratios eliminates so many statistical problems for the consumption function, it has been suggested that a similar procedure might be useful for estimating other aggregate demand and supply relationships. In general, this will not be the case. Estimates of several econometric models of the United States and other countries by the author show that the problems of simultaneity, multicollinearity, and serial correlation are by far the most severe for consumption functions.

[13] For a discussion of this, see E. Kuh and J. R. Meyer, "Correlation and Regression Estimates When the Data Are Ratios," *Econometrica*, Vol. 23, No. 4 (October, 1955), pp. 400–416.

used as an independent variable. However, this additional bias is thought to be small relative to the biases that have been removed by using ratio functions.

3.2 ADDITIONAL PITFALLS IN MEASURING THE MARGINAL PROPENSITY TO CONSUME

There have been literally hundreds of consumption functions estimated empirically, and we certainly have no intention of reviewing all of them. Instead, we set a few "ground rules" for all consumption functions and then examine the theoretical and empirical results that have been advanced within the framework of these basic qualifications.

1. Every consumption function should include present personal disposable income and past patterns of consumer behavior as independent variables. The latter are usually, but not always, represented by lagged consumption. We shall examine in some detail whether additional terms add to the explanation of consumption.

2. All variables should be measured in constant dollars. There are both economic and statistical reasons for this. Consumers make decisions in terms of their real consumption relative to their real income. If all money incomes and prices of goods and services were to double simultaneously, consumers would still spend the same proportion of their income.[14] On the other hand, if incomes were to double in the short run while prices stayed constant, the consumption/income ratio would decrease until individuals adjusted their spending patterns to the additional real income. From a statistical point of view, if income and consumption both rose only because of price increases, this would introduce yet another element of spurious correlation into the relationship between these two variables. The rise in money consumption and money income would both be due to price increases, suggesting a spurious positive correlation; meanwhile, consumers would be purchasing the same quantity of goods and services with the same real income.

It has sometimes been claimed that consumption and income should be measured in per capita constant-dollar income instead of total constant-dollar income. This is a relevant criticism for those economies with large immigration where the immigrants have a different marginal propensity to consume than other residents of the country. However, it makes virtually no difference which form is used for the U.S. economy. Some regression estimates we computed for both constant dollars, and per capita income showed no significant differences. This is in sharp contrast with the regression equations estimated in current dollars, where the additional bias was quite noticeable. This is

---

[14] This assumes that the money stock also doubles and the interest rate remains constant. The price of bonds will then remain at its original level.

illustrated by the equations in Table 3.2, all of which were estimated for the period 1929–1962 with the war years (1942–1945) omitted.

Perhaps a parenthetical remark is in order at this point about "good" or "bad" values of $\bar{R}^2$ (the fraction of the variance of the dependent variable explained by the regression equation). Some readers may be tempted to conclude that all the $\bar{R}^2$ listed above are very "good" because they are close to unity. However, the high values are due only to the very strong common trend among all the variables. The "naive" consumption function $C = -1.50 + 1.055C_{-1}$ has an $\bar{R}^2$ of 0.995; yet this function is useless for predicting turning points, estimating the effect of a tax cut or other changes in income, or estimating the value of the mpc. It will be useful only in those years in which consumption increases at its average rate during the sample period. In such cases no function is necessary for prediction. By comparison, all the ratio functions to be presented have a much lower $\bar{R}^2$ than the naive model because the trend has been removed, yet all of them do a much better job of explaining consumption patterns.

3. The correct deflator should be used for personal disposable income. The use of the consumption deflator as the correct deflator can be defended on at least two grounds. One argument is the "purchasing power" argument; personal disposable income ought to be deflated by a price index measuring the amount of goods that can be bought in physical terms. Unless consumer savings go directly into the purchase of capital goods, an unlikely occurrence given existing financial institutions, then the consumer price index is to be preferred over these indices, including elements of capital goods formation, such as the overall price deflator. Another argument stems from the neo-classical determination of consumer behavior in which individual consumption functions are homogeneous of degree zero in consumer prices and income. The same basic relationship ought to hold at a macroeconomic level.

In spite of this, some econometric studies have deflated income by the

TABLE 3.2   COMPARISON OF AGGREGATE AND PER CAPITA CONSUMPTION FUNCTIONS

		$\bar{R}^2$
Current dollars	$C = 2.28 + 0.799Y + 0.138C_{-1}$ $(0.050)\quad(0.057)$	0.999
Constant dollars	$C = 5.04 + 0.659Y + 0.280C_{-1}$ $(0.055)\quad(0.064)$	0.999
Constant dollars per capita	$C = 6.37 + 0.652Y + 0.261C_{-1}$ $(0.049)\quad(0.059)$	0.996

Note: Here and in Table 3.3, consumption *includes* purchases of durable goods.

TABLE 3.3 RESULTS OF USING DIFFERENT DEFLATORS FOR ESTIMATING THE CONSUMPTION FUNCTION

		Sample Period	Sum of Coefficients
Ball and Drake	$C = 0.57Y + 0.41C_{-1}$ $(0.06)\quad(0.07)$	1929–1960	0.98 (0.014)
Klein	$C = -4.93 + 0.56Y + 0.44C_{-1}$ $(0.07)\quad(0.07)$	1929–1962	1.00 (0.014)
Evans	$C = 5.04 + 0.66 + 0.28C_{-1}$ $(0.06)\quad(0.06)$	1929–1962	0.94 (0.019)

GNP deflator. This has been done by Klein in his annual models with only one price level,[15] although he avoids this practice in his quarterly models. It has also been attempted by Ball and Drake.[16] It can be shown that the use of the GNP deflator instead of the consumption deflator will *lower* the estimate of the short-run mpc but will *raise* the sum of the coefficients and hence the estimate of the long-run mpc.[17] This is illustrated in the equations given in Table 3.3. These results have additional significance because it was shown in Chapter 2 that if the sum of the coefficients is not significantly different from unity, the consumption function can be shown to be transformed from the original equation $C = kW$, where W is wealth. The estimate 0.98 is not significantly different from unity; the 0.94 figure clearly is, as is shown by the standard error estimates. Thus the use of an improper deflator for the personal disposable income not only biases both the short-run and long-run estimates of the mpc, but it suggests that consumption is a function of wealth instead of income. Other evidence presented shows that this is not true.

The use of the incorrect deflator in the consumption function of the Klein–Goldberger model has also led to other problems of interpretation. For example, Gardner Ackley has written:

> The only statistical study using annual data that has suggested a marginal propensity to consume as low as 0.5 is one by L. R. Klein and A. S. Goldberger. Their consumption function appears as follows:[18]
>
> $$C_t = -22.26 + 0.55W_t + 0.41P_t + 0.34A_t + 0.26C_{t-1} + 0.72L_{t-1} + 0.26N_t \cdots$$

[15] In particular, this method is used in the Klein–Goldberger model and later revisions of this model. The actual equation used in Table 3.3 was taken from L. R. Klein, "Problems in the Estimation of Interdependent Systems," in Wold, *op. cit.*, p. 32.

[16] R. J. Ball and P. S. Drake, "The Relationship Between Aggregate Consumption and Wealth," *International Economic Review*, Vol. 5, No. 1 (January, 1964), pp. 63–81.

[17] M. K. Evans, "The Importance of Wealth in the Consumption Function," *Journal of Political Economy*, Vol. 75, No. 4 (August, 1967), pp. 335–351.

[18] W is personal disposable wage income, P is personal disposable property income, A is personal disposable farm income, L is liquid assets, and N is population. All variables are in billions of constant dollars except population, which is in millions.

If we fit a regression in the simple form $C_t = aY_t + bC_{t-1} + d \cdots$ we obtain the following $C_t = 0.72Y_t + 0.17C_{t-1} + 82.2 \cdots$. It is difficult to explain, fully why the marginal propensity to consume is so much higher and the coefficient of lagged income so much lower than Klein–Goldberger's.[19]

As noted above, Klein's estimate is too low, because of the use of the GNP deflator for personal disposable income. This is unavoidable in a model with only one price level. His estimate of 0.50 for the yearly mpc is lower than the value of 0.56 given in Table 3.3, where the GNP deflator was also used, because of the inclusion of the population term. The per capita regression given in Table 3.3 shows that the inclusion of population in the consumption function should have virtually no effect on the value of the mpc. However, because consumption, income, and population all have similar trends, the problem of multicollinearity is present. Part of the increase in consumption, which is really due to rising income, is attributed to the growth in population. This problem can be partially rectified by relating movements in population and income and substituting this relationship into the consumption function. For the sample period of this model (1929–1952), an increase in personal disposable income of $1 billion in 1939 dollars was accompanied by an increase in population of about 0.4 million. Substituting 0.4 for N in the consumption function would raise the yearly mpc to almost 0.6.

However, this does not explain why Ackley should have obtained such a high value of the yearly mpc (which he simply designates as "the" mpc). There are at least two reasons why Ackley's estimate is undoubtedly too high. First, he ignores the simultaneity bias and uses ordinary least-squares estimates. Second, he omits 1941, a nonwar year in the United States, because it does not fit very well. This procedure is rather puzzling and can hardly be recommended for empirical research. Rejecting observations for arbitrary reasons can be a dangerous method of estimating functions and may result in severely distorted parameter estimates.

4. Functions that claim to explain long-run consumer behavior should show that the long-run mpc is equal to the apc. This relationship is stressed by the relative income hypothesis, the permanent income hypothesis, and the life-cycle hypothesis. It is very hard to justify the claim that once an individual receives extra income he will always continue to spend a smaller percentage of this income than of all his other income. Eventually this extra income must be combined with other sources of income and treated in the same way. The question of when "eventually" arrives is an empirical question to be determined by the lag structure of the consumption function being estimated. Failure to obtain this result may indicate either that the independent variables do not explain consumption adequately, or that the parameters are biased due to the statistical methods selected and do not measure what they are supposed

---

[19] G. Ackley, *Macroeconomic Theory* (New York: Macmillan, 1961), pp. 263–264.

to measure. As indicated earlier, the problem of biases is more likely to be prevalent in functions estimated in level form than in ratio form.

It should be pointed out that in general the estimate of the long-run mpc obtained from ratio functions will be almost identical to the apc and thus the ratio functions assume this result. Consider the function $C/Y = a + bZ$, where Z can be any relevant ratio variable in the consumption function. Because $a = \overline{(C/Y)} - b\bar{Z}$ (barred variables are sample-period mean values), then

$$(3.10) \qquad \frac{C}{Y} = a + bZ = \left(\overline{\frac{C}{Y}}\right) - b\bar{Z} + bZ = \left(\overline{\frac{C}{Y}}\right) + b(Z - \bar{Z})$$

If the long-run average value of Z is in fact equal to the average value of Z over the sample period, which is likely to happen, then in the long-run $Z = \bar{Z}$ and $C/Y = \overline{C/Y}$. In this case the long-run mpc will equal the apc. Thus the fact that $C/Y = \overline{C/Y}$ cannot be used to determine the usefulness of any ratio function. The usefulness of the test of whether the long-run mpc equals the apc is restricted to levels functions. Ratio functions also force what would be the constant term in the corresponding levels equation to be zero; thus levels functions with a small positive constant term will probably understate the long-run mpc.

We have examined some of the reasons various estimates of the consumption function give different results. At this point some of the consumption functions based on the theories developed in Chapter 2 are compared and the estimates of the short-run and long-run mpc's which they imply are examined. In particular, the empirical estimates of consumption functions based on the theories of Duesenberry, Friedman, and Modigliani will be analyzed.

3.3   ESTIMATES OF THE CONSUMPTION FUNCTION AND THE MARGINAL PROPENSITY TO CONSUME

The simplest function consistent with the basic qualifications outlined in the previous section is Friedman's permanent income hypothesis,[20] which can be written $C_t = kY_{p_t}$, where Y_p is permanent income. If a distributed lag of present and previous disposable personal income with geometrically declining weights is substituted for permanent income, which is the substitution used by Friedman, and the Koyck transformation is performed, the function is $C_t = (1 - \lambda)kY_t + \lambda C_{t-1}$, where λ is the ratio of the weights in two successive years. This is of course very similar to the simple function discussed extensively in the earlier sections of this chapter, but without the constant term.

Several extensions of this particular theory have been supplied, most of them

---

[20] M. Friedman, *A Theory of the Consumption Function* (Princeton, N.J.: Princeton University Press for NBER, 1957).

involving alternative substitutions of terms for permanent income. One such ingenious alternative has been suggested by Mincer.[21] His substitution incorporates the idea that permanent Y = measured Y + transitory Y. If we let Y = measured income and Z = permanent income, then

(3.11) $$C = dZ + a(Y - Z)$$

and thus

(3.12) $$C = aY + (d - a)Z = aY + bZ$$

or, in ratio form,

(3.13) $$C/Y = a + b(Z/Y)$$

The problem has thus been reduced from measuring permanent income to measuring the ratio of permanent to measured income. Mincer considers several variables that might measure Z/Y; the one that he thinks gives the most satisfactory results is population/man-hours (P/M). Ando and Modigliani[22] have used Mincer's general idea but have substituted labor force/employment (L/E) for P/M. Their ratio is preferable because it removes the effect of the declining trend in individual man-hours, which has no counterpart in the steady (or slightly increasing) C/Y ratio. The form of the permanent income hypothesis $C/Y = a + b(L/E)$ is also tested. One would not expect the lagged C/Y ratio to be significant in this function, because permanent income is already represented by a proxy variable.

Another extension of the permanent income hypothesis, which avoids the use of additional proxy variables for Z, has been developed by this author. Since $C = kZ$ in equilibrium, the consumption function can be written simply $C/Y = k$ when measured income equals permanent income. In estimating the actual consumption function one must in effect determine what happens when measured and normal income are not equal. When this is the case, the consumption function will be of the form $C/Y = k - a[(Y - Z)/Y]$. This is similar to other forms of the permanent income hypothesis except that it is now necessary to measure $Y - Z$ instead of Z or Z/Y.

It is assumed that the average individual expects to receive a certain increase in income during each time period; this expected increase may be set equal to the average percentage increase over the last t periods. Since this average changes very slowly over time, it can be approximated by the average percentage increase of income over the sample period. This component of the actual change in income is considered by each individual to be part of his permanent income. Any deviation from this average increase, positive or negative, will be considered as transitory income. The relationship of permanent and transitory

[21] J. Mincer, "Employment and Consumption," *Review of Economics and Statistics*, Vol. 42, No. 1 (February, 1960), pp. 20–26.
[22] Ando and Modigliani, *op. cit.*

income should properly be considered for past periods as well as the present. If the convenient specification is made that the importance of previous changes in income declines geometrically, we have the function

$$(3.14) \quad \left(\frac{C}{Y}\right)_t = k - a\left[\left(\frac{\Delta Y - \overline{\Delta Y}}{Y}\right)_t + \lambda\left(\frac{\Delta Y - \overline{\Delta Y}}{Y}\right)_{t-1}\right.$$
$$\left. + \lambda^2\left(\frac{\Delta Y - \overline{\Delta Y}}{Y}\right)_{t-2} + \cdots\right]$$

where barred variables are average values. This could be transformed directly into the form

$$(3.15) \quad \left(\frac{C}{Y}\right)_t = (1 - \lambda)k - a\left(\frac{\Delta Y - \overline{\Delta Y}}{Y}\right)_t + \lambda\left(\frac{C}{Y}\right)_{t-1}$$

but even in ratio form there will be a very high correlation between $(C/Y)_t$ and $(C/Y)_{t-1}$, which is likely to lead to distributed lag bias. It is preferable to transform the equation so that a four-quarter average of C/Y is obtained for the lagged term. This is accomplished by repeating the Koyck transformation for each of the four previous periods, as follows:

$$(3.16) \quad \tfrac{1}{4}\lambda\left(\frac{C}{Y}\right)_{t-1} = \tfrac{1}{4}\lambda k - \tfrac{1}{4}a\left[\lambda\left(\frac{\Delta Y - \overline{\Delta Y}}{Y}\right)_{t-1} + \lambda^2\left(\frac{\Delta Y - \overline{\Delta Y}}{Y}\right)_{t-2} + \cdots\right]$$

$$\vdots \qquad \vdots \qquad \qquad \vdots$$

$$\tfrac{1}{4}\lambda^4\left(\frac{C}{Y}\right)_{t-4} = \tfrac{1}{4}\lambda^4 k - \tfrac{1}{4}a\left[\lambda^4\left(\frac{\Delta Y - \overline{\Delta Y}}{Y}\right)_{t-4} + \lambda^5\left(\frac{\Delta Y - \overline{\Delta Y}}{Y}\right)_{t-5} + \cdots\right]$$

Subtracting these four equations from the original function, we obtain

$$(3.17) \quad \left(\frac{C}{Y}\right)_t = k\left(1 - \frac{1}{4}\sum_{i=1}^{4}\lambda^i\right) - a\left[\left(\frac{\Delta Y - \overline{\Delta Y}}{Y}\right)_t + 0.75\lambda\left(\frac{\Delta Y - \overline{\Delta Y}}{Y}\right)_{t-1}\right.$$
$$\left. + 0.50\lambda^2\left(\frac{\Delta Y - \overline{\Delta Y}}{Y}\right)_{t-2} + 0.25\lambda^3\left(\frac{\Delta Y - \overline{\Delta Y}}{Y}\right)_{t-3}\right] + \frac{1}{4}\sum_{i=1}^{4}\lambda^i\left(\frac{C}{Y}\right)_{t-i}$$

Since $\overline{\Delta Y}/Y$ is constant to a first approximation, these terms can be regrouped and the function simplified to

$$(3.18) \quad \left(\frac{C}{Y}\right)_t = k^* - a\left[\left(\frac{\Delta Y}{Y}\right)_t + 0.75\lambda\left(\frac{\Delta Y}{Y}\right)_{t-1} + 0.50\lambda^2\left(\frac{\Delta Y}{Y}\right)_{t-2}\right.$$
$$\left. + 0.25\lambda^3\left(\frac{\Delta Y}{Y}\right)_{t-3}\right] + \frac{1}{4}\sum_{i=1}^{4}\lambda^i\left(\frac{C}{Y}\right)_{t-i}$$

where

(3.19)
$$k^* = k\left(1 - \frac{1}{4}\sum_{i=1}^{4}\lambda^i\right) - a\sum_{i=0}^{3}\lambda^i\left(\frac{4-i}{4}\right)\overline{\left(\frac{\Delta Y}{Y}\right)}_{t-i}$$

This equation cannot be estimated by linear methods because of the simultaneous determination of a and λ in the change in income term and also the nonlinear way in which λ enters the lagged C/Y term. Although an iterative procedure could have been developed, we used a much simpler method by assuming λ is close to unity and estimating the equation directly. The numerical estimates obtained for this equation are[23]

(15.1)
$$\frac{C_{ns}}{Y} = 0.2273 - 0.4590\left[\left(\frac{\Delta Y}{Y}\right) + 0.75\left(\frac{\Delta Y}{Y}\right)_{-1} + 0.50\left(\frac{\Delta Y}{Y}\right)_{-2}\right.$$
$$\left. + 0.25\left(\frac{\Delta Y}{Y}\right)_{-3}\right] + 0.7232\,\frac{1}{4}\sum_{i=1}^{4}\left(\frac{C_{ns}}{Y}\right)_{-i} \qquad \overline{R}^2 = 0.825$$

where C_{ns} is the consumption of nondurables and services, billions of 1958 dollars, and Y is personal disposable income, billions of 1958 dollars. The time path of the mpc calculated from this function is given in Table 3.4. The method of calculation of these values is given in the appendix to this chapter.

The other functions that are included for comparison have already been discussed in Chapter 2. The original Duesenberry function was of the form $S/Y = a + b(Y/Y^0)$,[24] where Y^0 is peak previous income; this can be rewritten as $C/Y = (1 - a) - b(Y/Y^0)$. Later Duesenberry, Eckstein, and Fromm modified this function to include the effects of past values of the Y/Y^0 ratio.[25] Their revised function can then be written[26]

(3.20)
$$\left(\frac{C}{Y}\right)_t = (1 - a) - b\left[\left(\frac{Y}{Y^0}\right)_t + \lambda\left(\frac{Y}{Y^0}\right)_{t-1} + \cdots\right]$$

---

[23] Throughout the first part of this book, equations will be given that have been estimated by this author and L. R. Klein. These equations taken together form a new quarterly model known as the Wharton Econometric and Forecasting Unit (Wharton EFU) model. This model is presented in toto in Section 15.3. Equations with these numbers correspond exactly with those of Section 15.3. To provide empirical estimates of the various functions in the same context as the theoretical derivations, I have also included these equations in the chapters describing the individual functions of the model.

[24] J. S. Duesenberry, *Income, Saving, and the Theory of Consumer Behavior* (Cambridge, Mass.: Harvard University Press, 1949).

[25] J. S. Duesenberry, O. Eckstein, and G. Fromm, "A Simulation of the United States Economy in Recession," *Econometrica*, Vol. 28, No. 4 (October, 1960), pp. 749–810.

[26] *Ibid.*, p. 803. Actually their lag structure is of the form $C_t/Y_{t-1} = (1 - a) - b(Y_{t-1}/Y_{t-1}^0) + \lambda(C_{t-1}/Y_{t-2})$. Since present income is not included anywhere in the equation, this gives a first-period mpc of zero. This does not seem reasonable, so we have modified their function slightly and used it as given above.

TABLE 3.4 TIME PATH OF THE
VALUES OF THE MARGINAL
PROPENSITY TO CONSUME

Quarter No.	mpc
1	0.334
2	0.372
3	0.411
4	0.457
5	0.510
6	0.543
7	0.574
8	0.604
9	0.630
10	0.652
11	0.672
12	0.689
⋮	⋮
∞	0.789

After transformation, this becomes

$$(3.21) \qquad \left(\frac{C}{Y}\right)_t = (1 - a)(1 - \lambda) - b\left(\frac{Y}{Y^0}\right)_t + \lambda\left(\frac{C}{Y}\right)_{t-1}$$

It is somewhat easier to examine the implications of this function if the Y/Y^0 term is inverted; since this ratio is almost always close to unity, this will make very little difference. Thus the form of the function that we test is

$$(3.22) \qquad \left(\frac{C}{Y}\right)_t = (1 - a')(1 - \lambda) + b'\left(\frac{Y^0}{Y}\right)_t + \lambda'\left(\frac{C}{Y}\right)_{t-1}$$

This equation is designated as the DEF function. The Ando–Modigliani function is of the form[27]

$$(3.23) \qquad \left(\frac{C}{Y_L}\right)_t = a + b\frac{W_{t-1}}{(Y_L)_t} \qquad \text{or} \qquad \left(\frac{C}{Y_L}\right)_t = a' + b'\frac{W_{t-1}}{(Y_L)_t} + c'\left(\frac{L}{E}\right)_t$$

where Y_L is labor income and W is net worth (wealth) of households. This function is not directly comparable to the other functions for several reasons. First, labor income is used as the income variable instead of total personal disposable income. Second, the equation is estimated in current dollars

---

[27] Ando and Modigliani, *op. cit.*

instead of constant dollars. Third, it is estimated for consumption of non-durables and services plus use value of consumer durables.[28] Although an attempt has been made to reconcile these estimates with those obtained from other equations, some small differences may still exist.

It is of interest to compare both yearly and quarterly functions to see if the mpc of the first four quarters is approximately equal to the mpc estimated from the yearly function. This provides an additional check of internal consistency of the estimates and also may be useful in determining the approximate magnitudes of some of the biases. Since very few yearly observations have yet occurred in the postwar period, the annual functions are estimated for the period 1929–1962, omitting 1942–1946. Besides the actual equation estimates, estimates of $\bar{R}^2$, the Durbin–Watson statistic (d),[29] the yearly mpc, and the long-run mpc are given for each equation in Table 3.5. It should be stressed that all these consumption functions exclude purchases of consumer durables. The latter are treated separately in Chapter 6.

A wide variety of different hypotheses appear to be satisfied. The coefficients of the variables in all the consumption functions chosen for comparison are highly significant in all cases and give reasonable values of the short-run and long-run mpc's. The yearly mpc for the levels function is probably understated. This would appear to be a clear case of the distributed lag bias resulting in an underestimate of the income coefficient, particularly for nondurables and services. The Friedman–Mincer function yearly mpc may be understated because we have assumed that the labor force is unaffected by changes in income; this is not strictly true. The yearly mpc for the DEF function is somewhat higher than the other values obtained; this difference disappears when the quarterly functions are considered. From these estimates, we can say that the yearly mpc for nondurables and services is between 0.35 and 0.45.

We now consider the quarterly results for the postwar period. These equations are estimated for the period 1947–1962. The results, shown in Table 3.6, are quite different for these functions. The equations with the W/Y ratio and the labor force/employment ratio perform very poorly. When a lagged C/Y term is added to these equations, the other terms are clearly insignificant; when this was tried for the yearly functions, it was the $(C/Y)_{-1}$ term that was not significant. On the other hand, the levels, DEF, and Evans functions continue to give reasonable results, although the quarterly mpc of the levels function continues to be biased downward because of the distributed lag bias. The

---

[28] I originally intended to estimate this function on a comparable basis with the other functions. However, Albert Ando pointed out that this would not be a test of the Ando–Modigliani function but of some other hypothesis.

[29] The Durbin–Watson statistic measures the degree of serial correlation of the residuals. If positive serial correlation exists, the standard error estimates are biased downward and $\bar{R}^2$ is biased upward. If $d = 2.0$, no serial correlation exists; a value of $d < 1.4$ generally indicates positive serial correlation. For a further discussion of this statistic, see Johnston, *op. cit.*, chap. VIII. However, it should be pointed out that this statistic is biased upward toward the value of 2.0 if the lagged dependent variable is included in the regression; on this see Griliches, *op. cit.*

TABLE 3.5 COMPARISON OF
VARIOUS ANNUAL CONSUMPTION FUNCTIONS[a]

	$\bar{R}^2$	d	Yearly mpc	Long-Run mpc
1. $C = 0.280Y + 0.676C_{-1}$ $\quad(0.041)\quad(0.052)$	0.998	1.09	0.280	0.828
2. $C/Y = 0.343 + 0.440(L/E)$ $\quad\quad\quad\quad\quad(0.042)$	0.792	1.45	0.343	0.834
3. $C/Y = 0.104 - 0.402(\Delta Y/Y)$ $\quad\quad\quad\quad\quad(0.029)$ $\quad + 0.884(C/Y)_{-1}$ $\quad\quad(0.038)$	0.962	2.05	0.440	0.834
4. $C/Y = 0.209 + 0.267Y^o/Y$ $\quad\quad\quad\quad\quad(0.041)$ $\quad + 0.423(C/Y)_{-1}$ $\quad\quad(0.097)$	0.864	1.38	0.561	0.834
5. $C^*/Y_L = 0.602 + 0.085(W_{-1}/Y_L)$ $\quad\quad\quad\quad\quad\quad(0.003)$	0.959	1.53	0.447^b	0.834^b

[a] C, consumption of nondurables and services, billions of constant dollars; C^*, consumption of nondurables and services plus use value of consumer durables, billions of current dollars; Y, personal disposable income, billions of constant dollars; Y^o, peak previous income, billions of constant dollars; Y_L, disposable labor income, billions of current dollars; L, labor force, millions; E, employment, millions.

[b] Adjusted to be comparable with the other functions.

Source: Taken, with some modification, from M. K. Evans, "The Importance of Wealth in the Consumption Function," *Journal of Political Economy*, Vol. 75, No. 4 (August, 1967), pp. 335–351.

quarterly mpc for nondurables and services is approximately 0.3 to 0.35. Of some interest are the identical values of the quarterly mpc from the DEF and Evans functions.

The comparisons of the yearly mpc's taken from the annual functions and the quarterly functions are given in Table 3.7. It can be seen that in general there is substantial consistency, although the results are not exact.

The failure of the Ando-Modigliani and Friedman–Mincer functions to perform satisfactorily in the postwar period is primarily due to the period right after the war; this problem was discussed in Chapter 2. Recall that in the early postwar years, the C/Y ratio was very high even though the economy was near full employment, and the W/Y ratio was below its long-run average. The Friedman–Mincer function posits that the C/Y ratio will be high only in times of recession or depression and does not take into account the possibility that personal disposable income might decrease during periods of

TABLE 3.6   COMPARISON OF
VARIOUS QUARTERLY CONSUMPTION FUNCTIONS[a]

	$\bar{R}^2$	d	Quarterly mpc	Long-Run mpc
1. $C = 0.222Y + 0.738 \dfrac{1}{4}\sum\limits_{i=1}^{4} C_{-i}$ $\quad$ (0.030)$\quad$(0.038)	0.998	1.76	0.222	0.807
2. $C/Y = 0.606 + 0.189(L/E)$ $\qquad\qquad$ (0.158)	0.007	0.49	0.606	0.803
2a. $C/Y = 0.158 + 0.038(L/E)$ $\qquad\qquad$ (0.105)				
$\quad + 0.755 \dfrac{1}{4}\sum\limits_{i=1}^{4}\left(\dfrac{C}{Y}\right)_{-i}$ $\quad$ (0.083)	0.570	2.31	0.765	0.803
3. $C/Y = 0.227 - 0.459 \sum\limits_{i=1}^{4}\dfrac{4-i}{4}\left(\dfrac{\Delta Y}{Y}\right)_{-i}$ $\qquad\qquad$ (0.049)				
$\quad + 0.723 \dfrac{1}{4}\sum\limits_{i=1}^{4}\left(\dfrac{C}{Y}\right)_{-i}$ $\quad$ (0.051)	0.825	1.58	0.334	0.789[b]
4. $C/Y = 0.082 + 0.470(Y^0/Y)$ $\qquad\qquad$ (0.042)				
$\quad + 0.313 \dfrac{1}{4}\sum\limits_{i=1}^{4}\left(\dfrac{C}{Y}\right)_{-i}$ $\quad$ (0.071)	0.826	1.19	0.333	0.803
5. $C^*/Y_L = 0.815 + 0.046(W_{-1}/Y_L)$ $\qquad\qquad$ (0.014)	0.130	0.68	0.617[c]	0.803[c]
5a. $C^*/Y_L + 0.201 + 0.011(W_{-1}/Y_L)$ $\qquad\qquad$ (0.010)				
$\quad 0.766 \dfrac{1}{4}\sum\limits_{i=1}^{4}\left(\dfrac{C^*}{Y_L}\right)_{-i}$ $\quad$ (0.078)	0.658	2.09	0.152[c]	0.803[c]

[a] All the symbols are identical to those used in Table 3.5.
[b] Estimated 1948–1964.
[c] Adjusted to be comparable with the other functions.
Source: Taken, with some modifications, from M. K. Evans, "The Importance of Wealth in the Consumption Function," *Journal of Political Economy,* Vol. 75, No. 4 (August, 1967), pp. 335–351.

substantial inflation. Once full employment has been reached, further increases in *ex ante* demand will usually result in a redistribution of income through inflation, and thus a decrease in personal disposable income occurs. The Ando–Modigliani function does not consider the fact that in the short run, consumption and savings (which are additions to wealth) are likely to be

TABLE 3.7 COMPARISON OF VALUES OF
THE YEARLY MARGINAL PROPENSITY TO CONSUME

	Yearly mpc from Annual Functions	Yearly mpc from Quarterly Functions[a]
1	0.280	0.292
2	0.343	[b]
3	0.440	0.394
4	0.561	0.514
5	0.447	[b]

[a] Average of the mpc's for first four quarters.
[b] Dynamic structure not given by the functions, so these terms cannot be calculated.

substitutes rather than complements. Furthermore, in times of inflation the W/Y ratio is likely to decrease if a substantial amount of wealth is held in fixed-value assets. Although the nominal value of savings deposits and savings bonds accumulated by patriotic workers during the war rose 10 percent during the period 1945–1948, a rise in the general price level of 50 percent in the same period reduced the real value of these assets by almost one third. It is not likely that this decline was responsible for the very high C/Y ratios in the early postwar period. It is more likely that consumers based their spending patterns at least partially on previous higher levels of real income.

The foregoing examination would suggest that at least the aggregate implications of the life-cycle hypothesis are inconsistent with observed postwar behavior. As discussed in Chapter 2, the strict proportionality statement of this hypothesis ($C = kW$) requires that the yearly mpc be less than 0.2 and that the coefficients of the equation $C = aY + bC_{-1}$ sum to unity. Even when the estimate of the yearly mpc for nondurables and services is biased downward, it is still almost 0.3, and the values $a + b$ sum to significantly less than unity when the correct deflator for income is used. Furthermore, in the more generalized version of the hypothesis, the W/Y ratio explains very little of the fluctuations in the postwar C/Y ratio and is clearly insignificant when the lagged C/Y ratio is added to the function.

3.4   CONCLUDING COMMENTS ON THE CONSUMPTION FUNCTION

In this chapter, as in Chapter 2, we have tried to stress that there is no such monolithic concept as "the" marginal propensity to consume. Instead, the change in consumption resulting from a unit change in personal disposable income is different for every different time period, and it increases monotonically as the time span lengthens. This view of the mpc has been advanced most strongly by Friedman, but is also incorporated in the work of

Duesenberry, Modigliani, and others. Friedman also showed how this concept of consumer behavior logically leads to the conclusion that the long-run mpc must be equal to the apc. Although it is not possible to test this statement exactly because of the biases encountered in estimating the consumption function, the available evidence for time-series analysis does support this position.[30] It was also found that these biases can best be eliminated by estimating the consumption function in ratio form, a form that is also preferable from a theoretical point of view.

For policy purposes it may be of interest to examine the best estimates of the mpc at different time periods. It was found that for nondurables and services, the quarterly mpc was about 0.3 or 0.35, and the yearly mpc was between 0.35 and to 0.45. In general, the yearly mpc was about 0.1 higher than the quarterly mpc for corresponding functions, whatever the actual calculated values.[31] When these values can be compared to the apc for nondurables and services of 0.80, it is seen that the consumption function approaches its long-run equilibrium value very slowly, so that changes in income are likely to affect consumption patterns at a differential rate for several years. This has obvious implications for various types of fiscal policies, particularly tax cuts, which are discussed in the framework of overall multiplier analysis after other components of aggregate demand and supply have been considered.

It should again be mentioned that these figures do not represent the various values of the mpc for total consumption; purchases of consumer durables are not considered until Chapter 6. Because of the stock-adjustment nature of the consumer durable functions, the mpc for durables is likely to decrease over time and thus have an offsetting influence on the steadily increasing nature of the mpc for nondurables and services. Thus the question of the value of the mpc for total consumption cannot properly be answered until the separate nature of the consumer durable functions has been analyzed.

The function that we use in the Wharton EFU model (see p. 62, footnote 23) is based on the permanent income hypothesis. This theory has been found to agree more closely with observed consumer behavior than either the relative income or life-cycle hypotheses. However, a somewhat different empirical formulation than the one used by Friedman is suggested here. Because of severe statistical problems peculiar to estimating the consumption function, it is preferable to formulate the equation in ratio form and use a weighted average of lagged consumption. The short-run differences between transitory and permanent components of measured income are emphasized by using *changes* in actual and average income.

Consumption of nondurables and services has been found to be a function

---

[30] The results presented in Chapter 2 suggest that the permanent income hypothesis is verified by cross-section data as well, although these conclusions are not quite as strong.

[31] This does not include those functions which did not work for the postwar period.

of permanent income, usually represented as a weighted average of past incomes, and of the transitory elements of present income. Other variables sometimes suggested as determinants of consumption were found to have no significant effect, at least for the postwar U.S. economy. In particular, it was found that the stock of household wealth was not an additional determinant of consumption. Thus various asset effects which have suggested that the C/Y ratio increases when prices fall because of the greater real value of wealth have been found to have virtually no empirical support.[32] In this respect we have tested a rather elegant version of the wealth–income hypothesis; some simpler regressions we estimated, which simply correlate the C/Y ratio with the W/Y ratio, show even less effect of the latter term, which occasionally has a negative sign. So-called strategic components of wealth which were tried, such as liquid assets, also were not significant. In fact, additional evidence presented in Chapter 6 offers support for the hypothesis that consumption and liquid assets are substitutes rather than complements. Other variables that have sometimes been suggested for inclusion in the consumption function, such as income distribution between wages and property income, population, and family composition, also have little influence on aggregate time-series estimates.

In spite of the fact that the consumption function is a relatively simple function in the sense that it does not contain a large number of different terms, great care should be taken in formulating and estimating it correctly. Biased or distorted estimates may give radically different results when these functions are used for forecasting and policy simulation. Since the values of the mpc over time of these values are perhaps the most important parameters in policy decisions, accurate estimates of these values are particularly important.

---

[32] These effects are discussed briefly in Section 13.1.

APPENDIX to Chapter 3

Method of Calculating Values of the Marginal Propensity to Consume

The calculations of the short-run and long-run mpc's are not always apparent by inspection. Here we show how they are calculated for each equation. All calculations include relevant growth factors. The growth rate, λ, is taken to be 0.02 per year for the 1929–1962 functions and 0.0075 per quarter for the postwar calculations.

(A3.1) $$C = a + bY + dC_{-1} \qquad \text{s.r. mpc} = b$$

The l.r. mpc can be calculated by setting $C_{-1} = (1/[1 + \lambda])C$. Then

$$C\left(1 - \frac{d}{1 + \lambda}\right) = a + bY \qquad \text{and} \qquad \text{l.r. mpc} = \frac{b}{1 - (d/[1 + \lambda])}.$$

(A3.2) $$\frac{C}{Y} = a + b\frac{L}{E} \qquad \text{s.r. mpc} = a \text{ (we assume that } E = \alpha Y)$$

In the long run $L/E \cong \overline{(L/E)}$. Therefore,

$$\frac{C}{Y} = a + \left(\frac{\overline{L}}{\overline{E}}\right) \cdot b \qquad \text{and} \qquad \text{l.r. mpc} = a + \left(\frac{\overline{L}}{\overline{E}}\right) \cdot b$$

(A3.2a) $$\frac{C}{Y} = a + b\frac{L}{E} + d\left(\frac{C}{Y}\right)_{-1}$$

$$C = aY + \frac{b}{\alpha} \cdot L + d\left(\frac{C}{Y}\right)_{-1} \cdot Y$$

$$\text{s.r. mpc} = a + d\left(\frac{C}{Y}\right)_{-1} \qquad \text{taking } \left(\frac{\overline{C}}{\overline{Y}}\right)_{-1} \text{ at its mean value}$$

$$\text{l.r. mpc} = \frac{a + b\overline{(L/E)}}{1 - d}.$$

(A3.3) $$\frac{C}{Y} = a - b\left[\frac{\Delta Y}{Y} + 0.75\left(\frac{\Delta Y}{Y}\right)_{-1} + 0.50\left(\frac{\Delta Y}{Y}\right)_{-2} + 0.25\left(\frac{\Delta Y}{Y}\right)_{-3}\right] + d\frac{1}{4}\sum_{i=1}^{4}\left(\frac{C}{Y}\right)_{-i}$$

$$C = aY + b\left[\Delta Y + 0.75\Delta Y_{-1}\left(\frac{Y}{Y_{-1}}\right) + 0.50\Delta Y_{-2}\left(\frac{Y}{Y_{-2}}\right) + 0.25\Delta Y_{-3}\left(\frac{Y}{Y_{-3}}\right)\right]$$

$$+ d\left[\frac{1}{4}\sum_{i=1}^{4}\left(\frac{C}{Y}\right)_{-i}\right]Y$$

Therefore,

$$\Delta C \cong a\Delta Y - b[\Delta(\Delta Y) + 0.75\Delta(\Delta Y_{-1}) + 0.50\Delta(\Delta Y_{-2}) + 0.25\Delta(\Delta Y_{-3})]$$

$$+ \frac{d}{4}\left[\Delta C_{-1} + \Delta C_{-2} + \Delta C_{-3} + \Delta C_{-4} + 4\left(\frac{\overline{C}}{\overline{Y}}\right)\Delta Y - \left(\frac{\overline{C}}{\overline{Y}}\right)\Delta Y_{-1} - \left(\frac{\overline{C}}{\overline{Y}}\right)\Delta Y_{-2}\right.$$

$$\left. - \left(\frac{\overline{C}}{\overline{Y}}\right)\Delta Y_{-3} - \left(\frac{\overline{C}}{\overline{Y}}\right)\Delta Y_{-4}\right]$$

The s.r. mpc in the following periods, with $\overline{(C/Y)}$ taken at its mean value, are

t:
$$\left(\frac{\Delta C}{\Delta Y}\right)_t = a - b + d\left(\frac{\overline{C}}{Y}\right)$$

$t + 1$:
$$\left(\frac{\Delta C}{\Delta Y}\right)_{t+1} = a - 0.75b + 0.75\left(\frac{\overline{C}}{Y}\right) + \frac{d}{4}\left(\frac{\Delta C}{\Delta Y}\right)_t$$

$t + 2$:
$$\left(\frac{\Delta C}{\Delta Y}\right)_{t+2} = a - 0.50b + 0.50\left(\frac{\overline{C}}{Y}\right) + \frac{d}{4}\left[\left(\frac{\Delta C}{\Delta Y}\right)_t + \left(\frac{\Delta C}{\Delta Y}\right)_{t+1}\right]$$

$t + 3$:
$$\left(\frac{\Delta C}{\Delta Y}\right)_{t+3} = a - 0.25b + 0.25\left(\frac{\overline{C}}{Y}\right) + \frac{d}{4}\left[\left(\frac{\Delta C}{\Delta Y}\right)_t + \left(\frac{\Delta C}{\Delta Y}\right)_{t+1} + \left(\frac{\Delta C}{\Delta Y}\right)_{t+2}\right]$$

$t + 4$:
$$\left(\frac{\Delta C}{\Delta Y}\right)_{t+4} = a + \frac{d}{4}\left[\left(\frac{\Delta C}{\Delta Y}\right)_t + \left(\frac{\Delta C}{\Delta Y}\right)_{t+1} + \left(\frac{\Delta C}{\Delta Y}\right)_{t+2} + \left(\frac{\Delta C}{\Delta Y}\right)_{t+3}\right]$$

$t + j$:
$$\left(\frac{\Delta C}{\Delta Y}\right)_{t+j} = a + d(\tfrac{1}{4})\sum_{i=1}^{4}\left(\frac{\Delta C}{\Delta Y}\right)_{t+j-i}$$

These formulas are only approximate, because the growth in income has been neglected. Thus in the long run the formula $C/Y = a/(1 - d)$ must be modified to $(a - 2.5\lambda b)/(1 - d)$. For the yearly version of this function,

$$\frac{C}{Y} = a - b\left(\frac{\Delta Y}{Y}\right) + d\left(\frac{C}{Y}\right)_{-1}$$

the relationships are similar but easier. For the first year

$$\frac{\Delta C}{\Delta Y} = a - b + d\left(\frac{C}{Y}\right)$$

the second year

$$\left(\frac{\Delta C}{\Delta Y}\right)_{t+1} \cong a + d\left(\frac{\Delta C}{\Delta Y}\right)_t$$

and in the long run

$$\frac{\Delta C}{\Delta Y} = \frac{a - \lambda b}{1 - d}.$$

(A3.4)
$$\frac{C}{Y} = a + b\frac{Y^0}{Y} + d\left(\frac{C}{Y}\right)_{-1}$$

Therefore,

$$C = aY + bY^0 + d\left(\frac{C}{Y}\right)_{-1} \cdot Y$$

The s.r. mpc $= a + d\overline{(C/Y)}_{-1}$ [again take $\overline{(C/Y)}_{-1}$ at its mean value]. In the long run

$$\frac{C}{Y} = \left(\frac{C}{Y}\right)_{-1} \quad \text{and} \quad \frac{Y^0}{Y} = \frac{Y_{-1}}{Y} = \frac{Y}{(1 + \lambda)Y} = \frac{1}{1 + \lambda}$$

Therefore,

$$\frac{C}{Y} = a + \frac{b}{1 + \lambda} + d\left(\frac{C}{Y}\right) \quad \text{and} \quad \frac{C}{Y} = \frac{a(1 + \lambda) + b}{(1 + \lambda)(1 - d)}.$$

(A3.5)
$$\frac{C^*}{Y_L} = a + b\frac{W_{-1}}{Y_L}$$

This needs to be converted to C and Y to be comparable with other estimates of the short-run and long-run mpc:

$$\frac{\Delta C^*}{\Delta Y_L}\left(\frac{\Delta C}{\Delta C^*}\right)\left(\frac{\Delta Y_L}{\Delta Y}\right) = \left(a + b\frac{\Delta W_{-1}}{\Delta Y_L}\right)\left(\frac{\Delta C}{\Delta C^*}\right)\left(\frac{\Delta Y_L}{\Delta Y}\right)$$

Assume that

$$\frac{\Delta C}{\Delta C^*} = \left(\overline{\frac{C}{C^*}}\right) \quad \text{and} \quad \frac{\Delta Y_L}{\Delta Y} = \left(\overline{\frac{Y_L}{Y}}\right)$$

In general, these will be close approximations, because both C and C^* exclude purchases of durables and both Y_L and Y exclude highly cyclical corporate profits. Then

$$\frac{\Delta C}{\Delta Y} = a\left(\overline{\frac{C}{C^*}}\right)\left(\overline{\frac{Y_L}{Y}}\right) + b\frac{\Delta W_{-1}}{\Delta Y}$$

Let

$$a' = a\left(\overline{\frac{C}{C^*}}\right)\left(\overline{\frac{Y_L}{Y}}\right) \qquad b' = b$$

Then

$$\frac{\Delta C}{\Delta Y} = a' + b'\frac{\Delta W_{-1}}{\Delta Y}$$

s.r. mpc $= a'$

l.r. mpc $= a' + b'\left(\overline{\frac{W}{Y}}\right)$ (where barred variables are again mean values)

(A3.5a)
$$\frac{C^*}{Y_L} = a + b\frac{W_{-1}}{Y_L} + d\left(\frac{C^*}{Y_L}\right)_{-1}$$

$$\frac{C}{Y} = a' + b'\frac{W_{-1}}{Y} + d'\left(\frac{C}{Y}\right)_{-1}$$

where a' and b' are as above and $d' = d\overline{(C/C^*)}\overline{(Y_L/Y)}$.

$$C = a'Y + b'W_{-1} + d'\left(\frac{C}{Y}\right)_{-1} \cdot Y$$

s.r. mpc $= a' + d'\overline{\left(\frac{C}{Y}\right)}_{-1}$

l.r. mpc $= \dfrac{a' + b'\overline{(W/Y)}}{1 - d'}$

CHAPTER 4

FIXED BUSINESS INVESTMENT

4.1 THE MARGINAL EFFICIENCY OF INVESTMENT

The investment function, unlike the consumption function, had been widely discussed and analyzed before the time of the *General Theory*. The theory of investment behavior depends on the theory of optimal capital accumulation, which was given the most thorough pre-Keynesian treatment by I. Fisher.[1] Fisher assumed that the firm wanted to maximize its present value, i.e., the properly discounted flow of net receipts. This is the only criterion consistent with utility maximization. If it is assumed that there are perfect capital markets,[2] then the firm will maximize its present value if it invests in all projects whose present value is positive at the market rate of interest.

To demonstrate how this is accomplished, consider for a moment the two-period analysis.[3] Assume that the individual firm which wishes to invest has a preference function between current and future income, which can be represented by an indifference map and operates along production opportunity curves with diminishing marginal productivity of capital. The individual firm

---

[1] I. Fisher, *The Theory of Interest* (New York: Macmillan, 1930). Most of the essential ideas can be found in his earlier work, *The Rate of Interest* (New York: Macmillan, 1907).

[2] This assumes that the borrowing and lending rate are equal and that this rate is unaffected by the amount of borrowing or lending done by the individual firm.

[3] This treatment follows J. Hirshleifer, "On the Theory of Optimal Investment Decision." *Journal of Political Economy*, Vol. 66, No. 4 (August, 1958), pp. 329–352.

has a certain amount of income C_0 in period 0, which it can either consume or invest. It expects to earn returns R_1 on its investment in period 1. If there were no borrowing, the solution would be very simple. The firm would invest that amount which was determined by the tangency of the production possibility curve and the highest indifference curve. However, if borrowing is permitted, the firm can increase its utility by borrowing in period 0, earning returns on the productive assets purchased with borrowed funds, and then repaying the funds in period 1. By borrowing, the firm can expand its budget line in period 0. Consider a new budget line tangent to the production opportunity curve. This new higher budget line will then be tangent to a higher indifference curve, which will raise the firm's utility. This process is shown geographically in Figure 4.1, where the firm moves from u_1 to u_2 and earns income (C_{02}, R_{12}) instead of (C_{01}, R_{11}).

We now consider the gain in income in period 1 relative to the cost (foregone income) in period 0; in percentage terms this can be expressed as $(R_1 - C_0)/C_0$. All productive investment projects can then be ranked by this rate of return, which is what Fisher calls "the rate of return over cost."[4] Firms will continue to invest as long as this rate is greater than the market rate of interest, for in doing so they will continue to move to higher indifference curves.

The analysis becomes more complicated if it is extended to more than two periods. To maximize utility in this case, the rate of return over cost must be set equal to the market rate of interest between any two periods. If the market rate is changing, this can lead to many difficulties. The solution in general will not be straightforward and may involve substantial problems if firms cannot dispose of capital equipment after they once purchase it. The problem becomes much more manageable if we assume that (1) market interest rates are expected to remain constant over time, and (2) all net receipts over time from a given investment can be immediately and perpetually reinvested at the same internal rate of return as that earned by the investment. Then the problem reduces to the treatment given by Keynes.[5] We can then denote this rate of return earned by the investment by r; then if C_0 is the cost (supply price) of the capital good, we have

$$(4.1) \qquad C_0 = \frac{R_1}{1+r} + \frac{R_2}{(1+r)^2} + \frac{R_n}{(1+r)^n} + \frac{S_n}{(1+r)^n}$$

(S is the scrappage price). Here r is the rate of return that equilibrates costs and expected future returns. This is a well-known and popular formulation given in many textbooks. Keynes named this internal rate of return, which equilibrates costs and expected future returns, the *marginal efficiency of*

---

[4] Fisher, *op. cit.*, p. 168.

[5] This point is due to A. Alchian. See his "The Rate of Interest, Fisher's Rate of Return over Cost, and Keynes' Internal Rate of Return," *American Economic Review*, Vol. 45, No. 5 (December, 1955), pp. 938–943.

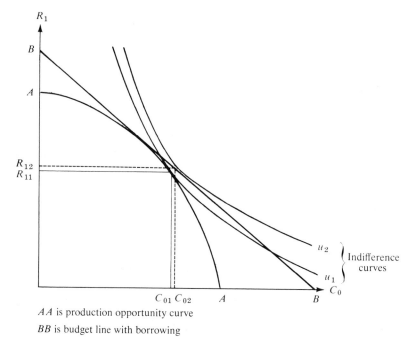

AA is production opportunity curve

BB is budget line with borrowing

Figure 4.1

capital (mec).[6] Keynes himself thought that his explanation was equivalent to the treatment given by Fisher. He states that "Professor Fisher uses his 'rate of return over cost' in the same sense and for precisely the same purposes as I employ the 'marginal efficiency of capital.' "[7] However, it should be pointed out that the two treatments are not equivalent unless assumptions 1 and 2 hold. In many cases it is not unreasonable to assume that they do hold. Businessmen often view expected future rates as being equivalent to present rates, and retained earnings can often be invested at the going rate of return which the firm is currently earning. For analytical purposes this simplified form is much easier to work with, and we do use it in developing additional relationships in this section. However, under certain circumstances the two criteria can lead to entirely different investment patterns; a number of these are discussed by Hirshleifer.

The formula favored by Keynes can be simplified in several ways. First, firms may expect that future returns will be the same for all years. Second, the capital good may have a scrappage price of zero. Third, the good may last a

[6] J. M. Keynes, *The General Theory of Employment, Interest, and Money* (New York: Harcourt Brace, 1936), p. 135.

[7] *Ibid.*, p. 141.

very long time, in which case the last terms, $R_n/(1 + r)^n$, will be very close to zero.[8] If a capital good satisfies all these criteria, then

$$(4.2) \qquad\qquad C = \sum_{i=0}^{\infty} \frac{R_i}{(1 + r)^i}.$$

Then $C = R/r$ or $r = R/C$. Although these may not be very realistic assumptions, this simplified formula stresses the obvious but important facts that r will rise when the expected rate of return rises and will fall when the present cost of the capital good rises. These relationships naturally hold for the general formula as well as the simplified case.

Every firm has many different investment projects it might undertake. Suppose that it knows the present cost and can estimate a stream of expected future returns for each project. If all such projects are ranked according to their rates of return over cost for a given market interest rate, the resulting schedule is known as the *marginal efficiency of investment* schedule (*meI*). If all firms in the economy do this and we aggregate the schedules horizontally, we will have an aggregate *meI* schedule.

We now need to employ the concepts of the *mec* and the *meI* to derive a meaningful investment demand schedule. This needs to be done in two steps. First, we can derive a relationship between the *mec* and the stock of capital; this is quite straightforward. If firms are maximizing profits, they will use more of a given factor as its price relative to other factors decreases. Holding other prices and output constant, this gives a negative relationship between the *mec* and the stock of capital. If the market rate of interest is substituted for the *mec*, this schedule becomes a demand curve for capital. These schedules are shown in Figure 4.2.

Let us assume that the current interest rate is i_t. Then the desired capital stock will be given by K^*, which is larger (*e.g.*) than the actual stock K_t. In a growing economy this will be the usual situation. Only if the interest rate were to rise to i_0 would there be no net investment. Since desired stock is greater than actual stock, Figure 4.1 tells us that net investment will be positive. But that is all it tells us. In particular, it does not say what the rate of investment will be. It indicates only the total amount of investment needed to close the gap between desired and actual capital stock, without suggesting whether this will occur in one day, one month, one year, or ten years. Additional information is needed to determine the rate of investment per unit time.

If there were no restraints on productive capacity or no increasing costs associated with faster delivery, all the desired extra capital goods could be purchased immediately and the economy could expand indefinitely. Of course this is not what happens. Instead, the faster that firms seek to increase their

---

[8] For example, if $r = 0.05$ and $n = 200$ years, $1/(1 + r)^n = 0.000058$; if $n = 300$, $1/(1 + r)^n = 0.00000042$.

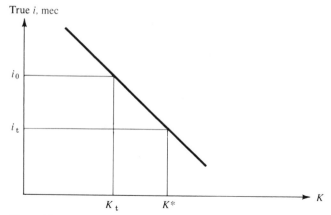

Figure 4.2

capital stock, the more expensive will be the per unit cost.[9] There are two main reasons faster expansion is more costly. First, internal increasing costs associated with integrating new equipment in a going concern rise as the disruption becomes more complete. Second, there is a limit to productive capacity in the capital goods industry. In many cases this limit takes the form of an increase in backlogged orders rather than a rise in the list price. In this case premiums may be paid for faster delivery. Although this factor may be inoperative if only one firm or possibly one small industry is affected, a change in the rate of interest or other general economic variables will affect a wide range of firms and thus affect the overall availability of capital goods.[10] The rise in cost due to an *ex ante* increase in demand for investment goods will lower the *meI* by reducing the rate of return over cost for each investment, *cet. par.* This can easily be seen by recourse once again to equation (4.1):

$$C = \frac{R_1}{1 + r} + \cdots + \frac{R_n}{(1 + r)^n} + \frac{S_n}{(1 + r)^n}$$

A rise in C with R_i and S constant must lower the value of r needed to equilibrate costs and returns. Thus the faster the rate of investment, the higher the per unit cost and the lower the efficiency of each investment. This accounts for the negative relationship between the *meI* and I. Furthermore, the faster the rate of investment, the more sharply costs will rise. This means that the *meI* curve slopes downward at an increasing rate (concave). To complete the shape of the

---

[9] This analysis was first developed by A. Lerner in his *Economics of Control* (New York: Macmillan, 1944), chap. 25.

[10] For a further discussion of these points, see R. Eisner and R. H. Strotz, "Research Study Two: Determinants of Business Investment," in Commission on Money and Credit, *Impacts of Monetary Policy* (Englewood Cliffs, N.J.: Prentice-Hall, 1963), pp. 73–85.

True i, meI

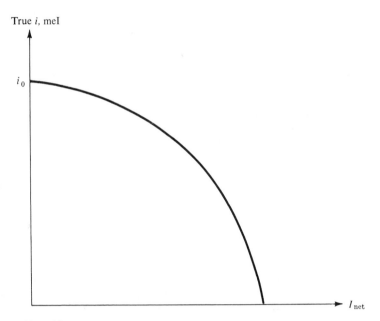

Figure 4.3

meI schedule, recall that at interest rate i_0 capital stock is in equilibrium, so there will be no net investment. If the market rate of interest is substituted for the meI, this becomes the *investment demand schedule*. These relationships are shown in Figure 4.3.

Again we stress that the negative relationship between the meI and investment occurs because an increasing rate of investment can be accomplished only at a higher unit cost, which reduces the rate of return that equalizes returns and costs. Given this schedule, the going market interest rate can then be used to determine the rate of investment. Since (under the assumptions given above) profit-maximizing firms continue to invest until the $meI = i$, a lower interest rate does cause firms to undertake projects that were previously not profitable. However, this happens in two steps. First, a lowering of the interest rate increases the desired capital stock. Second, an increase in the rate of investment lowers the meI through an increase in costs until it decreases to the level of the lower interest rate.

The cost variables we have discussed thus far influence the shape of the meI curve and cause it to be downward sloping at an increasing rate. However, we have not yet examined the variables that determine the level of the meI. These are discussed next; most of them affect expected future returns rather than costs.[11]

---

[11] The following discussion can be found in much greater detail in J. S. Duesenberry, *Business Cycles and Economic Growth* (New York: McGraw-Hill, 1958), chap. 4.

1. The most important variable affecting the returns to investment is the level of demand. An increase in demand will raise the *meI* by increasing the expected future returns earned by hiring an additional capital good. If the firm was previously on the margin between investing or not investing in an extra good, it will now make the positive decision. Conversely, a decrease in demand will result in a lowering of the *meI* schedule. Often this change is met by waiting until equipment is fully depreciated rather than by selling capital assets.

2. An increase in capital stock will lower the returns earned by each additional investment, *cet. par.*, which will lower the *meI* schedule. Thus increases in investment not matched by proportional increases in demand will eventually lead to a reduction in further investment. A decrease in capital stock will raise the *meI* schedule, but such decreases usually occur very slowly

3. The relative age of the capital stock may also influence the *meI* schedule. The rate of return over cost may be higher if new equipment is purchased than if old equipment continues to be used, even if the old equipment must then be sold or discarded at a zero price. This is particularly likely to happen in industries with very rapid technological development (for example, the airlines' transfer to jets). In such cases firms may invest even if they have excess capacity or do not expect future increases in demand.

4. The returns that firms expect to earn cannot be known with certainty. If capital equipment is specialized, the selling price of a used machine yielding returns per unit time of δ will be less than $1/k$ times the price of a new machine yielding returns $k\delta$. This will be especially true if firms try to sell machines during a general business recession. Partially because of this asymmetry in buying and selling prices, variability of expected future returns will lower the *meI* schedule.

The long-run addition to capital stock due to a lower interest rate will be the same regardless of the speed of the adjustment path. However, the rate of investment will depend on the change in the cost of capital goods. The *meI* and demand for capital schedules omit this consideration. These schedules show instead that a decrease in the rate of interest will increase the equilibrium K stock and then increase investment, but until a new equilibrium position is established they do not tell the amount by which investment will increase.

This argument need not be symmetrical. Since it is cheaper and easier to cancel a planned project than to order new capital goods, a rise in the interest rate could have a proportionately greater effect than a decline. On the other hand, the number of cancellations is effectively limited by the number of planned projects. It may be possible for firms to reduce their capital stock further by sales of assets only at prices so low that expected future returns are maximized by keeping idle equipment.

The effect of a change in the interest rate may be negligible or even nonexistent if substantial excess capacity exists. If the equilibrium capital stock increases from \$1200 billion to \$1350 billion because the interest rate falls but the actual stock is \$1400 billion, there may still be no increase in investment.

This example oversimplifies too much, for there are likely to be some firms in equilibrium even if the average firm is not. Even so, on balance one would expect to find a much reduced interest elasticity during periods of economic slack.

The amount of investment occurring at any given time thus depends on many factors besides the rate of interest. If we concentrate on the two most important variables affecting expected future returns, output and capital stock, and temporarily drop the effect of all other variables, we have the basis of the accelerator principle, which is examined next.

4.2   THE ACCELERATOR PRINCIPLE

The accelerator is firmly embedded in pre-Keynesian literature: its origins can be traced back to Aftalian, Bickerdike, and Hawtrey.[12] Probably the best-known early study is J. M. Clark's "Business Acceleration and the Law of Demand."[13] Clark studied fluctuations in railroad traffic and purchases of railroad cars. Although he made several qualifications, his main conclusions are clear: Orders for railroad cars lead movements in traffic, and orders for cars fluctuate more closely with the *change* in traffic than with the *level* of traffic. This is the simple or naive form of the acceleration principle, which posits a certain fixed relationship between capital and output. Stated symbolically, $K_t/O_t = \alpha$. Then $K_t = \alpha O_t$ and $(I_{net})_t = \alpha \Delta O_t$.[14] Thus the accelerator, when translated from a stock to a flow concept, does state that investment is proportional to the change in output. Stated in other terms, if output were to remain at a high level but did not continue to increase, net investment would eventually become zero. This is shown in Figure 4.4.

Clark stressed some of the qualifications of the naive accelerator in his article. His two main points were:

1. The accelerator is inoperative (or not fully operative) when excess capacity exists. In this case, we would retain the same general formal equation but would expect net investment to be positive only when excess capacity was relatively small.

---

[12] A. Aftalian, "La reálité des surproductions générales, essui d'une théorie des crises générales et periodiques," *Revue d'Economie Politique*, 1909. A later restatement of these views may be found in "The Theory of Economic Cycles Based on the Capitalistic Techniques of Production," *Review of Economic Statistics*, Vol. 9, No. 4 (October, 1927), pp. 165–170. C. F. Bickerdike, "A Non-Monetary Cause of Fluctuations in Employment," *Economic Journal*, Vol. 23 (September, 1914), pp. 357–370. R. G. Hawtrey, *Good and Bad Trade* (London: Constable, 1913).

[13] J. M. Clark, "Business Acceleration and the Law of Demand," *Journal of Political Economy*, Vol. 25, No. 1 (March, 1917), pp. 217–235.

[14] In these and the following transformations, we ignore the stochastic error component attached to each equation.

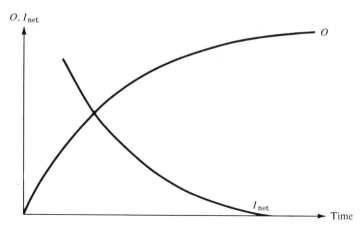

Figure 4.4

2. There are lags between ordering and actual delivery. Bottlenecks may occur in the production of investment goods, and shortages of key factor resources may occur.

The naive accelerator has been modified in other ways:

3. It is sometimes argued that businessmen do not know what their output will be during any given year. Thus they will base this year's capital requirements on last year's output. In this case, $K_t/O_{t-1} = \alpha$, $K_t = \alpha O_{t-1}$, and $(I_{net})_t = \alpha \Delta O_{t-1}$. This lag might also be partially due to delays in ordering and production.

4. As stated above, the change in capital stock is defined as net investment, but we actually observe gross investment. Thus it is argued that $I_t = (I_{net})_t + D_t = \alpha \Delta O_{t-1} + D_t$, where D equals replacement investment and is at least partially autonomous with respect to the change in output. A slight variant of this would be to write $I_t = \alpha \Delta O_{t-1} + A_t$, where A is totally autonomous investment.

Although these points are quite valid, the naive accelerator hypothesis adjusted in this manner is still untenable. Even if we test the function only near full capacity, include replacement investment, and allow for some lags in planning and delivery, the accelerator relationship gives very poor results. This is not to say that this theoretical principle is not a useful tool in the analysis of investment. However, the mold into which it has been cast, even with the above modifications, is still too rigid. We note that this particular relationship can be criticized empirically on at least two grounds.

1. Relationships of the form $I_t = \alpha \Delta O_t + \beta$ or $I_t = \alpha \Delta O_{t-1} + \beta$ invariably explain very little of investment, and the α's are often not significant.

2. In virtually all empirical studies, the value of α obtained from estimating investment functions is much smaller than the value of α obtained from measuring the average K/O ratio. This was the basis of the famous critique of

Kuznets[15]; he tested data for the railroad industry and found that the estimates of α were only one fifth to one half as large as would be expected. Furthermore, this evidence has been repeated in extensive testing for postwar data. While the yearly value of the aggregate K/O ratio is approximately 2.5,[16] the yearly estimate of α given by functions such as $I = \alpha\Delta O + \beta$ is always less than unity and sometimes as low as 0.1.[17]

In spite of these facts, the arguments for or against accelerator occupied a substantial part of the literature, with the argument largely unresolved for many years. Goodwin and Chenery[18] in independent research suggested a *stock-adjustment* model of the form $I_{\text{net}} = \mu$ (desired K_t − actual K_{t-1}), where μ represents the fraction of the gap between desired and actual stock that is filled at time t. If desired $K = \alpha O$, then $(I_{\text{net}})_t = \mu(\alpha O_t - K_{t-1})$. Here we find that investment is proportional to the *level* of output, although the basic accelerator ingredient, desired $K_t = \alpha O_t$, is still present. Chenery modified his function slightly by dividing through K_{t-1}, giving

$$\frac{(I_{\text{net}})_t}{K_{t-1}} = \delta\left(\frac{\alpha O_t}{K_{t-1}} - 1\right)$$

Chenery interprets O_t/K_{t-1} as a measure of capacity utilization (partially because of the way in which K was defined) and calls this function the *capacity principle*.

Goodwin and Chenery did not discuss the basic similarities in these three functions:

(4.3) $K_t = \alpha O_t$ or $\Delta K_t = (I_{\text{net}})_t = \alpha\Delta O_t$ (accelerator)

(4.4) $(I_{\text{net}})_t = \delta(\alpha O_t - K_{t-1})$ (stock adjustment)

(4.5) $\dfrac{(I_{\text{net}})_t}{K_{t-1}} = \delta\left(\alpha\dfrac{O_t}{K_{t-1}} - 1\right)$ (capacity)

In fact, Chenery tested (4.3) against (4.5) for six industries and reached the conclusion that in general the "capacity" model works better than the "accelera-

---

[15] S. Kuznets, "Relation Between Capital Goods and Finished Products in the Business Cycle," *Economic Essays in Honor of Wesley Clair Mitchell* (New York: Columbia University Press, 1935), pp. 209–269.

[16] S. Kuznets, *Capital in the American Economy* (Princeton, N.J.: Princeton University Press for NBER, 1961), pp. 80–81, table 6, col. 6.

[17] Whenever giving values of α, it is necessary to specify time units because α is the ratio of a stock to a flow. If quarterly figures were given for output, for example, α would be four times as large.

[18] R. M. Goodwin, "The Non-linear Accelerator and the Persistence of Business Cycles," *Econometrica*, Vol. 19, No. 1 (January, 1951), pp. 1–17. H. B. Chenery, "Overcapacity and the Acceleration Principle," *Econometrica*, Vol. 20, No. 1 (January, 1952), pp. 1–28.

tor" model.[19] This is an important conclusion and has been verified by numerous other research workers. However, today we would rephrase this comparison and say that the "capacity" version of the accelerator works better than the "change in sales" version.

The relationship between these various functions was first presented by Koyck in his *Distributed Lags and Investment Analysis*,[20] although the solution had been suggested earlier by Eckaus,[21] who argued that the acceleration principle was really the velocity principle (that is, that investment is proportional to the level of output). Koyck said that instead of assuming that $K_t = \alpha O_{t-1}$, it is more sensible to posit that capital stock is proportional to some weighted average of previous output which extends over many years. After a certain point, each previous year has a declining weight in this average. There are any number of particular lag structures that could express this fact; Koyck chose a structure with a series of geometrically declining weights. That is, if λ is between 0 and 1 (but probably much closer to 1), then

$$(4.6) \qquad K_t = \alpha(1 - \lambda)(O_t + \lambda O_{t-1} + \lambda^2 O_{t-2} + \cdots + \lambda^k O_{t-k} + \cdots)$$

Although this series could continue indefinitely, we assume that there will be some nth previous period beyond which λ^{n+j} will effectively be zero.

The large number of lagged output terms makes it very difficult to estimate this equation empirically in its present form. Koyck then proposed the following ingenious method of reducing the equation to manageable proportions.

Equation (4.6) can be rewritten at time $t - 1$ and multiplied by λ, so that

$$(4.7) \qquad \lambda K_{t-1} = \alpha(1 - \lambda)(\lambda O_{t-1} + \lambda^2 O_{t-2} + \cdots + \lambda^k O_{t-k} + \cdots)$$

Subtracting (4.7) from (4.6) gives

$$(4.8) \qquad K_t - \lambda K_{t-1} = \alpha(1 - \lambda)O_t$$

and all other terms cancel out. Rewriting this slightly, we have

$$(4.9) \qquad K_t = \alpha(1 - \lambda)O_t + \lambda K_{t-1}$$

We have already used a similar procedure to transform the consumption function (p. 19); it will be used for many of the other functions developed throughout this text. In general the transformation of an equation $Y_t = \alpha \sum_{i=0}^{\infty} \lambda^i X_{t-i}$ to the form $Y_t = \alpha X_t + \lambda Y_{t-1}$ has become known in the economic literature as a *Koyck transformation*.

---

[19] Chenery actually found that the capacity formulation worked better in four of the six industries, while the change in sales formulation worked better in the other two. However, Kuh and Meyer later showed that the results of the latter two cases were due to a spurious correlation introduced by ratios, and, when this was taken into account, the capacity formulation was superior for all six industries. See E. Kuh and J. R. Meyer, "Correlation and Regression Estimates When the Data Are Ratios," *Econometrica*, Vol. 23, No. 3 (July, 1955), pp. 400–416.

[20] L. M. Koyck, *Distributed Lags and Investment Analysis* (Amsterdam: North-Holland, 1954).

[21] R. S. Eckaus, "The Acceleration Principle Reconsidered," *Quarterly Journal of Economics*, Vol. 67, No. 2 (May, 1953), pp. 209–230.

It is a simple matter to change equation (4.9) so that investment is the dependent variable. Since $(I_{net})_t = K_t - K_{t-1}$, $K_t = (I_{net})_t + K_{t-1}$. Substituting the right side of this expression into (4.9) we have

(4.10) $$(I_{net})_t + K_{t-1} = \alpha(1 - \lambda)O_t + \lambda K_{t-1}$$

and

(4.11) $$(I_{net})_t = \alpha(1 - \lambda)O_t - (1 - \lambda)K_{t-1}$$

To convert to gross investment, we add depreciation (D) to both sides of the equation. Then

(4.12) $$(I_{net})_t + D_t = I_t = \alpha(1 - \lambda)O_t - (1 - \lambda)K_{t-1} + D_t$$

Depreciation is assumed to be proportional to last period's capital stock, or $D_t = \delta K_{t-1}$. Adding this to the above relationship we obtain

(4.13) $$I_t = \alpha(1 - \lambda)O_t - (1 - \lambda - \delta)K_{t-1}$$

We refer to this as the *flexible accelerator*.

For investment to be negatively correlated with existing capital stock, it is necessary that $(1 - \lambda) > \delta$. This conceivably might not hold, because we mentioned earlier that λ is quite close to unity. However, empirical evidence to be discussed later indicates that this is quite unlikely.

Thus by transforming the equation $K_t = \alpha(1 - \lambda)\sum_{i=0}^{\infty} \lambda^i O_{t-i}$ to a form in which investment is the dependent variable, we obtain the result that investment is positively related to the *level* of output and negatively related to capital stock.

Since the functions $I_t = \alpha(1 - \lambda)O_t - (1 - \lambda - \delta)K_{t-1}$ and $I_t = \alpha\Delta O_t$ are both accelerators, it is not surprising that the long-run response of investment to a change in output is similar for both functions. Consider a situation where output is rising at a declining rate and eventually stops increasing at a high level. According to the naive accelerator, net investment will be declining continuously over this period. According to the flexible accelerator, net investment will rise for several periods before the negative effect of the increased capital stock outweighs the positive effect of further increases in output. Both functions posit that eventually net investment will become zero and gross investment will be equal to depreciation. These functions are compared graphically in Figure 4.5.

One of the main criticisms of the naive accelerator was that the values of α obtained from the relationships $K = \alpha O$ and $I = \alpha\Delta O$ were so different. This inconsistency is easily remedied with the flexible accelerator, for the marginal coefficient of the unlagged output term is now $\alpha(1 - \lambda)$ instead of α. Since λ is probably between 0.8 and 0.9, $\alpha(1 - \lambda)$ will be only $\frac{1}{5}$ to $\frac{1}{10}$ the size of the average K/O ratio. As shown later, this agrees with a wide range of empirical results.

As suggested earlier, $I_t = \alpha(1 - \lambda)O_t - (1 - \lambda - \delta)K_{t-1}$ is also known as

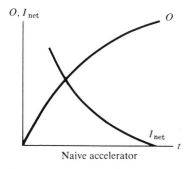

Naive accelerator

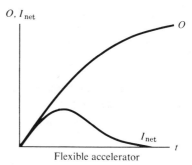

Flexible accelerator

Figure 4.5

the stock-adjustment principle and can be derived in a slightly different way. Suppose net investment is proportional to the difference between desired capital stock (K^*) this period and actual stock last period. Then we can write (as on p. 82).

(4.14)
$$(I_{net})_t = \mu(K_t^* - K_{t-1})$$

If desired stock is proportional to current output, then

(4.15)
$$(I_{net})_t = \alpha\mu O_t - \mu K_{t-1}$$

or

(4.16)
$$I_t = \alpha\mu O_t - (\mu - \delta)K_{t-1}$$

for gross investment. This is the same equation as the flexible accelerator with $1 - \lambda = \mu$.

We can also show the equivalence of the capacity form of the investment function (suggested by Chenery) and the flexible accelerator. The usual form of the capacity principle is written $(I_{net})_t = \beta C p_t$. Under certain circumstances this function is almost the same as $(I_{net})_t = \alpha(1 - \lambda)O_t - (1 - \lambda)K_{t-1}$. To show this, let $Cp \equiv$ actual O/full-capacity O. In general full capacity output (O_f) is a function of capital and labor inputs, but for the United States (at least) it is reasonable to assume that the limiting factor is capital. Then

(4.17)
$$(O_f)_t = \theta K_{t-1} \quad \text{and} \quad Cp_t = \frac{1}{\theta}\frac{O_t}{K_{t-1}}$$

We then have to show that

(4.18)
$$\alpha(1 - \lambda)O_t - (1 - \lambda)K_{t-1} = \frac{1}{\theta}\left[\beta\left(\frac{O_t}{K_{t-1}}\right) + \gamma\right]$$

where γ is an arbitrary constant. The ratio O_t/K_{t-1} can be expanded using the following approximation[22]:

(4.19)
$$\frac{O_t}{K_{t-1}} \cong \frac{1}{\overline{K}} O_t - \frac{\overline{O}}{(\overline{K})^2} K_{t-1} + \frac{\overline{O}}{\overline{K}}$$

where barred variables represent mean values. Thus the two formulations will be approximately equivalent if

(4.20)
$$\alpha(1 - \lambda) = \frac{\beta}{\theta} \frac{1}{\overline{K}} \quad \text{and} \quad 1 - \lambda = \frac{\beta}{\theta} \frac{\overline{O}}{(\overline{K})^2}$$

But these two equalities taken together imply that $\alpha = \overline{K}/\overline{O}$. Thus if the esti-mated value of α is equal to the average capital/output ratio, the capacity principle, flexible accelerator, and stock-adjustment principle formulations of the investment function are all equivalent.

In summarizing this section, we point out that very few economists now seriously consider the naive accelerator as a workable hypothesis. Because of the work of Koyck and empirical implementation of this form by several research workers, a properly modified accelerator hypothesis has come to be very widely accepted by economists. We may rightfully include the flexible accelerator among the fundamental relationships of a modern investment function, and pass at this point to other facets of investment analysis.

4.3   THE MARGINAL COST OF FUNDS

So far we have made the statements that firms will invest up to the point where the *meI* = *i*, and that the main determinants of the *meI* are out-put and capital stock; we have shown how these enter the investment function. Actually, the above equality is a convenient generalization that is not quite correct if capital markets are not perfect. Firms will invest until the rate of return on the last investment is equal to the *marginal cost of funds (mcf)* for this last investment. The *mcf* will be equal to the market interest rate only if the interest rate remains unchanged no matter how much the firm borrows and if there is no increasing risk attached to this extra borrowing. This is not a realistic assumption under any circumstances. The only organization in this country that can borrow an unlimited amount relative to its assets is the U.S. government. Although some firms do not need to borrow an amount that will affect either the rate at which they borrow or the internal risk factor, this is not true for the majority of firms. Thus it is necessary to derive a *mcf* schedule to determine how much firms will invest.

The importance of credit (as opposed to the value of the market interest rate) is also well embedded in the classical theories. In particular, an elastic

---

[22] L. R. Klein, *A Textbook of Econometrics* (Evanston: Row, Peterson, 1953), p. 121.

credit supply was stressed by the overinvestment theories (which will be discussed in Part II).[23] Later, in an article published a year after the *General Theory*,
Keynes stressed what he called the "finance motive."[24] He pointed out that
unless the banks made funds available for expansion of productive capacity,
the increase in investment could not take place. In another early article,
Kalecki discussed the "principle of increasing risk,"[25] in which he argued
that the true cost of borrowed funds to the firm increased as the debt/equity
ratio increased. However, the development of the mcf schedule followed
here is due to Duesenberry. The exposition here is essentially a review of
Duesenberry's contributions; the interested reader is referred to his treatment
at this point.[26]

Firms may finance investment in one of three ways. They may finance internally (either from retained profits or depreciation), they may borrow from
banks or through the bond market (both methods requiring fixed interest
payments), or they may borrow through equity financing (the stock market).
There are of course different costs and different risks inherent in each method
of financing. There is no risk attached to spending funds that the firm has
already received. It could loan these funds to other borrowers; it would then
earn the going rate of return, usually the market rate of interest. This loss of
revenue represents an imputed cost to the firm.

It is also possible for the firm to pay out these excess funds to its stockholders instead of loaning them to other borrowers. In this case it is argued
that the firm should do this if the rate of return that it can earn on possible
future projects is less than the average rate of return on equity capital. For only
this way will stockholders' equity be maximized. However, this argument is
severely mitigated by the differential tax treatment of dividends and capital
gains; dividends are taxed at rates that are at least twice as high as capital gains.
Thus the stockholders would have to receive a dividend yield at least twice as
great as the yield earned on internal projects or loans to other firms before it
could be profitable to them on an after-tax basis to have excess funds distributed as additional dividends. Primarily because of this reason, the imputed
cost of financing investment with internal funds is more closely related to the
yield on bonds than the yield on equities. Since this cost is very low relative
to the average payout on investment projects, it alone is unlikely to be a major
deterrent to investment.

If a large firm wishes to borrow to invest, it will probably be able to borrow
at almost the same rate that it could lend out excess funds. Thus the actual
interest cost of the loan will be no greater than the imputed loss on not lending

[23] See Chapter 12 for a list of these references.

[24] J. M. Keynes, "Alternative Theories of the Rate of Interest," *Economic Journal*, Vol. 47 (June,
1937), pp. 241–252, especially p. 248.

[25] M. Kalecki, "The Principle of Increasing Risk," *Economica*, [n.s.] Vol. 4 (November, 1937),
pp. 440–447.

[26] Duesenberry, *op. cit.*, chap. 5.

out money it already has. The true interest cost will be higher, however, because of the additional risk. This risk need not be and is often not reflected in the actual market interest rate at which the loan is negotiated. It is reflected in the extra imputed risk premium required to service additional debt relative to the earnings available.

If a firm is committed to a certain size payment for debt service and its profits decrease below the necessary covering point, it can continue to meet its interest payments only be reducing its retained earnings or surplus, reducing its dividend, or borrowing new funds to pay old debts. None of these is satisfactory from the firm's point of view. In the first case, dividends will stay constant, but potential investors will note that the firm failed to cover its dividend in the current quarter. If the dividend is actually reduced, the general reaction will be even less favorable. If the firm's net earning record is depressed, it may have to pay a higher rate of interest next time it borrows. If it uses equity financing, the value of its stock will be depressed and it will become more expensive to raise money through the sale of equities. If a firm has no outstanding stocks and hence does not finance through equity capital, it must either reduce its surplus or resort to additional borrowing. Loans made in such cases are apt to be at very high rates and on very unfavorable terms. Firms that increase their future debt payments increase the probability of possible retrenchment if future earnings fall. This extra risk factor must be included as part of the true interest cost of borrowing additional funds.

If this risk factor rises substantially, thus putting the true cost of borrowing well above the stated interest rate, one might expect firms to finance through the sale of equities, which have no concomitant compulsory payment. However, relatively few firms avail themselves of this "advantage"; 75 percent of external financing is done by bonds rather than stocks.[27] This occurs because equity capital is much more expensive than borrowing from banks or through the bond market. There are several reasons for this. The main difference is again due to differential tax treatment for bonds and stocks. Interest payments are deductible before corporate income tax; dividends are not. Since the corporate income tax is about 50 percent, this means that, *cet. par.*, a firm must earn twice as much pretax profit to service equity financing as bond financing. Some slight additional charges may arise from the cost of flotation and the fact that a large issue of stock may somewhat reduce the existing market value of these shares. In addition, if firms have only been paying out part of their after-tax earnings, and are expected to keep the same dividend/ earnings ratio on new issues of stock, this will further increase the amount they must earn to service equity capital. For example, a firm that had been paying out half of its after-tax profits as dividends would be expected to cover twice the dividend on its new stock also, which would redouble the cost of equity financing. If the dividend yield were equal to the bond yield, it would

---

[27] Securities and Exchange Commission, *Statistical Bulletin*, various issues.

cost four times as much to finance through equities if no risk were involved on bond financing. The advantage of equity financing is clearly that payments are not mandatory.

In 1964, the bond yield for industrial bonds was 4.52 percent, the prime (bank) rate was 4.5 percent, the average dividend yield on industrial stocks was 3.00 percent, the percentage of after-tax profits paid out in dividends was 46.6 percent, and the marginal corporate income tax rate was 50 percent. Thus for the average industrial firm (neglecting costs of flotation and repercussions in the market) the true cost of equity financing was $3.00/[(0.50)(0.466)] = 13$ percent. This compares to a bond interest cost of 4.5 percent plus risk premium. It is seen that this risk premium must be substantial before it is actually cheaper for firms to switch to equity financing. For public utilities, which generally have a higher payout ratio, the cost of equity capital will be correspondingly smaller.

With these considerations in mind, we can construct the marginal cost of funds schedule shown in Figure 4.6. Region A represents financing done by the firm from retaining earnings (RE) or depreciation (D). There is no risk factor involved in this region; the only cost of funds is the foregone interest that could be earned by investing the funds elsewhere. Thus the true cost of borrowing in region A is equal to the market interest rate. Region B represents financing done by borrowing from banks or bonds. The sharp rise in the true cost of borrowing is *not* primarily due to a rise in the market interest rate at which firms must borrow. It is due instead to the imputed risk factor which occurs with increased debt servicing. Region C represents financing done through equity capital. Here again there is no imputed risk, because the firm does not have to pay dividends. The gradual upward slope is due to the fact that as a firm offers more and more of its stock on the market, this will invariably depress its price and raise the yield that is paid.

The intersection of the *meI* and *mcf* schedules then determines investment, as shown in Figure 4.7. As stated earlier, the parameters of the *meI* curve are

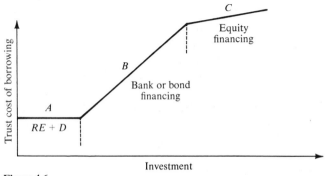

Figure 4.6

True i

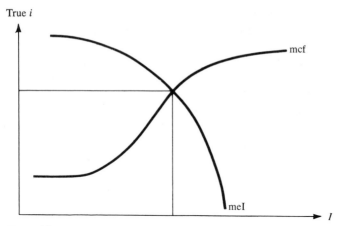

Figure 4.7

mainly output and capital stock, although age of the capital stock and variability of output will also affect its position to a lesser degree. The parameters
of the *mcf* schedule are profits minus dividends (retained earnings), depreciation, and the market interest rate.

It is sometimes claimed that the debt/liquid asset ratio is also a determinant
of the *mcf* schedule. In other variants, it is the debt/profit ratio that is important. If this were true, and firms had a large stock of liquidity (or a small
amount of debt), it would not matter whether cash flow were large enough to
finance investment plans and service debt charges. However, as long as the
firm's investment is at least partially financed by external funds, we argue that
it is the flow of funds rather than the stock which is the more important factor.
If external funds are used, their cost and availability depends in some degree
on the firm's credit rating. If the flow of earnings drops, the firm's credit rating
will be adversely affected in the market, and funds will be more expensive or
harder to obtain. This will be true even if the stock of funds is considered adequate by general market criteria.

It should be mentioned at this point that Duesenberry's explanation does
include the stock of debt as a determinant of the *mcf* schedule. The preceding
paragraph is based partially on the fact that most empirical evidence has shown
that whereas the flow of funds is an important determinant of investment, the
stock of funds measured in various ways is not. In one study, Meyer and
Glauber tested 17 different liquidity stock variables for possible consideration
in their investment function. They found that "the only liquidity measure ...
that seemed remotely related with investment was what might be called the
net quick monetary stock."[28] In an earlier well-known study by Meyer and

[28] J. R. Meyer and R. R. Glauber, *Investment Decisions, Economic Forecasting, and Public Policy*
(Cambridge, Mass.: Harvard University Press, 1964), pp. 92–93.

Kuh,[29] it was reported that the contribution of the liquidity stock to the explanation of investment was essentially zero. In Chapter 5 we shall examine more empirical evidence which suggests that liquidity or debt stocks are not important. Here we may assume that they do not significantly influence investment.

The possibility exists that the intersection of the *mel* and *mcf* schedules shifts over the business cycle. Since the *mel* depends primarily on output, it shifts out when output increases and shifts back when it decreases. This possibility is shown in Figure 4.8. Thus in a boom the interest rate would be important, whereas in a recession cash flow would be the important financial determinant of investment. This is known as the *bifurcation hypothesis*. The argument as stated, however, overlooks the fact that as output increases, profits and retained earnings increase. If output and cash flow increase in equal proportions, then we have the situation shown in Figure 4.9. This is known as the phenomenon of *synchronization* between output and residual funds.

This problem of synchronization has been the source of a good deal of discussion. The topic first received substantial attention in the article by Meyer and Kuh referred to above. In the first of many large-scale research projects on investment by firms (or industries), Meyer and Kuh examined investment patterns from 1946 to 1950. Their findings were that during 1946 and 1947 when demand was expanding rapidly, capacity was the most important determinant of investment. In our present terminology, the *mel* curve intersected the *mcf* curve well into region *B* during these years. During 1948 and 1949, when according to Meyer and Kuh "economic conditions stabilized or declined in several lines of activity," the *mel* curve shifted back to region *A*, at which time "the two liquidity flow variables, profits and depreciation expense, provided the best explanation of investment outlay."[30] The year

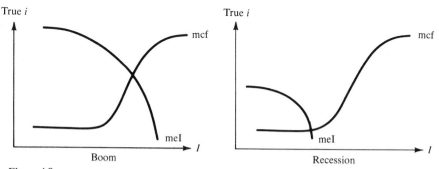

Figure 4.8

---

[29] J. R. Meyer and E. Kuh, "Acceleration and Related Theories of Investment: An Empirical Inquiry," *Review of Economics and Statistics*, Vol. 37, No. 3 (August, 1955), pp. 217–230.
[30] *Ibid.*, pp. 229–230.

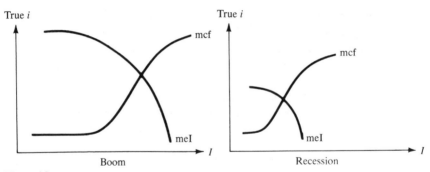

Figure 4.9

1950 was a "mixed" year and did not definitely fit into either region. Actually, it is quite unlikely that 1948 was a year in which the *meI* curve shifted back. However, the general pattern that was established conformed to the lack of synchronization. Meyer and Glauber[31] continued a similar type of study for the years 1951–1954. Their findings for the period are quite mixed; capacity-type variables do well in 1951, a boom year, but they also do well in 1954, a recession year, whereas liquidity variables provide only a "semiadequate explanation" of investment in 1954. Furthermore, Meyer and Glauber are quite disturbed by "the utter failure of any conventional model—accelerator, expectational, or fund flow—to explain investment in 1952."[32] These later results do not represent a very strong endorsement of the bifurcation hypothesis. Actually, much of the problem encountered by Meyer and Kuh and Meyer and Glauber stems from the unrealistic lag structures that both use. Both studies have no lag, or lags less than a year, for all financial variables.[33]

The synchronization hypothesis was also tested by Dhrymes and Kurz[34] for the sample period 1951–1960, using a more realistic lag structure. Their results are quite interesting and we comment on them at length on pp. 125–129. At the present we are concerned with their finding on the importance of profits in the investment function. According to the bifurcation hypothesis with correctly specified lags, profits should be significant in recession years *and the year after*; these would be 1954, 1955, 1958, and 1959 in the Dhrymes–Kurz sample. Profits were significant in all these years except 1959, where the coefficient of profits was positive but not quite significant. If no synchronization exists, then profits would *not* be significant in any of the other years. However, they are significant in 1953 and 1956 (years that bear no relationship to each other in their position in the cycle), and are positive, although not significant, in 1951, 1952, and 1957. Only in 1960 was the coefficient of

---

[31] J. R. Meyer and R. R. Glauber, *op. cit.*

[32] *Ibid.*, p. 135.

[33] This point is discussed in detail in Section 4.4.

[34] P. J. Dhrymes and M. Kurz, "Investment, Dividend and External Finance Behavior of Firms," in *Determinants of Investment Behavior* (New York: Columbia University Press for NBER, 1967), pp. 427–467.

profits actually nonsignificantly negative. From this study we can draw the conclusion that substantial synchronization probably does exist. Although it is not perfect, and there is some tendency for the *meI* curve to shift relative to the length of the horizontal part of the mcf curve, this tendency is not very marked.

The other claim of the bifurcation hypothesis—that the interest rate is an important determinant of investment only in boom years—needs closer examination. It is a familiar phenomenon, and economics students are taught from Samuelson on up, that monetary policy can be used to stop a boom but not a recession. This argument can easily be explained if the *meI* curve shifts relative to the *mcf* curve over the cycle. In the upswing, firms borrow from external sources, so that a rise in interest rates (or a tightening of credit) curtails investment appreciably. In a recession, firms invest less than the amount of their retained earnings plus depreciation, so changes in the cost or availability of external funds have a much smaller effect on investment.[35] However, if substantial synchronization exists, which is suggested by available empirical evidence, this argument will not hold because the intersection of the *meI* and *mcf* schedules occurs in the same relative position over the entire business cycle. In this case another explanation of the asymmetrical importance of monetary policy is necessary.

First it should be pointed out that the statements that monetary policy will not stop a recession and the one that monetary policy is ineffective in a recession do not always express the same idea. In the postwar period, the Federal Reserve Board has always lowered interest rates when it is apparent that the economy is in a recession. If policy is used in a unilateral direction during recessions, the two statements are equivalent. However, in 1931 and 1932, the Fed raised interest rates substantially to protect the position of the dollar even though the economy was in the midst of its most serious decline. There is evidence that this lowered the rate of investment in 1932 and 1933 even below the depressed levels that it would have ordinarily reached.[36] Although little expansion of capacity was taking place during these years, some modernization that might have occurred at low interest rates could well have been stymied by this rise.

The previous discussion suggests that during recessions a fall in the interest rate will not raise investment very much, but an increase will lower it

---

[35] Macroeconomic texts often discuss the case of the liquidity trap, in which interest rates are already at an institutional minimum and cannot fall further. We are assuming here that the interest rate can be changed and are examining the effects of such a change in investment. Furthermore, the "trap" case has not been the experience of the postwar U.S. economy.

[36] In a revised and up-dated version of the Klein–Goldberger model which was estimated from 1929 to 1963, the interest rate has a significantly negative sign in the investment function. If the long-term interest rate had stayed at its 1929 level, then (according to this function) investment would have been $3.6 billion, or 54 percent higher, than its 1933 level. If it had fallen to 3 percent investment would have increased by an additional $4.7 billion. The evidence for this period is necessarily scanty, because detailed national income data were not available then.

substantially. The explanation for this is to be found primarily in the shape of the *meI* curve at different interest rates rather than the region of intersection of the *meI* and *mcf* curves. We have already suggested in Section 4.1 that the *meI* becomes more inelastic at lower interest rates. This argument was based partially on the existence of production ceilings and thus needs some modification for recessions.

Suppose that the desired capital stock has dropped from 1400 to 1300 because of a decrease in demand. A decrease in the interest rate would raise the desired stock back to 1350, which is still not enough to cause positive net investment. A rise in the interest rate would lower desired capital stock to 1250, even further below the actual level. If all firms were previously in equilibrium and all are affected similarly by changes in output and the interest rate, then actual stock would be greater than desired stock for all firms and gross investment would be zero until depreciation reduced capital stock to the desired level.

This is not the way things happen, however. Gross fixed investment is always positive in recessions and even in depressions. Since not all firms are in equilibrium at any given time, there are some that want to increase their capital stock (or at least keep it at the same level) even with the decline in demand. Otherwise they would not invest at all. For these firms, a decline in the interest rate will lead to an increase in the rate of investment. This time the availability of capital equipment is a much less serious problem (although unfilled orders do not go to zero in recessions) but there are still increasing internal costs associated with introducing new equipment too rapidly. If during a recession a firm is integrating new equipment as rapidly as possible without incurring serious bottlenecks, a decrease in the interest rate is not likely to cause any further increase in the rate of investment. On the other hand, a rise in the interest rate will result in cancellation of those projects which were previously profitable. If the interest rate were to continue to rise, eventually

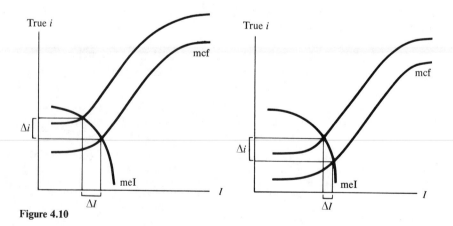

Figure 4.10

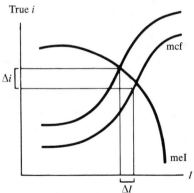
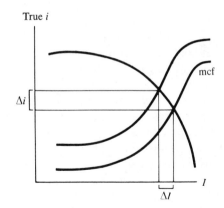

Figure 4.11

all firms would be in the position where their actual stock was greater than their desired stock. Thus an increase in the interest rate can have a substantial deterring effect on investment even during a recession by causing cancellations of those projects which would still be profitable at a low rate.

The concave slope of the *meI* schedule can thus be justified for recessions as well as booms. This means that if interest rates are high, the *meI* and *mcf* curves will intersect in a relatively elastic portion of the *meI* curve; if interest rates are low, the intersection will be in a relatively inelastic portion (Figure 4.10).

If the curves intersect in region *B* (Figure 4.11), the demonstration is quite similar. Thus even if synchronization of the *mcf* and *meI* curves does occur, we can still conclude that high interest rates will lower investment substantially, but low interest rates will raise it much less. It is not necessary to rely on the bifurcation hypothesis to explain this result.

4.4 LAG STRUCTURE FOR THE INVESTMENT FUNCTION

We have now combined the marginal efficiency of investment schedule and the marginal cost of funds schedule as strands of a useful theory of investment. It is now of prime importance to determine a lag structure for this function. As was previously discussed, the shape of the *meI* function is due in large part to the fact that firms cannot obtain additional capital goods immediately without incurring a much higher cost. The production lag of capital goods should be an essential ingredient in any complete theory of investment. The administrative or decision lag may also be quite important, because decisions to purchase capital goods may affect the firm's position for many years.

In early studies of investment, Klein[37] made investment a function of last year's profits, capital stock, and interest rate. However, many studies that followed neglected this lag structure and tried to make investment a function of variables with no lag or a very short lag. The rationale for this was presumably that investment decisions are based on expected future returns, and present conditions give the closest reading to future conditions. It has taken many painstaking man-years of research to establish the fact that investment decisions take time to make and that these decisions are based on past performance. Occasionally a study still appears in which investment is a function only of current output and other unlagged variables, but these attempts are becoming rarer and in any case no longer merit serious consideration. On an aggregate basis, we note that the first four quarters after any of the postwar recessions have always been marked by relatively low fixed business investment, even though output has increased rapidly. There is an asymmetry in this argument because recession years are bad years for investment. However, this is due to cancellations and cutbacks of plans already underway rather than a decrease in original plans before the downturn started. This is shown in Table 4.1. The only time in which investment was higher in the four quarters following the recession than during the recession was in the 1949–1950 period. However, the increase in 1950 actually strengthens our conclusion, not weakens it, because the rise was due to the Korean War. Investment in response to the Korean War demand was clearly a result of modifications of existing plans rather than of plans formulated while the recession was still underway. Investment plans are formulated a year ahead, and if the year in question is a recession year, plans for the following year call for lower investment. These plans are followed unless highly unusual exogenous disturbances, such as a war, change them in midstream.

The problem of the actual lag structure of investment, as apart from the relevant variables that should be included, was first studied by Koyck. We

TABLE 4.1   CYCLICAL BEHAVIOR OF FIXED BUSINESS INVESTMENT
(all figures are in billions of 1958 dollars)

	1948.4–1949.4	1953.3–1954.2	1957.4–1958.2	1960.2–1961.1
During recession	30.9	35.7	38.0	38.0
First four quarters after recession	33.2	35.5	33.9	38.0
Next four quarters after recession	35.2	40.4	37.3	40.9

[37] L. R. Klein, *Economic Fluctuations in the United States, 1929–1941*, Cowles Commission Monograph 11 (New York: Wiley, 1950). L. R. Klein and A. S. Goldberger, *An Econometric Model of the United States, 1929–1952* (Amsterdam: North Holland, 1955).

have presented an abbreviated version of the Koyck function in Section 4.2. In making this transformation, Koyck also paid close attention to the time response of investment to a change in output. In particular, he noted that the previous year's output often influenced investment more than the current year's output. Thus his function was actually written $K_t = \alpha O_t + \beta \sum_{i=0}^{\infty} \lambda^i O_{t-i-1}$, with $\beta > \alpha$ (or at least $\beta > \lambda\alpha$). This represented the first attempt to distinguish the contributions of present and past output.

An early postwar study by Friend and Bronfenbrenner[38] represents the first attempt to divide investment decisions into *original plans* and *realizations*. Their analysis centers around the investment anticipations series[39] in which firms were asked in January 1949 to state the amount of investment planned during the present year and then, in a special following survey, were asked not only to compare the anticipated and actual figures for 1949 but to list the reasons for the discrepancy. The reason cited most often was change in the sales outlook. In comparison, changes in the cost or availability of either debt financing or equity financing were mentioned by less than 1 percent of the respondents. Changes in supply conditions were mentioned about half as often as changes in sales outlook; most of the remaining reasons were listed as "routine error" or miscellaneous. Similar studies by Friend and his colleagues taken intermittently throughout the postwar period invariably lead to the same conclusion—changes in sales are important in modifying investment decisions, but changes in financial variables are not.[40]

The separation of investment decisions into original plans and modifications was given further treatment by Modigliani and others.[41] Continuing to work with anticipations, Modigliani *et al.* suggest the function $I = f(S, A_{-1})$ to explain investment, where S is sales and A_{-1} is the previous year's anticipations. Following the lead of Friend and Bronfenbrenner, they find that "sales are a sufficiently important variable to justify formulating and fitting a realization function for investment involving this variable alone ... the effect of current events other than sales is also not likely to be very pronounced."[42]

---

[38] I. Friend and J. Bronfenbrenner, "Business Investment Programs and Their Realization," *Survey of Current Business*, Vol. 30, No. 12 (December, 1950), pp. 11–22.

[39] These series, developed primarily by Friend, appear on a regular basis in the *Survey of Current Business*. They are discussed in much greater detail in Chapter 17.

[40] A survey that appeared in August, 1967, showed that even the unprecedented monetary squeeze of 1966 had very little effect on fixed business investment plans already in process. See J. Crockett, I. Friend and H. Shavell, "The Impact of Monetary Stringency on Business Investment," *Survey of Current Business*, Vol. 47, No. 8 (August, 1967), pp. 10–27.

[41] F. Modigliani and H. M. Weingartner, "Forecasting Uses of Anticipatory Data on Investment and Sales," *Quarterly Journal of Economics*, Vol. 72, No. 1 (February, 1958), pp. 23–54. F. Modigliani and K. J. Cohen, "The Significance and Uses of *Ex Ante* Data—A Summary View," in M. J. Bowman, ed., *Proceedings of the Conference on Expectations, Uncertainty, and Business Behavior* (New York : Social Science Research Council, 1958). Also by the same authors, *The Role of Anticipations and Plans in the Economy of the Firm, and Their Use in Economic Analysis and Forecasting* (Urbana : University of Illinois, 1961).

[42] Modigliani and Weingartner, *op. cit.*, pp. 39 and 50.

They also point out that investment is determined largely by variables lagged one year, and that current sales do not have a very large effect on investment. This agrees closely with both the regression equation estimates of Klein and Koyck and the survey results of Friend *et al.*

We are interested in determining the variables that influence investment plans as well as modifications, so for our purposes we shall use the relevant lagged endogenous variables instead of last year's anticipations. As will be seen in Chapter 17, these endogenous variables do contain substantial information not included in the yearly anticipations. However, whether lagged endogenous variables or anticipations are used, several important concepts clearly emerge from the work of Modigliani and his colleagues in this field.

1. Investment depends mostly on variables lagged one year or more. These represent conditions current at the time the original decision to invest was formulated.

2. A realization (or modification) function is necessary to explain the difference between anticipated and actual investment as reflected in changing market conditions. The term(s) in the realization function should have a very short lag to reflect recent changes.

3. Sales are the only important term in the realization function, because other variables (such as existing stock and financial conditions) are essentially initial conditions, which need not be included again.

This dichotomy between original plans and modification forms the basis of the investment function presented here.

The Modigliani–Weingartner article suggests, but does not specifically state, that sales of the previous year are of more importance than the current year in explaining investment, as was found by Koyck.[43] Explicit tests of this hypothesis were first undertaken by Eisner.[44] He retained the idea of a long distributed lag but estimated each term of this lag separately, giving the general form $\Delta I = a_0 + a_1 \Delta S + a_2 \Delta S_{-1} + \cdots + a_7 \Delta S_{-6}$ (all lags in years).[45] Some of the long-lagged years are of dubious significance, a point that is discussed later. However, this type of approach highlights the long lags that are essential to explain investment behavior correctly. In general, his findings are that $a_2 > a_1$.

Eisner's results necessitate the estimation of coefficients for several lagged sales terms, a process that often leads to statistical difficulties. If the level of sales is used, multicollinearity is likely to distort the results; if the change in sales is used, errors of measurement are likely to bias the parameter estimates

---

[43] This test cannot be performed explicitly, because their function does not contain an explicit lagged sales term.

[44] Eisner has written several articles on the investment function. However, the lag structure that he uses in all of them is the same. This first appeared in his "A Distributed Lag Investment Function," *Econometrica*, Vol. 28, No. 1 (January, 1960), pp. 1–30.

[45] Eisner's actual function, which is substantially more complicated, is discussed in Chapter 5.

downward.[46] A preferable alternative would be to use some generalized lag structure for which the response of investment over time to a change in output would first rise and then fall but which would require the estimation of only a few parameters. The geometric distribution suggested by Koyck is unsatisfactory in this respect because the weights decline continuously.

Just such a distribution, the Pascal distribution, was suggested by Solow[47]; it is a generalization of the geometric distribution and allows for weights that first rise and then fall. It can be written

$$(4.21) \qquad P(r, \lambda) = \binom{r + i - 1}{i}(1 - \lambda)^r \lambda^i$$

Mathematically, r and λ can take on any real values, but for economic relevance r is restricted to be a positive integer and $0 < \lambda < 1$. If $r = 1$, this reduces to the geometric distribution. For $\lambda \geq \frac{2}{3}$, this distribution will have rising and then falling weights for all $r \geq 2$. Solow works out some expressions that might be estimated, but in practice this method has not worked successfully. Thus we consider other methods that maintain the essential pattern of the Pascal distribution but present less formidable problems for empirical estimation.

One alternative formulation has been suggested by deLeeuw.[48] He tested the following three types of lag distributions[49]:

$$(4.22) \qquad I_t = a_1(O_t + \lambda O_{t-1} + \lambda^2 O_{t-2} + \cdots + \lambda^j O_{t-j})$$

This is, of course, the standard distributed lag function with geometrically declining weights, as used by Koyck. The weights start declining immediately from time t and are not permitted to rise first.

$$(4.23) \qquad I_t = a_2(bO_t + bO_{t-1} + bO_{t-2} + \cdots + bO_{t-j})$$

This is a rectangular distribution, in which the weights of all the output terms are equal back to $t - j$ and zero before that time.

$$\begin{aligned}(4.24) \qquad I_t = a_3[&O_t + 2O_{t-1} + 3O_{t-2} + \cdots + kO_{t-k+1} + (k - 1)O_{t-k} \\ &+ (k - 2)O_{t-k-1} + \cdots + O_{t-2k+2}]\end{aligned}$$

This is an inverted V distribution, where the weights first rise and then fall. DeLeeuw found that a peak of six quarters worked best for this distribution.[50]

These general shapes of those functions are shown in Figure 4.12; the graphs

---

[46] There is some evidence that this has happened in Eisner's results. He claims that the coefficients of the sales terms should sum to approximately unity. Yet he consistently gets totals that are between 0.6 and 0.7.

[47] R. M. Solow, "On a Family of Lag Distributions," *Econometrica*, Vol. 28, No. 2 (April, 1960), pp. 393–406.

[48] F. deLeeuw, "The Demand for Capital Goods by Manufacturers: A Study of Quarterly Time Series," *Econometrica*, Vol. 30, No. 3 (July, 1962), pp. 407–423.

[49] DeLeeuw's functions also include cash flow and the long-term bond yield. Since the lag structure for all variables in a given regression is identical, we omit these variables for ease of exposition.

[50] For this case the actual function would be $I = a_3(O_t + 2O_{t-1} + 3O_{t-2} + 4O_{t-3} + 5O_{t-4} + 6O_{t-5} + 7O_{t-6} + 6O_{t-7} + \cdots + O_{t-12})$.

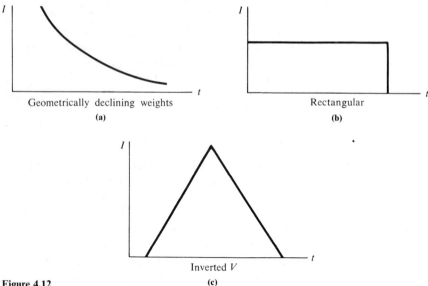

Geometrically declining weights

(a)

Rectangular

(b)

Inverted V

(c)

Figure 4.12

represent the time response of investment to a unit change in output. DeLeeuw found that the inverted V distribution gave substantially better fits than the other two distributions, thus adding an important piece of evidence to the growing accumulation that the effect of output on investment first rises, then falls.

The $\bar{R}^2$'s for the equations are:

Equation No.			Total Length of Lag
(4.22)	(4.23)	(4.24)	(Quarters)
	0.588	0.629	6
0.572	0.751	0.726	8
	0.667	0.817	10
	0.458	0.872	12
	0.348	0.865	14

It is clear that the fit of the inverted V distribution is superior and that it fits best for a total lag period of 12 quarters, implying a peak at 6 quarters. Note that even the rectangular distribution (implying constant weights for all quarters included) gives better results than a distributed lag distribution whose weights decline uniformly from time t.

So far we have placed the lag between changes in the endogenous variables and actual investment expenditures at a little over a year. Actually there are two separate lag sequences that should be noted. The first is the *administrative* or decision lag; this represents the time it takes from the change in endogenous variables to the formation of actual plans. Although this lag cannot be measured exactly, it is probably quite short—on the order of three to six months. This represents the time necessary to have plans approved by committees and worked out on the drawing boards. The second lag, which is the *appropriations* or production lag, is by far the larger of the two. This lag represents the time that elapses between the approval of the appropriations and the actual investment expenditures. Several studies have been made to determine the length of the appropriations lag. Mayer has found that the average time from the start of construction to completion is about 15 months. He mentions that this is corroborated by unpublished Department of Commerce data which show an average construction period of 13.1 months.[51] In an earlier study by Mayer and Sonenblum,[52] it was reported that the average lag during World War II and Korea was ten months. These were based on "estimated" finishing time and thus are somewhat understated.

Almon has explained the lag between appropriations and expenditures in a slightly different way. She computed the relationship between actual expenditures and appropriations lagged 0, 1, 2, 3, 4, 5, 6, and 7 quarters. The weights reported for total manufacturing are[53]:

0	0.068	4	0.157
1	0.122	5	0.127
2	0.156	6	0.084
3	0.168	7	0.038

The peak of this distribution is between three and four quarters, or just short of a year, which agrees fairly closely with the findings of Mayer. When the three- or six-month administrative lag is added, this sets the lag for original investment decisions at five to six quarters.

In a recent study, Sachs and Hart also considered the question of the length of the investment lag.[54] In an experiment in which the computer was essentially directed to find the lag structure that maximized the fit, a lag of six quarters was found to be the most important. Whenever lag structure has been a specific question, the evidence has pointed to a long lag of this length. In the complex area of investment functions, this is one of the few areas in which there is substantial empirical agreement. Functions that ignore these findings are apt to be of questionable use in explaining investment.

[51] T. Mayer, "Plant and Equipment Lead Times," *Journal of Business*, Vol. 33, No. 2 (April, 1960), pp. 127–132. These results were also reported in T. Mayer, "The Inflexibility of Monetary Policy," *Review of Economics and Statistics*, Vol. 40, No. 4 (November, 1958), pp. 358–374.

[52] T. Mayer and S. Sonenblum, "Lead Times for Fixed Investment," *Review of Economics and Statistics*, Vol. 37, No. 3 (August, 1955), pp. 300–304.

[53] S. Almon, "The Distributed Lag Between Capital Appropriations and Expenditures," *Econometrica*, Vol. 33, No. 1 (January, 1965), p. 188.

[54] R. M. Sachs and A. G. Hart, "Anticipations and Investment Behavior: An Econometric Study of Quarterly Time Series for Large Firms in Durable-Goods Manufacturing," in *Determinants of Investment Behavior* (New York: Columbia University Press for NBER, 1967), pp. 489–536.

We now propose an investment function that includes the principal determinants of both the *mei* schedule—output (O) and capital stock (K)—and the *mcf* schedule—the interest rate (i) and cash flow (L), which are both represented here with the single symbol F (for financial variables). The lag structure includes both variables influencing the original decisions with a five- to six-quarter lag and a modification function that enters with a short (one-quarter) lag. Algebraically this function can be represented as

$$(4.25)\quad K_t = a_0 + a_1 \sum \lambda^i S_{t-i-1} + a_2 \sum \lambda^{i\frac{1}{2}}(S_{t-i-5} + S_{t-i-6})$$
$$- a_3 \sum \lambda^{i\frac{1}{2}}(K_{t-i-5} + K_{t-i-6}) + a_4 \sum \lambda^{i\frac{1}{2}}(F_{t-i-5} + F_{t-i-6})$$

Using the Koyck transformation as before, and writing $t - 67$ as a subscript to represent an average of a six-quarter and a seven-quarter lag, we have

$$(4.26)\quad \lambda K_{t-1} = \lambda a_0 + a_1 \sum \lambda^{i+1} S_{t-i-2} + a_2 \sum \lambda^{i+1} S_{t-i-67}$$
$$- a_3 \sum \lambda^{i+1} K_{t-i-67} + a_4 \sum \lambda^{i+1} F_{t-i-67}$$

Subtracting (4.26) from (4.25) as usual, we have

$$(4.27)\quad K_t - \lambda K_{t-1} = a_0(1 - \lambda) + a_1 S_{t-1} + a_2 S_{t-56} - a_3 K_{t-56} + a_4 F_{t-56}$$

Since $K_t - K_{t-1} = I_{\text{net}}$, then

$$(4.28)\quad I_{\text{net}} = a_0(1 - \lambda) - (1 - \lambda)K_{t-1} + a_1 S_{t-1} + a_2 S_{t-56}$$
$$- a_3 K_{t-56} + a_4 F_{t-56}$$

We actually measure gross investment rather than net investment; the difference is depreciation, which we may assume to be proportional to lagged capital stock. The generalized investment function then reads

$$(4.29)\quad I_t = a_0(1 - \lambda) - (1 - \lambda)K_{t-1} + a_1 S_{t-1} + a_2 S_{t-56}$$
$$- (a_3 - \delta)(K_{t-56}) + a_4 F_{t-56}$$

Since movements in the capital-stock series closely follow a trend, it may be very difficult to get reasonable estimates for $(1 - \lambda)$ and $(a_3 - \delta)$ because of multicollinearity. However, this problem can be eliminated by substituting $(bCp_{t-1} + \gamma)$ for $a_1 S_{t-1} - (1 - \lambda)K_{t-1}$, where Cp_{t-1} is the rate of capacity utilization lagged one quarter and γ is some arbitrary constant. This is the same approximation that was used on p. 85 for a simpler version of this function. Using this approximation gives

$$(4.30)\quad I_t = a^* + bCp_{t-1} + a_2 S_{t-56} - (a_3 - \delta)K_{t-56} + a_4 F_{t-56}$$

where $a^* = a_0(1 - \lambda) - b(\bar{S}/\bar{K})$. On a priori grounds we would expect b and a_2 to be positive and a_4 to be positive for cash flow and negative for interest rates. We would also expect cash flow to be more important in the manufacturing sector and the interest rate to be more important in the nonmanufacturing sector, as discussed in Section 5.2. Not as much can be said about the sign of $\delta - a_3$, because it is composed of terms with different signs. In general, it will be negative (as shown), but if replacement investment is a relatively large part of capital stock, it might be positive. Although we do not wish to reject values of $\delta - a_3$ out of hand, this term usually has a negative sign.

It is instructive to trace out the time path of response of investment to a unit change in sales for this function. Sales at the original time of planning will have an important effect on investment plans; sales of previous periods may be considered to have geometrically decreasing weights. But sales immediately after the planning period will have very little additional importance in determining capital requirements. As time progresses from the original decision toward the present, sales will again have an increasingly important influence on investment. Graphically this relationship is shown in Figure 4.13. The result is an inverted W distribution which is similar to deLeeuw's inverted V distribution but is superior because it allows additional weight to be given to modifications of original appropriations.

We can also compare this time path of investment response to an increase in sales with those for other functions which have also been designed so that investment first rises and then falls. Such functions include the deLeeuw inverted V distribution, and functions by Jorgenson and Griliches and Wallace.[55] Also, we can use Almon's weights for the appropriations data after adding the administrative lag (set here at six months).

The time response of investment to an increase in sales for the above functions is plotted in Figure 4.14. Net, rather than gross, investment is considered, so that the nth-period response is zero. The weights on the vertical axis are normalized; that is, the sum of net investment from period 1 to n due to a unit change in sales is equal to unity.

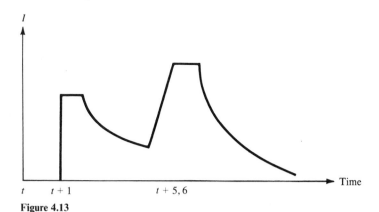

I

t   *t* + 1   *t* + 5, 6

Time

Figure 4.13

[55] D. Jorgenson, "Capital Theory and Investment Behavior," *American Economic Review Papers and Proceedings*, Vol. 53, No. 2 (May, 1963), pp. 247–259. Z. Griliches and N. Wallace, "The Determinants of Investment Revisited," *International Economic Review*, Vol. 6, No. 3 (September, 1965), pp. 311–329. The latter two functions are essentially accelerator functions that take into account "user cost of capital" and were designed with the problem of lag structure prominently in mind.

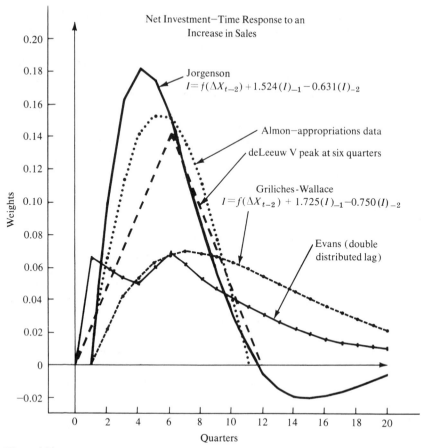

Figure 4.14

The functions seem to fall into two groups. One is formed by the Jorgenson, Almon, and deLeeuw functions, which peak fairly sharply and have zero weights in either the eleventh or twelfth quarter. The other group consists of the Evans and Griliches–Wallace functions, which stretch out over a much longer period of time. The Evans function is the only one with a double peak, a fact that is not too surprising when we consider that all the other functions except the Almon function were specifically formulated to give a single peak. It is interesting to note that in 1958 when sales dropped off sharply, cancellations were at their highest, giving additional support to the relationship between modifications in investment and sales with a short lag. Additional work that will relate the appropriations themselves to economic variables should be helpful in giving more information about the time path of investment with respect to sales.

There has often been some confusion about the role of financial variables in the double distributed lag function. As explained above, firms make their original investment decisions based on variables lagged slightly more than a year. These variables are output, capital stock, and financial variables (cash flow and interest rates). At the time of the original decisions, funds are committed at the then current rate of interest or out of existing cash outlays. Appropriations are then made and investment expenditures are spread out over the next year or two. Modifications of these original plans may take place because output or capacity utilization has changed. However, modifications in investment will *not* be influenced by changes in the market rate of interest or the firm's cash flow (*cet. par.*) because the funds have already been committed at the *then existing* rate of interest or out of *existing* internal financial resources. Changes in these variables after the funds have already been committed at stated terms will not influence modifications of the original plans. Thus, although it is important to have a double distributed lag for sales, it is equally important to realize that this is not necessary or even sensible for the financial variables. This point is often misunderstood. In a report on the manufacturing sector of the large-scale Brookings model,[56] an investment function with a lag structure patterned after the one described above was estimated to be

(4.31) $I_t = -0.86 + 0.0868X_{t-1} - 0.145K_{t-1} + 0.104X_{t-5}$
           $\qquad\qquad (0.0195) \qquad\quad (0.058) \qquad\quad (0.022)$

           $\qquad + 1.108i_{t-1} - 1.116i_{t-5}$
           $\qquad\quad (0.482) \qquad\; (0.439)$

where I = gross fixed business investment in the manufacturing sector, billions of 1954 dollars

$\quad X$ = gross output originating in the manufacturing sector, billions of 1954 dollars

$\quad K$ = capital stock in the manufacturing sector, billions of 1954 dollars

$\quad i$ = average corporate bond yield, percent

Both X_{t-1} and X_{t-5} are significant, and the parameter estimate of X_{t-5} is greater than X_{t-1}, as expected. For reasons that remain unclear, L (cash flow) was not included.[57] However, i_{t-1} was included; according to the above argument, this never should have been done. Owing to problems of identification, it is not surprising that the coefficient of i_{t-1} is positive; this is discussed later. When using this lag structure (as with many others) one must take care to understand the role of each variable correctly and not merely reduplicate the entire process of determining investment with a shorter lag.

---

[56] G. Fromm and L. R. Klein, "The Brookings-SSRC Quarterly Econometric Model of the United States: Model Properties," *American Economic Review Papers and Proceedings*, Vol. 55, No. 2 (May, 1965), pp. 348–361. The Brookings model is discussed in more detail in Chapter 18.

[57] When virtually the same equation was estimated by this author with L included with a lag of five to six quarters, it was highly significant (the coefficient was 2.7 times its standard-error estimate).

EXTENSIONS AND REFINEMENTS
OF THE BASIC
INVESTMENT FUNCTION

5.1   THE IMPORTANCE OF EXPECTATIONAL
VARIABLES IN THE INVESTMENT FUNCTION

There are many unsettled issues relating to the investment function that were not discussed in Chapter 4. This chapter considers some of the more important of these issues. At the outset the reader is warned that here, perhaps more than anywhere else in this text, the frontiers of econometric knowledge are rapidly expanding and changing; thus the answers to many of the problems are not yet at hand. The basic concepts developed in Chapter 4—the determinants of the marginal efficiency of investment, marginal cost of funds schedules, and a sensible lag structure—serve as a guideline for interpreting and explaining more complex phenomena of investment decisions. Even so, there are areas where the profession awaits more data and research before reaching any consensus.

One problem that has long confronted economists is the use of expectational variables as a determinant for explaining investment. As previously stated, the profit-maximizing businessman invests so that he maximizes the present value of the firm, which involves the same investment decisions as maximizing the properly discounted stream of future profits. Thus it has been argued that firms consider future expectations of variables such as prices and output, rather than past levels, as proper criteria for investment. The question examined in this section is whether investment predictions can be improved by using economic indicators that represent future events or whether investment decisions appear to be based entirely on past levels of the relevant variables. Three variables have been suggested to explain future patterns of capital spending: indices of buying plans, stock prices, and unfilled orders. The variables discussed in this section all affect modifications of investment decisions rather than original plans. Each of these variables will be considered in turn.

The buying-plans expectations will not be discussed fully until Chapter 17. Here only enough will be said to reach a conclusion on whether these data are helpful in explaining investment. These indices are compiled from actual statements of what businessmen plan to spend on new plant and equipment rather than reflections based on attitudes about the general business climate. Several indices are currently available; our discussion is restricted to the two principal ones. One is the Office of Business Economics—Securities and Exchange Commission (OBE-SEC) index of quarterly buying plans, available in December, March, June, and September for the first, second, third, and fourth quarters of the year. Recently, an attempt has been made to extend these expectations six months ahead, but this is not yet done for all quarters. The other is the McGraw-Hill yearly survey of buying plans, released during the first week in November of the previous year. Here we discuss only the OBE-SEC quarterly expectations series, because it has a better forecasting record. This is partially due to the obvious fact that the OBE-SEC forecasts are made for the next quarter only, whereas the McGraw-Hill forecasts are made for the next full year. On the other hand, the advantage of the OBE-SEC forecasts is not quite as large as it might at first seem. For one thing, the second-quarter estimates (for example) are prepared well before the first-quarter investment figures are known; thus the figures are really two-quarter forecasts. Second, there may be some problems in predicting quarter to quarter fluctuations that are smoothed over in the yearly figures.

The main point in introducing the buying expectations at this point is to test whether they contain additional information on investment spending which is not imparted by the endogenous variables used. If there is, one would expect that other variables in the equation should remain significant and the expectations should add additional information. Furthermore, the overall predictive accuracy of the equation ought to be improved. If the buying plans do add significantly to the explanation of investment, this may mean either that some variables explaining the past are missing or that some information about expected future variables is contained in the buying plans. Since the investment function has been closely scrutinized by several different authors recently from various points of view,[1] it is rather unlikely that some important

---

[1] Several of these studies are referred to quite often throughout the chapter and are cited here. References to these works will not be cited again in the chapter unless specific pages are indicated.

P. J. Dhrymes and M. Kurz, "Investment, Dividend, and External Finance Behavior of Firms," in *Determinants of Investment Behavior* (New York: Columbia University Press for NBER, 1967), pp. 427–467.

R. Eisner, "A Permanent Income Theory for Investment: Some Empirical Explorations,"

predetermined variables have been overlooked by all of them. We take the position that if expectations are important they do represent some information about future behavior.

For purposes of this discussion it is useful to divide investment into manufacturing and nonmanufacturing sectors. The reason for this will be discussed in detail in the next section. Using the type of investment function developed in Chapter 4 $[I = f(X_{-1}, K_{-1}, L_{-56}, X_{-56}, i_{-56})]$, anticipations make a significant net addition to predictive accuracy in the manufacturing sector but do not do so in the nonmanufacturing sector.[2] The usefulness of the expectations is somewhat marred by the fact that they perform most poorly at the turning points, indicating once more that businessmen's idea of the future is likely to be an extrapolation of the past and present. However, there is evidence that expectations are important in the manufacturing sector, so there is reason to explore other variables that have been used to explain expected future demand. Our discussion for the rest of the section will pertain only to manufacturing investment.

Fluctuations in the stock market have always been of interest to economists (among others) both for their own utilization and because they are sometimes thought to be a good leading indicator of aggregate economic activity, particularly investment. Stock market indices have been used in various investment studies. However, different reasons for including this variable have been used, so it is necessary to discuss these before proceeding to examine the relevance and possible significance of the stock market variable.

One approach is suggested by Grunfeld.[3] He argues that stock prices represent information about expected future profits. His study is done at the level of the firm, and the variable he uses is the market value of the firm.[4] Grunfeld argues that firms invest to maximize the present value of all future earnings of the firm, so that investment will be higher if this present value is high relative

---

American Economic Review, Vol. 57, No. 3 (June 1967), pp. 363–390.

M. K. Evans, A Study of Industry Investment Decisions," *Review of Economics and Statistics*, Vol. 49, No. 2 (May, 1967), pp. 151–164.

E. Kuh, *Capital Stock Growth: A Micro-Econometric Approach* (Amsterdam: North-Holland, 1963).

W. H. Locke Anderson, *Corporate Finance and Fixed Investment—An Econometric Study* (Boston: Harvard University Press, 1964).

J. R. Meyer and R. R. Glauber, *Investment Decisions, Economic Forecasting, and Public Policy* (Boston: Harvard University Press, 1964).

R. W. Resek, "Investment by Manufacturing Firms: A Quarterly Time Series Analysis of Industry Data," *Review of Economics and Statistics*, Vol. 48, No. 3 (August, 1966), pp. 322–333.

[2] See M. K. Evans and E. W. Green, "The Relative Efficacy of Investment Anticipations," *Journal of the American Statistical Association*, Vol. 61, No. 1 (March, 1966), pp. 104–116. Also see Chapter 17, pp. 466–467.

[3] Y. Grunfeld, "The Determinants of Corporate Investment," in A. C. Harberger, ed., *The Demand for Durable Goods* (Chicago: University of Chicago Press, 1960), pp. 211–266.

[4] Actually Grunfeld uses market value of equities plus book value (instead of market value) of bonds. But as he points out, this makes very little difference.

to the replacement cost of capital stock.[5] But this does not necessarily follow. Eisner has shown that firms with high profit to capital stock ratios do not invest more in the long run than firms with low profit to capital stock ratios. The fact that firms invest to maximize future profits does not necessarily imply that high future profits means greater investment. It is only if sales are high that more investment will be needed to maximize profits.

Grunfeld estimates regressions of investment on the value of the firm (essentially an index of stock prices), capital stock, the interest rate, and profits. He finds that the first three variables are important whereas profits are not. He states that the results "confirm very strikingly our main hypothesis that the value of the firm serves as a superior explanatory variable of investment to profit in either form" (i.e., current or lagged). He also states "the value of the firm incorporates expectations factors that are relevant for investment behavior."[6] However, since Grunfeld has concentrated on expected future profits instead of sales in his model, his equations do not contain any sales variables at all. With all due respect to Grunfeld's work, it does not seem at all reasonable to estimate an investment function without any type of sales term. All that he has shown is that the market value represents future expectations better than do profits. This in itself agrees with our decision to treat profits as a liquidity variable instead of an expectations variable. It is no surprise when this variable fails to work in a role where it does not belong. However, the use of the market value variable *instead* of any sales variable vitiates Grunfeld's results. There is little reason to believe that future profits as such are an important determinant of investment, and the significance of stock prices should not be tested in this context.

Another possibility that has been suggested is that stock prices measure the cost of equity capital. Often it is claimed that since equity financing typically accounts for a very small percentage of funds borrowed by manufacturing corporations (usually less than 15 percent) the price of equity capital is similarly unimportant.[7] Others claim that this is not the correct approach because it ignores the fact that the cost of investing retained earnings may be equal to the cost of equity instead of the market interest rate, since the firm can use retained earnings either for additional dividend disbursements or for additions to capital stock. Presumably it will do the former if it does not think it can earn an equivalent rate of return on the latter. In other words, the return on equity capital sets the minimum rate of return which the firm plans to accept on its investment projects. However, we have already shown in Chapter 4 how differential taxation severely mitigates this argument.

A third suggestion is that stock prices represent expected future output of the firm instead of expected future profits. Of course, these two hypotheses

---

[5] *Ibid.*, p. 225.
[6] *Ibid.*, pp. 263–265.
[7] See, for instance, Dhrymes and Kurz, *op. cit.*, and Resek, *op. cit.*, for this viewpoint.

are not unrelated. Movements in output are usually closely correlated with movements in profits. But although individuals may invest in stocks because they expect future profits to be high, businessmen invest in plant and equipment because they expect future output to be high. For the stock market to be an effective indicator of future investment, investors in the market must see future sales in the same light as the businessmen who invest in plant and equipment. Then an index of stock prices can be considered as a well-recognized and easily available variable for indicating the course of future sales. Stock prices in this sense form an index of informed opinion shared by investors in plant and equipment and knowledgeable investors in the market. Such an assumption implies that the market price is determined by long-run sales and not by short-run speculation, a view not shared by Keynes among others.[8] However, we shall assume that this is at least a reasonable assumption in order to test the feasibility of stock prices in a correctly specified investment function.

A fourth possibility is that an index of stock prices serves as a general business indicator and partially reflects current business sentiment about the economy as a whole. Of course, individual industry stock prices also reflect current business sentiment to a certain degree. Price/earnings ratios are invariably higher in booms than in recessions. However, it is possible that a change in overall stock market prices would be correlated with the investment of a given firm or industry even if its particular stock price had not changed. If this were the case, we would expect an overall indicator of stock prices to do somewhat better in explaining industry investment than individual industry stock prices.

Resek has recently tested stock prices as a proxy for expected output in individual industry investment functions. Of the 13 two-digit[9] manufacturing industries, stock prices are significantly positive in 11, which compares quite favorably with the results that 10 of 13 change in output variables and only 5 cash flow variables are significant with the correct sign. Resek also calculated the same equations without stock prices in order to assess the net effect of this variable. The addition of the stock price index increased the fit in 10 of the 13 equations; most óf these increases were rather substantial. The largest gains were in the food ($\bar{R}^2$ rose from 0.240 to 0.567), iron and steel (0.301 to 0.742), and other transportation (0.395 to 0.761) industries. The values of stock prices are quite significant, and half the t ratios are over 6.0. Some possible criticisms only tend to bolster Resek's findings.

1. All his variables are in ratio or percentage form except stock prices; thus this variable might well represent a trend factor. This type of problem bothered Eisner and Meyer and Glauber, who both used the change in stock prices. However, Resek tested for this possibility by inclusion of a trend. He

---

[8] J. M. Keynes, *The General Theory of Employment, Interest, and Money* (New York: Harcourt, Brace, 1936), pp. 154–156.

[9] OBE-SEC data on investment are available for 13 manufacturing industries classified by the Standard Industrial Classification (SIC) as two-digit industries. A list of these 13 industries will be given in Table 5.1.

found that in general a trend variable was not significant and in all cases had very little effect on the magnitudes of the coefficients of the other variables. The stock price index does not represent a trend factor in Resek's study.

2. Resek uses the Almon[10] lag structures, which are in the form of an inverted V and allow no decision lag. No modifications sales variable is included in his functions, so it is possible that the stock price index primarily represents modifications of existing investment decisions. However, this is not supported by the available evidence. The three industry investment functions that are most improved by the inclusion of an index of stock prices are food, iron and steel, and other transportation. Without the stock price variable, these three functions have poorer fits and more coefficients with incorrect signs than any of the other industry equations. When a sales modification variable is substituted for stock prices, these three functions are not improved very much and continue to give the poorest results.

In another study, Meyer and Glauber find that an index of stock prices is significant in the regression for total manufacturing but is not significant in the individual industry equations. The comparison is not entirely clear-cut, since Meyer and Glauber use the level of stock prices in the aggregate function and the change in stock prices in the individual functions.[11] What concerns us here is that they use the *overall* manufacturing stock price index in the *individual* industry equations, where it is almost uniformly nonsignificant.

This allows us to draw some conclusions about the role of stock prices as a general cyclical indicator. If the overall manufacturing stock price index had been significant in the individual industry equations, this would have been due to its importance as a general cyclical variable. In these equations, however, individual industry stock prices were important, whereas total manufacturing stock prices were not. This is confirmed by some of our own regressions. Thus the failure of Meyer and Glauber to find stock prices significant, far from negating their importance, allows us to distinguish between various alternative roles for this variable. We are left with the conclusion that stock prices either measure expected future output or cost of equity for individual firms. At this point we shall assume that at least part of the importance is related to expected future output and consider the question of equity capital cost in Section 5.3.

The evidence presented so far suggests that there is some information besides that contained in sales, capital stock, interest rates, and various measure of cash flow that businessmen utilize when making investment decisions. The importance of the expectations suggests that this variable exists. The use of an

---

[10] S. Almon, "The Distributed Lag Between Capital Appropriations and Expenditures," *Econometrica*, Vol. 33, No. 1 (January, 1965), pp. 178–196. See p. 101 for a further discussion of these lags.

[11] The reason for this switch is not given explicitly, except for some vague references to multicollinearity. However, one may speculate that the use of the levels of the stock price index negated importance of the cash flow variable, which they believe to be important. Another simpler reason may have been that the fit was better with changes instead of levels.

index of stock prices as a proxy for expected future output is one possible explanatory variable that may fill this role. Another variable that is sometime used is unfilled orders. Certainly these carry some information about future sales, because they measure the degree to which orders have been placed but not yet shipped. By describing the existing backlog of sales they may impart additional information about pressures on capacity. Resek reports that he tried unfilled orders but with very little success. However, he expected it to act as a supply limitation on investment rather than a spur to further investment. In his exposition, unfilled orders and investment would be negatively related, while according to our analysis they would be positively correlated. Furthermore, Resek points out that for his sample period (1954–1963) supply considerations were important only in 1955. Thus there is really very little reason to suggest a negative relationship between these two variables, but a positive relationship is quite reasonable.

The only available tests reported for this variable are those by Eckstein[12] and some by this author. Eckstein uses the deLeeuw function and preferred lag structure[13] and adds the ratio of the change in unfilled orders to sales ($\Delta U/S$) as an additional variable. He also adds an index of leading indicators in another equation. Of the two, the leading indicators probably correspond more closely to an index of stock prices. Eckstein finds that both variables improve the deLeeuw function considerably, with $\Delta U/S$ doing slightly better. He does not report results with both of these variables in the same equation. This would have given more of an indication whether the variables contain separate or overlapping information and, if the latter is true, which variable is more important.

The importance of both unfilled orders and stock prices in the investment function has been examined in detail in some work done by this author. In the aggregate manufacturing equation it was found that both these variables impart additional information to the explanation of investment when they are both included as well as when each is included separately. Evidently these variables impart different kinds of information about investment plans.

To test this hypothesis further we estimated separate regression equations for each industry for which unfilled orders figures are available and in all industries for stock prices. Unfilled orders are important in the iron and steel, nonferrous metals, and, to a lesser degree, other transportation (mainly aircraft) industries. They were not important in either the electrical or nonelectrical machinery industries. Detailed orders figures are not available for other industries, but, as these industries account for almost 80 percent of all unfilled orders, the omission does not seem too important.[14]

---

[12] O. Eckstein, "Manufacturing Investment and Business Expectations: Extensions of deLeeuw's Results," *Econometrica*, Vol. 33, No. 2 (April, 1965), pp. 420–424.

[13] These were discussed on p. 100.

[14] Another 10 percent of unfilled orders is accounted for by fabricated metal products, for which no investment figures are available.

Stock prices with a short lag (indicating a modifications variable) were significant at the 5 percent level in 8 of 13 industries. The results are less favorable to the stock price variable than those reported by Resek; the difference can be attributed to the inclusion of a modifications variable in our function. In industries in which unfilled orders are the strongest—iron and steel and nonferrous metals—stock prices are not at all important. Although the evidence is not too strong (since other transportation does not conform), it may be that industries consider either pressures on capacity that exist now or, alternatively, consider expected future output.

Without presenting a large number of regression equations at this point, we summarize our findings in general. Unfilled orders figures are available only for a few industries. They are important in those industries which have the largest percentage fluctuations in sales,[15] indicating that the slower-moving unfilled orders represent pressure of demand more accurately than do widely fluctuating sales. The fact that they were important only when sales were an unreliable indicator of capital requirements suggests that *unfilled orders impart information about current requirements of demand and not future requirements.* They are probably not a proxy for expected future output. Unfilled orders are important in the iron and steel, nonferrous metals, and other transportation-equipment industries, primarily because in these industries they are a better indicator of the permanent component of demand than the more usual sales variable. The importance of correctly indentifying permanent elements of demand has been stressed by Eisner, although he does not use an unfilled orders variable.

In a sense this represents a reversal of Eckstein's findings. He argues that "orders serve as direct evidence of a firm's future sales"[16] and are important for that reason. However, we find that the stock-price index takes care of this element and unfilled orders serve a different purpose—as a proxy variable for sales in those industries where transitory components of sales are the largest.

In general, a stock-price variable gives good results for the individual industry equations as well as for total manufacturing. Even though this variable is not significant in all industries, it is important in several. Furthermore, individual industry stock prices perform much better than an overall index. Stock prices are primarily a modifications variable; they are more often significant when included with a lag of one and two quarters than with a lag of five and six quarters. The evidence is not completely one-sided, however. The longer lag of stock prices gives better results than the shorter lag in three industries and is often significant. This means that stock prices may also influence original investment plans through their effect on the cost of equity capital. Stock prices contain information independent of unfilled orders both at the industry and aggregate levels. Whereas unfilled orders represent current needs, stock

---

[15] See Table 5.1 for these figures.
[16] Eckstein, *op. cit.*, p. 421.

prices represent mainly expected future needs. Both variables have their main effect on modifications rather than original plans; unfilled orders are never significant with a long lag.

In summary we draw the following conclusions about the existence and importance of expectational variables on manufacturing investment. First, firms consider expected future output in a way not measured by sales, cash flow, interest rate, and capital-stock variables. This is shown by the significant net addition made to predictions by the anticipations index. Second, this extra information is best captured by an index of stock prices, which is significant in over half the industries. Stock prices for individual industries work well but an overall index performs poorly in the industry equations. Third, unfilled orders, which have sometimes been suggested as another choice for an expectations variable, do not serve to project future demand but rather serve as a proxy for sales in those industries where sales contain largely transitory fluctuations. Finally, the projection of expected future output occurs mostly as a modification to existing plans, for original plans are based more explicitly on past performance.

5.2   INTERINDUSTRY DIFFERENCES

There is good reason to believe that profit-type variables are important determinants of investment for some industries, whereas interest rates are important for others. This has been argued by Duesenberry in connection with the explanation of his marginal cost of funds schedule as one of the determinants of investment. He says:

> A firm ... [which has] a cost-of-funds curve which slopes steeply upward as soon as investment exceeds retained earnings and depreciation by a relatively small amount ... tends either to rely entirely on internal funds and a relatively small amount of debt or to issue equities. It will issue equities, however, only when the marginal efficiency of investment is quite high. Such firms ... may be a majority among manufacturing firms.[17]

On the other hand, he argues that:

> Businesses which are safe both competitively and with respect to cyclical fluctuations can safely carry a good deal of debt. Public utilities are in the latter range.[17]

Such statements may well imply that a cash flow variable would be more important in the manufacturing sector and that the interest rate would be more important in the nonmanufacturing sector, of which public utilities are a substantial component. Furthermore, cash flow might reasonably be expected to be more important for some subsectors of manufacturing, whereas the interest rate would be more important in other subsectors.

---

[17] J. S. Duesenberry, *Business Cycles and Economic Growth* (New York: McGraw-Hill, 1958), p. 98.

There are other factors of secondary importance that may help to determine the relative importance of cash flow and interest rates on investment. However, these will act more on the elasticity of the *meI* curve than through the *mcf* schedule. For those industries in which equipment has a relatively short life, either through normal use or because of technological obsolescence, the interest cost will be a very small part of the total cost of the investment. Conversely, for those industries with equipment that has a relatively long life, the level of the interest rate will be more important in influencing investment decisions, as interest costs will represent most of the total cost of the capital equipment.

We can distinguish among the following cases of intersection of the *meI* and *mcf* schedules as given in Figures 5.1 to 5.4. In Figure 5.1 the *meI* curve intersects the *mcf* curve well to the left of the amount in internally generated funds. In most cases, the firm will spend its extra cash through expansion or diversification. However, some extremely large companies may feel it is not wise to pursue these alternatives. The auto companies seem to be in such a position.[18] In this case neither cash flow nor the interest rate will be an important determinant of investment, because the firm has more than enough internally generated funds to finance capital requirements dictated by levels of output.

In Figure 5.2 the *meI* curve intersects the *mcf* curve approximately where the latter begins to rise. In this case it rises quite sharply, so the amount of cash flow is an effective determinant of maximum investment. The *mcf* curve will turn up sharply for those firms whose profits fluctuate substantially, because there is great risk attached to these firms carrying substantial amounts of debt.

In Figure 5.3 the *meI* curve again intersects the *mcf* curve approximately where the latter begins to rise, but this time it rises at a much slower rate.

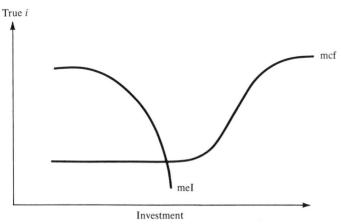

Figure 5.1

---

[18] *Ibid.,* p. 100.

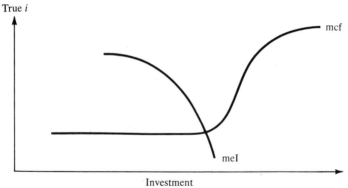

Figure 5.2

In this case there will still be a substantial additional true cost to borrowing externally, but fairly often the *meI* will be great enough to make this worthwhile. In such cases both cash flow and the interest rate might be important determinants of investment.

In Figure 5.4 the *meI* curve intersects the *mcf* curve well beyond the limit of internally generated funds. In this case the interest rate is an important determinant of investment but cash flow is not.

We would expect the greatest difference in the use of the cash flow and interest rate variables to occur between the manufacturing and nonmanufacturing sectors. However, it should be possible to distinguish some pattern even within the manufacturing sector. Duesenberry suggests that the slope of the marginal cost of funds schedule for a firm rises more sharply the more profits fluctuate cyclically. This in turn would be primarily due to fluctuations in output, caused by (1) cyclical fluctuations of the industry sales or (2) changing market position due to competition. Of the two, the first is found to be of greater importance. We omit the degree of competition (or monopoly) from further consideration

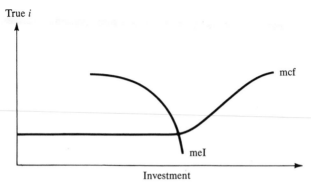

Figure 5.3

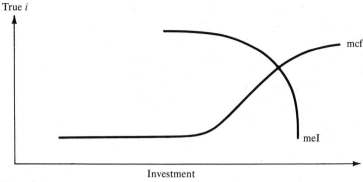

Figure 5.4

at this point. The relationship between fluctuations in capacity utilization[19] and the elasticities of cash flow and the interest rate is shown in Table 5.1.[20] A zero elasticity means that the term was dropped from the industry investment equation because of its nonsignificance.

The results that can be drawn from Table 5.1 are inconclusive. There is some relationship between the importance of the interest rate and fluctuations in

TABLE 5.1 RELATIONSHIP BETWEEN FLUCTUATIONS IN CAPACITY UTILIZATION AND FINANCIAL VARIABLES IN INDUSTRY INVESTMENT FUNCTIONS

Industry Classification	Standard Error of Capacity Utilization (Index No.)	Cash Flow Elasticity	Interest Rate Elasticity
20—Food	16	0.48	−0.33
22—Textiles	43		−0.71
26—Paper products	43	0.30	−0.54
28—Chemicals	35		
29—Petroleum	26	0.37	−0.78
30—Rubber	57	0.36	
32—Stone, clay, and glass	42		−0.48
331—Iron and steel	119		
333—Nonferrous metals	61		
35—Machinery	67		
36—Electrical machinery	62	0.31	
371—Autos	93		−1.77
372—Other transportation	110	0.46	

---

[19] Capacity utilization was used instead of sales to measure cyclical fluctuations rather than movements of a trend.

[20] This table is taken, with some modifications, from Evans, *op. cit.*, p. 158.

capacity utilization. If the automobile equation is omitted, there is a significant negative correlation between these variables.[21] Five of the six industries with smaller fluctuations have significant interest rate elasticities, but none of the industries with larger fluctuations do except for autos. The very high reported interest rate elasticity for the car investment equation, which is also found in the work of Resek and Locke Anderson, does not appear to be a reasonable result. As mentioned above, the large auto companies rarely borrow money for investment, because they generate internal funds in excess of those needed for capital requirements.

The relationship between cash flow and fluctuations in capacity utilization is not the one expected from the theory outlined above. Only two of the six highly cyclical capital goods industries (331 through 372) have a significant cash flow elasticity, whereas several of the industries with small cyclical fluctuations do. The latter finding is not unreasonable; the *meI* and *mcf* curves probably intersect in region *C* for those industries, because the interest rate is also significant in all cases except rubber. However, the failure to find a positive relationship between cash flow and investment for most of the highly cyclical capital-goods industries is rather surprising. Even if autos are excluded on the basis that neither financial variable should be significant (intersection in region *A*) the results are not very good. Particularly puzzling are the results for the steel industry. In supplementary experimentation with this particular industry to see if some significant cash flow variable could be found even at the expense of data mining, the results were always the same. Cash flow variables were nonsignificant and sometimes even negative. This is also the case for the studies of Resek and Locke Anderson, as reported in Section 5.3. Lags of up to three years were also tried on the possibility that a much longer lag structure existed for the steel companies than for other industries, but no correlation was found in this case either. The steel companies are constantly arguing that they need larger profits to have enough money for investment in new plant and equipment. On the basis of these studies, it would appear that the plea is really for higher profits alone, and that investment plans are determined by output requirements.

We now turn to the nonmanufacturing sector, where the results are much more clear-cut. Here cash flow is not significant for any of six categories,[22] whereas interest rate variables are significant for all industries except railroads. For the commercial and other sector, the spread between the long- and short-term interest rates is used instead of the level of the long-term rate. This variable is also used to explain investment in residential construction; commercial investment (which is mostly construction) is somewhat similar to residential

---

[21] The correlation coefficient between the standard error of capacity utilization and interest rate elasticity (excluding automobiles) is $r = 0.58$. This corresponds to a value of $F = 5.6$. The 5 percent significance level of (1, 11) degrees of freedom is 4.8.

[22] These are mining, railroads, other transportation, public utilities, communications, and commercial and other.

construction because both types of investment often obtain funds from the money market only after the needs of other business enterprises have been satisfied. The rationale for this term is described in Chapter 7.

The dichotomy between the manufacturing and nonmanufacturing sectors, plus the negative correlation between the interest rate and cyclical fluctuations for industries in the manufacturing sector (except for autos), verifies part of Duesenberry's hypothesis. On the other hand, although the cash flow variable is not significant in the nonmanufacturing sector and is significant in parts of the manufacturing sector, it does not give reasonable results in that sector.

Since the particular measure of cash flow we have used has not worked well, it seems logical to try alternative measures. This is the approach taken in the next section. However, before turning to this task, there is one problem that needs further clarification. Despite the generally poor showing of the cash flow variable in the individual industry equations, this term is often highly significant in the aggregate manufacturing investment function. Furthermore, the elasticity of the cash flow term in the overall equation is significantly higher than a weighted average of the elasticities in the individual equations. This does not happen for any of the other variables. It appears that total cash flow serves as a general cyclical indicator as well as a financial variable; when stock prices are added to the function this discrepancy disappears. We document this conclusion in the remainder of this section.

It has been noted for some time that the percentage of the variance of investment explained (as measured by $\bar{R}^2$) is higher for the aggregate manufacturing investment function than for the average of the individual functions; this is also true for the nonmanufacturing sector. This was discussed by Grunfeld in an early reference to the problem in view of the results he obtained.[23] The subject was pursued further by Griliches and Grunfeld and by Boot and deWit.[24] The same phenomenon has been noted by Meyer and Glauber, Locke Anderson, and the present author, even though widely differing forms of the investment function were used. A few brief comments on this phenomenon may be in order, although a statistical discussion of the problem is not called for here.

In very general terms there are three possibilities that may occur among the error terms of the individual industry equations for each given year:

1. The errors may be negatively correlated. In other words, positive and negative errors will on the average be evenly distributed for a given year. In the aggregate equation these errors are likely to cancel out, giving rise to a much better fit.

2. The errors may not be correlated. In this case the aggregate equation

[23] Grunfeld. *op. cit.*, pp. 248–255.

[24] Z. Griliches and Y. Grunfeld, "Is Aggregation Necessarily Bad?" *Review of Economics and Statistics*, Vol. 42, No. 1 (February, 1960), pp. 1–8.

J. C. G. Boot and G. M. deWit, "Investment Demand: An Empirical Contribution to the Aggregation Problem," *International Economic Review*, Vol. 1, No. 1 (January, 1960), pp. 3–30.

will probably have a smaller standard error because of the law of large numbers.

3. The errors may be positively correlated. They will tend to be mostly positive in one year and mostly negative in another year. In general, the average error of the aggregate equations will not be smaller unless one of the independent variables is serving as a general cyclical indicator. For example, investment for a certain industry might be high in a given year if *total* manufacturing profits (and cash flow) were high in the previous year, even if the cash flow of the particular industry itself had not been high.

A glance at the graph in Figure 5.5 clearly demonstrates that the residuals do tend to "bunch"; most of them are positive in good years and negative in bad years.[25] Yet the residuals of the aggregate function, fitted with the same

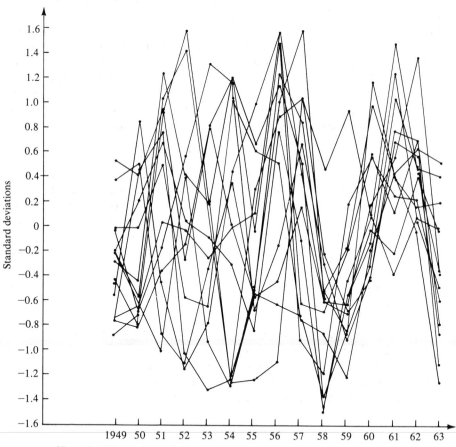

Normalized Errors (Annual Observations) of Two Digit Industry Investment Functions

Figure 5.5

[25] In 5 of the 15 years, 11 or more of the 13 industries had errors of the same sign. The probability that this would happen if the errors were randomly distributed is less than 0.0001.

variable, do not show this pattern. The implication is clear: One of the coefficients in the aggregate function is not a weighted average of the coefficients in the individual equations but is serving as a general cyclical indicator. This tendency is also noted by Boot and deWit, who find "a tendency toward positive correlation of the microdisturbances corresponding to separate firms, a feature which suggests that the individual firms' investments were subject to a common factor that is not introduced explicitly as an explanatory variable in the microregressions."[26]

We can get some estimate of which variable is acting in such a way by comparing the weighted elasticities of the individual industries with the aggregate function. Additional evidence on this point can be obtained by comparing the regressions estimated for total manufacturing investment with and without an index of stock prices. These comparisons are given in Table 5.2.

The inclusion of stock prices improves the investment equation in several respects. Besides increasing the goodness of fit, the capital stock term now enters with the correct negative sign. In every case the elasticities are now closer to the weighted averages of the individual functions, and in particular the cash flow elasticity decreases by almost half. In an aggregate function without stock prices, total cash flow serves as a general cyclical indicator as well as a financial variable. This does not occur in the individual functions, which accounts for the reduced level of significance for cash flow in the industry-investment equations.

TABLE 5.2 COMPARISON OF ELASTICITIES IN INDIVIDUAL AND AGGREGATE MANUFACTURING INVESTMENT FUNCTIONS

Variable	Weighted Average of Elasticities of Individual Investment Functions	Elasticities of Aggregate Function without Stock Prices	Elasticities of Aggregate Function with Stock Prices
Cp	1.73	1.94	1.65
S	1.19	0.72	1.07
L	0.18	0.36	0.23
i	−0.45	−0.33	−0.50
K	−0.64	—[a]	−0.72
SP			0.29

[a] The K term was dropped from this form of the equation because its parameter estimate was not significantly different from zero.

[26] Boot and deWit, *op. cit.*, p. 21.

5.3   ADDITIONAL LIQUIDITY PROBLEMS

Our analysis of Section 5.2 basically led to the conclusion that the cash flow variable is not a very important determinant of investment in the form in which it was included in the investment functions. Although cash flow was important in a number of industries, it generally was not significant in most of those manufacturing industries where one would expect it to be on a theoretical basis. When stock prices were included in an aggregate function, the importance of cash flow dropped considerably and the coefficient was then approximately equal to a weighted average of individual industry coefficients, which is quite small. Thus we are led to consider other formulations of the cash flow variable, in particular those which incorporate stocks of debts and assets.

In Chapter 4 it was argued that as long as the principle of increasing risk was valid, the true cost of borrowing an additional dollar increased after a certain value of the debt/asset ratio was reached. More specifically, it is the total stock of debt relative to the ability to service charges on this debt that is the relevant variable. Suppose, however, that the total stock of debt is kept approximately proportional to the ability to pay, and this ability to pay follows profits closely. Profits and cash flow are quite closely related, particularly in the short run, so debt is essentially proportional to cash flow. If this is the case, there is no need to include debt as a separate variable. This is implicitly the approach that we have been using up to now. However, since it has not worked particularly well, we ought to examine alternative specifications of the cash flow variable.

Duesenberry suggests that the debt/profit ratio is the relevant variable for explaining the increasing upward slope of the mcf schedule. However, he argues that for this purpose an average of past profits is more relevant than current profits.[27] A more common approach is to relate the ability to pay to the stock of assets. The use of the debt/asset (D/A) ratio in this context is suggested by Locke Anderson. He claims that "the amount of long-term debt which firms consider safe seems to depend primarily on the size of the firms' assets.... Firms appeared to take the limits quite seriously and to avoid actions which would push the debt beyond the limiting share of total capital."[28] Anderson later estimates this "limiting share" to be 18 percent.[29] Resek has also used a similar formulation of a liquidity variable in his investment function; he prefers the form $1/\{K - [(D - RE)/A]\}$, where K is a predetermined constant always greater than D/A and RE are retained earnings. Resek does not specify the value of K in his study. It is clear that as the D/A ratio increases toward the "limiting share," the true cost of additional borrowed funds becomes very expensive. The retained earnings variable represents recognition of the fact that if firms are near the safe D/A limit, they will finance only through

[27] Duesenberry, *op. cit.*, p. 95.
[28] Locke Anderson, *op. cit.*, pp. 41–42.
[29] *Ibid.*, p. 49.

internal funds unless the expected rate of return is very high. Resek might also have included depreciation with retained earnings as an additional source of internal funds. It is not clear how his failure to do so influences his results.

Locke Anderson uses a variable that he calls "long term debt capacity," which is the difference between 18 percent of the total assets and outstanding long-term debt at the beginning of the period. Essentially this amounts to using the difference between the actual and maximum allowable D/A ratios.[30] He does not include retained earnings or depreciation in this formulation, but introduces these explicitly as an additional variable.

Resek finds in his study that the D/A ratio works better than cash flow (L). However, he does not report his results, merely stating that multicollinearity was a problem between output, the change in output, and cash flow, and that all three of these variables behaved erratically when included together. He does report that L has a (correct) positive sign in 6 of 13 industries when included with output. His results show that the D/A ratio has the correct negative sign for 8 of 13 industries, 5 of which are significant. Locke Anderson finds that for a decision lag (that is, the time between changes in economic variables and the beginning of investment plans)[31] of three quarters his version of the D/A ratio is significant in five equations compared to only two for cash flow. In his aggregate manufacturing equation the t ratio for the D/A ratio is 3.4, whereas for cash flow it is only 0.6. However, for a decision lag of one quarter, both D/A and L are significant in five equations and the t ratio of D/A is only 1.4, whereas it is 2.9 for L. Although this does show that the lag structure makes some difference, it does not answer the question of which is the better variable or whether either should be included. Except for the low figure recorded by cash flow in Anderson's study with decision lag 3, there is no evidence at all that any one of the three variables—cash flow or either variant of the debt/asset ratio—is superior in explaining investment decisions. These results are summarized in Table 5.3 on p. 124.

Another approach to this problem is to examine the interindustry structure of these various liquidity variables. According to the hypothesis developed in Section 5.2, the cyclical capital-goods industries should be more sensitive to increasing debt/asset ratios than other firms. The record of these variables for the capital-goods industries is given in Table 5.4. There is no tendency at all toward the expected pattern in Resek's findings, where the D/A ratio is significant in only one of these six industries for both formulations of the function.

---

[30] The variable actually used is $\kappa A - D$, where $\kappa = (D/A)_{max}$. Therefore, $\kappa A - D = [(D/A)_{max} - (D/A)]A$, which can be linearly approximated by

$$\bar{A}\left[\left(\frac{D}{A}\right)_{max} - \frac{D}{A}\right] + A\left[\left(\frac{D}{A}\right)_{max} - \frac{D}{A}\right] + \text{const.}$$

[31] Locke Anderson's lag structure is developed by taking a 4 quarter average of the independent variables and then adding a "decision lag" of 1, 2, or 3 quarters to this average. This represents an average lag of $2\frac{1}{2}$ quarters plus the decision lag: if the latter is 3 quarters, this gives a total lag of $5\frac{1}{2}$ quarters, which agrees closely with the optimal lag estimated in Chapter 4.

TABLE 5.3 RELATIVE PERFORMANCE OF VARIOUS LIQUIDITY VARIABLES

Author	Study	Liquidity Variable Being Tested	Total No. Correct Signs (Maximum 13)	Total No. Significant (at 5% Level)
Resek	Stock prices excluded	Debt/asset ratio	8	5
Resek	Stock prices included	Debt/asset ratio	9	5
Locke Anderson	Decision lag of three quarters	Cash flow	6	2
Locke Anderson	Decision lag of three quarters	Debt/asset ratio	10	5
Locke Anderson	Decision lag of one quarter	Cash flow	10	5
Locke Anderson	Decision lag of one quarter	Debt/asset ratio	9	5
Evans	Inverted W distribution	Cash flow	9	6

Locke Anderson's findings are just a bit more encouraging for the D/A ratio, but only with the short lag. This is not a very convincing result in view of his statement that the decision lag of three quarters represents the best lag; such a lag also agrees with other work done on lag structures. While one might reasonably argue that cash flow would have some effect on investment in these industries, none of the available evidence supports this reasoning. While cash flow remains a relevant determinant of manufacturing investment, its effect is well scattered throughout the various industries. Since there is no additional information or explanation of investment to be gained by using D/A ratios, they are not included for further scrutinization in this chapter.

The role of short-term assets has also been examined by Locke Anderson, who is the only one to do so. Using reasoning similar to that used for the long-term debt and asset variables, he develops a relationship between desired and actual short-term liquidity. He suggests that cash, short-term government holdings, tax liabilities, outstanding short-term debt, and change in net current financial assets ought to be important variables in the investment function. However, because of wrong signs and insignificant coefficients, it becomes necessary to drop all the variables except short-term governments and tax liabilities. Locke Anderson attributes these wrong signs to spurious correlation caused by cyclical variability.

The magnitudes of the coefficients of the two remaining variables are almost equal and opposite in sign.[32] This suggests that all Locke Anderson is

---

[32] See, for instance, Locke Anderson's table of "most successful equations" (his p. 114).

TABLE 5.4   INDUSTRY COMPARISONS OF THE IMPORTANCE OF VARIOUS LIQUIDITY VARIABLES

Author	Study	Liquidity Variable Being Tested	331[a]	333	35	36	371	372	No. Significant
Resek	Stock prices excluded	Debt/asset ratio	NS[b]	WS	S		NS	WS	WS	1
Resek	Stock prices included	Debt/asset ratio	NS	NS	NS	S		NS	WS	1
Locke Anderson	Decision lag of three quarters	Cash flow	WS	NS	WS	WS	WS	NS	0
Locke Anderson	Decision lag of three quarters	Debt/asset ratio	NS	S	WS	S		NS	NS	2
Locke Anderson	Decision lag of one quarter	Cash flow	WS	NS	S		WS	NS	NS	1
Locke Anderson	Decision lag of one quarter	Debt/asset ratio	NS	S	WS	S	S	WS	3
Evans	Inverted W distribution	Cash flow	WS	NS	NS	S	WS	S	2

[a] Industry classification codes are given in Table 5.1.

[b] S, significant with the correct sign; NS, nonsignificant with the correct sign; WS, wrong sign.

measuring is the well-known phenomenon that short-term government assets are specifically put aside for tax liabilities and do not have any effect on investment. Locke Anderson himself discusses this phenomenon; he states that "in order to observe the cyclical behavior of these security holdings, it is necessary to take account of the practice of funding against tax liabilities with short-term government securities."[33] Furthermore, desired short-term liquidity is quite easily changed because firms can borrow for a short term without being committed to a long series of interest repayments or capital loss, as is the case with long-term debt. Owing to both the theoretical and empirical difficulties encountered in this area, the inclusion of short-term assets as a determinant of investment does not seem to be a very promising path to follow.

Another way to approach the problem of the role of internal funds in the investment function is to consider the fact that these funds are used for other purposes besides plant and equipment investment. In a very interesting and well-done study, Dhrymes and Kurz suggest that the investment function

---

[33] *Ibid.*, p. 16.

should be considered one of several simultaneous decisions made by top management of corporations. Firms make decisions to invest in plant and equipment and inventories, pay dividends, and borrow through the bond and stock markets at the same time. Thus investment decisions should be estimated as one of a number of jointly determined functions and not in isolation. From a statistical point of view, this raises the question of whether estimation ought to proceed by the method of ordinary least squares or whether simultaneous methods of estimation ought to be used. In most time-series work, where many of the variables have strong common trends, the difference has not been very large. However, Dhrymes and Kurz find substantial differences in the values and even changes in the signs of the parameter estimates when different methods of estimation are employed.

Basically the method they use is to estimate investment as a function of profits, sales, and alternative sources and uses of funds, which are dividends, external finance through borrowing, and short-term investment (mainly inventories). They then proceed to estimate dividends as a function of the same jointly determined variables and also estimate external borrowing in a similar way. In symbolic notation we have

(5.1)
$$Dv = f_1(\pi, N, I, EF)$$

$$I = f_2(\pi_{-1}, S - S_{-3}, N, Dv, EF)$$

$$EF = f_3(D/A, i, Dep, \pi, Dv, I)$$

where[34] Dv = dividends

I = plant and equipment investment

EF = external borrowing

π = profits

N = net short-term liquidity position (this is dominated by movements in inventory fluctuation)

S = sales

D/A = debt/asset ratio

i = interest rate

Dep = depreciation

It will be seen in this model that the D/A ratio, the interest rate, and depreciation will have an effect on investment only inasmuch as they influence the amount of external borrowing which is necessary. If the amount of internally generated funds is greater than the amount of planned investment, these funds will not represent a constraint on investments. Essentially this would be an intersection

---

[34] Dhrymes and Kurz, op. cit., pp. 455–457. We have changed and simplified their notation somewhat. All the variables they use are in ratio form, to eliminate the heteroscedasticity that would otherwise arise from the use of a cross-section sample. We have omitted these ratios to present the essence of their theory.

of the *meI* and *mcf* schedule in region *A* of the previous discussion. If, on the other hand, some external borrowing is needed, the amount of internal funds available is of some importance. It is also seen that investment depends directly on alternative uses of funds—short-term investment and divident payments.

The results of this study show that when all sources and uses of funds are taken into consideration, profits have a significant positive effect on investment. Dividends and inventory investment are clearly substitute uses for these funds and exert a negative effect on investment. Dhrymes and Kurz also argue that failure to trace this chain of causality has resulted in the finding that profits are not a significant determinant of investment in other cross-section studies, especially those of Eisner and Kuh. Suppose that profits are positively related to investment, and dividends are positively related to profits but negatively related to investment. Then an increase in profits will not raise investment if it is used to increase dividends. In the Dhrymes–Kurz system this will be reflected by the positive coefficient of profits and the negative coefficient of dividends in the investment function. In other systems, where the chain of causality is not so clearly traced, it will be reflected by a nonsignificant coefficient for profits.

Dhrymes and Kurz also include a variant of the *D/A* ratio and a variable representing interest rate (interest payments/amount of bond finance) in the external finance equation. The partial regression coefficient of external finance in the investment equation is itself rather weak; it is significantly positive in only three years and negative in four others. On balance it is clearly positive, because none of the negative terms is very large, but the link is still somewhat tenuous. In the external finance equation, both the *D/A* ratio and the interest rate ought to be negatively related. The inclusion of the *D/A* ratio is a failure—it is negative in five years and positive in five years, although some of the negative years are significant. Coupled with the weak coefficient of external finance in the investment equation, it would seem especially hard to build much of a case for that variable. On the other hand, the interest rate variable is negative in all ten years and significantly negative in most of them so that a stronger case exists here. This agrees with other findings of the effect of interest rates on investment, as discussed below.

Thus our assumptions about the *mcf* schedule can be modified to represent interactions among various sources and uses of funds. The study of Dhrymes and Kurz shows that, *cet. par.*, an increase in profits will raise investment; but *cet. par.* may be an invalid statement if alternative uses of funds are needed. Additional work in this area is presently being undertaken by Dhrymes, and the answers to these problems must await future results. Perhaps promising new light can be shed on the problem of cash flow in the investment function with the help of this excellent study. At a minimum it would suggest a careful analysis of inventory and dividend policies in the highly cyclical capital goods industries.

In Section 4.3 it was suggested that the bifurcation hypothesis might be one explanation of the role of cash flow in the investment function. That hypothesis stated that cash flow is the important financial variable during recessions, whereas the interest rate is important during booms. This cannot be tested very well by time-series analysis; continual cross-section analysis for several years is much better. This has been done in the Dhrymes–Kurz study for the period 1951–1960. According to the bifurcation hypothesis, cash flow would serve as an effective limit on investment in those years when general business activity was low, or, more accurately, in years when businessmen *think* that business activity is going to be low, because funds are committed a year in advance. Thus recession years and the following years should be those for which profits (or cash flow) are important. In the range of the Dhrymes–Kurz study these are 1954, 1955, 1958, and 1959. As was mentioned in Chapter 4, the coefficient of profits is positive and significant in all these years except 1959. However, it is also positive in all the years of the sample except 1960 and is additionally significantly positive in 1953 and 1956. Thus profits appears to be useful in explaining investment throughout the sample period.

There is some corroboration for this study. Using continual cross-section analysis for 1951–1954, Meyer and Glauber found that cash flow less the change in working capital was significant only for 1 and 3 industries out of 20 for 1951 and 1952, respectively, but was significant for 9 and 7 industries in 1953 and 1954, respectively. Thus the same pattern is observed even though a different concept and a questionable lag structure is used. For the period 1955–1958, Eisner found that profits were highly significant in 1955 and 1956, but not in 1957 and 1958. In the eight years covered by these studies, 1958 is the only year of disagreement.

The bifurcation hypothesis can also be tested in another way in the context of the Dhrymes–Kurz model—by examining the sign of the profits variable in the external finance equation. If business activity is low and profits and sales are down, according to this hypothesis, businessmen should be more hesitant to borrow, so that there should be a positive correlation between

TABLE 5.5   ADDITIONAL TESTS OF THE BIFURCATION HYPOTHESIS

	1951	1952	1953	1954	1955	1956	1957	1958	1959	1960
Prediction by bifurcation hypothesis	n[a]	n	n	p	p	n	n	p	p	n
Actual regression coefficient sign	n	p	n	p	p*	n*	p	p	n	p

[a] n, negative relationship, and p, positive relationship between profits and amount of external financing.

* Parameter estimate less than its standard error estimate.

TABLE 5.6 ADDITIONAL TESTS OF THE BIFURCATION HYPOTHESIS

	1951	1952	1953	1954	1955	1956	1957	1958	1959	1960
Predicted by bifurcation hypothesis	p[a]	p	p	O	O	p	p	O	O	p
Actual regression coefficient	O	p	p	p	O	n	O	n	O	O

[a] n, negative coefficient, and p, positive coefficient of external finance term in the investment function, if greater than its standard error; O, coefficient less than its standard error.

profits and external borrowing in recession years. In the boom, profits will not be a barrier, since the *mei* curve moves out relative to the *mcf* curve. Firms will determine their investment based on variables other than cash flow, so higher profits will lead to less external borrowing. Thus in boom years there should be a negative correlation. The evidence is shown in Table 5.5. Only six of the ten signs conform to a priori expectations, and if the least significant observations are omitted, only four of eight conform.

Another test that can be performed along the same lines is to compare the coefficient of the external finance variable in the investment function. It ought to be positive in boom years and not correlated either way in recession years (since then only internal funds ought to be important). We say zero correlation occurs if the parameter estimate is less than its standard error estimate. These results are presented in Table 5.6. Only four of the ten signs conform to a priori expectations. There is no evidence of the correlation posited by the bifurcation hypothesis in any of these tests or studies.

As was previously mentioned, the bifurcation hypothesis also states that interest rates should be an important determinant of investment in booms but not in recessions. Empirically it is difficult to measure interest rates charged to individual firms by banks; such figures are available only implicitly as total interest payments to banks divided by total outstanding bank loans. Even with this weak measure of interest rates on new loans, Dhrymes and Kurz find that the partial correlation between interest rates and investment is negative for all years of the sample. Again there is no finding for the bifurcation hypothesis. Meyer and Glauber, the chief proponents of such a theory, suggest finding the answer in time-series analysis by estimating separate functions for boom years and recession years. However, they, too, find the interest rate to be significantly negative in both equations. Furthermore, we have already argued that a slightly lower effect of the interest rate in the downswing might well be due to the increasing inelasticity of the *mei* at lower interest rates and not the relative shifting of the *mei* and *mcf* curves.

The interest rate is an important determinant of investment in all the recent studies in which it is included. Except for the studies of Kuh and Eisner, which do not include the interest rate, all other results considered here find that it is quite significant. In some respects this represents a turnabout from the 1950s, when it was often believed that the interest rate was not a significant determinant of investment. Griliches and Wallace have suggested that this is due to the fact that interest rates were fixed at low levels from 1946 to 1953; thus there was no statistical variability that could be measured and related to fluctuations in investment.[35] Although this may be part of the reason, the view that interest rates were found to be unimportant probably has been overstated. In several early works by Klein,[36] interest rates were generally found to be significant when included with a lag of one year. The fact that investment decisions take a while to make was incorporated in this early work in empirical model building. However, most early researchers neglected the question of lag structure and found only that the unlagged interest rate was not significant. This is still true; witness the wrong signs for the interest rate with a short lag in the investment functions of the Brookings model, as discussed in Chapter 4. Regardless of the reasons for a nonsignificant interest rate in many earlier investment functions, it is now generally considered to be an important determinant of investment.

Some regression estimates by this author show that the interest rate becomes more significantly negative in almost all cases when stock prices are added to the investment function. For aggregate manufacturing investment this can be seen in Table 5.2. There is no such definite relationship between stock prices and any other of the independent variables. This is what would be expected to occur if stock prices are an additional determinant of the cost of borrowed funds. Stock prices and interest rates both tend to reach their cyclical peaks shortly before the downturn of the cycle and their cyclical lows near the upturn of the cycle. But if stock prices are positively correlated with investment and interest rates are negatively correlated with investment, the absolute value of the interest rate coefficient will be biased downward if stock prices are omitted. The following possibilities may occur:

1. Stock prices are not at all important as a financing variable, because very little financing is done through equities. Financing constraints can be measured adequately with cash flow and the interest rate. In this case, stock prices still might be important as an expectations variable but would have no effect on the parameter estimates of other financing variables. This does not seem to be the case.

2. The relative importance of stock prices (as a financing variable) to the interest rate should be approximately equal to the amount of new issues raised

[35] Z. Griliches and N. Wallace, "The Determinants of Investment Revisited," *International Economic Review*, Vol. 6, No. 3 (September, 1965), p. 326.

[36] L. R. Klein, *Economic Fluctuations in the United States 1921–1941* (New York: Wiley, 1950). L. R. Klein and A. S. Goldberger, *An Econometric Model of the United States Economy, 1929–1952* (Amsterdam: North-Holland, 1955).

by equity financing relative to the total amount of new issues. In other words, if only one fourth of outside new money is raised through equity and three fourths by bonds (or banks), then the long-lag stock-price variable should have an elasticity of about one third that of the interest rate. This effect cannot be isolated and measured exactly, because stock prices with a short lag serve as an expectations variable, and short- and long-lag stock-price variables cannot both be included in the same time-series regression without serious problems of multicollinearity. However, in general we would expect the long-lag stock-price variable to be less important than interest rates and less important than the short-lag stock-price variable. This is what is observed in our studies.

3. Stock prices should be more important than interest rates, because firms must weigh the opportunity costs of retained earnings in terms of dividends rather than in terms of the interest rate. As previously mentioned, if the rate of return on a future project is not expected to be great enough to cover the yield on equity capital, then retained earnings should be paid out to the stockholders. In this case, the relative importance of stock prices to bond yields would be measured by the equity/debt ratio, not the new stocks issued/ new bonds issued ratio. Since the equity/debt ratio is greater than unity for the average of all manufacturing corporations, then stock prices with a long lag should be more important than interest rates. Although this represents an interesting alternative for describing the marginal cost of funds schedule, it is not supported by the facts.

4. The cost of borrowed capital is independent of the way in which it is financed. This is the Modigliani–Miller cost of capital hypothesis. Their Proposition I states that "The average cost of capital to any firm is completely independent of its capital structure and is equal to the capitalization rate of a pure equity stream of its class."[37] Essentially the reason given for this is that arbitrage will eliminate any difference in the market values of two firms worth the same amount. Therefore it makes no difference what bond/stock ratio the firm uses for financing. Since the firm is worth a given amount, it will be capitalized at only that one return consistent with its market value. This ratio cannot be altered by changing the way in which debt is marketed. Miller[38] has suggested that if this argument holds, the bond/stock ratio should be independent of interest rates, dividend yields, or their ratio. He suggests that the ratio

$$\frac{\text{new money issues through stocks}}{\text{total new money issues}}$$

---

[37] F. Modigliani and M. H. Miller, "The Cost of Capital, Corporation Finance and the Theory of Investment," *American Economic Review*, Vol. 48, No. 3 (June, 1958), p. 268.

[38] M. H. Miller, "Research Study Five: The Corporation Income Tax and Corporate Financial Policies," in Commission on Money and Credit, *Stabilization Policies* (Englewood Cliffs, N.J.: Prentice-Hall, 1963).

should be uncorrelated with

$$\text{(a)} \; \frac{1}{\text{dividend yield}}, \quad \text{(b)} \; \frac{\text{bond yield}}{\text{dividend yield}}, \quad \text{and}$$

$$\text{(c)} \; \frac{\text{bond yield adjusted for taxes}}{\text{dividend yield}}$$

The reason for the last ratio is that firms may prefer debt financing to equity financing because interest payments are deductible, whereas dividends are not. Thus the comparable cost of present-day debt service is really about half the stated interest rate.

Using Miller's own data and hypotheses for the same time period (1920–1956) he discusses, we obtained the results shown in Table 5.7. There it can be seen that *all* sets of calculations are significant at the 1 percent level except for the last run, which is still significant at the 5 percent level. We reran the bond yield after taxes calculation for two subperiods, the low-tax years and the high-tax years, the dividing point being 1941. It does not seem sensible to treat changes in the tax structure at that time as if they affected only the bond yield. Personal income taxes also rose at the same time that corporate income taxes rose, so that the tax advantage of capital gains from equities became much more important than it had been before. Because of this, investors were more willing to buy equities than previously, *cet. par.*, and the advantage of debt finance was partially offset. For these two subperiods the correlation between the (bond yield after taxes/dividend yield) ratio and the stock/bond

TABLE 5.7   RELATIONSHIPS AMONG DIVIDEND YIELD, BOND YIELD, AND NEW STOCK FLOTATION

Correlation of new money issues through stocks ÷ total new money issues, with:	$\bar{R}^2$	Time Period	F Statistic	Value of F Statistic at Level of Significance	
				5%	1%
$\dfrac{1}{\text{dividend yield}}$	0.264	1920–1956	12.5	4.1	7.4
$\dfrac{\text{bond yield}}{\text{dividend yield}}$	0.285	1920–1956	14.0	4.1	7.4
$\dfrac{\text{bond yield after taxes}}{\text{dividend yield}}$	0.184	1920–1956	7.9	4.1	7.4
	0.351	1920–1941	10.3	4.3	8.0
	0.363	1942–1956	7.4	4.6	8.9

Source: From M. H. Miller, "Research Study Five: The Corporation Income Tax and Corporate Financial Policies," in Commission on Money and Credit, *Stabilization Policies* (Englewood Cliffs, N.J.: Prentice-Hall, 1963), table V-A2, p. 448, and table V-A5, p. 452.

ratio is substantially higher and compares favorably with the other correlations reported.

There is a significant relationship between the ratio of new equity to new debt financing and the relative yields of bonds for stocks for all Miller's suggested tests. In a multivariate analysis this result would undoubtedly be much stronger, because other elements affecting this ratio would be properly specified. But even in this simple correlation test, the relationships are clearly significant. Thus there does not seem to be much gained by arguing that investment does not depend on the relative costs of financing. At a minimum the burden of proof is upon those who wish to show that there is no correlation.

5.4   THE DETERMINANTS OF INVESTMENT—STATISTICAL RESULTS AND CONCLUSIONS

We now summarize the results on investment functions and present empirical estimates. This is not a straightforward thing to do, because these functions are estimated in diverse forms. The results of earlier work on the investment function (through 1959) have been thoroughly discussed by Eisner and Strotz.[39] We do not review work covered in their article but concentrate on more recent investment functions. We have selected seven studies for inclusion: those of Eisner, Meyer and Glauber, Locke Anderson, Jorgenson, Griliches and Wallace, Resek, and this author.[40] All these have appeared in 1964 or later; although Eisner's early work in this area appeared in 1960,[41] we use his 1965 results.[42]

Because of the many different measures of output, cash flow, and investment which are used in these studies, plus the fact that some regressions are estimated in ratio form whereas others are not, we present the comparative statistics in terms of elasticities. A technical explanation of the calculations is found in the appendix to this chapter. Here we merely discuss the general formulation

---

[39] R. Eisner and R. H. Strotz, "Research Study Two: Determinants of Business Investment," in Commission on Money and Credit, *Impacts of Monetary Policy* (Englewood Cliffs, N.J.: Prentice-Hall, 1963).

[40] All these studies have been referred to earlier in the chapter except for D. Jorgenson. "Anticipations and Investment Behavior," chap. 2 in J. S. Duesenberry, G. Fromm, L. R. Klein, and E. Kuh, eds., *The Brookings Quarterly Econometric Model of the United States* (Chicago: Rand McNally, 1965).

[41] R. Eisner, "A Distributed Lag Investment Function," *Econometrica*, Vol. 28, No. 1 (January, 1960), pp. 1–30.

[42] Some other important studies that appeared recently are not included here, because they deal mainly with aspects of investment other than the actual estimating of the parameters. DeLeeuw's study, although very important because it establishes the inverted V type of distribution, is mainly concerned with the finding of an optimum lag structure, although the function quite sensibly includes capacity utilization, cash flow, and interest rate variables. Almon's study is entirely concerned with the lag between appropriations and expenditures. The study by Dhrymes and Kurz is primarily concerned with the interdependence of investment and other decisions of the firm. Kuh explores the microeconomic approach and does not actually estimate aggregate parameters.

of the different functions. For simplicity this exposition will include only the output term, but in all cases the elasticities for the other terms are calculated similarly. All elasticities are calculated at sample-period mean values unless otherwise stated. In all the examples we consider the case where output rises by one unit and stays at this new higher level.

1. The simplest form of the investment function used here is

$$(5.2) \qquad\qquad I_t = a + bO_{t-j}$$

The short-run (impact) elasticity of investment with respect to output (referred to throughout as e_{IO}^S) is $b \cdot (\bar{O}/\bar{I})$, where barred values are sample-period mean values. Investment keeps growing at rate b; capital stock keeps increasing, so one cannot calculate a finite long-run elasticity of output with respect to capital (symbol e_{KO}^L). This is the form used by Locke Anderson.

2. A very similar form in which investment keeps increasing monotonically is

$$(5.3) \qquad\qquad I_t = a + bO_{t-j} + cI_{t-j-1}$$

Here e_{IO}^S is again $b \cdot (\bar{O}/\bar{I})$ and the long-run elasticity of investment with respect to output (e_{IO}^L) is $[b/(1-c)] \cdot (\bar{O}/\bar{I})$. No e_{KO}^L can be calculated from this form either. This is the equation used by Meyer and Glauber.

3. $I_t = a + bO_{t-j} - \lambda K_{t-1}$. As shown in Chapter 4, this comes from the form

$$(5.4) \qquad\qquad K_t = b \sum_{i=0}^{\infty} \lambda^i O_{t-i-j}$$

Then

$$(5.5) \qquad e_{IO}^S = b \cdot (\bar{O}/\bar{I}) \qquad \text{and} \qquad e_{KO}^L = \frac{b}{1-\lambda} \cdot (\bar{O}/\bar{K})$$

This is the form used by Evans.

4. $I_t = a + \sum_{i=0}^{n} \mu_i \Delta O_{t-i}$, where μ_i have no preassigned values but will generally first rise and then fall. This function comes from the form

$$(5.6) \qquad\qquad K_t = \sum_{i=0}^{n} \mu_i O_{t-i}$$

and the elasticities are thus

$$(5.7) \qquad e_{IO}^S = \mu_0 \cdot (\bar{O}/\bar{I}) \qquad \text{and} \qquad e_{KO}^L = \sum_{i=0}^{n} \frac{\overline{\mu_i O_{t-i}}}{\bar{K}}$$

This is the form used by Eisner and Resek. In Resek's case the μ_i are the weights determined by Almon.

5. $I_t = a + bO_{t-j} + c(I_{t-1} - \delta K_{t-1})$, where δ = the depreciation rate. This function generally gives first rising weights (as cI_{t-1} gives successively larger

values to I_t) and then decreasing weights (as δK_{t-1} gives, on balance with cI_{t-1}, smaller values to I_t). This is the form used by Jorgenson and by Griliches and Wallace. Again $e_{IO}^S = b \cdot (\bar{O}/\bar{I})$. In the long run, Jorgenson derives his function so that e_{KO}^L is identically unity. Griliches and Wallace do not do this, so for their function

$$(5.8) \qquad e_{KO}^L = \frac{b}{\delta(1-c)+\delta} \cdot (\bar{O}/\bar{K})$$

In Table 5.8 we present estimates for the average percentage change in investment for one and two years following a 1 percent change in sales, cash flow, or the interest rate, which then stay at these new levels. The "peak" elasticity, which is the single quarter in which the impact elasticity is the highest, is also presented. After the peak, the weights again turn down for all functions except that of Locke Anderson, where they stay at this level. The peak elasticities are not calculated for the Meyer–Glauber function, because their weights increase monotonically. Long-run elasticities relative to the capital stock are also given where relevant (see p. 136).

The form of the Evans manufacturing investment function estimated in accordance with the theory developed previously is

$$(5.9) \qquad I_{pm} = -11.48 + 5.28 C_{p-1} + 0.0453\tfrac{1}{2}(X_{m-5} + X_{m-6})$$
$$\qquad\qquad\quad (0.66) \qquad\quad (0.0076)$$

$$+ 0.1888\tfrac{1}{2}(L_{m-5} + L_{m-6})$$
$$(0.0590)$$

$$- 1.539\tfrac{1}{2}(i_{L-5} + i_{L-6}) + 0.0783\tfrac{1}{2}(SP_{m-1} + SP_{m-2})$$
$$(0.366) \qquad\qquad\qquad (0.0214)$$

$$- 0.0309\tfrac{1}{2}(K_{m-5} + K_{m-6}) \qquad \bar{R}^2 = 0.874$$
$$(0.0107)$$

A slightly different function is actually used in the Wharton EFU model as given in Chapter 15. There we do not use the stock price index, in order not to have to predict it, and we incorporated the Almon weights. That function is

$$(15.4) \qquad I_{pm} = -17.45 + 24.59 C_{p-1} + 0.1308 \sum_{i=0}^{7} A_i(X_m)_{-i-2}$$
$$\qquad\qquad\qquad\quad (2.30) \qquad\qquad (0.0104)$$

$$+ 0.1644 \sum_{i=0}^{7} A_i(L_m)_{-i-2} - 1.158 \sum_{i=0}^{7} A_i(i_L)_{-i-2}$$
$$(0.0610) \qquad\qquad\qquad (0.292)$$

$$- 0.0248 \sum_{i=0}^{7} A_i(K_m)_{-i-2} \qquad \bar{R}^2 = 0.895$$
$$(0.0065)$$

TABLE 5.8   ELASTICITIES OF SELECTED INVESTMENT FUNCTIONS[a]

Equation No.[b]	Elasticities Relative to Investment				Elasticities Relative to Capital Stock
	Av. 1 yr	Av. 2 yr	Peak (in Quarter $t + j$)		Long Run
Output					
1	0.13	0.95	2.18	7 on	n.c.[c]
2	0.96	1.43	n.c.[d]		n.c.[c]
3	1.68	1.83	2.23	6	0.93
4	0.53	0.88	1.32	8	0.60[e]
5	0.57	2.32	4.96	7	1.00
6	1.75	2.06	2.95	3–6	0.64
7	1.79	1.35	2.25	3	n.c.[c]
	(0.92)[f]	(1.47)[f]			
Interest rate					
1	0.03	0.18	0.41		n.c.[c]
	(0.07)[g]	(0.49)[g]	(1.13)[g]		
2	0.08	0.24	n.c.[d]		n.c.[c]
3	0.00	0.22	0.50		0.16
4	0.35	0.59	0.86		0.38[e]
5	0.20	0.83	1.43		0.38[e]
7	1.42	1.22	1.78		n.c.[c]
	(0.83)[f]	(1.33)[f]			
Cash flow					
1	0.01	0.04	0.10		n.c.[c]
	(0.30)[h]	(0.58)[h]	(0.69)[h]		
2	0.36	0.54	n.c.[d]		n.c.[c]
3	0.00	0.10	0.23		0.07

[a] All values are taken from time-series estimates.
[b] Equations are as follows: 1, Locke Anderson; 2, Meyer and Glauber; 3, Evans; 4, Griliches and Wallace; 5, Jorgenson; 6, Eisner; 7, Resek.
[c] Cannot be calculated because of inappropriate form of the investment function (see the text).
[d] Weights in this function keep rising over time, so no "peak" can be established after which weights start declining.
[e] Values taken from Z. Griliches and N. Wallace, "The Determinants of Investment Revisited," *International Economic Review*, Vol. 6, No. 3 (September, 1965), p. 324.
[f] In Resek's functions, there is no lag at all between change in economic variables and the beginning of investment (that is, no decision lag). Some of the elasticities have been recalculated assuming the same parameter estimates but a two-quarter decision lag. It is clear that this is not an entirely valid procedure, because the parameter estimates themselves would undoubtedly change a little with a different lag structure.
[g] Use of the bond rate instead of the bill rate. The latter is used in Locke Anderson's "preferred" equation.
[h] Taken from Locke Anderson's function with decision lag equal to one quarter instead of three quarters.

Variables are defined as

I_{pm} = gross private domestic investment in the manufacturing sector, billions of 1958 dollars

C_p = index of capacity utilization, fraction

X_m = gross output originating in the manufacturing sector, billions of 1958 dollars

L_m = corporate cash flow (retained earnings plus depreciation) in the manufacturing sector, billions of 1958 dollars

i_L = average yield on long-term corporate bonds (Moody's), percent

SP_m = index of manufacturing stock prices (Standard and Poor's), 1958 = 100.0

K_m = capital stock in the manufacturing sector, billions of 1958 dollars

A_i = normalized Almon weights: $A = 0.074$, $A_1 = 0.132$, $A_2 = 0.170$, $A_3 = 0.183$, $A_4 = 0.171$, $A_5 = 0.138$, $A_6 = 0.091$, and $A_7 = 0.041$

Other functions used and calculating the elasticities will be found in the appendix to this chapter.

A few comments may be in order on the similarities and differences of the elasticities. The low impact elasticities of output for equations 1 and 4 in Table 5.8 are due to the time paths in these functions and do not reflect the fact that output is less important in the long run. For instance, Griliches and Wallace find that only 39 percent of the eventual change in investment has taken place two years after a change in output (or interest rates) has occurred. This does not seem very reasonable in view of the findings from other functions (for a time path of some of these functions, see Figure 4.14). It is also interesting to note that the two functions which have the most similar theoretical structure, equations 4 and 5, have the greatest differential in the two-year effect of output. We suggest that the average two-year output elasticity (for these two equations) of 1.6 is a reasonable value.

The interest rate elasticity is subject to a great deal of variability. The Jorgenson figure is not independently obtained, because the interest rate is combined with output and other variables in fixed proportions, so that the size of the interest rate elasticity is closely related to the output elasticity. Resek's elasticity seems very far out of line, although it is possible that all the others are wrong. This might have been due to the inclusion of stock prices in the model, but even in his version without stock prices, the elasticity is still greater than unity. It might also be partially a proxy for the trend, but Resek reports that the inclusion of a trend does not significantly alter his results.

Unfortunately, cash flow was not included in many of the models, so less information is available about its probable elasticity. Eisner uses gross profits instead of cash flow, which is different not only because taxes and dividends have not been deducted but because depreciation has not been added. He gets an elasticity for gross profits of approximately 0.30 (for a two-year average), which is not out of line with the other figures presented. Resek uses the term

$$\frac{1}{\text{const.} - [(\text{debt} - RE)/\text{assets}]}$$

but since no values of the constant are given, it is not possible to determine the elasticity of retained earnings (depreciation is still omitted). However, some reasonable estimates of the constant put the elasticity of retained earnings at less than 0.2. Since the highest estimate of cash flow elasticity in all these studies is smaller than the lowest estimate of output elasticity, there is not much question about which variable is more important. Of course, this does not mean that only one of them is important.

In spite of these differences in the functions, several conclusions emerge about manufacturing investment functions:

1. A change of 1 percent in output will produce an average change of $1\frac{1}{2}$ to 2 percent in investment over a two-year period.

2. A change of 1 percent in the interest rate will produce a change of between $\frac{1}{4}$ to $\frac{1}{2}$ percent in investment. A change of one *point* in the long-term interest rate, say from 4 to 5 percent, will change investment from 5 to 10 percent over a two-year period. Those who claim that monetary policy is ineffective (in all fairness, a dwindling group) must not be talking about the postwar U.S. economy. However, two important caveats are in order. First, the *long-term* rate must be affected, not merely the short-term rate. Second, the *lag* before interest rates start to have much of an effect is over a year. The reason for this is that a rise in interest rates will have no effect on projects already under way.

3. A change of 1 percent in cash flow will change investment from $\frac{1}{4}$ to $\frac{1}{2}$ percent. Changes in cash flow will not affect all manufacturing industries and will not affect nonmanufacturing investment at all.

A combination of conclusions 1 and 3 leads to the observation that a \$1 billion cut in personal income taxes will lead to an average of $\frac{1}{2}$ to $\frac{3}{4}$ percent increase in investment over a two-year period. A \$1 billion increase in corporate cash flow, either through a decrease in corporate income taxes or an increase in depreciation allowances, will lead to a $\frac{1}{4}$ to $\frac{1}{2}$ percent increase in investment over the same period. Thus if the aim of the government is to stimulate investment through fiscal policy, it will get more change, dollar for dollar, through cutting personal income taxes than corporate income taxes. Changes in the latter or liberalization of depreciation allowances must be defended on grounds other than stimulating investment or GNP.[43]

All the above results have been examined and tabulated only for the manufacturing sector. There has been some reluctance to estimate nonmanufacturing investment functions relative to the large numbers of studies which have been done for manufacturing. However, the results are substantially different for

---

[43] These multiplier values are discussed in greater detail in Chapter 20.

the two sectors, as was indicated in Section 5.2. It would be expected that cash flow would be less important and the cost and availability of credit more important for nonmanufacturing investment. This is in fact the case. An additional disaggregation within this sector is also necessary between very large firms which are prime customers for borrowing funds, such as those in the transportation, public utility, and communications industries, and those much smaller firms which receive residual supplies of credit, which undertake most commercial investment (stores and shopping centers) and investment of professional practices. In the first case, the level of interest rates would be the more appropriate financial variable; in the latter case, a term representing nonprice rationing of credit is needed. This is represented by the spread between the long-term and short-term interest rates.[44] We have found that a conglomerate function for all nonmanufacturing investment has only a weak interest rate term, whereas the functions separated in this way both have highly significant interest elasticities. A detailed sectoral analysis is given elsewhere[45]; here we merely present the results for the regulated and commercial and other sectors.

$$(15.5) \quad I_{pr} = 1.49 + 0.0140[(Z_{-1} + Z_{-2})/2] - 0.0043[(K_{r_{-1}} + K_{r_{-2}})/2]$$
$$\quad\quad\quad\quad\quad (0.0083) \quad\quad\quad\quad\quad\quad (0.0032)$$

$$+ 0.0429 \sum_{i=0}^{7} A_i Z_{-i-3} - 2.1042 \sum_{i=0}^{7} A_i (i_L)_{-i-3} \quad\quad \bar{R}^2 = 0.810$$
$$(0.0113) \quad\quad\quad\quad\quad (0.2645)$$

$$(15.6) \quad I_{pc} = -35.72 + 0.1742C_{-1} - 0.0563K_{c_{-1}}$$
$$\quad\quad\quad\quad\quad\quad (0.0278) \quad\quad (0.0170)$$

$$+ 0.0363 \sum_{i=0}^{7} A_i C_{-i-2} + 2.396 \sum_{i=0}^{7} A_i (i_L - i_s)_{-i-2} \quad \bar{R}^2 = 0.930$$
$$(0.0475) \quad\quad\quad\quad (0.461)$$

where I_{pr} = fixed business investment in mining and regulated industries, billions of 1958 dollars

Z = final sales in the private sector, billions of 1958 dollars

K_r = capital stock in mining and regulated industries, billions of constant dollars

i_L = average yield on corporate bonds (Moody's), percent

I_{pc} = fixed business investment in commercial and professional and other industries, billions of 1958 dollars

C = total consumption, billions of 1958 dollars

K_c = capital stock in commercial and professional, and other industries, billions of 1958 dollars

i_s = yield on 4- to 6-month prime commercial paper, percent

A_i = Almon weights; see p. 137.

---

[44] The rationale for this term is examined in Section 7.3.
[45] See Evans, *op. cit.*

All cash flow terms that were tried were nonsignificant and sometimes even negative, a result that has also been reported by Eisner.[46] All the output, capital-stock, and interest rate terms have the expected signs and in almost all cases are highly significant. The interest-rate elasticities for these functions (calculated at the mean values) are 0.50 and 0.43, the latter being calculated for a change in i_s with no change in i_L. It has been argued that since the elasticities are less than unity, it is technically correct to say that investment is interest-inelastic. Although this is of course true by definition, it gives a distorted connotation of the importance of interest rates on investment. A rise of 4 to 5 percent in interest rates, which is not an unusual increase, would lower total investment by a maximum of $4.9 billion, or over 11 percent at the mean value, when all lagged effects are included. This proportion is quite similar to the one found for the manufacturing sector.

In view of these results it may be possible to answer a few of the questions about investment functions that have permeated the literature.

1. "Accelerator," "capacity," or "stock-adjustment" model: As was shown in Chapter 4, these are closely related since they all come from the formulation $K_t = \sum \mu_i O_{t-i}$, where the μ_i may equal λ^i, as suggested by Koyck, but probably have a general Pascal distribution, first rising and then falling. In this case the Koyck transformation does not hold exactly; other methods of determining the μ_i are called for. The methods that have been tried include the double distributed lag and generalized lag operator.[47] We have also shown that from an empirical point of view these functions give similar results. The differences in short-run output elasticities are due to different lag structures rather than the different ways in which the output term is included. Furthermore, many of the equations contain more than one of these terms, combining a stock-adjustment formulation with an accelerator or capacity term.

2. "Profits" or "sales": Although this argument has been analyzed for some time, it was most strongly pressed by Eisner, who claimed that profits were only a proxy variable which lost virtually all significance when sales were included. Two papers in 1965 modified this sentiment to such a degree that its "either–or" form was obliterated. First, Dhrymes and Kurz showed that when the entire range of decisions of the firm was properly specified and appropriate estimating techniques were used, profits were a significant determinant of investment. Second, in time-series analysis, Eisner found that profits were in fact quite significant. This led him to the conclusions that "a partial resolution of the controversy over the role of past profits in investment . . . may be found in a suggestion that past profits have little to do with the long-run rate of investment but may affect its timing." He continues, "Firms and industries earning higher profits do not invest markedly more (over the long run), if at

[46] R. Eisner, "Investment Plans and Realizations," *American Economic Review Papers and Proceedings*, Vol. 52, No. 2 (May, 1962), pp. 190–203.

[47] This is used by Jorgenson: see the appendix, function 5.

all more, than firms and industries earning lower profits."[48] In other words, when long-term investment decisions are made, it is the production function that determines investment and not the profit rate. However, over the business cycle, fluctuations in investment are affected by profits and cash flow, although not nearly as much as sales. Cash flow continues to be an important short-run determinant of investment, although much less important than output.

3. Importance of the interest rate: In every study in which the interest rate was included (all except Eisner), it was definitely significant. One oddity is that Locke Anderson uses the bill rate instead of the bond rate. Since firms do not borrow at the bill rate, it must serve some other purpose. The usual explanation, and the one given by Locke Anderson, is that nonprice credit rationing is used and the bill rate measures tight money better than the bond rate. Maisel uses a similar argument for residential construction,[49] but it is more probable that builders, who borrow mainly from banks, face this restriction rather than industrial firms, which use the bond market much more frequently.

The interest rate elasticities cover a fairly wide range, but Resek's are by far the highest. Some of his individual industry elasticities are almost 4, which appears to be most unlikely. This would imply that a 25 percent increase in the interest rate (from 4 to 5 percent) would result in a 100 percent drop in investment in certain industries, mainly highly cyclical capital-goods industries, where one might expect the interest rate to be less important. However, even if some of the estimates are too high, the interest rate is clearly an important variable in the investment function.

4. "Future" or "past" demand: It is usually argued that while businesses make investment plans on what they expect future demand to be, these expected future plans are really based on past variables. To a very large extent this is true, but in the manufacturing sector it was found that expectations did make a significant net addition to predictions. Upon further exploration it was found that stock prices added to the predictive ability and also resulted in more reasonable coefficients for the rest of the variables in the equation. Unfilled orders were found to serve essentially as a proxy variable for permanent components of demand in those industries where there were large transitory fluctuations in sales. The role of profits, inasmuch as they are important, is clearly that of a liquidity variable (so that a long lag is implied) rather than as an expectations variable (implying a short lag).

5. General lag structure: Since the work of Eisner (1960), deLeeuw (1962), and Almon (1965), it has been generally recognized that there is a lag of a year or more between changes in economic variables and peak response of investment, and that the weights of this response first rise and then fall. This is the pattern used in all these studies except Meyer and Glauber, whose work was

---

[48] Eisner, "A Permanent Income Theory...," *op. cit.*, p. 17.
[49] S. J. Maisel, "Nonbusiness Construction," chap. 6 in *The Brookings Model...*, *op. cit.*

started before these studies were available. We also suggest that sales variables enter with both a long and short lag, the latter representing modifications of existing plans. Financial variables enter only with a long lag, because existing plans are not changed if the amount or cost of money changes after sums have already been committed.

6. Long-run homogeneity of the production function: Eisner has argued that if the production function is linear and homogeneous and there are constant long-run factor proportions and constant utilization of capacity, then the long-run elasticity of capital stock with respect to output will be unity. This implies a constant long-run capital/output ratio, which seems quite reasonable in view of the postwar experience. However, Eisner gets various results for the long-run capital–output elasticity which are about 0.6 or 0.7. Jorgenson also thinks that this long-run elasticity should be unity, but he derives his function so that it is identically so, and the hypothesis cannot be directly tested. It is likely that Eisner has significant biases because of errors in measurement resulting from his use of change-in-sales variables. When we use the level of sales instead of the change in sales, we obtain an elasticity close to the suggested 1.0 value. Although further results would be helpful, it is reasonable for the long-run capital–output elasticity to equal unity.

In summary, we now know enough about the investment function to make some definite statements about general lag structure and also output, interest rate, and cash flow elasticities. Although more work is needed on the investment function, particularly in the area of the marginal cost of funds schedule, it is now possible to assign reasonable values to key parameters for policy purposes, and to do this with a fair degree of confidence.

TECHNICAL APPENDIX to Chapter 5

In this appendix we present the actual functions used and show how the elasticities that appear in Table 5.8. are calculated

1. Locke Anderson

$$I_t = 0.1208(S - S_{max})_{t-4567} + 0.0856L_{t-4567}$$
$$\quad (0.0215) \qquad\qquad\qquad (0.1039)$$

$$\quad - 676(i')_{t-4567} + \text{other terms} \qquad \text{(p. 110, line 1 of table 7.1)}$$
$$\quad (100)$$

where S_{max} = previous maximum level of sales

i' = treasury bill rate

$t - 4567$ means average lag of 4, 5, 6, and 7 quarters; all quarters weighted equally

We assume that $S_{max} = \lambda K$, so that the coefficient 0.1208 is used for the calculation of sales elasticities. The time path of the response of investment to all variables is:

Quarter	Weight	Quarter	Weight	Quarter	Weight	Quarter	Weight
1	0	3	0	5	$\frac{1}{2}$	7	1
2	0	4	$\frac{1}{4}$	6	$\frac{3}{4}$	8	1

so that the first-year average reponse is $\frac{1}{16}$ of the coefficients and the average response over the first two years is $\frac{7}{16}$ of the coefficients. Mean values are given on p. 88 of Locke Anderson, *op. cit.*, so that elasticities at the mean are easily calculated.

2. Meyer and Glauber

$$I_t = 0.165L_{t-1} + 12.1Cp_{t-1} - 36.1i_{t-3} + 3.4\Delta SP_{t-1}$$
$$\text{(standard errors not given)}$$
$$\text{elas.}[0.257] \qquad [0.685] \qquad [0.165]$$

$$+0.823I_{t-2} + \text{other terms} \qquad \text{(p. 155, last line of table VII-5)}$$

The impact elasticities at the mean values are given by Meyer and Glauber, (p. 157, table VII-6) so that all that is needed is the time path over the first eight quarters, taking into consideration the $0.823I_{t-2}$ term:

	For L, Cp	For i		Average Weight	
Quarter	Weight			L, Cp	i
1	1.000	0.0	1 yr	1.407	0.500
2	1.000	0.0			
3	1.823	1.000	2 yr	2.093	1.430
4	1.823	1.000			
5	2.500	1.823			
6	2.500	1.823			
7	3.058	2.500			
8	3.058	2.500			

One additional problem is that Cp has to be changed to sales to get a sales elasticity. We have

$$Cp \cong \frac{S}{S_{max}} \quad \text{and} \quad S_{max} \cong \alpha K \quad \text{so } Cp \cong \frac{S}{\alpha K}$$

The Cp elas $= 12.1(\bar{S}/\alpha \bar{K} \bar{I}) = n_{Cp}$. Sales elas η_s would equal $b \cdot (\bar{S}/\bar{I})$, where $b = 12.1/\alpha K$ [since $S \cong (Cp)(\alpha K)$]. Thus $\eta_s = (12.1) \cdot \bar{S}/(\alpha \bar{K} \cdot \bar{I}) = \eta_{Cp}$. The two elasticities are the same as long as the above approximations hold.

3. Evans. The preferred function was given in the text. Impact elasticities are $S_{t-1}, 1.90$; $S_{t-56}, 1.07$; $L, 0.23$; and $i, 0.50$. Time paths of response are:

Quarter	S	i, L		Average Weight	
				S	i, L
1	1.000	0.0			
2	0.918	0.0			
3	0.843	0.0	1 yr	0.884	0.0
4	0.774	0.0			
5	0.992	0.500	2 yr	0.962	0.444
6	1.176	0.959			
7	1.052	0.881			
8	0.938	0.809			

To determine the long-run elasticities with respect to capital stock it is necessary to separate the Cp term into sales and capital-stock components. Recall from Chapter 4 that

$$aCp \cong a(S/K) \cong a\left(\frac{1}{\bar{K}} \cdot S - \frac{\bar{S}}{\bar{K}^2} \cdot K + \text{const.}\right)$$

Therefore, comparing the equation

$$K = b\sum \lambda^i S_{t-i-1} - c\sum \lambda^i K_{t-i-56} \quad \text{or} \quad I = bS_{t-1} - (1 - \lambda)K_{t-1} - (c - \delta)K_{t-56}$$

where $\delta = 0.025$, with

$$I = aCp - (c - \delta)K_{t-56} + \cdots$$

we have the relationships, as before,

$$b = \frac{a}{\bar{K}} = 0.0806$$

$$1 - \lambda = \frac{a\bar{S}}{\bar{K}^2} = 0.0818$$

We now have

$$K_t = 0.0806 \sum \lambda^i S_{t-i-1} + 0.0453 \sum \lambda^i S_{t-i-56} - 0.0559 \sum \lambda^i K_{t-i-56}$$

In the long run,

$$K = \left(\frac{0.0806 + 0.0453}{0.0818 + 0.0559}\right)S$$

Since $(\bar{S}/\bar{K}) = 1.016$, then $(\partial K/\partial S)(\bar{S}/\bar{K}) = 0.93$. Long-run elasticities for L and i are calculated in a similar way.

4. Griliches–Wallace

$$I_t = 0.0123 O_{t-2} - 0.8292 i_{t-2} + 0.7504(I_{t-1} - 0.025K_{t-1})$$
$$\quad (0.0027) \qquad (0.1959) \qquad (0.0373)$$

$$+ \ 0.00879 SP_{t-2} + \text{const.} \quad \text{(p. 318, Table 3, line 5)}$$
$$(0.00324)$$

Exact sources of data were given, so mean values and elasticities at the means were calculated by us. The time path is given on p. 321, table 4, col. 3, as follows:

Quarter	Weight	Impact elasticities: $O = 0.42$, $i = 0.28$ Average Weight (Relative to Impact Elasticities)	
1	0.000		
2	0.025		
3	0.044		
4	0.057	1 yr	1.26
5	0.068		
6	0.073	2 yr	2.10
7	0.076		
8	0.077		

These weights are normalized so that the cumulative effect on capital for all n periods is 1.000. Griliches and Wallace show that this function can be transformed to a form similar to Jorgenson's function (5) as follows: Write terms in O_{t-2}, i_{t-2}, and SP_{t-2} as $f(X_{t-2})$ and let NI equal net investment $(I_t - 0.025K_t)$. Then

$$I_t = f(X_{t-2}) + 0.75NI_{t-1}$$
$$I_t - 0.025K_t = NI_t = f(X_{t-2}) + 0.75NI_{t-1} - 0.025K_t$$

Then

$$NI_{t-1} = f(X_{t-3}) + 0.75NI_{t-2} - 0.025K_{t-1}$$

Therefore,

$$NI_t - NI_{t-1} = f(X_{t-2} - X_{t-3}) + 0.75NI_{t-1} - 0.025K_t - 0.75NI_{t-2} + 0.025K_{t-1}$$
$$NI_t = f(X_{t-2} - X_{t-3}) + 1.75NI_{t-1} - 0.025(K_t - K_{t-1}) - 0.75NI_{t-2}$$

Therefore,

$$NI_t = f(X_{t-2} - X_{t-3}) + 1.725NI_{t-1} - 0.75NI_{t-2} \quad \text{(p. 320)}$$

Long-run elasticities are supplied by Griliches and Wallace on p. 324, table 5, col. 3.

5. Jorgenson. Jorgenson's hypothesis is based on what he calls "the complete theory of investment behavior," which is

$$I_t = \mu(\theta)(K_t^E - K_{t-1}^E) + \delta K_{t-1} \quad \text{(p. 52)}$$

K_t^E is desired capital stock at time t and equals $\alpha(pO/c)$ (c is the user cost of capital). $\mu(\theta)$ is some power series in a lag operator and determines the weights for I due to a change in K_t^E. In particular, $\mu(\theta) = \gamma(\theta)/\omega(\theta)$, where $\gamma(\theta)$ and $\omega(\theta)$ are polynomials. Then

$$I_t = \frac{\gamma(\theta)}{\omega(\theta)}(K_t^E - K_{t-1}^E) + \delta K_{t-1}$$

Therefore,

$$\omega(\theta)(I_t - \delta K_{t-1}) = \gamma(\theta)(K_t^E - K_{t-1}^E)$$

Expanding the lag operators as polynomials, we have

$$(I_t - \delta K_{t-1}) + \omega_1(I_{t-1} - \delta K_{t-2}) + \cdots = \gamma_0(K_t^E - K_{t-1}^E) + \gamma_1(K_{t-1}^E - K_{t-2}^E) + \cdots$$

The $\omega(\theta)$ and $\gamma(\theta)$ are general polynomials that may have zero terms for one and two quarter lags and may have rising and falling terms. Both of these do occur, and Jorgenson's equations are:

Durable manufacturing:

$$I_t = 0.00099\Delta K_{t-3}^E + 0.00079\Delta K_{t-4}^E + 0.00054\Delta K_{t-5}^E$$
$$(0.00040) \qquad\qquad (0.00043) \qquad\qquad (0.00040)$$

$$+ 1.242(I_{t-1} - \delta K_{t-4}) - 0.394(I_{t-2} - \delta K_{t-5}) + 0.0256K_{t-3}$$
$$(0.142) \qquad\qquad (0.139) \qquad\qquad (0.0031)$$

Nondurable manufacturing:

$$I_t = 0.00058\Delta K_{t-6}^E + 1.220(I_{t-1} - \delta K_{t-4}) - 0.420(I_{t-2} - \delta K_{t-5})$$
$$(0.00029) \qquad\qquad (0.136) \qquad\qquad (0.134)$$

$$0.0184K_{t-3}$$
$$(0.0044)$$

Equations are from *The Brookings Model...*, *op. cit.*, pp. 691–692. As in Griliches–Wallace, the normalized weights of response are given [pp. 81–82, $\zeta(\theta)$ column]:

Quarter	Durables (46%)	Nondurable (54%)	Average Weight
1	0.0	0.0	
2	0.0	0.0	
3	0.058	0.0	
4	0.106	0.0	1 yr 0.0193
5	0.156	0.0	
6	0.157	0.129	2 yr 0.0742
7	0.140	0.166	
8	0.119	0.163	

These weights are actually the change in investment due to a change in the desired stock of capital, that is, $\partial I/\partial K^E$. They need to be multiplied by $\partial K^E/\partial O$ and $\partial K^E/\partial i$; the latter is given by Jorgenson (p. 88), whereas the former is shown below to be identically equal to unity.

To get elasticities (for example, for output) we need

$$\frac{\partial I}{\partial K^E} \frac{\partial K^E}{\partial O} \frac{O}{K^E} \frac{K^E}{I}$$

Since $K^E = \alpha pO/c$,

$$\frac{\partial K^E}{\partial O} = \frac{\alpha p}{c} \quad \text{and} \quad \frac{\partial K^E}{\partial O}\frac{O}{K^E} = \frac{\alpha pO}{cK^E} = \frac{K^E}{K^E} \equiv 1$$

Values of K^E (taken equal to K for purposes of calculating elasticities) and I are taken from figures supplied by Jorgenson. For long-run elasticities,

$$\frac{\partial K}{\partial K^E}\frac{\partial K^E}{\partial O}\frac{O}{K^E}\frac{K^E}{K} \quad \text{is just} \quad \frac{\partial K^E}{\partial O}\frac{O}{K^E}$$

which we showed is unity. $(\partial K^E/\partial i)(i/K)$ is taken from Griliches–Wallace, p. 324.

6. Eisner

$$\frac{I_t}{K_{t-1}} = \frac{0.037\Delta S_t^* + 0.201\Delta S_{t-1}^* + 0.126\Delta S_{t-2}^* + 0.099\Delta S_{t-3}^*}{(0.057) \quad\quad (0.055) \quad\quad\quad (0.044) \quad\quad\quad (0.042)}$$

$$\frac{0.119\Delta S_{t-4}^* + 0.022\Delta S_{t-5}^* + 0.034\Delta S_{t-6}^* + 0.385(\pi_t/K_{t-1})}{(0.042) \quad\quad\quad (0.044) \quad\quad\quad (0.035) \quad\quad\quad (0.187)}$$

$$+ \frac{0.110(\pi_{t-1}/K_{t-2})}{(0.091)} \quad\quad \text{(table 6, p. 28, Industry Time Series)}$$

N.B.: All lags are now in *years*.
In this equation

$$\Delta S_{t-i}^* = \frac{\Delta S_{t-i}}{\frac{1}{3}(S_{t-i} + S_{t-i-1} + S_{t-i-2})}$$

The sales elasticities are not straightforward because of the ratio form. We have (for first-year elasticity)

$$I_t = \mu_0 \frac{\Delta S_t \cdot K_{t-1}}{\frac{1}{3}\sum_{i=0}^{2} S_{t-i}}$$

Therefore,

$$\frac{\partial I_t}{\partial S_t} = \mu_0 \left[\frac{\frac{1}{3}\sum_{i=0}^{2} S_{t-i}K_{t-1} - \frac{1}{3}K_{t-1}\cdot \Delta S_t}{(\frac{1}{3}\sum_{i=0}^{2} S_{t-i})^2} \right]$$

Taking mean values and dropping subscripts (assume $\bar{S}_{t-i} \cong \bar{S}_{t-i-1}$),

$$\frac{\partial I}{\partial S}\frac{\bar{S}}{\bar{I}} \cong \mu_0 \left(\frac{\bar{S}\cdot\bar{K} - \bar{K}\cdot\Delta S/3}{\bar{S}^2}\frac{S}{\bar{I}} \right)$$

Assume that $\Delta S/3$ is very small relative to $\bar{S}$, so

$$\frac{\partial I}{\partial S}\frac{\bar{S}}{\bar{I}} \cong \mu_0 \left(\frac{\bar{K}}{\bar{S}}\frac{\bar{S}}{\bar{I}} \right) = \mu_0 \left(\frac{\bar{K}}{\bar{I}} \right)$$

An average figure of $\bar{K}/\bar{I}$ for gross fixed assets and investment at annual rates is 15. To convert to quarterly data, we use the following weights:

Quarter	Weight	Average Weight
1	0.037	
2	0.037	
3	0.201	1 yr 0.119
4	0.201	
5	0.201	2 yr 0.140
6	0.201	
7	0.126	
8	0.126	

The long-run elasticity is much simpler. We have (approximately)

$$\frac{\Delta K}{K} = \sum \mu_i \left(\frac{\Delta S}{S} \right)_{t-i}$$

Thus the $\sum \mu_i$ term is already an elasticity of capital stock with respect to sales.

7. Resek. Only elasticities are given (no coefficients) and only industry equations (no aggregate manufacturing equations) are given. An aggregate equation was constructed by us by taking weighted averages of the industry equations. They are all of the form

$$\left(\frac{I}{K} \right)_t = a + b_2 \left[\mu_i \left(\frac{\Delta O}{K} \right)_{t-i} \right] + b_3 [\mu_i(i)_{t-i}] + b_4(\mu_i L'_{t-i}) + b_5(\mu_i SP_{t-i})$$

where

$$L' = \frac{1}{\text{const.} - [(\text{debt} - RE)/\text{assets}]}$$

The μ_i are weights determined by Almon. We use the weights for total manufacturing for the purposes of determining the elasticities for the overall equation:

Quarter	Weight	
0	0.068	Weighted elasticities from Resek's equations:
1	0.122	
2	0.156	
3	0.168	O 1.54
4	0.157	i 1.39
5	0.127	L' 0.23
6	0.084	
7	0.038	The average weights for one and two years relative to these
8	0.000	elasticities are:
	0.919	
		1 yr 1.16
		2 yr 0.88

Although some of Resek's variables are in ratio form, the elasticity estimates are not appreciably affected. For output, $I/K = b'_2(\Delta O/K)$ and $I = b'_2\Delta O$ give the same elasticity. For the interest rate,

$$\frac{\partial(I/K)}{\partial i}\frac{iK}{I} = \frac{K(\partial I/\partial i) - I(\partial K/\partial i)}{K^2}\frac{iK}{I} = \frac{K - I}{K}\frac{\partial I}{\partial i}\frac{i}{I}$$

since $\partial I/\partial i = \partial K/\partial i$ for the first period. Since $(K - I)/K \cong 1$ for an impact elasticity, there is no appreciable difference between

$$\frac{\partial I}{\partial i}\frac{i}{I} \quad \text{and} \quad \frac{\partial(I/K)}{\partial i}\frac{iK}{I}$$

CHAPTER 6

CONSUMER DURABLES

6.1   GENERAL DETERMINANTS

As was indicated in Chapter 2, the determinants of purchases of consumer durables are much different from those of other consumption. Because of the particular nature of these goods, it has sometimes been suggested that a function explaining these purchases should be an adaptation of functions explaining consumption of nondurables and services and fixed business investment. Unfortunately, this gives a misleading impression of the type of consumer durables function that should be developed. In particular, the lag structures found in these other functions are quite inappropriate here. In the function for consumption of nondurables and services, lagged consumption is an important determinant of present consumption. This is explained through habit persistence or irreversibility of consumption patterns. In the fixed business investment function, there is a lag of a year or more between the time when economic variables change and the bulk of investment is actually undertaken. However, neither of these important relationships is found in a function explaining consumer durables. First, durable purchases are by their nature made only sporadically, unlike those purchases such as food, rent, and so on, which must be· made frequently at evenly spaced intervals. Past purchases of durables tend to have a negative rather than a positive effect on present purchases. Second, purchases of most durables can be made almost immediately, unlike fixed business investment, so that a long lag between income and purchases does not occur. The lag on income, if it exists at all, is found to be no more than one quarter. The only variables that appear with lags in the consumer durables function are those variables representing past purchases or possibly past commitments to repay. It is sometimes suggested that substantial lags may be involved in the decision process, because consumers must save to buy durables; businesses, it is claimed can always borrow in the capital markets. However, the true situation is more nearly reversed. Over 60 percent of new cars are purchased partially or entirely on credit, whereas only 25 to 30 percent of new plant and equipment is financed externally. Given the existing institutional arrangements for obtaining loans on durable goods, individuals stocks of savings have only a negligible role in determining the lag structure of the consumer-durables function. Thus superficial modifications of functions developed previously for other consumption and investment will not provide a satisfactory explanation for durable purchases. A different approach is necessary, although we shall continue to draw on some of the theory developed earlier.

It should be pointed out that by their nature, durable goods are not purchased to be used up themselves but for the flow of services they provide. The flow of services received from these goods, which is akin to the definition of consumption as used in Chapter 2, is not the definition of consumption entered in the national income accounts. The national income definition refers to gross additions to the stock of durables in much the same way that fixed business investment refers to gross additions to the stock of business capital. Just as the stock of capital is proportional to the firm's output, the stock of durables is proportional to an individual's income. Furthermore, just as both present and lagged output are important determinants of investment, both present and lagged income should be used to explain the level of the *stock* of consumer durables. Also, just as the purchases of consumer nondurables and services are proportional to permanent income, the stock of consumer durables is also proportional to permanent income. If it is again represented by a weighted average of present and past measured incomes, then

$$(6.1) \qquad (K_d)_t = \alpha \sum_{i=0}^{\infty} \lambda^i Y_{t-i}$$

By the now-familiar Koyck transformation, this gives[1]

$$(6.2) \qquad (C_d)_t = \alpha Y_t - (1 - \lambda - \delta)K_{d_{t-1}}$$

which states that purchases of durable goods depend positively on income and negatively on previous stocks.

Another possible relationship between income and capital stock can be written as $(K_d)_t = \alpha Y_t$, in which case $(C_d)_t = \alpha \Delta Y_t$. This is the naive accelerator

---

[1] For a detailed derivation of this relationship, see p. 83. As usual, K_d = stocks of consumer durables, C_d = purchases of consumer durables, and Y = personal disposable income.

for consumer durables. As was true in the investment sector, this form of the equation has repeatedly been found to be unsatisfactory and is not considered further.

Consumer theory asserts that the demand schedule for any given good or service is a function of its own price, income, prices of other goods and services, and attitudes and tastes. As is usual in estimating statistical demand functions, all other relevant prices are usually considered to be all other consumer prices, conveniently combined into the consumer price index. This function can be represented as

$$(6.3) \qquad (C_d)_t = a Y_t - b(K_d)_{t-1} - c\left(\frac{p_d}{p_c}\right)_t + d A_t$$

where p_d = price index of durable goods

p_c = consumer price index

A = variable representing attitudes and tastes

This is the basic form of the consumer-durables function that we shall consider.

The analysis of consumer behavior examined so far assumes that the consumer is faced with a rigid budget line determined by the present year's income. However, this cannot even be approximately true for durables, because the consumer may draw either on liquid assets or easily available consumer credit for assistance in financing his purchases. Of the two, available evidence (examined later) indicates that credit availability is by far the more important determinant. The influence of liquid assets on purchases of consumer durables is discussed below, where it is found that they are substitutes rather than complements. Adding credit terms (Cr), the exact nature of which are discussed later, the function becomes

$$(6.4) \qquad (C_d)_t = a Y_t - b(K_d)_{t-1} - c\left(\frac{p_d}{p_c}\right)_t + d A_t + e(Cr)_t$$

Finally, a variable representing supply conditions is also necessary. Such a term was not necessary for other components of consumption; if *ex ante* demand were higher than *ex ante* supply for these goods and services, price would rise until a new equilibrium would be reached. However, this has not always been the case for consumer durables, particularly in the years immediately following World War II. Durables were then in short supply at existing prices, but little attempt was made by the manufacturers to raise prices to the equilibrium level. Some "gray markets" existed and retail dealers received larger markups than usual, but many consumers waited, and the market price on new cars did not reflect the equilibrium price. For such types of situations, a dummy variable representing times of severe supply shortages is necessary to explain purchases of consumer durables properly, or else the entire equation will be misspecified. Although these periods occurred mainly in 1947 and 1948, they also happened during the major auto strikes of 1952 and 1964.[2]

Before proceeding to a more detailed explanation of some of these independent variables, we point out that it is analytically advantageous to subdivide purchases of consumer durables into autos and other durables. Although the theory developed to this point might apply equally well to both types of durables, the variables representing credit conditions, attitudes and tastes, and supply shortages have a sufficiently greater influence on autos to justify separate functions. Consumption of other durables can be explained adequately with the income, relative price, and stock variables; the other variables are found to be of virtually no importance. Thus the explanation and empirical implementation of the rest of this chapter will follow a pattern suggested by the two separate functions

(6.5)
$$(C_a)_t = f\left[Y_t, K_{a_{t-1}}, \left(\frac{p_a}{p_c}\right)_t, Cr_t, A_t, d_{st} \right]$$

(6.6)
$$(C_{na})_t = f\left[Y_t, K_{na_{t-1}}, \left(\frac{p_{na}}{p_c}\right)_t \right]$$

where subscript a = autos

subscript na = nonauto durables

d_s = dummy variable for supply shortages

All other variables are as defined above.

Up to this point we have purposely specified the credit and attitudes and tastes variables in an indefinite manner. We now turn to a detailed discussion of their importance in the autos function.

6.2   THE IMPORTANCE OF CREDIT

One of the major determinants of purchases of consumer durables is consumer instalment credit. The use of credit enables an individual to save after he has purchased a durable good instead of before. Given this interpretation, the role of credit has been formulated in two different ways. The formulation known as the "*burden*" *theory* states that debt contracted at any given time represents a burden that must later be repaid. According to this theory the availability of consumer credit does not change the total purchases of durables, but merely shifts the timing of them. Since consumers tend to buy durables when times are good, this theory also suggests that consumer credit

---

[2] It is always possible to estimate the function with these observations omitted from the sample period. There are two reasons we have not followed this procedure. First, it may be of interest to estimate the marginal importance of supply shortages. Second, as already discussed in Chapter 3, it may be a dangerous procedure to leave out those observations which do not fit very well.

contributes to the instability of the cycle. The other theory, which can be called the "*replacement*" *theory*, states that the use of consumer credit does increase purchases of consumer durables over the long run. Different versions of this theory suggest that durables are purchased either at the expense of other consumer items or at the expense of savings. These possibilities are not mutually exclusive, because both substitutions may occur.

The burden theory needs to be stated in a little more detail before it can be criticized properly. In the beginning of an upswing, purchases of consumer durables will rise, and new credit granted and credit outstanding will rise. Repayments will also rise, because they are some fixed proportion of credit outstanding. According to the burden theory, consumers will now have less money to spend on other purchases. This could lead to a recession by itself. Alternatively, if a recession has been started by other phenomena, the decrease in aggregate demand will be more serious than it would otherwise have been, because consumers are committed to larger repayments.

Patterns of durable purchases are apt to be highly cyclical, because they can easily be postponed during recessions. This would be true even if no credit were available. Thus to verify the burden theory it is necessary to show that the availability of credit heightens the cyclical pattern of durable purchases. Consumers may purchase *more* durables than they otherwise would during recessions if credit is more easily available then. The evidence examined in Section 6.6 suggests that this may be the case.

It is true that more cars will be purchased during the early stages of an expansion if credit is available than if it is not. But the burden theory holds only if the use of credit causes purchases of durables to be bunched at the beginning of the cycle to such an extent that this leads to destabilizing fluctuations in the economy and eventually to the next recession. If purchases early in the cycle lead to an expansion of income which leads to additional purchases and continued growth of the economy, then other explanations of the effect of instalment credit are needed.

A rather malignant spur of the burden theory, which actually belongs more to the realm of home economics than economics, suggests that if consumers would only save for their first durable purchases, they could then buy just as much as they would have purchased otherwise and save all the interest charges. If part of these additional savings were spent, total consumption would be increased. Thus one of the conclusions to be drawn from this theory is that the use of consumer credit actually decreases consumption. This is a little like saying that General Motors would be better off if they had never borrowed and had saved first before purchasing capital equipment. The analogy is not exact; businesses maximize profit, whereas consumers maximize utility. Furthermore, businesses can borrow at approximately the same rate as they can invest their funds, whereas consumers must pay a much higher rate. However, the alternative costs of saving compared to purchasing with credit must be considered. These include both the actual costs of using substitutes for durables and the opportunity cost of using saved funds. This opportunity cost may be substantially higher than the interest rate earned, for these funds can provide quick liquidity when necessary. Such liquidity may be able to be purchased elsewhere only at very unfavorable terms. When considering all these costs it may well be that it is actually cheaper to borrow and have the use of the services provided by a particular consumer durable than it is to save. In any case, alternative and opportunity costs must be closely examined before such statements about the benefits of savings make any sense.

The replacement theory of credit relies mainly on the premise that after an individual purchases a consumer durable, he is quite likely to replace it at some future date. It is unlikely that having once purchased the item, he will give it up. The irreversibility of consumer patterns of behavior is again important here. If the item were bought sooner than otherwise through the use of consumer credit, it will in general continue to be replaced earlier. This will add to the total stock of durables owned by an individual during his lifetime. If the durable were purchased when it otherwise would not have been, replacement will occur that otherwise would not have happened, again increasing the total stock. It is also possible that some people would never save enough to buy durables and that only through the use of consumer credit are these purchases ever made. This would suggest that durable purchases are made instead of savings, a viewpoint for which there is some empirical evidence. However, it is not necessary to accept the latter hypothesis to explain how the use of consumer credit permanently alters the amount of consumer durables purchased. This can be explained simply by noting the importance of the replacement phenomenon, which is entirely neglected by the simple burden theory.

Perhaps one of the reasons that the burden theory still enjoys some popularity is the companion thought that the ratio of consumer instalment credit to personal disposable income is exceeding some preassigned "prudent" limit; beyond this limit the great volume of repayments must cut into aggregate demand. This idea is buoyed partially by the fact that year after year *consumer credit becomes an increasing percentage of personal income.* Each year as this occurs, warning signs are seen and downturns in the economy are often forecast. Although the greatest outcry occurred after the 1955 boom in auto sales, more recent cases can be given. For example, *Business Week* has stated that "the only people who don't worry about the swelling volume of consumer debt apparently are consumers themselves."[3] The increasing debt/income ratio is still felt to be a precursor either of a rash of delinquencies or a drop in consumption, either of which will lead to a forthcoming recession. Yet several years ago it was pointed out in a brilliant article by Enthoven[4] that, far from exceeding some normal level of debt to income, the economy in 1955 was

---

[3] "Investment Credit Soars to a Record," *Business Week*, January 8, 1966, p. 46.

[4] A. Enthoven, "The Growth of Instalment Credit and the Future of Prosperity," *American Economic Review*, Vol. 47, No. 4 (December, 1957), pp. 913–929.

actually below this equilibrium level. The same conclusion is reached if his results are extended through 1964. Since the argument that overextensions of credit are a major cause of cyclical fluctuations is still pervasive, and since his explanation seems to have escaped many economists and others, it is reproduced here in some detail.

Enthoven's main argument stems from the situation that existed immediately after World War II: a full-employment economy with relatively large liquid assets, virtually no debt, and a severely depleted stock of consumer durables. In such a situation, it is quite likely to expect that debt outstanding would grow faster than income for a number of years until the economy reached some equilibrium debt/income ratio. The fact that the debt/income ratio continues to rise should in no way imply that consumers are overextending themselves; they are merely adjusting their debt to normal levels. Enthoven makes some simplifying although realistic assumptions about the economy which enable him to formulate a direct mathematical path to the equilibrium debt/income ratio. At the beginning of the period under consideration he assumes that

1. There is no consumer instalment debt outstanding.

2. Some change occurs in institutional structure and borrowers.

3. All borrowers are couples in the first year of marriage.

He also makes some general assumptions about the nature of the economy which allow aggregation from individuals to the total economy. These are:

4. All borrowers have the same average propensity to incur debt (that is, for a given income level, they will incur the same amount of debt).

5. The number of borrowers remains a constant percentage of the population.

6. The long-run income elasticity of consumer durables is unity. This means there will be no long-run substitutability of durables for other goods, or vice versa.

The latter group of assumptions can be easily verified. Various cross-section studies[5] suggest that relatively homogeneous groups (such as couples in their first year of marriage) do have approximately the same average propensity to incur debt. Enthoven shows in his article that the borrowers/population ratio (equal to the new married couples/population ratio) has remained almost constant over the postwar period. We show later in this chapter that the long-run income elasticity of demand for durables is very close to unity. The first three assumptions may at first seem rather stringent, but it is surprising how closely they do represent the immediate postwar period, particularly when only instalment credit is included (in particular, mortage credit is excluded). There was practically no instalment credit granted during the war, and almost all such debts contracted before 1942 had been paid. There were clearly some changes in the structure of borrowing and in the borrowers. For one thing,

---

[5] See, for instance, the cross-section studies on consumer durables referenced below.

credit controls were eased soon after the war ended. Furthermore, durable goods again became available. The return home of the armed forces and the transfer from military to civilian life certainly represented a great change in the position of borrowers.

The third assumption is not strictly necessary. It is included because Enthoven is trying to isolate the life-cycle effect in its pure form. In his pure life-cycle model, all borrowing is done by those individuals who have no debt. Thus an existing stock of debt, although it might hypothetically deter future borrowing for those people who are already in debt, actually has no effect on those people who actually *do* borrow, that is, the new households with no prior debt. Enthoven supposes that existing debt may have an inhibiting influence on future consumption of debtholders, so that he assumes they do no more borrowing. However, as discussed later, there is actually a positive relationship between outstanding debt and purchases of consumer durables. Thus Enthoven does not need to make this assumption to obtain his results.

Given these assumptions, Enthoven then generates the following model:

(6.7) $Y_t = Y_0(1 + r)^t$

(6.8) $N_t = \alpha Y_t$

(6.9) $R_t = b_0 N_t + b_1 N_{t-1} + b_2 N_{t-2} + \cdots + b_j N_{t-j}$

(6.10) $\Delta D_t = N_t - R_t$

where N = new borrowing of credit
      R = repayments of credit
      D = debt outstanding

Note that new borrowings are proportional only to current income. Thus unlike accumulated debt they do not rise relative to income over time.

Substituting $N_t = \alpha Y_t$ into the repayments equation gives

(6.11) $R_t = c_0 Y_t + c_1 Y_{t-1} + c_2 Y_{t-2} + \cdots + c_j Y_{t-j}$

The change in outstanding debt at each time period must then be

(6.12) $\Delta D_t = (\alpha - c_0) Y_t - c_1 Y_{t-1} - \cdots - c_j Y_{t-j}$

Since $Y_{t-j} = Y_0(1 + r)^{t-j}$ in general, then

(6.13) $\Delta D_t = (1 + r)^t \cdot Y_0 \cdot \left[(\alpha - c_0) - \dfrac{c_1}{1 + r} - \dfrac{c_2}{(1 + r)^2} - \cdots - \dfrac{c_j}{(1 + r)^j} \right]$

Since the expression in brackets is a constant, it can be written simply as *a*. Then since $Y_t = Y_0(1 + r)^t$, we have $\Delta D_t = a Y_t$, so that the *change* in debt outstanding is proportional to income. To get an expression for debt at any time

t it is necessary to calculate $D_t = \sum_{i=0}^{t} (\Delta D)_{t-i}$. We have

(6.14) $D_1 = aY_1 + D_0$ (assume a small initial stock of debt D_0), or

(6.15) $D_1 = a(1 + r)Y_0 + D_0$

(6.16) $D_2 = a(1 + r)^2 Y_0 + a(1 + r)Y_0 + D_0$

and, in general,

(6.17) $D_t = a(1 + r)^t Y_0 + a(1 + r)^{t-1} Y_0 + \cdots + a(1 + r)Y_0 + D_0$

Therefore,

$$(6.18) \qquad D_t = aY_0 \cdot \sum_{j=1}^{t} (1 + r)^j + D_0$$

and thus[6]

$$(6.19) \qquad D_t = \frac{a(1 + r)}{r} Y_0[(1 + r)^t - 1] + D_0$$

This can now be used to find the equilibrium debt/income ratio and the equilibrium rate at which debt will grow. We have

$$(6.20) \qquad \frac{D_t}{Y_t} = \frac{[a(1 + r)/r]Y_0[(1 + r)^t - 1] + D_0}{Y_0(1 + r)^t}$$

and, as $t \to \infty$,

$$(6.21) \qquad \frac{D_t}{Y_t} = \frac{a(1 + r)}{r}$$

By similar algebraic manipulations it can be shown that

$$(6.22) \qquad \frac{\Delta D_t}{D_{t-1}} = \frac{(1 + r)^t \cdot r}{(1 + r)^t - (1 + r) + (rD_0/aY_0)} = r \quad \text{as } t \to \infty.$$

---

[6] This can be shown by using some elementary results about partial sums. If S_x is a partial sum, then

$$S_x = x + x^2 + \cdots + x^t$$
$$xS_x = x^2 + \cdots + x^t + x^{t+1}$$
$$S_x(1 - x) = x(1 - x^t)$$

and

$$S_x = \frac{x(x^t - 1)}{x - 1}$$

In this case $x = 1 + r$, so that

$$S_r = \frac{(1 + r)[(1 + r)^t - 1]}{r}$$

as shown.

Thus the rate of growth of debt will asymptotically approach the rate of growth of income. However, when t is small, this growth will be much larger. For $t = 5$, for example, $\Delta D/D = 0.28$ for $r = 0.05$ and $D_0 = 0$.

Enthoven then proceeds to measure a and r from actual data. He uses personal income before taxes instead of disposable personal income, unlike most economists who have discussed this problem. Disposable personal income is probably the better measure, although a case can be made for before-tax income, since interest payments are deductible (for those individuals who itemize separately). However, we shall use personal income before taxes in order to compare our results more exactly with the findings of Enthoven. The results are almost the same regardless of which measure of income is used, because the before-tax income/after-tax income ratio has changed very little in the postwar period.

For the period 1946–1956, Enthoven found that r (the growth rate of money income) $= 0.0602$, and a (the change in debt for a given change in income) $= 0.0107$. This gives an equilibrium debt/income ratio of 18.8 percent. For comparison, in 1956 this ratio was only 9.7 percent. The economy's capacity to borrow was still quite a distance below its long-run equilibrium value. However, it is possible that the sample period Enthoven used was marked by a more rapid growth of income and credit than would be found in the long run, even when the assumptions of his model are taken into consideration. To test this possibility we reestimated his parameters for the period 1946–1964. It was found that $r = 0.0575$ and $a = 0.00956$, which results in an equilibrium debt/income ratio of 17.8 percent. While the ratio is somewhat lower, the difference is quite small.

Following the results of Enthoven, we have calculated in Table 6.1 the actual and predicted D/Y values for each year of the postwar period through 1964. This allows us to examine whether the ratio is actually following an asymptotic path toward the long-run equilibrium value, and also enables us to see how far along this path the economy has progressed.

The recession years are circled in Figure 6.1; note that on balance the debt/income ratio was higher than the trend value for the average of the four recession years. This gives a slight indication that the use of credit mitigates cycles rather than amplifies them. The years 1950 and 1955 are very far off, but both of these represent very unusual circumstances, as discussed in Section 6.5. The 1950 peak was due to "scare buying" because of the Korean War; many people wanted to buy durables regardless of how they were financed. In 1955 a substantial easing of credit terms led many people to use more credit than they had previously. Except for these two years, the trend D/Y ratio follows the actual values very well.

It might appear that the increase in debt slowed down considerably during the period 1958–1962. However, this was a period of high unemployment and therefore low purchases of durables (especially cars) and does not reflect a change in the patterns of use of instalment credit per se. In fact, note that in

TABLE 6.1   GROWTH OF DEBT/INCOME RATIO
DURING THE POSTWAR PERIOD[a]

Year	Actual Y	Trend Y	Actual D	Trend D	Actual D/Y, %	Trend D/Y, %
1945	171.1	171.1	2.46	2.46	1.44	1.44
1946	178.7	180.9	4.17	4.19	2.33	2.32
1947	191.3	191.3	6.70	6.02	3.50	3.15
1948	210.2	202.3	9.00	7.95	4.28	3.93
1949	207.2	214.0	11.59	10.00	5.59	4.67
1950	227.6	226.3	14.70	12.16	6.46	5.37
1951	255.6	239.2	15.29	14.45	5.98	6.04
1952	272.5	253.1	19.40	16.86	7.12	6.66
1953	288.2	267.6	23.01	19.43	7.98	7.16
1954	290.1	283.0	23.57	22.13	8.12	7.82
1955	310.9	299.3	28.91	24.99	9.30	8.35
1956	333.0	316.5	31.72	28.02	9.53	8.85
1957	351.1	334.7	33.87	31.22	9.65	9.33
1958	361.2	353.9	33.64	34.60	9.31	9.78
1959	383.5	374.3	39.25	38.17	10.23	10.20
1960	401.0	395.8	42.83	41.96	10.68	10.60
1961	416.8	418.6	43.53	45.98	10.44	10.98
1962	442.6	442.6	48.03	50.18	10.85	11.34
1963	464.8	468.1	53.75	54.65	11.56	11.61
1964	495.0	495.0	59.40	59.40	12.00	12.00

[a] The actual and trend values are graphed in Figure 6.1.

this period of "prudent" increases in debt, the economy experienced substantial underutilization of resources, whereas larger increases in the debt/income ratio have been accompanied by a sharp increase in the rate of growth of the economy. Far from causing distortions and recessions, increased use of consumer credit has been accompanied in recent years by a return toward full employment.

The simple burden theory, which states that fluctuations in the economy are caused partially by the use of consumer credit, appears completely fallacious. The use of instalment credit does increase aggregate demand in both the short and long run because replacement of durables rises and also because instalment buying is done partially at the expense of saving. Furthermore, although changes in credit terms may be destabilizing, the existence of credit availability itself is not. Smooth patterns of growth can occur if credit terms remain unchanged over the cycle.

There is substantial empirical evidence that the amount of debt outstanding is positively correlated with the purchase of consumer durables. This can be easily explained by referring to the replacement theory. Those individuals with relatively large stocks of durables need to replace them more often. Since

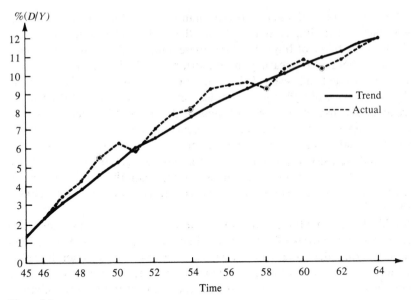

Figure 6.1

they have financed the original stocks with instalment credit, they return to the credit market for further financing. In a study designed in part to determine whether a consumer would use cash or credit to purchase a particular durable, Janet Fisher found that one factor—whether or not the consumer had previously used credit—accounted for over three quarters of the explained variance distinguishing the two groups.[7] She also found that those consumers with currently outstanding debts were much *more* likely to use credit than those with no instalment debt outstanding. In particular, she found that 71 percent of those individuals with debt outstanding at the beginning of 1957 had used further credit to purchase durables in 1957. On the other hand, only 35 percent of those individuals who had no present debt outstanding but had used credit one to ten years ago purchased durables on credit, and only 10 percent of those individuals who had not used credit in the past ten years used credit in 1957 to finance a consumer durable.[8] In a somewhat similar study, M. L. Lee found that higher levels of debt were positively related to the probability of borrowing to pay for a consumer durable, given that the decision to purchase had already been made.[9] In still another cross-section study, Klein and Lansing also found that "the existence of debt seems to be an indicator

---

[7] Janet A. Fisher, "Consumer Durable Goods Expenditures, with Major Emphasis on the Role of Assets, Credit, and Intentions," *Journal of the American Statistical Association*, Vol. 58, No. 3 (September, 1963), p. 654.

[8] *Ibid.*, p. 650.

[9] M. L. Lee, "An Analysis of Instalment Borrowing by Durable Goods Buyers," *Econometrica*, Vol. 30, No. 4 (October, 1962), p. 781.

more of a continuing willingness to buy than of an inability to pay for purchases. In fact, our finding is that the larger the debt in relation to income the greater the probability of buying."[10] All these studies add up to a clear case of the replacement factor negating any importance of the burden factor.

It could be argued that even if the stock of debt outstanding is positively related to purchases of consumer durables, repayments should still be negatively related, because these represent income that cannot be spent on goods and services and in particular cannot be spent on more durables. When the repayments variable was used in consumer durable functions, it was not significant and occasionally entered with the wrong sign. In other work we have found that it is stocks of durables, rather than the total amount of repayments, which have a significant negative effect on additional purchases of durables.[11]

It should also be mentioned that to a first approximation repayments are linearly related to the stock of debt outstanding, that is $R = \alpha D$.[12] Since a high level of outstanding debt does not cause fewer purchases of consumer durables, there is no reason for higher repayments to result in lower purchases as long as α remains constant. If α varies, that is, if the terms of the contract change, then this change in repayments may have a substantial effect on durable purchases. However, in this case it would be more appropriate to use the determinants of α in the durables equations rather than repayments themselves. This possibility is considered next.

We have presented a rather detailed theoretical and empirical discussion of the importance of debt to show that past commitments by individuals to use consumer instalment credit need not diminish future purchases of consumer durables, once the properly negative effect of stocks of these durables has been taken into account. However, the terms on which credit is available are quite important in determining purchases of durables, because these terms substantially alter the amount of savings which an individual must have in order to make the purchase. They also alter the relationship between repayments and debt outstanding. From this viewpoint, both the percentage of down payment and the number of months of the contract are important determinants of credit conditions. The finance charges, which will also influence the relationship between total repayments and debt outstanding, have only a slight influence on consumer purchases. This is both because consumers are generally assumed

---

[10] L. R. Klein and J. B. Lansing, "Decisions to Purchase Consumer Durables Goods," *Journal of Marketing*, Vol. 20, No. 2 (October, 1955), p. 130.

[11] M. K. Evans and A. Kisselgoff, "Demand for Consumer Instalment Credit and Its Effects on Consumption," *The Brookings Model: Some Further Results* (Chicago: Rand McNally, 1968).

[12] Repayments may also be positively correlated with income; that is, if income rises, prepayments may rise, while if it falls, payments may lag. In this case we could write $R = \alpha D + \beta Y$. But then $R - \beta Y = \alpha D$ can be substituted into the equation $C = \gamma Y - \delta R$; the equation then becomes $C = (\gamma - \delta\beta) \times Y - \delta\alpha D$. This reduces the repayments term to a pure debt effect. In general, $\delta\beta$ will be less than $\frac{1}{10}$ of γ, so that the parameter estimated of Y will still remain significantly positive.

to be notoriously interest-inelastic[13] and because these rates are quite sticky and have fluctuated very little in the postwar period.[14] The price of the durable itself, which of course also influences the cost, has already been included separately in the function but could be combined with the credit terms to form the average monthly payment. This can be closely approximated as[15]

$$(6.23) \qquad P = \frac{p_d(1 - D)(1 + F)}{M}$$

where P = an index of the average monthly payment

p_d = price index of the durable

D = percent of down payment

F = rate of finance charge

M = number of months of contract

One could enter each of the credit terms D, M, and F separately in the car equation and compute the relative efficacy of each one to see which influences purchases the most. However, there is a good reason for *not* doing this; as is discussed in Section 6.6, changes in the magnitude of these credit terms tend to offset one another in such a way that the monthly payment tends to remain constant. Thus the conglomeration of terms, which is the monthly payment, actually explains car purchases slightly better than these terms entered separately.

One improvement can be made in the monthly payment term by formulating it in constant dollars, as is done for the rest of the independent variables in the car equation. This would suggest that the term

$$(6.24) \qquad P^* = \frac{p_a(1 - D)(1 + F)}{p_c \cdot M}$$

would be a slightly better determinant of car purchases than the same term in current dollars. This does in fact turn out to be the case.

---

[13] This view is probably correct in view of the fact that consumers often have only a hazy notion of the interest rate they are paying. However, statistical evidence on this point must await greater fluctuations in the interest rates charged on consumer loans. We do not want to fall into the same trap as those economists who assumed that interest rates had no effect on investment because they estimated the investment function during a sample period when interest rates were unchanged.

[14] Over the period 1947–1962 the interest rate on consumer instalment credit stayed between 11.0 and 12.5 percent, See R. P. Shay, "New Automobile Finance Rates, 1924–1962," *Journal of Finance*, Vol. 18, No. 3 (September, 1963), pp. 461–493, for a series of these charges.

[15] This formula is not exact, for the interest should be compounded separately for each time period. For example, at a true interest rate of 12 percent, interest charges on a three-year loan equal 22 percent and for a four-year loan 28 percent. However, for our present purposes it is a close enough approximation.

[16] Unfortunately these figures are available only for cars. Some proxy variables were tried for other durables but without any success. Thus the rest of this part of the discussion refers only to cars.

Even though relative prices are already implicitly included in the constant-dollar monthly payment term, they ought to be included as a separate term in the car equation as long as (1) some consumers do not buy on credit and (2) changes in prices tend to be offset by changes in credit terms. Suppose that the relative price of cars increased by 10 percent and the number of months of the contract also increased enough so that P^* remained constant[17]: this could be accomplished only if the average existing length of contracts was not near its institutional maximum. Cash buyers would buy fewer cars; credit buyers might purchase the same number, but it is more likely that they would also buy fewer cars. In that case the p_a/p_c term should be included separately to denote a non-linear relation of the various components of the average monthly payment. Since a majority of new-car instalment contracts are presently written for 36 months and many lenders are reluctant to exceed this figure, a rise in the price of new cars would undoubtedly result in higher average monthly payments. But if P^* remained unchanged it would not be reasonable to argue that cash buyers have a high price elasticity of demand while credit buyers have none at all. Such considerations dictate the inclusion of a separate relative price term even when the average monthly payment already includes this variable.

6.3   ATTITUDES AND TASTES

A function explaining the purchases of automobiles which includes income, relative prices, stocks, and appropriate credit variables is still missing one important determinant. We have not yet made full use of the fact that durable purchases are postponable and that most people who already own a particular durable can continue to use it for another year or two. Thus during recessions consumers will not purchase nearly as many durables, and the ratio of consumer durable purchases to personal disposable income will fall substantially. This fact has been long noted. In an early study of car functions, Roos and Szeliski[18] attempted to meet this problem by making car purchases a function of "supernumerary" income, which they defined as the income left after paying for basic necessities such as food and rent.[19] Their idea was that this supernumerary income would be quite small in recessions and would

---

[17] Using the formula for average monthly payment as given, this would also imply a 10 percent rise in M. With actual compounding of interest, M would have to increase slightly more than 10 percent.

[18] C. F. Roos and V. Szeliski, "Factors Governing Changes in Domestic Automobile Demand," in *The Dynamics of Automobile Demand* (New York: General Motors Corporation, 1939), pp. 21–95.

[19] Roos and Szeliski actually measured supernumerary income as per capita disposable income minus $200 in 1923 prices. This allowance amounts to $400 in 1965 prices, or $1600 for a family of four. This is well below President Johnson's "poverty level," which may show how standards have changed.

explain the substantial drop in car purchases. Although this may have been a good idea for the interwar period, it is not relevant for the postwar years. Even in the most severe postwar recession (1958) personal disposable income hardly fell at all.[20] Part of this stability of income in recessions is due to the increase in unemployment compensation insurance; other stabilizing influences are social security payments, dividends, farm payments, and the graduated income tax. Since it is quite unlikely that transfer payments will be used to purchase new cars, we exclude them from the relevant income variable and use income minus transfer payments. However, percentage fluctuations in income minus transfer payments minus necessities are much smaller than percentage fluctuations in new-car purchases. One must also consider the crucial factor that when business turns down, many people will reduce their purchases of consumer durables *even if their own incomes are not reduced.*

Until recently, the major attempt used to explain this phenomenon was an exogenous attitudes index gathered by the Survey Research Center of the University of Michigan. This index is discussed in detail in Chapter 17. Here we just want to explain enough about it to illustrate its usefulness as a predictor of car sales.

The indices used by the Survey Research Center are designed to measure attitudes rather than buying plans. Questions are of the general type: What do you think next year will be like? or, are you better off now than a year ago?[21] An index of buying plans does exist, but we shall not discuss it here, because the Survey Research Center analysts themselves find that it does not add to predictive accuracy of durable purchases. The rationale behind the use of the attitudes index is that if consumers think times will be bad, they will not purchase durables even if they are not directly affected. One logical direction of inquiry is to examine whether the attitudes improve predictive accuracy significantly: If they do, one should examine whether the attitudes themselves can be explained by economic variables, which might then be substituted in their place.

Not surprisingly, the answers differ depending on what yardstick is used. It is clear that the Survey Research Center attitude index includes some non-income variables. If one relates consumption of durables to income alone, then the attitudes make a significant net addition to their explanation. This is the viewpoint taken by their analysts. But we take the position that it is relevant to judge the importance of the attitudes on the basis of a function already including other variables which belong in any reasonable durables function, instead of just a simple $C = f(Y)$ relationship.

Although we have suggested that a variable representing general cyclical movements appears to be important, very little work had been done in this

---

[20] From 1957.4 to 1958.2, personal disposable income in constant dollars fell only \$4.2 billion, or 1.3 percent; it started rising again in 1958.3.

[21] A complete list of these questions is given on pp. 461–462.

specific area until recently.[22] The unemployment rate was used by this author. In a thorough set of studies by Adams and others,[23] length of the work week and net accession rate of hiring were both found to represent essentially the same general cyclical characteristic, and each was found to work approximately as well as the others. When the unemployment rate is used in the car equation, the significance of the attitudes variable is much reduced.[24] Friend and Adams found that while the attitudes were helpful in explaining the 1955 boom, length of the work week explained auto purchases better than the attitude index for the period 1957–1962, and the attitudes did not improve the fit of the equation.[25] Since 1962 the record has not improved; the 1963–1965 figures are given in Table 6.2. In particular, the large dip in the attitude index in 1963.3 was not matched by a decline in car sales.

Friend and Adams found that length of the work week explained car purchases slightly better than did the unemployment rate for the period 1957–1962. Probably some combination of these variables which would still retain the inherently cyclical characteristics of both series would be an improvement. It is not clear which series should be preferred. Sometimes when production rises, the increase in man-hours is accomplished mainly through increased hours; other times it is done mainly through increased hiring (this is discussed in detail in Chapter 10). Thus neither series is an infallible indicator. However, the great majority of the time they move together.

The use of the unemployment variable might also contain some additional economic information as well as represent only cyclical attitudes. As mentioned earlier, transfer payments, which follow unemployment closely, are quite unlikely to be spent on cars. However, this can be taken into consideration by using the variable income minus transfers in the car equation, which is suggested above. Then unemployment is strictly a cyclical attitudinal variable.

Our discussion thus far has centered on cars, and it is natural to investigate whether cyclical attitudes affect purchases of other durables. Consumers are generally unwilling to enter into a contract for a payment of several thousand dollars when times are bad, but have much less reticence about buying an item for $250 or less. In this case, much less credit is used and the purchase is much more likely to be repaid over a shorter period of time. Furthermore, many nonauto durable items are small enough to be purchased with cash. It is even

---

[22] The first use of unemployment in a function explaining purchases of automobiles appears to be in M. K. Evans, *A Postwar Quarterly Model of the United States Economy, 1947–1960* (unpublished Ph.D. thesis, 1964).

[23] F. G. Adams, "Consumer Attitudes, Buying Plans, and Purchases of Durable Goods: A Principal Components, Time Series Approach," *Review of Economics and Statistics*, Vol. 46, No. 4 (November, 1964), pp. 347–355; I. Friend and F. G. Adams, "The Predictive Ability of Consumer Attitudes, Stock Prices, and Non-Attitudinal Variables," *Journal of the American Statistical Association*, Vol. 59, No. 4 (December, 1964), pp. 987–1005. F. G. Adams and E. W. Green, "Explaining and Predicting Aggregate Consumer Attitudes," *International Economic Review*, Vol. 6, No. 3 (September, 1965), pp. 275–293.

[24] Specific regression equations are discussed in Section 6.4.

[25] Friend and Adams, *op. cit.*, p. 999.

TABLE 6.2 COMPARISON OF SRC
ATTITUDE INDEX AND
PURCHASES OF NEW CARS

Quarter	C_{d-1}^e [a]	C_a [b]
1963.1	95.0	23.7
1963.2	94.8	24.1
1963.3	91.4	24.4
1963.4	96.2	24.9
1964.1	96.9	25.3
1964.2	99.0	26.0
1964.3	98.1	27.1
1964.4	100.2	24.6
1965.1	99.4	30.1
1965.2	101.5	29.2
1965.3	102.2	30.2
1965.4	103.2	29.9

[a] C_{d-1}^e, a 6-point index of attitudes, Fall, 1956 = 100.0, lagged one quarter; *Business Week*, Jan. 8, 1966, p. 38.
[b] C_a, purchases of automobiles, billions of 1958 dollars.

possible that cyclical attitudinal variables (such as unemployment) have some slight positive marginal effect on these purchases, instead of an additional negative effect. If this were the case, a rise in unemployment, *cet. par.*, would raise nonauto durable purchases slightly. Individuals who are personally unaffected by a slump in business activity but do not wish to purchase a car on credit during a recession would have more money available for purchasing other durables and may increase these purchases slightly. Although we do not want to overemphasize this point, it is supported by the available evidence.[26] It is safe to say that cyclical attitudinal variables do not greatly affect purchases of nonauto durables either way.

The empirical evidence suggests that the Survey Research Center index of attitudes can be explained by general cyclical variables such as unemployment. Except for 1955, these cyclical variables appear to be more useful in predicting purchases of cars than is the attitudes index. "Attitudes" have been reduced to a general cyclical phenomenon, but nothing has been said about tastes and the effects of model-year changeovers. The good year–bad year cycles of car purchases of the 1950s were sometimes thought to be due to the amount of restyling used in the new model year. With five good years in a row

---

[26] In some additional regressions calculated by us, unemployment had a nonsignificant positive sign in the equation for nonauto durables.

this argument has more or less disappeared. Although one make of car may gain at the expense of other makes because of a new design, there is no evidence at all to show that car sales were higher, *cet. par.*, in the years when most brands introduced new models than in years when only slight face-lifting occurred. The purchases of automobiles can be explained quite satisfactorily without resorting to any "taste" variable, once cyclical attitude variables are included.

6.4   EMPIRICAL RESULTS

The actual regression estimates are considered next. For the period 1948–1964 these are

$$(15.3)\quad C_a = 48.54 + 0.1346[Y - (Tr/p_c)] - 54.19(p_a/p_c) - 0.430Un - 4.129\delta_s$$
$$\qquad\qquad (0.0228) \qquad\qquad (10.20) \qquad (0.175) \qquad (0.458)$$

$$\qquad\qquad + 1.835Cr - 0.0744(K_a)_{-1} \qquad \bar{R}^2 = 0.916$$
$$\qquad\qquad (0.478) \qquad (0.0180)$$

$$(15.2)\quad C_{na} = -11.52 + 0.1570Y - 0.0574(K_{na})_{-1} \qquad \bar{R}^2 = 0.965$$
$$\qquad\qquad\qquad (0.0274) \qquad (0.0251)$$

where C_a = purchases of automobiles and parts, billions of 1958 dollars

$\qquad Y$ = personal disposable income, billions of 1958 dollars

$\qquad Tr$ = transfer payments, billions of current dollars

$\qquad p_a$ = implicit price deflator of automobiles and parts, 1958 = 1.00

$\qquad p_c$ = implicit price deflator for all consumption, 1958 = 1.00

$\qquad K_a$ = stock of automobiles, billions of 1958 dollars

$\qquad Un$ = percent unemployment

$\qquad d_s$ = dummy variable for supply shortages (used 1948.1–1949.1, 1952.3)

$\qquad Cr$ = dummy variable for credit conditions (-1 during Regulation W, 1 in 1955 and later years, and 0 elsewhere)

$\qquad C_{na}$ = purchases of other consumer durables, billions of 1958 dollars

$\qquad K_{na}$ = stock of other consumer durables, billions of 1958 dollars

It was indicated earlier that the constant dollar monthly payment would be a good term to use for credit conditions in the auto equation. Unfortunately the data are not yet available beyond 1962, so it is not possible to test the importance of this term for the entire sample period used to estimate the other consumer durable equations. However, for this truncated sample period the monthly payment term was highly significant, with a t ratio of 4.4. For the period after the expiration of credit controls (1953–1962) the t ratio of its coefficient was 6.0. These levels of significance are somewhat higher than those obtained by using the dummy variable. This suggests that we have captured a substantial part but by no means all the effect of changing credit conditions with this simplified dummy variable.

These functions were also estimated using one of the SRC attitude indices. The results were

(15.3a) $C_a = 30.27 + 0.1055[Y - (Tr/p_c)] - 47.54(p_a/p_c) - 0.097Un - 3.269d_s$
$\qquad\qquad$ (0.0265) $\qquad\qquad\qquad$ (10.59) $\qquad$ (0.234) $\qquad$ (0.609)

$\qquad\qquad + 0.899Cr - 0.0449(K_a)_{-1} + 0.120(C_d^e)_{-1} \qquad \bar{R}^2 = 0.917$
$\qquad\qquad$ (0.647) $\quad$ (0.0226) $\qquad$ (0.056)

(15.2a) $\qquad C_{na} = -14.19 + 0.1157Y - 0.0209(K_{na})_{-1} + 0.0552(C_d^e)_{-1}$
$\qquad\qquad\qquad\qquad$ (0.0370) $\quad$ (0.0333) $\qquad\qquad$ (0.0327)

$\qquad \bar{R}^2 = 0.964$

where C_{d-1}^e = 8-point SRC index of attitudes and buying plans, 1958 = 100 (lagged one quarter). The equations are little changed. The attitudes are significant (by a small margin) in the auto equation and are not significant in the other durables equation. The unemployment term becomes insignificant, suggesting that it and the attitudes variables explain the same general phenomena. The fits are virtually unchanged when the attitude index is added, indicating that the attitude index does not add any new information.

In most other studies of durable goods, capital-stock variables have either been ignored or have been found to be nonsignificant, but in this study they are quite significant and important. One reason for this may be the way in which capital stock is measured. In empirical time-series studies of durables, the stock is too often calculated either by merely counting units or by applying some straight-line depreciation rule, both being quite unsatisfactory. The only studies of consumer durables which seem to give this problem serious consideration are those by Gregory Chow.[27] As Chow points out, "much misunderstanding of the automobile market has come from the tendency to 'count cars.' The evidence . . . is strong that the market does not consider all cars to be equivalent."[28] Chow expresses the stock of cars in terms of new-car equivalents. The weights used in converting old cars to new-car equivalents are the different relative prices of cars t years old. Chow finds that the average annual rate of depreciation is 23 percent for the period 1920–1953 and that this rate fluctuates very little.[29]

An alternative method of estimating a constant annual average rate of depreciation is to assume that at the end of a certain number of years (for example, t years) a car is worth only scrap value, which is α of the original

[27] G. C. Chow, *Demand for Automobiles in the United States* (Amsterdam: North-Holland, 1957), and "Statistical Demand Functions for Automobiles and Their Use for Forecasting," in A. C. Harberger, ed., *The Demand for Durable Goods* (Chicago: University of Chicago Press, 1960).

[28] G. C. Chow, "Statistical Demand Functions . . .", *op. cit.*, p. 150.

[29] *Ibid.*, pp. 149–150.

value. Then if $1 - \lambda$ is the annual depreciation factor, $\lambda^t = \alpha$, and given reasonable values of t and α, λ can easily be calculated. Values that we choose are $t = $ ten years and $\alpha = 0.05$; t is converted to quarters because quarterly functions are being used, so that $\lambda^{40} = 0.05$, and $\lambda = 0.9288$. For four quarters, $\lambda = 0.744$, or $1 - \lambda = 0.256$, which is very close to the figure found by Chow. The identities

$$K_{a_t} = \sum_{i=0}^{40} \lambda^i C_{a_{t-i}} \quad \text{and} \quad K_{na_t} = \sum_{i=0}^{40} \lambda^i C_{na_{t-i}}$$

are then used to calculate the values of capital stock used in the regressions.

The short-run income and price elasticities for the functions without the attitude index (at the means) are given in Table 6.3. The long-run elasticities are obtained in the following way. Assume a unit change in income and no long-run change in the equilibrium values of relative prices, unemployment, or supply or credit conditions. Then

(6.25) $\Delta C_a = 0.1346\Delta(Y - Tr) - 0.0744\Delta K_{a-1}$

(6.26) $K_a = \sum_{i=0}^{40} \lambda^i C_{a_{t-i}} = C_{a_t} + \sum_{i=1}^{40} \lambda^i C_{a_{t-i}} = C_{a_t} + \sum_{i=1}^{41} \lambda^i C_{a_{t-i-1}} - \lambda^{41} C_{a_{t-41}}$

Therefore,

(6.27) $$K_a = C_{a_t} + 0.9288 K_{a_{t-1}} - 0.05 C_{a_{t-41}}$$

We assume that $0.05 C_{a_{t-41}}$ is approximately constant; since it is very small compared to C_a, changes in it will make almost no difference in the solution. Then

(6.28) $$\Delta K_{a_t} \cong \Delta C_{a_t} + 0.9288\Delta K_{a_{t-1}}$$

In long-run equilibrium all time subscripts can be neglected, so that

(6.29) $\Delta C_a = 0.1346\Delta(Y - Tr) - 0.0744\Delta K_a$

(6.30) $\Delta K_a = \Delta C_a + 0.9288\Delta K_a \quad \text{or} \quad \Delta K_a = \dfrac{\Delta C_a}{0.0712}$

TABLE 6.3   SHORT-RUN PRICE AND INCOME ELASTICITIES FOR CONSUMER DURABLES

	Price	Income
Cars	−3.1	2.2
Other durables	—	2.3

TABLE 6.4 LONG-RUN PRICE AND
INCOME ELASTICITIES FOR
CONSUMER DURABLES

	Price	Income
Cars	−1.5	1.1
Other durables	—	1.2

Therefore,

$$(6.31) \qquad \Delta C_a = 0.1346 \Delta(Y - Tr) - \frac{0.0744}{0.0712} \Delta C_a$$

Therefore,

$$(6.32) \qquad \frac{\Delta C_a}{\Delta(Y - Tr)} = \frac{0.1346}{1 + (0.0744/0.0712)} = 0.0658$$

Similarly, we find that

$$(6.33) \qquad \frac{\Delta C_{na}}{\Delta Y} = 0.0869 \qquad \frac{\Delta C_a}{\Delta(p_a/p_c)} = 26.50$$

The values after translation into long-run elasticities are given in Table 6.4. The long-run income elasticity is very close to unity for both cars and other durables, a result that would be expected from earlier discussions of the consumption function. The price elasticity for cars is also quite reasonable. However, there is little question that a relative price term in the equation for other durables should be significant; this point needs further discussion.

The failure to find a significant price elasticity may be due in part to a particularly severe index number problem. As usual, the price index for nonauto durables is a weighted average of the prices of various durables with the weights decided in some base year. For most consumer price indices this gives a reasonable estimate of the prices consumers are actually paying, but this is not so for nonauto durables. New products are constantly being introduced (for example, television sets, air conditioners, and, more recently, color television sets) which are bought in large quantities only when the price at which they are available is much lower than their original price. However, the weights used for these products when they are new is very small, so that the large drop in their prices which is concomitant with a large volume of sales is hardly reflected in the overall price index of durables. For example, prices of color television sets dropped approximately 20 to 25 percent in 1965. This was one of the main reasons for a very large increase in the number of sets sold. However, this decrease was not reflected in the price index for nonauto durables, because the weights given to color television sets was very small. Part of the explanation for the nonsignificant measured price elasticity may be due to this reason. No such problem exists with cars, where the basic unit has changed much less in the postwar period. Except for this one problem, all the other coefficients and elasticities seem to be quite reasonable.

It might also be noted that a short-run price elasticity of -3 for automobiles corresponds to the profit-maximizing position of $MR = MC$, since marginal costs are about two thirds of the manufacturer's price. Car manufacturers have also come to realize the high price elasticity of demand for their product. They do think that price increases were in large part responsible for relatively poor sales from 1956 to 1959 and that price stability was an important reason for continued high sales from 1962 to 1966. Stiffer government resistance to increased prices since that time may be another reason for smaller price increases than would have otherwise occurred.

6.5   THE PATTERN OF CONSUMER DURABLE PURCHASES OVER THE CYCLE

Up to this point we have discussed the determinants of purchases of consumer durables in some detail but have not said much about their pattern over the cycle. We have indicated that durables fluctuate over the cycle by a greater percentage than income or GNP, but we have developed no specific mechanism to suggest that the general cyclical pattern for durables differs from these other variables. However, under various circumstances there might be a decrease in the consumer durables/income ratio during the later part of the upswing of the cycle which would be due to the fact that consumers first purchase durable assets and later switch to liquid assets. This problem can be characterized by considering a consumer faced with the problem of distributing his current income among the following broad groups of purchases: nondurables and services, durables, money, liquid assets (savings accounts and so on, and bonds), equities, and other (real estate, and so on). At each point in time, the consumer must decide in what order he will purchase items in these groups. For the present, assume that purchases of nondurables and services are made on a regular basis and that funds for them are allocated first. Then attention can be concentrated on the division between durable, liquid, and other assets.

Assume that initially the economy is in equilibrium. Then the demand functions for all types of assets can be written in the form

(6.34) $$A_i = f\left(Y, \frac{p_i}{p_c}, K_i, S_i\right) \qquad (i = 1, \ldots, j)$$

where A_i = the ith asset

$\quad\quad p_i$ = price of the ith asset

$\quad\quad K_i$ = stock of the ith asset

$\quad\quad S_i$ = special factors that may affect the demand for the ith asset, such as credit conditions for buying cars, margin requirements for the stock market, loan-to-value ratio for purchasing real estate, and so on. However, we are holding these constant for this argument, so their particular nature is unimportant

As long as income rises at an equilibrium rate, each consumer will continue to purchase each asset in equilibrium quantities, which may vary among consumers.[30]

Now assume a recession occurs and income falls below its equilibrium level. Presumably both durable and other asset accumulations are foregone, but stocks of durables are more likely to be depleted through the simple expedient of not replacing them. We want to examine the order in which consumers acquire these foregone assets during the next upswing. Available evidence shows that they will choose durable assets first, ahead of liquid assets.[31] This may well be because the stock of durables was depleted by a greater percentage during the recession. As these stocks are brought back into equilibrium, consumers may then shift from durable to liquid and other assets, particularly liquid assets. From this viewpoint, durable and liquid assets are substitutes. If these liquid assets do not find investment outlets, there could be a slackening of aggregate demand which would cause the beginning of a recession.

This theory attained some popularity during the 1950s and particularly in 1955, when it was thought that consumer durables stocks had reached equilibrium at the expense of other types of assets, resulting in relatively poor durables sales (especially automobiles) in 1956 and 1957. This type of theory would also explain the widespread view of the 1950s that car sales could not stay at high levels two years in a row.

The record of car sales for selected years is given in Table 6.5. At the end of 1962, the good year–bad year pattern had existed for almost the entire postwar period. The only exception was 1960, when car sales rose very slightly over 1959, and the second half of 1960 was worse than the first half. Many people predicted a downturn in car sales in 1963 on this basis.

Things looked quite different at the end of 1965. Clearly the old alternate-year theory no longer holds. The record must be analyzed to see why car sales in the 1950s were never high in adjacent years. The changes in some of the

---

[30] Stated this way, the problem may appear to have some relation to the portfolio selection problem. However, we are discussing a fundamentally different problem—the one of timing in a dynamic framework rather than risk aversion in a static framework. Quite possibly a complete exposition of the problem would draw on both these elements.

[31] In the years following recessions, durable purchases increased $17\frac{1}{2}$ percent, while net financial saving (that is, liquid assets minus debt) increased by $4\frac{1}{2}$ percent.

TABLE 6.5   SEMIAUTONOMOUS CYCLE IN CAR SALES AND ITS CAUSES

Year	Car Sales, Constant \$	Car Prices (1958 = 1.00)	Monthly Payment, Constant \$	Unemployment Rate
1950	15.9	0.886	40.8	5.2
1951	13.3	0.935	49.9	3.3
1955	21.2	0.965	31.9[a]	4.4
1956	17.9	0.965	30.7	4.2
1959	19.0	1.032	30.8	5.5
1960	20.0	1.021	29.7	5.7
1962	21.8	1.009	32.7	5.5
1963	24.1	1.009	n.a.	5.5
1964	25.6	1.009	n.a.	5.2
1965	30.0	0.993	n.a.	4.6

[a] 1953, 38.0; 1954, 34.4.

independent variables in the car equation are listed in Table 6.5 for these years. Income and stock variables are not included because they followed the same pattern in all the pairs of years being considered.

The 1950–1951 subcycle was caused largely by a rise in the price of cars and the imposition of Regulation W, resulting in a severe tightening of credit conditions. Sales in 1950 were also buoyed by the "scare buying" at the beginning of the Korean War. The 1955–1956 subcycle was caused mainly by a very appreciable easing of credit terms, which actually began in 1954. Although car sales were rather high in 1954 by recession standards, the full effect of the easing of credit conditions did not manifest itself until 1955. From 1956 to the present, credit conditions have remained about the same; many people who bought cars in 1955 would not have done so at that time if credit conditions had not been eased. The 1955 experience is an example of how changes in the terms for instalment credit contracts can be destabilizing. From 1959 to 1960 car sales rose slightly in spite of an increase in the rate of unemployment. Seen with several additional years of hindsight, it appears that by this time the good year–bad year cycle of automobile sales was disappearing.

Thus if no large fluctuations occur in the variables affecting durables purchases, they are very likely to continue to increase throughout the upswing of the cycle. It is still important to examine the relationship between purchases of durables and other assets over the cycle to determine whether equilibrium levels of both are purchased throughout the upswing or whether there is a relative shift to liquid assets in the later stages of the cycle. To determine this it is necessary to state something more definite about the *order* in which various types of assets are purchased. The groundwork for such a study exists, although in quite a different context. Recent work by Pyatt[32] and Paroush[33] has suggested the following problem. Suppose that at any given time there is a certain probability that a household will buy a given durable, and this depends on the collection of durables already owned. Then it should be possible to form a correlation matrix relating those durables already owned to that durable good which is to be purchased next. This was done by Pyatt for a number of different consumer durables. He found that there was a definite order in which these items were purchased and that there were relatively few exceptions. In one of his studies[34] Pyatt obtained the results given in Table 6.6. Paroush conducted a similar study and found that a radio, gas cooker, refrigerator, and washing machine were purchased in that order. He suggests that this scheme could be used for market research.[35] Pyatt sees a much wider use for this general type of analysis, stating that "the analysis which we have developed is an analysis of the accumulation of attributes rather than of durable goods. Ownership of durable goods is only one type of attribute. Other types of attributes are being a consumer of particular commodities, being capable of answering particular examination questions, having the symptoms of some infection, and possessing the characteristics of a particular social class. The list could be continued almost indefinitely."[36] For our purpose, it is reasonable to ask whether this idea of priority patterns can be extended in a rather different way to encompass not only the difference between various durables, but between durable and other assets. Stratifying by income classes, one could see whether a certain amount of cash was preferred to a durable, savings bank asset, and so forth at different times during the cycle. This type of study could

TABLE 6.6 ESTIMATE OF THE PROBABILITY PATTERNS
DEFINED OVER A GROUP OF
FOUR DURABLE GOODS

Durable Good	Position in Order of Accumulation				Average Position
	1st	2nd	3rd	4th	
Cooker	0.990	0.009	0.000	0.001	1.013
Vacuum cleaner	0.006	0.903	0.087	0.004	2.090
Washing machine	0.004	0.062	0.697	0.237	3.167
Refrigerator	0.001	0.025	0.216	0.758	3.731

[32] F. G. Pyatt, *Priority Patterns and the Demand for Household Durable Goods* (Cambridge: Cambridge University Press, 1964).

[33] J. Paroush, "The Order of Acquisition of Consumer Durables," *Econometrica*, Vol. 33, No. 1 (January, 1965), pp. 225–235.

[34] Pyatt, *op. cit.*, p. 40.

[35] Paroush, *op. cit.*, p. 233.

[36] Pyatt, *op. cit.*, p. 136.

go far in determining whether there is some point during the cycle when consumers do switch from durable to liquid assets.

These priority patterns probably are not the same for each cycle, since different forces influence purchasing decisions. Pyatt did in fact find that the hypothesis of a constant realized probability pattern must be rejected. If so, it would be quite instructive to see if the various deviations in purchasing patterns did conform closely to changes in the independent variables in the regression equations for durable and other assets, and whether in fact such patterns would be approximately constant in the absence of exogenous shocks. Although such a study has not yet been undertaken, it commends itself as an area for future research. Data from consumer surveys may be used for this purpose.

In the absence of such a priority pattern study, we now look at other information regarding the complementarity or substitutability of nondurables and services, durables, present savings, and stocks of liquid assets over the postwar period. Other evidence which is available for cross-section and time-series data indicates that there is a slight negative relationship between consumer durables and liquid assets, although strong substitutability has not yet been established. There is clearly no positive relationship between the two, nor would we expect that there would be. In Chapter 2 several reasons were mentioned for liquid asset holdings not influencing consumption of nondurables and services. These reasons also apply here, as does the added substitutability relationship between purchases of durables and liquid assets.

At the cross-section level, all the studies referred to earlier support the fact that liquid assets are either uncorrelated or negatively correlated with purchases of consumer durables. Fisher found that "the relationship of savings account size and size of savings bonds to net outlays (on consumer durables) were quite small and not significantly different from zero."[37] Klein and Lansing "consistently" found that "liquid asset holdings are not closely associated with purchasing decisions" and in fact were negatively associated.[38] In time-series analysis, no positive relationship at all has been discovered between these two variables. Some regressions we calculated showed a nonsignificant negative relationship. Most time-series studies of consumer durables do not even discuss the role of liquid assets because of their unimportance.

The long-run relationship between the capital stock of durables and the stock of liquid assets also shows no correlation between the two. This is shown in Table 6.7, where business cycle averages have been tabulated to eliminate short-term fluctuations.

There is a slight upward trend in all ratios, but since 1959 L/Y has risen considerably, whereas K_a/Y and K_{na}/Y have remained constant. It can also be seen that although consumer durables purchases have been high relative to

[37] Fisher, op. cit., p. 655.
[38] Klein and Lansing, op. cit., p. 120.

TABLE 6.7   RELATIONSHIP OF STOCKS OF CONSUMER DURABLES AND LIQUID ASSETS

all figures are in billions of constant dollars (except the ratios)

Dates of Business Cycles	Stock of Autos[a]	Stock of Other Durables[a]	Income	Liquid Assets	$\dfrac{K_a}{Y}$	$\dfrac{K_{na}}{Y}$	$\dfrac{L}{Y}$
1950–1954	36.5	52.2	264.5	155.9	0.14	0.20	0.59
1955–1958	52.6	64.7	310.2	192.2	0.17	0.21	0.62
1959–1961	58.6	74.3	341.3	227.5	0.17	0.22	0.67
1962–1965	68.8	87.2	400.0	294.9	0.17	0.22	0.74

[a] Calculated from the equations $K_{a_t} = \sum_{i=0}^{40} \lambda^i (C_a)_{t-i}$ and $K_{na_t} = \sum_{i=0}^{40} \lambda^i (C_{na})_{t-i}$, where $\lambda = 0.9288$.

income in recent years, the ratio of capital stock to income has not changed, thus indicating that replacement demand is accounting for an increased share of sales.

The relationships among nondurables and services, durables, and current savings are a little more complex. In the initial discussion of priority patterns, we assumed that purchases of nondurables and services were determined before asset decisions were considered. Obviously, this is an oversimplification, because consumer durable purchases may be substituted either for nondurables and services or current savings. A comparison of fluctuations in the C_d/Y ratio with the C_{n+s}/Y and S/Y ratios is shown in Table 6.8. The comparison starts in 1949 because of the severe shortages of durables that existed during 1947 and 1948. The adjusted $\Delta Y/Y$ column is $\Delta Y/Y$ minus 3.7 percent, the average rate of increase of constant dollar personal disposal income over the sample period.

Little information can be drawn from Table 6.8 in its present form. In boom years C_d/Y and S/Y are relatively high and C_{ns}/Y is relatively low; the reverse is true in recessions. This follows directly from the results that the short-run income elasticities of durables and savings are greater than unity and of other consumption is less than unity and adds no new information. However, it masks the relationship we are trying to uncover. We must first determine what each yearly value of C_d/Y, C_{ns}/Y, and S/Y would be *if income were at an equilibrium level*. To do this we adjust C_d/Y and S/Y down and C_{ns}/Y up during booms and do the reverse during recessions.[39] These adjusted ratios will still differ substantially from year to year, but the differences will now be due to *nonincome* factors (for example, changes in relative prices, credit conditions, and so on). If C_d/Y is relatively high some year, for example, we can examine whether the extra expenditure on durables is reflected primarily in a decrease in other consumption or a decrease in saving.

When these adjustments are made, a rather striking negative relationship

TABLE 6.8 SUBSTITUTABILITY AMONG DURABLES,
OTHER CONSUMPTION, AND SAVING

Year	C_d/Y	S/Y	C_{n+s}/Y	$\Delta Y/Y$, %	Adjusted $\Delta Y/Y$, %
1949	0.123	0.062	0.815	0.4	−3.3
1950	0.139	0.076	0.785	8.1	4.4
1951	0.123	0.090	0.787	2.4	−1.3
1952	0.117	0.091	0.792	2.9	−0.8
1953	0.128	0.090	0.782	4.4	0.7
1954	0.127	0.081	0.792	1.0	−2.7
1955	0.146	0.075	0.779	6.2	2.5
1956	0.133	0.090	0.777	4.1	0.4
1957	0.131	0.088	0.781	2.1	−1.6
1958	0.119	0.090	0.791	0.9	−2.8
1959	0.131	0.077	0.792	4.3	0.6
1960	0.132	0.071	0.797	2.1	−1.6
1961	0.125	0.080	0.795	3.1	−0.6
1962	0.134	0.079	0.787	4.8	1.1
1963	0.140	0.074	0.786	3.5	−0.2
1964	0.144	0.085	0.771	6.8	3.1

appears between C_d/Y and S/Y as shown in Table 6.9. This table shows that there is a strong negative correlation between C_d/Y and S/Y, while there is very little correlation between C_d/Y and C_{n+s}/Y. This is confirmed by a rank correlation test, which shows that while there is a very significant negative relationship between S/Y and C_d/Y, there is actually a small nonsignificant *positive* relationship between C_{n+s}/Y and C_d/Y.[40] It does appear that durables purchases are in fact undertaken in place of savings and not in place of non-durables and services. Although this test is too crude to be applied unequivocally, it is indicative of the relationship between durable purchases and other spending and saving.

---

[39] The method of adjustment is as follows. Suppose that the mean value of $C_d = a_1$, of $C_{n+s} = a_2$, of $S = a_3$, and of $Y = a$. By definition, $a_1 + a_2 + a_3 = a$. If Y changes by one unit, then C_d will change by m_1, C_{n+s} will change by m_2, and S will change by m_3, where the m_i are marginal propensities to consume or save respectively; clearly, $m_1 + m_2 + m_3 = 1$. The new ratios will then be

$$\frac{C_d}{Y} = \frac{a_1 + m_1}{a + 1} \qquad \frac{C_{n+s}}{Y} = \frac{a_2 + m_2}{a + 1} \qquad \frac{S}{Y} = \frac{a_3 + m_3}{a + 1}$$

Then the change between the actual and average ratios, which is the amount of the adjustment, is given by

$$\Delta\left(\frac{C_d}{Y}\right) = \frac{a_1 + m_1}{a + 1} - \frac{a_1}{a} = \frac{(a_1 + m_1)a - a_1(a + 1)}{a(a + 1)} = \frac{m_1 - (a_1/a)}{a}$$

Going one step further, it can be shown that C_a and C_{na} are substitutes rather than complements. Furthermore, the large increases in the amount on instalment debt which occurs in the years when car sales are high does not discourage purchases of other durables in the following year. On the contrary, a very good year for car sales followed by a poor year implies that purchases of other durables will increase in the second year. For example, when the C_a/Y ratio fell from 0.0715 in 1955 to 0.0579 in 1956, the C_{na}/Y ratio rose from 0.0740 to 0.0747.

TABLE 6.9   ADJUSTED C_d/Y AND S/Y RELATIONSHIP

Year	C_d/Y	S/Y	C_{n+s}/Y
1955	0.143	0.068	0.789
1964	0.140	0.076	0.784
1963	0.140	0.075	0.785
1950	0.135	0.064	0.801
1960	0.134	0.076	0.790
1962	0.133	0.076	0.791
1956	0.133	0.089	0.778
1957	0.133	0.093	0.774
1959	0.132	0.075	0.795
1954	0.130	0.089	0.781
1953	0.127	0.088	0.785
1961	0.126	0.082	0.792
1949	0.126	0.072	0.802
1951	0.124	0.094	0.782
1958	0.122	0.098	0.780
1952	0.118	0.093	0.789

for $a \cong a + 1$. Similarly,

$$\Delta\left(\frac{C_{n+s}}{Y}\right) = \frac{a_2 + m_2}{a + 1} - \frac{a_2}{a} = \frac{m_2 - (a_2/a)}{a}$$

$$\Delta\left(\frac{S}{Y}\right) = \frac{a_3 + m_3}{a + 1} - \frac{a_3}{a} = \frac{m_3 - (a_3/a)}{a}$$

Substituting approximate yearly marginal propensities and sample period averages, we have $m_1 = 0.25$, $m_2 = 0.4$, $m_3 = 0.35$, $a_1/a = 0.13$, $a_2/a = 0.80$, $a_3/a = 0.07$, and $a = 300$. Thus

$$\Delta\left(\frac{C_d}{Y}\right) = \frac{0.25 - 0.13}{300} \qquad \Delta\left(\frac{C_{n+s}}{Y}\right) = \frac{0.40 - 0.80}{300} \qquad \Delta\left(\frac{S}{Y}\right) = \frac{0.35 - 0.07}{300}$$

per billion dollars of change in Y. To convert to percent, these figures must be multiplied by $3\frac{1}{3}$.

[40] The actual rank correlation coefficients are $r = -0.66$ for S/Y and C_d/Y, and $r = +0.07$ for C_{n+s}/Y and C_d/Y.

6.6   EXPLANATION OF CREDIT TERMS

It was shown in earlier sections of this chapter that the average monthly payment is an important determinant of car purchases, although credit conditions did not seem to have an important influence on purchases of other durables. To complete the explanation of car purchases, we shall discuss the relationships that explain the components of the average monthly payment and shall also indicate the possible magnitude of its importance on car sales. Functions will be developed for the percentage of down payment, average length of contract in months, and finance charges.[41]

Two contrasting views can be advanced for the explanation of credit terms. According to the first explanation, the supply of credit available to consumers is quite inelastic. When total credit becomes tighter, the amount of consumer credit offered is reduced accordingly, resulting in higher down payments and shorter average length of contracts. Credit scarcity could be measured both by some general measure of economic activity, whose fluctuations would represent the overall demand for credit, and by actual interest rates, which would rise when credit was scarcer. Short-term rates usually reflect this scarcity more sharply than long-term rates. This inelasticity would also be partially due to an implicit risk factor; during recessions when unemployment (or business failure) rates were high, less credit would be offered. If we let r stand for general terms of credit (of which down payment and average length of contract are two), then this hypothesis states that $r = a_0 - a_1 X - a_2 i - a_3 U$, where X is some general measure of production, i a general interest rate, and U a risk factor. In other words, r should be negatively related to all three determinants.

According to the other viewpoint, credit to consumers is highly elastic. In that case, scarcity in the general credit market has very little effect on the supply of consumer credit. Thus there would be a zero partial correlation between r and i. When general business conditions are good, consumers are more likely to use more credit at easier terms. This must be balanced against the fact that during recessions, when car sales are lower, dealers will offer easier credit terms to stimulate sales. The implicit risk factor of lending during recessions is overshadowed by the desire to lower the monthly payment and increase sales. If this theory were to be verified, then $r = a_0 + a_1 X + a_3 U$, $a_2 \cong 0$. The results, which were calculated for a fairly wide range of variables and specifications of the function, strongly suggest that the supply of instalment credit to consumers is highly elastic (in the empirical range which was tested) and that the second hypothesis explaining r is correct.

There are two additional problems to be considered with respect to this equation. One is the problem of lag structure, because changes made in r do not occur instantaneously but in response to changes in the automobile market

---

[41] The following section is taken, with some modifications, from Evans and Kisselgoff, *op. cit.*, pp. 24–27.

in the recent past. Theoretically, it is reasonable to use lags of up to one year, because both automobile manufacturers and dealers usually base their conclusions on whether business is good on a complete model year rather than on any one particular quarter. This suggests a lag structure of the form

$$(6.35) \qquad\qquad r_t = \alpha \sum \lambda^i Z^*_{t-i}$$

where

$$Z^* = \tfrac{1}{4}(Z_t + Z_{t-\frac{1}{4}} + Z_{t-\frac{1}{2}} + Z_{t-\frac{3}{4}})$$

Z is the general variable in the regressions explaining r, and all lags are now in years. The transformed equation becomes

$$(6.36) \qquad\qquad r_t = \alpha Z^*_t + \lambda r_{t-1}$$

For quarterly data, the r_{t-1} term can be approximated by r four quarters ago.

The other problem to be considered is the practical limits on down payment and length of contract. Most lending institutions will not lend very much over 100 percent of the dealer cost of a new car and are also reluctant to extend credit for more than 36 months. To do so would result in a substantial period of negative equity, especially for those contracts in which the percentage of down payment was near zero. Thus as the percentage of the car purchased on credit and the average length of contract approach 100 percent and 36 months, respectively, successive increases in these terms will become smaller and smaller for the same change in X and U. Such behavior can be closely approximated by approaching these limits asymptotically. Then

$$(6.37) \qquad\qquad \frac{1}{(r - r^*)_t} = \alpha \sum \lambda^i Z^*_{t-i}$$

and thus

$$(6.38) \qquad\qquad \frac{1}{(r - r^*)_t} = \alpha Z^*_t + \lambda \left(\frac{1}{r - r^*}\right)_{t-1}$$

where r^* is the maximum value of r. For purposes of estimation, this can be closely approximated by

$$(6.39) \quad (r - r^*)_t = \alpha \frac{1}{Z^*_t} + \lambda(r - r^*)_{t-1} \ \text{ and } \ r = \alpha \frac{1}{Z^*_t} + \lambda r_{t-1} + (r^*_t - \lambda r^*_{t-1})$$

Since r^* is defined as the maximum feasible value of r, it is in general the same for all periods. However, this does not hold for the period when Regulation W was in effect. A dummy variable is added to these regressions, which is unity when this regulation was in force and zero otherwise. This procedure also enables us to obtain an estimate of the marginal significance of Regulation W when the effect of other variables has been accounted for, instead of simply measuring the average drop which occurred in credit terms when this regulation was activated.

The estimates for these functions are

$$(6.40) \quad D = 74.39 - 4.37 d_{RW} - 22.51(1/Un^*) - 17.86(1/X_m^*) + 0.339 D_{-4}$$
$$\qquad\qquad (0.44) \qquad (4.45) \qquad\qquad (3.16) \qquad\qquad (0.084)$$

$$\bar{R}^2 = 0.967$$

$$(6.41) \quad M = 34.62 - 6.96 d_{RW} - 15.70(1/Un^*) - 14.09(1/X_m^*) + 0.357 M_{-4}$$
$$\qquad\qquad (0.48) \qquad (4.68) \qquad\qquad (2.58) \qquad\qquad (0.073)$$

$$\bar{R}^2 = 0.961$$

where $D = 100$ percent $-$ down-payment percentage

$M = $ average length of contract in months

$d_{RW} = $ dummy variable for Regulation W

$Un^* = \frac{1}{4}(Un_t + Un_{t-1} + Un_{t-2} + Un_{t-3})$, where $Un = $ percent unemployed

$X_m^* = \frac{1}{4}(X_{m_t} + X_{m_{t-1}} + X_{m_{t-2}} + X_{m_{t-3}})$, where $X_m = $ gross output originating in the manufacturing sector, billions of constant dollars

In particular, note that the imposition of Regulation W resulted in about a 4.4 percent increase in down payment and a seven-month decrease in the average length of contract.

Regulation W was in effect during most of World War II and was reimposed in late 1948 and during the Korean War. The fact that it was actually very effective and did cause consumers to change their buying patterns is widely believed to have accounted for its demise. It applied to all consumer goods purchased on instalment credit, but its major effect was on automobile purchases. The postwar dates and regulation conditions for purchases of automobiles are given in Table 6.10.

TABLE 6.10   DATES AND CONDITIONS OF REGULATION W

Date Effective	Minimum Down Payment for New Cars, %	Maximum Contract Length, months
9–20–48	$33\frac{1}{3}$	15–18[a]
3–7–49	$33\frac{1}{3}$	21
4–27–49	$33\frac{1}{3}$	24
6–30–49	Expired	
9–8–50	$33\frac{1}{3}$	21
10–16–50	$33\frac{1}{3}$	15
7–31–51	$33\frac{1}{3}$	21
5–7–52	Expired	

[a] 18-month loans could be granted on loans of over $1000; otherwise 15 months was the maximum.

A slightly different theoretical structure is necessary to explain the rate of finance charges. Although D and M are often varied by individual dealers for individual customers, the same is not true for finance charges. These are usually set by lending institutions and are invariant to particular consumers for any given period of time. There is some indication that changes in finance charges are used as a way to offset changes in D and M, although the leverage is small. When these variables are decreasing, thereby raising the monthly payment, there is a tendency for finance charges to be lowered to compensate for some of this increase. On the other hand, when D and M are rising, it is easier to raise finance charges without increasing the monthly payment. For example, during the Korean War when Regulation W was in effect and car sales were low, finance charges dropped from 12 to 11 percent. Although this is a small change relative to the total monthly payment, it does represent the lowest level of finance charges during the sample period. It also reflects some effort on the part of lenders to adjust the average monthly payment down after D and M were fixed by law. In the 1955–1956 period, when D and M were rising rapidly, there was a rise in finance charges from 11 to 12.5 percent. Again, this is not a large change but is representative of this general behavior. Such a rise does imply an increase of almost 3 percent in the monthly payment, or approximately $2.50 per month for a $2500 contract for 36 months.

The function explaining finance charges is

$$(6.42) \qquad F = 6.23 - \underset{(0.0103)}{0.0417\tfrac{1}{4}} \sum_{i=1}^{4} P_{-i} + \underset{(0.0833)}{0.6010F_{-4}} \qquad \bar{R}^2 = 0.697$$

where F is the interest rate charged on new-car loans, in percent, and P is the index of average monthly payment as defined in Section 6.2.

Finally, we consider the effect on car purchases of a change in credit conditions which is approximately equivalent to the change induced by the imposition of Regulation W. According to the equations given above, this implies an increase in down payment of 4.37 percent and a decrease in the average length of contract of 6.96 months. There will be a partially compensating decrease in finance charges of 0.70 percent. If there are no changes in the price of autos or the consumer price level, this would result in an increase in the average monthly payment index from 32.7 (1963.1 figures, the latest which were available) to 39.2. In an equation estimated for the period 1953–1962, the average monthly payment term has a coefficient of 0.9595.[42] Thus the drop of car sales would be 0.9595×6.5, or a decrease of $6.25 billion. In the long run this change would be reduced to $2.34 billion, still a substantial sum. Effects of this magnitude indicate why specific consumer credit controls such as Regulation W have not been used recently. If they are to be reactivated, it should be done only if there is a genuine need for such controls, for they are bound to have a sizeable effect on the whole economy.

---

[42] Evans and Kisselgoff, *op. cit.*, eq. (1d).

CHAPTER 7

INVESTMENT IN
RESIDENTIAL CONSTRUCTION

7.1 INTRODUCTION

The next component of aggregate demand to be considered is investment in residential construction, which includes houses and apartments. As will be demonstrated throughout this chapter, the determinants of residential construction are much different from those of fixed business investment. Residential construction essentially receives residual supplies of factor resources from other sectors of the economy, which results in a general countercyclical pattern. This pattern is compounded by the fact that, owing to the rather unusual way in which housing is included in the national income accounts, the actual residential construction figures measure the supply of housing instead of the demand.

In general, the national income accounts distinguish between the production and final sale of goods by classifying those goods which have been produced but have not yet been sold as inventories. If goods are produced and then immediately purchased, as is the case for many types of capital equipment, this classification problem does not exist. However, this is not the way in which the housing market operates. It is unusual for a dwelling unit to be started with the particular occupant already designated; instead, most houses and apartments are constructed for the general market, much like durable consumer goods, and sold at a later date. If the national income statistics for residential construction did follow the pattern of consumer goods, new houses and apartments would be separated into units actually sold and inventories. These could then be explained separately. However, investment in residential construction is recorded in the national income accounts as final demand at the time of actual construction, not at the time of purchase. Thus to explain short-term fluctuations in residential construction it is necessary to explain the supply of new dwelling units as well as the demand for these units.

Many functions explaining residential construction include both demand and supply elements without distinguishing which variables serve which purpose. In such cases it is not clear whether the short-run or long-run movements in housing investment are being explained. To avoid this problem, we first discuss the long-run determinants of the demand for housing. These primarily follow trend movements and in general do not fluctuate during the short cycle. The causes of short-run fluctuations in the supply of housing can then be considered separately and the relevant short-run function that explains these fluctuations can be developed.

7.2   LONG-RUN DETERMINANTS OF HOUSING

Before proceeding to the short-run cycle in housing, we note that there has been considerable work done on the existence and characteristics of a long cycle in housing, which is thought to be approximately 20 years.[1] These long cycles are supposed to have their origin mainly in changes in demographic and other exogenous factors. Proponents of long cycles usually assume that these exogenous disturbances have certain effects on the economy which are magnified in their effects on housing. These "shocks" may well be due to wars, immigration waves, development of previously virgin land because of railroads, or other similar phenomena. However, they do not appear to have had an important role in influencing residential construction investment since 1945. If the long-cycle hypothesis were to hold in the postwar period, the economy would have witnessed an extensive period of building after the war for ten years or so in order to catch up on wartime backlogs; after this, housing investment would have leveled off considerably and possibly declined. However, an examination of actual residential construction figures shows that no such movement has occurred. Although it is still possible for a major downturn to occur in housing, it will no longer be due to causes having their origin in World War II. The long-cycle hypothesis

[1] See A. H. Hansen, *Business Cycles and National Income* (New York: Norton, 1964) chap. 3, and J. S. Duesenberry, *Business Cycles and Economic Growth* (New York: McGraw-Hill, 1958), pp. 158–164, for discussion of these cycles and further references. For more recent work in this area, see M. Abromovitz, *Evidences of Long Swings in Aggregate Construction Since the Civil War* (Princeton, N.J.: Princeton University Press for NBER, 1964).

may have considerable historical interest but is quite unlikely to be a significant determinant of residential construction at present.

The demand for housing is determined by long-run factors, principally population or the number of households. In the long run the number of dwelling units is closely correlated with population; the way in which it is divided into family units is also of importance. This has led to the suggestion that the number of households, rather than population, is the relevant long-run demographic determinant of the demand for residential construction. If a household were defined as a unit with separate dwelling accommodations, then the number of households would tautologically be the correct variable. However, a household is usually defined as a separate spending unit; in that case several households may share common living quarters. This is more likely to happen during times of adverse economic conditions; in particular, young married couples may live with their parents longer before finding their own living quarters. Because of this possibility, the number of households is not an unequivocally better indicator of the demand for housing than is population. Another demographic variable, the family formation (marriage) rate, is even less satisfactory, for it is correlated with short-term economic indicators (for example, it decreases when unemployment rises), and thus includes elements of both short-run cyclical fluctuations and long-run trend movements. Population is not influenced by these short-run fluctuations, although its growth was severely diminished during the 1930's.

Several other variables have often been suggested as determinants of the long-run demand for housing, although they more properly belong in a short-run function. The most important of these are income, credit conditions, and the price of housing. Income is sometimes considered to be an important long-run determinant of housing in much the same way that population is. However, Grebler and Maisel point out that "per capita value of residential capital and demand for new construction in constant prices fluctuated within narrow margins and in 1950 was only slightly larger than in 1890."[2] This does not mean that the percentage of income spent on housing has been constant; the *actual amount* per capita has changed very little when price changes are taken into account. This can be contrasted to a growth in constant dollar per capita personal disposable income of 3.9 times from 1890 to 1960. This is illustrated in Table 7.1.

In view of the great disparity between long-run growth rates of personal disposable income and investment in housing, it should be clear that income does not belong in the long-run housing function.[3] If income is to be included

---

[2] L. Grebler and S. J. Maisel, "Determinants of Residential Construction: A Review of Present Knowledge," in Commission on Money and Credit, *Impacts of Monetary Policy* (Englewood Cliffs, N.J.: Prentice-Hall, 1963), p. 487.

[3] In some regression equations designed to measure the long-run housing function, it was found that the population term was always highly significant, whereas the income term was consistently nonsignificant and often had a negative coefficient.

TABLE 7.1. RESIDENTIAL CONSTRUCTION INVESTMENT PER CAPITA 1890–1960

Dates[a]	N^b	$p_h I_h^c$	p_h^d	I_h^e	I_h/N (index)
1889–1891	63.07	0.99	0.147	6.73	1.07
1899–1901	76.16	0.74	0.151	4.90	0.64
1909–1911	92.26	1.49	0.200	7.45	0.81
1919–1921	106.51	2.14	0.389	5.50	0.52
1929–1931	123.07	2.67	0.365	7.32	0.59
1939–1941	132.18	3.40	0.376	9.04	0.68
1949–1951	151.74	16.8	0.832	20.2	1.33
1959–1961	180.75	23.6	1.042	22.6	1.25

[a] Three-year averages are used to smooth out erratic year to year fluctuations that have little connection with the long-run relationships.

[b] N, population, in millions.

[c] $p_h I_h$, residential construction investment, billions of current dollars.

[d] p_h, index of residential construction costs, 1958 = 1.00.

[e] investment in residential construction, billions of 1958 dollars.

Source: Historical Statistics of the United States, tables A-2, p. 7; N-105, p. 386; and N-115, p. 393, for the period to 1929, and the *Survey of Current Business* for more recent data.

(as it finally is), it will be for reasons other than its long-term effect on residential construction investment.

Similar results can be tabulated showing that there is no long-run relationship between housing investment and credit conditions. The interested reader is referred to the work of Grebler and Maisel[4] for a summary of these findings and the relevant literature. Very briefly, there has been a great increase in the use of credit to purchase homes, both through easing of terms in the private market and the entry of the federal government into the mortgage field. Even though these developments have occurred, the real per capita value of housing has failed to rise very much. Although there has been a decided shift from rental units to home ownership because of easier credit conditions, this has had very little effect on the real per capita stock of dwelling units. For long-run determinants of residential construction, Grebler and Maisel find that "the absence of a strong growth trend in real terms in the face of a trend toward easier external financing emphasizes the importance of non-financial determinants."[5] Other studies have found that changes in the long-term bond yield or interest rate on mortgages have little or no effect on long-run housing investment. The same lack of any discernible relationship with residential construction investment has been reported for the relative costs of construction.

[4] Grebler and Maisel, *op. cit.*, pp. 487–490.

[5] *Ibid.*, p. 487.

7.3 THE EFFECTS OF CREDIT ON SHORT-RUN FLUCTUATIONS IN HOUSING

We now examine the short-run fluctuations in housing for the postwar U.S. economy. The general countercyclical pattern of residential construction investment is shown in Table 7.2. Technically, a countercyclical series is one that always moves in the opposite direction from aggregate economic activity. Although housing investment turns up almost as soon as GNP turns down, it continues its upturn for about a year after GNP starts to rise before contracting; the reasons for this asymmetry are discussed later. But since residential construction clearly moves in a different direction from GNP over most of the cycle, it is generally considered to be a countercyclical variable.

The results from Table 7.2 are suggestive but not conclusive, since the 1960–1961 cycle exhibits a slightly different pattern from the other cycles. Except for this latest cycle, residential construction investment rose (or remained constant) during recessions; it continued to rise rapidly during the first year of the boom, and then decreased. Plant and equipment investment, on the other hand, declined during all the recessions, continued to fall or rose slowly during the first year of the boom, and then rose more rapidly during the next year. The main exception to this pattern occurred during the Korean War. However, as explained in Chapter 4, this is clearly an example of existing appropriations being greatly speeded up at the beginning of hostilities. Since these appropriations were finished ahead of schedule where possible, the following year (when these projects would have ordinarily been completed) showed a slight decline in fixed business investment.

TABLE 7.2 CYCLICAL PATTERNS OF THE COMPONENTS OF FIXED INVESTMENT RELATIVE TO GNP
(all variables are in billions of 1958 dollars)

Recession Dates		Changes in Selected Variables During the Recessions			Changes During the Next Four Quarters			Changes During the Next Four Quarters After That		
Peak	Trough	ΔGNP	$\Delta I_h{}^a$	$\Delta I_p{}^b$	ΔGNP	ΔI_h	ΔI_p	ΔGNP	ΔI_h	ΔI_p
1948.4	49.4	−5.2	3.0	−5.8	46.8	3.9	7.3	18.6	−5.2	−0.6
1953.2	54.2	−14.3	1.2	−0.9	35.3	4.8	3.5	10.2	−3.2	4.3
1957.3	58.1	−17.7	0.0	−4.7	31.1	5.0	−1.1	21.6	−1.1	4.4
1960.1	61.1	−7.5	−2.8	−1.7	37.0	2.2	2.7	21.5	1.1	2.4

^{a} The I_h series excludes farm residential construction.
^{b} I_p = fixed business investment.

The other exception to this general pattern is the 1960–1961 recession. This latest observation might lead one to suspect that the pattern of housing over the cycle is changing, as was in fact the case for automobile sales. Therefore this cycle and all the turning points are examined in more detail later in the chapter. At this point the reader is asked to accept the general countercyclical nature of housing; confirmation is supplied later.

Most recent writers on the housing function have recognized that housing is sensitive to credit conditions and have singled out this variable as the major short-term determinant of residential construction. This relationship, developed mainly by Guttentag,[6] states that credit which home builders and home buyers receive is essentially a residual. Banks and financial intermediaries, including life insurance companies, also make loans for fixed investment and would rather service these business loans first. In a sense what is left over is then available to home builders.

Suppose as a first approximation that total credit available is constant over the business cycle, and that the only demand for credit is by residential builders and for fixed business investment. If the demand for credit for the latter is proportional to investment, and these loans are given a higher priority, there will be a clear tendency of the supply of credit to builders to be countercyclical. This is shown in Figure 7.1. The credit supply for consumer and business borrowing consists of credit made available through commercial banks, savings institutions and similar financial intermediaries, assets of life insurance companies, and the bond and stock markets. If anything, there is a slight tendency for total available credit to be countercyclical because of the behavior of monetary policy.

As noted in Chapter 6, the supply of credit to the consumer sector is almost completely elastic. Since purchases of consumer durables in general follow

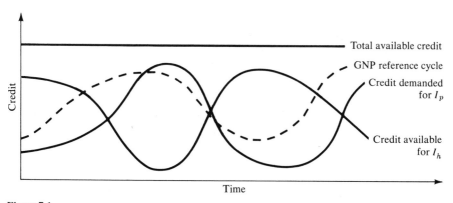

Figure 7.1

[6] J. M. Guttentag, "The Short Cycle in Residential Construction," *American Economic Review*, Vol. 51, No. 3 (June, 1961), p. 292.

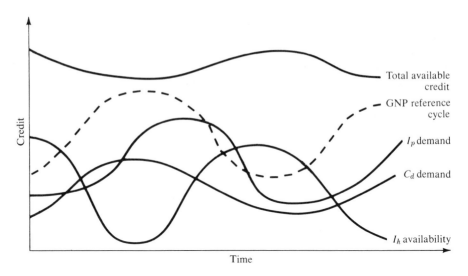

Figure 7.2

the business cycle, demand for this type of credit will also be highest at the peak of the boom, adding to the squeeze on credit for residential construction. All these elements of demand and supply for credit can be combined as shown in Figure 7.2, where it is shown that the amount of credit available to home builders is clearly lower during boom times and higher during recessions, at least for the type of cycles experienced in the postwar U.S. economy.

Although this countercyclical availability of credit for residential construction has been noted by most writers on the subject, there is substantial disagreement on the best way to represent this phenomenon empirically. Maisel uses the treasury bill rate,[7] which certainly must be a proxy variable, since home builders or buyers do not borrow at this rate. Alberts suggests the ratio of mortgage yields to bond yields,[8] whereas Suits suggests a measure of the difference between maximum FHA and VA rates and bond yields.[9] Neither of these latter two gives a very good measure of the cyclical characteristics of credit availability. The argument advanced by both Alberts and Suits is that mortgage yields fluctuate less over the cycle than do bond yields. When bond yields rise, lending institutions shift from residential mortgages into financing of business investment. While the idea of shifting from one

---

[7] S. J. Maisel, "A Theory of Fluctuations in Residential Construction Starts," *American Economic Review*, Vol. 53, No. 3 (June, 1963), p. 372.

[8] W. W. Alberts, "Business Cycles, Residential Construction Cycles, and the Mortgage Market," *Journal of Political Economy*, Vol. 70, No. 3 (June, 1962), p. 272.

[9] D. B. Suits, "Forecasting and Analysis with an Econometric Model," *American Economic Review*, Vol. 52, No. 1 (March, 1962), p. 114.

TABLE 7.3 RELATIONSHIP OF SHORT- AND LONG-TERM
INTEREST RATES OVER THE CYCLE

Peak[a]	Trough[a]	Short-Term Rate	Long-Term Rate
1953.3	1954.3	2.75	3.54
		1.36	3.13
1957.3	1958.2	3.95	4.44
		1.72	3.98
1960.1	1961.1	4.69	4.81
		3.02	4.54

[a] These are peaks and troughs for the short-term interest rate series rather than GNP. However, the dates are almost the same.

market to another over the cycle is of substantial importance, their argument is vitiated by the fact that bond yields themselves do not fluctuate very much over the cycle and are very slow to reflect changes in monetary stringency.

One good cyclical measure of the tightness of credit is the spread between short-term (commercial paper) and long-term (corporate bond yield) rates. In general, short rates will rise relative to long rates during booms and will fall during recessions. This is shown in Table 7.3 for the postwar period (the 1949 recession is omitted, because this was before the accord and interest rates were still pegged). This can be represented diagrammatically as shown in Figure 7.3.

The term structure of interest rates is discussed in Section 11.4. Here it may be said that the cyclical pattern of long- and short-term interest rates is due to expectations about capital gains. We assume that in the short run investors expect interest rates to stay at present levels or to continue to move

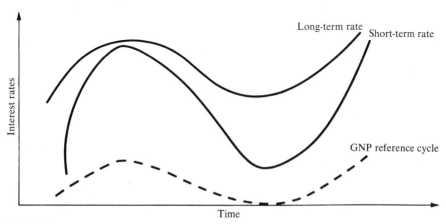

Figure 7.3

in the same direction, while in the long run they expect them to return to normal levels. If interest rates are high and rising, which generally occurs during booms, investors will expect zero or negative capital gains on short-term obligations but positive capital gains on long-term obligations. Thus long-term securities will be relatively more attractive, will sell at a higher price, and thus will carry a lower yield than short-term securities. During recessions when interest rates are low and falling, just the opposite pattern occurs. Investors will avoid long-term securities because of the fear of capital losses; this will depress their price and thus raise their yield relative to short-term securities.

The spread between the long-term and short-term interest rates represents a better measure of the tightness of credit than does the level of either interest rate. A long-term interest rate of 4 percent may be either high or low, depending on other current factors. If it is low, and associated with easy money, investors will expect this rate to rise. This will lead to capital losses, short-term securities will be preferred and the spread between the two rates will be large. On the other hand, if investors consider 4 percent to be a high rate, the opposite argument will apply and the spread will be small or even negative. Thus easy money through its effects on expectations about capital gains will lead to a large spread between the interest rates, and tight money to a small spread. As we have already argued, banks and other lending institutions will give higher priority to loans for business investment during periods of tight money. Other sources of supply for funds, such as the bond and stock markets, are effectively closed to all but the largest residential builders.

Another reason advanced to explain the general countercyclical nature of residential construction is known as the "*fixed-rate*" *theory*. This theory relies completely on the credit obtained by buyers and does not consider stringency of funds available to builders. Many buyers can finance the purchase of a new home with a mortgage either backed by a commercial or savings bank (a conventional mortgage) or insured by the federal government (a VA or FHA loan). If the state does not set a maximum rate on mortgages, the bank can charge any interest rate on the conventional loan which it thinks the consumer will accept, but the maximum rates on FHA and VA mortgages are fixed by law. If the average conventional rate is well above the maximum government-insured rates, which usually happens during periods of tight money, then lenders will not make VA and FHA loans. Those individuals denied loans are generally those who cannot afford a conventional down payment, so that they are effectively discouraged from entering the new housing market. The ceiling, or fixed, rate on the VA and FHA loans is thus enough to give housing its countercyclical nature, according to this theory, because it eliminates a sector of the potential housing market during boom times.

This analysis completely ignores the supply side of the market and the cost and availability of funds to builders. Perhaps even more serious, it also fails to take into account the fact that when credit is tighter, lending institutions are likely to screen prospective borrowers more carefully and exclude those with low or variable incomes, regardless of whether or not there is a ceiling interest rate. Those buyers who are supposedly shut out of the market during boom times because of the low ceiling rates on government-insured mortgages are the same buyers who would very likely be refused a loan anyhow because of selective sifting of customers and nonprice rationing of credit during boom times. Even if the FHA and VA mortgage rates were fully competitive with commercial rates, these marginal borrowers would undoubtedly be refused mortgages during periods of tight money. On the other hand, suppose that plenty of credit is available, short-term assets are bringing a relatively low rate of return, and the demand for funds for fixed business investment is relatively low. Then lending institutions will definitely lower their requirements to buyers and builders alike and make more loans available for residential construction whether or not these loans are government-insured. The fixed-rate theory focuses its attention on the wrong facet of credit availability, seeking to blame the low ceiling rates for keeping prospective borrowers out of the market, whereas in fact it is the general tightness of credit available to homebuilders and buyers which keeps them both out of the market.

Because of its many logical errors, the fixed-rate theory is not used very often any more to explain fluctuations in residential construction investment. However, since this theory enjoyed some measure of respectability during the 1950s, it should be briefly mentioned if only to examine its fallacies.

Another possible determinant of residential construction is the variety of exogenous credit controls used during the postwar period. Most of these controls affected borrowing terms for FHA and VA mortgages only. Changes in these terms were made almost exclusively in periods of tight money when most lending institutions were not servicing government-insured mortgage loans. The increases in interest rates and other changes in these loans which occurred during booms were still insufficient to make FHA and VA loans attractive to lenders, and thus had almost no effect on residential construction investment.[10]

The one change in credit conditions that might have influenced patterns of residential construction was the imposition of Regulation X in October, 1950. This regulation applied to all mortgages, not just those which were federally insured. It raised minimum down payments and tightened mortgage terms generally. The possibility of these controls was known to both builders

---

[10] Guttentag, *op. cit.*, argues that this was true in general, but that the tightening of terms in July 1950 did have a considerable effect, because "by eliminating no-down-payment loans under the VA program, this restriction struck a most sensitive nerve, since these loans had come to account for about three-fifths of all VA primary home loans on new homes at the peak of the 1949–50 housing boom." (p. 289). However, we would argue that by July, 1950, with the Korean War having already started, corporations were already expanding their investment plans and were quickly rounding up available sources of financing. Thus even if the regulation had not been changed, most of these borrowers would have soon been out of the market anyhow.

and buyers long before they were actually passed. Their main effect seems to have been a general speeding of construction and signing of contracts and mortgages at pre-Regulation X terms; subsequently less activity took place after the regulation was official. It is true that the late 1950–1951 downturn in housing was somewhat more severe than the other postwar downturns. However, this can be accounted for quite adequately by noting the very high rate of fixed business investment during the early Korean War. More conclusively, when the controls were relaxed in 1952, there was very little additional activity in residential construction investment. This contrasts sharply with the record purchases of cars in 1955 after Regulation W was discontinued. Thus, unlike consumer-durables purchases, exogenous credit controls probably exert little influence on fluctuations in residential construction investment.

7.4   OTHER SHORT-RUN DETERMINANTS OF HOUSING

Another important determinant of the volume of residential construction investment is the cost of construction. Variable costs, particularly labor costs, represent a very high proportion of total costs in this area. Even a modest change in labor costs will affect builders' profit margins appreciably, particularly because these changed costs are unlikely to be fully reflected in changed prices. The price of housing is determined by the demand for and supply of the total existing stock; additions within a year's time or less must necessarily be a miniscule percentage of the total. The amount of new dwelling units built is thus highly elastic with respect to construction costs. This differs sharply from the demand for industrial construction, which is quite price-inelastic. This is hardly surprising; the new dwelling unit being constructed by the residential builder represents virtually his entire cost of business, while an industrial building more likely represents only a small part of the total cost of that particular business. Thus here again the home builder is at a disadvantage when bidding for scarce factor resources.

This problem would be minimized if the supply of construction labor were itself very elastic, but just the opposite is true. The supply of trained construction workers is almost fixed in the short run, and given the existing institutional arrangements, it takes a considerable amount of time to train new workers. Furthermore, with current rigidly controlled apprentice programs, this training is likely to be quite small relative to the number of existing workers. In the industrial construction sector, moreover, construction workers have the advantage known to readers of elementary economics texts as "the importance of being unimportant."[11] This principle is often used to explain

---

[11] For those whose elementary economics needs refreshing, the demand curve for a factor will be more inelastic (1) the more inelastic is the demand curve for the product, (2) the lower is the cost of the factor relative to total cost, (3) the more essential the factor is, and (4) the more inelastic are the supply curves of substitute factors.

higher wages received by construction workers relative to the other workers. It also explains the fact that construction workers on industrial projects are paid more than those on residential projects.

This differential wage scale between industrial and residential construction workers induces an added flexibility of construction workers between the two sectors. As the demand for fixed business investment increases, some workers will switch from residential to industrial construction, since relatively more jobs are available at a higher wage rate. When fixed business investment declines to a relatively low level, these workers will return to work on residential construction and take the lower paying jobs which are available. Thus again the homebuilder is in the position of receiving a residual factor of production; he gets the construction workers which are not used on industrial jobs. Clearly industrial construction jobs are more plentiful during boom times and thus residential construction is lowered then.

These relationships are expressed graphically in Figure 7.4. When the demand for industrial construction shifts from D_1 to D_2, some workers and contractors will respond to higher wages in that area and leave the residential construction field. This actually leaves *fewer* workers available (at a higher wage) for residential construction.

A slight additional element of cyclicality is introduced into the analysis by considering the costs of construction relative to a price of rent index. When rents are high relative to construction costs, there is more incentive to build new houses and apartments. While construction prices rise during booms and fall during recessions relative to their trend values, rents are less affected by such short-run fluctuations. Unlike fixed business investment, where the price of products, labor, and capital tend to rise together, a rise in construction costs is likely to result in a high price relative to rents as well

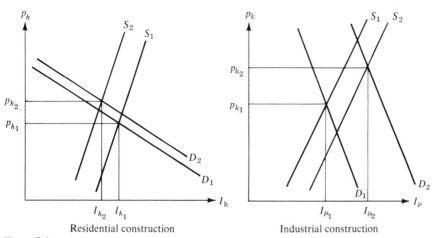

Residential construction   Industrial construction

Figure 7.4

as in absolute terms; the reverse is true for a fall in construction costs. In addition, when overbuilding has occurred, rent prices will decline, which has a negative effect on residential construction. We use the ratio of construction costs to rents as the relevant cost variable in explaining residential construction investment.

The fact that residential construction seems to be a residual in both the money and factor markets has led Alberts to observe that "periodic decreases in the use of resources elsewhere in the economy have induced compensatory increases in the use of resources in the housing industry; subsequent periodic increases in the use of resources elsewhere in the economy have induced compensatory decreases in the use of resources in the housing industry."[12]

We now consider the problem of the lag between decision and construction in the residential construction field. As stressed throughout this text, the lag structure, which is usually ignored in the static or equilibrium case, is quite important in determining the actual pattern of business cycles. The length of the cycle will depend in large part on the lags in the aggregate demand and supply equations. As in fixed business investment, we have two lags to consider: (1) the lag between the change in economic variables and the decision to build, and (2) the time necessary for actual construction. The second lag is easily estimated. According to an identity used by the Department of Commerce to allocate actual housing starts to residential construction expenditures in the national income accounts,

(7.1) $$(I_h)_t = 0.41(ST)_t + 0.49(ST)_{t-1} + 0.10(ST)_{t-2}$$

where ST represents housing starts and the lags are in quarters. This puts an average construction lag of approximately two months into the housing equation.

The first lag is discussed most thoroughly by Alberts; he suggests that the "planning-building" lag (as compared to "building-selling" lag) is three to four months;[13] this makes the total lag about two quarters. This is similar to results obtained by other workers in the area who have considered the lag structure. Maisel finds a lag of one quarter for costs and three quarters for interest rates in his starts equation,[14] which incorporates only the first lag. The difference in Maisel's lags are a little puzzling; probably builders obtain credit as early as they get cost estimates from subcontractors, but not six months earlier. Empirical tests that we computed show that the lag between housing investment and both the credit and cost variables is explained slightly better with a three-quarter lag than a two-quarter lag; both these were much better than alternative lag structures. Thus Alberts' figures are close to the lag we determine empirically. The small discrepancy represents the time between changes in economic conditions and the original decision by home

[12] Alberts, *op. cit.*, p. 274.
[13] *Ibid.*, p. 276.
[14] Maisel, *op. cit.*, p. 372.

builders to begin planning. Information is not likely to be received instantaneously in these areas.

It was mentioned earlier that income might be a short-run determinant of
residential construction expenditures, but this possibility has not yet been
examined. Many authors omit the term completely. Maisel[15] does not use it
at all in his equations; Alberts[16] thinks that it may have some importance,
but stresses that the shift of the demand for housing over the cycle, which is
based on income, is much smaller than shifts in the supply of housing. Grebler
and Maisel[17] list several examples of equations for housing which do not
contain an income term. The many assorted housing equations of Klein[18] in
his various models always contain an income term. His analysis has not
usually been given in terms of supply conditions, however, as variables such
as family formation rate and long-term interest rate, easily identifiable as
demand variables, are the ones usually included. However, in a 1963 revision
of the Klein–Goldberger model,[19] Klein has used a short-term rate in the
housing equation, and has suggested the correct role for income in that
equation. We can apply the anticipation–modifications synthesis, which was
the basis of the fixed business investment function lag structure, to the housing
function as well. If builders start their plans during a recession (a fairly likely
occurrence, as has been shown), and income begins to rise rapidly, they may
slightly alter original plans and either add more expensive options or speed
up existing construction, and vice versa for a fall in income. Thus income with
no lag at all or a very short lag is a relevant variable in the residential construction equation as long as it is used as a *modifications* variable, and not as a
long-run determinant of housing. In this role, income primarily affects the
value of housing rather than the number of units constructed. The proposed
housing function thus is of the form $I_h = f[Y, (p_h/p_r)_{-3}, (i_l - i_s)_{-3}]$, where the
lags are in quarters and housing and personal disposable income are in
constant dollars. The empirically estimated equation is

$$(15.7) \qquad I_h = 58.26 + 0.0249\,Y - 45.52(p_h/p_r)_{-3} + 1.433(i_l - i_s)_{-3}$$
$$ (0.0033) \qquad (4.76) \qquad\qquad (0.282)$$

$$\bar{R}^2 = 0.820$$

where I_h = investment in nonfarm residential construction, billions of 1958
    dollars

[15] *Ibid.*, p. 372.
[16] Alberts, *op. cit.*, pp. 272–273.
[17] Grebler and Maisel, *op. cit.*, pp. 496–505.
[18] L. R. Klein, *Economic Fluctuations in the United States, 1921–1941*, Cowles Commission
Monograph 11 (New York: Wiley, 1950); "A Postwar Quarterly Model: Descriptions and
Applications," in *Models of Income Determination* (Princeton, N.J.: Princeton University Press
for NBER, 1964); L. R. Klein and A. S. Goldberger, *An Econometric Model of the United States
Economy 1929–1952* (Amsterdam: North-Holland, 1955).
[19] L. R. Klein, *The Keynesian Revolution*, 2nd ed. (New York: Macmillan, 1966), p. 233.

Y = personal disposable income, billions of 1958 dollars

p_h = cost index of residential construction, 1958 = 1.00

p_r = rent index, 1958 = 1.00

i_l = long-term corporate bond yield, percent

i_s = short-term rate on commercial paper, percent

7.5   HOUSING INVESTMENT OVER THE CYCLE

About the time when the articles of Guttentag (1961), Alberts (1962), and Maisel (1963) were appearing, stressing the importance of supply conditions and the essentially countercyclical nature of residential construction investment, the evidence of the 1960–1961 cycle and its aftermath seemed to cast a great deal of doubt on these theories. Specifically, nonfarm residential construction rose from \$23.2 to \$24.2 from 1962 to 1963, largely due to a boom in apartment buildings, even though GNP rose from \$530 to \$551 (all figures in billions of 1958 dollars). At first this might seem to disprove the countercyclical argument. Opinion was divided whether the countercyclical theory no longer held, or whether the determinants of apartment building were quite different from single-family dwellings and could not be explained by the same analysis. When a mild downturn in residential construction did occur in 1964, it was then argued that apartments were "overbuilt," an argument which, it was claimed, also precluded the traditional arguments. Since these hypotheses were fairly widespread, and since housing did rise during 1963 when it might have been expected to fall, this matter deserves further attention.

Recall that the countercyclical nature of housing is not so closely related to movements in GNP as it is to movements in fixed business investment, because it is this sector with which it directly competes for factor resources. Thus only if fixed business investment increased faster than GNP during 1963 would there be any reason to expect residential construction investment to decrease. This simply did not occur. As long as excess resources exist in the economy, the theory developed in this chapter clearly states that there is no reason for housing to decline. This is the 1963 experience. However, once money tightened and fixed business investment became a relatively higher percentage of GNP, then residential construction declined. A striking verification of this theory occurred in 1966, when homebuilders virtually ran out of available sources of funds and successfully appealed to Congress to arrange the release of additional funds specifically earmarked for housing. Meanwhile residential investment plummeted 25 percent in seven months, while new housing starts fell an unprecedented 46 percent in the corresponding earlier seven-month period.

The continuing rise of housing through 1963 and the subsequent decline starting in 1964 can thus be explained in terms of the housing equation given above. Credit terms did not tighten and construction costs did not start to rise rapidly until mid-1963; with a three-quarter lag, these changes would not affect residential construction investment until early 1964, which is precisely what happened. Thus it is directly relevant to the above arguments to compare residential construction investment with fixed business investment rather than with GNP. The timing and sharpness of the decline in housing should be directly related to the proportion of resources utilized by the higher-priority fixed business investment category.

Until the 1960–1961 recession, the lag pattern between housing and other fixed investment was quite consistent. Housing turned up an average of two quarters after fixed business investment turned down; it turned down an average of three quarters after other investment turned up. The reason for the slightly shorter lag when fixed business investment turned down is due to the fact that cancellations can be made more quickly than additional appropriations, thus freeing resources for home builders more quickly. These figures are shown in Table 7.4.

Both the length of the lag for the downturn in residential construction investment and the amount of the decline can be directly related to the proportion of resources utilized by fixed business investment, as measured by the ratio of fixed business investment to gross national product (I_p/X). This is shown in Table 7.5.

We use the I_p/X ratio two years after recessions because actual investment at that time is the result of original plans made at the beginning of the upturn (five to six quarters earlier). These original plans, which include financing arrangements, are what cause housing to turn down soon after the boom begins.[20]

It is always a real problem to try to draw meaningful conclusions from only four observations. However, there does seem to be a definite relationship between both the length of lag and amount of decline in housing investment compared to the I_p/X ratio. This relationship is not linear but has the same

TABLE 7.4 RELATIONSHIP BETWEEN FIXED BUSINESS INVESTMENT AND RESIDENTIAL CONSTRUCTION AT TURNING POINTS

Downturn I_p	Upturn I_h	Lag, Quarters	Upturn I_p	Downturn I_h	Lag, Quarters
1949.1	1949.2	1	1950.1	1950.4	3
1953.3	1954.1	2	1955.1	1955.3	2
1957.4	1958.3	3	1958.4	1959.3	3
1960.3	1961.1	2	1961.3	1964.2	11

---

[20] It might also be noted that the collapse in the housing market in 1966 coincided with an I_p/X ratio of 0.111, the highest since 1948.

TABLE 7.5   RELATIONSHIP BETWEEN FIXED BUSINESS INVESTMENT
AND GNP

Year of Recession	I_p/X Ratio Two Years Later	Length of Lag	Drop in I_h During First Year of its Downturn, Billions of 1958 Dollars
1949	0.103	3	−6.7
1954	0.106	2	−6.1
1958	0.097	3	−4.5
1961	0.094	11	−1.4

general shape as a typical marginal cost curve: horizontal in the region where excess capacity exists and then sloping upward at an increasing rate. When investment is small enough relative to GNP so that there are substantial idle resources in the capital goods sector, changes in the I_p/X ratio have a very small effect on housing. As the ratio of fixed business investment to GNP increases, residential construction investment will become more and more sensitive to changes in this ratio. If this is the case, then the counter-cyclical nature of housing tends to stabilize the business cycle both at peaks and troughs.

In summary, we have shown in this chapter that the function explaining residential construction is really more of a supply function than a demand function for short-run fluctuations. The amount of residential construction investment has shown a definite tendency to act in a countercyclical fashion. This is due mainly to the fact that builders, in a crude sense, receive both residual credit and construction labor; however, these conclusions hold only in an economy which is near full employment. In more serious recessions, sufficient factor resources might well be available at all stages of the cycle. Furthermore, the demand for housing would certainly fall if population growth declined because of lower levels of real per capita income. But for the postwar U.S. economy, the countercyclical relationship of residential construction is likely to be an important component of the theory of the business cycle.

CHAPTER 8

INVENTORY INVESTMENT

8.1 GENERAL BACKGROUND

Throughout the postwar period, inventory investment has consistently fluctuated more than any other component of aggregate demand during recessions. For the four postwar recessions the average decline in GNP has been $10.0 billion and the average decline in inventory investment has been $7.4 billion, or almost three quarters. This pattern has occurred in each recession, as can be seen from the values given in Table 8.1. Because of this fact, the postwar business cycles are often called *inventory recessions*. Klein and Popkin[1] have shown that if 75 percent of the fluctuations in inventory investment could be controlled, the economy would not have had any postwar business recessions. Thus a meaningful understanding of the determinants and lag structure of inventory investment are essential to a full understanding of the business cycle and intelligent application of fiscal and monetary policy.

In spite of this, relatively little empirical investigation of inventory investment has taken place. Keynes spent very little time discussing inventories, since the great depression of the 1930s was clearly more than another inventory recession (although there are some suggestions that it started that

---

[1] L. R. Klein and J. Popkin, "An Econometric Analysis of the Postwar Relationship Between Inventory Fluctuations and Change in Aggregate Economic Activity," Part III of *Inventory Fluctuations and Economic Stabilization* (Washington D.C.: Joint Economic Committee, 1961), pp. 71–86.

TABLE 8.1 FLUCTUATIONS IN INVENTORY INVESTMENT
AND GNP DURING RECESSIONS

Recession Dates	Total Change in GNP	Total Change in ΔI_i
1948.4–1949.4	− 5.4	− 9.5
1953.3–1954.2	− 11.6	− 4.8
1957.3–1958.1	− 15.7	− 8.0
1960.2–1961.1	− 7.1	− 7.2

way and failed to "turn the corner"), and more fundamental work on the consumption and fixed-investment sectors was needed to explain the situation of the 1930s. The major prewar theoretical attempt to explain inventory investment was made by Metzler,[2] whose contributions are discussed below. The first major attempt to categorize inventories systematically was a monumental study done by Moses Abromovitz[3] for the NBER. This study deals with manufacturing inventories during the interwar (1919–1938) period. Unfortunately, many of the conclusions which Abromovitz draws from this study are blurred, because the only data available for this period were yearly data. Unlike other components of aggregate demand, inventory investment fluctuates very widely over the course of a year (in general) so that quarterly data are often needed to make more useful statements about inventory behavior. A quarterly study of manufacturing inventories has been provided for the postwar period by Stanback,[4] who draws many of the same conclusions about inventories as did Abromovitz. We should point out, however, that these studies are descriptive and do not give regression estimates. Also, these studies are made in terms of inventory stocks. When examining components of aggregate demand, we want to work with changes in stocks, just as we work with changes in stocks in fixed business investment, housing, and consumer durables.

Before examining some of the detailed evidence on inventory behavior, we ought to examine the basic reasons for holding inventories. Some of these are discussed next.[5]

(1) Transactions: This term is usually applied to the amount of money held by individuals and businesses for the needs of daily economic activity.

---

[2] L. A. Metzler, "The Nature and Stability of Inventory Cycles," *Review of Economic Statistics,* Vol. 23, No. 3 (August, 1941), pp. 113–129.

[3] M. Abramovitz, *Inventories and Business Cycles with Special Reference to Manufacturing Inventories* (New York: National Bureau of Economic Research, 1950).

[4] T. M. Stanback, Jr., *Postwar Cycles in Manufacturers' Inventories* (Princeton, N.J.: Princeton University Press for NBER, 1961).

[5] For a somewhat different list, see R. Eisner and R. H. Strotz, "Research Study Two: Determinants of Business Investment," in Commission on Money and Credit, *Impacts of Monetary Policy* (Englewood Cliffs, N.J.: Prentice-Hall, 1963), pp. 105–108.

There is a cost to holding money (the interest that could be earned) and there is a cost of not holding money (cost of transforming assets into money). Given these costs, each individual decides the optimal amount of money to hold relative to his purchases. It is sensible to describe the same type of mechanism for the holding of inventories. Each firm considers the costs of holding or not holding inventories and, having decided these, determines some optimal inventory/sales ratio α. Symbolically, $I_i = \alpha S$.[6] Presumably, α could vary with the costs of holding inventories. The costs could be the interest rate at which working capital is borrowed or the rate at which it could be lent. Since the former rate is usually higher than the latter, the amount of internal cash which the firm has may also be of importance. The costs of storage could conceivably also be important; this has not been studied on the aggregate level. Most studies have supported the position that α is invariant (or nearly so) with respect to interest rates and internal liquidity. We shall accept this viewpoint for the present and examine some of the evidence on this point later.[7]

(2) Speculative: Firms may desire to hold more inventories than they need for transactions purposes for two reasons. They may expect the price of stocks to rise, in which case they will receive capital gains, or they may expect certain materials to be in short supply in the future and wish to purchase them now. If we continue our analogy with the reasons for holding money, a resemblance can be drawn only with the first of these reasons. This has led some economists to suppose that the price motive is the important reason for inventory speculation. Although it is true that inventory investment and changes in the price level do move together, these movements are often accompanied by similar changes in sales and backlogs of orders. It is the partial correlation, rather than the simple correlation, which is relevant. The evidence presented later suggests that while the speculative motive for holding inventories is important, the possibility of future shortages rather than future price changes is the principal determinant of this motive.

(3) Buffer Stocks: Many times firms will incorrectly forecast sales in the coming time period (for example, quarter). In these cases it is likely that sales and inventory investment will move in opposite directions. If sales estimates are too low, extra sales will result in depleted inventories. Conversely, if sales estimates are too high, unintended inventories will accumulate. This may occur either because the firm's production (or ordering) schedule is inflexible, or because it may be cheaper to adjust production schedules gradually even if these schedules are flexible. A slack period may enable firms to store up extra stocks to meet peak demands better. In a peak period, production

---

[6] Throughout this chapter, I_i refers to stock of inventories and ΔI_i refers to inventory investment. S refers to sales unless otherwise stated.

[7] For the postwar U.S. period, α has averaged about 50 days of sales in manufacturing and 40 days in wholesale and retail trade.

smoothing will enable the firm to meet demand without purchasing additional capital equipment that will very seldom be used.

(4) Backlog of Demand: If manufacturing firms are shipping goods at a certain rate, but their backlog of orders is high, they will stock more inventories in response to this established demand than if the backlog is low. We define the change in the backlog of orders, or the *change in unfilled orders* (ΔU) as new orders minus shipments. When new orders are coming in faster than shipments are being made, firms will consider this increase in established demand as a reason to increase their inventories. The reverse will be true when new orders are being received more slowly than shipments are leaving.

These are the main reasons why firms hold inventories. Many discussions of inventory investment hinge on explanations of expectations and errors in forecasts. Although we agree that these are important, the expectations and errors are made with respect to sales and prices within the framework of the above categories. The specific ways in which they enter the functions will be spelled out next.

8.2   ACCELERATOR MODELS AND LAG STRUCTURE

In a very fine and now classic article, Metzler[8] develops a theoretical structure for inventory investment functions. He considers only the transactions demand, but does introduce expectations and errors into his model. Metzler considers production for both sales and inventory investment; we consider only the latter here. The complete Metzler model will be explored in Chapter 13, where the dynamic properties of his system are examined. For now it is sufficient to concentrate on his inventory investment equation. Since this model is rather complex, we first present the case of no expectations.

Metzler combines the simple transactions demand for inventory stocks with a stock adjustment model in which investment in any given period is equal to the *total* difference between desired and actual stocks. Algebraically this can be represented as

(8.1) $(\Delta I_i)_t = (I_i^d)_t - (I_i)_{t-1}$

(8.2) $I_i^d = \alpha S_t^e = \alpha S_{t-1}$

where I_i^d represents the desired inventory stocks and S^e represents expected sales. Note in particular that expected sales are equal to actual sales *last* period. This simplified assumption is modified below.

This model can be slightly expanded by noting that inventory stocks at time $t-1$ are equal to stocks at time $t-2$ less depletions during $t-1$. In

---

[8] Metzler, *op. cit.*

this simple model, depletions are equal to the change in sales, so that

(8.3) $$(I_i)_{t-1} = (I_i)_{t-2} - \Delta S_{t-1}$$

Substituting (8.3) and (8.2) into (8.1) yields

(8.4) $$(\Delta I_i)_t = \alpha S_{t-1} - (I_i)_{t-2} + \Delta S_{t-1}$$

This is the basic Metzler equation and provides a general lag structure from which to build. Note in particular that sales are lagged one period and inventory stocks are lagged two periods. As we shall see later, this is not the most common lag structure for inventory investment functions.

Metzler now introduces the elasticity of expectation η, defined as the ratio between the expected change in sales between periods t and $t - 1$ and the observed change in sales between periods $t - 1$ and $t - 2$. Algebraically, $\eta = \Delta S_t^e / \Delta S_{t-1}$. The value of η is usually restricted to values between 0 and 1. If $\eta = 1$, firms will expect the previous change in sales to continue in the same direction. If $\eta = 0$, firms will not take the previous change in sales into account when estimating present sales.

Adding expectations to the Metzler model, we now have

(8.5) $\quad S_t^e = S_{t-1} + \eta \Delta S_{t-1} \qquad$ (from the definition of η)

(8.6) $\quad (I_i)_{t-1} = (I_i)_{t-2} - (S_{t-1} - S_{t-1}^e) = (I_i)_{t-2} - \Delta S_{t-1} + \eta \Delta S_{t-2}$

Since

(8.7) $\quad (\Delta I_i)_t = (I_i^d)_t - (I_i)_{t-1} \qquad$ and $\qquad (I_i^d)_t = \alpha S_t^e$

this gives

(8.8) $\quad (\Delta I_i)_t = \alpha(S_{t-1} + \eta \Delta S_{t-1}) - (I_i)_{t-2} + \Delta S_{t-1} - \eta \Delta S_{t-2}$

Combining terms gives

(8.9) $\quad (\Delta I_i)_t = \alpha S_{t-1} + (1 + \alpha\eta)\Delta S_{t-1} - \eta \Delta S_{t-2} - (I_i)_{t-2}$

Thus when we introduce errors and expectations into the sample transactions demand model for holding inventories, we find that inventory investment depends on last period's sales, the change in last period's sales, the change in sales two periods ago, and inventory stocks two periods ago.

The Flexible Accelerator

One of the problems with the Metzler model is its assumption that firms adjust their inventory requirements completely within a given quarter. This problem can be remedied quite easily within the basic framework of the equation. The Metzler model states that $\Delta I_i = I_i^d - I_{i_{t-1}}$, implying that firms' investment in a given period is equal to the total difference between desired and actual stocks. It is more realistic to assume a partial adjustment; this was first tried by Klein.[9] The function then takes the form $\Delta I_{i_t} = \delta(I_{i_t}^d - I_{i_{t-1}})$, where δ represents the fraction of desired minus actual inventories that is adjusted each period. This equation is called the *flexible accelerator* by Lovell.[10]

Klein's early functions are somewhat different from the one suggested by Metzler (even without the expectations), because he uses yearly data; his function was first estimated for the interwar period, when quarterly data were not available. Klein's function is of the form

(8.10)
$$\Delta I_{i_t} = a_0 + a_1 S_t + a_2 p_t - a_3 I_{i_{t-1}}$$

The speculative motive is introduced by the inclusion of the price level, p; this term is found to be significant. The "flexibility" of the accelerator is found to be quite large. Far from completely adjusting within a quarter or two, Klein found that only 52 percent of the difference between desired and actual inventories was made up over an entire year.[11]

The Variable Accelerator

The next significant contribution to aggregate inventory investment functions is that of Paul Darling.[12] Darling starts with the basic Metzler equation (without the ΔS_{t-1} term), modified for the flexible accelerator. This gives the equation $\Delta I_i = c + \delta(\alpha S_{t-1} - I_{i_{t-2}})$. Darling suggests that α varies over the cycle; it is higher when the ratio of the change in unfilled orders to sales is higher, and vice versa. The coefficient α is effectively a *variable accelerator*, and

(8.11)
$$\alpha = b_0 + b_1 \left(\frac{\Delta U}{S}\right)_{t-1} \qquad (b_1 > 0)$$

where U = unfilled orders. Substituting this in the original equation, we have

(8.12)
$$\Delta I_i = c + \delta \left[b_0 S_{t-1} + b_1 \left(\frac{\Delta U}{S}\right)_{t-1} \cdot S_{t-1} - I_{i_{t-2}} \right]$$

or

(8.13)
$$\Delta I_i = c + \delta b_0 S_{t-1} + \delta b_1 \Delta U_{t-1} - \delta I_{i_{t-2}}$$

---

[9] L. R. Klein, *Economic Fluctuations in the United States, 1921–1941*, Cowles Commission Monograph 11 (New York: Wiley, 1950).

[10] M. Lovell, "Determinants of Inventory Investment," in E. F. Denison and L. R. Klein, eds., *Models of Income Determination* (Princeton, N.J.: Princeton University Press for NBER, 1964), p. 183. Much of this analysis is also contained in M. Lovell, "Manufacturers' Inventories, Sales Expectations, and the Accelerator Principle," *Econometrica*, Vol. 29, No. 3 (July, 1961), pp. 293–314.

[11] There is some evidence that this ratio has increased over time, indicating that inventory adjustments are now made faster. In an updated equation estimated through 1963, Klein found that 62 percent of this difference is adjusted in one year.

[12] P. G. Darling, "Manufacturers' Inventory Investment, 1947–1958," *American Economic Review*, Vol. 49, No. 4 (December, 1959), pp. 950–962.

In this way, unfilled orders are introduced into the equation. This represents the role of established demand in the explanation of inventory investment. Darling did not include a price term in his equation, but it is easy to modify his results to take this into account. If the variable accelerator α depends on the change in prices as well as the change in unfilled orders, then we can write

$$(8.14) \qquad\qquad \alpha = b_0 + b_1 \left(\frac{\Delta U}{S}\right)_{t-1} + b_2 \left(\frac{\Delta p}{S}\right)_{t-1}$$

Even though Darling's lag structure corresponds quite closely to Metzler's, and although he is "incorporating the basic ingredients of the accelerator part of the Metzler theory,"[13] he questions his results rather severely. In particular, he feels that the lagged inventory stock should have a shorter lag. As he explains, "the fairly long lag for I_i may result from the failure of the equation's variables to account for the differences between actual and intended investment. . . . The empirically determined lag of two quarters for I_i may provide a merely mechanical and coincidental offset. . . . The length of this lag is spurious in the sense that firms do not behave on the basis of this long lag."[14]

As will be shown later in this chapter, available empirical evidence does lead to the conclusion that a two-quarter lag on inventory stocks is indeed the correct one; however, we do not plan to apologize for this result. Darling's results appeared in 1959, before the work of Eisner and others stressed the long lag that appears in the fixed investment function and before economic research centered on the lag structure common to the simultaneous decisions of fixed business investment, dividends, and inventory investment.

In one sense the Darling study is a little unusual: inventory investment is not measured in constant dollars, as would be expected. Instead, the change in book value of inventories in current dollars is used. This measure includes changes in book value due to capital gains or losses besides the changes due to purchases or sales of inventories.[15] Since price changes are already included in the inventory investment figures, one cannot reasonably include prices as a separate variable and test for the speculative motive with this data. The usual modification of including inventory valuation adjustment for capital gains is necessary to transform this equation to one explaining the inventory investment component in the national income accounts.

---

[13] *Ibid.*, p. 950.

[14] *Ibid.*, pp. 953–955.

[15] This is strictly true only if inventories are not valued on a LIFO basis. According to U.S. Department of Commerce, *National Income, 1954 Edition* (Washington: Government Printing Office, 1954), p. 137, only about 10 percent of them are.

The Buffer-Stock Motive

So far we have traced the development of the inventory function through the following steps:

1. Stock adjustment $\Delta I_i = (I_i^d - I_{i_{t-2}})$
2. Flexible accelerator $\Delta I_i = \delta(I_i^d - I_{i_{t-2}})$
3. Variable accelerator $\Delta I_i = \delta(I_i^d - I_{i_{t-2}})$ where $I_i^d = \alpha S_{t-1}$ and

$$\alpha = b_0 + b_1 \left(\frac{\Delta U}{S}\right)_{t-1}$$

All these elements are used by Lovell although with a somewhat different lag structure. He also disaggregates inventories into two sectors, purchased materials and goods in process, and finished goods. The motives for holding inventories in each group are somewhat different. To see this, consider an unexpected increase in demand. In the first sector, orders will not immediately become sales, as the goods must still be produced. An increase in demand will not result in any immediate change in inventories; it will be reflected in increased unfilled orders, which will raise inventory investment with some lag.

Patterns of inventory investment in finished goods are quite different. An increase in demand will be immediately transformed into an increase in sales; unfilled orders are not of importance in this sector. Thus an unexpected increase in sales will at first result in a decrease in inventories, and, conversely, an unexpected decrease will result in additional inventories. As explained earlier, this unanticipated holding of inventories is known as the *buffer-stock motive*. As Lovell explains, "when sales exceed the anticipated level, the buffer of finished goods inventory carried in order to prevent runouts is depleted; on the other hand, when sales forecasts are unduly optimistic, unplanned inventory accumulation occurs. Only a firm fabricating goods to specific order escapes the problem."[16] In general, this motive is relevant only in the finished goods sector; increases in demand for purchased materials and goods in process are at first transmitted through increased orders rather than increased sales. Although there are circumstances in which the buffer-stock motive exists for these categories, as pointed out by Eisner, these situations are quite unusual.[17] The absence of a buffer-stock motive for purchased materials and goods in process is supported by empirical evidence.

Lovell's model for inventory investment is

(8.15) $(\Delta I_{ip})_t = \delta_1[(I_{ip})_t^d - (I_{ip})_{t-1}]$

(8.16) $(\Delta I_{if})_t = \delta_2[(I_{if})_t^d - (I_{if})_{t-1}] + \lambda[(\hat{S}_f)_t - (S_f)_t]$

---

[16] Lovell, "Determinants of Inventory Investment," *op. cit.*, pp. 193–194.

[17] R. Eisner, "Interview and Other Survey Techniques and the Study of Investment," in *Problems of Capital Formation: Concepts, Measurement, and Controlling Factors* (Princeton, N.J.: Princeton University Press for NBER, 1957), p. 569.

where

$$(I_{if})_t^d = \beta(\hat{S}_f)_t$$

and

$$(I_{ip})_t^d = \alpha_0(S_p)_t + \alpha_1(\Delta S_p)_t \qquad \alpha_0 = b_0 + b_1(U/S_p)_t$$

That is,

$$(I_{ip})_t^d = b_0 S_{p_t} + b_1 U_t + \alpha_1(\Delta S_p)_t$$

where subscript p = purchased materials and goods in process sector

subscript f = finished-goods sector

$\hat{S}_f$ = anticipations of sales in the finished-goods sector

Equation (8.15) is similar to that developed by Darling, except that the lags are shorter. The ΔS_p term is supposed to enter with a negative sign, because there may be a tendency for stocks to fall below the desired level when output is rising. Lovell does not discuss the choice of his particular lag structure. In the second equation, λ is a "production adaptation" coefficient that represents the degree to which businesses adjust their production schedules within any given time period (here, one quarter). If $\lambda = 1$, this means that producer plans are completely *inflexible*, that is, if $\lambda = 1$ and S_t is greater than $\hat{S}_t$, then ΔI_{it} would be reduced by the total amount of the extra sales. This would mean that producers had not changed their production schedules at all. If $\lambda = 0$, unexpected changes in sales will have no effect on ΔI_i; firms will be able to offset these changes completely. Presumably λ is between 0 and 1. We can rewrite equation (8.16) (dropping the f subscripts for convenience) as

(8.17) $$\Delta I_{it} = \delta(\beta\hat{S}_t - I_{it-1}) + \lambda(\hat{S}_t - S_t)$$

Adding and subtracting a $\delta\beta S_t$ term gives

(8.18) $$\Delta I_{it} = \delta\beta S_t + \delta\beta\hat{S}_t - \delta\beta S_t - \delta I_{it-1} + \lambda(\hat{S}_t - S_t)$$

(8.19) $$\Delta I_{it} = \delta\beta S_t + (\delta\beta + \lambda)(\hat{S}_t - S_t) - \delta I_{it-1}$$

Lovell then suggests an ingenious transformation that helps test the types of anticipations that firms make. Let $\hat{S}_t = \rho S_{t-1} + (1 - \rho)S_t$. If $\rho = 1$, firms will base their forecasts entirely on last period's sales. If $\rho = 0$, firms will base the forecasts entirely on this period's sales. As Lovell points out, this second alternative does *not* mean that firms are able to predict sales accurately. It does mean that whatever procedure they use is not biased; that is, the errors of prediction are random.[18] Substituting this in the above equation, we have

(8.20) $$\Delta I_{it} = \delta\beta S_t + (\delta\beta + \lambda)[\rho S_{t-1} + (1 - \rho)S_t - S_t] - \delta I_{it-1}$$

$$= [\delta\beta - (\delta\beta + \lambda)\rho]S_t + (\delta\beta + \lambda)\rho S_{t-1} - \delta I_{it-1}$$

$$= \delta\beta S_t - (\delta\beta + \lambda)\rho\Delta S_t - \delta I_{it-1}$$

---

[18] Lovell, "Determinants of Inventory Investment," *op. cit.*, p. 201.

By testing this function empirically and solving to determine the values of the structural coefficients, it would ordinarily be possible to find approximate values for ρ, which should indicate something about how firms make sales forecasts. However, in this particular formulation, it is impossible to solve for unique values of ρ and λ; only the value of the product $\rho\lambda$ can be obtained.

Lovell's estimate of this equation is[19]

$$(8.21) \qquad \Delta I_t = -258.2 + 0.0419S_t - 0.1315\Delta S_t - 0.1521I_{i_{t-1}}$$

which means that $\delta\beta = 0.042$, and therefore $0.042\rho + \lambda\rho = 0.13$. This means that *either* ρ or λ is close to zero. Either firms make their sales forecasts on the basis of this period's sales, or they are able to adjust their production schedules almost completely within a three-month period. Some sample values are:

λ	ρ
1.0	0.12
0.5	0.24
0.1	0.92
0.088	1.00

Lovell originally thought that λ was closer to unity than to zero, in which case ρ would be less than $\frac{1}{4}$. However, in a later paper[20] he was able to estimate λ by using anticipations data, and found that λ was only 0.11 for durables and 0.10 for nondurables. If these estimates are correct, then ρ is almost unity, and businessmen do in fact base their estimates of this period's sales on last period's sales. This is another piece of evidence in favor of the longer lag structure.

Some additional results on the time lag of expectations are available from a study by Bakony.[21] In the trade inventory equation, he suggests including a sales-expectation term of the form

$$(8.22) \qquad (S^e)_t = S_{t-4}\left(\frac{S_{t-1}}{S_{t-5}}\right)^w$$

where $(S^e)_t$ are sales expectations and $0 \leq w \leq 1$. Bakony constructs variations of $(S^e)_t$ for $w = 0, 0.5$, and 1.0, and then estimates various regression equations using the different variants of the $(S^e)_t$ term. He finds that the greatest percentage of trade inventory investment is explained by using the variant

---

[19] *Ibid.*, p. 204.

[20] M. Lovell, "Sales Anticipations, Planned Inventory Investment, and Realizations," in *Determinants of Investment Behavior* (New York: Columbia University Press for NBER, 1967), pp. 537–580.

[21] L. I. Bakony, *A Statistical Study of Trade Inventory Behavior*, September, 1963, mimeographed.

in which $w = 0$, implying that businessmen predict on the basis that this year's sales will be the same as last *year's*. These and other results lead Bakony to the conclusion that "the statistical evidence and the foregoing subjective considerations lead to a tentative acceptance of the naive expectations hypothesis $S_t = S_{t-4}$."[22] This is even a stronger statement than that implied by Lovell's finding, because the "naive-expectations" hypothesis is now based on a year, rather than a quarter. It does lend additional credence to the Lovell results that λ is close to zero and ρ is close to unity.

8.3   OTHER DETERMINANTS OF INVENTORY INVESTMENT

The role of changes in the price level in the inventory investment function is considered next. The existing evidence on this is somewhat mixed. Most of the functions discussed do not include a price term; for those which have tried it, Klein finds positive results[23] and Lovell finds negative results. Both use lag structures which are somewhat suspect; Lovell uses price changes one period *ahead* (as a proxy variable for the way in which businesses expect prices to move) and Klein uses prices of the present period. The correct method of introducing prices into the inventory equation is to include a price term[24] in the variable accelerator as was done previously and write

$$(8.23) \qquad \alpha = b_0 + b_1\left(\frac{\Delta U}{S}\right)_{t-1} + b_2\left(\frac{\Delta p}{S}\right)_{t-1}$$

Thus if price expectations are to influence inventory investment, they should work through the variable accelerator with the same lag as unfilled orders.

There is a good reason why Lovell found a negative correlation between inventory investment and present changes in prices. Besides considering a buffer-stock motive in sales, we might well consider one in prices. When firms find themselves with excess inventories, they may try to move stock by selling it at lower prices. If so, an increase in finished goods inventories relative to sales would result in a decrease in prices. Similarly, when sales are rising rapidly, firms may wish to stock up on inventories. However, if many firms want to do this, most will be frustrated for a while. Thus inventory investment will actually fall, but prices will rise as firms bid up the prices of available goods. Thus a negative partial correlation of the changes in present

---

[22] *Ibid.*, p. 22.

[23] L. R. Klein, "A Postwar Quarterly Model: Descriptions and Applications," in *Models of Income Determination* (Princeton, N.J.: Princeton University Press for NBER, 1964).

[24] The wholesale price index is used in some of the studies referred to in this chapter; others use the general price level. We believe that the former is more sensible when considering inventories (because the general price level contains, among other things, components for services and government expenditures) and have used it in all our computations reported here.

prices with inventory investment shows the relevance of the buffer stock motive in prices rather than determining whether expected changes in prices influence speculative purchases or sales of inventories.

The actual empirical coefficients of the change-in-price variables with various lags in the inventory investment functions are not easy to interpret, a fact that may have led to some confusion about the role of the speculative motive. According to our theory, the Δp_t term should be slightly negative, the Δp_{t-1} term positive (if the speculative motive holds), and the $\Delta p_{t-2}, \Delta p_{t-3}, \ldots,$ terms should have little effect. If these latter two terms are significant, they are probably proxy variables for some other explanatory determinant of inventory investment. For manufacturing and other (nonfarm) inventories, some results are given in Table 8.2. The results are at best suspect. Except for establishing a weak case for the speculative motive in the manufacturing sector, the highly significant price terms are different from what would be expected. In particular, only the longer-lagged Δp variables are significant in the manufacturing sector; sales terms with lags of this length were consistently nonsignificant.

All postwar regression estimates of inventory investment equations are heavily influenced by the early quarters of the Korean War, when inventory investment increased at an unprecedented rate. Prices and unfilled orders also rose very rapidly but sales did not continue to rise rapidly as the economy approached full capacity. If regressions are calculated for the 1952–1963 subperiod, the results are quite different, as shown in Part B of Table 8.2.

These results suggest that price speculation is not an important determinant of inventory investment. However, the highly significant relationships between manufacturing inventory investment and price changes with a long lag and nonmanufacturing inventory investment and price changes with no lag which

TABLE 8.2   SIGNIFICANCE OF VARIOUS PRICE TERMS
IN INVENTORY INVESTMENT EQUATIONS

Lag Term	Manufacturing Sector t Ratio	Nonmanufacturing Sector t Ratio
A. Including the Korean War period		
Δp	−1.9	3.9
Δp_{-1}	0.7	2.8
Δp_{-2}	4.2	1.8
Δp_{-3}	3.5	1.0
B. 1952–1963 subperiod		
Δp	−0.1	0.0
Δp_{-1}	1.0	−1.2
Δp_{-2}	1.3	−2.1
Δp_{-3}	0.4	−0.3

occurred during the Korean War period still need to be explained. The first correlation is greatly reduced when the change in unfilled orders with a long lag $(U_{-2} - U_{-4})$ is added to the inventory function. Furthermore, this latter term remains significant for the 1952–1963 subperiod.

The explanation of the $(U_{-2} - U_{-4})$ term is found in the speculative motive as it applies to hoarding of goods. A large change in unfilled orders, which represents a large change in expected future demand, will lead to a similar change in inventory investment. However, firms are likely to change their inventory requirements more than would be dictated by levels of demand if they expect future shortages to develop or to disappear. In these cases much larger fluctuations in inventory investment may develop.

None of this yet provides an explanation for the long lag in the unfilled-orders term. The reason is similar to the one that explains the negative correlation between unlagged prices and inventory investment in the manufacturing sector. When a sharp increase (for example) in orders occurs, firms will try to accumulate more inventories. However, as pointed out above, this will lead to a fall in inventory investment for a while until increases in production can match increases in shipments of raw materials and goods in process. Not until after this happens will the *ex ante* demand for increased inventories due to speculative hoarding actually result in a further increase in *ex post* inventory accumulation. This adjustment process is likely to take at least six months. The same argument applies when demand decreases. Firms try to reduce their inventories, but unintended inventory investment will take place for a while because sales are also declining. The change in unfilled orders with a long lag is thus a useful indicator of speculative demand in the manufacturing inventory investment function.

Quite a different line of reasoning must be used to explain the positive correlation between unlagged price changes and inventory investment in the nonmanufacturing sector, because the above argument asserts a negative correlation. This can best be done by considering sector differences and the interrelationship between sales in the manufacturing sector and inventory investment in the trade sector; this is deferred until Section 8.4.

Other possible influences on inventory investment mentioned at the beginning of the chapter are the possible cost and availability of funds as measured by interest rates and cash flow. Only a few studies have examined the importance of these variables on inventory investment; most of these show no significant relationships.[25] There are several theoretical reasons for this. As is well known, a large percentage of the total cost of fixed business investment may represent interest payments; this is almost never true for inventories. The internal risk factor on fixed investment is virtually absent for inventory investment, because firms are not committed to any long-term

---

[25] For a brief mention of these studies, see Eisner and Strotz, *op. cit.*, p. 226, and Lovell, "Determinants of Inventory Investment," *op. cit.*, pp. 212–214.

debt service. There is more of a short-term technical relationship between inventories and sales than between fixed business investment and production. A firm may work existing plant and equipment overtime or add additional man-hours in the short run; however, it often cannot produce its product without closely specified proportions of raw materials and goods in process. For all these reasons, it is not surprising that the interest rate and cash flow are not relevant determinants of inventory investment. As a further pragmatic note, we might mention that current computer programs used by many industries to control inventory stocks work exclusively with various stock/sales ratios and do not consider the cost or availability of funds.

Thus in the absence of virtually any theoretical or positive empirical evidence on the role of credit factors influencing inventory investment, we can state that links between the real and monetary sectors, however important they are in other parts of the economy, are of negligible importance here. The control of the cycle through monetary policy cannot be successfully implemented through direct action on inventory investment.

8.4   SECTORAL DIFFERENCES

We have alluded to some of the differences between manufacturing and nonmanufacturing inventory investment in Section 8.3. As was true for fixed business investment, this analysis can be considerably expanded, because the determinants of inventory investment in these two sectors are rather dissimilar. In general, manufacturing inventory investment is comparable to the "raw-material" and "goods-in-process" categories, while trade inventory investment is comparable to "finished goods."[26] Although there are other minor categories included with trade, these will have very little effect on the analysis.

Another reason for separating inventories this way is to show the inter-relationships between the two sectors. After manufacturers produce goods, they distribute them to wholesalers and retailers. If manufacturers' production schedules are synchronized with retailers' orders, and if sales expectations of retailers are correct, then all goods fabricated by manufacturers will be sold immediately by retailers. However, if either of these two conditions is not satisfied, a change in manufacturing output is likely to result in unanticipated changes in trade inventory investment. When we combine this additional reason for holding wholesale and retail inventories with the previous analysis, and consider an unanticipated increase (for example) in retail sales, the following series of events occurs.

---

[26] Certainly there are also finished goods in the manufacturing sector. However, we feel that the buffer-stock motive is much less important for manufacturers, because they do not sell directly to consumers. This hypothesis is verified by our empirical results.

First, inventory investment at the retail level will decrease as firms initially meet increased sales out of present stocks.

Second, retail firms' new orders due to these increased sales will be transmitted to the manufacturing sector. However, these new orders will not immediately become sales because of the time needed to manufacture these additional items and the existing backlog of orders. When the backlog of orders is sizable, the change in unfilled orders will also be substantial.

Third, when manufacturing firms find their backlog of orders has increased, their inventory investment in raw materials and goods in process will increase.

Fourth, when these new orders are turned into actual sales in the manufacturing sector, these sales may become additions to inventories in the retail sector.

These steps show that a lag exists between an increase in sales in the retail sector and inventory investment in that sector. New orders resulting from increased retail sales are not immediately turned into additional manufactured goods because of both production and decision lags. An example of this is contained in the report that "the auto industry is little concerned in the fourth quarter about customer acceptance of new models ... preferring to stock dealers and fleets at the end of the year and then taking a look at demand early in the first quarter."[27] This indicates that for at least one major industry, inventory stocks changed by unanticipated changes in sales are "adjusted" by a buffer-stock motive for one quarter before production schedules are changed.

The last step of this sequence also suggests that trade inventory investment is a function of the change in manufacturing output. But it must be stressed that this relationship is not an *ex ante* decision relationship but is instead an *ex post* realization relationship.

The reason for the unlagged price term in the trade inventory equation now becomes clearer. When large variations in production occur in the manufacturing sector (for example, due to the Korean War) they are likely to be accompanied by price variations in the same direction. If changes in manufacturing production are accompanied by substantial price changes, at these times there is an *ex post* relationship between movements in manufacturing prices and trade inventory investment. Although this condition has not occurred very often, it does explain the significant positive partial correlation that occurs between these two variables.

8.5   EMPIRICAL RESULTS

We have now discussed the various causes of inventory investment but have left unanswered several questions that should be examined empirically.

---

[27] *The New York Times*, September 8, 1964.

In particular, we wish to concentrate on the lag structure and see if empirical evidence can shed any light on this problem.

Before doing this it will be useful to discuss the concept of the equilibrium inventory/sales (I/S) ratio. This involves setting $\Delta I_i = 0$ and solving for the I/S ratio. Consider the simple function

$$(8.24) \qquad \Delta I_i = \delta(\alpha S_{t-1} - I_{i_{t-2}})$$

If $\Delta I_i = 0$, then $\alpha S_{t-1} = I_{i_{t-2}}$ and $I/S = \alpha$.[28] This estimated value of α can then be compared with the observed value. If α is a variable accelerator, the problem becomes a little more complicated. Then $\alpha = b_0 + b_1(\Delta U/S) + b_2(\Delta p/S)$ and takes on different values during different phases of the business cycle. If we want to get an average value of α over the postwar period, we can set $\Delta U/S$ and $\Delta p/S$ equal to their mean values and obtain an average value of α in that way.

One interesting test would be to compare the equilibrium I/S ratios that result from the various lag structures. There has been some confusion over the various values generated by different equations.[29] However, part of this problem arises from the fact that different measures of sales are used. In some cases the concept used is total sales (including interindustry sales), in other cases it is GNP, and in still other cases GNP less services. We have taken all these differences into account and have estimated the marginal equilibrium I/S ratio implied from each equation and the actual ratio for the exact variables used over the sample period 1948–1963.[30] The results are given in Table 8.3. Although it is true that the actual I/S ratios vary, this is because of different measures of sales which are used. What is important and relevant is that all the functions give results that are very close to the actual average values. Thus we are unable to tell which lag structure is superior on the basis of this test.

To facilitate a more exact comparison of these various lag structures, we could compare the functions directly for the same data and time period in order to assess the comparisons and conclusions more accurately. It soon

---

[28] Since we are considering an equilibrium solution that occurs when there are no further changes, we need not worry about the various lags, because $S_t = S_{t-1} = S_{t-2} = \cdots$ in equilibrium. Thus we can neglect subscripts for the purposes of this explanation.

[29] See, for instance, R. P. Mack, "Comment" on Lovell, "Determinants of Inventory Investment," *op. cit.,* pp. 225–226. She discusses "the wide variety among coefficients linking inventories to sales."

[30] These functions that were chosen are representative of those which have been estimated for postwar quarterly U.S. data. This list is not intended to be complete, but is supposed to include at least one example of all the reasonable lag structures that have been estimated. The actual functions, in the order listed above, are found in Darling, *op. cit.*; J. Duesenberry, O. Eckstein, and G. Fromm, "A Simulation of the United States Economy in Recession, *Econometrica,* Vol. 28, No. 4 (October, 1960), pp. 749–810. Lovell, "Determinants of Inventory Investment," *op. cit.,* p. 186. T. C. Liu, "An Exploratory Quarterly Econometric Model of Effective Demand in the Postwar United States Economy," *Econometrica,* Vol. 31, No. 3 (July, 1963), pp. 301–348. Klein, "A Postwar Quarterly Model: Descriptions and Applications," *op. cit.,* p. 16. The Evans functions are those listed on p. 219.

TABLE 8.3 COMPARISON OF EQUILIBRIUM VALUES OF I/S RATIOS

Function	Implied I/S Ratio	Actual I/S Ratio	Lag Structure	Sales Variable
Darling[a]	1.95	1.78	S_{-1}, I_{-2}	Manufacturing total sales
DEF	1.25	1.25	$S, \Delta S, I_{-1}$	
			ΔI_{-1}	GNP-ΔI_i-services
Lovell	0.81	0.83	$S, \Delta S, I_{-1}$	GNP
Liu	1.37	1.25	S, S_{-1}, I_{-1}	
			ΔI_{-1}	GNP-ΔI_i-services
Klein	0.89	0.83	S, I_{-1}	GNP-ΔI_i
Evans[b]	1.02	1.07	S, S_{-1}, I_{-2}	Output originating

[a] Manufacturing only; others all nonfarm inventory.
[b] Weighted average of manufacturing and nonmanufacturing functions.

becomes clear that not all of the six functions listed above need to be tested separately. Actually there are only two basic lag structures: the one carefully spelled out by Lovell $(S, \Delta S, I_{-1})$ and the one suggested here $(\Delta S, S_{-1}, I_{-2})$. The Klein and Darling functions are easily seen to be simpler versions of the Lovell and Evans functions, respectively.

A third apparent lag structure has been used by DEF and Liu. Their equations contain both $\Delta I_{i_{t-1}}$ and $I_{i_{t-1}}$ terms. There has been some confusion about the underlying structural formulation of these equations. It is not explicitly discussed by either author and an attempt at reconciliation with the more usual form (without $\Delta I_{i_{t-1}}$) by Lovell does not hold in general.[31] However, the derivation is quite straightforward if one makes the assumption that *desired* inventory stocks are proportional to a geometrically declining weighted average of past sales:

$$(8.25) \qquad (I_i^d)_t = \alpha(1 - \lambda) \sum_{i=0}^{\infty} \lambda^i S_{t-i}$$

Then we have

$$(8.26) \qquad (\Delta I_i)_t = \delta[(I_i^d)_t - I_{i_{t-1}}] = \delta\alpha(1 - \lambda) \sum_{i=0}^{\infty} \lambda^i S_{t-i} - \delta I_{i_{t-1}}$$

Using the Koyck transformation once again gives

$$(8.27) \qquad (\Delta I_i)_t = \delta\alpha(1 - \lambda)S_t + \lambda(\Delta I_i)_{t-1} - \delta(I_i)_{t-1} + \lambda\delta(I_i)_{t-2}$$

[31] Lovell has suggested (in "Determinants of Inventory Investment," *op. cit.*, p. 191) that the DEF function could have been taken from the form $\Delta I_{i_t} = a_0 + a_1 S_t + a_2 I_{i_{t-1}} + a_3 U_{t-1}$, which would have eliminated these difficulties. But unfortunately, the coefficients of the transformed equation are overidentified with respect to the original equation, and, unless severe nonlinear constraints are added, the two equations are quite different.

But $(I_i)_{t-2} = (I_i)_{t-1} - (\Delta I_i)_{t-1}$, so

(8.28) $(\Delta I_i)_t = \delta\alpha(1 - \lambda)S_t + \lambda(1 - \delta)(\Delta I_i)_{t-1} - \delta(1 - \lambda)(I_i)_{t-1}$

In equilibrium $\Delta I_i = 0$, so the I/S ratio is again α. The coefficients of the S_t and $(I_i)_{t-1}$ terms will both be multiplied by a factor of $(1 - \lambda)$ relative to the form without the $(\Delta I_i)_{t-1}$ term.

It is not immediately clear whether this equation is superior to one that does not contain the lagged inventory investment term. Standard statistical tests designed to measure the goodness of fit are partially invalidated by the inclusion of the lagged dependent variable. In some experimentation, DEF found that the inclusion of this term increased the fit but the resulting function missed the sample period turning points more often. A more serious drawback is the theoretical structure underlying the desired inventory stock function. *Actual* stocks are quite likely to depend on several previous periods of sales because of decision and production lags and imperfect adjustment between desired and previously existing stocks in any given time period. However, *desired* stocks are proportional to expected sales, which may depend on sales last period but are quite unlikely to depend on a long weighted average of previous sales. Because of these problems, we compare only Lovell's function with ours.[32]

Several different forms of inventory investment functions were tried incorporating ideas advanced by Lovell and those discussed in this chapter. Without reporting these results in detail, we can summarize them by stating that in all cases the fit was improved and the level of significance of the inventory stock term was higher when the longer lag structure was used. As would be expected from Table 8.3, there was not much difference in the implied value of the equilibrium I/S ratios, although where differences did appear they too generally favored the longer lag structure. Such results cannot be conclusive, and, as previously stressed, the comparison of equations on the basis of goodness-of-fit statistics alone is often misleading. However, we would argue that no evidence has appeared which suggests that the shorter lag structure is more realistic.

We now report on the estimated inventory investment functions that were found to be most satisfactory. A few minor adjustments have been made in the exact empirical choice of variables. First, we have used the change in unfilled orders, following Darling, instead of the level of unfilled orders used by Lovell. As discussed earlier, this variable is included twice in the equations; once with a lag of one to two quarters, and also with a lag of two to four quarters. The second (longer) lag represents possible shortages during the Korean War, as explained earlier.

---

[32] We wish to mention at this point that the use of Lovell's functions for a direct comparison does not imply a fundamental disagreement with his work. On the contrary, it is because he has formulated his ideas so clearly and precisely that an exact comparison is possible.

Second, we have included a dummy variable for steel strikes (for the manufacturing sector only). Usually this variable is $+1$ before strikes and -1 during strikes, but can be more flexible if necessary. If the steel strike lasts longer than most businessmen expect, so that restocking is necessary, this dummy variable might be -2 during the strike and $+1$ in the restocking period. Such an alternative was actually used for the 1959 steel strike. For actual *ex ante* forecasts in recent years, a value of $+\frac{1}{2}$ has been used in situations where a strike was thought to be likely. If it did not occur, a value of $-\frac{1}{2}$ was then assigned for the period during which excess inventories were being worked off. Whatever combination of values is used for the dummy variable, their sum always adds to zero, because a steel strike should not have any permanent effect on inventory investment, *cet. par.*

Third, we have used purchases of consumer durables as well as total sales originating in the nonmanufacturing sector for the trade inventory equation. Consumer durables are the most important group of purchases in determining trade inventory requirements.

The empirical estimates of the inventory investment functions specified in this way are

$$(15.8) \quad \Delta I_{im} = -5.03 + 0.0718 S_{m-1} - 0.0539 I_{im-2} + 0.422 \Delta U_{-1}$$
$$\phantom{(15.8) \quad \Delta I_{im} = -5.03 +} (0.0272) \qquad (0.0224) \qquad (0.083)$$

$$+ 0.203(U_{-2} - U_{-4}) + 2.074 STR \qquad \bar{R}^2 = 0.768$$
$$ (0.040) \qquad\qquad (0.603)$$

$$(15.9) \quad \Delta I_{in} = -14.94 + 0.0668(S_n)_{-1} - 0.1173(I_{in})_{-2} + 0.2180(C_d)_{-1}$$
$$\phantom{(15.9) \quad \Delta I_{in} = -14.94 +} (0.0456) \qquad (0.0476) \qquad (0.0634)$$

$$+ 0.3325 \Delta X_m + 40.43[p_m - (p_m)_{-2}] \qquad \bar{R}^2 = 0.610$$
$$ (0.0686) \qquad (11.82)$$

where I_{im} = inventory stocks in the manufacturing sector, billions of 1958 dollars, adjusted for inventory valuation adjustment

S_m = sales originating in the manufacturing sector, billions of 1958 dollars

U = unfilled orders, billion of 1958 dollars

STR = dummy variable for steel strike, $+1$ in 1952.2, 1959.2, 1960.1, -1 in 1952.3, -2 in 1959.3, and 0 elsewhere

I_{in} = inventory stocks in the nonmanufacturing sector excluding the government, farm, and residential construction sectors, billions of 1958 dollars, adjusted for inventory valuation adjustment

S_n = sales originating in the nonmanufacturing sector excluding the government, farm, and residential construction sectors, billions of 1958 dollars

C_d = purchases of consumer durables, billions of 1958 dollars

X_m = output originating in the manufacturing sector, billions of 1958 dollars

p_m = wholesale price index excluding food and farm products, 1958 = 1.00

In summary, we have shown that a lag structure of the form $\Delta I_{i_t} = f(S_{t-1}, I_{i_{t-2}})$ seems superior to one with shorter lags. Sales, inventory stock, and the change in unfilled orders are important explanatory variables in the inventory investment functions. On the other hand, interest rates and cash flow are not important or even correct variables in these functions. Finally, prices should be included only if they represent the buffer-stock motive and not if they represent the speculative motive.

CHAPTER 9

THE FOREIGN SECTOR

9.1   IMPORT AND EXPORT EQUATIONS

For the first dozen years of the postwar period, little attention was paid to the foreign sector when the analysis of macroeconomics was considered. Most attention was centered on the problem of full employment without inflation; what scanty reference was made to the balance of payments problem was usually set in the context of a "dollar-shortage" problem, that is, a surplus of gold held by the United States. However, starting in 1958 the nagging realization began that the United States had a negative liquidity balance every year for the past several years (except in 1957, when the Suez crisis raised exports far above their normal level). The balance of payments problem began to command more attention, until it is now one of the primary economic problems for government policy. The net foreign balance of exports minus imports is clearly not the same thing as the net gold flow; owing to the importance currently attached to the latter figure, a brief section (9.3) is included in this chapter to explain the difference between these figures.

It is now a generally accepted fact that imports are significantly related to movements in domestic aggregate economic activity; they rise rapidly during booms and decline during recessions. The price of imported goods relative to domestic goods is also an important determinant of imports, although documentation of the precise elasticity has proved to be a bit elusive. The price of imported goods is taken to be exogenous to the system, which is probably quite true, because there is likely to be very little short-run relationship between movements of prices in this country and prices abroad, except possibly for exogenous disturbances such as the Korean War. Exports are sometimes thought to be totally unrelated to other domestic activity, since they depend on income of other countries; however, this needs to be modified in two respects. First, exports (like imports) depend on relative prices, so that the price of domestic goods and services produced for export relative to the price of other countries' goods (approximated here by a price index of world trade) is an important variable in the export function. Second, changes in United States GNP and domestic imports change exports and GNP of other countries with which we trade; this may in turn affect our exports. The probable effect of this "feedback" for a two-country world is examined and realistic values for the United States and the rest of the world are used in Section 9.2.

It may be well at the outset to establish the general nature of the import and export functions by visual inspection, supplied in Figure 9.1. Both series are graphed in constant dollars. Imports show a marked decline in all recessions except, somewhat oddly, the 1958 recession, which was the most severe one in the postwar period; even so, they certainly decreased relative to the

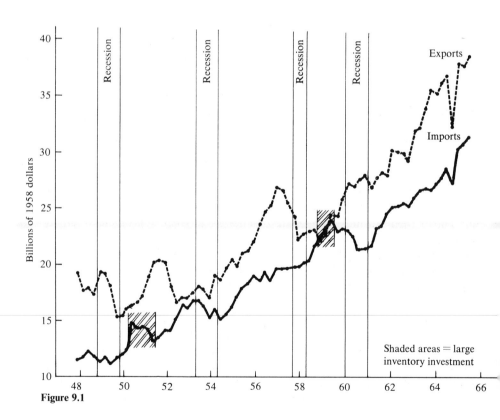

Figure 9.1

trend. The continued rise in imports in 1958 was undoubtedly due to substantial domestic price increases in the capital goods sector in the 1955–1959 period. However, the biggest fluctuations in imports have not been associated with recessions, but rather with periods of intensive inventory investment: the beginning of the Korean War and the 1959 steel strike. The large increase in inventories in the latter half of 1965, which was associated primarily with very strong overall aggregate demand, although the Vietnam situation had some additional effect, also resulted in strong import demand. These periods are also marked on the graph.

The relationship of exports to GNP is not as straightforward. First, it is necessary to exclude the large increase in late 1956 and early 1957, which was due to the Suez crisis, as mentioned above. The sharp downturns in 1963.1 and 1965.1 (which were partially matched by a decrease in imports) were due to dock strikes. These aberrations should not affect the rest of the analysis.

At first glance, there seems to be little relationship between recessions and declines in exports. Although there is at least one quarter during each recession when exports decrease, this is not very conclusive, because exports are higher in each recession period than they were in the previous four quarters, except in 1958. A more critical look at the data, however, reveals a very interesting and more useful relationship. It would be expected that there is some lag between a change in U.S. imports and a change in foreign countries' income, just as there is a substantial lag in the multiplier for this economy, as consumption patterns change slowly and investment decisions take time to make. If this were the case, exports would not start to decline until the recession in this country was well under way and would continue to decline even after the upturn had started in this country. This pattern is brought out in Table 9.1. The pattern does not conform exactly, because exports continued to rise slightly in the latter part of the 1954 and 1961 recessions. However, there was clearly a slowdown in export purchases at these times.

We now examine the function for the foreign sector in detail, starting with imports. There are several advantages to disaggregating imports into at least

TABLE 9.1   RELATIONSHIP BETWEEN EXPORTS AND GNP
DURING RECESSIONS

Beginning of Recession	Exports Previous Four Quarters	First Two Quarters of Recession	Change	Next Three Quarters of Recession	Change
1949.1	18.1	19.4	1.3	16.5	−2.9
1953.3	17.3	18.1	0.8	18.5	0.4
1957.4	26.4[a]	23.6	−2.8	23.2	−0.4
1960.2	24.7	27.5	2.8	27.8	0.3

[a] Artificially high due to the Suez crisis.

three groups: foodstuffs (crude and "manufactured," that is, processed), crude materials and semimanufactured goods (mainly metals and petroleum), and finished goods and services. All the equations are straightforward. The demand for imported food depends on income, population, and relative prices. This function is measured in per capita terms to minimize the multicollinearity between income and population. Crude and semimanufactured products are used almost exclusively in the manufacturing sector, so they are a function of output originating in that sector. This is also the sector in which imports increase when inventories are being built up, so the manufacturing output term should be divided into final sales and inventory investment. The latter term is found to be of great importance. Finished goods and services are purchased mainly by consumers, and thus are a function of personal disposable income. A lagged import term may also be relevant, because most of these purchases are similar to domestic consumption. The actual equations estimated are

(15.10) $$\frac{F_{if}}{N} = 0.0117 + 0.0064(Y/N) - 0.0041(p_{if}/p_f) \qquad \bar{R}^2 = 0.305$$
$$\qquad\qquad\quad (0.0013) \qquad\quad (0.0015)$$

(15.11) $$F_{im} = 3.51 + 0.0329S_m + 0.0960\Delta I_{im} - 2.14(p_{im}/p_m) \qquad \bar{R}^2 = 0.900$$
$$\qquad\quad (0.0022) \qquad (0.0194) \qquad (0.74)$$

(15.12) $$F_{ic} = -2.57 + 0.0293Y - 1.97(p_{ic}/p_c) + 0.6014$$
$$\qquad\qquad (0.0073) \quad (1.48) \qquad\quad (0.1109)$$

$$\frac{1}{4}\sum_{i=1}^{4}(F_{ic})_{-i} \qquad \bar{R}^2 = 0.989$$

where F_{if} = imports of foodstuffs, billions of 1958 dollars

p_{if} = price index of above, 1958 = 1.00

p_f = prices received by farmers, 1958 = 1.00

N = population, millions

F_{im} = imports of crude materials and semimanufactured goods, billions of 1958 dollars

p_{im} = price index of above, 1958 = 1.00

p_m = wholesale price index, 1958 = 1.00

S_m = final sales in manufacturing sector, billions of 1958 dollars

ΔI_{im} = manufacturing inventory investment, billions of 1958 dollars

F_{ic} = other imports (finished goods and services), billions of 1958 dollars

p_{ic} = price index of above, 1958 = 1.00

p_c = consumer price deflator, 1958 = 1.00

Y = personal disposable income, billions of 1958 dollars

Two forms of the equations are considered for F_{im} and F_{ic}, those with and without the lag term. The long-run income (sales) elasticity is just about the same for both forms of these equations, although this is not as true for the price terms. The long-run price elasticity is somewhat higher in the materials equation *with* the lagged import term, and is somewhat higher in the other imports equation *without* the lagged import term. For the following discussion, the equation with the lagged terms will be used, because these reflect what is known about habits in consumer behavior and purchasing patterns of businessmen. However, estimates of some of the elasticities taken from the alternative equations are also presented and discussed.

Income elasticities are discussed first. Just as was true for the consumption function, it is very important to distinguish between short- and long-run marginal propensities or income elasticities in the import function. These are a little harder to interpret in the latter case, because imports are a function of manufacturing sales and manufacturing inventory investment as well as personal disposable income. In the long run this makes little difference, since the shares of manufacturing and disposable income relative to GNP have stayed approximately constant, and changes in inventory investment tend to be very close to zero.[1] In the short run the problem is complicated somewhat. Considering yearly values as representative short-run values, a 1 percent change in GNP will be accompanied by a 0.8 percent change in personal disposable income and 1.5 percent change in manufacturing sales.[2] Manufacturing inventory investment certainly cannot be ignored in the short run; however, all elasticities are presented without including a separate inventory term, and its effects are analyzed separately. This is because the changes in manufacturing inventory investment with respect to a given change in aggregate economic activity vary widely, depending on orders, possibility of strikes, and other forces explained in Chapter 8.

The income elasticities for total imports (calculated at the mean values) are: short run (a), 0.83; short run (b), 0.85; long run, 1.54. Case (a) assumes all the independent income and sales variables change in the same proportion; case (b) assumes that they change according to the actual percentage figures given above. Since the difference is so small, it is not considered in the rest of the analysis.

The long-run income elasticity is rather unusual in that it implies that as income increases, imports will be an increasing share of GNP. Considerable detail was denoted in earlier chapters to showing that the long-run elasticities of consumption with respect to income, and capital stock with respect to output, were unity, implying that in the long run there would be no relative shifts of the percentage of consumption and investment composing GNP. This

[1] The slight decline in the manufacturing share of the economy may be of substantial interest in another context, but will have a negligible effect on the elasticity calculations here.

[2] These figures are taken from multiplier calculations based on the complete model, presented in Chapter 20.

finding was supported by the available figures for long-run trends. However, the same sort of relationship does not seem to be true for imports. To compound the confusion, imports as a percentage of GNP have declined historically. In the period 1929–1938,[3] when income was depressed and tariffs were much more restrictive than they are now, imports were 4.8 percent of GNP, a higher percentage than in the postwar period. Part of the answer to this seeming paradox is that the ratio of imports to GNP was at an historic low right after World War II and has increased steadily from that point to the present, as shown in Table 9.2. Note that current values are slightly above the 1929–1938 average of 4.8 percent and are approaching the 1929 value of 5.0 percent. Also note that the current ratio of imports/GNP compared to the 1947–1949 ratio is 1.38, or close to the estimated long-run income elasticity of 1.54. Thus both sets of figures are consistent, although they do not answer the question of whether the postwar trend of increasing imports relative to GNP will continue.

As stated previously, the short-run income elasticity of 0.8 relative to GNP excludes inventory investment. A change in 1 percent in GNP (about $4.5 billion for the postwar mean value) will on the average change manufacturing inventory investment by $0.1 billion over the period of a year. This raises the short-run elasticity to about 1.0. However, if the increase in GNP were due to a rise in defense expenditures, manufacturing inventory investment would increase by $0.3 billion, raising the income elasticity to 1.3.

Much of the recent econometric analysis of import and export functions for the United States (and other parts of the world) has been done by Rudolf Rhomberg. He has estimated the income elasticity of U.S. imports from Western Europe at 2.0 and from the rest of the world at 0.8.[4] If one third of our imports come from Western Europe and two thirds from the rest of the world (the 1965 figures), then his estimate of overall income elasticity is 1.2, which is close to our figure.

TABLE 9.2 GROWTH OF IMPORTS IN THE POSTWAR PERIOD

Business Cycle	Imports/GNP, %
1947–1949	3.55
1950–1954	3.85
1955–1958	4.39
1959–1961	4.75
1962–1965	4.90

[3] National income figures are not available before 1929, and figures after 1938 were distorted by the war.

[4] R. R. Rhomberg, "A Short-Term World Trade Model," mimeographed (presented at the First World Congress of the Econometric Society, September, 1965).

Ball and Marwah have estimated import functions of similar categories of imports for 1948–1958 and have found that the short-run income elasticity is 0.9 and the long-run elasticity is 1.6.[5] This latter figure is slightly too high because inventory investment was not separated from the output term, and thus the long-run figures include a spurious effect of inventories. When this adjustment is made, the long-run value is about 1.3.

It is possible that events of the early postwar years were significantly different from the rest of the period. Imports from war-ravaged Europe were sharply curtailed, and the Korean War period was also unusual because of shifting demand schedules due to speculation and a greater need for critical war materials. To test this, Rhomberg and Boissoneault estimated import functions for the United States for the period 1954–1961 and found that the income elasticities were somewhat lower and the price elasticities were somewhat higher. However, in assessing the forecasting ability of the equations estimated over the various periods, they state that "somewhat surprisingly, it is found that equations fitted to the shorter, and more recent, subperiod are not clearly superior to the regressions computed for the whole period ... there do not seem to be compelling reasons for shortening the sample period for purposes of the foreign sector equations."[6] We follow these findings and continue to discuss import and export equations estimated for the entire postwar period.

The close agreement of the income elasticities of the studies quoted above diverges a bit when price elasticities are estimated. The results are:

	Short Run	Long Run
Evans[a]	−0.4	−0.6
Evans[b]	—	−0.6
Rhomberg	—	−0.8
Ball–Marwah	−0.5	−1.0

[a] form of the functions with distributed lags.
[b] form of the functions without distributed lags.

Although there is some disagreement in the exact size of the parameter estimates, it should be noted that in all of these studies, the price elasticity for imports is less than or equal to unity. Thus an increase in the price of imports, *cet par.*, while it will increase the net foreign balance in *constant* dollars, will diminish it in *current* dollars and thus worsen the balance of payments.

[5] R. J. Ball and K. Marwah, "The United States Demand for Imports, 1948–1958," *Review of Economics and Statistics*, Vol. 44, No. 4 (November, 1962), pp. 395–401.

[6] R. R. Rhomberg and L. Boissoneault, "The Foreign Sector," in J. S. Duesenberry, G. Fromm, L. R. Klein, and E. Kuh, eds., *The Brookings Quarterly Econometric Model of the United States* (Chicago: Rand McNally, 1965), pp. 392–393.

We now consider the export sector. This, too, could properly be disaggregated in the same way as imports, but this would require some detailed figures on GNP components of foreign countries. Instead, an aggregative export function is estimated with an index of world trade as the relevant income variable. This partially reflects the effect of U.S. income (through the feedback mechanism) on our exports, except that the lag in this mechanism is not included. The ratio of the price for world trade to the price of exports is used for the relative price variable. The estimated equation is

$$(15.13) \quad F_e = -38.88 + 0.1665 X_{wt} + 34.33 (p_{wt}/p_e) + 0.4663 \frac{1}{4} \sum_{i=1}^{4} (F_e)_{-i}$$
$$(0.0128) \qquad (4.78) \qquad\qquad (0.0534)$$

$$\bar{R} = 0.976$$

where F_e = exports, billions of 1958 dollars

X_{wt} = quantity index of world trade, 1958 = 100.0

p_{wt} = price index of world trade, 1958 = 1.00

p_e = price index of U.S. exports, 1958 = 1.00

The estimated price and income elasticities (again at the means) are:

	Short Run	Long Run
Income	0.7	1.3
Price	−1.5	−2.8

The long-run income elasticity is almost the same as it is for imports. This implies that if GNP in this country and world trade grow at the same rate, the net foreign balance (of this country) will remain at the same percentage of GNP. This implies a slight improvement in the balance of payments, since the net foreign balance will increase in absolute terms. The high price elasticity is quite different from the import functions. Rhomberg and Boissoneault estimate a similar equation and find the long-run price elasticity to be −2.0, considerably lower than our estimate but still highly elastic.

If these elasticity estimates are close to the true values, they form an interesting if somewhat unhappy picture for the U.S. balance of payments. If prices of our exported goods grow faster than world export prices, our balance of payments will deteriorate; if prices of imported goods rise faster than domestic prices, our balance of payments will still deteriorate. On the other hand, if U.S. export prices increase less than world export prices, our balance of payments situation will improve. This is the path that must be taken; the United States cannot wait for rising foreign prices to correct this problem, for that is likely to make it worse.

It has often been argued that the country with the slower growth rate will have the balance of payments turn in its favor, since imports will increase more slowly than exports. However, this argument does not take into consideration the fact that the faster-growing country may have a greater elasticity of supply (perhaps because it is further away from full employment) and thus will have less price increase than the slower-growing country. Furthermore, an increase in the rate of growth in one country may not hurt its balance of payments situation if its exports growth to another country with a lower elasticity of supply. This interaction of income and price phenomena is considered next.

9.2　INTERNATIONAL TRANSFER OF ECONOMIC ACTIVITY

This has long been a favorite topic of business-cycle theorists; although recent references to this subject are not as voluminous as they used to be, articles still frequently appear on the subject.[7] The point of this section is not to develop any new theory but rather to get some actual empirical estimates for magnitude of this transfer using the estimates developed throughout the book and also some recent income and price elasticities computed by Rhomberg. For ease of exposition, some elementary multiplier analysis is developed for the foreign trade case. The reader unfamiliar with multiplier analysis may skip to Chapter 19, where it is developed in somewhat more detail. However, anyone who has followed the text this far should have no difficulty with this section.

To cover familiar ground first, neglect price effects and consider a very much oversimplified world with only two countries (the United States and the rest of the world), which have very simple aggregate demand functions. For instance,

$$(9.1) \quad C_1 = aX_1 \qquad\qquad C_2 = eX_2$$

$$(9.2) \quad I_1 = bX_1 \qquad\qquad I_2 = fX_2$$

$$(9.3) \quad M_1 = cX_1 \qquad\qquad M_2 = dX_2(= E_1)$$

$$(9.4) \quad E_1 = dX_2 \qquad\qquad E_2 = cX_1(= M_1)$$

$$(9.5) \quad C_1 + I_1 + G_1 + E_1 - M_1 = X_1 \qquad C_2 + I_2 + G_2 + E_2 - M_2 = X_2$$

and consider the effect of an increase in G_1 on $F_1 (= E_1 - M_1)$:

$$(9.6) \quad X_1 = (a + b - c)X_1 + dX_2 + G_1 \qquad X_2 = (e + f - d)X_2 + cX_1 + G_2$$

$$(9.7) \quad X_1 = \frac{dX_2 + G_1}{1 - a - b + c} \qquad\qquad X_2 = \frac{cX_1 + G_2}{1 - e - f + d}$$

$$(9.8) \quad \frac{dX_1}{dG_1} = \frac{1}{1 - a - b + c}\left(d\frac{dX_2}{dG_1} + 1\right) \qquad \frac{dX_2}{dG_1} = \frac{c}{1 - e - f + d}\frac{dX_1}{dG_1}$$

---

[7] For a list of some of these articles, see R. A. Gordon and L. R. Klein, eds., *Readings in Business Cycles* (Homewood, Ill.: Richard D. Irwin, 1965), international aspects section, p. 575.

$$(9.9) \quad \frac{dX_1}{dG_1} = \frac{1}{1 - a - b + c\left(1 - e - f + d\right)}\frac{dX_1}{dG_1} + \frac{1}{1 - a - b + c}$$

$$(9.10) \quad \frac{dX_1}{dG_1}\left[1 - \frac{cd}{(1 - a - b + c)(1 - e - f + d)}\right] = \frac{1}{1 - a - b + c}$$

$$(9.11) \quad \frac{dX_1}{dG_1}\left[(1 - a - b + c) - \frac{cd}{1 - e - f + d}\right] = 1$$

$$(9.12) \quad \frac{dX_1}{dG_1} = \frac{1}{(1 - a - b + c) - \dfrac{cd}{1 - e - f + d}}$$

If $d = 0$, that is, the feedback mechanism is not operative, this case reduces to the familiar multiplier.

It is easily shown for this case that if prices are unchanged an increase in X_1 must always decrease F_1 unless one of the marginal propensities to import is negative or one of the marginal propensities to spend is greater than unity.

$$(9.13) \quad \frac{dF_1}{dG_1} = \frac{dE_1}{dG_1} - \frac{dM_1}{dG_1}$$

$$(9.14) \quad \frac{dE_1}{dG_1} = d\left(\frac{dX_2}{dG_1}\right) = \frac{cd}{1 - e - f + d}\frac{dX_1}{dG_1}$$

$$(9.15) \quad \frac{dM_1}{dG_1} = c\left(\frac{dX_1}{dG_1}\right)$$

Therefore,

$$(9.16) \quad \frac{dF_1}{dG_1} = -c\frac{dX_1}{dG_1}\left(1 - \frac{d}{1 - e - f + d}\right)$$

which is less than zero unless one (or three) of the terms is negative, which is most unlikely.

Yearly values for the United States are $a = 0.4$,[8] $b = 0.2$, $c = 0.03$. Values for the rest of the world are a little harder to estimate. Rhomberg gives values for consumption and import functions (no investment functions) for Western Europe and no such functions for the rest of the world.[9] The value of e for Western Europe is also about 0.4, and other evidence suggests that this figure is fairly reasonable for other developed countries (Canada, Japan, and Australia), which together with Western Europe account for two thirds of U.S. world

---

[8] Note that this is *not* the mpc out of disposable income but out of GNP.

[9] These and the following empirical estimates are all taken from R. R. Rhomberg and L. Boisson-neault, "Effects of Income and Price Changes on the U.S. Balance of Payments," mimeographed (presented at the December, 1964, meeting of the Econometric Society), appendix.

trade. In underdeveloped countries the percentage of GNP going to disposable personal income is undoubtedly less than 70 percent, so even if the mpc = 1 in these countries, e would not be higher than 0.7; thus the average value of e (weighted by importance of world trade) is between 0.4 and 0.5. The value of f is likely to be lower than that for the United States, since more investment is planned by the government, and underdeveloped countries are less likely to have induced inventory fluctuations, so f is likely to be about 0.15. Taken together, $e + f$ is likely to be about the same as $a + b$, that is, about 0.6. The marginal propensity of Western Europe to import *from the United States* is estimated to be 0.06, although their total marginal propensity to import is much larger. This figure is also used for the rest of the world, in the absence of a better estimate. Thus

$$(9.17) \quad \frac{dF_1}{dG_1} = -c \cdot \frac{1}{(1 - a - b + c) - \dfrac{cd}{1 - e - f + d}} \left(1 - \frac{d}{1 - e - f + d}\right)$$

$$= -\frac{0.03}{0.43 - (0.0018/0.46)}\left(1 - \frac{0.06}{0.46}\right) = -0.065$$

so an increase in U.S. government expenditures of \$1 billion will increase imports by (about) \$0.075 billion and will increase exports (through the feedback mechanism) by \$0.01 billion, so that the net loss in the foreign balance is \$0.065 billion.

Things are quite a bit different when prices are considered. Prices enter two ways; both imports and exports depend on relative prices, and for balance of payment problems, the current dollar figure is relevant rather than the constant dollar figure. Then the model is

$$(9.18) \qquad C_1 = aX_1 \qquad\qquad C_2 = eX_2$$

$$(9.19) \qquad I_1 = bX_1 \qquad\qquad I_2 = fX_2$$

$$(9.20) \qquad M_1 = cX_1 - \lambda\frac{p_i}{p_e} \qquad M_2 = dX_2 + \mu\frac{p_i}{p_e}$$

$$(9.21) \qquad E_1 = dX_2 + \mu\frac{p_i}{p_e} \qquad E_2 = cX_1 - \lambda\frac{p_i}{p_e}$$

The term $p_i = \delta M_1$; that is, the price of our imports, which is rest-of-the-world exports, depends on the volume of imports. This is a supply equation. The term p_e is assumed not to vary and is fixed at unity, because Rhomberg *et al.* estimate the inverse of the supply elasticity of U.S. exports to be $\frac{1}{15}$, not significantly different from zero. This means that for practical purposes the supply curve for U.S. exports is almost perfectly elastic. Combining the equations for this version of the model gives

(9.22) $X_1 = aX_1 + bX_1 + dX_2 + \mu p_i - cX_1 + \lambda p_i + G_1$

(9.23) $X_2 = eX_2 + fX_2 + cX_1 - \lambda p_i - dX_2 - \mu p_i + G_2$

(9.24) $X_1(1 - a - b + c) = dX_2 + (\mu + \lambda)p_i + G_1$

(9.25) $X_2(1 - e - f + d) = cX_1 - (\mu + \lambda)p_i + G_2$

Therefore

(9.26) $\dfrac{dX_1}{dG_1} = \dfrac{1}{1 - a - b + c}\left[d\dfrac{dX_2}{dG_1} + (\mu + \lambda)\dfrac{dp_i}{dG_1} + 1\right]$

and

(9.27) $\dfrac{dX_2}{dG_1} = \dfrac{1}{1 - e - f + d}\left[c\dfrac{dX_1}{dG_1} - (\mu + \lambda)\dfrac{dp_i}{dG_1}\right]$

Also,

(9.28) $\dfrac{dp_i}{dG_1} = \delta\dfrac{dM_1}{dG_1} = \dfrac{\delta c}{1 + \lambda\delta}\dfrac{dX_1}{dG_1}$

Since $M_1 = cX_1 - \lambda p_i$,

(9.29) $\dfrac{dM_1}{dG_1} = c\dfrac{dX_1}{dG_1} - \lambda\delta\dfrac{dM_1}{dG_1}$

and

(9.30) $\dfrac{dM_1}{dG_1} = \dfrac{c}{1 + \lambda\delta}\dfrac{dX_1}{dG_1}$

Substituting the expressions for dX_2/dG_1 and dp_i/dG_1 in the equation for dX_1/dG_1,

(9.31) $\dfrac{dX_1}{dG_1} = \dfrac{1}{1 - a - b + c}\left\{1 + \dfrac{d}{1 - e - f + d}\left[c\dfrac{dX_1}{dG_1} - (\mu + \lambda)\dfrac{\delta c}{1 + \lambda\delta}\dfrac{dX_1}{dG_1}\right]\right.$
$\left. + \dfrac{(\mu + \lambda)\delta c}{1 + \lambda\delta}\dfrac{dX_1}{dG_1}\right\}$

Let

(9.32) $1 - a - b + c = m,\quad 1 - e - f + d = n,\quad \dfrac{(\mu + \lambda)\delta c}{1 + \lambda\delta} = p$

and

(9.33) $\dfrac{dX_1}{dG_1} = X'_1 \qquad \dfrac{dX_2}{dG_1} = X'_2$

(similarly for other variables). Then

$$(9.34) \qquad X_1' = \frac{1}{m}\left[1 + \frac{d}{n}(cX_1' - pX_1') + pX_1'\right]$$

Therefore,

$$(9.35) \qquad X_1' = \frac{1}{m} + \frac{X_1'}{m}\left(\frac{dc}{n} - \frac{dp}{n} + \frac{np}{n}\right)$$

$$(9.36) \qquad X_1'\left[1 - \frac{1}{mn}(dc - dp + np)\right] = \frac{1}{m}$$

$$(9.37) \qquad X_1' = \frac{1}{m - (1/n)(dc - dp + np)}$$

and

$$(9.38) \qquad X_2' = \frac{1}{n}(c - p)X_1'$$

By definition,

$$(9.39) \qquad \frac{dF_1}{dG_1} = F_1' = p_e E_1' + E_1 p_e' - p_i M_1' - M_1 p_i'$$

We have

$$(9.40) \qquad p_e' = 0 \qquad E_1' = dX_2' + \frac{\mu\delta c}{1 + \lambda\delta}X_1'$$

and

$$(9.41) \qquad p_i' = \frac{\delta c}{1 + \lambda\delta}X_1' \qquad M_1' = \frac{c}{1 + \lambda\delta}X_1'$$

Therefore,

$$(9.42) \quad F_1' = p_e\left(dX_2' + \frac{\mu\delta c}{1 + \lambda\delta}X_1'\right) - M_1\left(\frac{\delta c}{1 + \lambda\delta}\right)X_1' - p_i\left(\frac{c}{1 + \lambda\delta}\right)X_1'$$

$$= dX_2' + \frac{c}{1 + \lambda\delta}X_1'(\mu\delta - M_1\delta - 1)$$

($p_e = p_i = 1$, since they are index numbers). If there are no price terms, this reduces to

$$(9.43) \qquad F_1' = dX_2' - cX_1' = -cX_1'\left(1 - \frac{d}{n}\right)$$

which was given above.

At this point some numerical estimates are needed. From above,

(9.43) $a + b = 0.6$ $e + f = 0.6$ $c = 0.03$ $d = 0.06$

Therefore,

(9.44) $m = 0.43$ $n = 0.46$

1965 values of E and M (in billions of 1958 dollars) are about 30, so if the price elasticity of imports is 0.8, $\lambda \cong 25$; if the price elasticity of exports is 2.0 (using the lower estimate), $\mu \cong 60$.

The supply elasticity of rest-of-the-world exports is estimated by Rhomberg to be 2.5 for Western Europe and 1.2 for other countries, so the weighted average is 1.6. This means

(9.45) $$\frac{\Delta M_1}{\Delta p_i} \frac{p_i}{M_1} = 1.6$$

so

(9.46) $$\delta = \frac{\Delta p_i}{\Delta M_1} \cong \frac{1}{50}$$

Then

(9.47) $$\frac{(\mu + \lambda)\delta c}{1 + \lambda\delta} = p = \frac{(85/50)(0.03)}{1 + 0.5} \cong \frac{1}{30}$$

Solving numerically,

(9.48) $$X'_1 = \frac{1}{m - (1/n)(dc - dp + np)} = \frac{1}{0.43 - \dfrac{(0.0018 - 0.002 + 0.0153)}{0.46}}$$

$$\cong 2.5$$

(9.49)

$$X'_2 = (1/n)(c - p)X'_1 \cong 0.0$$

since $c \cong p$.

Because X_2 does not change at all, U.S. exports increase only through a favorable shift in relative prices. The size of this effect is

(9.50) $$\frac{\mu\delta c}{1 + \lambda\delta}X'_1 = \frac{0.036(2.5)}{1.5} = 0.06$$

Imports (in *current* dollars) increase by

$$\frac{c}{1 + \lambda\delta}X'_1(1 + M_1\delta) = \frac{0.03(2.5)}{1.5}(1.6) = 0.08$$

Thus the balance of payments deteriorates somewhat, but only by 0.02, compared to 0.065 in the case where prices did not change. The net foreign balance in constant dollars, which is equal to

$$\frac{\mu\delta c}{1 + \lambda\delta}X'_1 - \frac{c}{1 + \lambda\delta}X'_1$$

has actually improved by 0.01, since $\mu\delta > 1$. If the higher export elasticity of 2.8 ($\mu = 84$) were used, there would even be an improvement on current account of 0.004.[10]

This section has shown that the assertion that the balance of payments will turn against the faster-growing country is invalidated if the slower-growing country is already at full employment and the faster-growing country is not. In this case, an increase in GNP (and imports) of the faster-growing country will result in an increase in inflation rather than growth for the other country. The resulting shift in the terms of trade will increase exports and decrease the growth in imports of the country not yet at full employment. This is not an unrealistic example; Verdoorn and Post have shown that for the Netherlands at low rates of unemployment, an increase in exogenous expenditures has a negative multiplier. The rise in prices reduces the net foreign balance by more than the increase due to a rise in expenditures.[11]

This analysis may go a long way in explaining why the recent increase in the rate of growth in the United States did not result in a decrease in our net foreign balance, and also may account for the fact that a more rapid increase in our GNP has coincided with more rapid inflation in Western Europe. Thus if this country can keep export prices from rising, a continued rapid rate of growth need not cause a deterioration in the current account part of U.S. balance of payments.

9.3   BALANCE OF PAYMENTS PROBLEMS

In Sections 9.1 and 9.2 we examined the determinants of imports and exports and showed that the net foreign balance of goods and services need not turn against the faster-growing country if that country is not at full employment. This being the case for the United States, an increase in our surplus on current account for the 1959–1965 period occurred concomitantly with recent rapid growth and stable prices. Thus the increased concern about balance of payments deficits and the gold drain during that period was clearly due to increasing deficits in other sectors of the balance of payments. To

---

[10] All these figures are relative to a $1 billion increase in U.S. government expenditures.

[11] P. Verdoorn and J. J. Post, "Capacity and Short-Term Multipliers," in P. E. Hart, G. Mills, and J. K. Whitaker, eds., *Econometric Analysis for National Economic Planning*, Proceedings of the Sixteenth Symposium of the Colston Research Society (London: Butterworth, 1964), pp. 179–199.

analyze this problem it is necessary to comment briefly on the method of bookkeeping used for these accounts. After this, the trends in the major components are examined and their future possibilities discussed.

Unlike the rest of the national income accounting concepts and methods, which are widely adopted and generally accepted, there is no such homogeneity in the balance of payments accounts. The Economic Report of the President points out that since the accounts summarize a system of double-entry bookkeeping, the total net difference must always be zero. Thus "any surplus or deficit includes only selected payments and receipts. A variety of such measures has been used in recent years, including, among others, the "basic balance," the "balance on regular transactions," the "liquidity balance," and the "balance on official reserve transactions" ("official settlements"). No single concept is best for all analyses. The measure that is most appropriate for one country at one time may be less appropriate under other circumstances."[12] The accounting system discussed here will center on the liquidity balance (explained below), which is probably the most widely used.

The second major problem with the balance of payments figures is the nature of the balancing item, known as errors and omissions. The idea of introducing some such term to balance both sides of the accounts is also used in the overall national income accounts, where it is called the statistical discrepancy. However, the statistical discrepancy is very small compared to GNP; its average absolute value is $1.4 billion, only 0.3 percent of GNP. The average absolute value of the errors and omissions term is not large in itself ($0.8 billion), but is 3.4 percent of exports and 38.4 percent of the net foreign balance.[13] Even more important, the errors and omissions term was positive for every year during the period 1948–1959 (except for a miniscule −$0.02 billion in 1950) and has been negative in every year from 1960 to the present. This problem is discussed below in more detail.

Given that there are serious handicaps in drawing conclusions from the balance of payments accounts, we discuss very briefly the system of accounts presently favored by the government. For a more detailed treatment of these accounts, the reader is referred to any standard textbook on international trade.[14] The accounts are usually divided into:

1. Current account
   a. Balance of goods and services
   b. Remittances and pensions
2. Capital account
   a. Government grants and capital expenditures
   b. Long-term private capital movements

---

[12] Economic Report of the President (Washington: Government Printing Office, 1966), pp. 160–162.

[13] All these figures are based on data for 1948–1965 inclusive.

[14] See, for example, C. P. Kindleberger, International Economics (Homewood, Ill.: Richard D. Irwin, 1963), chap. 2.

c. Short-term private capital movements
   Less: Nonliquid foreign investment in the United States
3. Reconciling items
   a. Liquid holdings of U.S. assets by foreigners
   b. Change in U.S. reserve assets (mostly gold)
   c. Errors and omissions

The balance on goods and services is relatively straightforward to define, although it includes items such as income on direct investments which would not be included in domestic purchases of goods and services. The largest category is merchandise exports and imports excluding transfers under military grants, although the net surplus or deficit is quite large on some of the other items. For 1964 and 1965 the figures are as given in Table 9.3.

Because travel is listed separately, it at first appears to be an item that could be substantially reduced, and in fact a great deal of talk is currently heard about the travel gap. This is largely nonsense. No action has been planned to overcome the "coffee gap" ($1.1 billion), the "sugar gap" ($0.5 billion), or the "petroleum gap" ($1.4 billion), because there would be no point in doing so. However, these figures do not appear separately in the standard balance of payments accounts, so they are not brought to the attention of the average public (or average public servant) as often. There is no point in singling out one particular item in which this country has a deficit and suggesting that steps be taken to curtail purchases of this one item unless one is willing to make a value judgment that the marginal utility of the last dollar spent on (for example) coffee is greater than the marginal utility of the last dollar spent on tourism.

Remittances and pensions, the other major classification in the current account, raises no difficulties. Private remittances and government pensions and other transfers simply consist of money sent abroad by our citizens (or

TABLE 9.3 U.S. BALANCE OF GOODS AND SERVICES
FOR 1964 AND 1965 *(all figures are in billions of current dollars)*

	1964			1965		
	Exports	Imports	Net	Exports	Imports	Net
Merchandise	25.3	18.6	6.7	26.3	21.5	4.8
Transportation	2.3	2.5	−0.2	2.4	2.6	−0.2
Travel	1.1	2.2	−1.1	1.2	2.5	−1.3
Misc. services[a]	2.1	0.9	1.2	2.3	0.9	1.4
Military sales	0.8	2.8	−2.0	0.8	2.8	−2.0
Income on investment	5.4	1.4	4.0	6.0	1.6	4.4
	37.0	28.4	8.6	39.0	31.9	7.1

[a] Mainly insurance, fees, and royalties.

government) for charitable purposes, such as Care packages, donations to philanthropic organizations, and gifts to relatives in other countries.

We now consider the capital account. Government grants and capital are usually treated as follows:

1. Military grants of goods and services are netted out against the same item in exports, so goods and services which are merely transferred from this country to another country under a military grant are often not included in the balance of payments accounts.

2. Other grants of the government are entered as unilateral net transfers. Much of this is foreign aid.

3. Capital expenditures of government consist of direct loans to foreign governments and also loans made through the export-import bank and other similar international agencies. Some foreign aid is also included in here. Scheduled and nonscheduled repayments of loans are subtracted from these figures.

Private capital movements are somewhat more straightforward. They can be divided into direct investment abroad (for example, purchases of plant and equipment abroad paid for with U.S. funds), foreign securities to U.S. residents net of redemptions (including both bonds and equities), other long-term claims (investment in other long-term foreign assets not covered above), and short-term claims (such as finance company paper and other similar assets). This figure must be netted against foreign investment here and foreign purchases of U.S. long-term and short-term private securities. These figures are shown in Table 9.4. Note in particular the large swing in short-term claims, from −$2.1 billion in 1964 to $0.7 billion in 1965; this is discussed below.

TABLE 9.4 U.S. CAPITAL ACCOUNT AND UNILATERAL FLOWS FOR 1964 AND 1965   (*all figures are in billions of current dollars*)

	1964			1965		
	Credits	Debits	Net	Credits	Debits	Net
Remittances		0.8	−0.8		1.0	−1.0
Unilateral transfers						
of government		1.9	−1.9		1.8	−1.8
Government loans	0.6	2.3	−1.7	0.9	2.5	−1.6
Private capital:						
Direct investment		2.4	−2.4		3.3	−3.3
Foreign securities		0.7	−0.7		0.7	−0.7
Other long-term claims	0.7	1.3	−0.6	0.2	0.3	−0.1
Short-term claims		2.1	−2.1	0.7		0.7
Balance			−10.2			−7.8

Excluding purely military transactions, the net deficit in 1964 and 1965 in the government sector was −$3.6 billion and −$3.4 billion. However, to appraise this figure properly it is necessary to include an additional entry called "transactions involving no direct dollar outflow from the United States," which was $3.6 billion in both years. This represents the amount of U.S. government funds distributed in foreign countries which were spent back in this country; these funds represent no liquidity drain on this country. This figure has already been included in the figure of exports of merchandise and miscellaneous services, which accounts in large part for the surpluses in these categories. To get a true picture of the net gold flow due to nonmilitary foreign aid it is necessary to balance the −$3.6 billion and −$3.4 billion figures against the $3.6 billion figure which has already been added to exports. Seen in this light, it appears that foreign aid is not hurting our balance of payments problems and in fact in 1965 slightly helped them. Whatever else one has to say about foreign aid, it cannot be blamed for the gold outflow.[15]

The reconciling items are now considered. These are usually referred to as "below the line" in standard balance of payments accounting. These consist of (1) foreign holdings of U.S. liquid assets, (2) changes in U.S. official reserve assets (mainly, but not entirely gold), and (3) errors and omissions, which are substantial, as was mentioned earlier. The *liquidity balance* is defined as categories 1 and 2. The accounting identity connecting these items is:

surplus on current account	+	surplus on capital account	+	errors and omissions	+	increase in foreign holdings of U.S. liquid assets	+	Decrease in U.S. official reserve assets	≡ 0

These figures are shown for the postwar period in Table 9.5.

To see just what has been happening, it may be worthwhile to divide this period into subperiods of 1948–1957, when there was little worry about the gold drain, and 1958–1965, when this problem became more serious. Annual averages for these periods are given in Table 9.6.

As can be seen from the last two columns, the annual increase in the deficit, which is equal to the gold flow plus changes in foreign holdings of U.S. liquid assets, has increased from $0.9 billion to $2.8 billion, or $1.9 billion per year. However, $1.2 billion of the increase in the deficit, or almost two thirds of this change, can be attributed to a change from $0.6 billion to −$0.6 billion in the errors and omissions term. If this term had remained at $0.6 for both periods, the annual deficit would only have increased from $0.9 billion to $1.5 billion.

---

[15] It may seem unrealistic to argue that more than 100 percent of foreign aid is spent in this country. However, this is not the case, for the government loans figure includes a credit of $0.9 billion (in 1965), which represents interest payments on past loans. When this adjustment is made, it is seen that the proportion of 1965 foreign aid spent in the United States was 36/43, or 84 percent, a figure fully comparable with other estimates. Yet the $0.9 billion credit cannot be divorced from the foreign aid figure, because it is the result of previous government loans.

TABLE 9.5 SUMMARY BALANCE SHEET OF U.S. BALANCE
OF PAYMENTS   *(all figures are in billions of current dollars)*

Year	(1)[a]	(2)	(3)	(4)	(5)	(6)	(7)	(8)
1948	6.4	−4.9	−1.0	−0.1	−0.6	1.2	−1.7	0.7
1949	6.1	−5.6	−0.7	0.2	−0.6	0.8	−0.3	0.1
1950	1.8	−3.6	−1.1	−0.2	−0.5	0.0	1.8	1.8
1951	3.7	−3.2	−0.7	−0.1	−0.5	0.5	0.0	0.3
1952	2.2	−2.4	−0.8	−0.1	−0.5	0.6	−0.4	1.4
1953	0.4	−2.1	−0.4	0.2	−0.6	0.3	1.3	0.9[b]
1954	1.8	−1.6	−0.8	−0.6	−0.6	0.2	0.5	1.1
1955	2.0	−2.2	−0.7	−0.2	−0.6	0.5	0.2	1.0
1956	4.0	−2.3	−1.9	−0.5	−0.7	0.5	−0.9	1.8
1957	5.7	−2.6	−2.8	−0.3	−0.7	1.2	−1.2	0.7
1958	2.2	−2.6	−2.6	−0.3	−0.7	0.5	2.3	1.2[b]
1959	0.2	−2.0	−1.4	−0.1	−0.8	0.4	1.0	2.7
1960	4.1	−2.8	−2.2	−1.3	−0.7	−1.0	2.1	1.8[b]
1961	5.6	−2.8	−1.9	−1.6	−0.7	−1.0	0.6	1.8
1962	5.1	−3.0	−1.9	−0.5	−0.7	−1.2	1.5	0.7[b]
1963	5.9	−3.6	−3.0	−0.8	−0.8	−0.4	0.4	2.3
1964	8.6	−3.6	−3.7	−2.1	−0.8	−1.2	0.2	2.6
1965	7.1	−3.4	−4.1	0.7	−1.0	−0.6	1.2	0.1[b]

[a] (1) Surplus on current account; (2) surplus on movements of government grants and capital; (3) net credit of all long-term private assets netted against foreign investment in the United States; (4) credit of all short-term foreign assets; (5) remittances and pensions; (6) errors and omissions; (7) net decrease in U.S. official reserve assets (negative values represent increase); (8) change in foreign holding of U.S. liquid assets.

[b] Years in which net gold outflow was greater than net change in foreign holding of U.S. liquid assets.

By definition, the items that are included in errors and omissions are largely unknown. However, it is generally believed that this term consists mainly of unrecorded short-term capital movements and, to a lesser degree, unrecorded purchases of tourists abroad. Thus the negative balances recorded in these categories are probably lower than the true figures. But if the main increase in

TABLE 9.6 AVERAGES OF U.S. BALANCE OF PAYMENTS

	(1)[a]	(2)	(3)	(4)	(5)	(6)	(7)	(8)
1948–1957	3.4	−3.0	−1.1	−0.2	−0.6	0.6	−0.1	1.0
1958–1965	4.9	−3.0	−2.6	−0.7	−0.8	−0.6	1.2	1.6

[a] Same as in Table 9.5.

the balance of payments deficit is due to items of an unknown type, it may be somewhat unrealistic to single out any one sector for controls.

A second reason for the increased gold drain is the fact that foreigners have recently been much less willing to hold U.S. liquid assets and have demanded more gold for a given level of annual deficit than they did previously. If the average annual level of the deficit had remained the same for the period 1958–1965 but foreigners had held U.S. liquid assets in the same patterns as they did during 1948–1957, the yearly gold outflow would have been only $0.6 billion per year instead of $1.2 billion. For example, in 1958, 1960, 1962, and 1965 the net outflow of gold was greater than the increase in foreign holdings of U.S. liquid assets. In the 1948–1957 period, this happened only once, in 1953, and then by a very small margin. Thus a change in the propensity to hold U.S. securities, together with the large changes in errors and omissions, account for almost all the difference in the annual gold outflow between these two periods.

It may be a comforting armchair exercise to explain that the gold flow is really a matter of little consequence, meanwhile noting that the United States has lost $10 billion of gold in the last eight years. If this trend were to continue for the next eight years, the value of the dollar in international markets would become rather precarious. However, the United States is still much better off with the gold outflow due to these causes than if it were due to a loss of its competitive situation in world markets. This is clearly not the case, because the surplus of goods and services increased rather steadily through 1964. Thus if international capital markets can be convinced of the fact that the dollar is basically sound, and if the unfavorable trends in errors and omissions and holding of gold can be reversed, the net gold outflow would become much smaller without any changes in our international competitive situation.

Meanwhile it has been thought necessary to take short-term steps to stem the unfavorable balance of trade and thus convince the rest of the world that U.S. securities are a worthwhile asset to hold. The surplus on current account increased steadily from 1959 to 1964; it would clearly be advantageous to continue increasing this figure, but no controls have been suggested for imports except for those on travel. Government transfers, although negative, have not been increasing. Furthermore, owing to payments in kind and "buy American" and other tying arrangements, there is no net deficit in the balance of payments due to foreign aid; sometimes there is even a slight surplus. Remittances and pensions are not likely to be affected, and their growth has in any case been very slight.

The big increases in the balance of payments deficit have come in short-term and long-term capital movements. It is in these areas that the government has moved to curtail the outflow. These moves have taken several forms. At first the effort was made to raise short-term interest rates to attract foreign capital while holding long-term rates low in order to stimulate domestic investment. This was known as "operation twist". Although it did succeed in raising short-term rates, long-term rates also rose to the highest level since the 1920s, which might reasonably have been expected. Inasmuch as this program was supposed to attract foreign capital, it was of little success. Capital outflows continued to increase, so that more direct measures were deemed necessary.

Next was the introduction of the interest equalization tax in mid-1963, which reduced the effective interest rate earned on foreign securities to the rate obtainable in this country. In February 1965 this tax was also applied to most bank loans of a year or more made to developed countries. Furthermore, large corporations and banks were asked to observe voluntary guidelines and to reduce the outflow of direct foreign investment and short-term capital. These guidelines were continued and in some cases made more stringent in 1966. As can be seen from Table 9.4, these moves were unsuccessful in decreasing direct foreign investment but appeared to work quite well for other long-term claims and short-term claims. The guidelines appeared to be particularly successful for the latter category, which changed from − $2.1 billion in 1964 to $0.7 billion in 1965, as financial institutions recalled many of their foreign short-term holdings. However, it should be noted that the − $2.1 billion was much higher than the average figure of − $0.8, billion for the previous five-year period, so that part of the reversal was probably a natural reaction, particularly with tighter money in the United States in 1965. Further deterioration of both current and capital account in 1966 and 1967 led to mandatory controls in 1968.

Although these measures may be necessary to reverse the unfavorable balance of payments situation in the short run, they are clearly not to the long-run advantage of either the United States or the countries with which it trades. The restrictions in capital outflow should be removed as soon as it seems likely that the gold outflow will be diminished. In 1965, income on investments accounted for a net figure of $4.4 billion, larger in absolute value than the negative figure of − $4.1 billion due to long-term private capital movements. Although it is possible to decrease foreign investment in the short run without decreasing interest income very much, this clearly cannot continue in the long run, and the surplus on current account would dwindle substantially.

One of the benefits of international trade is factor price equalization. It is usually assumed that the price of capital (the interest rate) is equalized rather than the price of labor, since the former is generally assumed to be much more mobile than the latter. However, this explanation does not consider "guidelines" intended to hamper the process of capital movements. Higher interest rates in foreign countries occur because capital is scarcer there than in the United States. To maximize world production, capital should be transferred until the interest rate is equalized in all countries. Furthermore, the more capital that is kept in this country (and out of other countries), the greater will be the interest rate differential, and the more tendency there will be for small companies to evade the guidelines and for errors and omissions to increase more rapidly. Thus not only will the United States partially negate the benefits of international trade through the guidelines, but in the long run this is not likely to help the balance of payments situation. Vigorous steps should be taken to keep export prices down and convince the nations with which we trade that the dollar is sound, so that they will again hold more U.S. securities and demand less gold reserves. As soon as the guidelines have accomplished this, they should be removed.

CHAPTER 10

AGGREGATE SUPPLY COMPONENTS
AND FACTOR SHARES

10.1   PRODUCTION AND LABOR
REQUIREMENTS FUNCTIONS

The explanation of the causes of aggregate demand in the macro-economic system has been completed, but the determination of the economic activity is not yet finished. An explanation of aggregate supply and its factors is still necessary. These should be examined in some detail both because they are necessary to explain aggregate demand accurately and for their own interest. It has been shown in previous chapters how the components of aggregate demand depend considerably on relative prices, factor shares, and other variables determined primarily by supply considerations. Increasing importance and interest have recently centered on the explanation and prediction of product and factor prices, unemployment, and profits and other factor shares. As just one example, primary interest in the 1966 and 1967 forecasts focused on the degree of inflation and possible shortages of factor supplies rather than the actual value of constant-dollar GNP, although these are all mutually interdependent. Such questions are quite different from those asked in the early 1960s, when the main problem facing economists was to find the best combination of monetary and fiscal policy that would stimulate the economy sufficiently to reduce unemployment to at least an "interim level" of 4 percent.

It is still true that the determination of aggregate demand must occupy a central role in predicting the level of prices and other supply variables. During periods of substantial unemployment and steady industrial prices, when wage increases do not exceed productivity gains, a model of aggregate demand is likely to be able to predict gross national product just as well as a more complete model. The first quarterly econometric models of Klein, Duesenberry *et. al.*, and Liu[1] were designed in this manner. However as the economy has returned to near full employment in the mid-1960s it has become increasingly important to analyze the functions explaining aggregate supply.

Supply functions, or production functions, were examined by classical economists long before the determination of aggregate demand was considered. Although primary discussion of these functions was confined to the theory of the firm, the aggregate production function was an integral part of the classical system of income and price determination. As is usual when working with aggregate production functions, we consider only two factors of production, labor (L) and capital (K). Since gross national product (X) is a value-added concept, intermediate factors of production cancel out. Technological progress is often considered an additional determinant of output, and is usually assumed to be related to a time trend (t). Symbolically this can be represented as $X = f(L, K, t)$.

It has been observed that the relative shares of national product earned by labor and capital have been quite stable over many decades. Such an observation suggests the formulation of a production function in which factor shares are assumed to be constant. One particular such function, the Cobb–Douglas function,[2] is undoubtedly the best known and most widely used production function. It has the general form

$$(10.1) \qquad X = aL^{\alpha}K^{\beta}e^{\gamma t}$$

For purposes of estimation this function is written in the logarithmic form

$$(10.2) \qquad \log X = \log a + \alpha \log L + \beta \log K + \gamma t$$

It can easily be shown that under conditions of perfect competition and profit-maximizing behavior, α and β are equal to the shares of output received by labor and capital, respectively. First note that the marginal product of

---

[1] L. R. Klein, "A Postwar Quarterly Model: Descriptions and Applications," in *Models of Income Determination* (Princeton, N.J.: Princeton University Press for NBER, 1964). Although this model formally includes several supply and price variables, the functions explaining these variables were suppressed when actual predictions were made and predetermined values were substituted in their place. J. S. Duesenberry, O. Eckstein, and G. Fromm, "A Simulation of the United States Economy in Recession," *Econometrica*, Vol. 28, No. 4 (October, 1960), pp. 749–810. T. C. Liu, "An Exploratory Quarterly Econometric Model of Effective Demand in the Postwar United States Economy," *Econometrica*, Vol. 31, No. 3 (July, 1963), pp. 301–348.

[2] C. W. Cobb and P. H. Douglas, "A Theory of Production," *American Economic Review*, Vol. 18, No. 1 (March, 1928), pp. 139–165. P. H. Douglas, "Are There Laws of Production?" *American Economic Review*, Vol. 38, No. 1 (March, 1948), pp. 1–41.

each factor is proportional to its average product, since

(10.3)
$$\frac{\partial X}{\partial L} = aL^{\alpha-1}K^{\beta}e^{\gamma t} = \alpha\frac{X}{L}$$

(10.4)
$$\frac{\partial X}{\partial K} = aL^{\alpha}K^{\beta-1}e^{\gamma t} = \beta\frac{X}{K}$$

Rewriting these expressions yields the result that α and β are the elasticities of their respective factors relative to output, since

(10.5)
$$\alpha = \frac{\partial X}{\partial L}\frac{L}{X} \quad \text{and} \quad \beta = \frac{\partial X}{\partial K}\frac{K}{X}$$

For purely competitive profit-maximizing firms,[3]

(10.6)
$$\frac{\partial X}{\partial L} = \frac{w}{p} \quad \text{and} \quad \frac{\partial X}{\partial K} = \frac{r}{p}$$

so that under these conditions

(10.7)
$$\alpha = \frac{wL}{pX} \quad \text{and} \quad \beta = \frac{rK}{pX}$$

which are labor's share and capital's share of output in current prices. By definition α and β must sum to unity under these last assumptions, since $wL + rK \equiv pX$.

Even if we do not assume pure competition and profit maximization, the Cobb–Douglas function is unduly restrictive. In particular, it leads to the stringent result that the capital/labor ratio is strictly proportional to the factor price ratio. This can be shown as follows.

From above,

(10.8)
$$\frac{\alpha}{\beta} = \frac{\partial X/\partial L}{X/L} \left| \frac{\partial X/\partial K}{X/K} \right. = \frac{\partial K}{\partial L}\frac{L}{K}$$

Therefore,

(10.9)
$$\frac{K}{L} = \frac{\beta}{\alpha}\frac{\partial K}{\partial L}$$

Under cost minimization

(10.10)
$$\frac{\partial X/\partial L}{w} = \frac{\partial X/\partial K}{r} \quad \text{or} \quad \frac{\partial K}{\partial L} = \frac{w}{r}$$

---

[3] w, the wage rate; r, the unit price of capital; and p, product price level.

Therefore,

(10.11)
$$\frac{K}{L} = \frac{\beta}{\alpha}\frac{w}{r}$$

From this it follows that a given percentage change in $\partial K/\partial L$ (or w/r) will lead to an equal percentage change in K/L. If we convert to logarithms, the equation above becomes

(10.12)
$$\log\left(\frac{K}{L}\right) = \log\left(\frac{\beta}{\alpha}\right) - \log\left(\frac{\partial L}{\partial K}\right)$$

Then

(10.13)
$$\frac{d(\log K/L)}{d(\log \partial L/\partial K)} = -1$$

This last expression is known as the *elasticity of substitution* and is denoted by σ. The Cobb–Douglas function is thus said to have a unitary elasticity of substitution.

A more general class of production functions has been proposed for which the elasticity of substitution can take any (constant) value. Such a function is known as a constant elasticity of substitution (CES) production function.[4] This function is derived from the equation

(10.14)
$$\log\left(\frac{X}{L}\right) = \log a + \sigma \log w$$

where σ is the elasticity of substitution as given above. If we impose the constraints of pure competition and profit maximization, which themselves imply constant returns to scale, this function can be transformed to

(10.15)
$$X = \gamma[\delta K^{-\rho} + (1 - \delta)L^{-\rho}]^{-1/\rho}$$

where γ = efficiency parameter (scale factor)

δ = distribution parameter (and equals $a^{-1/\sigma}\gamma^{[(1-\sigma)/\sigma]-1}$)

ρ = substitution parameter (and equals $(1/\sigma) - 1$)

The derivation is not particularly straightforward and is relegated to the appendix to this section.

We want to establish that this is a more general form of the Cobb–Douglas function. This can be done as follows. First, the CES function reduces to the Cobb–Douglas form as $\sigma \to 1$ (that is, $\rho \to 0$). This is also shown in the appendix. The CES function is thus more general because σ can take on any real value. Second, factor shares need not be constant, as factor intensities vary. This follows directly from the fact that σ need not be unity.

[4] K. J. Arrow, H. B. Chenery, B. S. Minhas, and R. M. Solow, "Capital-Labor Substitution and Economic Efficiency," *Review of Economics and Statistics*, Vol. 43, No. 3 (August, 1961), pp. 225–250.

So far we have posited that the σ in the CES function is the same elasticity of substitution that was defined earlier, but we have not yet shown this. If we rewrite the CES function as $X^{-\rho} = \gamma^{-\rho}[\delta K^{-\rho} + (1 - \delta)L^{-\rho}]$ and differentiate, we get

(10.16)
$$-\rho X^{-\rho-1}\frac{\partial X}{\partial L} = \gamma^{-\rho}[-\rho(1 - \delta)L^{-\rho-1}]$$

(10.17)
$$-\rho X^{-\rho-1}\frac{\partial X}{\partial K} = \gamma^{-\rho}(-\rho\, \delta K^{-\rho-1})$$

which can be reduced to

(10.18)
$$\frac{\partial X}{\partial L} = (1 - \delta)\gamma^{-\rho}\left(\frac{X}{L}\right)^{\rho+1}$$

(10.19)
$$\frac{\partial X}{\partial K} = \delta\gamma^{-\rho}\left(\frac{X}{K}\right)^{\rho+1}$$

Therefore,

(10.20)
$$\frac{\partial X/\partial L}{\partial X/\partial K} = \frac{\partial K}{\partial L} = \frac{1 - \delta}{\delta}\left(\frac{K}{L}\right)^{\rho+1}$$

Taking logs,

(10.21)
$$(\rho + 1)\log\left(\frac{K}{L}\right) = -\log\left(\frac{1 - \delta}{\delta}\right) - \log\left(\frac{\partial L}{\partial K}\right)$$

and

(10.22)
$$\frac{d(\log K/L)}{d(\log \partial L/\partial K)} = -\frac{1}{1 + \rho} = -\sigma$$

To show how factor shares vary, we use the equilibrium conditions that

(10.23)
$$\frac{\partial X}{\partial L} = \frac{w}{p} \qquad \frac{\partial X}{\partial K} = \frac{r}{p}$$

Then

(10.24)
$$(1 - \delta)\gamma^{-\rho}\left(\frac{X}{L}\right)^{\rho+1} = \frac{w}{p}$$

(10.25)
$$\delta\gamma^{-\rho}\left(\frac{X}{K}\right)^{\rho+1} = \frac{r}{p}$$

and

(10.26)
$$\frac{wL}{pX} = (1 - \delta)\gamma^{-\rho}\left(\frac{X}{L}\right)^{\rho}$$

(10.27)
$$\frac{rK}{pX} = \delta\gamma^{-\rho}\left(\frac{X}{K}\right)^{\rho}$$

In particular, note that for $\rho > 0$ $(0 < \sigma < 1)$ a decrease in X/L (average productivity of labor) will decrease labor's share, and similarly for capital. This agrees with typical marginal productivity theory. As firms move along the rising part of their marginal cost curves, they use more labor per unit of output. Since prices rise faster than wages, labor's share will fall if the substitution of labor for capital is less than proportional to the change in factor prices. In recessions, output falls more than capital stock, the X/K ratio decreases, and capital's share falls.

The CES function as it was derived has one drawback which the Cobb–Douglas function does not. The former function is derived under the assumption of constant returns to scale, whereas no such restriction is imposed on the latter function. However, the CES function has been modified to take into account the absence of constant returns to scale and also absence of perfect competition, so that is not a serious problem.[6]

There is, however, a more serious question about the applicability of the CES function for business cycle analysis. It posits that fluctuations in factor shares move in the same direction as fluctuations in average productivity (around a trend). Yet virtually all accumulated empirical evidence shows that there is an inverse relationship between labor's share and average productivity of labor. Labor's share is always larger in recessions and smaller in booms. This is a consistent and well-documented relationship; one needs only to look at the percentage change in wages and profits in recession years and boom years to verify this.[7] Yet labor productivity invariably decreases in recessions and increases sharply when the upturn begins. This occurs primarily because of hoarding of labor during recessions. This may be partially due to the quasi-fixed nature of overhead workers,[8] but there appears to be hoarding of production workers as well because of the costs of hiring and firing.[9]

---

[5] These add identically to unity, since

$$(1 - \delta)\gamma^{-\rho}\left(\frac{X}{L}\right)^{\rho} + \delta\gamma^{-\rho}\left(\frac{X}{K}\right)^{\rho} = 1 \rightarrow \gamma^{-\rho}[\delta K^{-\rho} + (1 - \delta)L^{-\rho}] = X^{-\rho}$$

which is identical to the expression given above for the CES function.

[6] See, for instance, P. J. Dhrymes, "Some Extensions and Tests for the CES Class of Production Functions," *Review of Economics and Statistics*, Vol. 47, No. 4 (November, 1965), pp. 357–366.

[7] Figures on income distribution, which are similar although not identical, are presented in Section 10.6.

[8] W. Y. Oi, "Labor as a Quasi-Fixed Factor," *Journal of Political Economy*, Vol. 70, No. 6 (December, 1962), pp. 538–555.

[9] Edwin Kuh, "Cyclical and Secular Labor Productivity in United States Manufacturing," *Review of Economics and Statistics*, Vol. 47, No. 1 (February, 1965), pp. 1–13.

Neither the Cobb–Douglas nor the CES function is suitable for explaining the short-term fluctuations in factor shares and average productivity that are observed to occur. This happens primarily because firms do not immediately adjust their short-run position to the one suggested by static microeconomic theory. There are lags in both hiring and firing of all factor resources as well as in pricing and output decisions.

To integrate these developments into the existing framework of the production function, consider the comparison of $a = (\partial X/\partial L)(L/X)$, labor's share actually received at any point in the business cycle, with $\alpha = \overline{(\partial X/\partial L)(L/X)} = wL/pX$, the long-run equilibrium share under pure competition. Then we would expect the following.

In recessions, $a > \alpha$. X fluctuates more than L.[10] Owing to the costs of hiring and firing, excess labor is kept on the job when output decreases. When it increases again, L changes very little, since men already on the job work again at normal efficiency.

In times of increasing output but some unemployed resources, $a = \alpha$. No hoarding of labor occurs, and there is a negligible upward slope in the marginal cost curve.

In the peaks of full-employment booms, $a < \alpha$. This is due to diminishing marginal returns or profits inflation, that is, a tendency for prices to rise faster than wages. L changes faster than X; this is due both to reduced efficiency of existing workers because of substantial overtime and to lower efficiency of new workers who must be trained and are likely to be of poorer quality.

Graphically the negative relationship between a and capacity utilization (Cp) is shown in Figure 10.1. This can be approximated linearly by the simple function

$$(10.28) \qquad a = d_0 - d_1 Cp \qquad \text{with} \qquad d_0 - d_1 \overline{Cp} = \alpha$$

Similarly for capital's share,

$$(10.29) \qquad b = e_0 + e_1 Cp \qquad \text{with} \qquad e_0 + e_1 \overline{Cp} = \beta$$

These relationships can now be used in the production function. Our analysis at this point is restricted to the Cobb–Douglas function. Although it would be possible to incorporate these modifications into the CES function, this would involve a thorough revision of its derivation, which is not undertaken here.

There are at least two ways to substitute the capacity utilization term into the Cobb–Douglas function. One is to assume

$$(10.30) \qquad X = AL^a K^b e^{\gamma t} = AL^{(d_0 - d_1 Cp)} K^{(e_0 + e_1 Cp)} e^{\gamma t}$$

---

[10] The reader is reminded here that L refers to man-hours demanded, not employment or the labor force.

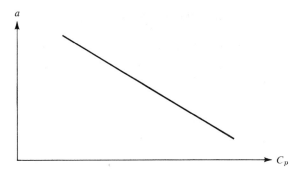

Figure 10.1

Then

(10.31) $\log X = \log A + (d_0 - d_1 Cp) \log L + (e_0 + e_1 Cp) \log K + \gamma t$

This could be linearized to the form

(10.32) $\log X = \log A + \alpha \log L + \beta \log K + Cp(e_1 \log \overline{K} - d_1 \log \overline{L}) + \gamma t$

Another possibility is to assume that

(10.33) $X = AL_u^\alpha K_u^\beta e^{\gamma t} = A(L \cdot Cp)^\alpha (K \cdot Cp)^\beta e^{\gamma t}$

where L_u and K_u are utilized labor and capital. Then

(10.34) $\log X = \log A + \alpha \log(L \cdot Cp) + \beta \log(K \cdot Cp) + \gamma t$

This could also be linearized, but in this case it makes more sense to consider the $L \cdot Cp$ and $K \cdot Cp$ terms themselves as estimates of utilized labor and capital.

A slight variant of the above is to argue that the inclusion of the utilization factor is more important for capital than for labor, since the labor term has already been adjusted by using man-hours. Then we would have

(10.35) $\log X = \log A + \alpha \log L + \beta \log(K \cdot Cp) + \gamma t$

The exact form of the transformation is an empirical question; our results show that the last equation gives the most reasonable results. Regression estimates will be presented in Table 10.1.

One additional improvement was found to be the use of an actual measure of average productivity instead of a time trend for the technological progress factor. For the manufacturing sector, productivity has increased approximately 2.8 percent per year for the period 1947–1949 and 3.6 percent per year for the period 1960 to the present.[11] One might think that the substitution

---

[11] These figures are taken from the *Economic Report of the President*, and represent business cycle averages (averaging done by us).

of one trend for another would make very little difference. However, it turns out to be crucial in specifying the equation correctly.

Since we have chosen the Cobb–Douglas function partially on the basis of its relative simplicity, there may also be some cause for considering the even simpler production function which is linear in the variables instead of in their logarithms. This function can be written

$$(10.36) \qquad X = f + gL + hK + jt$$

Under conditions of pure competition and profit maximization, $\partial X/\partial L = w/p = g$, so $wL/pX = g(L/X)$ and factor shares do vary with factor intensities. However, this function assumes that the elasticity of substitution is infinite. This can be shown by demonstrating that this function is the limiting case of the CES function as $\sigma \to \infty$. This proof is also given in the appendix.

It may seem like an extreme position to state that a change in factor prices will have an infinite effect on the ratio of factors demanded. Although the linear production function may be easier to work with, particularly in combination with complete models, there is little else to recommend it. Almost all empirical studies that have been undertaken with the CES production function show that σ is less than unity.[12] If these results are valid, the linear production function is further away from reality than the Cobb–Douglas function.

However, Nelson has argued that for at least the short run the value of σ makes very little difference in predicting output for reasonable values of α and β.[13] Ignoring higher-order terms, changes in output for a CES production function can be expressed as

$$(10.37) \qquad \dot{X} = \dot{A} + (1 - \delta)\dot{L} + \delta\dot{K} + \tfrac{1}{2}\delta(1 - \delta)\frac{\sigma - 1}{\sigma}(\dot{K} - \dot{L})^2$$

where A is the level of technology and the dots above the variables represent percentage changes.[14] Assume that $\sigma = \tfrac{1}{2}$, $\delta = \tfrac{1}{3}$, and $\dot{K} - \dot{L} = 0.03$. Then the yearly error in $\dot{X}$ that would occur by assuming $\sigma = 1$ (the Cobb–Douglas function would be

$$(10.38) \qquad \frac{1}{2}\cdot\frac{1}{3}\cdot\frac{2}{3} - \left(\frac{\frac{1}{2}}{\frac{1}{2}}\right)\cdot(0.03)^2 = -0.0001$$

compared to a yearly growth rate of about 0.04. Even over a 20-year period this would give a cumulative error of only 5 percent in the prediction of the change in output. Furthermore, this error remains small as $\sigma \to \infty$.

---

[12] See, for example, the studies cited by Arrow, Chenery, Minhas, and Solow and by Dhrymes.

[13] R. R. Nelson, "The CES Production Function and Economic Growth Projections," *Review of Economics and Statistics*, Vol. 47, No. 3 (August, 1965), pp. 326–328.

[14] This formula and the following example are taken from M. Nerlove, *Notes on Recent Empirical Studies of the CES and Related Production Functions*, Stanford: Stanford University, Technical Report 13, July, 1965, pp. 2–3. Nerlove's paper compares the results of several recent estimates of CES functions.

The question of whether the linear production function gives reasonable results can thus be treated primarily as an empirical one. For this reason estimates are given for both the linear and Cobb–Douglas production functions in Table 10.1. At first glance the results might appear to be similar. However, note that in the linear production functions for manufacturing, the capital stock term has an incorrect negative sign in one equation and is not significantly different from zero (at the 5 percent level) in the other. The Cp term also has an incorrect positive sign.[15] Both these difficulties are eliminated when the Cobb–Douglas functions are used. The reader might also note that the comparable $\bar{R}^2$ are almost identical, yet the nature of the functions are quite different. This is a striking example of the relative worthlessness of $\bar{R}^2$ as a measure for selecting the "best" equation when other criteria are not also considered.

Both ordinary least squares (OLS) and two-stage least squares (TSLS) estimates are presented for some of the equations, since the results differ considerably. This can be seen from the equations in Table 10.1. Results are also included for both the manufacturing and the nonmanufacturing sectors. Cyclical fluctuations are not as important in the latter sector; furthermore, much greater difficulties exist in measuring capacity utilization for many areas of nonmanufacturing. For these reasons this term has been omitted in that sector, and as a result the functions are somewhat simpler.

The logarithmic forms of the production functions suggest that there are constant returns to scale in manufacturing and increasing returns to scale in nonmanufacturing industries. These results are in agreement with other studies, in which the production functions were estimated in somewhat different forms.[16] The elasticity of almost unity for the man-hours term in the latter equation suggests that firms are operating on the constant part of their average variable cost curves, which is quite a reasonable finding for regulated and trade industries.

In the form in which the production functions are written, it appears that output is determined by the size of the labor force, capital stock, and the state of technology. If all factor resources are being fully utilized, these functions are used to determine maximum output for each sector. If the economy is not operating at maximum output, actual output is determined by aggregate demand. These production functions then determine the number of man-hours demanded for a given output, capital stock, and technology. For this reason these functions are sometimes rewritten with utilized labor (or man-hours) as the dependent variable and are known as *labor-requirements* functions. Although this form of the function may better emphasize its use

---

[15] If we substitute $d_0 - d_1 Cp$ in place of g in the function $X = f + gL + hK + jt$ and linearize, the Cp term enters with a negative sign.

[16] See, for example, R. G. Bodkin and L. R. Klein, "Nonlinear Estimation of Aggregate Production Functions," *Review of Economics and Statistics*, Vol. 49, No. 1 (February, 1967), pp. 28–44.

TABLE 10.1   ESTIMATION OF VARIOUS PRODUCTION FUNCTIONS[a]

	$\bar{R}^2$
(OLS) $X_m = -3.77 + 3.074(Nh)_m - 0.1195(K_m Cp) + 9.846Cp + 13.08t$ (1.356) (0.0494) (2.653) (0.87)	0.975

(OLS) $X_m = -12.84 + 4.415(Nh)_m + 0.0608(K_m Cp) + 4.469Cp$
    (1.087)   (0.0353)   (1.911)
  $+ 10.54\text{prod}$
  (0.52)
	0.983

(OLS) $\ln X_m = 0.567 + 0.7046 \ln (Nh)_m + 0.2803 \ln (K_m Cp)$
    (0.1327)   (0.0524)
  $+ 0.6273\text{prod} - 0.0198 \ln Cp$
  (0.0368)   (0.1225)
	0.984

(OLS) $\ln X_m = 0.568 + 0.6874 \ln (Nh)_m + 0.2828 \ln (K_m Cp)$
    (0.0780)   (0.0511)
  $+ 0.6317\text{prod}$
  (0.0249)
	0.984

(15.14) (TSLS) $\ln X_m = 0.645 + 0.7547 \ln (Nh)_m + 0.2402 \ln (K_m Cp)$
    (0.0889)   (0.0574)
  $+ 0.881\text{prod}$
  (0.037)
	0.984

(OLS) $X_n = -4.49 + 6.287(Nh)_n + 0.1680K_n + 0.2353t$ (1.093) (0.0611) (3.3356)	0.979
(OLS) $X_n = -4.71 + 5.683(Nh)_n + 0.1324K_n + 2.679\text{prod}$ (1.087) (0.0265) (1.414)	0.980

(OLS) $\ln X_n = 1.002 + 0.7684 \ln (Nh)_n + 0.2893 \ln K_n$
    (0.1535)   (0.0332)
  $+ 0.104\text{prod}$
  (0.050)
	0.980

(15.19) (TSLS) $\ln X_n = 0.270 + 0.9897 \ln (Nh)_n + 0.2755 \ln K_n + 0.082\text{prod}$ (0.2108) (0.0371) (0.084)	0.976

[a] X, gross output originating, billions of 1958 dollars; N, employment, millions; h, hours worked per week, 40 hours = 1.00; K, capital stock, billions of constant dollars; t, time trend; prod, productivity trend (see the text); Cp, index of capacity utilization, percent; m, manufacturing sector; n, nonmanufacturing sector.

and help to delineate the flow of causality better in a complete model, it has little to recommend it from an empirical point of view. If maximum likelihood methods of estimation were used, the choice of dependent variable would be irrelevant. However, when two-stage least squares is used, the transformed results are drastically inferior; this has been confirmed by repeated trials on our part. The main problem arises because of the possible ambiguity of the sign of the $K \cdot Cp$ term. If we transform

$$(10.39) \qquad \log X = \log a + \alpha \log L + \beta \log(K \cdot Cp) + \gamma t$$

to

$$(10.40) \qquad \log L = \frac{1}{\alpha}[\log X - \log a - \beta \log(K \cdot Cp) - \gamma t]$$

the $\log(K \cdot Cp)$ term should clearly have a negative sign. However, a rise in X will lead to a rise in Cp; since L and X are positively correlated, this often leads to a spurious positive correlation between L and $K \cdot Cp$. If total capital stock is used instead of utilized stock this problem disappears, but the overall equation is much poorer. Labor requirements functions are estimated by Kuh in the Brookings model;[17] he uses total capital stock but also includes employment lagged one quarter, which sometimes appears with a coefficient greater than unity. This does not seem to be a satisfactory result, although Kuh claims it is not necessary to "strain" to get a "sensible interpretation" for the value of this lagged term.

These production functions, and especially the one for the manufacturing sector, can also be used to derive an index of capacity utilization (Cp), which is itself used together with the capital stock as one of the independent variables. Cp can be defined as

$$(10.41) \qquad Cp = \frac{\text{actual output}}{\text{maximum output}}$$

where maximum output is calculated by using the estimated values of a, α, β, and γ in the function

$$(10.42) \qquad \log X = \log a + \alpha \log L + \beta \log(K \cdot Cp) + \gamma t$$

but this time inserting values for the total labor force (possibly adjusted for some frictional unemployment) and fully utilized capital stock. Such a method has also been used for CES production functions. This method works well for the entire economy provided good figures are available for existing capital stock. For individual sectors of the economy, it is necessary to allocate the labor force among these various sectors in the proportion in which they would be hired at full employment. This allocation is likely to shift over time, so one must establish peak periods and interpolate the allocation between these peaks. But this introduces a problem that exists when the peaks do not represent true maximum output.

The other principal method of measuring maximum output is simply to connect peak points by trend lines which then represent maximum output at

---

[17] E. Kuh, "Income Distribution and Employment over the Business Cycle," in J. S. Duesenberry, G. Fromm, L. R. Klein, and E. Kuh, eds., *The Brookings Quarterly Econometric Model of the United States Economy* (Chicago: Rand McNally, 1965), p. 244.

other points in the cycle. This used to be the method used to estimate the Wharton School capacity index. The obvious problem with this approach is that some of the peak points will not represent true maximum output. This was particularly true of the 1959 peak in the postwar U.S. economy. An adjustment was needed in this case for several industries.[18] In any case, the measurement of maximum output still remains a difficult and somewhat hazy area of quantitative economics.[19]

APPENDIX to Section 10.1

In this appendix we first derive the CES production function. Then we show how certain specified values of σ lead to special cases of the function usually known by other names.[20] In particular,

$\sigma = 1$ gives a Cobb–Douglas function
$\sigma = \infty$ gives a linear production function (straight-line isoquants)
$\sigma = 0$ gives a fixed-proportion or Leontief function (right-angle isoquants)

As stated in the text, the CES function is derived from the equation

$$\log(X/L) = \log a + \sigma \log w$$

Since $X = wL + rK$,

$$w = \frac{X}{L} - r\frac{K}{L} = \frac{X}{L} - \frac{dX}{dK}\frac{K}{L}$$

Therefore,

$$\log\left(\frac{X}{L}\right) = \log a + \sigma \log\left(\frac{X}{L} - \frac{dX}{dK}\frac{K}{L}\right)$$

$$\frac{X}{L} = a\left(\frac{X}{L} - \frac{dX}{dK}\frac{K}{L}\right)^{\sigma}$$

$$\left(\frac{X}{L}\right)^{1/\sigma} = a^{1/\sigma}\frac{X}{L} - a^{1/\sigma}\frac{K}{L}\frac{d(X/L)}{d(K/L)}$$

Therefore,

$$\frac{d(X/L)}{d(K/L)} = -\frac{a^{-1/\sigma}(X/L)^{1/\sigma}}{K/L} + \frac{X/L}{K/L}$$

---

[18] For a full description of this method and the adjustments made, see L. R. Klein and R. S. Preston, "The Measurement of Capacity Utilization," *American Economic Review*, Vol. 57, No. 1 (March, 1967), pp. 34–58.

[19] For a comparison of several indicators of capacity utilization, see A. Phillips, "An Appraisal of Measures of Capacity," *American Economic Review Papers and Proceedings*, Vol. 53, No. 2 (May, 1963), pp. 275–292.

[20] The analysis here follows Arrow, Chenery, Minhas, and Solow, *op. cit.* An alternative and somewhat more general proof can be found in Murray Brown, *On The Theory and Measurement of Technological Change* (Cambridge: Cambridge University Press, 1966), appendix A.

or

$$\frac{d(X/L)}{X/L - a^{-1/\sigma}(X/L)^{1/\sigma}} = \frac{d(K/L)}{K/L}$$

The left side can be expanded to

$$\frac{d(X/L)}{X/L} + \frac{[a^{-1/\sigma}(X/L)^{\frac{1}{\sigma}-2}]\, d(X/L)}{1 - a^{-1/\sigma}(X/L)^{\frac{1}{\sigma}-1}}$$

To integrate the second term on the left side, let

$$1 - a^{-1/\sigma}\left(\frac{X}{L}\right)^{\frac{1}{\sigma}-1} = z$$

Then

$$-a^{-1/\sigma}\left(\frac{1}{\sigma} - 1\right)\left(\frac{X}{L}\right)^{\frac{1}{\sigma}-2} d\left(\frac{X}{L}\right) = dz$$

in which case

$$\int \frac{1}{X/L} d\left(\frac{X}{L}\right) - \int \frac{\sigma}{1-\sigma}\frac{dz}{z} = -\int \frac{1}{K/L} d\left(\frac{K}{L}\right)$$

$$\ln\left(\frac{X}{L}\right) - \frac{\sigma}{1-\sigma}\ln\left[1 - a^{-1/\sigma}\left(\frac{X}{L}\right)^{\frac{1}{\sigma}-1}\right] = \ln\left(\frac{K}{L}\right) - \frac{\sigma}{1-\sigma}\ln\beta$$

Therefore,

$$\frac{K}{L} = \frac{X}{L}\left[1 - a^{-1/\sigma}\left(\frac{X}{L}\right)^{\frac{1}{\sigma}-1}\right]^{-(\sigma/1-\sigma)}\beta^{(\sigma/1-\sigma)}$$

or

$$\frac{K}{L} = \frac{X}{L}\left[1 - \alpha\left(\frac{X}{L}\right)^{\rho}\right]^{-1/\rho}\beta^{1/\rho}$$

where $\rho = (1/\sigma) - 1$ (as in the text) $\alpha = a^{-1/\sigma}$, and β is a constant of integration. Therefore,

$$\beta\left(\frac{K}{L}\right)^{-\rho} = \left(\frac{X}{L}\right)^{-\rho} - \alpha$$

$$\left(\frac{X}{L}\right)^{-\rho} = \beta\left(\frac{K}{L}\right)^{-\rho} + \alpha$$

Therefore,

$$\left(\frac{X}{L}\right) = \left[\beta\left(\frac{K}{L}\right)^{-\rho} + \alpha\right]^{-1/\rho}$$

$$X = (L^{-\rho})^{-1/\rho}\left[\beta\left(\frac{K}{L}\right)^{-\rho} + \alpha\right]^{-1/\rho}$$

so that

$$X = [\beta K^{-\rho} + \alpha L^{-\rho}]^{-1/\rho}$$

If we choose an efficiency parameter γ and let $\delta = \alpha\gamma^{\rho-1}$, the function can be rewritten

$$X = \gamma[\delta K^{-\rho} + (1 - \delta)L^{-\rho}]^{-1/\rho}$$

as in the text. However, this last step is not necessary to derive a CES function.

To show what happens when $\sigma = 1$, we can integrate the function

$$\log\left(\frac{X}{L}\right) = \log a + \log w$$

The method is identical but the algebra is much simpler when $\sigma = 1$. We have (following the above derivation)

$$\frac{X}{L} = a\left(\frac{X}{L} - \frac{dX}{dK}\frac{K}{L}\right)$$

$$\frac{d(X/L)}{d(K/L)} = -\frac{a^{-1}(X/L)}{K/L} + \frac{X/L}{K/L}$$

Therefore

$$\frac{d(X/L)}{(X/L)[1 - (1/a)]} = \frac{d(K/L)}{K/L}$$

$$\frac{a}{a-1}\ln\left(\frac{X}{L}\right) = \ln\left(\frac{K}{L}\right) + \frac{a}{a-1}\ln\beta$$

where β is again a constant of integration. Therefore,

$$\left(\frac{X}{L}\right)^{\frac{a}{a-1}} = \frac{K}{L}\cdot\beta^{\frac{a}{a-1}}$$

$$\frac{X}{L} = \beta\left(\frac{K}{L}\right)^{(a-1)/a}$$

$$X = \beta L^{1/a}K^{(a-1)/a}$$

which is the Cobb–Douglas function with constant returns to scale.

The fixed-proportion or Leontief function is even simpler, because there $\sigma = 0$. Thus we have

$$\log\left(\frac{X}{L}\right) = \log a \quad \text{or} \quad \frac{X}{L} = a \quad X = aL \text{ for } K > K_0$$

We can also write

$$\log\left(\frac{X}{K}\right) = \log b \quad \text{or} \quad \frac{X}{K} = b \quad X = bK \text{ for } L > L_0$$

This simply means that when there is excess capital, output is uniquely determined by labor, and vice versa. This gives rise to a right-angled isoquant for which profit-maximizing firms produce only at the corner. A change in factor prices for a given output will then have no effect on the ratio of factors demanded. There is no substitutability of one factor for another when their relative prices change.

The same method of integration cannot be used as $\sigma \to \infty$. However, this presents no particular problem. Since $\rho = (1/\sigma) - 1$, $\sigma \to \infty$ implies that $\rho \to -1$ and thus $X = (\beta K^{-\rho} + \alpha L^{-\rho})^{-1/\rho}$ simply becomes $X = \beta K + \alpha L$, the linear production function.

10.2   OTHER DETERMINANTS OF EMPLOYMENT AND UNEMPLOYMENT

The variable representing the demand for labor in the production function is man-hours rather than employment, because the former more closely represents the actual amount of labor input demanded. Thus to explain employment (and unemployment) it is necessary to develop a separate function explaining hours worked (for example, per week). Although in general hours and employment will move together over the cycle, there are several distinct features of an hours function that need to be explained.

1. Hours worked can serve as a much better buffer to changes in output than can employment. When the level of output changes, hours can be adjusted much more easily and at much less cost than employment. A large part of this is due to the additional costs associated with hiring and firing. If increases or decreases in output continue, and the expectation increases that these changes are permanent, then changes in employment are likely to replace changes in hours. Thus hours worked are likely to be a function of the change in output as well as the level of output.

2. When output increases, the decision of whether to increase man-hours by hiring more men or working the existing employees more hours depends largely on the relative costs of each alternative. The lower the wage rate is, *cet. par.*, the more overtime will be used, because the additional cost of extra hours will be relatively lower. Thus hours are likely to be negatively correlated with the wage rate. Offsetting this somewhat may be the fact that as the economy approaches full employment and wage rates rise at a faster rate (as explained in Section 10.3), it may be very hard to find additional skilled workers, so that some businesses find it necessary to increase overtime even at high wage rates. But this problem can be met by making hours worked positively related to capacity utilization as well as negatively related to wage rates.

3. The negative relationship between hours and wage rates may also be partially explained by the income effect. As wage rates increase, workers may prefer to take part of their extra income in leisure (less overtime). It is not possible to distinguish statistically between these two possible effects of the wage rate on hours. However, even if this entire relationship is due to the income effect, it is a small effect; a 10 percent increase in the wage rate, *cet. par.*, would result in a decrease in the work week of slightly less than one hour.

We have the following estimated sectoral equations:
Manufacturing:

(15.16) $h_m = 0.797 + 0.00076X_m + 0.00126\Delta X_m + 0.1906Cp$
                          (0.00021) (0.00044) (0.0423)

                          $- 0.0126wr_m$ $\bar{R}^2 = 0.711$
                          (0.0050)

Nonmanufacturing:

(15.20) $h_n = 1.186 + 0.0155Cp - 0.0391wr_n$ $\bar{R}^2 = 0.963$
                   (0.0235) (0.0011)

where h = index of hours worked per week, 40 hours = 1.00
      X = gross output originating, billions of 1958 dollars
      Cp = index of capacity utilization, percent
      wr = yearly wage rate, thousands of dollars per year
      m = manufacturing sector
      n = nonmanufacturing sector

As is readily apparent, the functions are quite different. This is due mainly to the cyclical nature of hours worked (and output) in the manufacturing sector and the absence of cyclical fluctuations in nonmanufacturing hours worked. This latter category, consisting mainly of trade, regulated industries, and service industries, shows virtually no fluctuations over the cycle but rather a slight long-run downward trend. The small (nonsignificant) Cp term undoubtedly represents the fact that as the economy nears full employment, it is harder to find additional workers in both the manufacturing and non-manufacturing sectors, and thus workers in both sectors are more likely to work overtime.

So far we have explained employment of wage and salary earners in the private nonfarm sector. Several other types of employment must be considered before the rate of unemployment (Un) is determined, by the identity

(10.43) $$Un = \frac{N_L - N_s - N_g - N_f - N_e}{N_L}$$

where Un = unemployment rate, percent
      N_L = civilian labor force
      N_s = number of nonagricultural self-employed
      N_g = number of government workers, excluding military
      N_f = number of agricultural workers (employers and employees)
      N_e = number of employees in the private nonfarm sector

The number of government workers, the number of farm workers, and the number of self-employed are considered to be exogenous. The rationale for the first choice is clear; the number of government employees depends on government purchases of goods and services, which are also exogenous. But it is sometimes argued that there is an endogenous component to fluctuations in the number of self-employed and farmers. A countercyclical pattern has been suggested on the grounds that relatively more of these workers will leave their present occupations and seek new job opportunities in times of full employment. However, no such support for this hypothesis is revealed

**TABLE 10.2   CYCLICAL PATTERNS IN THE NUMBER OF
SELF-EMPLOYED AND AGRICULTURAL WORKERS**

Period	Average Annual Change in Self-Employed, %	Average Annual Change in Agricultural Workers, %	Average Annual Unemployment, %
1947–1953	− 1.6	− 3.8	4.0
1953–1957	3.4	− 1.3	4.3
1957–1963	3.4	− 3.8	5.8

in Table 10.2. Although the countercyclical argument asserts that the change in employment for self-employed and other agricultural workers should have been almost the same for the periods 1947–1953 and 1953–1957 and less for the period 1957–1963, the actual figures present a different picture. Other exogenous and institutional factors are necessary to explain movements in these employment figures, because there does not appear to be any relationship between these figures and aggregate economic activity. When the year to year changes are considered, the same pattern emerges. In fact, farm employment dropped 6.1 percent in 1958, although overall unemployment rose from 4.3 to 6.8 percent, and this in spite of the fact that farm income rose almost 10 percent in 1958.

However, there is a definite pattern to the way in which growth in the labor force corresponds to the overall unemployment rate. This can best be seen by examining the increase in the civilian *labor force* (not employment) in the years following each postwar recession, as shown in Table 10.3. Except for the shortage of labor that occurred during the Korean War, when the civilian labor force slightly decreased, there is a very definite inverse relationship

TABLE 10.3   CYCLICAL PATTERNS IN CIVILIAN LABOR FORCE

Business Cycle Troughs	Increase in Labor Force First Four Quarters After Recession, %	Increase in Labor Force First Eight Quarters %	Average Un First Four Quarters %	Average Un Next Four Quarters, %
1949.4	3.57	4.10[a]	5.3	3.3
1954.2	2.66	6.48	5.1	4.2
1958.1	1.49	3.37	6.7	5.3
1961.1	1.18	2.26	6.4	5.6

[a] Growth somewhat lowered because of many Korean War draftees.

between the rate of unemployment and the growth of the labor force. Furthermore, it should be noted that while the civilian labor force decreased during the Korean War, the total labor force rose much more rapidly than usual. Thus in a function explaining participation in the labor force, it is more reasonable to express the participation rate (relative to population) as a function both of unemployment and the relative size of the armed forces. This leads to the general functional form

$$(10.44) \qquad \frac{N_L^M}{N} = f\left(Un, \frac{N_g^M}{N}\right)$$

where the superscript M denotes that the armed forces are included in both the labor force and government employee figures.

The relationship between participation rates and unemployment can be refined a little more. As unemployment gets very low, people enter the labor force at an increasing rate. The most obvious example of this was during World War II, when housewives and semiretired people entered the labor force. As unemployment gets very large, the participation rate will converge asymptotically to some minimum rate that will exist even with widespread unemployment. Additional changes in the unemployment rate when it is already quite large will have almost no effect on the participation rate. This nonlinear relationship can be represented by a positive correlation between the participation rate and the reciprocal of unemployment. Finally, there has been a slight negative trend in the participation rate in the postwar period as students stay in school longer and workers retire earlier. The estimated relationship is

$$(15.23) \qquad \frac{N_L^M}{N} = 0.4255 + 0.0169 \frac{1}{(0.0095)\,\frac{1}{4}\sum_{i=0}^{3}(Un)_{-i}}$$

$$+ 0.1139(N_g^M/N) - 0.000478t \qquad \bar{R}^2 = 0.952$$
$$ (0.1020) (0.000020)$$

where N_L^M = total labor force, millions
$ N_g^M$ = size of armed forces, millions
$ N$ = population, millions
$ Un$ = percentage of unemployment
$ t$ = time trend

Although this type of function has not been included in most of the econometric models currently available,[21] it is of considerable importance.

---

[21] The Brookings model might have been a notable exception to this statement; a whole chapter is entitled, "The Labor Force and Marriages as Endogenous Factors." In this chapter, S. Lebergott disaggregates the labor force into several age–sex classifications and develops participation ratio functions for each of them. However, as explained on p. 514, these functions were dropped from the form of the model actually used for simulations, and predetermined

It should be noted that the unemployment rate, as high as it was in 1962 and 1963, would have been 1.1 percent higher if the labor force had grown at the same rate as it did in 1959–1960, and would have been 4.2 percent higher, or, almost 10 percent, if the labor force had grown at the same rate as it did in 1955–1956. These are not negligible magnitudes.[22]

10.3   WAGE RATES AND PHILLIPS CURVES

In Sections 10.1 and 10.2 we showed how aggregate supply conditions determine the amount of employment and unemployment as well as setting ceilings on production and employment. In the remaining sections of this chapter we discuss the determination of factor shares and fluctuations in income distribution over the cycle. Any such examination needs to include an explanation of the wage bill, defined as employment times the wage rate. Having explained the former, we now turn to an investigation of the latter.

The wage rate functions developed here, which are similar to those in use elsewhere, are basically disequilibrium functions that relate changes in wage rates to excess demand in the labor market. If we were considering an equilibrium model, wages would be determined by the intersection of demand and supply curves for labor, such as shown in Figure 10.2.

In this case, shifts in either the demand or supply curve for labor could change wages. If, on the other hand, changes in the wage rate were related

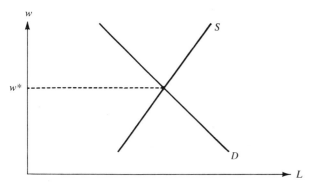

Figure 10.2

values of labor force participation ratios were used instead. A similar function can be found in L. R. Klein, "A Postwar Quarterly Model: Descriptions and Applications," in *Models of Income Determination*, Studies in Income and Wealth, Vol. 28, (Princeton, N.J.: Princeton University Press for NBER, 1964). However, the labor-force equation, like some of the other supply side equations, was always suppressed, and predetermined estimates were substituted in its place.

[22] T. F. Dernberg and K. T. Strand supply an independent estimate of "over 9 percent" unemployment in 1962–1963 if earlier growth rates of the labor force had continued, in their "Hidden Unemployment 1953–1962: A Quantitative Analysis by Age and Sex," *American Economic Review*, Vol. 56, No. 1 (March, 1966), pp. 71–95.

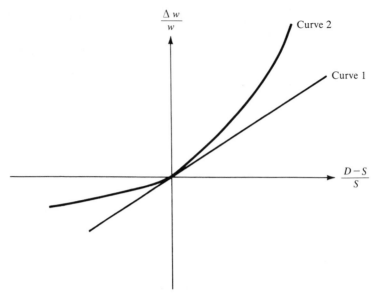

Figure 10.3

to the excess demand for labor, it would not be necessary to specify whether the demand curve or supply curve for labor has shifted.[23] Graphically this can be represented as shown in Figure 10.3. In this diagram curve 1 shows that percentage changes in the wage rate are proportional to the excess demand for labor. Curve 2 shows a nonlinear relationship which suggests that as the excess demand for labor becomes negative, wages do not change very much.

It should be noted that an excess demand for labor of zero certainly does not mean zero unemployment; instead it means that the number of vacant jobs is equal to the number of unemployed. A close relationship between changes in excess demand for labor and changes in unemployment exists only when excess demand is negative. Then for each further decrease in the excess demand for labor, there is likely to be the same increase in unemployment. However, the result is much different if there is positive excess demand for labor. An increase in the excess demand for labor may result in no change at all in unemployment, unless the job that is demanded can be filled by someone who is currently unemployed. As the excess demand for labor continues to increase, it will lower unemployment less and less. No matter how great the excess demand for labor becomes, unemployment can never be less than zero. This relationship between the excess demand for labor

---

[13] The exposition in this section follows R. G. Lipsey, "The Relation Between Unemployment and the Rate of Change of Money Wage Rates in the United Kingdom, 1862–1957: A Further Analysis," *Economica*, Vol. 27 (February, 1960), pp. 1–31.

and unemployment is shown in Figure 10.4. Combining this with *either* curve 1 or curve 2 in Fig. 10.3 gives a nonlinear relationship between *changes* in the wage rate and the *level* of unemployment. This relationship, as shown in Figure 10.5, is known as a *Phillips curve*.[24]

Phillips has used this curve to determine that for the United Kingdom a rate of $5\frac{1}{2}$ percent unemployment is needed if wages are to be held steady, and a rate of $2\frac{1}{2}$ percent unemployment is needed if prices are to be held steady; this would mean that wages would rise by the same percentage as productivity increases, estimated to be 2 percent per year. Samuelson and Solow have estimated a similar curve for the United States and have found a more pessimistic figure of $5\frac{1}{2}$ percent unemployment necessary for price stability, assuming that productivity increases at $2\frac{1}{2}$ percent annually.[25]

Phillips originally estimated such a function for the period 1861–1913. He then claimed that the same relationship which was fitted for that period did a very good job explaining wages during 1948–1957, if unemployment was lagged seven months. From this he drew the conclusion that since this relationship has remained approximately constant since 1861, the emergence of unions has had virtually no effect on the determination of wage bargains. This view has been criticized by Lipsey, who claims that a function estimated for the period 1923–1939 and 1948–1957 explains wages much better.

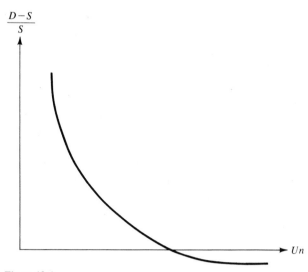

Figure 10.4

---

[24] A. W. Phillips, "The Relation Between Unemployment and the Rate of Change of Money Wage Rates in the United Kingdom, 1861–1957," *Economica*, Vol. 25 (November, 1958), pp. 283–299.

[25] P. A. Samuelson and R. M. Solow, "Analytical Aspects of Anti-Inflation Policy," *American Economic Review Papers and Proceedings*, Vol. 50, No. 2 (May, 1960), pp. 177–194.

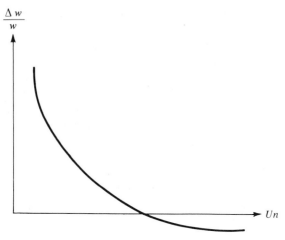

Figure 10.5

Furthermore, Lipsey shows that least-squares regression estimates for various periods are significantly different, thus rejecting the hypothesis that the same function holds for the entire period.

There are several refinements to the Phillips curve which are introduced at this point.

1. Wage decisions are based on *previous* levels of relevant economic variables. Wage bargainers do not change their stated demands because of current movements in economic indicators, and their demands are not based on what they think future economic activity will be.

2. Changes in prices are at least as important as unemployment in determining changes in the wage rate. This is neglected in the Phillips curve.

3. Lagged changes in wages are negatively correlated with present changes in wage rates. Since contracts are based on previous performance of the economy, they are likely to fall short of the actual equilibrium level in years after recessions and are likely to exceed this equilibrium level in years following a rapid increase in economic activity or prices. Part of the discrepancy which thus arises will be corrected in the following year.

4. The degree of nonlinearity between changes in the wage rate and unemployment is an empirical question and needs to be examined further. The relationship $\Delta w = f(1/Un, 1/Un^2)$ suggested by Lipsey may not be the best empirical choice.

5. Profits have often been suggested as another important determinant of the change in wages. This point needs serious consideration. However, it ought to be cleared up at the outset that there is no sense talking about the role of profits in determining the change in the wage rate until the rest of the function is properly specified. So this point is considered last.

Since wage bargains are usually determined yearly (although some important contracts cover a multiyear span), the change in wages should cover a yearly span, so that $(w_t - w_{t-4}) = f(Un, \Delta p, \ldots)$. Some economists have suggested that there is no lag between changes in the independent variables and changes in wage rates. However, this does not follow from the way in which wage bargains are determined. Furthermore, some empirical experimentation strongly suggests that variables lagged up to a year explain the change in wage rates better than do unlagged variables. Change in wage rates are found to depend on the average level of unemployment over the past year but not including the present quarter. Bargaining talks ordinarily take several weeks to several months, and demands during the talks are not changed on the basis of new developments in economic activity during the course of bargaining.

Changes in the price level are another very important determinant of changes in wage rates. For one thing, automatic cost of living clauses are included in many contracts; this is probably of greater importance in manufacturing than in other sectors of the economy. More important, wage earners will bargain to retain their share of national income, particularly if it has been eroded by rising prices. The money illusion of workers suggested by Keynes is largely absent in today's bargaining.[26] One of the most commonly heard criticisms of wage–price guidelines is that they ought to be adjusted upward to include price increases. Although such a move would destroy the usefulness of such guidelines, the suggestion does convey the importance workers attach to the reduction of their relative position through inflation. During the period February 1965–February 1966, the average worker found that his take-home pay in real terms had not increased at all, even though real national income had grown by over 4 percent; it was precisely this type of situation that prompted the strong demand for large wage increases starting in latter 1966.

Schultze and Tryon[27] have suggested that wage increases based on last year's unemployment and price changes are likely to "overshoot" their mark, so that large wage increases will be followed by gains that are smaller than usual. They found a strong tendency for this negative lagged term in all sectors of the economy except regulated industries, where it was negative but not significant. For overall analysis of the business cycle, this is an important finding, because it may tend to amplify cyclical tendencies that exist elsewhere in the economy.

We now return to the problem of the nonlinearity of the unemployment term. As originally formulated, this nonlinearity arose from the fact that unemployment decreases more and more slowly as the excess demand for labor increases. This idea can be expressed another way. Generally speaking,

---

[26] Lipsey has noted that the importance of the price variable in the wage equation has increased markedly in the postwar period.

[27] C. L. Schultze and J. S. Tryon, "Prices and Wages," in *The Brookings Model..., op. cit.,* p. 327.

employers prefer to hire young (but settled) married men. This group can best be approximated (given the available statistics) by married men age 25 to 34. Call the unemployment rate for this group U^*. The relationship between Un and U^* is shown in Figure 10.6. When overall unemployment is high, the rate for each group is about the same, although $Un - U^*$ is generally positive. However, as unemployment decreases and a "tighter" labor market starts to develop, almost all workers in the U^* group are hired and the gap between this group and the rest of the labor force widens.

Using this form of the nonlinear relationship and including the other terms previously suggested gives the following empirical estimate for the manufacturing sector:

$$(15.17) \quad wr_m - (wr_m)_{-4} = 0.050 + \underset{(0.0234)}{0.1481} \frac{1}{4} \sum_{i=1}^{4} (Un - U^*)_{-i}$$

$$+ \underset{(0.521)}{4.824}(p_{c-1} - p_{c-4}) - \underset{(0.0705)}{0.1946}[(wr_m)_{-4} - (wr_m)_{-8}]$$

$$\bar{R}^2 = 0.657$$

where wr_m = yearly wage rate in the manufacturing sector, thousands of dollars per year

$\quad p_c$ = implicit deflator of consumer purchases, 1958 = 1.00

$\quad Un$ = overall percentage of unemployment

$\quad U^*$ = percentage of unemployment, married males age 25 to 34

As has been previously noted for other functions presented in this chapter, the nonmanufacturing sector does not follow the same general cyclical pattern as does the manufacturing sector; this is also true for the wage equation. It is found that changes in nonmanufacturing wages follow manufacturing wages and consumer prices and also have a tendency to be negatively

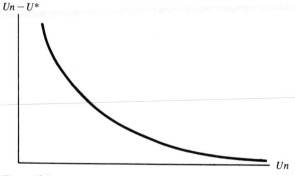

Figure 10.6

correlated with the previous year's wage changes. This equation is

$$(15.21) \quad wr_n - (wr_n)_{-4} = 0.176 + 0.3019[wr_m - (wr_m)_{-4}]$$
$$(0.1286)$$

$$+ 1.298[(p_c)_{-1} - (p_c)_{-4}] - 0.4741[(wr_n)_{-4} - (wr_n)_{-8}]$$
$$(0.777) \qquad\qquad\qquad (0.1154)$$

$$\bar{R}^2 = 0.330$$

We must still explain the relationship between $Un - U^*$ and Un as shown in Figure 10.6. For low values of Un the gap between Un and U^* will narrow, because as Un goes to zero, so will U^*. However, for most of the sample period, the relationship between $Un - U^*$ and Un shown above is of the form

$$(Un - U^*)Un = k + b(Un)$$

$$Un - U^* = b + \frac{k}{Un}$$

$$U^* = Un - b - \frac{k}{Un}$$

The actual estimated equation is

$$(15.22) \qquad U^* = -5.42 + 1.231Un + 8.929 \frac{1}{\frac{1}{4}\sum_{i=0}^{3}(Un)_{-i}}$$
$$(0.083) \qquad (2.939)$$

$$+ 0.3245 \frac{1}{4}\sum_{i=1}^{4}(U^*)_{-i} \qquad \bar{R}^2 = 0.929$$
$$(0.0899)$$

The approximate shape of this empirically estimated function is given in Figure 10.7. Note that the spread between Un and U^* starts to decrease for Un less than 3 percent. This reflects the fact that as unemployment goes to zero, U^*, and hence $Un - U^*$, must also go to zero.

We now consider the role of profits in the wage equation. The basic argument as stated by Schultze and Tryon is that "profits play an independent role ... an increase in profits above some long-run 'normal' for the industry is quite likely to find its way into increased wages."[28] The second half of their statement is correct, but the first half is not. The appropriateness of the statement hinges on what is meant by "normal" profits. If profits are increased by expanding output and holding prices steady, capital's share ought to increase at the same rate as labor's share (unless the process started in a recession when labor was being hoarded, in which case labor's share was above equilibrium). However, if profits are increased through profits inflation or through diminishing returns (demand-pull) inflation, then wage

---

[28] Schultze and Tryon, *op. cit.*, p. 315.

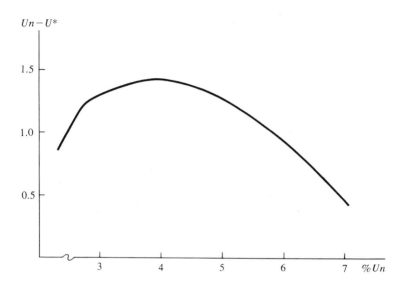

Figure 10.7

earners will bargain for a share of the increased profits. In other words, wage earners will bargain for a share of the increased profits *when these profits have risen through an increase in prices*; otherwise they will not. This relationship is completely captured by the price term in the wage equation. Profits, when added, make no net contribution and in fact have a slightly negative sign in the regressions we computed.

Since this conclusion is of considerable importance for business cycle theory, it may be of interest to examine some of the other work in this area. We can reject out of hand those studies which correlate the change in wages only with profits. It is true that there is a positive zero-order (that is, simple) correlation between the change in wages and both the change in profits and the level of profit rates. But this does not take into account the collinearity between profits and unemployment and between profits and prices, which is certainly considerable. There is not much to be gained from beating this dead horse, and it would not be mentioned at all except that articles continue to appear making just this mistake.

In a thorough study of the role of profits in the wage equation for the United Kingdom, Lipsey and Steuer conclude that

> the United Kingdom observations in the post-war period are consistent with the unemployment theory, but not with the profits theories which we have tested. Rather than being able to explain away the observed relation between wage and unemployment by an association between unemployment and the real causal factor, profits, we have found just the reverse: it is possible to explain away almost all the observed relation-

ship between wage changes and profits by means of a correlation between profits and unemployment.[29]

In view of this rather strong statement, it is a bit odd to find Schultze and Tryon claiming that "many theories of wage rate behavior give a significant role to profits as an explanatory variable. The empirical studies of . . . Lipsey and Steuer confirm this."[30] Schultze and Tryon find that the profit rate is significant only for contract construction and durable manufacturing and further state that when the equations were updated, the durable manufacturing profit coefficient lost significance. This is hardly a very strong finding for this variable. In sharp contrast, the consumer-price-index variable was highly significant in all sectors except contract construction and trade, and these difficulties were rectified when the updated sample was used.

A few other points about the wage function are worth noting. In his original article, Phillips found a tendency for wage increases to be greater when unemployment was decreasing, *cet. par.*, than when it was increasing, so that the rate of change of unemployment would be an additional term in the wage-rate equation. Lipsey has shown that this effect will occur if unemployment decreases faster in one sector of the economy than another sector during the upswing, while it increases at the same rate in both sectors during the downswing. This can be interpreted as a crude measure of structural unemployment, for if there were mobility between jobs in different areas and of different types, the unemployment rate would tend to be equalized among different industries. If demand rose faster in one sector of the economy than another, people would move to that sector. It may be supposing too much to argue that unskilled assembly-line workers could move into highly skilled service professions requiring long training, if not a high degree of intelligence. But within the manufacturing sector the significance of the change of the rate of unemployment variable should be a reasonable (although not perfect) measure of the degree of structural unemployment. This term should have a negative sign, because wages should rise faster, *cet. par.*, when unemployment is decreasing. However, in several regressions that we calculated, this term had a positive sign in all cases and sometimes was even significantly positive.

It is true that the absence of the correct negative sign cannot be taken as a very strong test of no structural unemployment; the test is unquestionably a crude one. In fact, no one regression or set of regressions can provide a definitive answer to the question of how much structural unemployment exists in the economy today. Yet undoubtedly those committed to the view that most of the present unemployment is structural will again denounce econometrics and point out that the computers which put all these people

---

[29] R. G. Lipsey and M. D. Steuer, "The Relation Between Profits and Wage Rates," *Economica*, Vol. 28, No. 2 (May, 1961), p. 150.

[30] Schultze and Tryon, *op. cit.*, p. 314.

out of work now spew forth meaningless results showing that indeed no such thing has occurred.

The empirical results do suggest that the specter of structural unemployment is largely illusory. Those who had argued that unemployment could not drop below 4 percent in the present economy quickly revised some of their arguments when the February 1966 unemployment rate fell to 3.7 percent and stayed below 4 percent for over a year. There are some illiterate 55-year-old former coal miners and sharecroppers who cannot be retrained for any available jobs, but these are a very small percentage of the total unemployed. We believe that if the government were to use fiscal policy to lower the unemployment rate to 3 percent, virtually all so-called structural unemployment would disappear. But even at unemployment rates between $3\frac{1}{2}$ and 4 percent, the "hard core" of unemployment has turned out to be surprisingly malleable.

We now consider the results these functions give in terms of Phillips-curve analysis and the wage–price spiral. In doing so we shall concentrate on the equilibrium values, so that the specific lag structures can be disregarded. It should be kept in mind, however, that the changes discussed here are *not* instantaneous, and will in general take several years before adjustment is complete.

Considering the Phillips curve first, the wage rate equations can be combined and simplified (performing all indicated operations at the sample means) to

$$(10.45) \qquad \frac{\Delta w}{w} = 0.0230 + 0.0139(Un - U^*) + 0.409\frac{\Delta p}{p}$$

First assume that the price term is inoperative; that is, prices do not rise even if unit labor costs increase. This assumption, which is dropped below, is usually made implicitly in Phillips-curve analysis by the simple expedient of neglecting the price term. For this case, some of the values are tabulated in Table 10.4. If overall productivity increases at 2 percent per year, it will be

TABLE 10.4   RELATIONSHIP BETWEEN UNEMPLOYMENT AND WAGE-RATE CHANGES

Un, %	$\frac{\Delta w}{w} \times 100$
8.0	2.0
7.0	3.1
6.0	4.1
5.0	5.0
4.0	5.4

necessary to have 8 percent unemployment for price stability; if the annual productivity increase is $2\frac{1}{2}$ percent, unemployment will still have to be $7\frac{1}{2}$ percent. If a more moderate goal of 2 percent price increase per year is acceptable, unemployment will still need to be at 6 or $5\frac{1}{2}$ percent, respectively. These results are more pessimistic than those reported by Samuelson and Solow.

However, this is not the whole story. If percentage wage increases exceed productivity gains, unit labor costs and price will rise, thus raising wages further. The wholesale price index equation can be rewritten in simplified form as

$$(10.46) \qquad \frac{\Delta p}{p} = 0.79 \frac{\Delta w}{w} + \text{other terms}$$

Thus a 1 percent increase in wage rates due to a decrease in unemployment would eventually raise prices by 1.17 percent and wages by an additional 0.48 percent. This is in fact a very mild wage–price spiral, much less severe than economists have sometimes believed. But it does result in price increases in addition to those indicated above. Including the effects of the wage–price spiral gives the following modified results, shown in Table 10.5. With the slight additional effects of the wage–price spiral, the results are even less favorable. Even at unemployment rates of 6 percent, prices are likely to rise at over 2 percent per year. Although it is true that manufacturing prices are likely to remain steady at 6 percent unemployment because productivity increases in that sector are about 4 percent annually, other prices will still continue to rise.

If these figures are too pessimistic, it is by a small margin. In the 10 "high-unemployment" years (5 percent or more) of the postwar period (through 1964), unemployment has averaged 5.8 percent and prices have risen 1.5 percent annually. In the eight "low-unemployment" years, unemployment has averaged 3.8 percent and prices have risen 3.4 percent annually. These figures

TABLE 10.5 MODIFIED UNEMPLOYMENT WAGE-RATE RELATIONSHIPS

Un, %	$\dfrac{\Delta w^a}{w}$	$\dfrac{\Delta w}{w} - 2\%$	$1.17\left(\dfrac{\Delta w}{w} - 2\%\right)$	$\dfrac{\Delta w}{w} - 2\frac{1}{2}\%$	$1.17\left(\dfrac{\Delta w}{w} - 2\frac{1}{2}\%\right)$
8.0	2.0	0.0	0.0	-0.5	-0.6
7.0	3.1	1.1	1.3	0.6	0.7
6.0	4.1	2.1	2.5	1.6	2.2
5.0	5.0	3.0	3.5	2.5	2.9
4.0	5.4	3.4	4.0	2.9	3.4

^{a} All $\Delta w/w$ multiplied by 100.

are very close to those given in Table 10.5 for a $2\frac{1}{2}$ percent increase in productivity. Unfortunately there is no supporting evidence even for the relatively pessimistic findings of Samuelson and Solow that price stability can be reached at $5\frac{1}{2}$ percent unemployment. The price increase of $3\frac{1}{2}$ percent in 1966 while unemployment hovered around the 4 percent level suggests that this situation is unlikely to improve in the near future.

10.4   PROFITS

It is unnecessary from a theoretical viewpoint to estimate both wage bill and profit functions in the context of a complete model. If profits are defined as an economic residual, that is, $\pi = pX - T_B - D - W - RI$,[31] then estimating all these other variables leaves the profit figure as a residual magnitude. It would be possible to treat depreciation, rent and interest, or indirect business taxes as a residual; however, this would make very little sense either from a theoretical or empirical point of view. The first two are accounting magnitudes determined by tax laws or past contracts, whereas the latter is clearly related to output and the relevant tax laws and should be estimated in that manner. Profits are clearly the only sensible residual. Why, then, a separate profits function?

In the first econometric model built by Tinbergen, profits were considered to play the primary role in determining the movements and fluctuations of the entire economy. However, in work by Klein and others, this notion of the importance of profits was eliminated and they appeared only as a residual. In a somewhat similar vein, there are no functions explaining profits in the Brookings model, although they do appear occasionally as independent variables in the system. To understand the theory of the business cycle as it is presented here, however, it is necessary to understand the relationship between profits and wages over the cycle and the effect this has on aggregate demand. Although this aspect of cyclical behavior has been neglected by some writers, it is of considerable importance in influencing cyclical patterns that have their origin in aggregate demand.

There is an additional reason for including a profits function from a fore-casting point of view. The actual statistical relationship that adds up factor shares to obtain gross national product includes the statistical discrepancy. This term may be quite large (it has been as high as $5 billion) and may

---

[31] These symbols for factor shares, used throughout the rest of the chapter, are defined as:

π = corporate profits before corporate income taxes
pX = gross national product
T_b = indirect business taxes
D = depreciation
W = compensation of employees
RI = rent and net interest

change substantially from quarter to quarter. Because of these erratic shifts in the statistical discrepancy, much better predictions of profits (and dividends and retained earnings) will ordinarily be obtained from a separate profits function than from the residual calculation.

It might appear from the factor-share identity stated above that an increase in wages by some given amount will decrease profits by the same amount. However, this statement is very misleading, because it neglects the interaction among wages, prices, and profits. Consider the effect on profits of an economy-wide increase in the wage bill with no accompanying productivity increase (profits can include unincorporated business income as well as corporate profits here). Such an increase may seem unlikely but in fact occurs regularly when the rate of social security contributions of employers rises.

Assume some simplified functions of the form $W \equiv wL$, $L = bX$, so that $W = wbX$.[32] The wage rate depends only on lagged variables, as shown in the previous section. Assume that D and RI are proportional to the capital stock (K) over the short run, and that $T_b = \tau(pX)$, where τ is the tax rate. Then

$$(10.47) \qquad \pi = (1 - \tau)pX - (wb)X - rK$$

For purely competitive profit-maximizing firms,

$$(10.48) \qquad p = \frac{1}{\alpha}MC = \frac{w}{\alpha MPP_L}$$

where $1/\alpha$ is the markup factor. If firms are producing on the horizontal part of their MC curves, then

$$(10.49) \qquad p = \frac{w}{\alpha APP_L} = \frac{wL}{\alpha X} = \frac{wb}{\alpha}$$

Therefore,

$$(10.50) \qquad \pi = (1 - \tau)wb\left(\frac{1}{\alpha} - 1\right)X - rK$$

---

[32] The symbols used in this discussion that are not given in footnote 31 are defined as:

MR = marginal revenue
MC = marginal costs
AC = average costs
MPP_L = marginal physical product of labor
APP_L = average physical product of labor
p = price
q = quantity
e = elasticity of demand
w = wage rate
r = interest rate
X = output
L = man-hours
K = capital stock
α = elasticity of labor with respect to output

Assume that X does not change when w does; that is, there is no change in aggregate demand through the redistributive effects of the change in prices. (This assumption is dropped below.) Then

$$(10.50) \qquad \frac{\partial \pi}{\partial w} = (1 - \tau)(bX)\left(\frac{1}{\alpha} - 1\right)$$

$$> 0 \qquad \text{as long as } 1/\alpha > 1$$

Thus as long as there is no change in aggregate demand and wages are fully passed along, an *increase* in overall wages will *raise* overall profits. The assumptions of pure competition and the horizontal part of the MC curve are made only to simplify the exposition; they do not affect the basic results. However, the markup factor must be greater than unity for this result to occur.

Consider next the same equation on an industry basis with an industry-wide increase in wages. The question of changing demand can now no longer be ignored. Again we have:

$$(10.51) \qquad \pi = (1 - \tau)b\left(\frac{1}{\alpha} - 1\right)(Xw) - rK$$

$$(10.52) \qquad \frac{\partial \pi}{\partial w} = (1 - \tau)b\left(\frac{1}{\alpha} - 1\right)\left(X + w\frac{dX}{dw}\right)$$

Since $w = (\alpha/b)p$, and thus $dw = (\alpha/b)dp$,

$$(10.53) \qquad \frac{\partial \pi}{\partial w} = (1 - \tau)b\left(\frac{1}{\alpha} - 1\right)X\left[1 + \frac{p(dX)}{X(dp)}\right] = (1 - \tau)b\left(\frac{1}{\alpha} - 1\right)X(1 + e)$$

Thus if the elasticity of demand for the industry product(s) is less than unity and the markup factor is greater than unity, a change in wages will change profits in the same direction.

In almost all cases the elasticity of demand facing an individual firm will be much greater than unity, so this conclusion will be reversed if only one firm in an industry faces an increase in wages. However, this situation is unusual; industry-wide wage increases are likely to be the rule rather than the exception. The demand for many industries is certainly not inelastic; for example, the price elasticity of demand for cars has already been estimated by us to be approximately -3.0. In general, the more elastic the demand for the product, the less likely it is that wage increases will be passed on as higher prices. On the other hand, some of the increase is likely to be passed on unless the demand curve is completely elastic. Since wages have almost tripled in the postwar period but labor's share has remained about the same, almost all wage increases in excess of productivity gains have eventually been passed along in the form of higher prices. The price equation estimated by us does suggest that for manufacturing, α is less than unity in the short run but becomes greater than unity after about two years and eventually approaches the full markup value of 1.5.

Thus for firms in an industry with an inelastic demand curve, profits will rise when wages rise faster than productivity. To see how wage earners come out, refer back to the equation $W = WBX$. Then

$$(10.54) \qquad dW = b[wdX + Xdw], \quad \text{or}$$

$$(10.55) \qquad \frac{dW}{dw} = bX\left[\frac{wdX}{Xdw} + 1\right]$$

since $\qquad \dfrac{w}{dw} = \dfrac{p}{dp},$ then

$$(10.56) \qquad \frac{dW}{dw} = bX(1 + e)$$

Thus the total wage bill will increase with an increase in wages if the elasticity of demand is less than unity. The same conditions which results in an increase in profits also results in an increase in the wage bill. However, this result must be tempered by the degree to which the overall price level rises, which would partially decrease the gain of the workers in real terms. In an extreme situation, if wage–price movements originating in a "key" industry were widely copied, the wage and price level could rise proportionately in all industries, so that workers' real wages remained unchanged. If aggregate output and employment then fell because of the price increase,[33] labor would actually be worse off in real terms. However, the idea of one wage–price change spreading to the entire economy in the same proportion is unlikely, so wage earners receiving wage increases in excess of productivity gains will probably get a higher total wage bill in both money terms and real terms as long as the demand for the product they produce is inelastic.

Before leaving readers with the impression that one way for businessmen to raise profits is to raise wages, we should point out that the necessary criterion of inelasticity of demand is likely to be quite stringent, particularly in the long run. If the price of one particular product continues to increase relative to other products, buyers are more and more likely to use different products or alternative sources of supply (such as foreign producers) as substitutes. These changes may take time to occur, thus giving a distorted short-run picture of a very inelastic demand for this product. However, when new sources of supply and substitutes are found, there is likely to be a great deal of switching away from the higher-priced product, revealing a much higher long-run elasticity of demand. Consideration of the long-run elasticity of

---

[33] The reasons this might occur are discussed in Section 13.1.

demand as the relevant value for pricing decisions will be discussed in Section 11.1.

Probably no industry follows this pattern of increasing elasticity of demand over time more closely than the steel industry. In the period 1954–1958, the now infamous "open door" policy was followed, in which steel wages increased by an average of 7 percent per year and steel prices increased by an average of 6.2 percent per year. Wage increases appeared to be granted quite easily as long as they could be passed along in price increases. Profits (as a percentage of stockholder's equity) averaged 13.5 percent after taxes for 1955–1957. However, starting in 1958, users of steel began shifting to foreign producers and substitute materials, and steel profits began a sharp decline, reaching a low in 1962 of only 5.5 percent; they have increased slightly since then. Although 1958 was a recession year in which steel profits would have been expected to drop, they have not yet recovered. The steel industry has changed from a high-profit industry to a low-profit industry. In 1965 their profits were only 9.7 percent, well below the all-manufacturing average of 13.0 percent. Of 22 major categories of manufacturing investment, steel had the lowest profit rate of all, except for paper, which was 9.4 percent.[34] This occurred in a capital-goods boom year when steel profits would ordinarily be higher than normal. Furthermore, the net export surplus of steel decreased from $700 million in 1955 to $70 million in 1965; production of steel has only increased 11 percent in this 10-year period, whereas production of nonferrous metals has increased 42 percent during the same period. Meanwhile, the number of production workers in the steel industry has dropped more than 10 percent. The short-term gains of both steel companies and steel unions have turned into long-term losses.

Having explored some aspects of the role of profits in the overall economy, we now proceed to derive a profits function. Again we have

(10.57) $\pi = pX - W - RI - D - T_b = (1 - \tau)pX - W - rK$

Again define the wage bill $W \equiv wL$, where $w = f(Un_{-1}, p_{c_{-1}})$, as was shown in Section 10.3, and $L = bX$. Since both unemployment and the consumer price level are closely tied to the level of aggregate economic activity, the wage-rate function can be approximated by $w = f(pX_{-1})$. These substitutions give

(10.58) $\pi = (1 - \tau)pX - bX \cdot f(pX_{-1}) - rK$

By a standard linear approximation

(10.59) $bX \cdot f(pX_{-1}) = bX[\overline{f(pX_{-1})}] + f(pX_{-1}) \cdot \overline{bX} + c_1$

---

[34] The profit figures are taken from the *Quarterly Financial Report for Manufacturing Corporations*; other figures are from the *Survey of Current Business*.

Write $(1 - \tau)pX = apX + cpX$, where $a + c = 1 - \tau$. Then

(10.60) $\pi = apX + X[cp - f(\overline{pX_{-1}}) \cdot b] - \overline{bX} \cdot f(pX_{-1}) + c_1 - rK$

(10.61) $cpX = c(\bar{p}X + \overline{X}p + c_2)$

so that

(10.62) $\pi = apX + X[c\bar{p} - f(\overline{pX_{-1}}) \cdot b] - b\overline{X} \cdot f(pX_{-1})$
$$+(c\overline{X})p + c_1 + c_2 - rK$$

The point of the additional transformation $1 - \tau = a + c$ is to identify the sign of the coefficient of X as positive instead of negative. In general the quantity $c\bar{p} - f(\overline{pX_{-1}}) \cdot b$ will be positive if c is greater than $f(\overline{pX_{-1}}) \cdot b$, where the latter is labor's share of output, or approximately 0.65. This implies that a is less than 0.25 ($\tau = 0.1$), which it is in all the equations which we estimated. Writing this in somewhat simplified form gives

(10.63) $\pi = a'pX + b'p + c'X - d'(pX_{-1}) - f'K + g'$

If we define capacity utilization rate $Cp = $ actual X/maximum X, and maximum X is a function of the capital stock, then $Cp = \theta(X/K)$. The $c'X$ and $-f'K$ terms can be combined into a Cp term to give

(10.64) $\pi = a'pX + c''(Cp) - d'(pX)_{-1} + b'p + g'$

This is the form of the profits function which is used.

One problem still needs to be settled. In this derivation, the lagged output term is included because it represents the negative effect of wages. But it has been argued above that increased wages are not likely to have an adverse effect on profits. Thus except for those industries which do not pass along increases (and decreases) in unit labor costs, other interpretations for the importance of this term need to be suggested. One may be the increases in fixed costs that arise from higher capital expenditures due to higher sales which cannot be passed on as easily. These costs would occur a year or so after sales and profits rose, since this is the average lag for investment purchases. Another important reason is that there might be an increase in the number of firms entering purely competitive industries in response to higher profits and sales. Although there is no direct way to measure the lag between increased sales and new entrants, it seems reasonable to assume about a year's time for this lag. This suggests the possibility, which is explored at some length in a paper by this author,[35] that the interpretation for the lagged output term may be different for oligopolistic industries and competitive industries. This would lead to different forms of the profit function for different

---

[35] M. K. Evans, "An Industry Study of Corporate Profits," *Econometrica*, Vol. 36, No. 2 (April, 1968). The general approach in this section follows that paper.

classes of market structure. For the total economy and for the total manufacturing sector, however, the general structure presented above holds. The empirical results are

$$(10.65) \qquad \pi = -2.45 + 0.0745pX + 55.19Cp - 36.26$$
$$ (0.0029) \qquad (7.19) \qquad (\ 7.01)$$

$$\times \tfrac{1}{4}\left(\tfrac{1}{2}Cp_{-2} + \sum_{i=3}^{5} Cp_{-i} + \tfrac{1}{2}Cp_{-6}\right) \qquad \bar{R}^2 = 0.949$$

$$(10.66) \qquad \pi_m = -3.42 + 0.1767S_m + 44.45Cp - 0.0727S_{m-4}$$
$$ (0.0125) \qquad (10.82) \qquad (0.0135)$$

$$+ 15.85\Delta p_m \qquad \bar{R}^2 = 0.968$$
$$(5.29)$$

where π = total corporate profits, billions of current dollars

pX = gross national product, billions of current dollars

Cp = index of capacity utilization, percent

π_m = manufacturing corporate profits, billions of current dollars

S_m = total sales in the manufacturing sector, billions of current dollars

p_m = wholesale price index, 1958 = 1.00

10.5   OTHER FACTOR SHARES

As has previously been noted several times there is a definite cyclical pattern to the shift of relative factor shares, which has very important implications for business cycle theory and policy. The cyclical distribution between wages and profits may intensify cyclical movements whose origins are in the real sector, or may even be a cause of fluctuations in the economy. This theory is not new; in fact, it formed the basis of many of the pre-Keynesian theories of the cycle, some of which are discussed in Part II. However, this phenomenon has sometimes been neglected in the postwar period. This can be traced partially to the development of econometric models that were estimated entirely in constant dollars or had only one price level. But the importance of the supply side of econometric models is again becoming apparent.

The main point examined here is how spendable income (disposable income to individuals, cash flow to corporations) is distributed to individuals and businessmen over the cycle, because this will affect aggregate consumption and investment. The relevant identities to be considered are[36]

$$(10.67) \quad DPI = \frac{W + P + F + R + IN + Dv + Tr - \text{SocSec} - Tp}{p_c}$$

$$(10.68) \quad L = \frac{\pi - T_c - Dv + D}{p_k}$$

and

$$(10.69) \quad W + P + F + R + IN + \pi + D + T_b = \text{GNP}$$

Prices are of importance in this distribution of income for several reasons. First, capital-goods prices fluctuate more than consumer prices over the cycle. Second, prices are an important determinant of both wage rates and profits. Third, tax functions are always in money terms. Thus during inflation the percentage of GNP going to the government sector will increase. This will adversely affect both consumption and investment, which will be helpful during the inflationary period but may eventually depress the economy if economic activity decreases but prices stay at their highest previous levels.

To explain the distribution of income between DPI and L it is necessary to explain the determinants of several terms in these identities which have not been previously discussed.

Taxes are simply taken to be proportional to the income on which they are based. A great many institutional subtleties can be built into these functions, but these are not treated in this text. For our purposes, we use functions of the form

$$T_p = a_0 + a_1(PI - Tr)$$

$$T_c = b_0 + b_1(\pi - IVA)$$

$$T_r = c_0 + c_1 Un + c_2 t$$

$$T_b = d_0 + d_1 NI + d_2 t^{37}$$

---

[36] Variables not previously defined in this chapter are:

DPI	= disposable personal income
P	= unincorporated business income except farms
F	= unincorporated business income of farms
R	= rents and royalties
Dv	= dividends
Tr	= transfer payments, including interest on the government debt
SocSec	= social security contributions of employers, employees, and self-employed
T_p	= personal tax and nontax payments
p_c	= price of consumer goods
L	= cash flow of corporations plus depreciation of unincorporated businesses
T_c	= corporate income taxes
p_k	= price of capital goods
IN	= net interest income

The choice of equations is obvious for the most part. Personal taxes depend on personal income except transfer payments, and corporate taxes depend on corporate profits including capital gains, that is, not adjusted for inventory valuation. Transfer payments are generally of two types: social security and other retirement or disablement payments, which are not affected by cyclical disturbances but have tended to grow rather steadily (although often in discrete intervals) over time; and unemployment compensation insurance, which obviously varies with unemployment but has also tended to grow over time. Indirect business taxes could also be made a function of the various types of consumption and investment rather than a function of total national income, as done here. The time trend in this function represents rising rates of taxation (such as on gasoline, liquor, tobacco, real estate, and so on) rather than greater coverage of these taxes.

A simplified form of the depreciation function is used here, although it too could depend on intricacies of the tax laws. Depreciation allowances are usually calculated on an original cost basis; some sort of accelerated declining balance method of write-off is usually used. One such case would be the use of geometrically declining weights (constant percentage write-off of the remaining value). In this case the function would be

$$(10.70) \qquad D = \alpha \sum_{i=0}^{n} \lambda^{i}(p_{k}I)_{t-i}$$

where n would depend on the average estimated life. Dummy variables are included for major changes in the tax laws, such as in 1962.[38]

Other factor shares are considered next. Farm income is treated exogenously, since it depends heavily on farm support prices, the weather, and U.S. export and foreign policy. Since P is similar in some respects to π, one might argue that the same type of function could be used to explain both. However, capacity utilization has little meaning for many segments of P, such as income from professional practices, and is very difficult to measure for other parts of P, such as wholesale and retail outlets. Similarly, the role of lagged output is quite difficult to interpret in a function explaining P. A much simpler function, $P = e_0 + e_1(pX)$, is defective because it does not allow for both cyclical and long-run relationships between P and pX. There is almost a proportional change of P to short-run fluctuations in pX, but in

---

[37] Additional definitions are:

PI	= personal income
IVA	= inventory valuation adjustment
Un	= unemployment
NI	= national income
t	= time trend

[38] Tax and depreciation function estimates are not given here because of frequent changes in the tax laws.

the postwar period P has been a steadily declining proportion of pX, dropping from over 9 percent in the early postwar years to recent levels of less than 6 percent. One way to take this into account in the function is to include a time trend. Since the inclusion of this trend is apt to distort the parameter estimate of the pX term because of multicollinearity, this function could also be estimated in first differences. However, quarter to quarter movements are apt to contain large erratic fluctuations relative to the true change. Another possibility would be to write

$$(10.71) \qquad P - \frac{1}{4}\sum_{i=1}^{4}(P)_{t-i} = e_1\left[pX - \frac{1}{4}\sum_{i=1}^{4}(pX)_{t-i}\right] + e_2$$

This could be estimated in the form

$$(10.72) \qquad P = e_1\left[pX - \frac{1}{4}\sum_{i=1}^{4}(pX)_{t-i}\right] + \frac{1}{4}\sum_{i=1}^{4}(P)_{t-i} + e_2$$

where the term $\frac{1}{4}\sum_{i=1}^{4}(P)_{t-i}$ need not be constrained to unity, although it should be close to that value.

Rent and net interest[39] payments are treated somewhat differently, although the final form of the estimated equation is similar. Both types of income are earned from holding some type of asset; the pricing decision is determined at the beginning of the contract and normally remains unchanged for the life of that contract. Thus it should be possible to write identically $R \equiv p_r(K_b + K_L)$, where p_r is a correctly weighted average of all past and present rents, K_b the stock of all buildings rented, and K_L the amount of all land from which rents and royalties are earned. K_L is almost constant, because the amount of land used in this way changes very little.

The linear approximation of this function is

$$(10.73) \qquad R = \overline{p_r}(I_b) + \overline{(K_b + K_L)}\Delta p_r$$

An alternative assumption is that the rent index gives more weight to present rents than past rents. In that case the function would be

$$(10.74) \qquad R_t = \sum_{i=1}^{\infty}\lambda^i(p_rI_b)_{t-i} + p_r(K_L)_t$$

Using the Koyck transformation for an average of the past four quarters (because of extremely high multicollinearity between R_t and R_{t-1}) gives

---

[39] Government interest paid is treated exogenously in this system. It could be made a function of the maturity structure of government debt and interest rates on government securities, but this is not done here. Imputed interest paid by consumers is also treated exogenously.

$$(10.75) \quad R_t = [(p_r I_b)_t + 0.75\lambda(p_r I_b)_{t-1} + 0.50\lambda^2(p_r I_b)_{t-2}$$
$$+ 0.25\lambda^3(p_r I_b)_{t-3}] + K_L(p_{r_t} + 0.75\lambda p_{r_{t-1}} + 0.50\lambda^2 p_{r_{t-2}}$$
$$+ 0.25\lambda^3 p_{r_{t-3}}) + \frac{1}{4}\sum_{i=1}^{4} R_{t-i}$$

For $\lambda \cong 1$ and additional linearization of the multiplicative terms we have

$$(10.76) \quad R_t = f_1(\Delta I_{b_t} + 0.75\Delta I_{b_{t-1}} + 0.50\Delta I_{b_{t-2}} + 0.25\Delta I_{b_{t-3}}$$
$$+ f_2(\Delta p_{r_t} + 0.75\Delta p_{r_{t-1}} + 0.50\Delta p_{r_{t-2}} + 0.25\Delta p_{r_{t-3}}$$
$$+ f_3(p_{r_t} + 0.75 p_{r_{t-1}} + 0.50 p_{r_{t-2}} + 0.25 p_{r_{t-3}})$$
$$+ \frac{1}{4}\sum_{i=1}^{4} R_{t-i}$$

where $f_1 = 2.5\overline{p_r}$, $f_2 = 2.5\overline{I_b}$, and $f_3 = K_L$. Unfortunately this function does not work very well. This may be due to the smoothed nature of the rent data; it may also be due to the difficulty of measuring I_b correctly (I_h was actually used as a proxy variable). The ΔI_b term was not significant, but, given the extremely smooth nature of the rent series, it is rather doubtful whether any other variable that fluctuates as much as investment does would have been successful. The p_r term was also not significant; this is probably because p_r does not represent the price of rents and royalties received from land to any meaningful degree. The Δp_r term was significant, and the lagged R_t term had a coefficient very close to unity, which partially justified the assumption that $\lambda = 1$.

A similar transformation can be used for the net interest equation. Again we can write identically

$$(10.77) \qquad\qquad IN \equiv \sum i \cdot B$$

where i represents the interest rate at which the bonds or other liabilities (bills or notes) were originally issued and B represents the face value of bonds or other liabilities issued at that rate. Assume that the bonds are proportional to outstanding capital stock, and also assume that at each point of time the maturity distribution is identical within each class of investment, so that at time $t - i$, λ^i of the bonds are still outstanding. Then

$$(10.78) \quad IN = \sum_{i=0}^{\infty} \lambda_1^i (i_L \cdot I_p)_{t-i} + \sum_{i=0}^{\infty} \lambda_2^i (i_m \cdot I_b)_{t-i} + \sum_{i=0}^{\infty} \lambda_3^i (i_f \cdot C_d)_{t-i}$$

where i_L is the interest rate for plant and equipment spending, i_m the interest rate for mortgages, and i_f the interest rate for financing of consumer durable purchases. The usual Koyck transformation is unsuitable unless $\lambda_1 = \lambda_2 = \lambda_3$, which is quite unlikely. However, continuing to treat these terms separately, and using the same type of transformation as for the rent equation, the equation can be transformed without too much distortion to the form

$$(10.79) \quad IN = g_0' + g_1' \sum_{i=0}^{3} \frac{4-i}{4}(i_L \cdot I_p)_{t-i} + g_2' \sum_{i=0}^{3} \frac{4-i}{4}(i_m \cdot I_h)_{t-i}$$

$$+ g_3' \sum_{i=0}^{3} \frac{4-i}{4}(i_f \cdot C_d)_{t-i} + \frac{1}{4}\sum_{i=1}^{4} IN_{t-i}, \qquad \lambda \cong 1$$

Linearizing as was done with the rent equation gives

$$(10.80) \quad IN = g_0 + g_1 \left[\sum_{i=0}^{3} \frac{4-i}{4}(\Delta I_p + \Delta I_h + \Delta C_d)_{t-i} \right]$$

$$+ g_2 \left[\sum_{i=0}^{3} \frac{4-i}{4}(\Delta i_L)_{t-i} \right] + \frac{1}{4}\sum_{i=1}^{4} IN_{t-i}$$

assuming that quarter to quarter movements in all the interest rates are approximately the same (this last is not strictly true, as was shown in Chapter 7). Again, as with the rent figures, the interest figures are very smooth, so that no correlation was found with either the investment term used above or any of its components. Even the Δi_L term was not significant, so the equation was reduced to a pure regression, and was not used. The estimates of the other share functions are

$$(15.32) \quad PB = 1.24 + 0.0607(\Delta pX + 0.75\Delta pX_{-1} + 0.50\Delta pX_{-2})$$
$$\qquad\qquad (0.0067)$$

$$+ 0.25\Delta pX_{-3} + 0.9529 \, \frac{1}{4}\sum_{i=1}^{4}(PB)_{-i} \qquad \bar{R}^2 = 0.992$$
$$\qquad\quad (0.0112)$$

$$(15.33) \quad RI = -0.57 + 23.08(\Delta p_r + 0.75\Delta(p_r)_{-1} + 0.50\Delta(p_r)_{-2})$$
$$\qquad\qquad (7.97)$$

$$+ 0.25\Delta(p_r)_{-3} + 1.0614 \, \frac{1}{4}\sum_{i=1}^{4}(RI)_{-i} \qquad \bar{R}^2 = 0.998$$
$$\qquad\quad (0.0091)$$

where PB = income of unincorporated business enterprises, billions of current dollars

pX = gross national product, billions of current dollars

RI = net rent, royalty, and interest income, billions of current dollars

p_r = index of rent prices; 1958 = 1.00

Dividends are considered next. The standard dividend function was developed by Lintner, who states:

> The question that comes up first—and usually continues to be the dominant issue—is "Is there any sufficient reason to change it, and if so, by how much?" not "How much should we pay this quarter (or this year)?" considered *de novo*. . . . Current dividend

distributions are primarily determined by last year's dividends and current profits. The net effect of other factors, insofar as not systematically reflected by current profits and lagged dividends, is small and random.[40]

Darling has suggested that profits plus depreciation is a more reasonable variable than profits alone, since it is total cash flow which determines dividends.[41] This adjustment would explain the supposedly low dividend/profit ratio in the early postwar period. Due to rapid inflation, depreciation (based on original cost) was well below replacement prices, so that accounting profits were much higher than true profits. However, the ratio of dividends to profits plus depreciation was actually slightly higher in the early postwar period than it is currently. The use of profits plus depreciation also gives a much more reasonable short-run marginal payout ratio and a long-run marginal payout ratio very close to the average ratio, which seems quite sensible. The empirical estimate of this function is

$$(15.34) \quad Dv = 0.17 + \underset{(0.0122)}{0.1103}(P_{ca} + D_m + D_r + D_c) + \underset{(0.0576)}{0.5289} \frac{1}{4} \sum_{i=1}^{4} (Dv)_{-i}$$

$$\bar{R}^2 = 0.990$$

where Dv = corporate dividend payments, billions of current dollars

P_{ca} = corporate profits after taxes, billions of current dollars

D_m = depreciation for manufacturing investment, billions of current dollars

D_r = depreciation for regulated and mining investment, billions of current dollars

D_c = depreciation for commercial and other investment, billions of current dollars

The generalized Lintner hypothesis has recently been questioned by Dhrymes and Kurz in the same study that was discussed in some detail in Chapter 5. Their argument is that the maximization of profits through optimal hiring of factor resources (labor and capital) is more important than keeping the dividend constant in the short run. But firms using equity financing will find it much more expensive to borrow funds if they cut their dividend payment, particularly in good times, when profits should be high. Although we agree that purchasing of additional capital stock is of primary importance when output increases, many firms find that this can be done without sharply increasing the cost of capital only by using equity financing. If the dividend per share is to be kept constant, the total amount of dividend payments will

---

[40] J. Lintner, "Determinants of Corporate Savings," in W. W. Heller *et. al.*, eds., *Savings in the Modern Economy* (Minneapolis: University of Minnesota Press, 1953).

[41] P. G. Darling, "The Influence of Expectations and Liquidity on Dividend Policy," *Journal of Political Economy*, Vol. 65, No. 3 (June, 1957), pp. 209–224.

rise; the total cost of the additional capital needs dictated by rising output may be minimized by increasing dividends rather than reducing them.

10.6   INCOME DISTRIBUTION OVER THE CYCLE

We now consider the cyclical fluctuation of income shares. Early in the cycle, firms are likely to raise prices due to an increase in the degree of monopoly power, which occurs if the demand curve for the firms' products shifts out parallel to itself. They may also raise prices if they are operating on the rising part of their marginal cost curve. This increase in price will increase profits substantially. Since dividends adjust slowly to changes in profits, a greater than proportional amount of after-tax profits will be retained. While prices have risen somewhat, the price of capital goods will not have risen more than the prices of other goods. Planning of investment will be made on the basis of current capital-goods prices.

As the upward movement of the economy continues, prices begin to rise at a more rapid rate. This is due to several factors. First, wages start to rise faster than productivity as wage earners bargain for a share of the increased profits that resulted from firms raising prices. This rise in unit labor costs is at least partially passed on in the form of higher prices. Problems of diminishing marginal returns may become more severe and the increase in labour productivity will then slow down. This problem will be particularly acute in the construction sector of the economy, where prices will rise most rapidly; the price of capital goods will then rise more rapidly than other prices. As the price of these goods rises, depreciation allowances based on original cost become more and more inadequate. Dividends will also rise relative to gross profits (including depreciation), further lessening the availability of funds.

Thus less funds (as a percentage of output, and thus of capital requirements) are available to businessmen both in current and constant dollars, but especially the latter. This will cause some decline in investment plans, which will decrease new orders and inventory investment and thus aggregate demand. With some shifting back of the demand curve for their products, firms will not be able to pass along as much of the increased labor costs, which are in turn due to higher wage bargains based on the previous year's increase in prices and low rates of unemployment.

Thus the firm has less cash flow in real terms for several reasons: (1) the growth in output has become much smaller or possibly even negative; (2) wages have increased faster than productivity, but these increases are harder to pass along in the face of slackening demand; (3) dividends continue to rise, since they are based mainly on past profits; and (4) prices of capital goods have increased faster than average product prices, so that funds which were regarded as adequate at the time of planning may not be so when the investment is completed; this is particularly true for depreciation reserves.

TABLE 10.6   DISTRIBUTION OF DISPOSABLE INCOME SHARES
OVER THE CYCLE

First Quarter of Recession	Av. of Recession Quarter + Next Two Quarters	Av. of Next Four Quarters	Av. of Next Four Quarters After That	Av. of Remaining Quarters
A. Wage share (as a percentage of GNP)				
1949.1	51.88	48.42	49.64	50.20
1953.3	51.19	50.16	50.44	50.60
1957.4	51.67	50.88	—[a]	—[a]
1960.2	51.08	50.50	49.98	50.57[b,c]
				50.35[d,c]
B. Rentier share				
1949.1	20.61	19.00	18.42	17.65
1953.3	17.90	17.33	16.93	16.88
1957.4	17.62	16.75	—[a]	—[a]
1960.2	16.67	16.50	16.39	16.30[b]
				16.10[d]
C. Profit share (cash flow)				
1949.1	10.76	11.92	9.91[e]	9.91[e]
1953.3	10.35	11.84	11.49	11.30
1957.4	10.86	11.48	—[a]	—[a]
1960.2	10.79	11.42	11.43	11.63[b,c]
				12.08[d]
D. Profit share, constant dollars $\left(\dfrac{L}{p_k} \div \dfrac{GNP}{p}, \% \right)$				
1949.1	11.66	12.77	10.53	10.49
1953.3	10.92	12.38	11.69	11.25
1957.4	10.84	11.42	—[a]	—[a]
1960.2	10.90	11.56	11.68	11.92[b]
				12.47[d]

[a] short cycle; insufficient observations for these columns.
[b] For period 1963.4–1964.4.
[c] Increase due to income tax cut.
[d] For period 1965.1–1965.4
[e] Low values due to excess profit tax.

Not much has been said about the effect of this cyclical pattern on disposable income and consumption. Short-run variations in income are largely reflected in savings, including purchases of consumer durables. Since the short-run mpc is much lower than the apc, short-run fluctuations in disposable income do not affect consumption very much. It is the much more volatile fixed business investment sector that is most affected by this cyclical pattern of increasing and then decreasing cash flow.

The cyclical shift of income received by various factor shares is shown in Table 10.6. Disposable income is divided into two groups, which are (1) wage and salary income plus transfers minus taxes and (2) rentier income: dividends, rent, and interest income, and unincorporated business income, all minus taxes. Although the last category undoubtedly contains some labor income, no imputation to labor was calculated for purposes of this table. Rentier income is separated from wage and salary income because it behaves differently in both cyclical and secular aspects. Although rentier income increases as a share of GNP in recessions and decreases in the early stages of booms, it continues to fall in the latter stages of the boom, but not as much. There has also been a secular downward trend in the share of rentier income during the postwar period. Whereas wage and profit shares have stayed approximately constant over the postwar period, the rentier share has dropped; the increase has gone to the government share (taxes less transfers). This does not invalidate the usual constant long-run factor shares argument, because that argument applies to shares earned, not shares received after taxes and transfers.

The cyclical shift of wages and profits is well documentated in this table, with the most recent period deviating only in the sense that stability of factor shares existed for several years; this is discussed below. In each of the previous three cycles, profits were lowest in the recession and the two quarters immediately following; they were highest in the next period and then gradually declined over the remainder of the cycle. Wages were highest in recessions and the following two quarters, lowest in the next period, and then gradually increased.

These conclusions have not yet taken into consideration the fact that p_k fluctuates more over the cycle than does p_c (or prices generally). To assess the possible importance of this additional fact, we measure both L and GNP in constant dollars, the respective deflators being p_k and p. These results are shown in part D of Table 10.6. Clearly a substantial profit squeeze has developed toward the end of each cycle except for the most recent period.

We now consider the post-1961 period. It was pointed out above that the first step in the cyclical shift of income was the decision of firms to raise prices when labor costs had not increased. However, this decision was noticeably absent for the latest period until the middle of 1965. The increase in the wage share in 1964 can be attributed to the substantial tax cut of that year and not to a decrease in the profit share, which also increased. While the major part of the extension of this upswing was clearly due to the tax cut and increased defense spending, it is not unreasonable to argue that the wage–price stability and lack of fluctuations in the profit share were also partially responsible for the longevity of this expansion. The profit squeeze that finally did occur in 1967 was accompanied by depressed demand in the private sector; only rapid increases in government spending ($9 billion in 1967.1 alone) kept the economy from another recession at that time.

CHAPTER 11

PRICES, MONEY,
AND INTEREST RATES

11.1   DETERMINATION OF THE GENERAL PRICE LEVEL

The aggregate demand and supply functions examined thus far have been formulated largely in real terms. Yet relative prices are important determinants both of various components of demand and distribution of factor shares. To obtain a complete picture of national income determination, it is necessary to provide an endogenous explanation of both absolute and relative prices.

Because prices are necessarily in money terms rather than real terms, most treatments in this area link together discussion of prices and money. The quantity theory provides a direct link; even if this link is later shown to be quite tenuous, it usually serves as a starting point for the theory of aggregate price determination. Our treatment is somewhat different; we start with the Keynesian hypothesis, develop this fully, and then return to alternative varieties of price determination which are often suggested. Although money has an important influence on the economy, we argue that this effect is manifested primarily through the interest rate rather than the price level. The discussion of the role of money in the economy is thus relegated to a later section in this chapter.

Although the Keynesian theory of income determination is primarily noted for its solution in real terms, the basic type of price equation suggested by Keynes is stated quite clearly. "In a single industry its particular price-level depends partly on the rate of remuneration of the factors of production which enter into its marginal cost, and partly on the scale of output. There is no reason to modify this conclusion when we pass to industry as a whole."[1] The type of equation in which prices are proportional to variable costs is usually known as a markup equation. We first develop a markup equation modified by the influence of changes in the level of output, at the level of the firm, and then aggregate to the sectoral level. Presumably the aggregation could be carried to the economy level, but not as smoothly. Primary consideration will be given to manufacturing firms at this point; other sectoral price levels are discussed in Section 11.3. Agricultural firms do not individually determine the price of their products; in the usual terms, they are price takers, not price makers. Prices of firms in regulated industries are set by government agencies; these prices are supposed to result in a normal rate of return. The prices of service industries are almost entirely determined by the wage rates in these industries; the prices of trade industries are usually determined by a certain percentage markup of manufactured goods. Thus if one can explain wage rates and prices of manufactured goods, prices of the service and trade sectors can be easily determined.

If the firm maximizes short-run profits, it produces where $MR = MC$.[2] Since

$$(11.1) \qquad MR = \frac{p\,\Delta q + q\,\Delta p}{\Delta q} = p\left(1 + \frac{1}{e}\right)$$

the firm produces where $p(1 + 1/e) = MC$, or $p = (e/[e + 1])(MC)$. If marginal costs consist entirely of labor, then

$$(11.2) \qquad p = \frac{e}{e + 1}\,MC = \frac{e}{e + 1}\,\frac{w}{\partial X/\partial L}$$

Other variable costs are marked up very similarly and need not be considered separately here. If the firm is producing on the constant part of its MC curve, then this expression simplifies to

$$(11.3) \qquad p = \frac{e}{e + 1}\,\frac{wL}{X} = \frac{e}{e + 1}\,\frac{W}{X}$$

where W/X are unit labor costs.

However, if this were actually the case, all purely competitive firms producing on the constant part of the MC curve would be making equilibrium losses equal to the amount of capital costs. In imperfect competition they would be making losses if $1/(e + 1) < rK/W$. This problem is usually skirted in

---

[1] J. M. Keynes, *The General Theory of Employment, Interest, and Money* (New York: Harcourt, Brace & World, 1936), p. 294.
[2] The symbols used here are the same as those given in footnote 32, Chapter 10.

elementary economics textbooks by stating that the MC includes a "normal" profit. A more reasonable alternative is to consider long-run normal prices, which include capital and other costs fixed in the short run, in the pricing decision. One way to do this is to consider explicitly the shares of output accruing o both labor and capital. If the firm's production function is of the Cobb–Douglas form, $X = aL^{\alpha}K^{\beta}e^{\gamma t}$, then for pure competition and profit-maximizing behavior,

$$(11.4) \qquad \frac{\partial X}{\partial L} = \frac{w}{p} = \alpha \frac{X}{L} \qquad \text{and thus} \qquad p = \frac{1}{\alpha}\frac{W}{X}$$

Here again α is about $\frac{2}{3}$, so that the *full markup factor* is about $1\frac{1}{2}$. This equation states that a given percentage change in unit labor costs will result in the same percentage change in prices, because

$$(11.5) \qquad \frac{\partial p}{\partial (W/X)}\frac{W}{pX} = \frac{1}{\alpha}\alpha = 1$$

The equation $p = (1/\alpha)(W/X)$ is similar to a short-run pricing equation except that capital costs are included by means of the factor $1/\alpha$ when the degree of markup is being determined.

In imperfect competition the results are very similar; we have

$$(11.6) \qquad \frac{\partial X}{\partial L} = \frac{w}{MR} = \frac{w}{p[(e+1)/e]} = \alpha\frac{X}{L}$$

Therefore,

$$(11.7) \qquad p = \frac{1}{\alpha}\frac{e}{e+1}\frac{W}{X}$$

Labor's share, which is defined to be wL/pX, is thus equal to $\alpha[(e+1)/e]$. This may at first appear to lead to some difficulties. If $e = -1$, it would appear that labor's share is zero. However, if a profit-maximizing firm produces where $e = 1$, this implies that $MR = MC = 0$, and thus labor's share is zero for a Cobb–Douglas production function, in which the MC/AC ratio is always constant. Under standard assumptions, no profit-maximizing firm would produce in the region $-1 < e < 0$, so labor's share would never be negative.

We now examine some of the properties of the price function

$$(11.8) \qquad p = \frac{1}{\alpha}\frac{e}{e+1}\frac{W}{X}$$

It is sometimes argued that the factor $(1/\alpha)(e/e + 1)$ remains almost constant, so that it is only necessary to explain unit labor costs to explain prices. Although this may have substantial validity in the long run, it is the short-run fluctuations in these parameters that are considered at this point.

The price level will rise (for example) if one or more of the following occur:

1. The demand curve for a product shifts out and the firm is operating on the rising part of its marginal cost curve. This is usually known as *demand-pull inflation.*

2. The level of the marginal cost curve shifts upward. This is usually known as *cost-push* or *wage-push inflation,* because wages are usually the principal component of variable costs.

3. The elasticity of demand decreases at each price because of a shift in the demand curve. This would result in an increase in the degree of monopoly power, represented in the price equation as $e/(e + 1)$.[3] This possibility has not received as much attention as the first two, but is usually called *profits inflation.* If this occurs, prices will rise *even though marginal costs have remained unchanged.* It is our contention that much of the postwar inflation can be explained only with reference to profits inflation.[4]

The first two cases may be represented as shown in Figures 11.1 and 11.2. Case 3 may have several possibilities. One is that the new demand curve will intersect the old curve at the same price but with a steeper slope, as shown in Figure 11.3. If this did occur, it would probably be due to change in tastes or in the price or availability of substitute goods. However, this case seems unlikely.

Another possibility is that the demand curve shifts out parallel to itself, as shown in Figure 11.4. Then prices will rise without any changes in costs. It can easily be shown that the elasticity of demand has decreased, and thus the

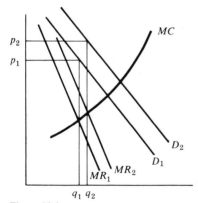

Figure 11.1

---

[3] This is similar to, but not the same as, Lerner's degree of monopoly power $1/e$.

[4] This idea is not new; it can be traced back at least as far as R. Harrod's *The Trade Cycle* (Oxford: Clarendon Press, 1936), especially pp. 75–76. Harrod even names this principle the Law of Diminishing Elasticity of Demand. Yet this idea has almost become submerged in the mass of arguments about demand-pull versus cost-push inflation. One more recent treatment of profits inflation can be found in G. Ackley, *Macroeconomic Theory* (New York: Macmillan, 1961).

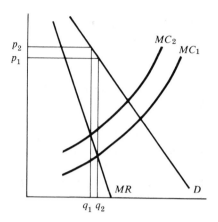

Figure 11.2

degree of monopoly power has increased, at every price, merely by considering the definition of elasticity

$$(11.9) \qquad\qquad e = \frac{\Delta q}{\Delta p}\frac{p}{q}$$

The slope $\Delta q/\Delta p$ has stayed the same (by definition, since the demand curve has shifted parallel to itself) and at any given p, q has increased, so e has decreased. Since $e < 0$, a drop in e will raise $e/(e + 1)$.[5]

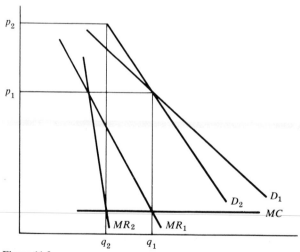

Figure 11.3

---

[5] Perhaps this can be seen most easily by a numerical example. If e goes from -3 to -2, $e/(e + 1)$ goes from $-3/-2$ to $-2/-1$, or an increase from $1\frac{1}{2}$ to 2.

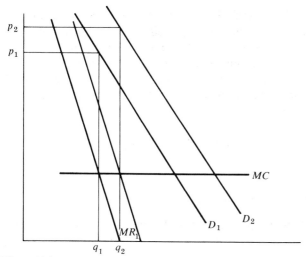

Figure 11.4

Sometimes it is argued that the demand curve does not shift out parallel to itself, but shifts so that it is iso-elastic: that is, the elasticity at any given price remains unchanged. In this case the price would be independent of the level of demand. This possibility is shown in Figure 11.5.

Unfortunately, the question of how the slope of the demand curve changes as the curve shifts is a very complicated one to answer empirically, because the usual linear regression techniques that assume a constant slope are immediately invalidated. To determine the slope at various levels of income one would need several observations for each level of income. If income were constantly changing, this becomes all but impossible from an empirical point of view. However, on theoretical grounds it seems more logical to suggest the parallel

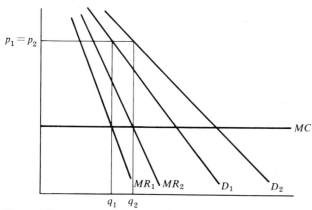

Figure 11.5

shift rather than the iso-elastic shift. If consumers (and producers) are less price conscious at higher income (and output) levels and more price conscious at lower levels, then the parallel shift of the demand curve has greater validity. If so, profits inflation could be an important cause of rising prices.

A more generalized price-markup equation can be given in the case where the MC/AC ratio is not constant and the MC curve has a changing slope in the relevant pricing region. Then

$$(11.10) \qquad p = \frac{1}{\alpha}\frac{e}{e+1}MC = \frac{1}{\alpha}\frac{e}{e+1}\frac{w}{MPP_L}$$

and

$$(11.11) \qquad MPP_L = APP_L - \theta(Cp)\cdot APP_L$$

where $\theta(Cp)$ varies directly with Cp. The relationship may or may not be linear; this is an empirical question that is examined later. This more general pricing equation can be written

$$(11.12) \qquad p = \frac{1}{\alpha}\frac{e}{e+1}\frac{W}{X}\frac{1}{1-\theta(Cp)}$$

Linearizing this gives

$$(11.13) \qquad p = \left[\frac{1}{\alpha}\frac{e}{e+1}\frac{1}{1-\theta(Cp)}\right]\frac{W}{X} + \left[\frac{1}{\alpha}\frac{e}{e+1}\frac{W}{X}\right]\frac{1}{1-\theta(Cp)}$$

$$+ \left[\frac{1}{\alpha}\frac{W}{X}\frac{1}{1-\theta(Cp)}\right]\frac{e}{e+1} + \left[\frac{e}{e+1}\frac{W}{X}\frac{1}{1-\theta(Cp)}\right]\frac{1}{\alpha}$$

Since the *average* value of $1/[1 - \theta(Cp)]$ is probably very close to unity, the coefficient for unit labor costs ought to be very close to the inverse of labor's share, or about $1\frac{1}{2}$.

There is a definite tendency for α to vary inversely with Cp; this was discussed in some detail in the Section 10.1. This can be expressed as

$$(11.14) \qquad \frac{1}{\alpha} \cong b_1 Cp$$

Rewrite $e/(e+1)$ as $1/[1 + (1/e)]$ and note that $1/e = (\Delta p/\Delta q)(q/p)$. If it is assumed that $\Delta p/\Delta q$ is constant for any given p,

$$(11.15) \qquad \frac{1}{e} = -b_2 q \cong -b_2' Cp$$

If $1 - \theta(Cp)$ is close to unity, then

$$(11.16) \qquad \frac{1}{1-\theta(Cp)} \cong 1 + \theta(Cp)$$

Combining these gives

(11.17) $$p = a_0 + a_1 \frac{W}{X} + a_2 Cp + a_3 \theta(Cp)$$

The last term may be linear, in which case the function reduces still further. It may increase at an increasing rate (substantial diminishing marginal returns), or it may be zero below some specified Cp level, such as when $MC = AVC$.

The price function discussed so far has assumed that prices are in equilibrium and that complete adjustment has been made. Actually this is not any truer for prices than any of the other variables we have considered, so an adjustment process is needed. A standard hypothesis is to assume that the change in prices in any given period is proportional to the difference between desired prices and last period's prices. Symbolically, $\Delta p = \delta(p^* - p_{-1})$, where now

(11.18) $$p^* = a_0 + a_1 \frac{W}{X} + a_2 Cp + a_3 \theta(Cp)$$

(p^* is the equilibrium price level). Therefore,

(11.19) $$\Delta p = \delta\left[a_0 + a_1 \frac{W}{X} + a_2 Cp + a_3 \theta(Cp) \right] - \delta p_{-1}$$

and

(11.20) $$p = \delta a_0 + \delta a_1 \frac{W}{X} + \delta a_2 Cp + \delta a_3 \theta(Cp) + (1 - \delta) p_{-1}$$

Prices are generally a very smooth series, so that when using quarterly data it is better for statistical reasons to take an average of the previous year's prices instead of last quarter's price. Otherwise the parameter estimate of the lagged term is likely to be severely biased upward. In any case, the importance of this term should not be overrated. Firms are likely to adjust prices quickly to changes in unit labor costs and capacity utilization. While a distributed lag is implied by this equation, almost half of any adjustment takes place during the first quarter.

An alternative approach to the dynamic structure above has been suggested by Schultze and Tryon.[6] They decompose unit labor costs into its components of wage rates and average productivity, and hypothesize that firms will pass along increases in wage rates almost immediately but may hesitate about adjusting prices due to quarter to quarter changes in productivity, caused partially by short-run hoarding of labor, strikes, or miscalculations in production scheduling. Schultze and Tryon thus suggest that $p^* = \alpha[w\overline{(L/X)}]$, where $\overline{X/L}$ is a 12-quarter moving average of output per man-hour, and $w\overline{(L/X)}$ is

---

[6] C. L. Schultze and J. S. Tryon, "Prices and Wages," in J. S. Duesenberry, G. Fromm, L. R. Klein, and E. Kuh, eds., in *The Brookings Quarterly Econometric Model of the United States* (Chicago: Rand McNally, 1965), chap. 9.

defined as "normal" unit labor cost. Then

$$(11.21) \qquad p = \alpha\left[w\left(\frac{\bar{L}}{X}\right)\right] + \delta\left[w\left(\frac{L}{X}\right)\right]$$

where the last term represents the current adjustment to changes in productivity. The equation is actually written in the form

$$(11.22) \qquad p = (\alpha + \delta)\left[w\left(\frac{\bar{L}}{X}\right)\right] + \delta\left[w\left(\frac{L}{X} - \frac{\bar{L}}{X}\right)\right]$$

but this makes no difference in the estimates.

This equation gives an implicit dynamic structure which is similar to ours in that there is a general distributed lag adjustment. However, their adjustment procedure differs in two ways. First, all changes in wage rates are immediately passed on in price changes. This may not be entirely true, especially for those changes which are due to changes in the percentage of overtime worked. Second, their estimates state that changes in productivity are passed along very slowly, particularly in the nondurable sector of manufacturing, where the $\delta[w(X/L) - w(\bar{X}/\bar{L})]$ term is not significant. This means only $\frac{1}{12}$ of any change in productivity in that sector is passed along in the current quarter, which seems too low. Both versions give long-run values of α which are very close to the actual value of 1.5 observed for the manufacturing sector in the postwar period; Schultze and Tryon get 1.49 and we get 1.32.

We next consider the possible form and significance of the $\theta(Cp)$ term. Schultze and Tryon suggest some "normal" capacity rate exists which is again a 12-quarter moving average, and that the marginal cost curve has a kink at this point. However, they have very little success with this term. One difficulty is that the point of discontinuity keeps shifting, although it should be some constant percentage of total available capacity. An alternative idea is to take some fixed rate of capacity utilization (denoted, say, by Cp_*) where the marginal cost curve is likely to begin rising, and put the kink there. This was tried by us but the additional term was not significant. A third possibility is the use of a quadratic (or possibly higher-order) relationship for capacity utilization rates above the kink, so $\theta(Cp) = (Cp - Cp_*)^n$. However, this did not work for various reasonable values of Cp_* and n, and in fact for $n = 1, 1.5, \ldots, 3$, this term was consistently nonsignificantly negative.

On the basis of this somewhat scanty evidence, we conclude that there is no important nonlinearity between the price level and the rate of capacity utilization. This does not mean that there is no nonlinear relationship between the price level and the level of aggregate economic activity. As the unemployment rate decreases, we have seen that wage rates rise at an increasing rate, which will accelerate increases in the price level. However, the net addition of a specific nonlinear capacity term is not significant. This suggests that firms base their pricing policies on a certain percent markup over *average* cost, not marginal cost. When average variable costs are constant and are thus equal to marginal costs, it makes no difference which cost firms use as the basis for their price. The differentiation appears only when marginal costs start rising and are thus above average variable costs. One might argue that this represents a deviation from short-run profit-maximizing behavior. Although this may be so, it probably does not represent a deviation from longer-run profit maximization. Long-run elasticities of demand for most products are much higher than short-run elasticities; a substantial rise in the price of a product may cause an intensified search by the buyers for alternative products or sources of supply, particularly foreign producers. In this light it is reasonable to interpret the elasticity of demand in the price mark-up equation

$$(11.23) \qquad \frac{P}{MC} = \frac{1}{\alpha} \frac{e}{e+1}$$

as a *long-run* elasticity of demand. Firms will not change their markup ratio every time a temporary or erratic shift occurs in the demand curve, but will adjust to changes which they believe will last for a longer time. This type of behavior is sometimes referred to as "administered prices," which are supposedly set by fiat and have little to do with demand and supply. However, if firms see slumps in business activity as quite temporary, with the long-run elasticity of demand unchanged, there will be little impetus to lower prices in recessions. On the other hand, when these firms do produce on the rising part of their marginal cost curves, they raise prices only by the percentage increase in average costs, not marginal costs. Although raising prices to cover the cost of the last unit in times of short supply may be good advice for elementary economics students to give on exams, it may be very poor advice for firms that stand to lose many long-time customers (to rivals who do not follow such textbook behavior), which may set in motion wage demands for a share of the increased profits, and which in times of national crisis invite the epithets "unpatriotic" and "war profiteer."

As a further attempt in introducing nonlinearities into the price equations, Schultze and Tryon try as an additional variable the difference between the actual inventory/output ratio and its trend value. They find that this term is significantly negative, which is not unreasonable, because excess inventories will have a depressing effect on prices. However, the entire importance of this term is due to events in the early Korean War period, when the inventory/output ratio was extremely low and speculative buying bid up prices substantially. Some regressions run without this special period show no such effect. Rather than include this relationship of doubtful causality, we have included a dummy variable for the period 1950.3–1951.1 to represent this period of speculative buying. Our estimated equation is

$$(15.18) \qquad p_m = -0.170 + 0.5418(W_m/X_m) + 0.2465C_p + 0.0429\delta_{KW}$$
$$\qquad\qquad (0.0890) \qquad\qquad (0.0361) \qquad (0.0063)$$

$$+ 0.6064 \ \frac{1}{4} \sum_{i=1}^{4} (p_m)_{-i} \qquad \bar{R}^2 = 0.982$$
$$(0.0703)$$

where p_m = price index of manufacturing sector, which is the same as the wholesale price level except farm and food products, 1958 = 1.00

W_m = manufacturing sector total wage bill, billions of current dollars

X_m = gross output originating, manufacturing sector, billions of 1958 dollars

Cp = index of capacity utilization, percent

d_{KW} = dummy variable, 1 for 1950.3–1951.1, 0 otherwise

11.2 THE CAUSES OF INFLATION: A HISTORICAL PERSPECTIVE

Our treatment of the determination of the price level has concentrated on the importance of unit labor costs, although this explanation has been considerably expanded by including elements of demand-pull and profits inflation. Although early references can be found for all these causes of inflation, the type of function presented here is of fairly recent vintage. In choosing this method of approach to the treatment of price determination, we have by-passed some of both the traditional and more recent alternatives that have been proposed.[7] We examine some of these theories with particular reference to the periods during which they were most widely accepted. Many of these hypotheses were developed to explain a particular event and have been found to be of little use for other situations and time periods. Although this is an occupational hazard common to much of economic theorizing, the problem seems particularly severe for theories of the price level.

In the nonclassical world, the price level was assumed to be determined by the money stock. There was always a definite relationship between prices and wages—that the real wage was equal to the marginal physical product of labor. This relationship was not thought to be sufficient to determine the absolute price level, because wages were flexible. However, if wages were rigid, then they did determine prices even in the classical system.

The equation of exchange, $MV = pX$, was transformed from an identity to a meaningful economic relationship by assuming that V was an institutional

---

[7] For a more traditional treatment which covers demand-pull, cost-push, and combination theories of inflation, the reader is referred to the comprehensive article by Martin Bronfenbrenner and F. D. Holzman, "Survey of Inflation Theory," *American Economic Review*, Vol. 53, No. 4 (September, 1963), pp. 593–661.

constant. If *M* decreased (for example) and prices and wages were flexible, output would stay the same and all changes would be reflected in prices. If the economy was not at full employment, wages and prices would continue to fall until output and employment returned to equilibrium levels. If prices and wages were rigid downward, output would decrease and unemployment would persist. Since this case was dismissed, the money stock determined the price level.[8]

In the 1930s, the emphasis shifted to the determination of output to the neglect of prices. In the immediate postwar period when prices rose more than 15 percent per year, economists generally agreed that demand-pull inflation was occurring. Spending was based in part on higher previous levels of income, and long queues appeared for consumer durables which were only slowly becoming available. Wages, especially union wages, clearly lagged behind increases in prices.

At the beginning of the Korean War, wholesale prices rose 12 percent in six months, an annual rate of over 25 percent per year. This was clearly due to speculative forces. Since prices then stayed quite stable from 1951 to 1955, there was hope of full employment without inflation. However, in many respects the stability of prices from 1951 to 1955 was illusory. Speculative buying had temporarily bid up prices substantially, but when the demand curve for these products moved back to normal (nonspeculative) levels, prices fell very slightly or not at all. This led to short-lived excess profits that were eroded by excess profits taxes and substantial increases in unit labor costs. The upward movement in commodity prices which would have occurred more gradually during a period of high capacity utilization and full employment happened very suddenly. The price level in 1955 was approximately the same with the Korean War as it would have been without it; the different shape of the time path led to an illusory view of price stability.

The 1955–1957 period, when wholesale prices rose by over 4 percent per year, resulted in a substantial difference of opinion about the causes of inflation, because the economy never got below 4 percent unemployment and was clearly not running at as high a level of capacity utilization as it had in 1946–1948 or 1950–1953. Some economists believed that this phenomenon was strictly a manifestation of cost-push inflation; wages rose faster than increases in marginal productivity, so prices increased. However, more intelligent analysis included the fact that elements of increased demand also had some effect on increased prices. The arguments which combined elements of demand-pull and cost-push with additional explanations can be broadly divided into two groups. One type of analysis claimed that full capacity utilization was reached

[8] The reason economists do not now think that downward flexibility of prices and wages will cause a return to full employment is because velocity will decrease when aggregate demand (and interest rates) decrease. However, the point of this discussion is not to explain the workings of the classical system but rather to point out that there has always been a definite relationship between wages and prices.

in key industries such as steel and autos, and the wage and price increases in those industries reflected demand-pull situations; these patterns were then widely copied.[9] Furthermore, since steel is used in so many other industries, this variable cost was marked up all along the line.[10] An important assumption of this "key-industry" argument is that workers try to narrow wage differentials between industries; large wage increases in one industry due to conditions of excess demand, higher profit rates, or greater productivity increases will be imitated in other industries even if no such conditions occur there. However, it is a simple matter to show that this is not the case. In manufacturing, wage rates in the highest-paying industries rose 5.2 percent annually for the 1955–1958 period, whereas the annual rate of increase in the lowest-paying industries was only 2.6 percent.[11] The wage gap widened instead of narrowed; there was no evidence of the "spillover" effect required by this argument. This sort of evidence, coupled with the fact that steel and auto prices have risen less than the average of all wholesale prices since 1958, has resulted in a short life for this particular theory.

Another suggested explanation of the 1955–1957 inflation, known as income inflation, had been developed in the early postwar years[12] but received renewed attention at this time. This analysis suggests that at or near full employment various groups—labor, businessmen, or rentiers—attempt to raise or maintain their real incomes by increasing their money incomes. There is an attempt to try and split up more than 100 percent of the total product. If one of these groups upsets the existing equilibrium, the other groups will try to regain their previous position by inflationary tactics. If it is argued, in addition, that this initial disturbance from equilibrium occurs because firms increase their percentage markup when business conditions improve, this hypothesis is seen to resemble the profits inflation theory developed in the previous section. An additional embellishment to this theory was added in the case of the steel industry, where both labor and business tried to increase their share of national

---

[9] This argument was developed most thoroughly by C. L. Schultze in "Recent Inflation in the United States," *Joint Economic Committee Study Paper No. 1* (Washington: Government Printing Office, 1959).

[10] O. Eckstein and G. Fromm have suggested that 40 percent of the rise in the entire wholesale price level for the period 1947–1958 was due to the increase in steel prices alone. See their "Steel and the Postwar Inflation," *Joint Economic Committee Study Paper No. 2* (Washington: Government Printing Office, 1959). Their figure is overestimated because it does not consider the use of foreign steel or other substitute products but does give some indication of the importance of steel prices in the overall price level.

[11] Corresponding price rises were 4.5 and 0.5 percent, respectively. The highest-paying industries were steel, petroleum, autos, ordnance, and aircraft; the lowest-paying were textiles, apparel, and leather.

[12] M. Reder, "The Theoretical Problems of a National Wage-Price Policy," *Canadian Journal of Economics*, Vol. 14, No. 1 (February, 1948), pp. 46–61. J. S. Duesenberry, "Mechanics of Inflation," *Review of Economics and Statistics*, Vol. 32, No. 2 (May, 1950), pp. 144–149. F. D. Holzman, "Income Determination in Open Inflation," *Review of Economics and Statistics*, Vol. 32, No. 2 (May, 1950), pp. 150–158.

income by large wage and price increases. In this case labor seemed to be pushing against an open door, because their wage demands were so easily accepted and passed on as higher prices.

The year that was probably the watershed year for choosing between theories of price behavior was 1958. This was clearly the most severe postwar recession; the industrial production index fell by 14 percent, but wholesale prices actually rose slightly. This diverse behavior of prices and output can be explained with our choice of price function as follows:

1. In 1957 the economy was far enough away from full capacity so that it was close to the horizontal part of the marginal cost curve. Thus a movement back along this curve in 1958 would not have any appreciable effect on prices.

2. Since wages depend on last year's rate of unemployment and price level (as discussed in Chapter 10), they were still rising at a faster rate than productivity. This shifted the marginal cost curve upward.

3. The elasticity of demand increased at each price (if the demand curve shifted parallel to itself), which would reduce the degree of monopoly and the markup factor and decrease prices.

Causes 2 and 3 tend to offset each other; from the movement of prices in 1958, it appears that these offsetting influences were about equal.

Another view is that there were no offsetting influences; rather "administered prices" merely stayed at their former level. Since then, downward revision on prices of several steel and other metal products (mainly to meet foreign competition) had vitiated the usefulness of this concept.[13]

Thus, starting in 1959, the importance of wages in determining the price level began to become generally recognized. Soon the wage–price guidelines were formulated by the Council of Economic Advisors,[14] and today most of the discussion of price stability is framed in terms of wage policy.

Not much has been said so far about the influence of the money stock on the price level. This is partially because modern-day practitioners of the quantity theory stress that for most of the postwar period both in the United States and abroad monetary policy has been passive. The central government has undertaken to increase the stock of money to that extent which will guarantee full employment, even if this means accepting the inflationary patterns set by business and labor. The increase in prices for a given real output can be maintained only by a larger money stock. Some draw from this the conclusion that the government is responsible for inflation; if it would only abandon its public commitment to full employment, labor and business would behave

---

[13] In early 1966, some of the steel companies completely abolished any price listing on some of their products, such as wire rods, to meet foreign competition. These are hardly administered prices.

[14] The first formulation is found in the 1962 report, pp. 83–88. Subsequent reports have continued to refer to these guidelines, although the exact measures of acceptable wage increases found in the earlier reports have been dropped.

in a more reasonable manner, and full employment without inflation would result.[15]

During the years of the postwar period when the money stock did not passively expand to ensure full employment, primarily 1955–1957, prices nevertheless rose rather rapidly. This would seem to negate the direct relationship between changes in the money stock and the price level. However, it was argued that the 1955–1957 period was characterized by a "velocity inflation" that was supposedly due to a belated adjustment to wartime (World War II, not Korea) increases in the money stock and the general upward trend in interest rates.[16] Since velocity is defined so that $MV = PX$, a rise in P with X steady or increasing and M decreasing must clearly result in an increase in V. But a need to find a new explanation for every postwar business cycle explaining why the previous version of the quantity theory did not hold has reduced its efficacy as a possible determinant of the price level.

The use of unit labor costs as the primary determinant of manufacturing prices is of substantial validity for the postwar U.S. economy. However, the type of function we have chosen is not useful in all situations. First, it is not useful in times of hyperinflation, whereas the quantity theory is; however, this clearly does not apply to the postwar United States economy. Second, it does not explain sharp increases in prices due to speculative buying, such as the one occurring at the beginning of the Korean War; but it is very doubtful whether other theories explain this either. Third, it does not explain periods following the lifting of price controls which had kept prices far below equilibrium levels, such as in 1946–1947. Perhaps the large stock of money accumulated during the war would help to explain the rapid price increase that did occur. However, with the relaxation of price controls and backlogged demand for consumer and producer durables, no theory which does not explicitly include these effects is likely to predict prices for such periods very accurately.

One of the reasons that there is so much disagreement about the causes of inflation even among those who think that unit labor costs are a significant determinant of prices is that the three causes of inflation we have included in our function seldom happen *seriatim*, but instead occur simultaneously. Just at the time when firms are likely to be operating on the rising part of their marginal cost curves, the demand curve is likely to be shifting out, thus raising the degree of monopoly power, and wage earners are most likely to be bargaining for increases exceeding productivity gains. Thus what actually happens may be similar to the situation shown in Figure 11.6. As we move from situation 1 to situation 2, it is clear that prices will rise. The quantity may also increase,

[15] M. Friedman, "Some Comments on the Significance of Labor Unions for Economic Policy," in D. M. Wright, ed., *The Impact of the Union* (New York: Harcourt, Brace & World, 1951), pp. 204–234. W. A. Morton, "Trade Unionism, Full Employment and Inflation," *American Economic Review*, Vol. 40, No. 1 (March, 1950), pp. 13–39.

[16] R. T. Selden, "Cost-Push versus Demand-Pull Inflation, 1955–1957," *Journal of Political Economy*, Vol. 67, No. 1 (February, 1959), pp. 1–20.

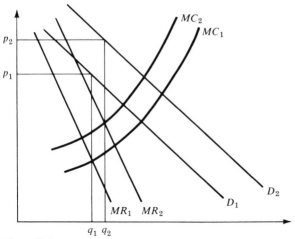

Figure 11.6

although this is far from certain. It is not at all clear what happens to profits. Since this is the way things really happen, it is sometimes difficult to "sort out" the various causes of inflation. The rising part of the cost curve is the part most likely to be associated with wage increases that are greater than productivity gains, so elements of demand-pull and cost-push are quite likely to occur together.

Some writers have gone further than this. They state that wage rates and aggregate expenditures are a function of the same variables. They argue that at least two of the three causes always occur together and it is not possible to single out any one cause of inflation at any given time. In this view, demand-pull and cost-push cannot be separated as causes of inflation, because they always occur together.[17] While this may be a likely occurrence there seems to be no particular advantage (except possibly for simplicity) of tying all these effects together in a single package. It is useful to analyze each effect separately, while realizing that they often occur simultaneously.

11.3   DETERMINATION OF SECTOR PRICE LEVELS

The wholesale price level, which was explained in Section 11.1, serves as the basis for determining the other price levels in the model. These are needed for three reasons. First, sector prices are needed for each component of aggregate demand in order to convert constant-dollar values into current-

---

[17] The strongest proponent of this view is S. Weintraub; for example, "The Keynesian Theory of Inflation: The Two Faces of Janus," *International Economic Review*, Vol. 1. No. 2 (May, 1960) pp. 143–155. The view is also found in R. J. Ball, *Inflation and the Theory of Money* (Chicago: Aldine, 1965).

dollar values. Second, relative price terms are used in several of the aggregate demand functions, such as consumer durables, housing, exports, and imports. Third, it is necessary to explain the differential movements of consumer goods prices and capital goods prices over the cycle, because this difference was used in explaining the redistribution of national income over the cycle.

Retail prices of consumer goods (autos, other durables, and nondurables except food) are considered first. It is assumed that retailer's margins do not fluctuate cyclically, although they may shift slowly over time. Thus quarter to quarter movements in retail prices of consumer goods will follow similar movements in wholesale prices, although there may be a slight lag in the full markup adjustment. In a multisector model, the wholesale price of each category of goods would be determined by unit labor costs and capacity utilization rates in each industry. This is the approach used by Schultze and Tryon in the Brookings model. These prices would then be converted to retail prices by the appropriate markup factors. However, for a less detailed structure of the economy, it is assumed that movements in the prices of autos, other durables, and nondurables except food all follow movements in the general wholesale price level (excluding food and farm products).

The price of consumer services is considered next. Many items in the consumer services classification are really imputations; these include imputed rent and interest, the net costs of insurance (premiums paid minus claims), and banking and brokerage services; it is hard to define a price level for these services even at a conceptual level. It is also very difficult to estimate a price level for contributions made to religious, educational, or charitable organizations. The prices of services supplied by public utilities and other regulated industries can be measured, but they tend to stay fixed for long periods of time (with the exception of airline fares). These services account for two thirds of total expenditures of consumer services. Although it would be possible to construct a price index for the remaining components of consumer services, there are still substantial difficulties in measuring and explaining quarterly (or yearly) movements in many of these prices. Thus for short-run movements, the price of consumer services is considered to be a trend, so that changes in this series are taken to be constant.

The price of food is considered to be exogenous, as are other components of the farm sector. However, a large proportion of changes in the consumer price level are often attributable to the price of food, so that some knowledge of the latter is essential when forecasting movements in the former. Movements in the price of food often accentuate or mask true movements of all other prices in the economy. Since food prices are determined by exogenous forces, they are not the relevant prices for consideration in policy purposes. For this reason the wholesale price level excluding food and farm products is often used as a guide to policy decisions.

The prices of imported goods and services are also exogenous, because they are determined by price relationships in other countries. However, the price of exports may be an important variable in the system, particularly when the effect of various monetary and fiscal policies are assessed on the foreign balance. Since the largest part of U.S. exports are manufactured products (although food exports have recently been increasing), changes in export prices follow changes in wholesale prices, again with a very slight lag.

Investment prices are treated somewhat differently than consumer prices. As explained in Chapter 7, the supply curve for fixed investment is much more inelastic than for consumer goods; this is particularly true for the labor component of construction. The demand curve for fixed *business* (but not residential) investment is also more inelastic than that for consumer goods, so that small shifts in the demand or supply curves for fixed business investment are likely to have substantially greater effects on the price of these goods than would be true in the consumer-goods sector. This inelasticity is represented in the price of capital goods (p_k) equation by the term I_p/X; this represents the proportion of gross national product being used in fixed business investment. It might be thought that the term I_h/X would be the relevant variable in the price of residential construction (p_h), but this is not the case. Since housing receives *residual* labor, a high I_h/X ratio may mean that the demand for construction labor on industrial jobs is low and therefore more workers are available for residential construction. The price of residential construction is more volatile than other capital goods prices, and changes in both I_p and I_h are reflected quickly in changes in p_h. Both these components of fixed investment are equally important in determining the change in p_h, since both represent demand for the same factors of production. The relative movements of p_k, p_h, and p_c (the consumer price index) during recessions and booms are shown in Figure 11.7.

The estimated price equations are

(15.40) $\Delta p_{ns} = 0.0039 + 0.063\Delta p_m + 0.130\Delta p_{m-1} + 0.088\Delta p_f$ $\bar{R}^2 = 0.672$
$\qquad\qquad\qquad\quad (0.075)\qquad (0.052)\qquad\quad (0.014)$

(15.41) $\Delta p_{na} = -0.0031 + 0.768\Delta p_m + 0.238\Delta p_{m-1}$ $\bar{R}^2 = 0.682$
$\qquad\qquad\qquad\qquad (0.143)\qquad (0.116)$

(15.42) $\Delta p_a = 0.0012 + 0.597\Delta p_{m-1}$ $\bar{R}^2 = 0.549$
$\qquad\qquad\qquad\quad (0.125)$

(15.43) $\Delta p_k = -0.0332 + 0.792\Delta p + 0.3915(I_p/X)$ $\bar{R}^2 = 0.564$
$\qquad\qquad\qquad\quad (0.143)\quad\ (0.1192)$

(15.44) $\Delta p_h = -0.0017 + 1.265\Delta p + 0.00143$
$\qquad\qquad\qquad\quad (0.206)\qquad (0.00037)$

$\qquad\qquad\qquad \times [(I_p + I_h) - (I_p + I_h)_{-2}]$ $\bar{R}^2 = 0.439$

(15.45) $\Delta p_e = -0.0022 + 0.646\Delta p_m + 0.488\Delta p_{m-1}$ $\bar{R}^2 = 0.496$
$\qquad\qquad\qquad\quad (0.233)\qquad (0.189)$

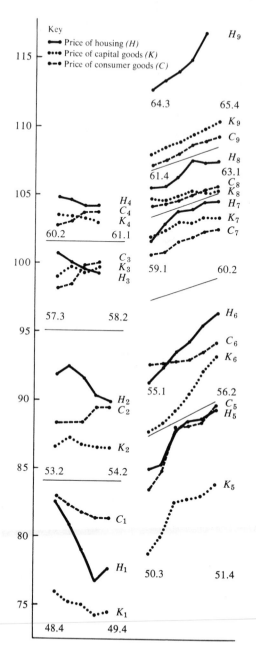

Figure 11.7

where p_{ns} = implicit deflator for consumer nondurables and services, 1958 = 1.00

p_m = wholesale price index, 1958 = 1.00

p_f = index of prices received by farmers, 1958 = 1.00

p_{na} = implicit deflator of consumer durables except autos and parts, 1958 = 1,00

p_a = implicit deflator of autos and parts, 1958 = 1.00

p = implicit GNP deflator, 1958 = 1.00

p_k = implicit deflator for fixed business investment, 1958 = 1.00

p_h = implicit deflator for residential construction, 1958 = 1.00

p_e = implicit deflator for exports, 1958 = 1.00

I_p = fixed business investment, billions of 1958 dollars

I_h = residential construction, billions of 1958 dollars

X = gross national product, billions of 1958 dollars

11.4   THE MONETARY SUBSECTOR

Since the time of the *General Theory*, most analysis of the monetary sector has centered around the Keynesian liquidity preference function. In its simplest form, this function states that the private sector (individuals, businessmen, and financial institutions) holds money for two principal reasons. The first is the transactions demand. Each unit of the private sector holds cash balances which are proportional to its average transactions. It is assumed that the proportion of money held to average transactions depends primarily on institutional factors such as the length of time between paychecks, corporate income tax payments, and other factors that change very slowly over time (except for revisions in the tax laws). A similar motive, holding money for precautionary purposes, is quantitatively unimportant and is usually included with transactions balances. The other principal reason for holding money is known as the speculative demand. According to the earlier neoclassical theory, no one would hold more money than he needed for transactions purposes because the rate of return on money was zero, whereas the rate of return on savings deposits, bonds, or other interest-earning assets was always greater than zero. However, Keynes pointed out that if interest rates were very low relative to normal levels, bond prices would be very high and future capital losses highly probable. In such circumstances it would be more profitable to hold money with its zero rate of return and invest the money a few years later at higher interest rates. Consider the alternative purchases of a 20-year bond which is currently paying 2 percent interest but is expected to (and does) pay 4 percent in following years. If the individual buys a bond now at 2 percent, he earns (discounting future earnings) per dollar of invested income:

$$\frac{0.02}{1.02} + \frac{0.02}{(1.04)^2} + \cdots + \frac{0.02}{(1.04)^{20}} + \frac{1.00}{(1.04)^{20}}$$

which equals 0.7292. If he waits a year and then invests he earns

$$\frac{0.04}{(1.04)^2} + \frac{0.04}{(1.04)^3} + \cdots + \frac{0.04}{(1.04)^{20}} + \frac{1.00}{(1.04)^{20}}$$

or 0.9628. An individual who buys a bond this year, sells it next year at a capital loss, and reinvests it in a bond paying 4 percent will still only earn 0.7292 because of the large capital loss he will receive.

Individuals and businesses can always invest in short-term securities that will carry no capital losses. This would imply that short-term rates on riskless securities would fall almost to zero in periods of substantial excess liquidity. During the 1930s interest rates on short-term government bills did fall as low as 0.07 percent, or a yearly return of only 70 cents per $1000 invested. The costs of handling the transactions were more than this for all but the largest investors.

It should be pointed out that today most of the speculative demand originates in the financial sector. Individuals can almost always direct their funds to federally insured savings institutions, earn the specified (positive) rate of return, and convert to other assets when desired with no capital loss. However, the problem of excess reserves in the banking sector will certainly not be mitigated by deposits of one bank in another bank. Commercial banks and other lending institutions need to find outlets for loans outside the banking sector and may not wish to make additional loans when interest rates are considered to be depressed. The substantial increase in excess reserves during each postwar recession suggests that the speculative motive is substantial.

These considerations suggest that the lower the interest rate, the more money would be held as an asset and the less would be spent for bonds. The demand for money can then be written

(11.24) $$M = kpX - \lambda pi$$

or, writing it in terms of *real cash balances*,

(11.25) $$\frac{M}{p} = kX - \lambda i$$

The price level is always included in the transactions demand, because transactions holdings are proportional to money income, but it is not always included in the speculative demand. However, the price term is necessary in both parts of the equation if we assume no money illusion on the part of the holders of money. If the price level were not included, the demand for money function would imply that changes in the price level (or, in an extreme case, change in the monetary unit) would induce people to hold a different amount of money as an asset even though the same amount of real income was being used to purchase the same amount of goods and services. Since we have rejected money illusion on the part of individuals in the aggregate demand and wage functions, it seems entirely reasonable to do so in the demand for money function.

Since this type of function has gained general acceptance, a number of writers, spearheaded by Patinkin,[18] have made an effort to show that the enlightened classical writers, particularly Wicksell,[19] really specified this type of a demand for money function instead of the equation of exchange, $MV = pX$. We do not argue this doctrinal point except to comment that the liquidity-preference function seems generally accepted by almost all present-day economists. Such a formulation denies the cyclical stability of the ratio of GNP to the money stock as promulgated by the "old" quantity theory. Since even acknowledged quantity theorists now talk about "velocity inflation," there is not much to be gained by rehashing this point once again.

There are, however, still a few points of disagreement about the interpretation of the liquidity-preference function. Most economists have argued that this function determines the rate of interest. The demand for money must always be equal to the supply of money *ex post* and the latter is largely exogenously determined, so if the price level and aggregate demand are determined by other considerations, this equation determines the interest rate. Although there is substantial agreement that it does so in most circumstances, it may not at times of full employment or times of deep depressions.

According to Wicksell (and given modern dress by Patinkin), at full employment the rate of interest is determined by the marginal productivity of capital and the propensity to save, and not by the money stock. Changes in the money stock will be reflected entirely in changes in the price level. This is of course the primary claim of the quantity theorists. However, even the advocates of this theory claim that this is a long-run equilibrium position. In the short run, where adjustments from one equilibrium position to another are occurring and inflexible product and factor prices exist, there is little question that tightening of the money supply does raise interest rates. In fact, this is the primary purpose of monetary policy and has an important role in causing the turning points of the cycle. For a decrease in the money stock to have no effect on the interest rate would require an immediate proportional reduction in prices, which is most unlikely at the peak of a boom. Thus in what follows we can concentrate on the actual short-run movements and dismiss the theoretical long-run relationships which have yet to be observed.[20]

---

[18] D. Patinkin, *Money, Interest, and Prices*, 2nd ed. (New York: Harper & Row, 1966), particularly appendix E.

[19] K. Wicksell, *Interest and Prices* (translated by R. F. Kahn from *Geldzins und Guterpreise*) (London: Macmillan, 1936).

[20] Only the difficulty in measuring the marginal productivity of capital keeps us from making a stronger statement about the observed postwar relationship between the money stock (M) and the interest rate (i). If we consider the three postwar full employment periods of 1946–1948, 1951–1953, and 1964–1966, we find that the aggregate savings ratio is very similar for all periods and

During deep depressions, Keynes argued that there was a minimum rate of interest which represented the lowest rate of return that any lender would be willing to take on a bond. Below this rate of interest no one would be interested in further lending. Thus additional increases in the money stock would have no effect on the level of GNP. This phenomenon is commonly known as the *liquidity trap*. Such an argument has been countered by assuming that some of the extra money added to real cash balances would be spent on goods and services regardless of the level of the interest rate. We have argued at some length in the chapters on consumption and investment, however, that stocks of money or other liquid assets have at most a negligible effect on these components of aggregate demand.

Many attempts have been made to estimate demand for money functions of the form $M/p = f(X, i)$, sometimes on an aggregate basis, more often on a sectoral basis (households, business, and so on). Early attempts to estimate this function often included a nonlinear interest rate term in an effort to estimate the region of the liquidity trap. Results by Tobin[21] and Klein and Goldberger,[22] based mainly on the depression years, did show evidence of a minimum rate of interest at about 2 percent. However, repeated attempts to estimate this type of function with postwar data have not been particularly successful.

Modern econometric research in monetary theory and policy has tended to deemphasize the speculative motive in the demand for money equations and stress instead the endogenous nature of the money supply. No longer is the stock of money treated as if it were determined independently of other monetary variables. Instead, interest rates and general economic activity, together with the action of the Federal Reserve System, jointly determine the money supply.

To give these ideas a more specific formulation we present a simplified discussion of a monetary sector model which follows the much more detailed studies of deLeeuw[23] and Goldfeld[24]. Both analyses consider the effect of financial intermediaries, but to simplify the exposition we consider only currency (C), demand deposits (D) and time deposits (T), the sum of which is

---

that there is a strong inverse relationship between M/GNP and the long-term bond yield. If the Wicksell-Patinkin theory holds, it would have to be argued that the marginal productivity of new capital equipment was lower in the immediate postwar period, when much of the capital equipment was old and obsolescent, than in the most recent period when the average age of the capital stock was much smaller. This seems most unlikely.

It can be protested that these are not truly long-run periods, but it would seem as a minimum that the burden of proof would be on those who posit no correlation to find long-run periods where the interest rate stayed the same in spite of large fluctuations in the M/GNP ratio.

[21] J. Tobin, "Liquidity Preference and Monetary Policy," *Review of Economic Statistics*, Vol. 29, No. 2 (May, 1947), pp. 124–131.

[22] L. R. Klein and A. S. Goldberger, *An Econometric Model of the United States Economy, 1929–1952* (Amsterdam: North-Holland, 1955).

[23] F. deLeeuw, "A Model of Financial Behavior," in *The Brookings Model ...*, *op. cit.*, chap. 13.

[24] S. M. Goldfeld, *Commercial Bank Behavior and Economic Activity* (Amsterdam: North-Holland, 1966).

defined as the money stock. We have

(11.26) $M_j = f_j(Y, X, i_j, i_k)$ $j = C, D, T$

where M_j is the jth component of the money stock

   Y is personal disposable income

   X represents other economic activity variables (principally investment and corporate cash flow)

   i_j and i_k are own and substitute rates of interest

The inclusion of interest rates in this function does not imply a liquidity trap. Instead it says that when the rates of (for example) time deposits are higher, time deposits will increase relative to other forms of holding liquid assets and stocks of money and other liquid assets will decrease.

We now relate the demand for money to the supply of money and Federal Reserve System policy variables. Instead of treating the entire money stock as exogenous, we center on one particular aspect over which the Fed has close control. We assume that the Fed can determine the level of *free reserves* (that is, excess reserves less borrowing from the Fed).

The problem of commerical banks' portfolio balance as it applies to free reserves is considered next. Their reserve position is most directly affected as follows: It will increase if demand and time deposits increase, decrease if loans increase, and decrease if reserve requirements increase. Reserve requirements can change if either the base (deposits) or the required reserve ratio changes. The latter is obviously at the discretion of the Fed, but the former is not. If deposits increase (for example), the decrease in reserve position will be more than offset by the increase in deposits, so on balance reserve position will be improved. We can treat net additions to loanable funds (after deducting increased reserves) and required reserve ratios separately. These considerations suggest the following *partial* function for determining the reserve position of banks:

(11.27) $FR = g(D(1 - k), L, k)$

where $FR =$ level of free reserves

   $L =$ commercial loans

   $k =$ required reserve ratio

Assume that banks are initially in equilibrium and there is an increase in loans. The Fed can control the level of free reserves through open-market operations and the discount rate. The banks can either borrow at the discount window or sell short-term government securities. Although they can do other things as well, for practical purposes these account for the great majority of short-term transactions.

Banks are supposedly discouraged from borrowing from the Fed except to meet unexpected short-term contingencies. Nevertheless there is some interest elasticity with respect to the discount rate.[25] If the discount rate is substantially below the yield that can be earned on short-term U.S. government securities, commerical banks will prefer to borrow from the Fed instead of selling these securities. Thus the lower the discount rate relative to short-term interest rates, the lower will be the level of free reserves if the Fed does not take offsetting measures.

It is quite probable, however, that the Fed will want to keep free reserves close to their previous level. In that case it will reduce borrowing at the discount window. Banks will then have little recourse other than to sell some of their short-term securities. This will depress the market price and thus raise short-term interest rates. In this chain of events, then, a tightening of money (either through increased demand for loans or explicit monetary policy) causes banks to sell government bills, which raises the interest rate on these bills. This is, of course, not a new result but it explicitly incorporates bank behavior and Federal Reserve policy moves into interest-rate determination.

To recapitulate, the amount of required reserves held by the banks depends on the required reserve ratio and the demand for money, which in turn depends on various types of income and interest rates. The level of free reserves is controlled closely by the Fed through their monetary policy tools. Commercial banks will make loans and buy other securities depending on demand and relative yields. They will then balance their accounts by borrowing at the discount window or trading short-term government securities. The tighter money is, the more government bills must be sold by the banks and the higher interest rates will go.

The degree of monetary stringency is thus seen to depend both on general economic activity and monetary policy. Among the general economic activity variables, the amount of deposits, corporate liquidity, and the demand for loans (primarily a function of investment) are the most important. All the three major Federal Reserve policy tools help to determine the money supply. Open-market operations are used to control the level of free reserves. The level of the discount rate determines to some extent whether banks sell short-term securities or draw down their excess reserves. The required reserve ratio determines the overall level of reserves for given demand and time deposits.

In addition, the discount rate may influence short-term rates directly. To examine this possibility more closely we discuss the exact nature of the discount rate in the free reserves equation. It has already been shown that banks will prefer to decrease their reserves by a greater amount the larger the (positive) spread between short-term interest rates and the discount rate, and they will sell more bills the smaller this spread. Because there is often considerable hesitancy about continued borrowing from the Fed, one would not expect the effects of changes in each interest rate to be symmetrical. A change of 1 percent in the short-term rate should have a greater effect on banks' reserve

---

[25] *Ibid.,* pp. 43–50.

position than a change of 1 percent in the discount rate. Empirical evidence on this point is discussed below. But changes in both rates exert an influence on bank behavior.

A glance at Figure 11.8 shows that there is a strong simultaneous movement between changes in the two rates; no leads or lags are apparent. Even a finer reading obtained with monthly data gives the same result.[26] Because of the concurrent changes in both series, the direction of causality cannot easily be determined. On the one hand, it could be argued that higher levels of the short term rate relative to the discount rate result in increased borrowing pressures at the discount window. To reduce this pressure the Fed follows already established market behavior by raising the discount rate. On the other hand, the Fed might want to decrease the amount of borrowing and *initiate* a tighter monetary policy. Then the Fed would raise the discount rate even though other interest rates were remaining constant. Banks would then find that the differential rate of return between holding bills and borrowing from the Fed had decreased, so they would sell more bills. However, this would depress the price of bills further and thus raise the short-term interest rate. It is possible that the spread between the two rates would remain unchanged. In this case the Fed would have raised short-term interest rates by increasing the discount rate.

Without specifying the direction of causality between the discount rate and the short-term rate, the free reserves function can now be written

$$(11.28) \qquad\qquad FR = f[D(1 - k), L, k, i_d, i_s]$$

The function estimated by deLeeuw is[27]

$$(11.29) \qquad \frac{\Delta FR}{(D + T)_{-1}} = -0.00156 + 0.00235i_d - 0.00216i_s$$

$$+ 0.053 \frac{\Delta[D(1 - k) + T(1 - k')]}{(D + T)_{-1}} - 0.387\left(\frac{FR}{D + T}\right)_{-1}$$

(no standard errors for the coefficients are given). k' is the required reserve

---

[26] Some results we computed showed that there is a high positive correlation between changes in the discount rate in a given month and changes in the bill rate during the previous month, the current month, and the following month, but virtually no correlation with changes during two months before or two months after. However, most of the time the bill rate was steady until the discount rate changed. If anything, this would suggest that the discount rate usually leads market rates. Typical examples of this would be the increase of $\frac{1}{2}$ percent in the discount rate in September 1959; the bill rate had been 3.25, 3.24, and 3.36 percent before this increase and rose to 4.00 percent in September. In the opposite direction, a $\frac{1}{2}$ percent decrease in the discount rate in June 1960 moved the bill rate from previous monthly levels of 3.44, 3.24, and 3.39 percent down to 2.64 percent in the same month. Similar examples can be found in the 1957–1958 period.

[27] These functions represent a revision of work done for the original version of the Brookings model and are found in G. Fromm and P. Taubman, *Policy Simulations with an Econometric Model* (Washington, D.C.: The Brookings Institution, 1968), appendix II.

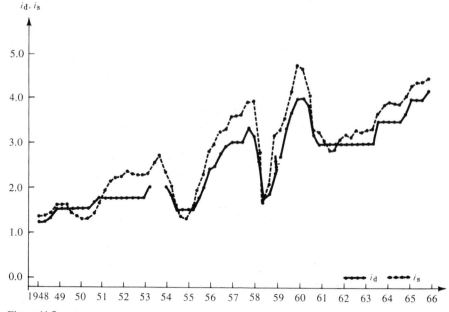

Figure 11.8

ratio on time deposits and all other variables are as defined above. Goldfeld estimates separate functions not only for excess reserves and borrowing at the discount window, but for city and country banks. If we disregard the lagged reaction terms that are present in all his equations we can aggregate and obtain the following equation[28]:

$$(11.30) \quad \Delta FR = 0.0673\Delta\left(D + \frac{FR}{k}\right) - 0.172\Delta L + 0.193i_d - 0.245i_s + \text{lagged terms}$$

Standard errors are reported by Goldfeld but are not applicable for the above equation, because it represents an average of four separate equations.

If $k \cong 0.16$, we can solve through for FR in Goldfeld's equation and obtain

$$(11.31) \quad \Delta FR = 0.333i_d - 0.422i_s + 0.116\Delta D - 0.297\Delta L$$

DeLeeuw's results can be made comparable to this by multiplying through by $\overline{D + T} = \$150$ billion. This gives

$$(11.32) \quad \Delta FR = 0.353i_d - 0.324i_s + 0.053\Delta[D(1 - k) + T(1 - k')] - 0.387FR_{-1}$$

The interest-rate effects are quite similar in magnitude. Although Goldfeld's function shows a slightly larger effect for i_s, the result is reversed in deLeeuw's findings. The coefficients of the ΔD terms are not entirely comparable, because deLeeuw includes the additional factor $1 - k$ but Goldfeld does not.

---

[28] Goldfeld, *op. cit.*, p. 131.

Furthermore, deLeeuw does not include a separate term for commercial loans. In an earlier version he included loans in the $D(1 - k) + T(1 - k')$ term so that it had the identical coefficient of 0.053. This is much lower than the effect found by Goldfeld. Unfortunately this term was not included separately so that its marginal contribution could be assessed more precisely. In any case it would seem that the loans variable is the least important term in the free-reserves function.

We have already stressed that in this monetary subsector model, free reserves can be closely controlled by the Fed. Since this is the case, it may be more appropriate to recast this equation in the form

$$i_s = f(i_d, FR, [D(1 - k) + T(1 - k')])$$

It should be pointed out that the way in which the function was derived implies no direction of causality between i_s and i_d but merely states that changes in both rates occur simultaneously. A further simplifying assumption is to use the identity that $D(1 - k) + T(1 - k') = RR$ (required reserves) as a means for substituting RR directly in the equation. Then

(11.33) $i_s = f(i_d, FR, RR)$

or

(11.34) $i_s = f(i_d, FR/RR)$

thereby treating FR/RR as a single policy variable. This eliminates having to estimate extra functions for D and T which are not used elsewhere in the system but is unrealistic in the sense that it does not allow required reserves to vary endogenously. On the other hand, it may be sensible to argue that the Fed controls the ratio of free reserves to required reserves rather than the level of free reserves, because the former more accurately gauges the degree of monetary stringency. This is the approximation used for our simplified short-term interest rate equation. The empirically estimated function is

(15.46) $i_s = 0.42 + 0.994i_d - 0.0895(FR/RR)$ $\bar{R}^2 = 0.961$
                    (0.034) (0.0118)

where i_s = rate on prime commercial paper, four to six months, percent

   i_d = discount rate at the Federal Reserve Bank of New York, percent

   FR = ratio of free reserves to required reserves for commercial banks, percent

Note in particular that the coefficient of i_d is almost identically unity. This is in agreement with the results of deLeeuw and Goldfeld. Although this particular function undoubtedly represents an oversimplification, it does agree with the results of more detailed and sophisticated studies of the monetary subsector that the short-term interest rate is primarily determined by Federal Reserve policy variables.

The determination of the long-term rate of interest (usually the long-term corporate bond yield) can be treated in a number of ways. Virtually all methods link the long-term rate to present and expected levels of the short-term rate. One standard way, known as the *expectations hypothesis*, states that the long-term rate is an average of expected future short-term rates and that long-term borrowers have to be offered a premium against the risk that interest rates will rise (and the price of bonds will fall) in the future. The problem is estimating the risk factor. DeLeeuw has suggested the following interpretation.[29] When current rates are above some long-run average, investors may expect them to fall and receive capital gains. On the other hand, when they are above this average, investors may also expect them to continue to rise in the near future. If investors expect capital losses, the differential between long and short rates will widen; investors will have to be compensated for their expected losses. If they expect capital gains, the differential will narrow. Thus the spread between long- and short-term interest rates will be positively correlated with recent movements in interest rates and negatively related with more distant movements. DeLeeuw has estimated the following function based on this pattern of behavior[30]:

$$(11.35) \qquad i_L - i_s = 1.399 + 3.161 \underset{(0.661)}{\left\{ i_L - 0.550 \left[\sum_{i=1}^{11} (0.45)^{i-1} \cdot i_{L-i} \right] \right\}}$$

$$- 4.455 \underset{(0.511)}{\left\{ i_L - 0.261 \left[\sum_{i=1}^{11} (0.75)^{i-1} \cdot i_{L-i} \right] \right\}} + \text{other terms}$$

The first term, which is more heavily weighted with recent values, is positively correlated with the spread between interest rates, whereas the second term, which gives relatively more importance to more distant values, is negatively correlated with the spread.

A much simpler form is simply to assume that expectations are neutral and the long-term rate is just proportional to a weighted average of past short-term rates, where the weights decline geometrically. This gives

$$(15.47) \qquad i_L = 0.21 + \underset{(0.028)}{0.086 i_s} + \underset{(0.037)}{0.889(i_L)_{-1}} \qquad \bar{R}^2 = 0.972$$

This sacrifices some information about expectations but has done well for predictive purposes.

---

[29] F. DeLeeuw, "A Model of Financial Behavior," in *The Brookings Model . . . , op. cit.,* p. 500.
[30] *Ibid.,* p. 477.

PART 2

COMPLETE THEORIES
OF
THE CYCLE

CHAPTER 12

PRE-KEYNESIAN THEORIES
OF THE BUSINESS CYCLE

12.1 AN OUTLINE OF THE BASIC CLASSICAL SYSTEM

In this part of the book, the individual equations that were previously discussed will be combined into a theory of the business cycle. Since cyclical fluctuations that have similar characteristics continue to occur, the way in which the various components of aggregate demand and supply combine to generate these repetitive patterns can be traced. It would be possible to proceed directly to a theory consisting of the functions that were examined and tested in Part 1. However, it is often quite difficult to trace individual cyclical forces in a model of 50 or more variables. For this reason it is first useful to explain the nature of cyclical fluctuations with simplified systems containing only a few variables. These systems are not realistic enough to be used for accurate predictions: empirical relationships must be added to any such basic structure to develop a model that both explains cyclical fluctuations and predicts them accurately. However, basic forces such as the accelerator which tend to cause fluctuations are an integral part of larger models, even if these forces are somewhat submerged and diffused. Unlike other branches of aggregate economics, many of the important ideas of business cycle theory were developed in the pre-Keynesian period, so that it is still relevant to examine some of these early theories.

In spite of the classical dogma that equilibrium positions were exclusively those of full employment, the business cycle was a recurring scene on the economic landscape, perhaps even more than today, so that considerable attention and effort was directed to the explanation of its causes and methods of control. Since almost all business cycle theorists (except for the under-consumptionists) were hampered by the tenets of the classical school, it is relevant to present briefly the outline of the aggregate economic system as envisaged by these classical economists. We shall then describe some of the more important theories of the cycle which were developed within this frame-work. Although many of the individual assumptions of the classical economists were in error, many useful principles of the business cycle were developed; these contributions are discussed in later sections of this chapter.

The two basic pillars of the aggregate classical theory are Say's law and the quantity theory. *Say's law* states that supply creates its own demand; the only reason that an individual works is to purchase goods and services with the remuneration he receives. In a barter economy, Say's law does in fact hold. An individual receives no money, only goods. He would work to produce these goods either if he expected to use them himself, or if he planned to trade them for some other goods, but for no other reason; thus he would not hoard them. The price ratio between goods would be determined by the demand and supply for these goods, and equilibrium prices would always be reached which would clear the market. If one good commanded a higher price than another good with identical production costs, some individuals would stop producing the lower-price good and start producing the higher-priced good. This would continue until the equilibrium price of both goods was the same. In similar fashion, the market-clearing mechanism would ensure that all goods would either be used or traded at some positive price. The possibility of some good being traded at a zero or negative price is summarily dismissed.

A similar argument prevails when money is introduced into the system *if* the same assumptions hold for money as for all other goods: it is never hoarded and can always be loaned at a positive price. Thus while individuals now receive remuneration for their work in money instead of goods and services, this serves only to facilitate trading and has no effect on the fundamental underlying relationships. Since money itself is barren, no one will want to hold more money than is necessary for brief transactions purposes. Instead, each individual will trade money for goods and services instead of bartering.

None of this is intended to preclude the possibility of saving. On the contrary, if an individual wishes to save, he can always loan his savings to some business-man or financial intermediary who will in turn invest these funds; thus the money will always be spent. The rate of interest at which these funds are loaned will, like every other price, depend on the demand and supply of the commodity, which in this case is savings. An increase in supply or a decrease in demand will lower the interest rate. However, no matter how much the demand and supply schedules shift, the classical economists argued that there would always be a positive equilibrium rate of interest which would clear the market. Many pages of the classical literature were devoted to explaining studiously how another bridge could be built, another tunnel drilled, or another railroad-track grade leveled if only the interest rate were low enough. As this rate approached zero, the annual return of these projects could always become greater than the yearly interest cost. Thus every individual receiving income would either spend it himself or loan it (perhaps through financial intermediaries) to someone else who would use the funds for investment. Therefore, full employment was always assured.

The statement that aggregate demand equals aggregate supply, or equivalently that investment equals savings, must of course always hold *ex post*. That is simply an accounting identity. But Say's law states that these relationships also hold *ex ante*. The amount people produce (aggregate supply) must be equal to the amount people *plan* to buy (aggregate demand) or else they would not produce it in the first place.

The other tenet of the classical theory, the *quantity theory*, states that the money stock is proportional to the money value of all transactions, which is equal to the price level times the physical volume of output. This is often written $MV = pX$, where V is the transactions velocity of money. Stated this way, the equation is an *ex post* identity and contains no explanatory value. The transformation from an identity to a functional relationship comes from the assumption that V is an institutional constant. Its value is determined by the nature of the banking system and the interval at which workers are usually paid; it does not fluctuate with the business cycle. The explanation for the constancy of V is similar to the explanation of Say's law. Neither individuals, businessmen, or financial intermediaries want to hold money that earns a zero rate of return. Any money not held for transactions purposes would always be lent out and used for some productive purpose. For this reason there would never be any idle cash balances or excess reserves, and a given amount of money would always support the same amount of money transactions. If, furthermore, the physical volume of output were fixed at the full-employment level, then changes in the money stock would be reflected only in changes in prices, in which case the quantity theory simplifies to $M = Kp$.

Say's law, together with the available factor resources and state of technology, thus determined the physical output of an economy at any given time. The quantity theory determined the overall price level. This price level was independent of the costs of production and depended only on the money stock. The wage rate, like any other price, would then be adjusted until the demand for labor was equal to the supply for labor. In purely competitive markets, all firms hire workers until the marginal physical product of the last man is equal to the real wage. Thus if there were an excess supply of labor because of (for example) technological improvement or growth in the labor force, money wages would be bid down by competitive forces. This would result in a fall in prices, which would be equal to the fall in wages if firms were operating on the constant part of their marginal cost curve, and less than the fall in wages if they were operating on the rising part of their marginal cost curves. In either case, both wages and prices would fall. Since the flow of money, MV, stays constant, the flow of money transactions, pX, must also stay constant. But if prices fell, the same nominal amount of money will purchase more goods and services. This would increase output and provide jobs for those currently unemployed. If this process did not produce sufficient jobs to return the economy to full employment, wages and prices would fall further and output would increase still more. The process would continue until full employment was reached. Only if wages or prices were rigid would there be unemployment, for then there would be an insufficient increase in output. It is sometimes claimed that the classical theorists ruled out these rigidities on the basis that they were unrealistic. This is not completely true, for as we shall see almost all the classical business cycle economists incorporated the rigidity of wages into their theories. However, they did argue that if unemployment were large enough, wages and prices would finally become flexible downward and a new full employment situation would be reached. Although there are certain advantages to wage earners and businessmen not adjusting their wages and prices downward in the short run, these advantages would soon disappear if the depression became more serious.

Thus, using the tools of Say's law, the quantity theory, and flexible prices and wages, the classical economists established that a position of full employment would always be reached in equilibrium. The key assumptions in this chain of causality are that people would always prefer to invest their idle cash balances at a positive rate of return instead of keeping them and earning a zero rate of return: and that there were always sufficient investment outlets for all these funds at some positive rate of return. Note that this conclusion has been reached without specifying anything about the shape of the consumption and investment functions except to say that the latter is interest-elastic at low interest rates. Thus the Keynesian consumption function, while a crucial tool (with proper modification) for explaining the general structure of the economy, is irrelevant in determining whether an equilibrium position can be reached at less than full employment.

Because it was not an integral part of the system, the classical economists had very little to say about the shape of the consumption function: it was usually referred to as the savings function, because of the more direct relationship between savings and investment. Some theorists suggested that savings depended positively on the interest rate, so less would be saved at a lower rate, but this was not a crucial part of the theory. Many other economists believed that savings was independent of other economic variables; it depended on such attributes as general thriftiness, degree of forethought, and the level of civilization. In any case, it definitely was not thought to be a function of either personal or national income.

This view has been extensively criticized by everyone who can refer to the myriad of studies showing a definite relationship between consumption and income. Yet the classical relationship merits a word of attention, if only before discarding it that much more forcefully. The classical savings function can be interpreted in two ways: Either the *absolute* level of savings or the *rate* of savings is independent of the level of income. In the first case, the rate of savings would decrease as population expanded and technology advanced, eventually leading to the classical stationary state where both savings and investment are zero. This is clearly a most unrealistic situation and bears very little resemblance to an economy with cyclical fluctuations. In the other case, the economy would continue to grow at a rate determined jointly by the savings rate and the rate of technological advancement. Although the classical economists were in general not concerned with the problems of growth, a function which suggests that the savings rate is independent of income is much closer to reality for the long run (for example, from cycle to cycle, or about four years or more) than the naive consumption function $C = a + bY$, $a > 0$, $b < 1$. It will be recalled that this naive consumption function predicted depression and eight million unemployed after World War II, instead of the substantial inflation that actually occurred. Thus for an economy that is continually near full employment, a savings function such as the classical economists used, interpreted in this way, was not far from describing actual behavioral trends. The long-run constancy (or maybe even slight upward trend) of the C/Y ratio attests to the fact that the naive Keynesian consumption function is not useful for explaining consumer behavior.

The basic elements of the classical system can be completed with the introduction of a labor supply function, which states that the amount of people seeking work is an increasing function of the real wage. This function has sometimes been used to argue that if the real wage declined sufficiently, enough people would leave the labor force to restore the economy to full employment. This is not only a very poor argument but totally unnecessary: it was shown above how full employment can be reached even if the labor supply is fixed. Furthermore, although the labor supply function may have some elasticity near full employment because marginal workers may be affected when all regular workers are already hired, it has almost no effect when there is substantial unemployment and regular members of the labor force are seeking jobs. In addition, the classical full employment position did *not* necessarily occur by a lowering of the real wage. Wages and prices would fall equally if firms were operating on the constant part of their marginal cost curves: then the increase in demand would occur because prices were cheaper and more could be bought with the same amount of money.

In functional notation, this system can be expressed as

$$C = \bar{C} \quad [\text{or } C = C(i)] \qquad MV = pX$$

$$I = I(i) \qquad\qquad L = L\!\left(\frac{w}{p}\right) \qquad (\text{or } L = \bar{L})$$

$$C + I = X \quad (\text{or } I = S) \qquad V = \bar{V} \text{ (institutional constant)}$$

$$X = X(L, K, t) \qquad\qquad M = \overline{M} \text{ (exogenously determined)}$$

$$\frac{\partial X}{\partial L} = \frac{w}{p} \qquad\qquad\qquad \Delta K = I$$

The interactions between these variables can also be traced on a standard multi-quadrant graph. In Figure 12.1 we show how the economy moves from one equilibrium position (denoted by 1's) to a new equilibrium position (denoted by 2's) when additional workers enter the labor force. In these diagrams we have assumed the supply of labor to be originally fixed at L_1. The level and slope of the production function determine total product (output) X and marginal product equal to the real wage (w/p). Quite separately, the money stock determines money output. The money output/real output ratio

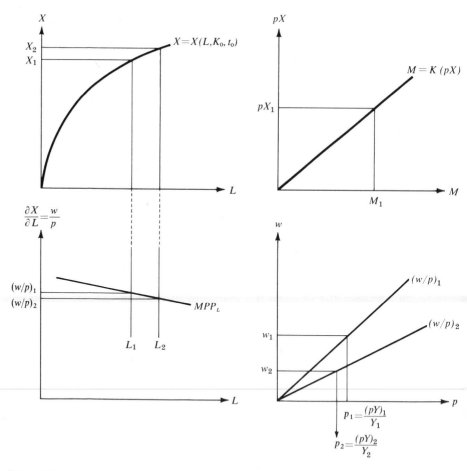

Figure 12.1

determines the price level, and the money wage equals the real wage times the price level.

If the economy always returned to full-employment equilibrium in this rather painless fashion, it might seem that the classical economists would have been hard pressed to develop a theory of the business cycle, particularly in terms of a recurring pattern generated by endogenous forces rather than in terms of exogenous shocks such as labor movements, new gold discoveries, or other diverse phenomena. As a matter of fact, it is necessary only to remove the crucial (and unrealistic) assumptions about idle cash balances, and it becomes almost, but not quite, as plausible to generate cycles in the remaining classical framework as it is in the Keynesian framework. First, the business cycle theorists realized that excess reserves did accumulate during depressions and that important reasons for the beginning of the upturn were an excess of loanable funds and low interest rates. Second, most theorists realized that investment was partially influenced by expectations, and that the same interest rate was less likely to generate as much investment in a depression as in a boom. Third, the lag of wages behind prices was noted by almost all analysts of the business cycle and was included in many of their theories. These cannot be considered Keynesian theories, for the concept of the multiplier is entirely absent. Statements such as "the increase in investment will raise total demand by almost the full amount of this increase" are fairly common. But given the fact that this important tool was missing, these theories form an important if sometimes shaky basis for later business cycle research.

It is not possible to separate all the classical theories of the business cycle into mutually exclusive categories, because most of them contain overlapping ideas. However, for purposes of exposition they may be categorized as follows:

(1) Monetary demand theories of the cycle. These theories hold that fluctuations in the interest rate and availability of loanable funds are responsible for fluctuations in investment, and thus of the economy. Turning points would not occur if changes in monetary conditions did not cause them.

(2) Nonmonetary demand theories of the cycle. These theories state that there is a maladjustment between the amount of capital stock and the amount of consumer demand, so that the investment/total demand ratio must be changed to return to equilibrium. These changes are enough to cause turning points, which may be accentuated by monetary factors. Many of these theories are related to various versions of the acceleration principle.

(3) Supply theories of the cycle. Fluctuations in the costs of doing business and profit margins are the main factors affecting economic activity. The change in profit margins, through its effect on expectations, is sufficient to cause the turning points. Although investment is the main component of aggregate demand affected, a change in profits may result in a change in the amount of funds available for all types of credit transactions and thus affect many components of aggregate demand.

The reader is hereby cautioned that the rest of this chapter is not intended to present a thorough coverage of the pre-Keynesian business cycle theories; for this, the reader is referred to the classic *Prosperity and Depression*.[1] Furthermore, no attempt will be made to establish a one-to-one correspondence between each idea and its author, although the most important references will be noted.[2] Instead, this chapter is intended to be an outline of the important ideas of classical business cycle theory which are still useful today, set in the general framework in which they were originally developed.

12.2   MONETARY DEMAND THEORIES OF THE CYCLE

The simplest of these theories, due primarily to R. G. Hawtrey,[3] is sometimes called the "purely monetary theory"; it is little more than an extension of the quantity theory, although it does include the idea that excess reserves do exist during depressions. Hawtrey's principal argument is that since $MV = pX$, no cyclical fluctuations would occur if MV could be stabilized over the cycle. He realizes that this is much more difficult than merely stabilizing M, the "stock of money": the "flow of money" must also be stabilized. However, if this could be accomplished, the business cycle could be controlled.

At the beginning of the upturn, there is an excess of credit and bank reserves, and interest rates are low. Hawtrey argues that low interest rates will stimulate investment in *working* capital (that is, inventories) rather than affecting fixed capital. Even a 1 or 2 percent change in the interest rate will have a substantial effect on inventory investment. This is true, according to Hawtrey, because the capital stock/sales ratio for inventories is much higher than the stock/sales ratio for fixed investment. This increase in inventory investment will stimulate production, which will increase aggregate demand; this in turn will raise sales, which will lead to more inventory investment, and the boom will continue upward. Meanwhile, increases in the flow of money are helping expand this boom. The money stock is increasing because of central bank policy. Although the early stages of the upswing would really be the correct time for the central bank to take precautionary and deflationary measures, this does not occur. The central bank sees no reason to discourage the boom as long as excess reserves are still plentiful. At the same time, velocity is also expanding, because bankers are now lending some of the idle cash balances that accumulated during the previous recession. The boom also gains momentum because prices begin to rise, which increases profits. This causes businessmen to increase their

---

[1] G. Haberler, *Prosperity and Depression*, 4th ed. (Cambridge, Mass.: Harvard University Press, 1958).

[2] For more complete references, see R. A. Gordon, *Business Cycles*, 2nd ed. (New York: Harper & Row, 1961), or A. H. Hansen, *Business Cycles and National Income*, expanded ed. (New York: Norton, 1964).

[3] An easily available summary of Hawtrey's views can be found in "The Trade Cycle," reprinted in *Readings in Business Cycle Theory* (Philadelphia: Blakiston, 1944).

orders for inventories, as they expect demand to keep rising and also wish to accumulate stocks before they become more expensive and in shorter supply. Thus increases in the money stock, transactions velocity, and price level all cause an increase in output.

There is an additional reason credit is so easily available. Increases in the wage rate lag behind increases in prices and output. Income distribution in the early stages of the upturn shifts in favor of businesses, who then find additional liquidity available in the form of retained earnings. Since labor income is rising more slowly than national income, cash for transactions purposes will not increase very much and will grow more slowly than the growth in the money stock. Thus the increase in the demand for transactions balances is smaller than the total increase in the flow of money, and the liquidity of the banks is increased even further.

This expansion could continue indefinitely if it were not for the limitations the central bank must ultimately apply to the growth of the money stock. These restrictions may occur for several reasons. If a given country is on the domestic gold standard, as England was at Hawtrey's time, the total amount of money will be limited by the amount of gold reserves. In time of inflation, these reserves are likely to be depleted, as rising prices raise imports and lower exports. For countries not on the domestic gold standard, the reserve requirements that the commercial banks must observe may finally stop the increase in credit. In these or other cases, the central bank will eventually be forced to restrict the growth of output and prices of the economy by tightening the supply of credit. By this time, too, wages are likely to have risen as much as prices, so that profit margins will be decreased and cash drawn out of the banking system for transactions purposes will have increased. Whether or not these all occur at the same time, the effect on credit is likely to be substantial when all of them finally do happen. Interest rates then rise sharply, and inventory investment is sharply curtailed.

Once the upper turning point has been reached, the economy rapidly spirals downward. A decrease in inventory investment results in less production, less sales, and still less inventory investment. Merchants are left with excess inventories on their shelves, they cancel already existing orders, and the downward movement of the economy is accelerated.

Since businesses no longer want to borrow as much as they did previously, banks are left with excess reserves. Merchants repay past loans instead of borrowing to buy goods, so that additional excess reserves flow into the banking system. This results in a reduction of interest rates, which again spurs the economy into another boom. Meanwhile, since wages lag prices both on the upswing and downswing, they are still falling at the beginning of the upturn. This means that less cash is needed for transactions, and more money is available for lending by the banking system. Because of this large supply of excess loanable funds, banks invariably overreact and lend more than enough money than would be necessary to return the economy to equilibrium. They overreact similarly in their contractions of credit at the upper turning point, so that the pattern of the business cycle continues to occur. To control the cycle, Hawtrey recommends that banks lend only that amount of money which would correspond to the equilibrium demand. However, he admits that this is a very difficult thing for individual banks to do *ex ante*; this job should be undertaken by the central bank and accomplished with the tools of the discount rate and open-market operations. Today Hawtrey would surely add the reserve ratio requirements of commercial banks as another useful tool. He feels that cycles can be conquered by monetary tools alone and that supplementary fiscal policy is not necessary.

Hawtrey's theory has some interesting and useful ideas. He correctly identifies inventory investment as the component of aggregate demand that fluctuates the most over the business cycle. His idea that wages lag behind prices, causing a shift in income distribution over the cycle, is a worthwhile one which is also found in many other pre-Keynesian theories. However, his link between inventory investment and the interest rate is one that has found almost no empirical support. Furthermore, his failure to suggest even a crude accelerator and mention that inventory investment is likely to be related to the changes in sales instead of the level of sales reduces the credence of his overall theory. His complete reliance on monetary variables leads him to an unrealistic theory of the cycle.

Another variant of the monetary demand theories of the cycle is known as the monetary overinvestment theories. These are associated mainly with Hayek and other members of the Austrian school.[4] Much of the analysis was developed by Wicksell,[5] but Wicksell himself believed that the turning points were caused by real factors rather than monetary factors, and thus is not included in this category. These theories state that an elastic credit supply is necessary for an upturn to begin, and is important in causing the upper turning point to occur. However, movements originating in the real sector of the economy, particularly fixed business investment, also help to cause the cyclical fluctuations.

The synopsis of this theory can be presented rather briefly. When interest rates are below equilibrium levels, fixed business investment will increase at a rate greater than can be supported by the total level of aggregate demand. Thus the economy will be "top heavy" with investment goods. For a number of reasons, there is not enough credit to continue all these projects, so interest rates rise, credit must be rationed, and some investment projects are discontinued. This leads to a general downturn that continues until excess credit finally leads to lower interest rates and a new upswing in investment begins.

---

[4] F. A. Hayek, *Prices and Production*, 2nd ed. (London: George Routledge, 1935). Also see his "Price Expectations, Monetary Disturbances and Maladjustments," reprinted in *Readings in Business Cycle Theory, op. cit.*

[5] See K. Wicksell, *Lectures on Political Economy, Vol. II* (London: Macmillan, 1935), pp. 190–214.

It can be seen that there is really not a great deal of difference between this theory and the "purely monetary" theory, except that fixed investment instead of inventory investment is affected. However, there are a few new ideas introduced which should be examined.

The concept of the equilibrium interest rate, or *natural rate* as it is called by Wicksell, who developed this general analysis, merits further attention. It is defined as the rate at which the demand for loanable funds is equal to the supply of savings *ex ante*. These demand and supply schedules in turn depend on the marginal productivity of capital and the savings rate. This natural rate needs to be compared not to the market rate of interest but to the market rate less the percentage changes in prices, or what Wicksell calls the *real rate*. The natural rate of interest fluctuates over the cycle, so it would be necessary to set the real rate equal to the natural rate at all times to keep investment at an equilibrium level. This would eliminate cyclical fluctuations in the economy.

However, bankers do not adjust their actual loan rates to some desired equilibrium level, but rather lower their rates as excess reserves accumulate. As the market rate continues to decrease, the demand for credit increases and exceeds the supply of savings available from current income. This supply of savings is supplemented by credit created by the banking system; this is inflationary because *ex ante* aggregate demand—spending from current income (equals production) plus past savings—is greater than *ex ante* aggregate supply. Thus if the market rate drops below the natural rate, prices will rise. The level of investment will rise above equilibrium not only because of low interest rates, but because of rising prices, since a rise in prices diminishes the real value of the funds which must be repaid.

By creating "cheap money," the banking system is directing resources from the consumer-goods industries into the capital-goods industries. A lower rate of interest encourages more capital-intensive and more roundabout methods of production, which in equilibrium will earn insufficient rates of return to justify their existence. Too large a proportion of the resources of society go into the production of capital goods. Since the economy is at full employment throughout this analysis, an increase in one sector must mean a decrease in the other sector. Such a misapportionment of resources is known as a *vertical maladjustment*. The allocation of the factors of production to the two sectors does not correspond to the future distribution of demand between consumption and investment. The maladjustment is vertical because it occurs between the "higher" (capital goods) and the "lower" (consumer goods) stages of production, in the nomenclature of the Austrian school.

The production of consumer goods has been curtailed by the transfer of resources to the capital-goods sector. For a while the demand for consumer goods will also be curtailed, because wages rise more slowly than prices and real incomes of workers decrease. Fixed-income recipients will also have decreased real incomes because of the rise in prices. The income lost by these two groups will be gained by entrepreneurs, who have a high rate of saving.

The transfer of income away from a group of the economy with a low savings rate (thus curtailing consumption) to one with a high savings rate (thus increasing investment) by means of inflation is known as *forced savings.*

Entrepreneurs are thus induced to build more capital-intensive processes of production because of lower effective interest rates and excess liquidity, which is supplied by the creation of inflationary credit through the banking system and forced savings by consumers. As with the previous version of the monetary demand theories, the expansion could continue indefinitely if the expansion of credit were not retarded. Here again the banking system is unwilling or unable to continue the expansion of credit. However, the supply of credit is also tightened for several other reasons. In the latter stages of the cycle, wages rise faster than prices, so that forced saving is reduced and profit margins are smaller. As consumers increase their real income, the demand for consumer goods will increase. These industries will then bid factor resources away from the capital-goods industries. This will result in an overall rise in factor costs in the economy, and inasmuch as these are not passed on in the form of higher prices, profit margins will be reduced further. Also, businessmen will actually be consuming capital because accounting depreciation allowances (based on original cost) will be insufficient to meet the costs of new machines purchased at current prices. Thus the amount of savings available will be insufficient to finance the existing investment projects. This is known as a *shortage of capital.* Note that if individuals would save more, or if the money supply could be expanded further, the boom could continue indefinitely. Monetary factors are, therefore, responsible for the upper turning point.

This shortage of capital will cause some projects to be discontinued and will keep others from starting. When this happens, output and prices will begin to fall. When prices fall, the real rate becomes higher than the market rate. Since the market rate is quite high at the end of the boom, the real rate now becomes greater than the natural rate. Investment is further discouraged, sales and production decline, and prices continue to fall. This process of deflation and depression continues to spiral downward.

Eventually excess reserves will accumulate in the banking system, which will reduce the market rate of interest to a level below the natural rate of interest. Prices are also likely to stop falling after a while because of the mechanism of the quantity theory: for a given stock of money a stable value of velocity (not distorted by inflationary creation of credit) will result in stable prices. However, this process is likely to occur very gradually, quite unlike the sharp change in economic activity associated with the upper turning point.

As is probably evident to the reader by now, this theory has many weak points. Besides the uncertain nature of the lower turning point, which is somewhat remedied by the nonmonetary overinvestment theories, several points of the explanation of the upswing are unrealistic. Still inherent in the overall argument is the statement that the boom could continue indefinitely if credit could be expanded indefinitely. Also seriously in error is the argument that an increase in the production of capital goods can occur only if there is a decrease in the production of consumer goods. Except for periods of overfull employment (such as World War II), consumption and investment have both grown during boom periods, although not necessarily at the same rate. There has been little bidding away of resources from one sector to another, except possibly in the construction industry.

12.3   NONMONETARY DEMAND THEORIES OF THE CYCLE

These theories can usefully be divided into two categories: the nonmonetary overinvestment theories and the underconsumption theories. Both sets of theories are fundamentally in agreement with each other and with the monetary theories about the pattern of the upswing, once it has started. Although the nonmonetary theories usually ignore monetary factors, they implicitly assume that the credit supply is sufficiently elastic to allow investment to expand to the point where it will turn down because of other factors. If this were not the case, the upper turning point would then be dependent on monetary factors, in which case the theory would reduce to the type previously discussed. It is assumed that excess reserves are retained by the banking system during the previous depression, and there is no reticence by bankers to augment the supply of loanable funds during the boom. However, the upper turning point is caused by the fact that investment has been increasing at an unsustainable rate, and therefore excess capacity has appeared in some industries. Investment decreases in these industries; this decrease spreads to the rest of the economy and causes a depression. Note the difference between this and the monetary theories, which stressed that the boom could continue indefinitely if only enough credit were available.

The most involved statement of the strict overinvestment theory has been given by Spiethoff.[6] To explain the phenomenon that there is both excess capacity in one type of investment goods and a shortage of capital (lack of savings) in another type of investment goods, he has separated so-called durable capital goods (such as railroads, steel mills, machine-tool factories, and so on) from indirect consumption goods (such as steel, cement, bricks, lumber, and so on). It is the second classification of goods whose production is disrupted by a shortage of capital, as explained next.

In the early stages of the boom, low interest rates, high liquidity, and an increase in business optimism lead to a high rate of investment. However, these

---

[6] M. Tugan-Baranowski and G. Cassel are often considered part of the same school. However, inasmuch as their explanations of the upper turning point depend more on monetary factors, they are more correctly classified with the monetary overinvestment theorists. Spiethoff's theories can be found in "Business Cycles" (translated and abridged from the original "Krisen") in *International Economic Papers*, No. 3 (1953), pp. 75–171.

goods do not immediately appear on the market, because there is a long gestation period for capital goods. Meanwhile, rising prices and high profit margins induce more entrepreneurs to produce more of these same investment goods which have not yet appeared on the market.

After the gestation period, the additional durable capital goods are ready for use, which greatly increases the production of indirect consumption goods. The demand for durable capital goods now decreases due to a variety of reasons discussed below, most of them based on some form of the acceleration or stock-adjustment principle.

The supply of indirect consumer goods increases at the same time that the demand for them decreases. Savings has decreased because of rising wages and inefficient methods of production, so that the greater demand is now for final consumer goods (food, clothing, and services). However, these are not available. Factor resources were bid away from these industries early in the upswing when the demand for capital goods was much greater. Thus a situation exists where there is an overproduction of indirect consumer goods but an underproduction of final consumer goods. Spiethoff is quite definite in stating that this is not a general overproduction. On the contrary, there has been a misallocation of resources because of below-equilibrium levels of the interest rate. Consumers cannot buy what they want, yet excess capacity exists in other industries.

This situation could be stopped if consumers were to forego their demand for consumer goods and supply savings to the indirect consumer-goods industries. However, it *cannot* be rectified by an injection of more credit into the economy. This would only result in an increase in the production of more and more indirect consumer goods, and would still leave a shortage of consumer goods. Furthermore, the longer this imbalance is prolonged, the worse it is likely to get. Unless consumers will increase their savings rate, the economy must wait for a restructuring of industry in which the balance between capital-goods and consumer-goods production will correspond to the demand in these two sectors. Thus there is just as much of a vertical maladjustment here as there was in the monetary overinvestment theories. However, here the demand for durable capital goods declines, leading to excess capacity in the indirect consumer-goods industries. There is surplus and shortage at the same time because the economy does not maintain its high savings rate.

Another variant of the nonmonetary overinvestment theories omits the distinction between durable capital goods and indirect consumer goods and concentrates on excess capacity in capital-goods industries, which leads to a slackening of demand for further investment in those industries and thus a general slackening of demand. One theory developed along these lines, due in different forms to Wicksell[7] and Schumpeter,[8] stresses the role of innovations

---

[7] Wicksell, *op. cit.* Also see his "The Enigma of Business Cycles" (translated from a lecture originally given in 1907), *International Economic Papers*, No. 3 (1953), pp. 58–74.

[8] J. Schumpeter, *The Theory of Economic Development* (Cambridge, Mass.: Harvard University Press, 1934).

and cyclical shifts in what we now would call the marginal efficiency of investment schedule. The Wicksellian doctrine is that fluctuations occurred in the
difference between the market rate and the natural rate, the latter being determined by the marginal productivity of capital and the savings rate. Fluctuations
in the natural rate, which were due to real causes rather than monetary causes,
primarily influenced cyclical fluctuations of the economy. Thus Wicksell
believed that real causes were responsible for the turning points of the cycle,
and that the upswing was started by the discoveries of new and improved
methods of production, in other words, an increase in the marginal productivity of capital. This led to many new investment opportunities, which were
exploited because the natural rate of return rose above the market rate. After
these new opportunities had been exhausted, additional investment projects
offered a much lower rate of return, so that many of them were not undertaken
at the going market interest rate. This decrease in investment caused a decline
in the economy. The lower turning point would occur when sufficient new
opportunities returned with high rates of return. This theory was expanded by
Schumpeter, who spoke of the herdlike nature of entrepreneurs to take advantage of a new process or product which had been shown to be successful.
Although inventions are likely to occur at evenly spaced intervals, business
optimism and psychology suggest that many entrepreneurs are likely to invest
in these new inventions *en masse*. Spiethoff himself used an argument somewhat
similar to this, but with sinister overtones. Since existing investment opportunities are constantly being depleted in the home country, it is necessary for cap-
italism to seek out investment opportunities which still exist in neighboring
countries not as highly developed and to carry the "good life" to these countries.

A slight variant of these theories in the acceleration principle itself. As
explained in Chapter 4, this principle states that there is a constant ratio
between capital stock and sales in a given industry. Thus a 10 percent increase
(for example) in sales would require a 10 percent increase in capital stock.
This would involve a large amount of investment at first, which would then
decrease to zero unless additional increases in sales were forthcoming, thus
causing a downturn. Those theorists which propounded the theory of the
accelerator were unable to see how the downturn would set in motion forces
that would eventually lead to another upturn. Consequently, many of the
reasons for the turning points were borrowed from other theories. However,
here again the downturn was caused by a lack of aggregate demand and a
downward shift of the marginal efficiency of investment schedule, not by a
shortage of savings or credit.

These nonmonetary theories have stressed that a decrease in demand for
further investment is the principal reason for the beginning of the downturn,
although at the same time consumer goods were in short supply. However,
suppose the argument is turned around and it is assumed that the investment
goods are built mainly to produce consumer goods. Then when the gestation
period is finished and these new machines reach the market, there will be an
excess of consumer goods. The price of consumer goods, which had been bid

up previously because of a shortage, will now fall precipitously as merchants try to sell their goods but consumers do not buy all these extra goods. If the savings rate could only be decreased (instead of increased) so that people would buy more, the depression could be averted. This is essentially the argument of the underconsumption theorists.

Since the state of the U.S. economy during the past 40 years has often been in a situation where total capacity far exceeds the amount of aggregate demand, one might think that the underconsumption theory has much to recommend it. But there are some questionable links in its chain of reasoning. The under-consumptionists all claim that the C/Y ratio declines in the downturn; people do not want to buy what is being offered. Actually, the C/Y ratio is higher in recessions than in booms, higher in the later part of booms than the earlier part, and reached its highest level (of slightly greater than unity) during the depression of the 1930s. The empirical evidence would seem to oppose the theory suggested by the underconsumptionists. However, there are some points worth exploring in this theory.

The most naive and untenable version of this theory states that due to technological advancement there is always a tendency for production to in-crease faster than demand. A theory in which *ex ante* supply and demand are never equal is just as bad if not worse than a theory in which *ex ante* supply and demand are always equal. The principal mistake made by this kind of reasoning is the failure to realize that the total value of any product produced is fully paid out in factor shares: wages, profits, rent and depreciation, and taxes. Only if individuals or businessmen (or possibly the government) decide for some reason that they do not want to spend the money which they have received will there be the possibility of *ex ante* supply exceeding demand. Thus for the underconsumption theories to have any validity, they must demonstrate that there is a shift in the aggregate marginal propensity to spend which causes the beginning of a decline.

One such view has been advanced by Hobson,[9] who argues that this phenom-enon occurs because of great inequality of income distribution. Employees as a group have very limited income, and thus purchasing power, relative to the total economy. In the early stages of the upswing, the very substantial share of national income retained by the entrepreneurs does not endanger full employ-ment, because these earnings are spent on investment. When new investment plans are completed, consumers cannot buy the goods which are turned out at prices that will enable businessmen to make a profit, because the consumers, as a group, do not have the aggregate purchasing power. When this occurs, investment is decreased further, leading to a depression.

Although the situation described by Hobson could conceivably occur, it is unlikely that it would happen today. In mature economies, a substantial middle class with a high average propensity to consume probably provides the

---

[9] J. A. Hobson, *The Industrial System*, rev. ed. (London: Longmans, Green, 1910).

necessary stimulus to consumption. In developing economies where income distribution is much more skewed, a high rate of growth has been able to be maintained, as new investment opportunities have continued to appear. Further-more, many investment goods turn out more investment goods, for which there is still a great need. The main problem in developing economies is generally the lack of consumer goods, not a glut of them. Hobson's views are logically defensible, however, and the situation he describes may have been a contributing factor to the 1929 downturn.

The other reasonable possibility of the underconsumption theories is that as aggregate supply and aggregate income increase, consumers spend a smaller and smaller proportion of their income. Thus as more and more goods gradually came on the market, some but not all would be taken at the going price. This idea that the savings rate increases as income increases is closely related to Keynes' statement of the marginal propensity to consume, and in fact the views of the underconsumptionists can be expressed very well by Figure 12.2, often alleged to be a somewhat simplified but useful explanation of the Keynesian system of income determination. Because of this, we digress a minute to indicate Keynes' views on the subject. In discussing the underconsumption theories, Haberler notes that Keynes, "while not himself primarily an advocate of the underconsumptionist thesis . . . has forged, in the concept of the 'propensity to consume' an instrument apt for the purposes of the under-consumptionist theory."[10]

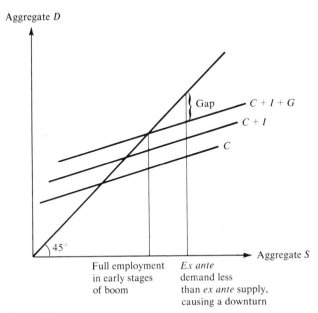

Figure 12.2

[10] Haberler, *op. cit.*, p. 111.

Keynes himself had this to say about the underconsumptionists:

> It may be convenient at this point to say a word about the important schools of thought which maintain, from various points of view, that the chronic tendency of contemporary societies to under-employment is to be traced to under-consumption. ... these schools of thought are, as guides to practical policy, undoubtedly in the right. ... Practically I only differ from these schools of thought in thinking that they may lay a little too much emphasis on increased consumption at a time when there is still much social advantage to be obtained from increased investment. ... But this is a practical judgment, not a theoretical imperative. ... For it is unlikely that full employment can be maintained, whatever we may do about investment, with the existing propensity to consume.[11]

There is very little way in which this paragraph, and particularly the last sentence, can be interpreted as a correct statement. All empirical evidence suggests that the propensity to consume has remained virtually unchanged from the 1930s to the present, yet there have been periods of full and even overfull employment in the last 30 years. Although there clearly has not been full employment for the entire postwar period, this is because investment decreased as a percentage of GNP, not consumption. "Whatever we may do about investment" for these less than full-employment periods was mainly a tight-money policy designed to curb aggregate demand through its effect on investment. It worked.

What, then, can be said for this latter version of the underconsumption theory? Certainly the short-run (for example, yearly) marginal propensity to consume is substantially less than the long-run marginal propensity to consume, which is equal to the average propensity to consume. Thus if consumers do receive a large increase in their incomes, they will save a substantial proportion of this extra income in the short run. If this savings is not met by opportunities for investment, it could conceivably cause a downturn. Yet this is not what actually causes recessions.

The solution to this problem lies in the interaction of the multiplier and the accelerator, the critical missing ingredient of all pre-Keynesian business cycle theories. When incomes are rising rapidly, and the savings rate is high, investment is also increasing rapidly because of the acceleration principle (a distributed lag accelerator will not greatly modify this line of reasoning). At the end of the boom, the rise in income is much slower because fewer new investment projects are being undertaken, so that the increases in income are less than the average increases and thus the savings rate is lower than the average. This conclusion cannot be drawn from the naive Keynesian consumption function, but follows immediately when adjustments are made for past patterns of consumer behavior. Thus at the end of the boom, the ratio of consumption to income is rising instead of falling, and thus cannot be responsible for the downturn. Instead, the decrease in investment, which is no longer as profitable, is still responsible.

---

[11] J. M. Keynes, *The General Theory of Employment, Interest, and Money* (New York: Harcourt Brace & World, 1936), pp. 325–326.

There is actually one interesting case where the accelerator and the under-consumption theories amount to almost the same thing, and this is the case of consumer durables. Unlike other consumption, the ratio of consumer durables to income appears to decline slightly in the later stages of the boom. This would be suggested by the accelerator, since the stock of consumer durables should be proportional to disposable income. However, there is a decline in these purchases relative to income, which is what the underconsumptionists state. Thus although the ratio of consumption of nondurables and services to income increases in the later stages of the upturn, lack of purchases of consumer durables at that time may be of considerable importance in causing the upper turning point.

In general, however, the underconsumptionists saw new machines spewing forth great quantities of all types of consumer goods, which could not be bought by consumers. What they neglected to see was the concomitant decrease in investment goods, which led to a decrease in aggregate purchasing power. For example, during the early stages of the boom, production might consist of $25 of investment and $75 of consumption. After the new machines have been completed and are producing additional consumer goods, total production of the economy might be $5 of investment and $90 of consumption. In concentrating on the rise in consumer goods, the underconsumptionists completely neglected the decline in aggregate demand caused by a reduction in investment.

It is clear that in these circumstances investment does not decrease because of a lack of savings, and there is clearly no capital shortage such as occurred in the overinvestment theories. A decrease in the savings rate would increase aggregate demand and thus avert the downturn. In this sense the underconsumptionists and Keynes were quite correct in analyzing the deflationary effects of savings, particularly at a time when investment was beginning to decrease. Thus the underconsumption analysis is of considerable value. However, it is not a theory of the cycle because it does not explain the turning points. It does explain how, once the upper turning point has been reached, it is less rather than more savings that would return the economy to full employment; however, it errs in assuming that a decrease in the consumption/income ratio is responsible for the turning point, and the fact that Keynes was enamored of this explanation because of his failure to take into consideration the effect of past patterns of consumer behavior on present consumption unfortunately does not make it any more correct.

What are the relative strengths and weaknesses of these various pre-Keynesian theories? Although they contain some unconvincing and extraneous details, these theories do suggest that certain favorable conditions combine to induce an expansion in investment which is greater than the equilibrium level. The end of the boom is signaled by a decrease in the rate of investment, whether this is due to insufficiency of credit, lack of savings, or the disappearance of further investment projects earning a rate of return higher than the market rate of interest.

The closest example of a modern theory probably is due to Wicksell, who explained how periodic shifts in the marginal efficiency of investment schedule (what he called the natural rate of return) caused investment and thus aggregate production to fluctuate over the cycle. However, exogenous shocks were still necessary to start the economy in an upswing. Although the monetary theorists were able to explain the lower turning point in terms of low interest rates and excess reserves, we have suggested that the investment function is quite inelastic at low interest rates, so that an actual shift of the function would undoubtedly be necessary to restart an upward movement in the economy. However, as pointed out previously, their theories suffer from a lack of any multiplier analysis and the combination of the multiplier with the accelerator. This problem is particularly serious in explaining the lower turning point, which was generally left unexplained by the classical economists.

12.4   SUPPLY THEORIES OF THE CYCLE

The theories presented in this section, due to Wesley C. Mitchell,[12] are categorized as supply theories because the principal factors causing the turning points—costs of doing business, profit margins, and income distribution—are essentially supply phenomena. Although it is clear that these factors must affect the various components of aggregate demand in order to cause cyclical fluctuations, there is not a direct and unique correspondence between changes in these supply factors and changes in one particular area of aggregate demand, such as fixed business investment. Instead, the leveling off or decrease in the profit rate is likely to affect general business conditions, so that many components of demand are likely to be affected, although not all equally. As Mitchell states, "since the quest for money profits by business enterprises is the controlling factor among the economic activities of men who live in a money economy, the whole discussion must center about the prospect of profits."[13]

Retail merchants are generally the first beneficiaries of the upturn, once it has started. Since they have let their stocks decrease during slack times, they increase their orders to wholesalers, who in turn place new orders with manufacturers. This chain of increased business activity diffuses through all sectors of the economy and creates an atmosphere of general business optimism.

One notable fact about the early stages of an upswing is the increase in profit rates. Overall profits rise partially because of the increase in sales, but primarily because unit profits increase. This happens because average costs are steady or even decreasing while prices rise. There is a marked decline in average fixed

---

[12] W. C. Mitchell, *Business Cycles and Their Causes* (Berkeley: University of California Press, 1941).

[13] Mitchell, *op. cit.*, p. xi.

costs as the rate of capacity utilization increases with the rising level of sales. Other fixed, or supplementary costs, will remain at levels negotiated during the previous depressions, and thus are likely to be below equilibrium levels. Interest costs will also be low, because bankers will hesitate to raise interest rates while substantial excess reserves continue to exist. Average variable costs will probably rise somewhat, but less than the rise in prices. Although the price increases for raw materials and goods in process may be greater than the price of finished goods, these represent only a small part of total costs. This will be more than offset by the lag in wage rates, as noted by several other theorists. Finally, freight rates will not rise at the beginning of the boom, because they are regulated and adjust very slowly.

Several reasons are advanced by Mitchell for the lag in wages. Unlike commodity prices, which are impersonally determined at the price which clears the market, there is some concept of a "just" wage below which a man cannot reasonably support his family. Since wages do not fall as much as prices in depressions, there is little pressure to raise them early in the expansion. Laborers themselves would be least likely to push for substantial wage increases at this time. Their weekly paychecks have increased because of a rise in hours, as short work-weeks have ended. The cost of living has not increased very much in the recent past, so that there is currently no erosion of purchasing power. Furthermore, workers would prefer to wait until their personal savings are replenished before becoming militant about further pay increases.

This increase in business sales and profits has taken place without a concomitant increase in fixed business investment, which was considered by most of the other theorists to be of central importance. Instead, Mitchell keenly notes that the increase in investment does not begin until the upturn is clearly under way. Only when sales and profits rise will entrepreneurs begin to formulate plans for greater investment. Furthermore, not much new investment is likely to be undertaken as long as excess capacity exists. Although the upturn is eventually accompanied by a greater than equilibrium rate of investment, it lags the general upturn and thus cannot be responsible for the turning points.

The very forces that led to an upturn in business activity and an increase in the rate of profit eventually cause this upturn to come to an end. Costs begin to rise faster than prices, profit margins decline, and credit tightens. In particular, the decreasing rate of profit in some firms and industries reduces the amount of credit which they can borrow, and thus forces them to curtail some of their activities. This curtailing of credit is the focal point of Mitchell's theory, and is discussed below in detail. However, since this is caused by a decrease in profit margins, the reasons for this decline must be examined first.

There are several reasons for costs to rise more rapidly in the later stages of the boom, and these are documented carefully by Mitchell. The decline in average fixed costs stops as businesses near full capacity. Further production takes place only with the addition of new machinery. Since prices are rising, particularly in the industrial sector, this new machinery is likely to be substantially more expensive than the old machinery that it is replacing. Other fixed costs, such as rent, insurance, and salaries are likely to be negotiated upward after a prolonged period of prosperity. Interest rates will rise sharply as excess reserves are depleted and the demand for credit increases.

Average variable costs also continue to rise. This is partially due to rising wage rates and higher costs of materials, but is principally caused by decreasing efficiency in all lines of production. The quality of labor deteriorates for several reasons. As full employment is reached, either marginal workers with poor work habits or new workers requiring training must be hired: in either case, output per man-hour diminishes. Overtime labor, besides costing more, is less efficient, as fatigue increases with the longer working day. Steady workers are less afraid of discharge when business is prosperous and the labor market tight: they are likely not to work as industriously, so that their efficiency also decreases.

The increase in overall demand results in the reactivation of inefficient enterprises that had been closed during the previous depression. These firms, besides operating at a higher level of average costs, bid for available factor resources and help to raise the cost of labor and raw materials still further. There is also a declining efficiency of management when business is booming, so that quality control is likely to decrease and spoiled work becomes a greater percentage of total output.

In spite of all these cost increases, firms would maintain their profit margins if they could pass these increases on to the customer in the form of higher prices. Why does this happen? The classical economists (except possibly for Wicksell) would argue that prices are determined by the quantity theory and not by the costs of production. However, Mitchell is not satisfied with such sophistry. Although admitting that "this analysis has a certain academic interest," he hastens to state that it "does not really bear upon the problem at hand."[14] In the early stages of an upswing, firms appear to have no problem raising prices faster than costs: in the later stages, therefore, additional factors must intervene to slow down this rate of increase.

Here Mitchell relies on an ingenious device. While it is true that most firms can continue to pass along cost increases in the form of higher prices, there will be specific reasons why others cannot. Then "an actual or even a prospective decline of profits in a few important industries suffices to create financial difficulties of grave concern to all industries."[15] Thus even if only a few industries cannot retain their profit margins, this is likely to have an unsettling effect on the whole economy.

One important class of industries that cannot pass along cost increases is the regulated industries, in particular the public utilities and the railroads. Other products, such as newspapers or small fair-traded items, may continue

---

[14] *Ibid.*, p. 54.
[15] *Ibid.*, p. 58.

to sell at prices which bring at least normal profits over the entire cycle but which result in decreased profits in the later stages of the boom.

There may also be a great increase in supply in certain industries, so that in these industries prices will decline at the same time that costs are rising. Supply may also be increased somewhat by the fact that firms cannot hold as large a stock of inventories as they had planned because of higher interest rates and tighter credit. These goods are then "dumped" on the market, further depressing prices. This happens only in a few industries, however, and is not a general glut on the market, such as the underconsumptionists would advocate. Mitchell does not reject their argument out of hand: he does examine it, but finds it to be at odds with the available statistics. If the upper turning point were marked primarily by an oversupply of consumer goods, one would expect their prices to fall the most. However, it is raw material prices that tend to fall in the later stages of the boom, whereas consumer prices continue to rise even into the depression.

Thus it is the regulated industries and the raw-material producing firms that are most likely to suffer a falling profit rate. Since market structure in these industries is likely to be oligopolistic, those large firms which are affected are likely to be important enough to influence general business sentiment. Although not all the firms in these industries need show a decline in profits, the fact that many of them do is enough to begin a decline in business confidence, manifested by a refusal to extend as much credit as previously. This point is discussed next.

The entire upswing has been largely financed by an extension of credit to consumers and businessmen alike. For at least the latter group, this use of borrowed funds is not really a voluntary action. "When the increase in business made possible by the use of borrowed funds adds more to profits than the interest adds to costs, borrowing becomes compulsory in sharply competitive trades."[16] The amount of credit that can be obtained through banks, bonds, and equities depends largely on the expected future rate of profit. As long as the profit rate and the stock market continue to rise, generating an atmosphere of steady business optimism, firms can continue to capitalize on these expected future profits. However, if the profits of a few large companies decrease, the whole feeling of optimism is likely to be punctured, and many firms cannot borrow as much as previously, even though their own profits have not been adversely affected. A very clear example of this can be found in the fluctuations of the stock market, where the fear of lower profits of one particular branch of industry often affects almost all listed issues, even though many of them continue to keep their profit rate steady or increasing. Thus the encroachment of costs on profits (possibly aggravated by the existence of overcapacity) of only a few key industries is sufficient to cause a general tightening of lending standards and availability of credit to all. Businesses begin to concentrate more on remaining solvent rather than expanding their sales further, and this, together

---

[16] *Ibid.*, p. 63.

with a noticeably increased pessimism about the future course of business, is enough to cause a reduction in new orders. This reduction spreads throughout the economy, causing a downturn in much the same way that an increase in new orders causes an upturn.

As the depression lengthens, certain corrective forces are in action which set the stage for the beginning of the next upturn. Prices and interest rates fall as the demand for goods and for borrowed funds decreases. Efficiency increases as marginal workers are dismissed and inefficient plants go out of business. Other fixed costs, which may have continued to rise after the upper turning point, finally are readjusted downward. This is partially due to the great decrease in construction costs.

However, all these adjustments will be insufficient to increase profit margins enough to cause a turning point unless there is some increase in aggregate demand. This does occur for several reasons. First, there is the operation of the acceleration principle in the inventory investment and consumer durables sectors. Second, trend influences, such as population, increase consumption of nondurables and services somewhat. Today this would be explained by the relative or normal income hypotheses, but Mitchell was correct in noting that these types of consumption continued to rise during most recessions. Third, and most important, the demand for new construction increases before the rest of the economy turns up. This is due primarily to the fact that credit is now plentiful and construction costs are relatively low, although demand is mildly stimulated by whatever increases occur in the consumer sector. Thus Mitchell states that the demand for construction depends on consumption, ease of obtaining credit, and the relative costs of construction. This is almost identically the functions for industrial and residential construction used in the model presented here. Yet it is only in the last few years that the general counter-cyclical nature of construction, especially residential construction, has been generally noted and similar functions have been empirically estimated.

Thus the end of the depression is signaled by the return of inventories to normal levels, the downward readjustment of high fixed costs and outstanding indebtedness, the decreasing of variable costs faster than the decline in prices, and some small increase in aggregate demand. This situation will then lead to an increase in orders, which will begin a new upswing.

Several aspects of Mitchell's analysis are valuable in a modern theory of the business cycle. One of these is the realization that changes in demand are transmitted through new orders. Another is that fixed investment, while accounting for most of the fluctuations in the economy, lags the cycle. Another is the essentially countercyclical nature of construction. Still another, also mentioned by other theorists, is the lag of wages behind prices and the resultant shift of income distribution over the cycle. One possible drawback to his theory is that while the accelerator is quite important in causing the lower turning point, it has virtually no influence on the upper turning point. This is quite different from the other theorists who used the accelerator to explain the upper turning point. It is also generally agreed that the accelerator is relatively inactive in periods of excess capacity. This, however, applies to the accelerator related to fixed business investment, whereas Mitchell applies it to inventories.

Today we live in a world that has smoother flows of liquidity, and the probability of a financial crisis is almost nonexistent. It is very doubtful that 90-day loans will again reach an average rate of 12 to 16 percent or that currency will demand a premium of 4 percent, such as occurred in the 1907 panic. Credit terms are less likely to be cut quite so rapidly or so deeply. The real aspects of the boom at the upper turning point are apt to be more important, and the financial aspects somewhat less important, than described by Mitchell. However, his theory does present many important elements that can be included within a general Keynesian framework.

CHAPTER 13

THE BASIC
KEYNESIAN SYSTEM

13.1   THE STATIC FRAMEWORK

This chapter presents a brief view of the basic Keynesian system which will be used as a foundation for a more sophisticated and empirically orientated explanation of fluctuations in the postwar U.S. economy. The material discussed in this chapter is primarily based on three very famous articles, to which the reader is referred: Hicks's "Mr. Keynes and the Classics: A Suggested Interpretation,"[1] Samuelson's "Interactions Between the Multiplier Analysis and the Principle of Acceleration,"[2] and Metzler's "The Nature and Stability of Inventory Cycles."[3]

In the *General Theory*, Keynes was mainly concerned with the task of demonstrating the existence of an equilibrium output at less than full employment, and thus devoted very little time to the problems of the business cycle as such. In his one chapter on the subject, he suggested that fluctuations in the marginal efficiency of investment schedule due to changes in expectations and fluctuations in patterns of consumer spending due to the changes in wealth (clearly a reference to the 1929 stock market crash) were the main causes of the cyclical behavior of the economy. He did not delineate any well-defined mechanism

---

[1] J. R. Hicks, *Econometrica*, Vol. 5, No. 2 (April, 1937), pp. 147–159.

[2] P. A. Samuelson, *Review of Economics and Statistics*, Vol. 21, No. 2 (May, 1939), pp. 75–78.

[3] L. A. Metzler, *Review of Economics and Statistics*, Vol. 23, No. 3 (August, 1941), pp. 113–129. These articles will not be cited again in this chapter unless a specific page reference is given.

by which the economy generates cycles, and, except for one paragraph, he ignored the problem of inventory fluctuations, which are of particular importance in the postwar business cycles. However, any more complicated theory of the cycle must clearly be based on the general Keynesian framework; thus the necessity to examine it at this point. First it will be shown how a simplified Keynesian system, without lags, is used to determine the equilibrium value of GNP. Then it will be shown how the inclusion of lags leads to endogenous cyclical fluctuations of that system.

The outline of the basic Keynesian system is set out in algebraic formulation, with the classical system recopied here for easy comparison. All the symbols are the same, except for the introduction of N (employment) as distinct from L (labor force). In the classical system these were always identical in equilibrium.

	Classical	*Keynesian*

$$\text{Classical} \qquad\qquad\qquad\qquad \text{Keynesian}$$

$$C = C(i) \quad \text{or} \quad C = \bar{C} \qquad\qquad C = C(X)$$

$$I = I(i) \qquad\qquad\qquad\qquad I = I(X, i)$$

$$C + I + G = X \qquad\qquad\qquad C + I + G = X$$

$$X = X(L, K, t) \qquad\qquad\qquad X = X(N, K, t) \quad \text{or}$$

$$N = N(X, K, t)$$

$$\frac{\partial X}{\partial L} = \frac{w}{p} \qquad\qquad\qquad \frac{\partial X}{\partial N} = \frac{w}{p} \quad \text{or} \quad p = \frac{w}{\partial X / \partial N}$$

$$L = L\left(\frac{w}{p}\right) \quad \text{or} \quad L = \bar{L} \qquad\qquad w = w_0 \quad \text{or} \quad \Delta w = w(\Delta p, Un)$$

$$MV = pX \qquad\qquad\qquad \bar{M}_s = M_D = kpX - \lambda pi$$

$$M_D = \bar{M}_s; \quad V = \bar{V} \qquad\qquad\qquad Un = L - N$$

The most important difference in the two systems is that national income is determined by aggregate demand in the Keynesian system rather than by technological considerations in the classical model. Thus the production function, instead of determining output, determines the amount of labor demanded for a given output, capital stock, and state of technology. It thus becomes the demand function for labor. The function $\partial X / \partial N = w/p$, although almost identical to the classical function $\partial X / \partial L = w/p$, now determines the price level instead of the demand for labor and can be rewritten in the form of a price-markup equation, as done above. A second important difference is that the stock of money no longer determines the level of output or prices, but, together with the aggregate demand equations, determines the interest rate. Even this is not true if the interest rate is at some irreducible minimum level.

A third difference is the inflexibility of the wage rate downward. In the formulation of his theory, Keynes stated that workers will not work below some specified money wage, presumably the one at which they are currently employed. After specifying the supply of labor function in money terms, he said that workers have money illusion and employers do not. An increase in the price level while the money wage stayed constant would lower the real wage, thus increasing employment while keeping workers satisfied. In actual practice there has been found to be a decided lack of money illusion among workers, as witnessed by the popularity of automatic escalator clauses which adjust wages up by the same percentage as price increases. It is sometimes argued that this floor on money wages alone prevents the economy from returning to a full-employment equilibrium position, and thus the solution of the Keynesian and classical systems are the same if prices and wages are perfectly flexible. This is nonsense. As shown below, there is little if any reason for the equilibrium output of the economy always to be at full employment even if wages are perfectly flexible. Thus this third difference is not of major importance, and we concentrate on the first two. Other differences will become apparent as the system is examined in more detail.

The modern defenders and apologists of the classical system and the quantity theory point with great emphasis to the wholesale destruction of money during the 1929–1933 period as a major cause of the Great Depression.[4] This view can be accepted by most economists, provided they do not subscribe to the entire classical liturgy. According to the theory outlined in Chapter 12, $MV = pX$ means that if prices are flexible, a given percentage drop in the money stock will be matched by an equal percentage decrease in prices, so that the level of real output will remain unchanged. It might appear that a decrease in the stock of money, coupled with rigid prices in the real world, was a primary force causing the depression. However, this is not so. In the 1929–1933 period, the money stock and the price level *both* decreased by approximately one fourth,[5] so that velocity must have decreased by approximately the same percentage as real output. Faced with rapidly decreasing demand and a pervading atmosphere of deep pessimism, investment plans were drastically curtailed and remained at low levels even when demand started to rise again as a result of the great amount of excess capacity. Thus in this most serious depression, prices and wages were for the most part flexible; yet one fourth of the labor force was unemployed. The interest rate clearly did not serve its function of equating investment and savings at a full-employment level.

It should be pointed out that the Federal Reserve System actually *raised*

---

[4] See, for instance, Milton Friedman and Anna Schwartz, *A Monetary History of the United States, 1867–1960* (Princeton, N.J.: Princeton University Press for NBER, 1963), chap. 7.

[5] The money stock declined 25 percent (both excluding and including time deposits) while the implicit GNP deflator fell 22 percent; consumer prices fell 27 percent. Manufacturing hourly wages fell 21 percent. Figures are from the *Historical Statistics of the United States* (Washington: Government Printing Office, 1957).

interest rates in 1931, to protect the international position of the dollar. The yield on highest-grade (Aaa) corporate bond yields rose to a high of over 5 percent, and medium-grade (Baa) bond yields went to 9.3 percent. Undoubtedly these increases in interest rates made the decline in economic activity much more severe than it otherwise would have been. However, by 1936 these rates had dropped to 3.2 and 4.8 percent, and the economy was still far from full employment.

In view of the inability of the interest rate to equate savings and investment at a full-employment level of output, Keynes suggested that full-employment levels of these curves might intersect only at an interest rate below any actual rate that could ever be reached. This would occur if there existed some irreducible minimum long-term rate that would not be lowered no matter how much the money stock increased. This concept is the famous liquidity trap, which arises from the generalized idea of the liquidity-preference function, considered next.

The classical economists thought that individuals and businessmen would hold money only for transactions purposes; they would never hold idle cash balances, or hold money itself as an asset. The reason for this, as explained previously, was that everyone would always prefer a positive interest rate earned from some asset other than money to the zero interest rate earned on money itself. However, Keynes showed that this was not always true. When interest rates became very low, the expectation increases that they will soon rise toward a normal level. Since interest rates and the price of bonds are inversely related, a rise in interest rates means capital losses for bondholders. These losses will be realized only if bondholders sell before the maturity date is reached. However, there will still be additional income foregone for those investors who keep the low-yield bonds and therefore do not purchase other higher-yield bonds available when interest rates again rise. At some very low long-term interest rate (often alleged to be about 2 percent, but never explicitly stated by Keynes) investors would weigh the probable interest gains against the probable future losses, and decide not to invest. This holding of money in idle cash balances is known as the speculative demand for money. Thus the demand for money depends both on the money value of output and on the level of the interest rate; it may be held both for transactions purposes or in idle cash balances for speculative purposes, if the interest rate is low enough.

Given that such an irreducible minimum interest rate existed, Keynes then claimed that full-employment investment and savings schedules would under certain circumstances intersect at an interest rate below this minimum. Diagrammatically this can be represented as shown in Figure 13.1.

The idea of the liquidity trap has often been taken as an article of faith and many heated arguments have arisen about whether it constitutes the crucial difference between the classical and Keynesian systems. However, a somewhat different approach would be merely to state that under certain circumstances, full-employment investment and savings schedules will not intersect at *any*

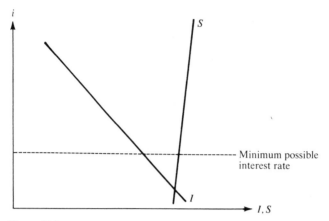

Figure 13.1

positive interest rate. This is likely to be true if the marginal efficiency of investment schedule is inelastic at low interest rates. This is shown in Figure 13.2. In this case the crucial significance of the liquidity trap vanishes and the question of whether such a trap exists and the level of the interest rate at which it occurs reduces to a mildly interesting empirical question.

It should be obvious that the savings–investment diagram of Figure 13.2 cannot continue to be used without substantial modification. The interest rate must always be positive, but *ex post* investment and savings are equal by definition. This problem can be solved only by shifting the investment and savings curves. In the Keynesian system, investment and savings are both a function of aggregate income; this differs completely from the classical system, where aggregate income was fixed and these schedules were determined by technological

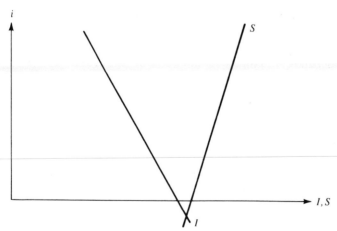

Figure 13.2

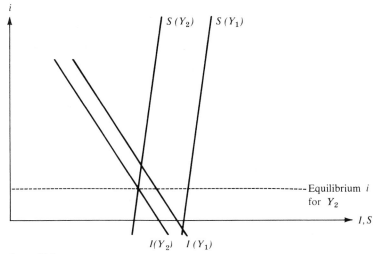

Figure 13.3

and institutional considerations. Thus every time income changes, the investment and savings schedules must shift. The amount that they shift will depend on the value of the mpc and the mpI (marginal propensity to invest). If *ex ante* investment is less than *ex ante* savings, income will decrease and both the investment and savings schedules will shift to the left. This is shown in Figure 13.3 within the framework of Figure 13.2. The relationships between savings and income and between investment and income are of great importance for determining how much these schedules shift and therefore what the equilibrium level of income is. However, the reason for the existence of an equilibrium level below full employment is not that consumption and investment depend on income, but rather that the investment function is interest-inelastic at low rates of interest. The disturbance away from equilibrium originally started because of a decrease in the marginal efficiency of investment schedule. As was shown in Chapter 12 this view was also held by many classical economists. However, none of them thought that the investment schedule might shift so far that it would not intersect the savings schedule at any realistic rate of interest. Since this does occur, the slopes of the consumption and investment functions relative to income are then needed to determine the level of aggregate income.

It might be conceivable that a decrease in income would shift the investment schedule to the left at least as much as the savings schedule. In this case no positive equilibrium income would ever be reached. Similarly, an increase in income would set off further increases which would also result in no finite equilibrium solution. For this reason it is always assumed that the investment schedule shifts less for any given change in income than the savings schedule, in other words, that the mpI < mps. For obvious reasons this is called the *stability condition* for a simple Keynesian system, and is exactly equivalent to the inequality that mpc + mpI < 1, or that the simple multiplier is finite.[6]

The crucial argument, then, in the invalidation of the classical system is that investment is not always equal to savings, *ex ante*, at some positive rate of interest. Once this follows, there will be idle cash balances, velocity will fluctuate cyclically, and the stock of money will no longer be proportional to money output even if prices are completely flexible. Thus the quantity theory will be invalidated and aggregate demand functions depending on income will be necessary to determine the equilibrium level of gross national product.

In the Keynesian system consumption (or savings) does not depend on the interest rate and the relationship between investment and the interest rate is relatively weak at low interest rates. Thus, in the simplest analysis of the Keynesian system, particularly for under-full-employment equilibria, investment and savings can be made a function of income only and not the interest rate. Then aggregate income can be determined directly from the intersection of the investment and savings schedules, instead of shifting the schedules every time a different (given) income occurs. This can be shown as in Figure 13.4. Note that the savings curve has a greater slope (with respect to income) than does the investment curve; this is again the stability condition. If the slopes were identical, the equilibrium level of national income would be indeterminate; if they were reversed, there would be no stable finite solution.

Adding aggregate income (Y) to both sides of the *ex post* identity yields the even more familiar "45°" or "Samuelson cross" diagram shown in Figure 13.5. Since $I = S$, then

(13.1) $$I + Y = S + Y$$

and

(13.2) $$Y = I + Y - S$$

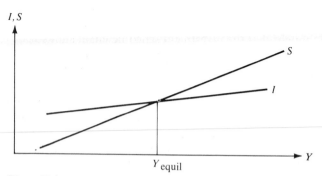

Figure 13.4

---

[6] Since mpc + mps ≡ 1, mpI < mps implies that mpI < 1 − mpc, or mpI + mpc < 1.

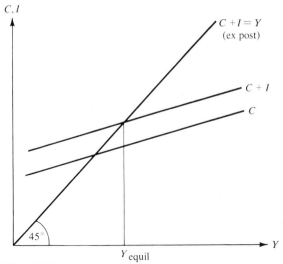

Figure 13.5

Therefore,

(13.3)
$$Y = I + C$$

Although there is little doubt of pedagogical usefulness or popularity of this diagram, the fact of the matter is that it eliminates the effect of the interest rate (it also eliminates the effect of the price level). It was Hicks who showed how national income and the interest rate could be determined simultaneously on a single diagram: this is considered next.

Let us return to the diagram in which the investment and savings schedules were a function of the interest rate. Assume an exogenous shift in national income due to a change in government spending. The I and S schedules will then shift in accordance with this new level of income. Since the savings schedule always shifts more than the investment schedule, higher incomes will always be associated with lower interest rates on this graph, and lower incomes will always be associated with higher interest rates. Thus if we combine the locus of all the points of intersection of the I and S schedules at various levels of income, we obtain a curve that is downward-sloping when plotted with interest rates on the vertical axis and *income* on the horizontal axis. This is Hicks's IS curve; it represents the intersection of the investment and savings schedules at all levels of interest rates and national income. This is shown in Figure 13.6. A little manipulation will show that the IS curve will be horizontal if the mpI = mps; its slope will be smaller the greater the difference between the mpI and the mps; and its slope will be smaller the more interest-inelastic is the investment schedule. It is assumed here that savings are very interest-inelastic.

This curve tells us what investment and savings will be for any given level of the interest rate and national income. It does not by itself tell us what these

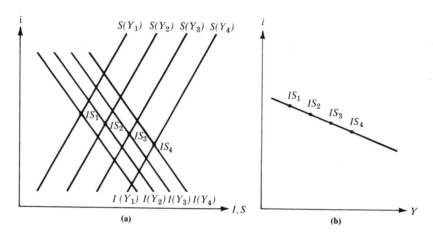

Figure 13.6

levels are. To ascertain this it is necessary to graph the liquidity preference function on the same graph. This function determines the interest rate, which in turn partially determines investment. Then the size of the multiplier is used to determine what national income will be. Actually the liquidity preference function includes a price term, but Hicks's analysis assumes constant prices, and we shall do the same for now.

The demand for money consists of the transactions (and precautionary) demand, which is proportional to total money income, and the speculative demand, which is negatively related to the interest rate. For a given money stock, the greater the increase in income, the more money will be held for transactions purposes, and therefore the less money will be held for speculative purposes, that is, held in idle cash balances. Since less money is now available for lending, the interest rate will rise. Thus the liquidity preference function will slope upward and to the right when plotted against interest rates and national income. Higher income will mean higher interest rates for a given stock of money.

At some high rate of interest, no one will want to hold speculative balances of money any more. In fact, investors will expect interest rates to fall, so they will earn capital gains by buying securities. At this point, further increases in *ex ante* aggregate demand will result only in higher interest rates and higher prices—but not in higher real incomes. We are back in the classical world.

On the other hand, as national income and interest rates fall, the speculative demand for money will increase. Idle cash balances and excess reserves will continue to accumulate. Ordinarily this would tend to drive interest rates down further. However, they cannot fall below the irreducible minimum, so the economy is now in the liquidity trap. Further increases in the money stock will not lower the interest rate nor will they increase national income. The liquidity preference function of this shape is Hicks's *LM* function and it can be combined with the *IS* function to determine jointly national income and the interest rate, as shown in Figure 13.7. Hicks then claims that Keynes considered only the part of the *LM* curve that is the liquidity trap, and draws from this the conclusion that Keynes's *General Theory* is a theory of depression only.

Clearly for the Keynesian framework to be useful, it should also give reasonable results near full employment as well as during recessions and depressions. However Hicks, while criticizing Keynes for not having a sufficiently general theory, did show that an under-full-employment equilibrium position could be reached. Again, the existence of the liquidity trap is not necessary. It is easy to envisage an inelastic *IS* curve that reaches a zero interest rate before full employment.

This diagram can be conveniently used to show the effects of fiscal and monetary policy for the so-called "Keynesian," "intermediate," and "classical" (full employment) ranges of the economy. Consider first an expansionary fiscal policy. This may occur through an increase in government spending, consumer spending (personal income tax cuts), or investment spending (corporate income tax cuts or liberalization of depreciation guidelines). All such moves will shift the *IS* function out by an amount $\Delta S/(1 - \text{mpc} - \text{mpI})$, where ΔS is the initial increase in spending.

If the economy is in the liquidity trap, an increase in spending will raise GNP by the full amount of the multiplier times the original increase. This is the simple example of the multiplier given when the interest rate is not considered in the system. In the intermediate range, GNP will rise, but not by the full amount of the multiplier. Interest rates will rise, investment will decrease somewhat, *cet. par.*, and this will decrease GNP by a multiplied amount. If the economy is at full employment and there are no idle cash balances, the money stock cannot expand further, the additional purchasing cannot be financed,

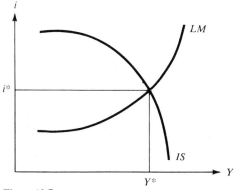

Figure 13.7

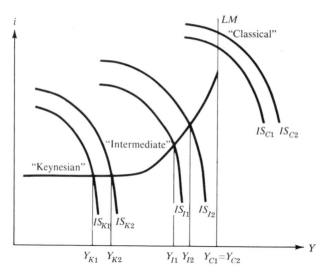

Figure 13.8

and there will be no change in real output. Instead, the components of GNP will be rearranged by inflation. Thus further expansionary fiscal policy will have no effect on real income if the economy is already at full employment. These various stages are shown in Figure 13.8.

The results are just the opposite for monetary policy. In the liquidity trap, an increase in the money stock will add to idle cash balances without decreasing the interest rate. It will thus have no effect on investment, and no effect on aggregate demand. In the intermediate range, an increase in the stock of money will result in more idle cash balances for the same income, and thus a lower interest rate. The amount that GNP will increase then depends on the interest elasticity of the investment function. If there is no relationship between investment and the interest rate, monetary policy will still fail to increase GNP. However, in the more usual case, a lower interest rate will increase investment, which will then increase GNP by the multiplier effect. This increase in income, however, will lead to an increased transactions demand for money and thus a somewhat higher interest rate than the one that existed immediately after the change in monetary policy. The net effect on the interest rate after income and the transactions demand for money have increased must also be considered. In the classical, or full-employment situation, only monetary policy will increase real output. An increase in the money stock will make available more money with which to finance increased expenditure. The interest rate may decrease, but in the true classical system it will not. In the classical system, *ex ante* investment and saving were always equal in equilibrium, so that a change in investment would be matched by an equal change in saving.

If this were the case, the *IS* curve would be horizontal, and thus there would be no drop in the interest rate.

It is of course possible that an increase in fiscal policy will be matched by monetary policy sufficient to keep the interest rate at the same level. In this case both the *IS* and *LM* curves would move out, and income would increase by the additional change in spending times the full multiplier.

In summary, Figures 13.8 can be used to show how fiscal and monetary policy change the equilibrium level of aggregate income and the interest rate. When used alone, fiscal policy is effective everywhere except where the *LM* curve is completely vertical, that is, where there are no idle cash balances. This is usually associated with a period of full employment, although this need not be the case. The efficacy of fiscal policy alone will become less and less powerful as fewer and fewer idle cash balances exist, but is a good tool to use when the economy is in a recession or depression. Monetary policy when used alone is effective everywhere except where the *LM* curve is completely horizontal (the liquidity trap) or the investment function is completely interest-inelastic (usually during recessions or depressions). This leads to the familiar statement that monetary policy is better at stopping booms than stopping recessions.

It should be pointed out that although the quantity theory is invalidated by this explanation except when no idle cash balances exist, this by no means negates the importance of money in the system. However, instead of positing a direct link between the quantity of money and the value of money output, it is now shown how the quantity of money influences the interest rate. At periods at and near full employment, this influence, and the resulting influence on investment, can be substantial. There is little doubt of this. However, it is also possible that times do occur when additional increases in the money stock will not lower the interest rate, or additional decreases in the interest rate will not increase investment. It is these possibilities that the classical economists refused to consider.

The main criticism of the Hicks explanation of the Keynesian system is that it omits equations determining employment, wages, and prices. One of the key problems, which has only been alluded to briefly, is the effect that wage cuts will have on aggregate demand and thus on employment. It will be recalled in the classical system that an equal percentage cut in wages and prices resulted in an increase in aggregate demand through the working of the quantity theory. Since MV remained constant, a drop in p resulted in an increase in X and thus an increase in employment.

In the Keynesian system we again assume profit maximization by firms and either perfect competition or no change in the degree of monopoly, so that a given percentage decrease in wages is reflected in the same percentage decrease in prices. Since real wages remain the same, there is no incentive for entrepreneurs to hire more workers unless aggregate demand increases. Aggregate demand is no longer determined by the quantity theory, however, but rather by the consumption and investment functions. There will be an increase in C

or I only if real income increases (leaving aside, for the moment, the effect of the interest rate). But there is no reason for real income to increase in this simple system. Certainly the real income of laborers has not changed. Entrepreneurs are selling the same number of goods at the same markup, so their real income has not changed either. So to a first approximation, a change in the money wage will only result in a change in the price level to the same degree, and there will be no increase in aggregate demand.

There are, however, several secondary effects that should be considered. One is the effect of these changes on the interest rate. According to the liquidity-preference theory,

$$(13.4) \qquad M = kpX - \lambda pi \qquad \text{or} \qquad i = \frac{1}{\lambda}\left(kX - \frac{M}{p}\right)$$

Thus if M is held constant, a decrease in p will result in a decrease in i for a given X. This will increase investment, cet. par., and thus raise GNP. There are, of course, the usual problems with this analysis. In a depression, the economy is likely to be in a very elastic region of the LM curve, if not the actual liquidity trap, and the investment function is most likely to be interest-inelastic. Furthermore falling prices are likely to have a very pessimistic effect on the marginal efficiency of investment schedule, shifting it backward so that the small gain due to a lower interest rate may be more than compensated for by the wave of pessimism. For all these reasons, the effect of a fall in prices on the interest rate is likely to be negligible.

Another effect of the decrease in prices may be a redistribution of real income in favor of fixed-income groups and away from entrepreneurs. The former group is generally considered to have a higher mpc than the latter group, because their income fluctuates less. However, this is likely to be offset if a decrease in prices leads to large-scale defaults of fixed contracts, which would also decrease the real income of fixed income groups. Again, the decrease in prices is likely to have a pessimistic effect on investment.

This effect would probably be a lot stronger if there were no defaulting of fixed contracts. As it is, a decrease in prices of assets will benefit creditors but will hurt debtors, so that on balance there will be no change unless debtors and creditors have different marginal propensities to consume. There is, however, a class of debt that is backed by the government—money and government securities. When the price level decreases, the real value of these assets will increase with no offsetting decrease in the private sector of the economy. In this way, people will feel wealthier and thus will raise their propensity to consume. This is often known as the Pigou, or real-balance, effect.[7]

In a way, this is only a slight extension of the Cambridge cash balance form of the quantity theory, which is usually written $M/p = kX$. Then as p drops,

[7] A. C. Pigou, "The Classical Stationary State," Economic Journal, Vol. 53, No. 4 (December, 1943), pp. 343–351.

people need to keep less money for transactions purposes and are likely to spend more of it, thus raising aggregate demand. However, given the insignificant magnitude of the empirical relationships between consumption and money, liquid assets, or total wealth, it can safely be said that this effect is of negligible importance. It is sometimes claimed that this relationship makes it theoretically possible for full employment to be reached by wage cuts. However, the same claim can be made for the first two reasons, which at least have stronger empirical support.

A fourth effect is that a decrease in prices will decrease imports and increase exports, thus increasing GNP, and vice versa for increasing prices. If the decrease in prices does not diminish aggregate demand for other reasons, this will have a definite effect on GNP. However, the size of this effect should not be overstated for a largely closed economy such as the United States. If the short-run price elasticities of imports and exports are about 0.5 and 1.5, respectively, and both imports and exports are about 5 percent of GNP, then a 50 percent change in prices would only change GNP in constant dollars by 5 percent initially, or by about 10 percent after multiplier effects (assuming a short-run multiplier of 2). Furthermore, the "beggar-my-neighbor" policies of the 1930s, designed to increase aggregate demand of a given country by raising exports and lowering imports, in effect exporting the recession abroad, did not accomplish their objective but resulted in a degeneration of foreign trade into bilateral trade agreements. So in practice this method worked very poorly.

Although all these reasons are plausible under certain sets of circumstances, a decrease in prices is quite unlikely to have much, if any, effect on aggregate demand. However, these reasons (except for the third one, the Pigou effect) are likely to be much more effective when prices are rising. Then they are liable to have a relatively stronger effect in decreasing aggregate demand. One of the reasons for this is the asymmetry of expectations about changes in prices. Although falling prices are almost universally pessimistic, rising prices are not always accompanied by unequivocal optimism. Many businessmen believe that the excesses of investment engendered by an initial rise in prices and profits will eventually lead to excess capacity and thus a decrease in aggregate demand. Whether this is right or not, it is representative of much popular opinion and does affect expectations. It should also be recalled that a rising price level (particularly near full employment) is much more likely to raise the interest rate than a falling price level (in a depression) is likely to lower it. Inasmuch as rising price levels are accompanied by output near or at full employment, investment will be more interest-elastic and thus the effect of rising prices on GNP is also likely to be greater for that reason.

An autonomous change in the wage rate, then, is likely to have little effect on the rest of the system. Whatever slight effect it does have on the interest rate and on aggregate demand is more likely to occur for an increase in wages than a decrease.

This system can be represented graphically, although not as simply as before. We must take note of the fact that the *IS* and *LM* curves are both functions of the price level. A rise in the price level is likely to shift the *IS* curve back slightly, as long as the increase in optimism engendered by the price rise has little effect on investment. A rise in the price level will also move the *LM* curve back, because the transactions demand for money is proportional to money output. The price level must be determined by other variables in the system and then used to find the exact position of the *IS* and *LM* curves. Since the real and monetary systems are interrelated, this process is likely to take several steps.

The demand for labor, wage rate, and price-markup equations can be added to the *IS–LM* diagram, as shown in Figure 13.9. Assume that the system is initially in equilibrium, with G_0 the level of autonomous expenditures and M_0 the money stock. Also assume that p_0 has already been determined to be the equilibrium price level. Then the levels of the interest rate and national income are found in diagram (a). The level of national income, X_0, is then used to find the number of laborers demanded, N_0, in diagram (b). The wage rate that workers will bargain for at each level of employment is shown in diagram (c).

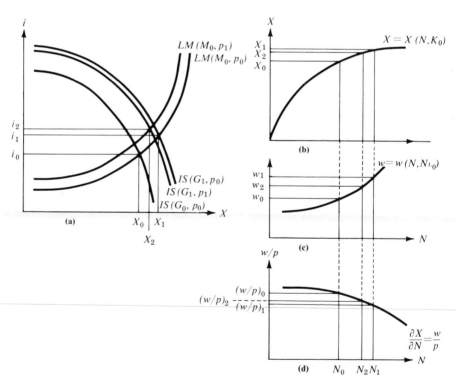

Figure 13.9

This is *not* a traditional labor supply function which states that more workers will enter the labor force as the *real* wage increases. Instead, it states that as employment increases (and unemployment decreases), wage earners will bargain for higher *money* wages. Actually, money wages are also a function of the price level: when prices rise, wage bargains will increase further. This is accounted for by the rising slope of the wage-rate equation, for prices will rise with a constant money wage when the economy approaches full employment and enters the region of diminishing marginal productivity. On the other hand, the supply of labor is considered here to be fixed at N_{L_0}, which is determined by demographic factors. Although there is a slight increase in the labor force near full employment which may be important in determining short-run fluctuations in the unemployment rate, such secondary considerations are best ignored in such a highly aggregated description of the economy. An exogenous increase in the labor force would increase unemployment and lower the wage and price level. This would increase output and employment somewhat, but not nearly enough to absorb the additional entrants into the labor force.

Once the money wage rate has been determined, the price level can be determined from the price mark-up equation. In diagram (d) this equation is transformed somewhat, so that the real wage is determined. However, given the money wage, the value of the price level (p_0) is immediately obvious.

Now consider an increase in autonomous expenditures to a level G_1. At the old price level, the *IS* curve will shift out by an amount $(G_1 - G_0)/(1 - \text{mpc} - \text{mpI})$, and the *LM* curve will remain unchanged. This will determine new values i_1, X_1, N_1, w_1, $(w/p)_1$, and p_1. Prices have risen for two reasons: the money wage rate has risen at a higher level of employment, and the spread between wages and prices has risen because of diminishing marginal productivity. This new higher price level will shift the *IS* and *LM* curves back slightly, which will determine new (lower) levels of X_2, N_2, w_2, and p_2. Only the interest rate may rise; whether it rises or falls depends on the slopes of the *IS* and *LM* curves. Since these curves depend on p_1, and another price level p_2 is being determined, the *IS* and *LM* curves will shift out very slightly, determining new values X_3, N_3, w_3, and p_3. This process will continue until the further changes in the price level are small enough to be ignored, when a new equilibrium position will be reached for all variables of the system.

This, then, is the basic statics of the simplest Keynesian system. Such a system without lags cannot explain endogenous cyclical fluctuations of the economy. To do that it is necessary to introduce elements of the accelerator and a definite lag structure into the system. To see how such systems can cause fluctuations, wages, prices, employment, and the interest rate are set aside for the moment, and only fluctuations in real variables are considered. When this mechanism has been explained, product and factor prices and factor shares can then be reintroduced into the system to form a modern theory of the business cycle.

13.2   INTERACTION BETWEEN THE MULTIPLIER AND THE ACCELERATOR AS AN ENDOGENOUS GENERATOR OF BUSINESS CYCLES

The interaction between the multiplier and accelerator was made famous in an article on that subject by Samuelson. This article marked the first step to integrate Keynesian theory with older business cycle theory, particularly the accelerator. In doing so, Samuelson supplied the critical missing link, an endogenous explanation of how movements of the economy during one cycle could generate further cycles. As we have seen, all previous nonmonetary theories of the cycle were forced to rely on primarily exogenous elements to explain the lower turning point.

The original simple model used by Samuelson was

$$C = \alpha Y_{t-1}$$

$$I = \beta(C_{t-1} - C_{t-2})$$

$$C + I + G = Y$$

However, following Hicks,[8] a second version of this model has become more common: we shall discuss his version:

$$C = c Y_{t-1}$$

$$I = v(Y_{t-1} - Y_{t-2})$$

$$C + I + G = Y$$

Movements of Y around its equilibrium value (denoted by lower case letters) after an initial exogenous shock may exhibit the characteristics shown in Figure 13.10. The shape of the time path of Y depends on the values of c and v. In general, the greater the value of v, the greater the chance of an explosive path of Y; the greater the value of c, the less likely it is that oscillations will occur. In the following analysis it is always assumed that $0 < c < 1$, and $v > 0$.

Before exploring the algebra of the solution, we discuss how this simple model generates cycles under a wide range of conditions. No cycles can occur with only first-order lags, and no cycles can occur without an accelerator relationship. In other words, the model

$$C = c Y_{t-1}$$

$$I = v(Y_t - Y_{t-1})$$

$$C + I + G = Y$$

---

[8] J. R. Hicks, *A Contribution to the Theory of the Trade Cycle* (London: Clarendon Press, 1950).

or the model

$$C = cY_{t-1}$$

$$I = v(Y_{t-1} + Y_{t-2})$$

$$C + I + G = Y$$

(a) Damped nonoscillatory

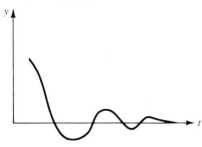

or

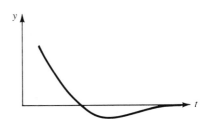

(b) Damped oscillatory

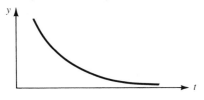

(c) Explosive oscillatory

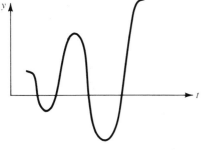

(d) Explosive nonoscillatory

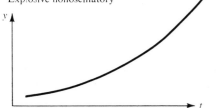

Figure 13.10

can never generate cyclical fluctuations as long as c and v are positive. In the first case, the system can be reduced to the form $y_t = ay_{t-1}$ (lower case letters represent deviations from equilibrium value), so that y_t is always a fixed proportion of y_{t-1}. This system will return to equilibrium if $a < 1$ and will diverge if $a > 1$. In the second case, the system can be reduced to the form $y_t = ay_{t-1} + by_{t-2}$. If a and b are both positive, increasing values of y can only be followed by additional increases, and there is no possibility of a downturn in y at any time.

Thus both second-order lags and an accelerator are needed to generate cycles. The multiplier itself is not needed to cause cyclical fluctuations. In fact, as the value of c increases, the chance of cycles is diminished. The model

$$I = v(Y_{t-1} - Y_{t-2})$$
$$\bar{C} + I + \bar{G} = Y$$

will generate cycles for any value of v between 0 and 4. However, the inclusion of the multiplier brings more realism to this simple model and results in cycles that are more similar to those which actually occur.

With or without a consumption function, two periods after an exogenous shock (for example, an increase in G) has raised Y, the $-vY_{t-2}$ term will have a negative effect on investment. Unless the accelerator is very strong or unless the mpc is very close to unity, this will result in a slight decrease in investment and a slowing down in the rate of increase in Y. This will ordinarily be enough to decrease I, and ΔY, still further. A turning point is soon reached and ΔY becomes negative. As soon as this happens, forces are already set in motion to reverse this fall in Y. The low values of Y mean that the term $-vY_{t-2}$ will have less and less of a negative effect on investment, so that investment will stop decreasing as rapidly. When this occurs, ΔY will increase, I will increase, and the economy will again turn up. This process will be repeated until the system either reaches a new equilibrium or continues to fluctuate so wildly that negative values of Y are reached. Clearly these explosive situations are not realistic, and it is easily shown that for reasonable empirical estimates of c and v, the system will always return to equilibrium.

This process can be illustrated with some numerical examples given in Table 13.1. However, before actual values of c and v are selected, something must be said about time units, since v related the *level* of investment to the *change* in income. Considerable confusion has arisen on this point, because in the long run v is also the capital-output ratio, which is about 2.5. Yet in a system where consumption depends on income last period and investment depends on the lagged change in income, the time periods cannot realistically be longer than a year and may be as short as one quarter. We have stressed in Chapter 4 that investment depends on the change in income for many previous years, not just one year. The marginal change in investment for a unit change in income of the previous year, far from being 2.5, is certainly less than 0.5.

TABLE 13.1 EXAMPLES OF THE INTERACTION OF THE MULTIPLIER AND THE ACCELERATOR

	A. Damped, No Oscillations; $c = 0.5$, $v = 0.05$				B. Damped, Oscillations; $c = 0.5$, $v = 0.8$				C. Explosive, Oscillations; $c = 0.5$, $v = 1.5$				D. Explosive, No Oscillations; $c = 0.5$, $v = 3.0$			
	C	I	G	Y	C	I	G	Y	C	I	G	Y	C	I	G	Y
Y_{-2}	50	0	50	100	50	0	50	100	50	0	50	100	50	0	50	100
Y_{-1}	50	0	50	100	50	0	50	100	50	0	50	100	50	0	50	100
Y	50	0	60	110	50	0	60	110	50	0	60	110	50	0	60	110
Y_{+1}	55	0.5	60	115.5	55	8.0	60	123	55	15	60	130	55	30	60	145
Y_{+2}	57.7	0.3	60	118.0	63	12.8	60	135.8	65	30	60	155	72.5	90	60	222.5
Y_{+3}	59.0	0.1	60	119.1	67.9	7.8	60	135.7	77.5	37.5	60	175	111.2	232.5	60	403.7
Y_{+4}	59.5	0.1	60	119.6	67.9	0.0	60	127.9	87.5	30	60	177.5	171.9	363.6	60	595.5
Y_{+5}	59.8	0	60	119.8	63.9	−6.2	60	117.7	88.8	3.7	60	152.5	297.8	755.4	60	1113.2
Y_{+6}	59.9	0	60	119.9	58.9	−8.2	60	110.7	76.2	−37.5	60	98.7				
Y_{+7}	60.0	0	60	120.0	55.3	−5.6	60	109.7	49.4	−80.7	60	28.7				
Y_{+8}	.	.	.	.	54.8	−0.8	60	114.0	14.4	−105.0	60	−30.6				
Y_{+9}	.	.	.	.	57.0	3.4	60	120.4	−15.3	−89.0	60	−44.3				
Y_{+10}	.	.	.	.	60.2	5.1	60	125.3	−22.2	−20.6	60	17.2				
Y_{+11}					62.7	3.9	60	126.6	−8.9	40.7	60	91.8				
Y_{+12}					63.3	1.0	60	124.3	45.9	163.5	60	269.4				
Y_{+13}					62.2	−1.8	60	120.4	134.7	266.4	60	461.1				
Y_{eq}	60	0	60	120	60	0	60	120	—	—	—	—	—	—	—	—

In the long run, v would be about 2.5, but in that case, when the time period is five years or more, investment would depend on the *unlagged* change in income and no cycles at all would be generated. This point is often overlooked.

For this theory to be a workable hypothesis that can be used in conjunction with other phenomena to generate a business cycle theory, instead of just an interesting mathematical theory, reasonable values of c and v should produce damped cycles with cycle lengths approaching those actually observed. It is not clear whether the lags referred to are quarter or years, and whether I is I_p or ΔI_i. However, it is reasonable to try alternative interpretations to see what results are obtained. The actual method for solving second-order difference equations is presented in the appendix to this chapter. The main steps of the method will be sketched and the principal results tabulated and discussed in the text.

Although the lag structure used by Samuelson is reasonable, there is no explicit discussion of the choice of lags in his article. Several other lag structures suggest themselves as being equally realistic, and one of the tests of usefulness for this model is that the results ought not to change greatly if one of the lags is slightly altered. To determine whether this is true we have reformulated the model in a number of different ways and calculated the behavior of the model with these alternative assumptions. This list is not meant to be exhaustive, but rather to provide sufficient alternatives to see how the results of the model change for different lag structures.

Case I (original formulation):

$$C = cY_{-1}$$

$$I = v(Y_{-1} - Y_{-2})$$

$$C + I + G = Y$$

$$Y - (c + v)Y_{-1} + vY_{-2} = 0$$

The solution is

$$Y_t = \overline{Y}_t + A_1\rho_1^t + A_2\rho_2^t$$

where $\overline{Y}_t$ is the equilibrium solution, A_1 and A_2 are arbitrary constants determined by initial conditions, and

$$\rho_{1,2} = \frac{(c + v) \pm \sqrt{(c + v)^2 - 4v}}{2}$$

where only the dominant root ρ_1 is of concern. There will be cycles if $4v - (c + v)^2 > 0$, or $(1 - \sqrt{1 - c})^2 < v < (1 + \sqrt{1 - c})^2$. The system will be damped if $v < 1$, and explosive if $v > 1$. This is graphed in Figure 13.11. For reasonable values of c and v see Table 13.2. The values of c may seem somewhat low, but recall that c is the marginal propensity to spend out of GNP, and thus would never be higher than $\frac{2}{3}$, even in the long run. The values of v,

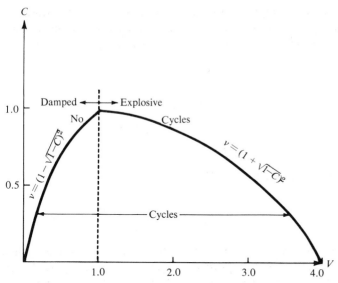

Figure 13.11

with and without inventories, are essentially the values determined by the empirical studies in Part I.

All four sets of assumptions generate damped cycles, but the length of the cycles implied is a bit unwieldy. In particular, the yearly cycles seem too long compared to the actual record. Although the quarterly cycles appear to be too short, this can be interpreted somewhat differently and is discussed below.

TABLE 13.2   VALUES OF c AND v, Case I

Assumption	Values	Behavior	Length of Cycle	Amplitude[a] (Fraction of $\bar{Y} - Y_0$)
Yearly lags, no inventories	$c = 0.40$ $v = 0.15$	Damped cycles	8 years	0.4
Yearly lags, inventories	$c = 0.40$ $v = 0.25$	Damped cycles	7 years	0.5
Quarterly lags, no inventories	$c = 0.30$ $v = 0.05$	Damped cycles	10 quarters	0.2
Quarterly lags, inventories	$c = 0.30$ $v = 0.35$	Damped cycles	6 quarters	0.6

[a] The amplitude represents the amount that the first cycle overshoots the new equilibrium relative to the difference between the new equilibrium value $\bar{Y}$ and the original value Y_0.

At any rate, none of the assumptions gives cycle lengths very close to observed behavior. This may primarily be due to the fact that consumption depends only on lagged income, which is not really the case. This suggests the next case, which is

Case II.

$$C = cY$$

$$I = v(Y_{-1} - Y_{-2})$$

$$C + I + G = Y$$

$$Y(1 - c) - vY_{-1} + vY_{-2} = 0$$

$$\rho_{1,2} = \frac{v \pm \sqrt{v^2 - 4v(1 - c)}}{2(1 - c)}$$

There will be cycles for $4v(1 - c) - v^2 > 0$, or $0 < v < 4(1 - c)$. The system will be damped for $v/(1 - c) < 1$; explosive for $v/(1 - c) > 1$. Graphically this is shown in Figure 13.12. Values are as given in Table 13.3. All the assumptions give the same cycle length in terms of the unit of the lags, which is a bit unusual. Although the length of the cycle generated by the yearly lags seems reasonable, if a little long, the quarterly cycles are clearly much too short. This does raise the question of a subcycle dominated by inventory investment, which is explored further in the other cases.

Since consumption depends on past as well as present income, a logical choice is to expand the model to the following:

Case III.

$$C = c_1 Y + c_2 Y_{-1}$$

$$I = v(Y_{-1} - Y_{-2})$$

$$C + I + G = Y$$

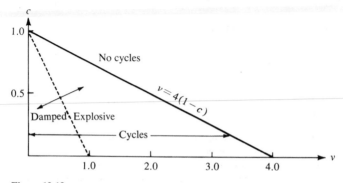

Figure 13.12

TABLE 13.3   VALUES OF c AND v, Case II

Assumption	Values	Behavior	Length of Cycle	Amplitude
Yearly lags, no inventories	$c = 0.35$ $v = 0.15$	Damped cycles	5 years	0.5
Yearly lags, inventories	$c = 0.35$ $v = 0.25$	Damped cycles	5 years	0.6
Quarterly lags, no inventories	$c = 0.20$ $v = 0.05$	Damped cycles	5 quarters	0.2
Quarterly lags, inventories	$c = 0.20$ $v = 0.35$	Damped cycles	5 quarters	0.6

$$Y(1 - c_1) - (c_2 + v)Y_{-1} + vY_{-2} = 0$$

$$\rho_{1,2} = \frac{(c_2 + v) \pm \sqrt{(c_2 + v)^2 - 4v(1 - c_1)}}{2(1 - c_1)}$$

Cycles will occur if

$$4v(1 - c_1) > (c_2 + v)^2$$

or

$$-(c_2 + 2c_1 - 2) - \sqrt{(c_2 + 2c_1 - 2)^2 - c_2^2} < v < -(c_2 + 2c_1 - 2)$$

$$+ \sqrt{(c_2 + 2c_1 - 2)^2 - c_2^2}$$

This is somewhat harder to interpret than the previous two cases, particularly in two dimensions. For $c_1 = c_2$, this reduces to

$$-(3c - 2) - \sqrt{(3c - 2)^2 - c^2} < v < -(3c - 2) + \sqrt{(3c - 2)^2 - c^2}$$

The stability condition does not involve c_2: the system will be damped if $v/(1 - c_1) < 1$ and explosive for $v/(1 - c_1) > 1$.

Some of these results are shown in Figure 13.13, including an additional result for $c_2 = 0.1$. Similar results would be obtained for other values of c_2 in this neighborhood. Values are as given in Table 13.4. Evidently the distributed lag on income in the consumption function does not change the results too much. This is not too surprising, because the multiplier is a stabilizing influence.

The next obvious step is to add a distributed lag on investment, leading to:

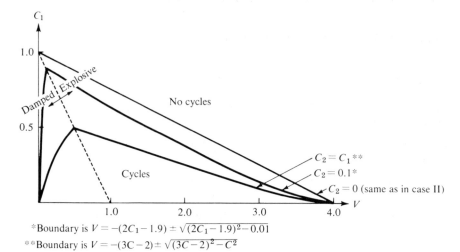

*Boundary is $V = -(2C_1 - 1.9) \pm \sqrt{(2C_1 - 1.9)^2 - 0.01}$

**Boundary is $V = -(3C - 2) \pm \sqrt{(3C - 2)^2 - C^2}$

Figure 13.13

TABLE 13.4   VALUES OF c AND v, Case III

Assumption	Values	Behavior	Length of Cycle	Amplitude
Yearly lags, no inventories	$c_1 = 0.35$ $c_2 = 0.15$ $v = 0.15$	Damped cycles	6 years	0.5
Yearly lags, inventories	$c_1 = 0.35$ $c_2 = 0.15$ $v = 0.25$	Damped cycles	6 years	0.6
Quarterly lags, no inventories	$c_1 = 0.15$ $c_2 = 0.10$ $v = 0.05$	Damped cycles	5 quarters	0.2
Quarterly lags, inventories	$c_1 = 0.15$ $c_2 = 0.10$ $v = 0.35$	Damped cycles	5 quarters	0.6

Case IV.

$$C = c_1 Y + c_2 Y_{-1}$$

$$I = v_1(Y - Y_{-1}) + v_2(Y_1 - Y_{-2})$$

$$C + I + G = Y$$

$$Y(1 - c_1 - v_1) - (c_2 - v_1 + v_2)Y_{-1} + v_2 Y_{-2} = 0$$

$$\rho_{1,2} = \frac{(c_2 - v_1 + v_2) \pm \sqrt{(c_2 - v_1 + v_2)^2 - 4v_2(1 - c_1 - v_1)}}{2(1 - c_1 - v_1)}$$

It is even more difficult to give a simple interpretation to this case. For ease of exposition, set $c_1 = c_2 = c$ and $v_1 = v_2 = v$. Then this case reduces to

$$\rho_{1,2} = \frac{c \pm \sqrt{c^2 - 4v(1 - c - v)}}{2(1 - c - v)}$$

Then cycles will occur if

$$4v(1 - c - v) - c^2 > 0$$

or

$$\frac{(1 - c) - \sqrt{1 - 2c}}{2} < v < \frac{(1 - c) + \sqrt{1 - 2c}}{2}$$

For these simplified assumptions, the system will be damped if $v/(1 - c - v) < 1$ and explosive if $v/(1 - c - v) > 1$. These can be reduced to $v < (1 - c)/2$ and $v > (1 - c)/2$. This case is graphed in Figure 13.14.

Since $c_1 \cong c_2$ is a more reasonable approximation than $v_1 \cong v_2$, we proceed under the assumption that the former equality holds, and then graph several different values of v_1 and v_2, as shown in Figure 13.15. Note that the scale of the graph has been changed substantially as the relevant damped region becomes smaller with the introduction of a distributed lag accelerator. As v_2 increases, the damped region continues to diminish, and at $v_2 \geq 1$ all solutions would explode. This is of course the same condition that held for case I. However, for relevant values of the c's and v's, the system stays well within the damped oscillatory region, as shown in Table 13.5. Although the boundary conditions have changed substantially in Case IV, there is very little difference in the results for relevant values of the parameters. It would be possible to explore

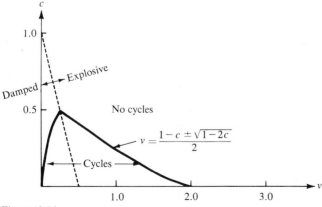

Figure 13.14

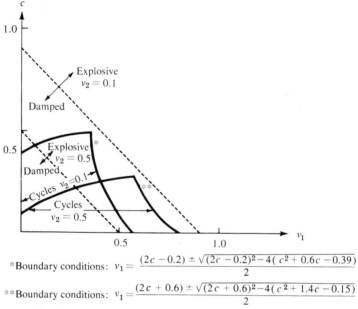

*Boundary conditions: $v_1 = \dfrac{(2c - 0.2) \pm \sqrt{(2c - 0.2)^2 - 4(c^2 + 0.6c - 0.39)}}{2}$

**Boundary conditions: $v_1 = \dfrac{(2c + 0.6) \pm \sqrt{(2c + 0.6)^2 - 4(c^2 + 1.4c - 0.15)}}{2}$

Figure 13.15

other cases with more complicated lag structures, but such an exercise rapidly loses its value as a pedagogical device. We have explored enough cases to suggest that the results of the model are not likely to vary a great deal when reasonable changes are made in the lag structure.

One puzzling feature of the model, which was alluded to earlier, is the fact that the yearly lags generate cycles of about five years, whereas the quarterly lags generate cycles of approximately five quarters. This suggests the possibility

TABLE 13.5   VALUES OF c AND v, Case IV

Assumption	Values	Behavior	Length of Cycle	Amplitude
Yearly lags, no inventories	$c_1 = 0.35 \quad v_1 = 0.10$ $c_2 = 0.15 \quad v_2 = 0.15$	Damped cycles	5 years	0.5
Yearly lags, inventories	$c_1 = 0.35 \quad v_1 = 0.30$ $c_2 = 0.15 \quad v_2 = 0.10$	Damped cycles	4 years	0.5
Quarterly lags, no inventories	$c_1 = 0.15 \quad v_1 = 0$ $c_2 = 0.10 \quad v_2 = 0.05$	Damped cycles	5 quarters	0.2
Quarterly lags, inventories	$c_1 = 0.15 \quad v_1 = 0.10$ $c_2 = 0.10 \quad v_2 = 0.20$	Damped cycles	5 quarters	0.5

of a very short subcycle dominated by inventory investment being super-imposed on the longer cycle dominated by fixed business investment. If this were in fact the case, and other forces causing the upturns and downturns were asymmetrical, this could provide an explanation of the fact that periods of contraction (that is, peak to trough) have averaged just over a year in the postwar period, while booms have been much longer than a year. In any case, whether this is true or not, a large number of elements will have to be added to the interaction between the multiplier and the accelerator before any theory of the business cycle can be constructed. The inherent mechanism in these terms that generates cycles is certainly not in itself a complete theory of the cycle.

13.3   MULTIPLIER–ACCELERATOR ANALYSIS APPLIED TO INVENTORY INVESTMENT

Since the question of an inventory subcycle was raised in the last section, it is of considerable interest to examine such a cycle by itself while treating all fixed investment as autonomous. Such a model has been developed by Metzler, in what today still remains one of the classic articles on business cycles. Our treatment of the Metzler model will be slightly different from the treatment used for the Samuelson (or Samuelson–Hicks) model. Although Samuelson chose a reasonable lag structure, he did not explicitly justify it, so that it seemed sensible to experiment with other forms of the model. On the other hand, Metzler analyzes the lag structure that he chooses in great detail; it is a crucial part of his model, and to depart from his lag structure would be to change the essence of the model. Several cases of the Metzler model are considered, as it is useful to show how the addition of various terms influences the results. However, all but the last case represents an intermediate step in the model, so stability conditions and oscillatory regions will not be analyzed. The interested reader is referred to the original Metzler article for many of the intermediate results.

Case I. In this simplest case, inventory investment is passive. No attempt is made to adjust inventories to a specified level. The only sector of the economy that is related to income is production of consumer goods, u_t, which depends on last period's sales. The latter is equal to GNP (Y_t) times the marginal propensity to consume out of GNP, β. Thus

$$u_t = \beta Y_{t-1}$$

All other spending is autonomous and is denoted by v_0, so that if

$$Y_t = u_t + v_0$$

then

$$Y_t = \beta Y_{t-1} + v_0$$

This simple model cannot generate cycles, as discussed in the last section.

Case II. Inventories are maintained at a normal level. Production for inventory investment, S_t, is given by

$$S_t = \text{actual sales in } t - 1 - \text{anticipated sales in } t - 1$$

$$S_t = \beta Y_{t-1} - \beta Y_{t-2}$$

Here anticipated sales in t are simply equal to actual sales in $t - 1$.

If actual sales last period were equal to anticipated sales, there will be no inventory investment this period. If sales last period were higher than anticipated, S_t will be positive, as firms attempt to bring inventories back up to normal levels: if they were lower, S_t will be negative. We then have

$$Y_t = u_t + S_t + v_0$$

$$u_t = \beta Y_{t-1}$$

$$S_t = \beta(Y_{t-1} - Y_{t-2})$$

so that

$$Y_t = 2\beta Y_{t-1} - \beta Y_{t-2} + v_0$$

Since we define $0 < \beta < 1$, this model will always give damped oscillations.

Case III. The first two cases have been unrealistically simple. The model assumes greater realism with the introduction of the elasticity of expectation, η. In this version of the model, inventories are passive, but an attempt is made to adjust production of current consumer goods: this adjustment is equal to some fraction η of the change in sales last period. This can be represented as

$$u_t = \beta Y_{t-1} + \eta(\beta Y_{t-1} - \beta Y_{t-2})$$

| production this period | sales last period | elasticity of expectation | change in sales last period |

The term η is defined as the ratio of expected change in sales this period to the actual change in sales last period, and is usually assumed to be between 0 and 1. If $\eta = 1$, firms will always expect the change in this period's sales to be equal to last period's change, and, if $\eta = 0$, previous changes in sales will have no effect on anticipated sales this period.

Since inventories are passive for this case, the model is simply

$$Y_t = u_t + v_0$$

Therefore,

$$Y_t = (\beta + \eta\beta)Y_{t-1} - \eta\beta Y_{t-2} + v_0$$

The solution of this system will always be damped, and will oscillate unless η is very small.

Case IV. The last two cases are now combined. Firms adjust both inventories and production for consumer goods. Although the equation for the latter is the same as in Case III, the inventory investment equation is somewhat changed. We had (from Case II)

$$S_t = \text{actual sales in } t - 1 - \text{anticipated sales in } t - 1$$

Actual sales are still βY_{t-1}, but anticipated sales are now $\beta Y_{t-2} + \eta(\beta Y_{t-2} - \beta Y_{t-3})$: that is, they include an extra anticipations term. Thus

$$S_t = \beta Y_{t-1} - \beta Y_{t-2} - \eta\beta(Y_{t-2} - Y_{t-3})$$
$$u_t = \beta Y_{t-1} + \eta\beta(Y_{t-1} - Y_{t-2})$$

from Case III, so that the complete system is now

$$Y_t = (2 + \eta)\beta Y_{t-1} - (1 + 2\eta)\beta Y_{t-2} + \eta\beta Y_{t-3} + v_0$$

This introduces a third-order difference equation, but the results are similar to the second-order equations given for other cases of this model. The system will produce damped oscillations unless β and η are both close to unity, in which case explosive oscillations will result.

Case V. The analysis is now expanded to include an accelerator for inventory investment: the elasticity of expectations term is dropped for the moment. The accelerator (in a stock-adjustment form with complete adjustment) states that

inventory investment in t = desired inventories in (t) − actual stocks of
inventories in
$(t - 1)$

Actual stocks in $t - 1$ are equal to desired stocks minus unintended depletions during $t - 1$. Depletions are in turn equal to the change in sales during $t - 1$, or $\beta Y_{t-1} - \beta Y_{t-2}$. Thus

$$S_t = \text{desired inventories in } (t) - \underbrace{(\text{desired stocks in } (t - 1) - (\beta Y_{t-1} - \beta Y_{t-2}))}_{\text{actual stocks in } (t - 1)}$$

The relationship from which the accelerator is derived states that

$$\frac{\text{inventory stocks}}{\text{sales}} = \alpha \qquad \text{or} \qquad \text{stocks} = \alpha \,(\text{sales})$$

Desired stocks in $t - 1$ are thus $\alpha(\text{sales}_{t-2}) = \alpha\beta Y_{t-2}$. Desired stocks in t are $\alpha(\text{sales}_{t-1}) = \alpha\beta Y_{t-1}$. Therefore,

$$S_t = \alpha\beta Y_{t-1} - \alpha\beta Y_{t-2} + \beta(Y_{t-1} - Y_{t-2})$$

Completing the rest of the model,

$$u_t = \beta Y_{t-1}$$

Therefore,

$$Y_t = (2 + \alpha)\beta Y_{t-1} - (1 + \alpha)\beta Y_{t-2} + v_0$$

Here α is an average stock/sales ratio rather than the marginal capital/output ratio v used in the Samuelson model. Thus the possibility of explosive oscillations is somewhat greater in this model, although still unlikely.

Case VI. The adjustment of inventories to normal levels, the elasticity of expectations, and the accelerator are now combined in this final version of the Metzler model. If $\eta = 0$, this reduces to Case V: if $\alpha = 0$, it reduces to Case IV: and if both are zero, it reduces to Case III.

From Case IV we have the following:

$$u_t = (1 + \eta)\beta Y_{t-1} - \eta\beta Y_{t-2}$$

$$(Sr)_t = \beta Y_{t-1} - \beta(1 + \eta)Y_{t-2} + \eta\beta Y_{t-3}$$

It is now necessary to combine the accelerator and the elasticity of expectations. Since one kind of inventory investment, adjustment to normal levels, is already included in this model, denote inventory investment due to the accelerator as S_a. Then

$$(S_a)_t = \text{desired inventories in } (t) - \text{desired stocks in } (t - 1)$$

(Desired inventories)$_t$ are now equal to α (expected sales)$_t$, which equals $\alpha[\beta Y_{t-1} + \eta(\beta Y_{t-1} - \beta Y_{t-2})]$. Similarly (desired inventories)$_{t-1}$ are now equal to $\alpha[\beta Y_{t-2} + \eta(\beta Y_{t-2} - \beta Y_{t-3})]$.
Therefore,

$$(S_a)_t = \alpha[\beta Y_{t-1} + \eta(\beta Y_{t-1} - \beta Y_{t-2})] - \alpha[\beta Y_{t-2} + \eta(\beta Y_{t-2} - \beta Y_{t-3})]$$

This can be simplified to

$$(S_a)_t = \alpha\beta[(1 + \eta)Y_{t-1} - (1 + 2\eta)Y_{t-2} + \eta Y_{t-3}]$$

Metzler thus combines (1) the multiplier (production of consumer goods), (2) replacement inventory investment (adjustment to unexpected sales), and (3) the inventory accelerator, all of which depend on the elasticity of expectations, to form his final version of the model. Since

$$Y_t = u_t + S_t + (S_a)_t + v_0$$

$$u_t = (1 + \eta)\beta Y_{t-1} - \eta\beta Y_{t-2}$$

$$(Sr)_t = \beta Y_{t-1} - \beta(1 + \eta)Y_{t-2} + \eta\beta Y_{t-3}$$

$$(S_a)_t = \alpha\beta[(1 + \eta)Y_{t-1} - (1 + 2\eta)Y_{t-2} + \eta Y_{t-3}]$$

the equation to be solved is

$$Y_t = [(1 + \eta)(1 + \alpha) + 1]\beta Y_{t-1} - [(1 + 2\eta)(1 + \alpha)]\beta Y_{t-2}$$
$$+ (1 + \alpha)\eta\beta Y_{t-3} + v_0$$

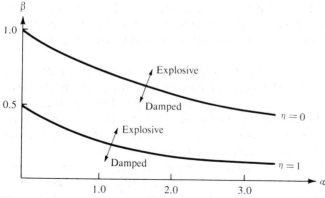

Figure 13.16

Before attempting a partial solution of this equation, it is crucial to consider the time periods involved in order to obtain reasonable empirical estimates of α, β, and η. As in the Samuelson model, this is important because α is the ratio of a stock to a flow. If the time period is one month, α will be 12 times as large as if the time period is one year. Although Metzler does not identify the exact length of the time periods, it is quite reasonable to suppose that they are about one quarter.

For the entire postwar period, inventory stocks have equaled between 40 and 50 days of manufacturers' and distributors' sales. Thus for one quarter, inventory stocks/sales $= \frac{1}{2}$. However, in this model inventories are related to GNP, not total sales. Because of double counting, GNP is equal to about $\frac{2}{3}$ of sales of goods, so that at quarterly rates inventory stocks/GNP $= \frac{1}{2}\frac{3}{2} = \frac{3}{4}$. The estimate for α is thus $\frac{3}{4}$. The estimate for β is not just the usual marginal propensity to consume but, as in the Samuelson model, the marginal propensity

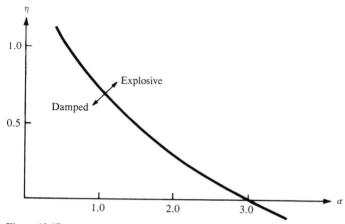

Figure 13.17

to consume out of GNP. For a lag of one quarter, $\beta = \frac{1}{4}$. Metzler states that β will certainly be greater than $\frac{1}{2}$, but that must be in the long run. For the period of a year, β would be only 0.35, in which case the system would be stable for all $\eta < 1$.

Given that $\beta = \frac{1}{4}$, the time path of Y will always be oscillatory for all values of α and η between 0 and 1. However, these cycles may not always be damped. For $\eta = 1$ and $\beta = \frac{1}{4}$, $\alpha > 0.7$ will give explosive cycles. On the other hand, if $\eta = 0$, then damped cycles will occur for all $\alpha < 3$. These results are shown for $\eta = 0$, $\eta = 1$, and various values of α and β in Figure 13.16. For $\beta = \frac{1}{4}$ and various values of α, η, the relationship is shown in Figure 13.17.

The question of whether this system generates damped or explosive cycles thus depends on the value of η, which is much harder to measure than α or β. If the value of η is in fact near unity, explosive cycles would result. However, if this were to occur, businessmen would eventually see that larger and larger booms were followed by deeper and deeper recessions, and this would clearly reduce their elasticity of expectations. Thus this model essentially contains a self-damping mechanism. If explosive cycles were to start, the inherent nature of these cycles would soon cause a great decrease in the elasticity of expectations, and return the economy to a region of damped oscillations once again.

APPENDIX to Chapter 13

Solution of Second-Order Difference Equations

In deriving the solution, we shall use the Case I Samuelson model as an actual example. However, the method presented is general and can be used to solve any second-order linear difference equation.

When solving the system

$$C_t = cY_{t-1}$$

$$I_t = v(Y_{t-1} - Y_{t-2})$$

$$C_t + I_t + G_t = Y_t$$

and substituting,

$$cY_{t-1} + v(Y_{t-1} - Y_{t-2}) + G_t = Y_t$$

first find the *particular* solution that satisfies all Y. This is done by setting $Y_t = Y_{t-1} = Y_{t-2} = \overline{Y}$. Then

$$C = c\overline{Y}$$

$$I = 0$$

$$C + I + G = \overline{Y} = G + c\overline{Y}$$

$$\overline{Y} = \frac{G}{1 - c}$$

This equilibrium solution of Y is of course the case of the simplest multiplier.

Next, consider deviations around the equilibrium value, $y_t = Y_t - \overline{Y}$. The solution is actually analyzed in terms of these deviations, the path by which Y_t converges to or diverges from equilibrium. Since Y_t and $\overline{Y}$ both satisfy the difference equation

$$cY_{t-1} + v(Y_{t-1} - Y_{t-2}) + G_t = Y_t$$

or

$$Y_t - (c - v)Y_{t-1} + vY_{t-2} = G_t$$

then $y_t = Y_t - \overline{Y}$ will satisfy the *homogenous* equation

$$y_t - (c - v)y_{t-1} + vy_{t-2} = 0$$

To solve this equation, choose values $y_t = y_0\rho^t$ and find the particular values of ρ that will satisfy the equation. Then

$$y_0\rho^t - y_0\rho^{t-1}(c - v) + y_0\rho^{t-2}v = 0$$

Dividing by $y_0\rho^{t-2}$ gives

$$\rho^2 - \rho(c - v) + v = 0$$

This ordinary quadratic equation can be solved by the usual formula.

$$x = \frac{-b \pm \sqrt{b^2 - 4ac}}{2a}$$

to obtain roots ρ_1 and ρ_2. The solution is then of the form

$$y_t = A_1\rho_1^t + A_2\rho_2^t$$

Since $y_t = y_t - \bar{Y}$,

$$Y_t = \bar{Y} + A_1\rho_1^t + A_2\rho_2^t$$

where A_1 and A_2 are arbitrary constants determined by initial conditions. Since we have defined ρ_1 to be the dominant root, ρ_2 will not influence the solution as t gets large. Y_t will converge to $\bar{Y}$ as t gets large if $\rho_1 < 1$, and will diverge if $\rho_1 > 1$. The "knife-edge" solution of $\rho_1 = 1$ is mathematically feasible but economically unrealistic.

In certain systems it may be possible that $\rho_1 < 0$, in which case cycles can be generated from the above equation. However, we have assumed throughout that c and v are always positive. Thus ρ_1, which equals $[(c + v) + \sqrt{(c + v)^2 - 4v}]/2$, will always be positive as long as $(c + v)^2 - 4v > 0$. Cycles will occur only when the quantity under the radical is negative. In this case it is necessary to use some transformations for complex numbers. In general

$$\rho_1 = -\frac{b}{2a} + \frac{i\sqrt{4ac - b^2}}{2a}$$

and

$$\rho_2 = -\frac{b}{2a} - \frac{i\sqrt{4ac - b^2}}{2a}$$

where $i = \sqrt{-1}$. These can be more easily written in the form $\rho_1 = x + iy$ and $\rho_2 = x - iy$; these are called *conjugate complex numbers*.

It is convenient to transform ρ_1 and ρ_2 to polar coordinates, which can be illustrated on an Argand diagram, shown in Figure 13.18. On the Argand diagram

$$x = r\cos\theta$$

$$iy = ri\sin\theta$$

and

$$x^2 - (iy)^2 = x^2 + y^2 = r^2$$

The homogeneous solution of the system

$$y_t = A_1\rho_1^t + A_2\rho_2^t$$

can now be written

$$y_t = B_1(x + iy)^t + B_2(x - iy)^t$$

where B_1 and B_2 are new arbitrary constants. Transforming to polar coordinates,

$$y_t = B_1(r\cos\theta + ri\sin\theta)^t + B_2(r\cos\theta - ri\sin\theta)^t$$

$$= r^t[B_1(\cos\theta + i\sin\theta)^t + B_2(\cos\theta - i\sin\theta)^t]$$

$$r = \sqrt{x^2 + y^2}$$

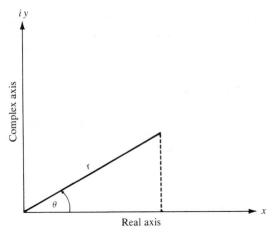

Figure 13.18

and since $x = -b/2a$ and $y = \sqrt{4ac - b^2}/2a$,

$$r = \sqrt{\frac{b^2}{4a^2} + \frac{4ac - b^2}{4a^2}} = \sqrt{\frac{4ac}{4a^2}} = \sqrt{\frac{c}{a}}$$

Thus the values of c and a will determine the value of r, which determines the amplitude of the cyclical path of y_t. If $r < 1$, the system will converge; if $r > 1$, it will diverge (we may always take the positive value of r).

This expression for y_t can be considerably simplified. First, by Demoivre's theorem,

$$(\cos \theta + i \sin \theta)^t = \cos \theta t + i \sin \theta t$$

Therefore,

$$y_t = r^t[B_1(\cos \theta t + i \sin \theta t) + B_2(\cos \theta t - i \sin \theta t)]$$

$$= r^t[(B_1 + B_2) \cos \theta t + i(B_1 - B_2)\sin \theta t]$$

Let $K_1 = B_1 + B_2$ and $K_2 = i(B_1 - B_2)$. Then $y_t = r^t(K_1 \cos \theta t + K_2 \sin \theta t)$. Now let $K_1 = K \cos \varepsilon$, $K_2 = K \sin \varepsilon$, by another arbitrary switch of contants. Then

$$y_t = r^t[(K \cos \theta t \cos \varepsilon + K \sin \theta t \sin \varepsilon)]$$

$$= r^t[K \cos(\theta t - \varepsilon)]$$

by a standard trigonometric identity. The two constants are now K, which depends on the size of the initial displacement away from equilibrium, and ε, a phase constant that depends on the part of the cycle the economy was in when the displacement occurred.

Since $x = r \cos \theta$,

$$\cos \theta = \frac{x}{r} = -\frac{b}{2a} \cdot \left| \sqrt{\frac{c}{a}} = \frac{-b}{2\sqrt{ac}} \right.$$

Finally the period of the cycle is given by $2\pi/\theta$, where θ is measured in radians.

To find the general solution, combine the particular and homogeneous solutions to get $Y_t = \bar{Y} + K \cdot r^t \cos(\theta t - \varepsilon)$ and, at $t = 0$ and $\varepsilon_0 = 0$, $K = Y_t - \bar{Y}$. Thus the complete solution is

$$Y_t = \bar{Y} + (Y_t - \bar{Y})r^t[\cos(\theta t - \varepsilon)]$$

To solve third-order difference equations it is necessary to solve a cubic equation and then proceed as above. Although this presents no theoretical difficulties, the solution of the cubic is likely to become very involved and tedious, particularly for equations of the type found in the Metzler model. In practice, graphical solution is a more satisfactory way to proceed for cubic and higher-order difference equations.

CHAPTER 14

POST-KEYNESIAN THEORIES
OF THE CYCLE

14.1   EXTENSIONS OF THE ACCELERATOR

The simple models presented in Chapter 13 contain some elements of realism, but a large gap still remains between these elementary combinations of the multiplier and accelerator and modern business cycle theory. Some of the developments bridging this gap will be examined in this chapter. In most cases the analysis will center on the real sector; factor and product prices are generally omitted or mentioned as an afterthought in these theories. These variables will be reinstated when a more complete theory of the cycle is considered.

The first model that is discussed was formulated by Michal Kalecki.[1] This model is technically not a post-Keynesian model, because it appeared a year before the *General Theory*. However, it contains many Keynesian elements in its formulation and is much more similar to other post-Keynesian theories than to pre-Keynesian literature. Kalecki develops a consumption function with a marginal propensity to consume and a stock-adjustment investment function. This model has led Klein to comment that "the Keynesian system as a mathematical model would have come into being without Keynes.... Eventually the theorists would have seen through the matter and given Kalecki's pre-General Theory model its full due."[2] Like the work of Tinbergen, which was

---

[1] M. Kalecki, "A Macro-dynamic Theory of Business Cycles," *Econometrica*, Vol. 3 (1935), pp. 327–344. Later, slightly modified versions of Kalecki's theory are not considered here.

[2] L. R. Klein, *The Keynesian Revolution*, rev. ed. (New York: Macmillan, 1966), p. 224.

progressing at the same time,[3] Kalecki made profits the variable of primary importance in the system. Only in later cycle theory was income distribution excluded.

In Kalecki's model, national income is equal to wages plus profits; spending by capitalists depends on profits, whereas spending by working people depends on wages. Working people are assumed to do no saving; their consumption is equal to their wages, and no explicit function is included for this component of aggregate demand. Capitalists spend their profits either on consumption or investment goods. These functions can be written

$$(14.1) \qquad\qquad C_1 = \lambda P + a$$

$$(14.2) \qquad\qquad I_0 = \alpha P - \gamma K$$

where C_1 = purchases of consumer goods by capitalists
$\quad\ \ P$ = gross profits (that is, including depreciation)
$\quad\ \ I_0$ = *orders* of investment goods
$\quad\ \ K$ = capital stock

As can be seen, the investment function is of the stock-adjustment form, except that profits are used instead of sales for the principal independent variable. The consumption function is very similar to the Keynesian consumption function, with $0 < \lambda < 1$, $a > 0$, the main difference being that it applies only to capitalists and not to all consumers.

This much of the model already includes some dynamic structure, since $I = dK/dt$. However, the cyclical nature of the solution to this model is due primarily to the lag between investment *orders* and actual *production*. Let θ be the average gestation period of all investment. Then production at time t, $I_p(t)$, is given by

$$(14.3) \qquad\qquad I_p(t) = \frac{1}{\theta} \int_{t-\theta}^{t} I_0(\tau)\, dt$$

In other words, production at time t is equal to the average amount of orders received over the last θ periods (for example, months).

The system can be closed by adding the equations $P = C_1 + I_p$, that is, gross profits are either consumed or invested, and $C_1 + I_p + C_2 = Y$, where C_2 is the consumption of employees, which is equal to total wages.[4]

In equilibrium $I_p = I_0 = I$, so that

$$(14.4) \qquad Y = a + \lambda P + I + C_2 = a + (1 - \lambda)C_2 + \lambda Y + I$$

---

[3] J. Tinbergen, *Statistical Testing of Business-Cycle Theories II: Business Cycles in the United States of America, 1919–1932* (Geneva: League of Nations, 1939).

[4] Although he does not state so explicitly, Kalecki assumes that profits and wages are both a fixed proportion of national income.

Therefore,

$$(14.5) \qquad Y = \frac{a + (1 - \lambda)C_2 + I}{1 - \lambda}$$

Thus if the time path of I can be found, the value of Y at any time can be easily determined by the above equation. The problem thus reduces to solving the equations for investment orders, which are

$$(14.6) \qquad I_0(t) = \alpha P(t) - \gamma K(t - \theta)$$

$$(14.7) \qquad I_0(t) = \alpha C_1 + \alpha I_p(t) - \gamma K(t - \theta)$$

$$(14.8) \qquad I_0(t) = \alpha C_1 + \frac{\alpha}{\theta} \int_{t-\theta}^{t} I_0(\tau) \, d\tau - \gamma K(t - \theta)$$

Differentiating this expression gives

$$(14.9) \qquad \frac{d(I_0(t))}{dt} = \frac{\alpha}{\theta}[I_0(t) - I_0(t - \theta)] - \gamma I_0(t - \theta)$$

or

$$(14.10) \qquad \frac{d(I_0(t))}{dt} = \frac{\alpha}{\theta} I_0(t) - \left(\frac{\alpha}{\theta} + \gamma\right) I_0(t - \theta)$$

This is the equation that must be solved to find the time path of I_0 and thus of Y. It is of the mixed difference-differential type, which is somewhat awkward to solve. The method of solution is not given here; a full treatment can be found in Allen.[5] However, some of the general results are discussed here.

Equation (14.10) can be somewhat simplified by taking $\theta = 1$. This can be done without loss of generality. The resulting time periods are then measured in units of θ instead of months or years. This gives

$$(14.11) \qquad \frac{dI_0}{dt} = \alpha I_0(t) - (\alpha + \gamma) I_0(t - 1)$$

The period of oscillation is $2\pi/\omega$, where ω is related to the constants of the investment equation by the relationship[6,7]

$$(14.12) \qquad \frac{\omega}{\tan \omega} + \log \frac{\sin \omega}{\omega} = \alpha - \ln(\alpha + \gamma)$$

---

[5] R. G. D. Allen, *Mathematical Economics*, 2nd ed. (London: Macmillan, 1959), chap. 8. Allen's treatment is highly recommended for those who prefer a more mathematical approach to these theories.

[6] *Ibid*, p. 256.

[7] There are actually multiple solutions for $\omega > \pi$, but since these imply cycles of less than two periods, they are not of interest here. Since $\sin \omega/\omega \to 0$ as ω increases, these very short cycles will be heavily damped.

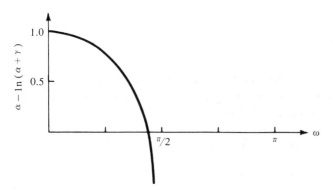

Figure 14.1

Graphically this can be represented as shown in Figure 14.1. The stability condition is given by

$$(14.13) \qquad A = \ln(\alpha + \gamma) + \ln\left(\frac{\sin \omega}{\omega}\right) < 0$$

Since $\alpha + \gamma$ is almost always less than unity and $\sin \omega/\omega < 1$ for all $\omega > 0$, this expression will almost always be negative; thus the system is generally stable.

Kalecki himself does not give a general solution but solves only for the "knife-edge" case, that is, $A = 0$. He finds $\alpha = 0.95$ and $\gamma = 0.12$. The length of the cycle is 10θ periods. Kalecki estimates θ to be 0.6 years, so the cycle length is six years. Although his estimate of γ is not unreasonable, α is certainly too high. Even if firms were to invest all their cash flow without a lag, which is unlikely, they still must pay taxes and distribute dividends. Certainly $\alpha = 0.5$ represents an upper limit. Values of $\alpha = 0.5$, $\gamma = 0.1$ give $\omega = 77°$ (1.35 radians) and thus $2\pi/\omega = 4.5$ periods.

If a more realistic value of θ equal to one year is taken, reasonable values of α and γ give cycle lengths similar to those actually observed. The stability condition is easily satisfied and the cycles are heavily damped. If α is much lower, say 0.2, the results are almost the same. Although small changes in the value of α near unity cause large changes in the cycle period $2\pi/\omega$, substantial changes in α for values less than 0.5 make very little difference in the cycle length.

There are several interesting features of the Kalecki model. It is the first one to specify a Keynesian-type consumption function, although the function applies only to capitalists. The assumption that capitalists save (almost) all their income and workers spend all theirs can be expanded into a growth model in which the rate of capital formation depends on income distribution. The most important development in this model is the replacement of the naive accelerator by the stock-adjustment principle (which, as has been shown previously, is equivalent to a distributed lag with geometrically declining weights).

The introduction of a lag between orders and production is also of considerable relevance and importance. All these ideas are important elements of a more comprehensive theory of the cycle.

The next model considered here is one developed by Nicholas Kaldor.[8] The consumption (or savings) function depends on income, and the investment function is again of the stock-adjustment type. The main innovative feature of this model is the use of nonlinear consumption and investment functions, a feature that has been widely copied and expanded by more recent theorists.

Kaldor's point of departure is the familiar *IS* diagram discussed in Chapter 13. As pointed out previously and shown in Figure 14.2, if *mpI* < *mps*, stable equilibrium will occur, and if *mpI* > *mps*, unstable equilibrium will occur. However, cycles do not occur in either case, although fluctuations are certainly observed to exist in reality.

In both these cases the *I* and *S* curves are linear with respect to income. However, if certain sections of these curves were nonlinear, there might be some regions where *mpI* < *mps* and other regions where *mpI* > *mps*. In this case, GNP might move back and forth between multiple equilibria, causing cyclical fluctuations. This is the essence of Kaldor's theory.

The investment function is likely to be income-inelastic at low levels of income because of the existence of excess capacity. It is also likely to be inelastic at very high levels of income because of the high costs of construction and the high costs and increased difficulty of borrowing. The investment function modified in this way has the shape shown in Figure 14.3.

It is also likely that the savings function is nonlinear. In what can be regarded as an early version of the permanent or normal income hypothesis, Kaldor argues that the *mpc* for each dollar of additional income will be high when income is at normal levels, but it will be very low (and thus the *mps* will be high) both at very low levels of income and at very high levels of income. When

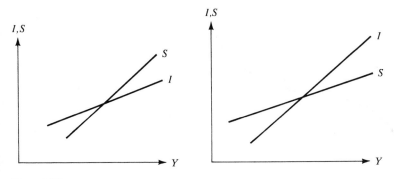

Figure 14.2

[8] N. Kaldor, "A Model of the Trade Cycle," *Economic Journal*, Vol. 50 (March, 1940), pp. 78–92.

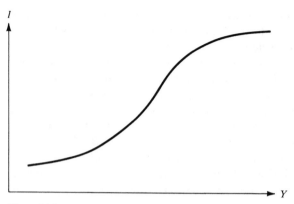

Figure 14.3

income is very low, people will try to maintain former standards of living, so that a further decrease in income will be accompanied by almost the full amount of decrease in savings. When income is very high, further increases in income will be accompanied by a very large proportional increase in savings, as individuals do not expect these high levels of income to continue. On the other hand, when income is increasing at a normal rate, most of every additional dollar will be spent. Such a savings function is shown in Figure 14.4.

When the *I* and *S* curves are combined, it can easily be seen that there are multiple equilibria. At points *A* and *B* in Figure 14.5, *mpI* < *mps*, so these are stable equilibria corresponding to high and low levels of GNP. Point *C* represents an unstable equilibrium, so the economy is unlikely to remain there very long.

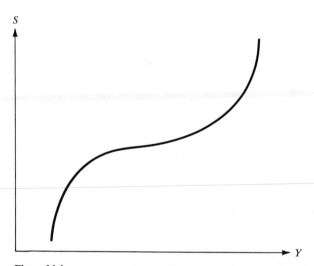

Figure 14.4

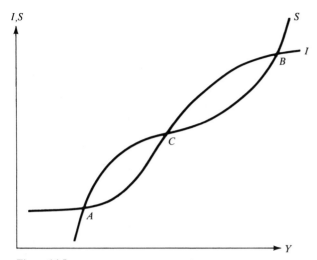

Figure 14.5

The I and S curves drawn here are short-run curves and will shift over time. At a high level of income, investment will increase more rapidly and thus capital stock will continue to grow. After a while additions to capital stock will shift the investment curve down. This is simply the stock-adjustment principle expressed verbally; algebraically we could write $I = aY - bK_{-1}$, where $\Delta K = I$. Kaldor suggests that the savings curve will shift up at high levels of income over time. This is similar to the underconsumptionist viewpoint and is unlikely to hold unless it applies to purchases of consumer durables. It is more likely that the slope of the savings curve will be reduced as people become more used to the high level of income and thus save a smaller proportion of it. However, this slight modification does not affect the general nature of the argument. The explanation will still hold if only the I curve shifts and the S curve remains stable.

Assume that the economy is currently at point B. There will be a tendency over time for the I curve to shift downward and the S curve either to flatten out or shift up. This will tend to move point C closer to point B until they eventually coincide. When this occurs, the economy is in a position of unstable equilibrium. Since deflationary pressures are at work, the economy will move downward from this unstable equilibrium toward point A, a new stable position at a much lower level of income. At this low income, investment will be smaller than depreciation, so capital stock will decrease. This will tend to raise the I curve. At low levels of income the S curve will either fall (as stocks of durables are depreciated and the demand increases for more new purchases) or flatten out. These shifts will now move point C closer to point A until they coincide, at which point the economy will return to point B. This process can continue indefinitely. One complete cycle is diagrammed in Figure 14.6.[9]

---

[9] *Ibid.*, p. 84.

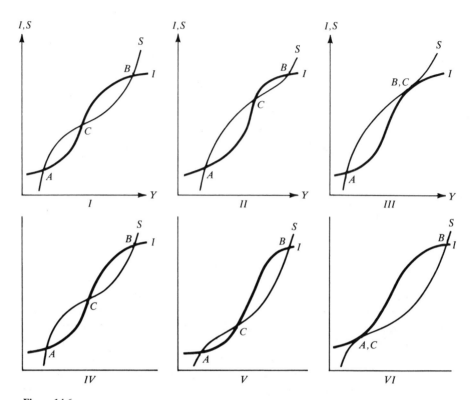

Figure 14.6

The cycles that continue to be generated by this mechanism need not all be of the same length, nor do the expansions and contractions need to be symmetrical. These characteristics will depend on the exact slopes and the rate at which the I and S curves shift. It is also possible that no cycles occur. For example, if the I curve fell very gradually at high levels of income and the S curve flattened out, point B might always stay at a higher level of income than point C, and a stable equilibrium would be established at B. However, this is quite unlikely, because the longer income stays at a high level, the more likely it is that the accumulation of capital stock will have a depressing effect on future investment.

The mechanism of the Kaldor model is both simple to understand and quite ingenious. The nonlinearities of the investment function due to excess capacity and restrictions on sources of cash flow are of crucial importance in explaining the cycle. The construction of a consumption function with different values of the *mpc* at increasing and decreasing levels of income is necessary to explain the differences between short- and long-run effects of income on consumption. Although it is necessary to quantify this model to obtain actual values of the functions at different phases of the business cycle, Kaldor's model represents a definite advance in cycle theory and suggests a plausible outline on which to build.

The idea of a nonlinear investment function was pursued further by Goodwin in a series of articles.[10] Goodwin uses real factors, rather than monetary factors, to explain the nonlinearities of the investment function. Again using the stock-adjustment principle, Goodwin argues that desired capital stock, K^*, is proportional to GNP, and investment is proportional to the difference between desired and actual capital stock. When this difference is positive, gross investment increases as fast as possible, limited only by the productive capacity of the capital-goods industry. When desired and actual capital stock are equal, gross investment is equal to replacement demand, and when desired capital stock is less than actual capital stock, gross investment is zero, and thus net investment is negative by the amount of the scrappage rate.

However, desired capital stock is never equal to actual capital stock. As long as the desired stock exceeds the actual stock, investment is increasing at a rapid rate and thus GNP is also growing at a rapid rate. As soon as actual stock reaches the desired level, the level of investment decreases, GNP decreases, and thus desired capital stock decreases. At the very time when equilibrium is reached, desired stock falls below actual stock, and gross investment drops to zero as excess capacity is worked off. The amount of investment can be related to the difference between desired and actual capital stock as shown in Figure 14.7. This results in the pattern for GNP shown in Figure 14.8. The oscillations continue in this fashion and there is no tendency to move toward an equilibrium value.

Such a crude model is clearly unrealistic, and several modifications are made in it by Goodwin. One change is to introduce "growth" into the model by means

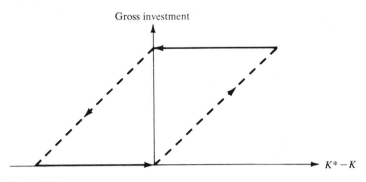

Figure 14.7

[10] R. M. Goodwin, "Secular and Cyclical Aspects of the Multiplier and the Accelerator," in *Income, Employment and Public Policy: Essays in Honor of Alvin H. Hansen* (New York: Norton, 1948), pp. 108–132; "The Non-Linear Accelerator and the Persistence of Business Cycles," *Econometrica*, Vol. 19, No. 1 (January, 1951) pp. 1–17; "A Model of Cyclical Growth," in E. Lundberg, ed., *The Business Cycle in the Postwar World* (London: Macmillan, 1955).

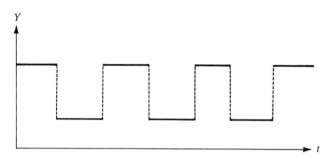

Figure 14.8

of a time trend. Desired capital stock is then a function both of GNP and of technological progress. This does not eliminate the discontinuities in the income path, but does allow for some asymmetry, because the upturns are now longer and the downturns shorter than before. Investment is still constrained to grow at the maximum possible rate during the upswings and the minimum rate (zero) during the downswings, but it now takes more time to reach desired capital stock when the economy is growing and less time to work off the excess capacity when GNP is falling. The time path of income will depend on how the rate of technological progress affects the maximum rate at which the economy can grow. If this rate is independent of technological change, the time path of GNP will look like the pattern shown in Figure 14.9. If, however, the economy can grow at a more rapid rate along the ceiling as technology improves, the path will be slightly modified, as shown in Figure 14.10.

The discontinuities in the income path can be eliminated by the use of lags and by the inclusion of further nonlinearities in the accelerator. Two types of lags are used by Goodwin. The first is the lag in production (supply) relative to demand. This can be written

$$(14.13) \qquad \frac{dY}{dt} = -\lambda(Y - Z)$$

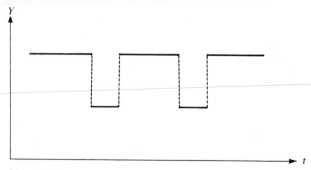

Figure 14.9

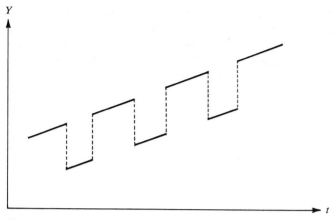

Figure 14.10

where Y = aggregate supply and Z = aggregate demand (*ex ante*). The second lag is the lag in demand relative to supply conditions, and is the same as Kalecki's orders-deliveries lag. This can be written

$$(14.14) \qquad\qquad I_p(t) = I_0(t - \theta)$$

where I_p and I_0 are deliveries and orders of investment goods, respectively, as previously.

An additional nonlinearity is added which states that the accelerator has much smaller values for extreme values of changes in GNP. This is shown for the general nonlinear function in Figure 14.11. This is very similar to the nonlinear accelerator of Kaldor. The only difference is that here investment is

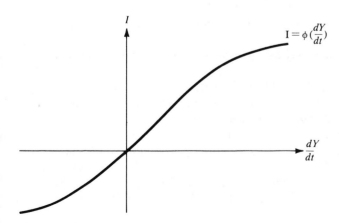

Figure 14.11

a function of the change in GNP, whereas Kaldor makes investment a function of the level of GNP. Goodwin does not specify the form of ϕ, nor does he give any particular reason for this type of nonlinearity. The reasons, however, may be thought to be those suggested by Kaldor, which are excess capacity in recessions and financial and cost factors in booms.

Listing the equations of the Goodwin model, we have

$$C = cY + b$$

$$I = \phi \left[\frac{dY(t - \theta)}{dt} \right]$$

$$C + I + A = Z$$

$$Z = Y + \frac{1}{\lambda} \frac{dY}{dt}$$

Combining these gives

(14.15) $$Y + \frac{1}{\lambda} \frac{dY}{dt} = cY + b + \phi \left[\frac{dY(t - \theta)}{dt} \right] + A$$

or

(14.16) $$Y = \frac{1}{1 - c} \left\{ \phi \left[\frac{dY(t - \theta)}{dt} \right] - \frac{1}{\lambda} \frac{dY}{dt} \right\} + \frac{A + b}{1 - c}$$

It can be seen that this equation is of the mixed difference-differential type, as was true for the Kalecki model. Furthermore, since the form of ϕ is not given, an analytic solution is not possible.[11] However, certain general characteristics can be observed. For the most general case, that is, the one with all lags, nonlinearities and technical progress included:

1. There is a trend rate of growth determined by the rate of technological progress.

2. The cycles are definitely asymmetric, with the upswings longer than the downswings.

3. The amplitude of the cycle is independent of the initial conditions. In linear models the amplitude will always depend on the size of the initial shock.

4. The system is inherently explosive, yet the ceilings and floors and nonlinearities keep the cycle in the same range.

All these characteristics differ substantially from the simple multiplier–accelerator models, which were intended primarily to show how cycles could occur rather than to trace out the time path of an actual cycle. Enough examples have been presented to show that with the addition of lags (particularly on the

---

[11] Phase diagrams are given by Goodwin for certain reasonable shapes of ϕ in his *Econometrica* article, *op. cit.* They are further discussed by Allen, *op. cit.*, chap. 9.

supply side), nonlinear accelerators, and growth in some context, the multiplier–accelerator models can be greatly modified and made asymmetrical. With proper assumptions about the values of the parameter estimates, the time periods of the cycle do approximate the length actually observed.

Aside from the nonlinearities, the principal difference of the Goodwin model from those examined earlier is the introduction of "growth" through a time trend. However, a more complex explanation of growth than this is in order. To examine this question more closely, we now turn to a model in which growth is the primary factor and cyclical fluctuations are secondary.

14.2   THE HARROD–DOMAR MODEL

The theories presented in Section 14.1 suggest a multitude of possibilities for cyclical fluctuations, but little attention is given to the variables responsible for growth. The Harrod–Domar model,[12] on the other hand, concentrates on the explanation of the rate of growth of the economy and to a large extent neglects cyclical fluctuations, although not quite so much as has sometimes been supposed.

Since this model is primarily concerned with growth rates, it seems appropriate to begin our discussion with the equation defining the actual growth rate. From this consumption and investment functions can be formulated. We have $g \equiv s/v$, where $g = (Y - Y_{-1})/Y_{-1}$, the rate of growth of GNP, s is the savings rate S/Y_{-1}, and v is the capital/output ratio

$$(14.17) \qquad v = \frac{K}{Y} = \frac{\Delta K}{\Delta Y} = \frac{I}{Y - Y_{-1}}$$

Therefore,

$$(14.18) \qquad \frac{s}{v} = \frac{S/Y_{-1}}{I/(Y - Y_{-1})} = \frac{Y - Y_{-1}}{Y_{-1}}$$

which is identically equal to g. These definitions can be transformed into consumption and investment functions:

$$C = Y - S = Y - sY_{-1}$$

$$I = v(Y - Y_{-1})$$

---

[12] The source usually cited for Harrod's version of the model is R. F. Harrod, *Toward a Dynamic Economics* (London: Macmillan, 1948), lecture 3. However, an earlier and more comprehensive statement of the model is given in "An Essay in Dynamic Theory," *Economic Journal*, Vol. 49 (March, 1939), pp. 14–33. Domar's version appeared independently in "Capital Expansion, Rate of Growth, and Employment," *Econometrica*, Vol. 14, No. 2 (April, 1946), pp. 137–147.

Therefore,

$$Y - sY_{-1} + v(Y - Y_{-1}) = Y$$

$$\frac{Y}{Y_{-1}} = \frac{s}{v} + 1$$

$$\frac{Y - Y_{-1}}{Y_{-1}} = \frac{s}{v}$$

This gives an exponential rate of growth $\rho = s/v$ as defined above. The time path of Y is simply a moving equilibrium that generates no cycles. As such, it is the simplest model that has been considered here, although the functions are not substantially different from the Samuelson model.

The interpretation given to the value of v, however, is quite different from before. It is not the amount of investment that will result from a change in one unit of output; instead, it is the extra amount of capital actually used per extra unit of output. In other words, it has the full value of the capital/output ratio, which is about 2.5, rather than the first-year change in investment resulting from a unit change in output, which is about 0.3. Since this is the interpretation given, it may be more accurate to write $\Delta Y = (1/v)I$; that is, the change in output is dependent on the addition to capital stock. This is in fact the interpretation given by Domar. The term $1/v$ can thus be taken to be the actual change in output, *ex post*, for a given amount of investment.

So far this seems to be a straightforward theory explaining the rate of growth in the economy, which is $\rho = s/v$. There are no cycles, and therefore the economy continues to grow at this rate every year. For actual values of $s \cong 0.10$ and $v \cong 2.5$, the rate of growth is about 4 percent per year, which is close to the observed value. However, the growth rate defined in this way is in general *not* the equilibrium growth rate; furthermore, there is no tendency for the economy to return to the equilibrium path.

To show this Harrod states what he calls his *fundamental equation*:

$$(14.19) \qquad\qquad g_w = \frac{s}{v_w}$$

where g_w is the *warranted* rate of growth. The warranted rate is defined as that rate of growth at which all producers are satisfied that they have produced just the right amount of investment for the output that has occurred. They will thus be induced to continue to invest just that amount which will maintain the current rate of growth. This is very similar to an equilibrium rate of growth, but Harrod hesitates to use that term, because the equilibrium is an unstable one. The term v_w is interpreted as the optimal capital/output ratio, which will be different from the actual capital/output ratio if output does not grow at the expected rate.

Suppose that the economy has previously been in moving equilibrium with growth rate g_w. In period t, assume that output grows at a faster rate than previously, owing to some exogenous force. Since investment is a function of the change in output, it would seem that it should also increase. However, this will not occur, because investment must always be equal to savings *ex post*, and savings depends only on the income of the previous period. Thus the only thing that can happen is that v, the capital/output ratio, decreases. In other words, output grows at a faster rate than the capital stock. In algebraic terms, $v < v_w$ occurs simultaneously with $g > g_w$, since $g = s/v$ and $g_w = s/v_w$.

Since the capital stock is below equilibrium levels, the rate of investment will increase in the next period but not by enough to close the gap between desired and actual capital stock. In fact, the gap will widen, because the increased investment will lead to increased output—but investment must always be equal to savings, which depends on income of the previous period. As long as $g > g_w$ and the savings rate remains unchanged, $v < v_w$: that is, the capital/output ratio will always be below its optimum level, so the economy will never return to equilibrium. Furthermore, the higher the actual growth rate relative to the warranted growth rate, the greater the difference between the actual and optimum capital/output ratios. An initial disturbance, no matter how small, will start the economy on a steadily diverging path from equilibrium growth.

Exactly the same argument can be made in the opposite direction. If the growth of the economy is decreased, there will be excess capital stock. This will result in a decrease in investment in the next period, which will decrease output still further. Excess capital stock will increase, investment and output will continue to decrease, and the economy will diverge further and further from equilibrium.

Although the Harrod–Domar model contains a multiplier and an accelerator, the results are certainly much different from all the other multiplier–accelerator models examined previously. The reason for this is to be found in the lag structure. Whereas in other models investment was a function of the lagged level or change of output, investment here is a function of the unlagged change in output. In addition, savings plans are always realized. This is quite different from the assumption that consumption plans are realized, which would leave *ex post* savings free to fluctuate with investment. These two factors combine to force investment to be equal to savings *ex ante* as well as *ex post*. Although *ex post* savings and investment must be equal by definition, *ex ante* savings and investment are usually free to assume different values. In the familiar IS diagram, $I = S$ *ex post* means only that the two curves must intersect at some positive value, whereas $I = S$ *ex ante* means that the slopes of the two curves must be identical. In this case the solution for GNP is indeterminate and a slight disturbance from equilibrium will result in no positive solution at all.

There are two main ways in which the theory can be modified. One method is to change the lag structure so that the model gives cyclical fluctuations.

Even if this is done, the cycles will be explosive for values of v in the neighborhood of 2.5, so that nonlinear constraints will be necessary. This approach is taken by Hicks, whose modifications are discussed in Section 14.3. The other possibility is to let the values of s and v vary over the cycle; this is in effect another way of introducing nonlinearities into the system.

When the actual growth rate exceeds the warranted growth rate, the divergence from equilibrium continues until the warranted rate rises to the actual rate. This can happen either because the savings rate rises or the optimal capital/output ratio falls. Both of these are likely to occur when income rises rapidly. Since actual income is higher than normal income, the mpc is likely to decrease. As existing investment projects are undertaken, the amount of capital per unit of output is likely to fall, although the equilibrium stock of capital is likely to keep rising as long as income increases. These are essentially the arguments used by Kaldor.

A second possibility is that not all investment depends on the change in income, but that some investment depends on the level of income and some is truly autonomous. Then we could write

$$(14.20) \qquad I = v_1 \Delta Y + v_2 Y_{-1} + v_3$$

$$(14.21) \qquad v_1 + v_2 + v_3 \neq v$$

Since $I = S$,

$$(14.22) \qquad s Y_{-1} = v_1 \Delta Y + v_2 Y_{-1} + v_3$$

or

$$(14.23) \qquad \frac{s}{v_1} = \frac{\Delta Y}{Y_{-1}} + \frac{v_2}{v_1} + \frac{v_3}{v_1} \frac{1}{Y_{-1}}$$

Therefore,

$$(14.24) \qquad g_w = \frac{\Delta Y}{Y_{-1}} = \frac{s - v_2 - v_3/Y_{-1}}{v_1}$$

The accelerator term is likely to be more fully operative when income is increasing rapidly, particularly when the actual growth rate exceeds the warranted growth rate. At such time v_1 is likely to increase relative to v_2 and v_3/Y. It may not be obvious what effect this has on g_w, for an increase in v_1 will lower g_w, whereas a decrease in v_2 and v_3/Y will raise it. However, it can be shown by calculating dg_w/dv_1, dg_w/dv_2, and dg_w/dv_3 that for values $v_2 > 1$, $s - v_2 - v_3/Y > 0$ (which must be the case for $g_w > 0$), and $dv_i/dv_j < 0$ (that is, an increase in one type of investment results in a decrease in the other types), an increase in v_1 increases g_w, whereas an increase in v_2 or v_3 decreases g_w. Thus if the actual growth rate continues to exceed the warranted growth rate, it is likely that the latter will eventually rise to the level of the former, causing a reversal in the pattern of income growth.

Another refinement of this formula can be made by including the foreign sector. The identity $I = S$ then becomes $I + E = S + M$, or

(14.25) $sY_{-1} + mY_{-1} = v_1 \Delta Y + v_2 Y_{-1} + v_3 + E$

Therefore,

(14.26) $$\frac{v_1 \Delta Y}{Y_{-1}} = s + m - v_2 - \frac{v_3}{Y_{-1}} - \frac{E}{Y_{-1}}$$

or

(14.27) $$g_w = \frac{\Delta Y}{Y_{-1}} = \frac{s + m - v_2 - (v_3/Y_{-1}) - (E/Y_{-1})}{v_1}$$

As income increases, the excess of imports over exports increases, and $m - E/Y_{-1}$ increases. This also has the effect of raising the warranted rate and thus eventually causing a downturn.

Using this analysis, the view that a high savings rate leads to a higher growth rate can be reconciled with the view that a higher savings rate is deflationary. Since $g_w = s/v_w$, a rise in the savings rate will increase the warranted growth rate. Recall that if the economy is already at the warranted rate, it will continue to grow at that rate in the absence of exogenous forces. However, if the actual growth rate $g = s/v$ does not increase as fast as the warranted rate, that is, $g < g_w$, then $v > v_w$. Attempts will then be made to reduce investment and capital stock, and the economy will spiral downward.

If the savings rate does increase, it can be asked why the economy does not in fact grow at the warranted rate. To answer this question Harrod introduces a third rate of growth, the *natural growth rate*, denoted g_n. This is the maximum rate at which the economy can grow and is determined by population, technological change, and the existing capital stock. If the warranted rate rises above the natural rate—if the rate of growth needed to keep the economy at equilibrium is greater than the maximum rate actually attainable—then $g_n < g_w$, $v > v_w$, the actual capital/output ratio will be greater than the optimal ratio, investment will decrease, and there will be constant deflationary pressures on the economy. On the other hand, if the savings rate is low, $g_n > g_w$ and inflationary pressures will occur. Thus in situations where $g_n < g_w$, it would be advisable to lower g_w, and where $g_n > g_w$ it would be advisable to raise g_w. In mature economies the former is more likely to be the case, so emphasis should be placed on *lowering* the warranted rate of growth. This could be accomplished either by lowering s or raising v_w. Both could be accomplished in a number of ways, but, in particular, government deficits will lower s and lower interest rates will raise v_w. Lower interest rates lower the warranted rate of growth, making it easier for the natural and actual growth rates to approach it and return the economy to equilibrium.

Although the Harrod–Domar theory is pathbreaking in that it makes the rate of growth one of the endogenous variables of the system instead of ignoring it or making it a time trend, the elements of the business cycle are neglected. A theory built on the Harrod–Domar theory of dynamic equilibrium but also incorporating cyclical fluctuations has been attempted by Hicks and is considered next.

14.3   HICKS'S THEORY OF THE CYCLE

The project of combining the interaction of the nonlinear accelerator and the multiplier with the growth theory of the Harrod–Domar model was undertaken by J. R. Hicks.[13] The linear version of the mathematical model developed by Hicks is almost identical to the Samuelson model discussed earlier. For this reason, this general type of model is sometimes known as the Samuelson–Hicks model. However, to lump them together is a distortion of the economic content of both models. Samuelson states that his model is "strictly a *marginal* analysis to be applied to the study of small oscillations" (original italics). Hicks's model, on the other hand, is largely concerned with the problem of growth and of a moving equilibrium, and his model should be approached in that spirit.

The ingredients of Hicks's model are similar to other models that have been discussed here: a consumption function, an induced investment function with a nonlinear accelerator, and autonomous investment. Inventory investment is presumed to have a role in shaping the time path of the cycle, although an explicit function for this form of investment is not given. Finally, the use of ceilings and floors is introduced as a primary determinant of the turning points of GNP.

The consumption function is considered first. As in the Samuelson model, it is of the form $C = cY_{t-1}$. There are two reasons given by Hicks for the lag of consumption behind income. One is simply the lag of expenditures behind receipts. The other is the lag of nonwage personal income behind changes in GNP. This is a little different from the lag of wages behind profits which was quite common in the pre-Keynesian theories. Hicks believes that changes in wages do not lag behind changes in national product, but that changes in salaries, rent and interest payments, and dividends do lag. These nonwage elements are enough to make consumption a function of previous income, and Hicks considers them to be the principal determinant of the overall lag in the consumption function. The argument cannot be very well taken, because wages account for a great deal more of personal income than do nonwage payments, and if the former does not lag national income, a stronger case should be made for having consumption a function of present income. At any rate,

---

[13] The formulation of Hicks's theory as an outgrowth of the Harrod–Domar model is clearly shown in his "Mr. Harrod's Dynamic Theory," *Economica*, Vol. 16 (May, 1949), pp. 106–121. A full statement of Hicks's theory is made in his *A Contribution to the Theory of the Trade Cycle* (London: Clarendon Press, 1950).

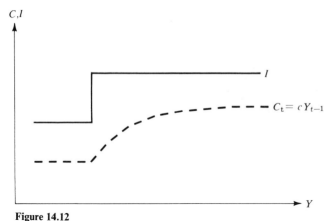

Figure 14.12

the function is of a familiar form, and a change in autonomous investment will result in the time path for consumption shown in Figure 14.12. The idea of consumption rising gradually to a change in income instead of changing completely in the first period is a valid and necessary assumption for reasonable consumer behavior. However, other lag forms, particularly $C = f(Y, C_{-1})$ are also available for this purpose, instead of having consumption depend only on one lagged value of income.[14]

Of more interest is the case of moving equilibrium, where autonomous investment continues to grow at a constant rate. In this case consumption will always be below the level which it would reach in the static case. Actual saving will be greater than the static equilibrium value, and the rate of saving will be greater the larger the rate of growth. If investment should decrease after rising for some time, consumption would still increase for one or more periods. If investment continued to decrease, consumption would be greater and savings would be smaller than in static equilibrium.

These concepts are shown in Figure 14.13. GNP is plotted on the vertical axis and investment and savings (which must be equal *ex post*) on the horizontal axis. The "S line" represents the amount of savings (and investment) that would occur for each level of income in static equilibrium. As long as investment and income are increasing along the path AB, savings are greater than the equilibrium level. After a while, suppose investment stops increasing. For a while income will still increase, because of the lag in the consumption function. If investment stays stationary for several periods, consumption and savings will finally reach their equilibrium levels; this is the simple static case. However, it is quite likely that investment may decrease soon afterward. Even so, income may continue to rise for a while, again because of lags in the consumption function.

---

[14] It should be mentioned that Hicks does consider a generalized consumption function of the form $C = f(Y, Y_{t-1}, \ldots, Y_{t-j})$ in the mathematical appendix, and uses it to derive more general results which are basically similar.

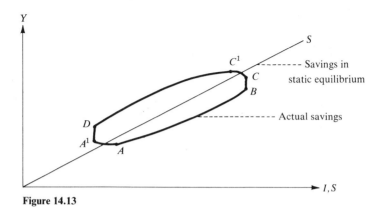

Figure 14.13

This is represented in the segment CC'. From C' to D both investment and income will be decreasing. Finally investment becomes stationary again; income still continues to fall from D to A'. As investment continues to increase, income still falls for a short while from A' to A before beginning to rise once more.

This pattern of consumption relative to a moving equilibrium of income has some elements in common with the permanent-income hypothesis developed later. Hicks does suggest that the savings line should pass through the origin, in which case the equilibrium rate of saving is independent of the level of income. The actual pattern of consumer behavior envisioned by Hicks is thus more complex than the simple function $C = cY_{-1}$ would suggest; this is due to the inclusion of a growth factor. The consumption function, however, has a damping influence on cycles. It is necessary to turn to the investment function to understand how cyclical fluctuations are generated.

Hicks next considers the accelerator in isolation. A unit change in output causes an increase in gross investment over time in the general shape of an inverted V, the increase eventually returning to zero. At first net and gross investment increase by the same amount. However, once the additional investment has been completed, capital stock becomes greater, and depreciation is greater. Thus a return to zero gross investment results in negative net investment equal to the amount of the added depreciation. This negative net investment continues until the capital goods are replaced. This is likely to happen all at once for machines purchased at the same time, because they would all have approximately the same life. The process continues with each peak somewhat smaller than the previous one, until the pattern finally dies out. If there are several such cycles superimposed on one another, the damping occurs even more quickly. This is shown in Figure 14.14.

It is important to note that the argument is not symmetrical. If output decreases, there is a limit to the amount that investment can fall, set by the fact that gross investment cannot be less than zero and net investment cannot be

net I

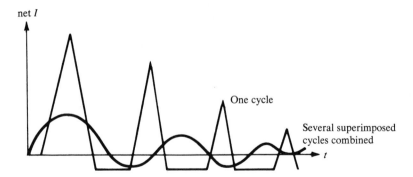

One cycle

Several superimposed
cycles combined

t

Figure 14.14

more negative than the depreciation rate. Therefore, in the case of a down-turn, gross investment may be zero for a long time until all the excess capacity has been worked off. There is no sharp peak corresponding to the rise in investment, and for that reason downturns are likely to be longer than upturns.

Inventory investment is considered next. A change in output will at first induce a change in inventory investment in the *opposite* direction. This represents the lag between orders and production. Until production schedules can be modified to meet the changing demand, inventory stocks will serve as a buffer. If demand increases, stocks will be depleted; if it decreases, excess stocks will accumulate. Once production can be changed, there will be a rapid acceleration of inventory investment, after which it will return to an equilibrium rate of change which is zero if the change in income is zero.

No particular shape for autonomous investment is specified by Hicks at this point. It is assumed to have a certain trend but is liable to fluctuate around this trend. If in fact autonomous investment, induced investment, and consumption all grow at a constant rate, the system will remain in moving equilibrium, with the growth rate equal to s/v. However, in the Harrod formulation all investment was induced, so it was a relatively simple matter to have investment and consumption grow at constant rates. However, once autonomous investment is introduced into the system and fluctuations are allowed, the property of moving equilibrium disappears. Although Harrod considered the possibility of autonomous investment, he did not consider the possibility of fluctuations in this type of investment.

It now remains to put these various components together and examine the nature of the resulting cycle. Leaving aside the nonlinearities for the moment, the system in its simplest form can be written

$$C = cY_{-1}$$

$$I = v(Y_{-1} - Y_{-2})$$

$$C + I + A = Y$$

The solutions of this model have been explored earlier, so it is not necessary to do so here. However, the reader will recall that the system is damped for $v < 1$ and explosive for $v > 1$. The introduction of inventory investment changes the path of GNP somewhat but does not materially alter the conclusions.

The first step away from this simple model is to include the rate of growth (g). In this case it can easily be shown that the resulting equation used to calculate the time path of GNP is

$$(14.28) \qquad y_t = \frac{1 - s + v}{1 + g} y_{t-1} - \frac{v}{(1 + g)^2} y_{t-2}$$

The system will be explosive for $v > (1 + g)^2$, which is quite similar to the earlier result. More important is the value of v to be expected. Hicks takes v to be the average capital/output ratio, as does Harrod, which means that it is substantially in excess of unity. The cycles are, therefore, explosive. It is because of this that the nonlinearities assume their great importance. The existence of a ceiling stops the upward progress of the boom, and the restraint that gross investment cannot be less than zero stops the progress of the depression. Thus the cycle has an inherently explosive nature but is contained by the ceilings and floors of the economy.

It is now possible to trace through the path of output over a typical cycle. For this case, assume that autonomous investment, which had previously grown at a constant rate, increases by an additional unit and continues to grow at the same rate. Also assume that the economy was previously in equilibrium, which means that A had been growing at a constant rate for a long enough time so that all fluctuations in I and C had disappeared. The economy then grows at an increasing rate, as traced out in several examples in Chapter 13. However, before the boom reaches its natural peak, it is likely to encounter the ceiling. For a while the economy will creep along the ceiling. However, movement along this ceiling represents a decreased amount of induced investment relative to the previous stage of the cycle. For this reason induced investment must turn down even further, because ΔY is decreasing. Thus the economy moves along the ceiling only for the amount of time of the investment lag; it then begins to turn down. Since the accelerator is explosive, it might be expected to cause a very rapid and sustained decrease in investment. However, this is not what happens. Instead, the value of the accelerator becomes zero, and the rate of decrease is limited by the rate of depreciation. Although the accelerator may continue to work for inventory investment, this is a small part of the total accelerator. The total amount of disinvestment that is necessary to return capital stock to an equilibrium level will indeed take place, but it will happen in a much more gradual manner, so that the slump is likely to be much longer than the boom. Autonomous investment will continue and will keep income from falling further, but meanwhile the gradual process of decumulation must continue to occur. Note that the time of the depression is not a function of the parameters of the model but of the depreciation rate and the degree to which autonomous investment continues to advance. Finally, all excess capacity will be worked off and the economy will settle into an equilibrium determined by autonomous investment and the size of the multiplier. Since autonomous investment continues to rise, income will continue to rise. But this will cause an increase in induced investment, so income will begin to rise at a more rapid rate, and thus the economy will rise toward the ceiling again, and the whole process will be repeated. One complete cycle is diagrammed in Figure 14.15.

There are now several modifications that can be superimposed on this basic pattern. First, the initial shock may be small enough or the distance between equilibrium and full employment may be large enough that the economy turns down before it hits the ceiling. Two possibilities could occur. One might be a series of "free" oscillations (that is, undisturbed by nonlinearities) which would build up until the economy did in fact reach the ceiling. The other possibility, which is fairly likely, is that because the accelerator becomes inoperative during the downswing, the forces causing cyclical fluctuations will be arrested. Then at the beginning of each upswing the cyclical process will begin anew and, coupled with the relatively mild upward start, will be insufficient to cause the economy to reach the ceiling. In that case we would have a potentially explosive situation, and yet one where the ceiling is never (or rarely) reached because other forces in the economy are not strong enough to generate a large enough boom. Both of these may be considered to be reasonable alternatives.

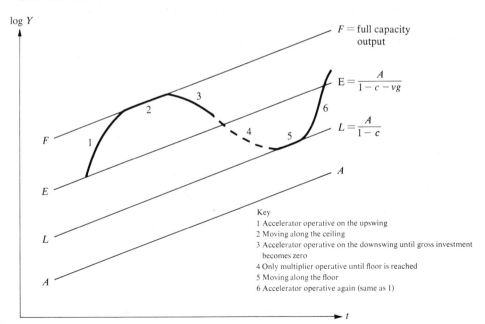

Key
1 Accelerator operative on the upswing
2 Moving along the ceiling
3 Accelerator operative on the downswing until gross investment becomes zero
4 Only multiplier operative until floor is reached
5 Moving along the floor
6 Accelerator operative again (same as 1)

Figure 14.15

The foregoing represents the main structure of Hicks's theory. He now proceeds to introduce monetary variables into the system. They enter into income determination primarily in the downswing and act mainly on autonomous investment. Monetary policy does not in general cause the downturn. However, the decrease in profits associated with the beginning of the downturn will almost always lead to an increase in the liquidity preference schedule and a resulting decrease in loanable funds. The monetary stringency causes a decrease in autonomous investment. This will lower income faster than would otherwise be the case. After the period of financial tightness has passed, autonomous investment will return to its previous level. Since income has already fallen most of the distance to the depression equilibrium level (determined by LL), the rest of the slump will be very short. However, this argument still states that excess capital stock must be fully depreciated before the depression is ended. This modification is shown graphically in Figure 14.16.

There are many interesting features of Hicks's theory, and it gains some realism when modified by cycles that turn down before the economy reaches the ceiling and by the use of monetary factors. However, at least two of the basic assumptions of the model cannot be reconciled with the facts: these are the statements that $v > 1$ for a time lag of one year or less and that the downswing is at least as long as the upswing. These are the two points on which Hicks has received most of his criticism. All the available empirical evidence on the investment function shows that the response of investment to a change in output is spread over many periods, so that damped cycles, rather than explosive cycles, actually result. The second point is even further removed from the real world. The relatively small decline in fixed business investment during the postwar recessions is almost entirely due to cancellations and contractions of existing plans. There is a lag of one year or more between original investment

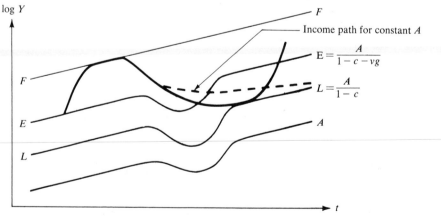

Figure 14.16

decisions and actual investment; since the average postwar recession has lasted slightly less than one year, the following expansion has already started before plans made to disinvest have very much effect. The decrease in capital stock in all the postwar recessions except 1958 has been negligible.

The role of the monetary factor is also confused in this theory. On the one hand, Hicks argues that the effect of tight money on autonomous investment tends to shorten the length of the contraction. On the other hand, he argues, as do most other economists, that the protracted length of the contraction from 1929 to 1933 was due largely to monetary disaster. As will be shown in Chapter 15, the incompatibility between these two views can be reconciled if one admits that monetary stringency evolves before the upper turning point is reached and is a contributing factor to the downturn. Then the easing of monetary policy when the recession is underway will lead to increases in certain types of investment, which will help to end the recession. If monetary policy remains tight, investment will continue to fall sharply, and the contraction may be prolonged for months or even years. Although Hicks considers the possibility that monetary factors do help cause the downturn, he distinctly believes that the downturn is caused by real rather than monetary factors. In any case, it is the return to monetary ease that is primarily responsible for ending the contraction and not the decumulation of capital stock.

In the author's view, Hicks's theory is best described as "suggestive." There are a number of worthwhile ideas that can be incorporated into modern business cycle theory, but the main outline of his theory needs substantial modification. One should be able to explain the growth of the economy without having to rely on paths that basically diverge from equilibrium, which is characteristic of both the Harrod–Domar and the Hicks models. Furthermore, one should incorporate the fact that the expansionary phase of the cycle is much longer than the contractionary phase. A promising alternative approach which incorporates these features is one that uses "ratchets" to explain both the cyclical and secular aspects of GNP movements. This approach, developed by Duesenberry, Smithies, and others, is considered next.

14.4   EXPLANATION OF THE CYCLE AND THE TREND WITH THE USE OF RATCHETS

We now come to a model capable of generating both cyclical fluctuations and growth through the operation of endogenous forces. There are actually several models treating this problem in a similar way. Here we follow the treatment of Smithies.[15] His model is

$$C = (1 - \alpha_1)Y + \alpha_2\overline{Y}$$

[15] A. Smithies, "Economic Fluctuations and Growth," *Econometrica*, Vol. 25, No. 1 (January, 1957), pp. 1–52.

$$I = \beta_1 Y_{-1} + \beta_2 \bar{Y} - \beta_3(Y_{f-1} - \bar{Y}) + k'$$

$$C + I = Y$$

$$Y_f - Y_{f-1} = \sigma I_{-1} - D_1 - D_2 + l'$$

$$D_1 = \delta_1 Y_{f-1}$$

$$D_2 = \delta_2(Y_{f-1} - Y_{-1})$$

where $\bar{Y}$ = peak previous level of GNP

Y_f = full-capacity GNP

D_1 = ordinary (physical) depreciation

D_2 = additional obsolescence

$1/\sigma$ = capital/output ratio

One improvement should be noted right away. The capital/output ratio, $1/\sigma$, is distinctly different from the marginal investment/output ratio, which is a combination of β_1, β_2, and β_3. Thus the troublesome problem of the interpretation of v in the equation $I = v(Y_{-1} - Y_{-2})$ is no longer an issue here.

The equations themselves are relatively straightforward. Consumption is a function of present and peak previous income. Induced investment is positively related to present and peak previous income and negatively related to excess capacity, and autonomous investment grows at a constant rate. The change in full-capacity output is proportional to the amount of gross investment minus depreciation and obsolescence and the growth in technology. Depreciation is subdivided into two components, representing the secular and cyclical components, respectively. The actual wearing out of machines is proportional to capital stock. When capacity utilization is high obsolescent machines will be retained and D_2 will be low or negative; in time of recessions, only more modern machinery will be kept and D_2 will be relatively high. Thus additional obsolescence is countercyclical and acts as a stabilizing influence on the economy.

Owing to the inclusion of the ratchet terms, there is a wide range of solutions. In general, the solutions can be divided into regions where the ratchet is not operative $(Y > \bar{Y})$ and regions where it is operative. These are referred to by Smithies as state I and state II, respectively. If the economy is to grow over time, it must be in state I part of the time; it will be in state II part of the time if there are any oscillations.

To find the solution in state I, that is, without the ratchet effect, set $Y = \bar{Y}$ in the consumption function and $Y_{-1} = \bar{Y}$ in the investment function.[16] Then the first three equations can be combined into

(14.29) $(1 - \alpha_1 + \alpha_2)Y + (\beta_1 + \beta_2 + \beta_3)Y_{-1} - \beta_3 Y_{f-1} + k' = Y$

---

[16] This treatment follows Smithies, *op. cit.*, part IV.

Therefore,

(14.30) $$Y = \frac{\beta_1 + \beta_2 + \beta_3}{\alpha_1 - \alpha_2}Y_{-1} - \frac{\beta_3}{\alpha_1 - \alpha_2}Y_{f-1} + \frac{1}{\alpha_1 - \alpha_2}k^t$$

and the last three equations can be solved as

(14.31) $$Y_f - Y_{f-1} = \sigma I_{-1} - \delta_1 Y_{f-1} - \delta_2(Y_{f-1} - Y_{-1}) + l^t$$

and, setting $I_{-1} = (\alpha_1 - \alpha_2)Y_{-1}$ gives

(14.32) $$Y_f = (1 - \delta_1 - \delta_2)Y_{f-1} + [\sigma(\alpha_1 - \alpha_2) + \delta_2]Y_{-1} + l^t$$

The trend terms will be useful later but are neglected at this point in order to examine whether the model can generate a growth pattern with endogenous forces alone. Dropping the trend terms and further simplifying the notations, we have

(14.33) $$Y = aY_{-1} + bY_{f-1}$$

(14.34) $$Y_f = cY_{-1} + dY_{f-1}$$

These two equations can be combined into a second-order difference equation in Y. By substituting $Y_{f-1} = (1/b)(Y - aY_{-1})$ we get

(14.35) $$Y - (a + d)Y_{-1} + (ad - bc)Y_{-2} = 0$$

Substituting $\rho^t = Y_t$ and solving for the roots of this equation gives

(14.36) $$\rho_{1,2} = \frac{a + d \pm \sqrt{(a + d)^2 - 4(ad - bc)}}{2}$$

Therefore,

(14.37) $$\rho_{1,2} = \frac{a + d \pm \sqrt{(a - d)^2 + 4bc}}{2}$$

To determine the region in which cyclical fluctuations occur it is necessary to see where the discriminant $(a - d)^2 + 4bc < 0$. Switching back to the parameters of the original model,

(14.38) $$D = (a - d)^2 + 4bc = \left[\frac{\beta_1 + \beta_2 + \beta_3}{\alpha_1 - \alpha_2} - (1 - \delta_1 - \delta_2)\right]^2$$

$$- 4\beta_3\sigma - \frac{4\beta_3\delta_2}{\alpha_1 - \alpha_2}$$

It would be quite awkward to evaluate this eight-dimensional function in the relevant area, so some simplifications are in order. First note that in the version of the model with no exogenous investment (that is, no trend term), $I = S$ implies

(14.39) $$\beta_1 Y_{-1} + \beta_2 \bar{Y} - \beta_3(Y_{f-1} - \bar{Y}) = \alpha_1 Y - \alpha_2 \bar{Y}$$

Furthermore, in equilibrium

(14.40) $$Y_{-1} \cong \bar{Y} \cong Y_{f-1} \cong Y$$

so that

(14.41) $$\beta_1 + \beta_2 \cong \alpha_1 - \alpha_2$$

Gross investment is about one quarter of gross private product, so that $\alpha_1 - \alpha_2 = 0.25 : \beta_1 + \beta_2$ cancels against $\alpha_1 - \alpha_2$ and need not be considered separately.

Since the K/O ratio is approximately 2.0, $1/\sigma = K/O = 2$ and $\sigma = 0.5$. The normal depreciation rate $\delta_1 = D/Y = 0.1$. Substituting in these values gives

(14.42) $$D = (4\beta_3 + 0.1 + \delta_2)^2 - 2\beta_3 - 16\beta_3\delta_2$$

We restrict $\delta_2 > 0$, $\beta_3 > 0$. Furthermore, $\delta_2 < 0.1$, because this is the depreciation rate for additional obsolescence, which is unlikely to be greater than the rate for normal depreciation. For $0 < \delta_2 < 0.1$, $D < 0$ for β_3 approximately between 0 and 0.1, which also seems reasonable.[17] The minimum value of D is given along the line $\beta_3 = \frac{1}{4}\delta_2 + \frac{1}{32}$.

An examination of the roots indicates explosive behavior for both cyclical and noncyclical behavior. Explosive oscillations will occur if

(14.42) $r^2 = ad - bc = (1 + 4\beta_3)(0.9 - \delta_2) + 0.5\beta_3 + 4\beta_3\delta_2 > 1$

which occurs if $\beta_3 > \frac{1}{41}$ when $\delta_2 = 0$ and $\beta_3 > \frac{2}{41}$ when $\delta_2 = 0.1$. Explosive nonoscillatory behavior (steady growth) will occur if

(14.43) $$\rho_1 = \frac{a + d + \sqrt{(a - d)^2 + 4bc}}{2} = 1 + \frac{4\beta_3 - \delta_1 - \delta_2}{2} + \sqrt{\frac{D}{2}} > 1$$

which occurs if $\beta_3 > 2.1/32$ when $\delta_2 = 0$ and $\beta_3 > 0.1$ when $\delta_2 = 0.1$.

Thus for reasonable values of the parameters, explosive cyclical fluctuations will occur. However, small shifts in these parameters could produce steady growth or possibly damped oscillations. Note that in this model it is possible to get a mildly explosive pattern of income even with the marginal investment/ output coefficient far below unity.

In the case of steady growth, the economy could grow at the following rates:

1. The warranted growth rate, in which case $Y = Y_f$ for all time periods and the economy is always in moving equilibrium. To find the rate of growth

---

[17] The exact inequalities are $D < 0$ for $0.3/32 < \beta_3 < 2.1/32$ for $\delta_2 = 0$ and $\frac{1}{40} < \beta_3 < \frac{1}{10}$ for $\delta_2 = 0.1$.

implied in this situation, refer back to the equation defining Y_f, which is

(14.44) $$Y_f = (1 - \delta_1 - \delta_2)Y_{f-1} + [\sigma(\alpha_1 - \alpha_2) + \delta_2]Y_{-1}$$

Since $Y = Y_f$ in this case,

(14.45) $$Y = [\sigma(\alpha_1 - \alpha_2) + (1 - \delta_1)]Y_{-1}$$

and

(14.46) $$\frac{Y - Y_{-1}}{Y_{-1}} = \sigma(\alpha_1 - \alpha_2) - \delta_1$$

This is the warranted rate of growth when gross investment is considered rather than net investment. Our values of $\sigma = 0.5$, $\alpha_1 - \alpha_2 = 0.25$, and $\delta_1 = 0.1$ give a growth rate of $2\frac{1}{2}$ percent per year, very close to the observed long-run behavior of 3 percent per year in constant dollars.

2. Persistent exhilaration, in which case $Y > Y_f$ and $g > g_w$.

3. Persistent excess capacity, in which case $Y < Y_f$ and $g < g_w$. Cases 2 and 3 are very unlikely to continue for a long time, because small shifts in the savings rate will cause a shift to cyclical fluctuations. This will occur because the model is operative in the region very near the boundary between cyclical and noncyclical behavior. This is quite unlike the Harrod–Domar model, in which small shifts in s and v have a negligible impact on the difference between g and g_w.

So far the model does not seem too different from the other models that have been examined, although the results thus far do seem more reasonable. However, when income declines and thus falls below the peak previous level, the ratchet effect becomes operative and a different variant of the model is solved to determine the time path of GNP. The model is different for several reasons. First, the combination of the parameters in the difference equation to be solved is changed. Second, the values of the parameters themselves may change somewhat. Third, the ratchet term, which is independent of time, must also be included in the solution as a separate influence.

With the ratchet terms treated separately and the trends still omitted, the first three equations are now combined into

(14.47) $$(1 - \alpha_1)Y + \alpha_2\bar{Y} + \beta_1 Y_{-1} + \beta_2\bar{Y} - \beta_3(Y_{f-1} - \bar{Y}) = Y$$

Therefore,

(14.48) $$Y = \frac{\alpha_2 + \beta_2 + \beta_3}{\alpha_1}\bar{Y} + \frac{\beta_1}{\alpha_1}Y_{-1} - \frac{\beta_3}{\alpha_1}Y_{f-1}$$

The last three equations remain the same, except that now $I_{-1} = \alpha_1 Y_{-1} - \alpha_2\bar{Y}$. This gives

(14.49) $$Y_f = (1 - \delta_1 - \delta_2)Y_{f-1} + (\sigma\alpha_1 + \delta_2)Y_{-1} - \sigma\alpha_2\bar{Y}$$

As before, these can be written for ease of exposition as

(14.50) $$Y = a'Y_{-1} + b'Y_{f-1} + r\overline{Y}$$

and

(14.51) $$Y_f = c'Y_{-1} + d'Y_{f-1} + s\overline{Y}$$

Substituting $Y_{f-1} = (1/b')(Y - a'Y_{-1}) - (r\overline{Y}/b')$ gives

(14.52) $$Y - a'Y_{-1} - r\overline{Y} = b'c'Y_{-2} + d'(Y_{-1} - a'Y_{-2}) - d'r\overline{Y} + b's\overline{Y}$$

and

(14.53) $$Y - Y_{-1}(a' + d') + Y_{-2}(a'd' - b'c') = \overline{Y}[r(1 - d') + sb']$$

The solution to this equation is of the form

(14.54) $$Y = A_1\rho_1^t + A_2\rho_2^t + R\overline{Y}$$

where $\rho^t = Y_t$ for no cycles, $Y = Ar^t(\cos\theta t + \varepsilon) + R\overline{Y}$ for cycles,[18] and

(14.55) $$R = \frac{r(1 - d') + sb'}{1 - (a' + d') + a'd' - b'c'}$$

It can easily be shown that R is always positive for relevant values of the parameters, so the ratchet effect always raises GNP above the level that would otherwise be reached during the downswing.

It has been shown thus far that under reasonable circumstances, the economy will be subjected to mildly explosive oscillations, and on the downswing the pattern of GNP will be modified by the existence of ratchets that retard the decline of consumption and investment and thus of GNP. After the lower turning point has been reached and the expansion begins again, three possibilities may occur.

1. The economy may rebound vigorously enough so that GNP will reach a higher level than it had previously. Then the economy will again be in state I. This may continue, and the economy will fluctuate between state I and state II. Endogenous growth will occur without the use of trends, and the cycles will be asymmetrical.

2. The cycles may be damped so that the economy remains in state II and continues to oscillate around a stationary equilibrium value of GNP.

3. The cycles may be explosive but the ratchet will be so weak that each depression trough will be lower than the previous one. In this case the model will behave almost as if it were continually in state I, and GNP will again fluctuate around a stationary equilibrium value.

There are thus two necessary conditions for endogenous fluctuating growth (without the use of trends). First, there must be explosive cycles in both state I and state II. Second, the ratchet effect must be strong enough to keep each

---

[18] For the details of this transformation, see the Appendix to Chapter 13.

trough at a higher level of GNP than the previous one. We now examine the parameters of the model to see whether these conditions are fulfilled.

The values of σ, δ_1, and δ_2 are unchanged. However, we can no longer make the assumption that $Y = \bar{Y}$, so a different method must be used to determine the values of the α_i and β_i. The yearly $mpc = 1 - \alpha_1$ is about 0.6, so $\alpha_1 \cong 0.4$. In the investment function take $\beta_1 = \beta_2 = 0.1$, which corresponds to the values of these coefficients at full capacity.

For cyclical fluctuation it is necessary that

(14.56) $$D' = (a' - d')^2 + 4b'c' < 0$$

$$= \left(\frac{\beta_1}{\alpha_1} - 1 + \delta_1 + \delta_2 \right)^2 - 4\beta_3\sigma - 4\frac{\beta_3\delta_2}{\alpha_1}$$

$$= (\tfrac{1}{4} - 1 - 0.1 - \delta_2)^2 - 2\beta_3 - 10\beta_3\delta_2$$

For $\delta_2 = 0$, $D' < 0$ if $\beta_3 > 0.21$. For $\delta_2 = 0.1$, $D' < 0$ if $\beta_3 > 0.1$. It is hard to assign an exact empirical estimate to β_3, but some wide limits can be estimated. If the change in investment in any given period is only proportional to the change in income, $\beta_3 = 0.1$. If the total change in income is due to the change in investment, $\beta_3 = 0.9$. If equilibrium consumption equals $\tfrac{3}{4}$ of gross private production and the yearly mpc is 0.6, then $\beta_3 = \tfrac{1}{2}$. It seems that actual values of β_3 are likely to be well within the range of cyclical fluctuations.

For explosive fluctuations it is necessary that $(r')^2 = a'd' - b'c' > 1$, and therefore

(14.57) $$(r')^2 = \frac{\beta_1}{\alpha_1}(1 - \delta_1 - \delta_2) + \beta_3 + \frac{\beta_3\delta_2}{\alpha_1} > 1$$

This becomes

(14.58) $$(r')^2 = \tfrac{1}{4}(0.9 - \delta_2) + \tfrac{1}{4}\beta_3 + \tfrac{5}{2}\beta_3\delta_2 > 1$$

For $\delta_2 = 0$, $(r')^2 > 1$ if $\beta_3 > 1.55$. For $\delta_2 = 0.1$, $(r')^2 > 1$ if $\beta_3 > 1.07$. It is clear that the cycles are damped rather than explosive, and by a substantial amount ($r = 0.6$ for $\delta_2 = 0.1$, $\beta_3 = 0.5$). Thus, whereas cycles are usually mildly explosive in state I, they are definitely damped in state II. This should not be surprising, because the inclusion of the ratchets clearly lowers the marginal propensities to consume and invest; part of these expenditures now depend on peak previous income. Furthermore, the stronger the ratchet, the more damped are the state II cycles, so there is no easy way out of the problem.[19] If the cycles are not explosive in state II, the economy can never rise above the peak previous level of income, and thus can never return to state I. Income will then continue to fluctuate around some depression level determined by the strength of the ratchet. Although this may have been an

---

[19] It can also be shown algebraically that for the same values of the parameters of the model, $(r')^2$ will always be less that r^2.

approximation to the way the economy behaved during the 1930s, it is clearly not a satisfactory explanation for the postwar economy.

The only way out of this problem is to argue that as the depression level of income persists, the ratchet effect will get smaller and smaller as the memory of the peak previous income becomes dimmer. In effect, the model would revert back to state I. But this would take a very long time and is not a satisfactory solution to the problem either.

There is a further serious problem with this model. Even if both state I and state II generate explosive cycles, the effect of the ratchet will be not only to dampen the depression *but also to lengthen it*. The reasons are similar to Hicks's theory; with a slower decrease in income, excess capacity will not disappear as fast. Thus it will take longer until investment and GNP turn up again. Algebraically this can be seen by noting that if $(r')^2 < r^2$, $\cos \theta' > \cos \theta$, and therefore $\theta' < \theta$ and $2\pi/\theta' > 2\pi/\theta$. Thus one of the problems the ratchet effect was supposed to eliminate is actually intensified. The cycle is indeed asymmetrical, but the downswings are longer than the upswings instead of vice versa.

Summarizing to this point, the following solutions can occur:

1. Continued growth without cycles, which may be equal to, greater than, or less than, the warranted growth rate. This is a possible, although not very interesting or realistic solution.

2. Fluctuations between state I and state II, both states explosive. This is the most interesting case, for it generates both cycles and endogenous growth. Unfortunately the parameters of the model are not even close to those needed for this solution. Furthermore, the downturns are longer than the upturns.

3. Fluctuations between state I and state II, but with such a weak ratchet effect that the economy reaches a new low in each downturn and thus no growth occurs. This is as unlikely as case 2 for realistic values for the parameters of the model and has little resemblance to the present economy.

4. Damped fluctuations contained within state II, which gradually converge to a depression level of income determined by the strength of the ratchet.

None of these is a plausible solution. However, the model can be salvaged by reinstating the trend variables, which were included in the original statement of the model but have not yet been introduced into the analysis. Consider trends in investment and full-capacity income combined with damped oscillations. The net effect will be to raise the level of income in state II and thus bring the economy back into state I, where cycles will be stronger and will probably be mildly explosive. Thus with the inclusion of trends, the economy is more likely to progress to state I. As shown by Goodwin and Hicks, the introduction of a trend will tend to make the upswings longer and the downswings shorter, conforming more closely to patterns observed in the real world.

The theory presented by Smithies is very flexible; for different values of the parameters of the model, one may get continued growth, explosive cycles with asymmetrical expansions and contractions or damped cycles which may also be asymmetric. Yet except for the explicit influence of trends, it is the removal of excess capacity that is responsible for the lower turning point. The ratchet effect keeps income from falling as fast in the downturn as it otherwise would, but it also keeps excess capacity from being removed as fast, so that in the absence of trends, the downturn will still be longer than the upturn. The combination of ratchets and trends can provide a path of GNP containing both cycles and growth, but this result is mitigated by the fact that reasonable growth cannot be generated endogenously for actual values of the parameters of the model. If one has damped cycles and introduces an exogenous growth trend, it is a simple matter to generate observed patterns of behavior without the use of ratchets.

The principal fault of this theory, then, must lie in the fact that investment will not turn up until a great deal of excess capacity has been worked off. Observed postwar behavior shows that the economy turns up before capital stock declines very much at all, and capacity utilization is usually at its low point when the expansion begins. An alternative course is to argue that factors *other* than excess capacity (that is, other than the accelerator) are partially responsible for turning points. One such choice might be monetary factors. It might also be argued that since the accelerator is distributed over many periods (except possibly for inventory investment), it leads to damped cycles. Much of the cyclical behavior of the economy would then be due to monetary or other factors.

It would be possible to build a multiplier–accelerator model incorporating distributed lag consumption and investment functions and monetary variables and evaluate the cyclical patterns of that model. However, there are severe diminishing marginal returns to pursuing this line of approach in greater detail. The algebra, although not complex, becomes quite cumbersome. Handy second-order difference equations are no longer adequate to determine the solution in models with more realistic and complicated lag structures. Instead, it would seem at this point to state a more general theory of the cycle, estimate this theory empirically, and examine its behavior by actual simulation. Such a theory of the business cycle is attempted in Chapter 15.

THE WHARTON EFU MODEL AND ITS CYCLICAL IMPLICATIONS

15.1   THE PATTERN OF AGGREGATE ECONOMIC ACTIVITY DURING THE CYCLE

The model presented in this chapter is a combination of some of the most important ideas of previous theories with the empirical information on choice of variables and lag structure that was examined in detail in Part I. Many of the ideas developed elsewhere in the book are simply collected here and arranged in proper order, instead of deriving new material at this point.

Before presenting any theory of the cycle, one should have a clear idea of the overall pattern of aggregate economic activity during a typical cycle. Although no two cycles are identical, they contain sufficient repetitive patterns so that useful generalizations about previous cycles can be helpful in explaining future cyclical behavior. Both the general time path of the cycle and the pattern of various different components of aggregate demand and supply during the course of the cycle need to be considered.

Pre-Keynesian students of the business cycle often found it useful to separate the different parts of the cycle into periods of "prosperity" or "boom" and periods of "depression" or "slump." The former were almost universally associated with rising incomes and full employment, whereas the latter signified declining incomes and rising unemployment. However, during the decade of the 1930s, this distinction proved to be no longer useful. The period from 1933 to 1937 was, until the present, the longest peacetime expansion on record, yet unemployment never fell below 14 percent. Under the older nomenclature, one would hesitate to call this either a boom (because of the high unemployment) or a depression (because of steadily rising incomes). Because of such problems, identification of the stages of the cycle has shifted to the use of the less colorful but more exact terms "expansion" and "contraction." To assign definite time intervals to these categories it is quite important to specify peaks and troughs correctly. Some of the problems inherent in this specification are discussed in Chapter 16; for now we assume that statistical problems are absent and the peak can be defined as the last time period during which aggregate economic activity (measured in real terms) increases, and the trough as the last time period during which it decreases.

The cycle is sometimes represented as a smooth sine curve taken relative to a trend. In this case not only are the period of expansion and contraction easily identifiable, but four stages of the cycle can be observed. The period of expansion below the trend line is known as "recovery" and above the trend line as "prosperity"; the period of contraction above the trend line is known as "recession" and below the trend line as "depression." Such a description of a cycle is shown in Figure 15.1.

This terminology is troublesome for at least two reasons. First, the use of the terms "prosperity" and "depression" lead to the sort of problems mentioned above. Second, the difference between a "recession" and a "depression" is often likely to be marred by political oratory; to the party in power, any stage of the downturn is a recession, but to the party out of power, the entire downturn must certainly be a depression. There is a more basic reason, however, for not using this description: the cycle is definitely asymmetrical. These four stages, if they can in fact be identified, are not all of the same length. Furthermore, the path of GNP over the cycle does not follow a sine curve but is quite likely to have substantial periods where it grows at the same rate as the trend and thus has no curvature at all. If the simplified representation of the cycle

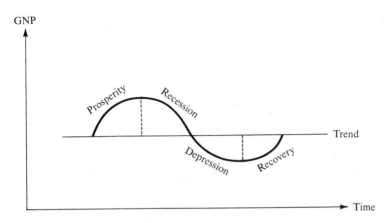

Figure 15.1

is to follow empirically observed behavior, it is more relevant to choose three periods, as follows:

Phase 1. Rapid growth of the economy (greater than the trend rate) coinciding with the beginning of the upturn.

Phase 2. A decline in the rate of growth to the trend rate, ending in the upper turning point.

Phase 3. A decrease in aggregate economic activity, cumulating in the lower turning point.

If no major exogenous forces (such as the beginning or ending of war, major changes in tax rates, and so on) influence GNP during the cycle, the typical observed pattern has been that phase 1 lasts approximately one year, phase 2 lasts one to two years, and phase 3 lasts one year. This accounts for the average three- to four-year length of the business cycle as measured since 1854. It will also be noted that the expansion phase is two to three years, whereas the contraction phase is only one year. This pattern is presented graphically in Figure 15.2.

Seen in this light, there are really three turning points. The first is the change from a rapid growth rate to a trend growth rate. The second is the actual downturn, and the third is the actual upturn. In this case, the simple multiplier–accelerator analysis cannot be used, for it posits a constantly decreasing rate of growth of GNP when it is above the trend, and a constantly increasing rate of growth of GNP when it is below the trend. There is a substantial period during which GNP grows at approximately the trend rate, which must also be explained. As shown in Chapter 14, Hicks explained the turning point from phase 1 to phase 2 by the use of ceilings. Although it is certainly true that an economy that was growing faster than the trend rate when it reached the ceiling would have to slow down, this has not been the reason for the turning points in the postwar U.S. economy. If the theory developed here is to be at all realistic, an alternative explanation to the ceiling must be advanced. As was shown in Chapter 14, Smithies and others use ratchets to explain the asymmetry of the business cycle. Yet it can be shown that consumption and investment functions

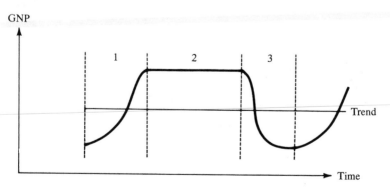

Figure 15.2

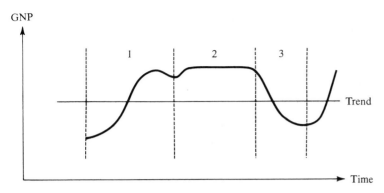

Figure 15.3

which are symmetric with respect to income changes can still be incorporated in a model that will generate asymmetrical behavior.

In spite of the fact that the expansion period is two to three times as long as the contraction, there is still a certain symmetry inherent in the time path of GNP. The downturn and lower turning point that comprise phase 3 are mirrored to a certain extent in the rapid increase and slight turning point that comprise phase 1. If Figure 15.2 were to be drawn in slightly more detail, a dip at the end of phase 1 would become apparent, as shown in Figure 15.3. There is definitely a period about four to five quarters after the initial upturn, during which GNP grows at a slower rate than not only the period before but also the period immediately afterward. The cause of this slowdown is very similar to the cause of the upturn after four to five quarters of contraction. The main difference is that at the end of phase 1 there are strong forces responsible for the continuation of expansion, whereas at the end of phase 3 there are usually no strong forces responsible for the continuation of contraction. It is possible that the expansionary forces carrying the economy from phase 1 into phase 2 are absent; then the cycle becomes a two-year cycle. This happens very seldom, but it is possible.

This slight period of slowdown is not an isolated phenomenon but has occurred in every postwar period of expansion. It is in fact this problem that has caused so many of the "leading indicators" to turn down much too early, a problem that is examined in some detail in Chapter 16. The record can be seen from the evidence given in Table 15.1.

It is also possible that the forces causing contraction might in certain circumstances still be present at what would ordinarily be the end of phase 3, so that the economy would continue to spiral downward. This is indeed what occurred in the period from 1929 to 1933. What now appears to be an incredible succession of blunders on both monetary and fiscal policy, complicated by international problems, kept deflationary pressures on the economy for four years. However, the institutional nature of the U.S. economy has changed sufficiently

TABLE 15.1   AVERAGE GROWTH PER QUARTER OF GNP
DURING UPTURN FOLLOWING RECESSION

(all figures are in billions of 1958 dollars)

Recession Year	Quarters 1–5	Quarters 6–8	Quarters 9–11
1949	9.7[a]	2.5[a]	5.0[a]
1954	8.1	1.0	2.7
1958	7.1	—[b]	—[b]
1961	9.0	4.7	6.3

[a] The beginning of the Korean War slightly prolonged the first phase of the cycle.

[b] Short cycle—GNP turned down by the eighth quarter.

so that this series of events is most unlikely to occur again. Thus, although the 1929 depression is still a phenomenon of interest to economists in general and business-cycle economists in particular, we shall sidestep it at this point and concentrate on the framework found in the postwar U.S. economy.[1] From the amount of detail and disaggregation presented in Part I it should be obvious that any theory of the business cycle developed here will include more than a "consumption" and "investment" function. At a minimum, aggregate demand should be divided into consumer durables, consumer nondurables and services, fixed business investment, residential construction, inventory investment, net foreign balance, and government purchases of goods and services. It is also necessary to introduce relationships for factor shares and prices and product prices, as will become evident below.

All the Keynesian and post-Keynesian theories of the cycle that have been examined here use the accelerator as the single most important cause of cyclical fluctuations. Our treatment will not differ in this respect. However, it should be noted that several different components of aggregate demand are explained by means of an accelerator, each with a different lag structure, a different optimal capital/output ratio, and a different time response. An accelerator could be used to explain any component of aggregate demand for which stocks of goods exist. This would include consumer durables, fixed business investment, and inventory investment. This list might logically be extended to include residential construction; however, in the short run this is influenced more by supply factors, so the accelerator is invalid here. Certain types of imports are subject to influences of the accelerator; however, in general, imports are treated

---

[1] L. R. Klein and M. R. Norman have used a revised version of the Klein–Goldberger model estimated for the period 1929–1964 to simulate the period 1929–1933 with present-day tax and transfer functions and easy monetary policy to see what the time path of the economy might have been. They find that some downturn still would have occurred, but it would have been much milder and shorter.

more like consumer nondurables and services. All these accelerator relationships are developed using the stock-adjustment form, $I_t = aX_t - bK_{t-1}$, so the destabilizing nature of the naive accelerator $I_t = \alpha\Delta X_t$ is blunted. This means that cyclical fluctuations will be even more damped than the simple examples given in Chapter 13. However, the accelerator is still important enough to be instrumental in causing turning points.

The most volatile component of aggregate demand is inventory investment. Purchases of consumer durables also respond rapidly to short-run changes in income. The short-run effect of the accelerator for plant and equipment investment is much weaker because of the long lag between a change in output and the resulting change in fixed business investment. Thus of all the accelerators, the one for fixed business investment is certainly no more important than the others, even though it has been assigned a central place in cycle theory. In fact, fixed business investment is not directly accountable for the turning points; it lags the cycle. It is important in prolonging the rise in GNP at the end of phase 1, however, and in determining the amplitude of the cycle itself.

15.2   BEHAVIOR OF THE COMPONENTS OF GNP DURING THE CYCLE

Having discussed the broad outlines of the cycle, we now follow the path of GNP in detail, noting which components are responsible for the increases and declines of the economy. We begin at the point at which the upturn has just started.

At the beginning of the upturn, the largest changes in economic activity are centered in the inventories and orders sectors. Although new orders do not turn up before the cycle does, they rise very rapidly as soon as the upturn starts. There is also a rapid rise in purchases of consumer durables. Although consumer durables account for only about 15 percent of total consumer spending, they account for almost *half* of total wholesale and retail inventory stocks. Furthermore, durable manufacturing inventories account for 60 percent of total manufacturing inventories, although some of this is due to capital goods. Thus large increases in consumer durables purchases will have a sizable effect on total inventory investment.

There is little change in other sectors of aggregate demand. Since fixed business investment lags the cycle, it will still be decreasing in the early stages of the boom, although the rate of decrease will be much slower. Some components of fixed business investment, such as commercial construction, may turn up at this point, but this is not enough to offset declines in manufacturing and public utility investment. Residential construction continues at a high level; however, this high level was reached in the later stages of the contraction and thus does not represent a further increase. Consumption of nondurables and services follows the increase in income. The net foreign balance, inasmuch as there is any movement at all, will probably decline slightly. Exports are likely to be slightly less as the effects of our recession are felt in foreign economies. The components of imports that follow inventory investment will increase substantially; other components will not increase very much.

As shown in Chapter 10, the early stages of the expansion are almost always marked by a cyclical peak in the profits/GNP ratio. This is *not* the same thing as saying that personal disposable income does not rise rapidly. What happens is that profits rise even faster than the rapid increase in GNP, and the wage bill does not rise quite as fast. The rapid rise in profits occurs for several reasons. Both total sales and profit margins increase. The latter occurs both because prices rise while average variable costs (mainly unit labor costs) remain steady or decline, and because excess capacity decreases, lowering average fixed costs. Prices are likely to rise because the elasticity of demand decreases in the boom, so that profit-maximizing firms will raise their prices even if unit labor costs (and other variable costs) have remained unchanged. Productivity increases are likely to be large at the beginning of an upturn, but wages are not likely to rise very fast, because they depend on the previous year's rate of unemployment and change in the consumer price level.

In the postwar period, GNP in *constant* dollars has grown at an average of $7\frac{1}{2}$ percent during the first year of the expansion. This is, of course, much higher than the trend growth rate. The demand for labor will increase at about that rate minus the rate of increase in productivity, so that labor income is likely to grow at 7 to 8 percent if wages increase at the same rate as marginal productivity. Even if they do not, the increase in labor income is still substantial. Profits have increased by 28 percent on the average during the first year of the expansion. Although there is clearly a cyclical redistribution of total income away from wage earners and fixed-income recipients toward profits, this is of modest enough magnitude so that real personal disposable income rises more rapidly in the early stages of the expansion than it does over the average of the business cycle. There will be little immediate effect of this slight price increase and income redistribution, although it will be of considerable importance in the next phase of the cycle because it affects wage bargains and investment.

This first, very rapid period of growth comes to an end after about one year because of a decrease in the rate of inventory investment. This depends on two separate and rather different factors. One is the accelerator mechanism. The other is the pattern of the backlog of orders, a very important determinant of inventory investment.

Firms have trimmed their backlog of orders to minimum manageable levels during the previous recession. When the increase in new orders starts, there will be some increase in shipments, but not by the full amount of the increase in orders. This occurs for two reasons. First, if a large number of new orders is placed all at once, it may be several months before production can be completed and shipments are made. Second, even if the placement of new orders is not bunched, firms will want to increase their backlog of orders to some optimal

Orders

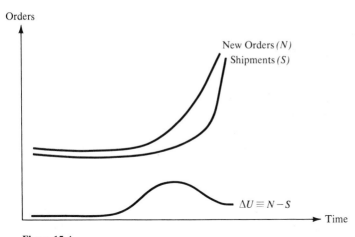

New Orders (N)

Shipments (S)

$\Delta U \equiv N - S$

Time

Figure 15.4

level relative to production scheduling. Thus at first new orders will increase faster than sales. After this optimal level of unfilled orders has been reached, shipments will start to accelerate. Thus ΔU, the change in unfilled orders, decreases. This process is shown diagrammatically in Figure 15.4.

Two separate causes are thus responsible for the marked decrease in the amount of inventory investment at the end of the first year of the expansion. This decline will slow down the rate of growth of GNP and personal disposable income, which will slow down the increase in consumption, particularly for consumer durables. These are certainly sufficient reasons for the rate of growth to decrease: as was shown in the simple multiplier–accelerator models, a cycle of five quarters dominated by inventory investment is a possibility. The force responsible for keeping the upturn going is fixed business investment, which depends primarily, although not exclusively, on lagged variables.

The fixed business investment function is essentially of the form $I_p = f(Cp, X_{-1}, F_{-1})$, where the lags are in years and F represents financial variables; these include corporate cash flow, the level of interest rates, and some measure of "tight money." At the beginning of the second phase (corresponding to the beginning of the second year of the expansion) all these variables will have an expansionary effect on investment. As previously explained, last year's output has been increasing very rapidly. Capacity utilization rates will be at a cyclical high both because of the rapid growth of the economy during the past year and because fixed business investment has not been very high, so that capital stock has not increased very rapidly. Profit rates in the previous year were also at a cyclical high. Because fixed business investment up to this point has been low, interest rates are low and monetary ease prevails. Thus the beginning of the second phase is initiated by a substantial rise in fixed business investment. The amplitude of this rise will be primarily determined by the rate of capacity utilization at which the economy is operating at the beginning of the second phase. If there is substantial excess capacity, investment probably will not increase very much, but even so should show a noticeable upturn from the levels of the previous recession. Even if the demand for investment for purposes of expansion is rather small, the demand for investment for modernization is likely to be substantial, with cash flow high and money easy to borrow. It should be mentioned that concomitant with this increase in fixed business investment, there will be a decrease in residential construction. However, the drop in the latter will be small (in absolute terms) compared to the rise in the former, so that on balance total fixed investment still rises sharply.

The rapid initial surge of growth in income has subsided; the economy now continues to grow at a trend rate. The accelerator relationships in inventory investment and purchases of consumer durables which tend to cause a further decrease in the rate of growth are offset by the fact that fixed business investment continues to increase for many quarters after the initial change in income. This was shown in Chapter 5, where several functions were cited in which investment first rises and then falls in response to an initial change in the level of income. Of the other components of aggregate demand, consumption of nondurables and services grows at the trend rate, and there is no reason for the net foreign balance to change very much unless the growth rates or price changes of the United States and countries with which it trades are very different.

After a year or two, the economy will begin to turn down if there are no exogenous forces acting to give income an added boost. Obvious examples of these are tax cuts and increased expenditures for government defense. The forces leading to the downturn are of two kinds, largely separate in nature. One is the combined influence of the accelerators. There has been a general deflationary influence of the accelerators in consumer durables and inventory investment. When the accelerator relationship also causes fixed business investment to turn down, which is about six quarters into the second phase, the combined effect is usually enough to cause a turning point and accelerate any decline in income. Note that the timing of the decline of six quarters, which was taken from study of the lag structure of the investment function, corresponds almost exactly with the average length of phase 2 of the cycle. This would lead one to believe that in the absence of any other effects, there would still be a downturn at this time. However, given the actual values of the marginal capital/output ratios for these functions, the decline that would occur would be quite modest, with a very gradual decrease in GNP, rather unlike the observed postwar recessions. Additional elements are needed to explain the sharp, if brief, decline in GNP.

Virtually all the upper turning points of the business cycles have been characterized by monetary stringency. During the second phase of the cycle, the idle cash balances that existed throughout the first phase almost always disappear. This phenomenon is due to two different causes. One is the reduction in corporate cash flow in constant dollars. The other is the conscious pressure of the central banking system to tighten money to prevent further inflation. These are considered in turn.

Recall that the later stages of the first phase were marked by a rise in prices although unit labor costs were steady or decreasing. When wage earners bargain in the following year, they will demand money wage increases greater than productivity gains in order to keep real wage increases equal to productivity gains. This will result in further price increases. However, as the rate of increase of demand slows down, the demand curve will not shift out as fast, making it harder for firms to raise prices as readily. Recall that if the elasticity of demand is greater than unity, firms will lose total revenue by raising prices. Since prices cannot be passed along as easily, profit rates are likely to fall. Furthermore, increases in total capacity that occur will make it harder for firms to raise prices in purely competitive and noncollusive oligopolistic industries.

This is not the only problem facing firms. Corporate cash flow (L), which is defined as

$$L = \frac{\text{after-tax corporate profits} - \text{dividends} + \text{depreciation}}{\text{price of capital goods}}$$

will decrease in the latter stages of the expansion. Profits are not rising as rapidly as previously, but dividends will continue to increase because they are based largely on lagged profits. Depreciation allowances are based on original cost instead of replacement cost, so they will rise much more slowly than the actual cost of new machines if the price of capital goods is rising rapidly. Since the supply curve is more inelastic for capital goods, particularly construction, than for consumer goods, the price of capital goods rises more rapidly than other goods in the later stages of the expansion. The greater the increase in fixed business investment, the greater the rise in capital-goods prices, and the greater the eventual cash squeeze on firms.

Because of this inflation, the monetary authorities will try to tighten money, which will result in a rise in interest rates and nonprice credit rationing. This will happen at approximately the same time as the profit squeeze and thus intensify the liquidity problem of businesses.

Another sector of the economy that must be examined at this stage of the cycle is the orders sector. An increase in the amount of available capacity (and thus a decrease in utilization rates) results in quicker processing of orders. Thus even if new orders continue to be received at the same rate, unfilled orders will decrease as shipments increase. Since the level of unfilled orders has decreased, there will be less demand for inventories, and inventory investment will fall sharply. It is this decrease in unfilled orders and inventory investment which is largely responsible for the sharp nature of the downturn that is actually observed. The relatively smooth nature of the distributed lag accelerator would produce a very gradual downturn. Monetary stringency does cause fixed business investment to decline faster. But the existence of excess capacity, and its effect on the backlog of orders and inventory investment, is the principal reason the downturn is usually quite steep. Once it has started, new orders decline, unfilled orders decline further, and inventory investment decreases further. The economy continues to decline and the resulting contraction phase is likely to last about one year.

To explain why the contraction lasts only a year instead of continuing as long as the expansion does it is necessary to explain the asymmetry of the fixed business investment function considered above. At the end of the second phase and beginning of the third phase, capacity utilization rates have decreased, money is tight, interest rates are high, and corporate cash flow in real terms has decreased. The only independent variable with an expansionary effect on investment is lagged output. Thus even if there were not a downturn in GNP, fixed business investment would be likely to decrease. The asymmetry in fixed business investment—it lags the cycle at the upturn but is almost coincident at the downturn—is due primarily to financial factors. While the economy grows at a trend rate during the second phase of the cycle, loanable funds become more expensive and harder to obtain.

At the end of the contraction, lagged output has fallen substantially. Although capacity utilization has also declined, the decline may be proportionately smaller than the decline in output because capital stock has also decreased somewhat. On balance the financial factors are more favorable at the end of the contraction than at the end of the expansion. Although profits have certainly fallen, easier monetary conditions clearly prevail, and interest rates are much lower than they were during the previous year. Thus at the end of the third phase, investment is not likely to continue to decrease rapidly, unlike the rapid increase at the end of the first phase. This asymmetry is one of the main reasons the downturn does not continue.

The other forces that slow down the rate of decrease in GNP are similar to the ones that caused the transition from phase 1 to phase 2 and are centered in the orders–inventories sector. Even if new orders decrease very rapidly, shipments will also decrease just as rapidly after a while and the change in unfilled orders will rise toward zero. This will also increase inventory investment from a negative amount toward zero. At least as important, easy money and the low relative costs of construction will result in an increase in residential construction. This will give further impetus to a rise in GNP. Purchases of consumer durables are likely to remain at low levels throughout the recession, because many individuals will be unwilling to purchase these items, particularly cars, as long as business conditions remain unfavorable. Thus the initial upturn depends on two main things: the slowing down of the decrease in unfilled orders and inventory investment, and the easing of monetary policy, permitting a rise in residential construction and a reduction in the decline in fixed business investment. Although the upper turning point would occur even without monetary stringency, the lower turning point probably would not occur as soon as it does without monetary ease. Eventually the combined elements of the accelerator would lead to a cessation of the decline in GNP, but this would be likely to take as long as the expansion phase, that is, more than two years.

At first glance this may seem contradictory to the statement made earlier in this text and elsewhere that monetary policy is more effective in stopping booms than in stopping recessions. However, this is not the case. First, we have suggested that monetary policy is effective in stopping booms. Although the expansion would end because of real factors, tight money makes the following recession more serious. Second, once interest rates are at low levels and there are plenty of excess reserves in the banking system, *additional* lowering of rates or *additional* increases in the stock of money are likely to have little effect on investment and thus on aggregate demand. This is primarily because of the small interest elasticity of investment at low interest rates rather than the existence of the liquidity trap. However, this statement holds only after an easy-money position has been reached. If money were to stay tight, and if interest rates were to stay high in the region where there was a substantial interest elasticity of investment, any downturn in GNP that had already started would be much larger. It is doubtful if the other forces in the economy would have enough effect to cause an upturn after only one year.

It is quite plausible in this connection to argue that the 1929–1933 contraction was due in large part to continued monetary stringency which prohibited even a modest slowdown in the rate of decline of fixed investment. The turning point in mid-1929 was undoubtedly caused by the accelerator mechanism manifested as excess capacity, and the downturn was magnified by the stock market crash in October. However, for the first year of the downturn there was a widespread feeling that the contraction might not last significantly longer than had been the case for the other interwar recessions. The 1920–1921 recession, following the speculative excesses of World War I, was quite severe but also very brief, and the economy returned to full employment shortly afterward. It was only when the continued stringency of monetary policy caused investment to continue to decelerate at the same high rate for two years that widespread failure of commercial and financial enterprises and wholesale destruction of money led to unparalleled wage and price cuts and to mass unemployment that remained until World War II.

It should be pointed out that changes in the institutional framework of the United States in the postwar period with respect to transfer payments and other automatic stabilizers clearly will lessen the magnitude of any downturn. Since personal disposable income stays higher than it would otherwise be, the slump is largely confined to investment and consumer durables. In most of the postwar recessions, consumer purchases of nondurables and services have not declined at all. However, the fact that contractions are no longer as severe does not in itself explain why the downturn is much shorter than the upturn. Continued monetary stringency in the contraction would very likely prolong the downturn for at least another year, although its ultimate severity would certainly be much milder than the great depression.

Suppose that monetary conditions were to remain easy throughout the cycle. In this case the transition from tight to easy money at the beginning of the contraction, which is largely responsible for the termination of the downturn, would not occur. Then it might be argued that the contraction, although mild, would last approximately as long as the expansion. However, this is probably not the case. Given the relatively small values of the accelerator coefficients which have been estimated empirically, an exogenous force of the size occurring in the postwar U.S. economy would lead to only one turning point and then a nonoscillatory path toward the equilibrium value. In other words, the cyclical mechanism would be heavily damped and would not continue to generate future cycles. Either changes in monetary conditions or exogenous forces are necessary to continue generating cycles, although endogenous forces will produce one and possibly two turning points after the initial shock has occurred.

Since monetary policy has historically been tightened whenever inflation occurs, and this pattern seems unlikely to change in the near future, easy monetary policy throughout the cycle would require stable prices. This would mean that firms would not raise their prices when their demand curves shifted out, and wageearners would not bargain more vigorously when demand for labor was higher. This would be a most interesting situation, but in the absence of rigidly controlled and enforced wage–price guidelines probably belongs in a book of fables. There is almost certainly going to be upward pressure on product and factor prices in full-employment situations, and this is almost certain to lead to stringent monetary policy. This will intensify the downward movement in investment, lead to a recession, cause a reversal to easy monetary policy, and thus lead to an upturn after about one year of contraction.

In summary, there are three main phases of the business cycle. In the first phase, output grows much more rapidly than the trend value. This phase is ended by a decrease in inventory investment and a declining rate of increase in consumer durables. The second phase, during which GNP grows at the trend level, lasts for about $1\frac{1}{2}$ years, and is ended by three factors. One is the cumulative aspects of accelerators for inventory investment, consumer durables, and fixed business investment. The second is a decrease in corporate cash flow in constant dollars and a tighter money policy. This occurs primarily because of a rise in prices, followed later by a rise in unit labor costs. The third is the existence of excess capacity, which reduces backlogs of orders and decreases inventory investment sharply. The third phase of the cycle, the downturn, lasts about a year. It ends because inventory investment becomes less negative, and certain components of fixed investment, mainly residential construction, increase. The latter is made possible by the easy money policy that begins as soon as the recession starts.

15.3   THE WHARTON ECONOMETRIC AND FORECASTING UNIT MODEL

We are now in a position to present the empirical estimates of a model of the postwar U.S. economy that is based on the analysis of individual functions given in Part I and overall cyclical theory given in Part II. This model, known as the Wharton Econometric and Forecasting Unit model (Wharton EFU model), has been developed jointly by the present author and L. R. Klein. It is an outgrowth of two earlier quarterly models, one constructed by the author[2] and the other by Professor Klein.[3] Most of the equations of this model have already been listed in Part I, where the specific components of aggregate demand and supply were analyzed. The complete list of equations, including tax and transfer functions and identities, is given later in this section.

The properties of the time path generated by the Wharton EFU model are examined in detail in Chapter 20. Here we include a brief note on its general cyclical behavior. If steadily increasing government expenditures and no change in the stringency of monetary policy are used as exogenous assumptions, the time path of the model shows a slight inventory subcycle of five or six quarters but no other cyclical fluctuations are apparent. If actual historical data are used for the exogenous assumptions, however, a much different picture is readily apparent. In one simulation experiment, the model was solved continuously for 48 quarters for the period 1952.3–1964.2. In each case the actual values of all exogenous variables were used, but all lagged values were generated internally by the solution and no adjustments of any kind were made for the entire period. The model correctly tracked the downturns in 1954, 1958, and 1960 and even reflected the minor decline in 1956. It further tracked actual economic conditions in that it did not turn down anywhere else.[4] The quarter to quarter correspondence was not precise in many cases, a major example being the failure of the model to follow the full extent of the 1955–1957 capital-goods boom. However, it did reflect all turning points correctly and did not predict any spurious ones. Experiments of this sort indicate that exogenous changes in fiscal and monetary policy are in large part responsible for the postwar cyclical pattern that has occurred. These effects are measured explicitly in Chapter 20.

---

[2] M. K. Evans, *A Postwar Quarterly Model of the United States Economy, 1947–1960*, unpublished Ph.D. thesis, 1964.

[3] L. R. Klein, "A Postwar Quarterly Model: Descriptions and Applications," in *Models of Income Determination*, Studies in Income and Wealth, Vol. 28 (Princeton, N.J.: Princeton University Press, 1964), pp. 11–30. Additional details on the antecedents of the Wharton EFU model can be found in M. K. Evans and L. R. Klein, *The Wharton Econometric Forecasting Model* (Philadelphia: University of Pennsylvania, 1967), chap. 1.

[4] The details of this and similar simulations are given in M. K. Evans and L. R. Klein, "Experience with Econometric Analysis of the American 'Konjunktur' Position," a paper prepared for the conference, *Is the Business Cycle Obsolete?*, mimeographed, 1967.

Because the specification of the Wharton EFU model has been explained in detail in Part I, we do not repeat the explanation of each of the equations at this point but instead limit ourselves to a capsule overview of the entire system. Equations (15.1)–(15.3) comprise the consumption functions; in all of these consumption depends on personal disposable income and past patterns of consumer behavior. In the car equation relative prices, the rate of unemployment, and dummy variables for supply and credit conditions are additional independent variables. In equations (15.4)–(15.6), fixed business investment is explained as a function of lagged output, capital stock, and financial variables. The lag structure in these equations is given by the Almon weights plus an additional lag between changes in economic conditions and the beginning of appropriations. Equation (15.7) states that residential construction is a function of income, relative prices, and credit conditions.

Equations (15.2)–(15.5) and (15.7) are also given in alternative forms that use anticipatory data. An index of consumer attitudes is used in the consumer-durables equations, the OBE-SEC investment intentions are used in the fixed business investment equations, and lagged housing starts are included in the residential construction function. These alternative equations have proved to be of limited usefulness thus far because they can only predict one quarter ahead in most cases.

Equations (15.8) and (15.9) are inventory investment functions for the manufacturing and nonmanufacturing sectors, respectively. Sales and lagged inventory stocks are important in both sectors. Unfilled orders and a dummy variable for steel strikes are used as additional independent variables in the manufacturing sector equation. Changes in output originating and prices in manufacturing and the level of consumer durable purchases are added to the equation explaining nonmanufacturing inventory investment. Equations (15.10)–(15.13) comprise the foreign sector and complete the explanation of aggregate demand. Income and relative prices are important in all the equations, and the lagged dependent variable is also included in the functions for other imports (mainly consumer goods and services) and for exports.

Equations (15.14)–(15.23) determine aggregate supply conditions in the model. Equation (15.14) is the production function for the manufacturing sector; output originating depends on utilized labor and capital and a measure of productivity. Since output is determined later in the model, this equation actually determines employment in the manufacturing sector. Equation (15.15) uses the *same coefficients* as (15.14) but introduces *total* available labor and capital as the independent variables. This gives a measure of full capacity output for manufacturing which can then be related to actual output to form an index of capacity utilization. Equation (15.16) explains hours worked in manufacturing as a function of output, the change in output, the index of capacity utilization, and the wage rate, all for the manufacturing sector. The wage rate [Equation (15.17)] is in turn a function of lagged values of the spread between the overall unemployment rate and the rate for males aged 25–34, lagged changes in the consumer price level, and changes in the wage rate during the preceding year. Manufacturing prices [Equation (15.18)] depend on unit labor costs and capacity utilization.

Equations are also estimated for the nonmanufacturing sector (excluding agriculture, housing, and government) for output originating, hours worked, and the wage rate. Nonmanufacturing output depends on man-hours and capital stock in that sector and an overall productivity trend. Hours worked depend on manufacturing capacity utilization and nonmanufacturing wage rates. The latter follow manufacturing wage rates and also depend on lagged changes in the consumer price level and changes in nonmanufacturing wages during the previous year. No equation is used to derive full capacity estimates of output in nonmanufacturing because of the difficulties in defining that concept for this part of the economy. A price level equation is not estimated for this sector because the price of output originating in the nonmanufacturing sector is determined as a residual.[5]

Equations (15.22) and (15.23) close this part of the system. First the unemployment rate of males aged 25–34 is explained as a nonlinear function of the overall unemployment rate. Then the labor force participation rate is determined as a nonlinear function of unemployment, the size of the armed forces, and a time trend.

Equations (15.24)–(15.35) explain income distribution and factor shares. Depreciation functions for the various sectors depend on capital stock and changes in the tax laws. Indirect business taxes, corporate income taxes, and personal income taxes depend on national income, corporate profits, and personal income less transfer payments respectively. Transfer payments depend on the number of unemployed and a time trend representing increased coverage. Income of unincorporated businesses depends on current dollar GNP, rental and interest income depends on a price of rent index, and dividend payments depend on gross profits after taxes. All these last three functions are transformed so that the lagged dependent variable appears as an additional explanatory variable. Finally, inventory valuation adjustment depends on changes in the wholesale price index.

Equations (15.36)–(15.39) are needed to close the real part of the system. An empirical approximation is used to relate annual retained earnings in the manufacturing sector to total annual retained earnings. This function is then used to generate quarterly figures for manufacturing retained earnings, because these figures are not available in the national income accounts. Equation (15.37) relates output originating in the manufacturing sector to the various relevant components of aggregate demand. Equation (15.38) connects output originating in housing (explicit and implicit rental payments) to housing stock and personal disposable income. In equation (15.39), the change in

---

[5] If the overall price level is determined elsewhere in the system (as explained below), one sector price equation is determined by identity when all the others are known.

unfilled orders is a function of the change in sales originating in the manufacturing sector and government defense spending.

The remaining stochastic equations deal with price formation and interest-rate determination. In equations (15.40)–(15.45), various sector prices depend on present and previous changes in the wholesale price index plus various factors affecting individual sectors. In particular, prices of capital goods depend on the amount of investment in recent periods. Equations (15.46) and (15.47) relate the short-term interest rate to the discount rate and the ratio of free reserves to required reserves, and the long-term interest rate to a weighted average of present and previous short-term rates.

Most of the identities [equations (a)–(cc)] serve only to define one symbol in terms of others for ease of presentation. However, a few of the equations do determine key variables not explicitly estimated stochastically in the system. For example, equation (a) determines the overall price level, given sector prices and quantities that are determined elsewhere. The GNP deflator is defined as the ratio between current and constant dollar GNP and is not estimated directly. Since the sum of factor shares must equal the sum of aggregate demand, which has already been estimated in the system, one factor share must be a residual. In equation (e), corporate profits before income taxes is defined in this way. The rest of the identities are sufficiently straightforward not to require additional comment.

All the stochastic equations and identities of the Wharton EFU model are given in the next pages, followed immediately by definitions of all the variables in alphabetical order. Unless specifically noted, all the stochastic equations have been estimated by two-stage least squares, using 12 principal components as the exogenous instruments, for the period 1948.1–1964.4. Each stochastic equation is followed by the multiple coefficient of determination adjusted for degrees of freedom ($\bar{R}^2$), the standard error estimate of the residual variance adjusted for degrees of freedom (S_e), the Durbin–Watson statistic (d), and a reference to the original discussion of the function in this book. The standard error estimates of the coefficients are given parenthetically for all cases except the constant terms. A value of $d < 1.4$ indicates significant positive auto-correlation of the residuals, which means that the standard error estimates are biased downward and $\bar{R}^2$ is biased upward. Since d is less than 1.4 in many of the equations, the relative goodness-of-fit statistics should be interpreted with additional caution.

STOCHASTIC Equations of the Wharton EFU Model

Equation No.	Equation	$\bar{R}^2$	S_e	d	Page Ref.

(15.1)
$$\frac{C_{ns}}{Y} = 0.2273 - 0.4590 \left[\frac{\Delta Y}{Y} + 0.75\left(\frac{\Delta Y}{Y}\right)_{-1} \right.$$
$$\hphantom{xxxxx} (0.0485)$$
$$+ 0.50\left(\frac{\Delta Y}{Y}\right)_{-2} + 0.25\left.\left(\frac{\Delta Y}{Y}\right)_{-3} \right]$$
$$+ 0.7232 \ \frac{1}{4} \sum_{i=1}^{4} \left(\frac{C_{ns}}{Y}\right)_{-i}$$
$$\hphantom{x} (0.0512)$$

$\bar{R}^2 = 0.825$, $S_e = 0.0048$, $d = 1.58$, Ref. 62

(15.2)
$$C_{na} = -11.52 + 0.1570Y - 0.0574(K_{na})_{-1}$$
$$\hphantom{xxxxx} (0.0274) \hphantom{xx} (0.0251)$$

$\bar{R}^2 = 0.965$, $S_e = 0.94$, $d = 1.29$, Ref. 168

(15.2a)
$$C_{na} = -14.19 + 0.1157Y - 0.0209(K_{na})_{-1} + 0.0552(C_d^e)_{-1}$$
$$\hphantom{xxxxx} (0.0370) \hphantom{xx} (0.0333) \hphantom{xxxx} (0.0327)$$

$\bar{R}^2 = 0.964$, $S_e = 0.95$, $d = 1.28$, Ref. 169

(15.3)
$$C_a = 48.54 + 0.1346[Y - (Tr/p_c)] - 54.19(p_a/p_c)$$
$$\hphantom{xxxx} (0.0228) \hphantom{xxxxxxxx} (10.20)$$
$$- 0.430Un - 4.129\delta_s + 1.835Cr - 0.0744(K_a)_{-1}$$
$$(0.175) \hphantom{xx} (0.458) \hphantom{xx} (0.478) \hphantom{xx} (0.0180)$$

$\bar{R}^2 = 0.916$, $S_e = 1.27$, $d = 1.13$, Ref. 168

(15.3a)
$$C_a = 30.27 + 0.1055[Y - (Tr/p_c)] - 47.54(p_a/p_c)$$
$$\hphantom{xxxx} (0.0265) \hphantom{xxxxxxxx} (10.59)$$
$$- 0.097Un - 3.269\delta_s + 0.899Cr$$
$$(0.234) \hphantom{xx} (0.609) \hphantom{xx} (0.647)$$
$$- 0.0449(K_a)_{-1} + 0.120(C_d^e)_{-1}$$
$$(0.0226) \hphantom{xxx} (0.056)$$

$\bar{R}^2 = 0.917$, $S_e = 1.26$, $d = 1.06$, Ref. 169

(15.4)
$$I_{pm} = -17.45 + 24.59Cp_{-1} + 0.1308 \sum_{i=0}^{7} A_i(X_m)_{-i-2}$$
$$\hphantom{xxxxx} (2.30) \hphantom{xxxxx} (0.0139)$$
$$+ 0.1644 \sum_{i=0}^{7} A_i(L_m)_{-i-2} - 1.158 \sum_{i=0}^{7} A_i(i_L)_{-i-2}$$
$$(0.0610) \hphantom{xxxxxxxx} (0.292)$$
$$- 0.0248 \sum_{i=0}^{7} A_i(K_m)_{-i-2}$$
$$(0.0065)$$

$\bar{R}^2 = 0.895$, $S_e = 0.68$, $d = 0.58$, Ref. 135

(15.4a)
$$I_{pm} = -11.43 + 15.62Cp_{-1} + 0.0892 \sum_{i=0}^{7} A_i(X_m)_{-i-2}$$
$$\hphantom{xxxxx} (1.86) \hphantom{xxxxx} (0.0105)$$
$$+ 0.1069 \sum_{i=0}^{7} A_i(L_m)_{-i-2} - 0.0271 \sum_{i=0}^{7} A_i(K_m)_{-i-2}$$
$$(0.0416) \hphantom{xxxxxxxx} (0.0044)$$
$$+ 0.3954ANP_m - 0.3201 \sum_{i=0}^{7} A_i(i_L)_{-i-2}$$
$$(0.0454) \hphantom{xxxx} (0.2189)$$

$\bar{R}^2 = 0.953$, $S_e = 0.46$, $d = 1.17$, Ref. ——

Equation No.	Equation	$\bar{R}^2$	S_e	d	Page Ref.
(15.5)	$I_{pr} = 1.49 + 0.0140[(Z_{-1} + Z_{-2})/2] - 0.0043$ $\qquad (0.0081) \qquad\qquad\qquad (0.0032)$ $\times [(K_{r_{-1}} + K_{r_{-2}})/2] + 0.0429 \sum_{i=0}^{7} A_i Z_{-i-3}$ $\qquad\qquad\qquad\qquad (0.0113)$ $- 2.1042 \sum_{i=0}^{7} A_i(i_L)_{-i-3}$ $\quad (0.2695)$	0.810	0.55	0.65	139
(15.5a)	$I_{pr} = -0.40 + 0.0061[(Z_{-1} + Z_{-2})/2] - 0.0082$ $\qquad\quad (0.0083) \qquad\qquad\qquad (0.0034)$ $\times [(K_{r_{-1}} + K_{r_{-2}})/2] + 0.0443 \sum_{i=0}^{7} A_i Z_{i-3}$ $\qquad\qquad\qquad\qquad (0.0108)$ $- 1.5519 \sum_{i=0}^{7} A_i(i_L)_{-i-3} + 0.1647 ANP_n$ $\quad (0.3291) \qquad\qquad\qquad (0.0612)$	0.828	0.52	0.79	——
(15.6)	$I_{pc} = -35.72 + 0.1742C_{-1} - 0.0563K_{c_{-1}} + 0.0363$ $\qquad\qquad (0.0278) \quad (0.0170) \qquad (0.0475)$ $\times \sum_{i=0}^{7} A_i C_{-i-2} + 2.396 \sum_{i=0}^{7} A_i(i_L - i_s)_{-i-2}$ $\qquad\qquad\qquad (0.461)$	0.930	1.05	0.73	139
(15.7)	$I_h = 58.26 + 0.0249Y - 45.52(p_h/p_r)_{-3}$ $\qquad\qquad (0.0033) \quad (4.76)$ $+ 1.433(i_L - i_s)_{-3}$ $\quad (0.282)$	0.820	1.15	0.36	197
(15.7a)	$I_h = 33.65 + 0.0101Y - 26.48(p_h/p_r)_{-3}$ $\qquad\qquad (0.0017) \quad (2.44)$ $+ 0.261(i_L - i_s)_{-3} + 0.00851I^s_{h-1}$ $\quad (0.146) \qquad\qquad (0.00054)$	0.964	0.51	1.63	——
(15.8)	$\Delta I_{im} = -5.03 + 0.0718S_{m-1} - 0.0539I_{im-2}$ $\qquad\qquad\quad (0.0272) \qquad (0.0224)$ $+ 0.422\Delta U_{-1} + 0.203(U_{-2} - U_{-4})$ $\quad (0.083) \qquad\quad (0.040)$ $+ 2.074STR$ $\quad (0.603)$	0.768	1.62	1.20	219
(15.9)	$\Delta I_{in} = -14.94 + 0.0668(S_n)_{-1} - 0.1173(I_{in})_{-2}$ $\qquad\qquad\quad (0.0456) \qquad\quad (0.0476)$ $+ 0.2180(C_d)_{-1} + 0.3325\Delta X_m$ $\quad (0.0634) \qquad\quad (0.0686)$ $+ 40.43[p_m - (p_m)_{-2}]$ $\quad (11.82)$	0.610	1.33	1.59	219

Equation No.	Equation	$\bar{R}^2$	S_e	d	Page Ref.
(15.10)	$\dfrac{F_{if}}{N} = 0.0117 + 0.0064(Y/N) - 0.0041(p_{if}/p_f)$ $(0.0013)(0.0015)$	0.305	0.0014	1.69	224
(15.11)	$F_{im} = 3.51 + 0.0329S_m + 0.0960\Delta I_{im} - 2.14(p_{im}/p_m)$ $(0.0022)(0.0194)(0.74)$	0.900	0.32	0.76	224
(15.12)	$F_{ic} = -2.57 + 0.0293Y - 1.97(p_{ic}/p_m) + 0.6014$ $(0.0073)(1.48)(0.1109)$				
	$\times \dfrac{1}{4}\sum_{i=1}^{4}(F_{ic})_{-i}$	0.989	0.41	0.79	224
(15.13)	$F_e = -38.88 + 0.1665X_{wt} + 34.33(p_{wt}/p_e)$ $(0.0128)(4.78)$				
	$+ 0.4663\,\dfrac{1}{4}\sum_{i=1}^{4}(F_e)_{-i}$ (0.0534)	0.976	0.89	1.26	228
(15.14)	$\ln X_m = 0.645 + 0.7547\ln(Nh)_m + 0.2402\ln(K_m Cp)$ $(0.0889)(0.0574)$				
	$+ 0.881\text{prod}$ (0.037)	0.984	0.024	0.82	254
(15.15)	$\ln X_m^c = 0.645 + 0.7547\ln N_m^C + 0.2402\ln K_m$				
	$+ 0.881\text{prod}$				
(15.16)	$h_m = 0.797 + 0.00076X_m + 0.00126\Delta X_m + 0.1906Cp$ $(0.00021)(0.00044)(0.0423)$				
	$- 0.0126wr_m$ (0.0050)	0.711	0.0081	1.61	259
(15.17)	$wr_m - (wr_m)_{-4} = 0.050 + 0.1481\,\dfrac{1}{4}\sum_{i=1}^{4}(Un - U^*)_{-i}$ (0.0234)				
	$+ 4.824(p_{c-1} - p_{c-4})$ (0.521)				
	$- 0.1946[(wr_m)_{-4} - (wr_m)_{-8}]$ (0.0705)	0.657	0.0568	1.03	268
(15.18)	$p_m = -0.170 + 0.5418(W/X)_m + 0.2465Cp$ $(0.0890)(0.0361)$				
	$+ 0.0429\delta_{KW} + 0.6064\dfrac{1}{4}\sum_{i=1}^{4}(p_m)_{-i}$ $(0.0063)(0.0703)$	0.982	0.0098	0.60	300
(15.19)	$\ln X_n = 0.270 + 0.9897\ln(Nh)_n + 0.2755\ln K_n$ $(0.2108)(0.0371)$				
	$+ 0.082\text{prod}$ (0.084)	0.976	0.022	0.55	254
(15.20)	$h_n = 1.186 + 0.0155Cp - 0.0391wr_n$ $(0.0235)(0.0011)$	0.963	0.0069	0.78	260

Equation No.	Equation	$\bar{R}^2$	S_e	d	Page Ref.
(15.21)	$wr_n - (wr_n)_{-4} = 0.176 + 0.3019[wr_m - (wr_m)_{-4}]$ (0.1286) $+ 1.298[(p_c)_{-1} - (p_c)_{-4}]$ (0.777) $- 0.4741[(wr_n)_{-4} - (wr_n)_{-8}]$ (0.1154)	0.330	0.0539	0.59	269
(15.22)	$U^* = -5.42 + 1.231Un + 8.929 \dfrac{1}{\frac{1}{4}\sum_{i=0}^{3}(Un)_{-i}}$ $\quad\quad (0.083) \quad (2.939)$ $+ 0.3245 \dfrac{1}{4}\sum_{i=1}^{4}(U^*)_{-i}$ (0.0899)	0.929	0.38	1.21	269
(15.23)	$\dfrac{N_L^M}{N} = 0.4255 + 0.0169 \dfrac{1}{\frac{1}{4}\sum_{i=0}^{3}(Un)_{-i}}$ $\quad\quad\quad (0.0095)$ $+ 0.1139(N_G^M/N) - 0.000478t$ $(0.1020) \quad\quad (0.000020)$	0.952	0.0023	0.59	262
(15.24)	$D_m = 0.29 + 0.0467 \sum_{i=0}^{N}(p_k I_{pm} - D_m)_{-i} + 2.952\delta_1$ $\quad\quad (0.0009) \; i=0 \quad\quad\quad (0.159)$	0.988	0.43	0.28	——
(15.25)	$D_r = 1.27 + 0.0205 \sum_{i=0}^{N}(p_k I_{pr} - D_r)_{-i} + 0.249\delta_1$ $\quad\quad (0.0003) \; i=0 \quad\quad\quad (0.071)$	0.994	0.17	0.15	——
(15.26)	$D_c = 3.54 + 0.0281 \sum_{i=0}^{N}(p_k I_{pc} - D_c)_{-i}$ $\quad\quad (0.0006) \; i=0$	0.962	0.56	0.21	——
(15.27)	$D_h = 2.08 + 0.0116 \sum_{i=0}^{N}(p_h I_h - D_h)_{-i}$ $\quad\quad (0.0001) \; i=0$	0.993	0.25	0.07	——
*(15.28)	$T_b = -2.90 + 0.0721NI + 0.3839t$ $\quad\quad (0.0113) \quad\quad (0.0557)$	0.994	0.71	0.27	——
*(15.29)	$T_c = -4.26 + 0.46(P_{cb} - IVA)$				
*(15.30)	$T_r = -2.95 + 1.565(U_N \cdot N_L^C/100) + 0.5069t$ $\quad\quad (0.113) \quad\quad\quad\quad (0.0059)$	0.997	0.42	1.43	——
*(15.31)	$T_p = -12.8 + 0.153(PI + SCI - Tr)$				
(15.32)	$PB = 1.24 + 0.0607(\Delta pX + 0.75\Delta pX_{-1} + 0.50\Delta pX_{-2}$ $\quad\quad (0.0067)$ $+ 0.25\Delta pX_{-3}) + 0.9529 \dfrac{1}{4}\sum_{i=1}^{4}(PB)_{-i}$ $\quad\quad\quad\quad\quad (0.0112)$	0.992	0.47	0.66	285
(15.33)	$RI = -0.57 + 23.08[\Delta p_r + 0.75\Delta(p_r)_{-1} + 0.50\Delta(p_r)_{-2}$ $\quad\quad (7.97)$ $+ 0.25\Delta(p_r)_{-3}] + 1.0614 \dfrac{1}{4}\sum_{i=1}^{4}(RI)_{-i}$ $\quad\quad\quad\quad\quad (0.0090)$	0.998	0.33	0.66	285

Equation No.	Equation	$\bar{R}^2$	S_e	d	Page Ref.
(15.34)	$Dv = 0.17 + 0.1103(P_{ca} + D_m + D_r + D_c)$ $\qquad (0.0122)$ $\qquad + 0.5289 \; \dfrac{1}{4} \displaystyle\sum_{i=1}^{4} (Dv)_{-i}$ $\qquad (0.0576)$	0.990	0.31	1.26	**286**
(15.35)	$IVA = 0.08 - 219.33\Delta p_m$ $\qquad\qquad (13.40)$	0.785	0.98	2.32	——
†(15.36)	$RE_m = -1.12 + 0.5810\,RE$ $\qquad\qquad\quad (0.0461)$	0.908	0.48	0.80	——
(15.37)	$X_m = -2.40 + 0.2213C_{ns} + 1.133C_d + 0.526I_p$ $\qquad\qquad (0.0442) \qquad (0.206) \qquad (0.203)$ $\qquad + 0.397\Delta I_i + 0.385G_d$ $\qquad (0.124) \qquad (0.038)$	0.983	3.25	0.63	——
(15.38)	$X_h = -7.30 + 0.0093 \displaystyle\sum_{i=0}^{N} \left(I_h - \dfrac{D_h}{P_h} \right)_{-i} + 0.1321\,Y$ $\qquad\qquad (0.0024) \qquad\qquad\qquad\qquad\quad (0.0125)$	0.995	0.67	0.42	——
(15.39)	$\Delta U = -0.55 + 0.344\Delta S_m + 0.670\Delta G_d + 6.61\delta_{UW}$ $\qquad\qquad (0.196) \qquad (0.155) \qquad (1.58)$	0.440	2.70	1.54	——
(15.40)	$\Delta p_{ns} = 0.0039 + 0.063\Delta p_m + 0.130\Delta p_{m-1} + 0.088\Delta p_f$ $\qquad\qquad\quad (0.075) \qquad (0.052) \qquad\quad (0.014)$	0.672	0.0028	1.50	307
(15.41)	$\Delta p_{na} = -0.0031 + 0.768\Delta p_m + 0.238\Delta p_{m-1}$ $\qquad\qquad\quad (0.143) \qquad (0.116)$	0.682	0.0064	1.30	307
†(15.42)	$\Delta p_a = 0.0012 + 0.597\Delta p_{m-1}$ $\qquad\qquad\quad (0.125)$	0.549	0.0020	1.56	307
(15.43)	$\Delta p_k = -0.0332 + 0.792\Delta p + 0.3915(I_p/X)$ $\qquad\qquad\quad (0.143) \qquad (0.1192)$	0.564	0.0047	1.67	307
(15.44)	$\Delta p_h = -0.0017 + 1.265\Delta p + 0.00143$ $\qquad\qquad\quad (0.206) \qquad (0.00037)$ $\qquad \times [(I_p + I_h) - (I_p + I_h)_{-2}]$	0.439	0.0075	1.71	307
(15.45)	$\Delta p_e = -0.0022 + 0.646\Delta p_m + 0.488\Delta p_{m-1}$ $\qquad\qquad\quad (0.233) \qquad (0.189)$	0.496	0.0105	1.46	307
(15.46)	$i_s = 0.42 + 0.994i_d - 0.0895(FR)$ $\qquad\qquad (0.034) \qquad (0.0118)$	0.961	0.19	1.02	317
(15.47)	$i_L = 0.21 + 0.086i_s + 0.889(i_L)_{-1}$ $\qquad\qquad (0.028) \qquad (0.037)$	0.972	0.12	1.79	318

* Estimated for shorter time periods due to changes in tax laws.
† Estimated yearly.

IDENTITIES

(a) $p_{ns}C_{ns} + p_{na}C_{na} + p_aC_a + p_kI_p + p_kI_{pf} + p_hI_h + p_m\Delta I_i + p_f\Delta I_{if} + p_gG + p_eF_e$

$\qquad - p_{if}F_{if} - p_{im}F_{im} - p_{ic}F_{ic} = pX$

(b) $C_{ns} + C_{na} + C_a + I_p + I_{pf} + I_h + \Delta I_i + \Delta I_{if} + G + F_e - F_{if} - F_{im} - F_{ic} = X$

(c) $NI = pX - T_b - D_m - D_n - D_h - D_f - SD$

(d) $PI = NI - P_{cb} + D_v + T_r + I_{gc} - SocSec$

(e) $P_{cb} = NI - W_m - W_n - W_f - W_g - PB - FF - RI$

(f) $Y = (PI - T_p)/p_c$

(g) $X = X_m + X_n + X_h + X_f + X_g$

(h) $p_n = \dfrac{pX - p_mX_m - p_hX_h - p_fX_f - p_gX_g}{X_n}$

(i) $W_m = wr_m \cdot h_m \cdot N_m$

(j) $W_n = wr_n \cdot h_n \cdot N_n$

(k) $U_n = \dfrac{N_L^M - N_m - N_n - N_g^M - N_g^c - N_f - N_e}{N_L^M - N_g^M} \times 100$

(l) $p_c = \dfrac{p_{ns}C_{ns} + p_{na}C_{na} + p_aC_a}{C_{ns} + C_{na} + C_a}$

(m) $I_p = I_{pm} + I_{pr} + I_{pc}$

(n) $\Delta I_i = \Delta I_{im} + \Delta I_{in}$

(o) $S_m = X_m - \Delta I_{im}$

(p) $S_n = X_n - \Delta I_{in}$

(q) $C_d = C_a + C_{na}$

(r) $P_{ca} = P_{cb} - T_c - IVA$

(s) $RE = P_{ca} - Dv$

(t) $p_kL_m = RE_m + D_m$

(u) $Cp = X_m/X_m^c$

(v) $K_a = \displaystyle\sum_{i=0}^{40} (0.929)^i C_{a-1}$

(w) $K_{na} = \displaystyle\sum_{i=0}^{40} (0.929)^i C_{na-i}$

(x) $K_m = \displaystyle\sum_{i=0}^{60} (0.953)^i I_{pm-i}$

(y) $K_n = \displaystyle\sum_{i=0}^{60} (0.953)^i (I_{pr} + I_{pc})_{-i}$

(z) $K_r = \sum_{i=0}^{N} \left(I_{pr} - \frac{D_r}{p_k}\right)_{-i}$

(aa) $K_c = \sum_{i=0}^{N} \left(I_{pc} - \frac{D_c}{p_k}\right)_{-i}$

(bb) $Z = X - \Delta I_i - \Delta I_{if} - G$

(cc) $C = C_{ns} + C_{na} + C_a$

LIST OF VARIABLES

$*A_i$	distributed lag weights (Almon weights) for investment functions. Normalized weights are $A_0 = 0.074$; $A_1 = 0.132$; $A_2 = 0.170$; $A_3 = 0.183$; $A_4 = 0.171$; $A_5 = 0.138$; $A_6 = 0.091$; $A_7 = 0.041$
$*ANP_m$	first investment anticipations of manufacturing firms, billions of 1958 dollars
$*ANP_n$	first investment anticipations of nonmanufacturing firms, billions of 1958 dollars
C	total consumption, billions of 1958 dollars
C_a	purchases of automobiles and parts, billions of 1958 dollars
C_d	purchases of consumer durables, billions of 1958 dollars
$*C_d^e$	index of consumer anticipations, 1958 = 100 (Survey Research Center)
C_{na}	purchases of consumer durables except automobiles and parts, billions of 1958 dollars
C_{ns}	purchases of consumer nondurables and services, billions of 1958 dollars
Cp	Wharton School index of capacity utilization
$*Cr$	dummy variable for consumer credit terms: -1 when Regulation W was in effect; 0 otherwise before 1955; 1 in 1955.1 and later
$*d_1$	dummy variable for change in depreciation tax laws: 0 before 1962; 1 in 1962.1 and later
$*d_{KW}$	dummy variable for Korean War: 1 in 1950.3–1951.1; 0 elsewhere
$*d_s$	dummy variable for supply shortages in automobiles: 3 in 1948.1–1948.2; 2 in 1948.3–1948.4; 1 in 1949.1 and 1952.3; 0 elsewhere
$*d_{UW}$	dummy variable for unfilled orders: 1 in 1950.3 and 1951.1; -1 in 1953.3–1953.4; 0 elsewhere
D_c	depreciation for commercial and other investment, billions of current dollars
$*D_f$	depreciation for farm investment, billions of current dollars
D_h	depreciation for residential construction, billions of current dollars
D_m	depreciation for manufacturing investment, billions of current dollars
D_r	depreciation for regulated and mining investment, billions of current dollars
D_v	dividends, billions of current dollars
F_e	exports, billions of 1958 dollars
$*FF$	income of unincorporated businesses, farm sector, billions of current dollars
F_{ic}	imports of goods and services except food products, raw materials, and semi-manufactured goods, billions of 1958 dollars

F_{if}	imports of crude and manufactured food products, billions of 1958 dollars
F_{im}	imports of nonfood crude materials and semimanufactured goods, billions of 1958 dollars
*FR	net free reserves as a percentage of total required reserves
*G	government purchases of goods and services, billions of 1958 dollars
*G_d	government purchases for national defense, billions of 1958 dollars
h_m	index of hours worked in the manufacturing sector, 40 hours $= 1.00$
h_n	index of hours worked in the nonmanufacturing sector, 40 hours $= 1.00$
*i_d	discount rate, percent
*I_{gc}	interest paid by government and consumers, billions of current dollars
I_h	investment in nonfarm residential construction, billions of 1958 dollars
*I_h^s	private nonfarm housing starts, thousands
I_i	stock of nonfarm inventories, billions of 1958 dollars, arbitrary origin
*I_{if}	stock of farm inventories, billions of 1958 dollars, arbitrary origin
I_{im}	stock of manufacturing inventories, billions of 1958 dollars, arbitrary origin
I_{in}	stock of nonmanufacturing nonfarm inventories, billions of 1958 dollars, arbitrary origin
i_L	Moody's average yield on bonds, percent
I_p	nonfarm investment in plant and equipment, billions of 1958 dollars
I_{pc}	plant and equipment investment in commercial and other industries, billions of 1958 dollars
*I_{pf}	farm investment in plant and equipment, billions of 1958 dollars
I_{pm}	manufacturing investment in plant and equipment, billions of 1958 dollars
I_{pr}	regulated and mining investment in plant and equipment, billions of 1958 dollars
i_s	short-term interest rate on four- to six-month commercial paper, percent
IVA	inventory valuation adjustment, billions of 1958 dollars
K_a	stock of automobiles, billions of 1958 dollars
K_c	stock of commercial and other investment, billions of 1958 dollars, arbitrary origin
K_m	stock of manufacturing investment, billions of 1958 dollars
K_{na}	stock of consumer durables except automobiles, billions of 1958 dollars
K_n	stock of nonmanufacturing nonfarm private investment, billions of 1958 dollars
K_r	stock of regulated and mining investment, billions of 1958 dollars, arbitrary origin
L_m	cash flow in the manufacturing sector, billions of 1958 dollars
*N	total population, millions
*N_e	self-employed except agriculture, millions
*N_f	number of farm workers, millions
*N_g^c	number of civilian government employees, millions

$*N_g^M$	number of military personnel, millions
NI	national income, billions of current dollars
N_L^M	total labor force including armed forces
N_m	manufacturing employees, millions
N_m^c	manufacturing labor force, millions
N_n	nonmanufacturing nonfarm private employees, millions
p	implicit GNP deflator, 1958 = 1.00
p_a	implicit deflator for automobiles, 1958 = 1.00
PB	nonfarm unincorporated business income, billions of current dollars
p_c	implicit consumption deflator, 1958 = 1.00
P_{ca}	corporate profits after taxes, billions of current dollars
P_{cb}	corporate profits before taxes adjusted for IVA, billions of current dollars
p_e	implicit deflator for exports, 1958 = 1.00
$*p_f$	prices received by farmers, 1958 = 1.00
$*p_g$	implicit deflator for government purchases, 1958 = 1.00
p_h	implicit deflator for nonfarm residential construction, 1958 = 1.00
PI	personal income, billions of current dollars
$*p_{im}$	implicit deflator for nonfood material imports, 1958 = 1.00
p_k	implicit deflator for nonresidential fixed business investment, 1958 = 1.00
p_m	implicit deflator for gross output originating in the manufacturing sector, 1958 = 1.00 (identical with wholesale price level excluding food and farm products)
p_n	implicit deflator for gross output originating in the nonmanufacturing nonfarm private sector, 1958 = 1.00
p_{na}	implicit deflator for consumer durables except automobiles, 1958 = 1.00
p_{ns}	implicit deflator for consumer purchases of nondurables and services, 1958 = 1.00
$*p_r$	price index of rent, 1958 = 1.00
$*prod$	productivity trend: increases at 2.8 percent per year through 1959 and 3.6 percent per year 1960 to 1964
$*p_{wt}$	price of world trade, 1958 = 1.00
RE	retained earnings, billions of current dollars
RE_m	retained earnings of manufacturing corporations, billions of current dollars
RI	rent and net interest paid, billions of current dollars
$*SCI$	social security contributions of individuals, billions of current dollars
$*SD$	statistical discrepancy plus subsidies less current surpluses of government enterprises, billions of current dollars
S_m	sales originating in the manufacturing sector, billions of 1958 dollars

S_n	sales originating in the nonmanufacturing nonfarm private sector, billions of 1958 dollars
*SocSec	social security contributions of employers, employees, and self-employed, billions of current dollars
*STR	dummy variable for steel strike: $+1$ in 1952.2, 1959.2, and 1960.1; -1 in 1952.3; -2 in 1959.3; 0 elsewhere
*t	time trend, 1948.1 $= 1$
T_b	indirect business taxes and business transfers, billions of current dollars
T_c	corporate income taxes, billions of current dollars
T_p	personal tax and nontax payments, billions of current dollars
Tr	transfer payments, billions of current dollars
U	unfilled orders, billions of 1958 dollars
U^*	unemployment rate of males age 25 to 34, percent
Un	unemployment rate, percent
*W_f	wage bill for farm workers, billions of current dollars
*W_g	wage bill of government employees, billions of current dollars
W_m	wage bill of manufacturing employees, billions of current dollars
W_n	wage bill of nonmanufacturing nonfarm private employees, billions of current dollars
wr_m	wage rate of manufacturing employees, thousands of dollars per year
wr_n	wage rate of nonmanufacturing employees, thousands of dollars per year
X	gross national product, billions of 1958 dollars
*X_f	gross output originating in the farm sector, billions of 1958 dollars
*X_g	gross output originating in the government sector, billions of 1958 dollars
*X_h	gross output originating from rent, billions of 1958 dollars
X_m	gross output originating in the manufacturing sector, billions of 1958 dollars
X_m^c	maximum gross output originating in the manufacturing sector, billions of 1958 dollars
X_n	gross output originating in the nonmanufacturing nonfarm nonrent private sector, billions of 1958 dollars
*X_{wt}	index of world trade, 1958 $= 100.0$
Y	personal disposable income, billions of 1958 dollars
Z	final sales in the private sector, billions of 1958 dollars

* Denotes an exogenous variable.

METHODS OF FORECASTING AND CONTROLLING THE CYCLE

FORECASTING WITH
LEADING INDICATORS:
THE NATIONAL BUREAU METHOD

16.1   GENERAL DESCRIPTION OF THE INDICATORS

The purpose of the first two parts of this book has been to develop and explain a model of the postwar U.S. economy that is both based on sound theoretical principles and forecasts accurately. Before examining the properties and characteristics of the model that has been constructed, it is useful to consider some other widely used methods of forecasting. These alternative methods may give predictions that are superior to those generated by an econometric model, or such a model may be improved by using additional information which reflects shifts in exogenous variables (such as attitudes) or in institutional arrangements (such as wage–price guidelines). Since a large part of business forecasting relies on methods other than econometric models, it is instructive to discuss some of these methods.

The first method to be examined is the use of leading indicators, developed by the National Bureau of Economic Research (NBER). Essentially this method consists of analyzing the behavior of many economic time series over the course of business cycles, determining the dates of turning points for these cycles, and then grouping series with noticeable cyclical characteristics into leading, coincident, or lagging indicators, depending on whether they usually lead, move with, or lag behind cyclical movements of aggregate economic activity.

The roots of this process go back to Wesley C. Mitchell's pioneering work *Business Cycles*,[1] written in 1913. In this work, part of which was described

---

[1] W. C. Mitchell, *Business Cycles* (Berkeley: University of California Press, 1913).

in Part II, Mitchell analyzed the behavior of many economic series over the business cycle and set the stage for later work. The formal analysis of various types of indicators was undertaken in response to a request to measure the possible severity and length of the 1937 recession. The type of statistical indicators desired and a list of those most nearly fitting these requirements were first issued in a release by Mitchell and Arthur F. Burns, *Statistical Indicators of Cyclical Revivals.*[2] A much more comprehensive report, *Measuring Business Cycles,*[3] was issued by Burns and Mitchell in 1946. Although the list of leading, coincident, and lagging indicators continues to be modified and updated, these reference works represent the basic approach to the subject, which is now considered in greater detail.

The classification of indicators by the NBER depends on determining *reference cycles*. Reference cycle peaks and troughs represent the approximate dates when aggregate economic activity reaches its cyclical high and low levels. Numerous problems exist in trying to obtain one or more series that will serve as unequivocal indicators for reference cycles. For purposes of the NBER method, monthly data are needed, although some quarterly series are used. At the time of Mitchell and Burns' original study, GNP was available only annually, although it is of course now available quarterly; some attempts have even been made to interpolate it monthly, although these figures are not yet generally accepted. Mitchell and Burns originally favored GNP in current dollars as the most reliable indicator, as opposed to some physical measure such as industrial production or employment. This was based on the belief that prices, as well as output, had a regular cyclical pattern. However, since prices have risen in the past two recessions, this is no longer the case. The dates of postwar reference cycles have been based on constant-dollar magnitudes rather than current-dollar magnitudes in those few instances where there has been a difference. At present the single most important indicator for determining reference cycles is the industrial production index. If the criterion is selected that a peak has been reached when changes in the next three months are all downward, and a trough has been reached when changes in the next three months are all upward, then the peaks and troughs of the postwar reference cycles and the industrial production index coincide almost identically. Peaks and troughs are not necessarily the highest and lowest points during a cycle, although they are usually quite close to these extreme values.

The only problem with using the industrial production index as an unequivocal measure of reference peaks and troughs is that it has a tendency to turn down for several months at times when much of the economy is still rising. This happened in 1952, 1956, and 1959, all of which happened to be

---

[2] W. C. Mitchell and A. F. Burns, *Statistical Indicators of Cyclical Revivals*, Occasional Paper 69 (New York: National Bureau of Economic Research, 1938).

[3] A. F. Burns and W. C. Mitchell, *Measuring Business Cycles* (New York: National Bureau of Economic Research, 1946).

years of steel strikes, although the downturns were influenced by other factors as well. It has become customary to consider any downturn to be a recession only if current-dollar GNP turns down for more than one quarter; this eliminates these "quasi-cycles." Final sales, retail sales, and personal income are used as corroborative indicators. Although these indices are helpful in determining whether a peak or trough has occurred, they are not as useful as the industrial production index in determining the timing of peaks and troughs. Employment (and unemployment) are also used to determine reference cycles. All postwar recessions have been marked by substantial increases in unemployment, which has not been the case for the quasi-cycles. However, these series are not used for determining the timing of the reference cycles either. There has been a slight tendency for the downturn in unemployment to lag the upturn in industrial production. Essentially, the exact turning points of reference cycles of the postwar period are determined by movements in the industrial production index, and a cycle is said to have occurred if there are large fluctuations in industrial production and unemployment and an actual decrease of more than one quarter in current-dollar GNP.

The general characteristics of the reference cycles can be summarized briefly. The NBER list of reference cycles started in December 1854; from that date to the present there have been 26 cycles with average characteristics as given in Table 16.1.[4] From this table it can be seen that the average

TABLE 16.1 GENERAL CHARACTERISTICS OF REFERENCE CYCLES

	Duration in Months			
	Contraction Peak to Trough	Expansion Trough to Peak	Entire Cycle	
Average All Cycles			Trough to Trough	Peak to Peak
26 cycles, 1854–1961	19	30	49	49
10 cycles, 1919–1961	15	35	50	54
4 cycles, 1945–1961	10	36	46	46
Average, peacetime cycles				
22 cycles, 1854–1961	20	26	45	46
8 cycles, 1919–1961	16	28	45	48
3 cycles, 1945–1961	10	32	42	42

[4] All figures in this chapter are taken from *Business Cycle Developments*, a monthly publication of the Department of Commerce. Supervision of this publication is done by Julius Shiskin, Chief Economic Statistician of the Bureau of the Census, who has been instrumental in developing many of the mathematical techniques now used to analyze the indicators.

length of reference cycles is just about four years, and there is no indication that this length is either increasing or decreasing (although when the current upturn is included, the postwar average will be considerably lengthened). The cycles are clearly asymmetrical, with the average expansion about twice as long as the average contraction, and are becoming more asymmetrical, the longest postwar contraction being 13 months. Cycles are almost always $2\frac{1}{2}$ years or longer; only 1 of the 26 cycles, the short but severe cycle of 1920, was briefer than this (it was 28 months). Fifteen of the 26 cycles are between 34 and 48 months, with the median value equal to 44 months, almost exactly equal to the average peacetime cycle.[5]

Once the dates of reference cycles have been determined, it is possible to classify different series as leading, roughly coincident, or lagging indicators. Originally Burns and Mitchell analyzed 487 different series and finally selected 71 by the criteria discussed below. This list has been updated and modified periodically and presently contains 30 leading, 15 coincident, 7 lagging indicators, and 28 other indicators of importance, for a total of 70. Diffusion indices (discussed below) are also included in a separate list. In the original selection, a series had to lead, be coincident, or lag at no less than two thirds of the reference cycle turning points to be classified as that type of indicator. In general this criterion has continued to be used.

Of these indices, the leading indicators are by far the most important for economic analysis. Coincident and lagging indicators are also useful; the coincident indicators define reference cycles and indicate the stage of the cycle where the economy currently is, and lagging indicators are similarly useful for confirmation of the fact that a cyclical peak or trough has been reached. But the main purpose of the NBER approach is to indicate coming turning points through early warning signals and to gauge the amplitude of the forthcoming downturn or upturn. Thus the major effort in this approach has been to select good leading indicators. Mitchell and Burns list the following 11 criteria, which they used to differentiate ideal leading indicators from others.[6]

1. The longer are its average leads at past revivals.
2. The more uniform are these leads in occurrence and length.
3. The closer its specific cycles come to having a one-to-one correspondence to business cycles.
4. The more clearly defined are its specific cycles.
5. The less intense are its erratic movements in comparison with the amplitude of its specific cycles.
6. The fewer are the changes in the direction of its month-to-month movements.

---

[5] These figures are all based on trough to trough dates.

[6] Mitchell and Burns, *op. cit.*, p. 173.

7. The smaller and more regular are the seasonal variations that have to be "eliminated" before the specific cycles can be studied.
8. The larger are the number of past revivals covered by the series.
9. The farther back in time any irregularities in conformity to business cycle revivals have occurred.
10. The broader is the range of activities represented by the series.
11. The more stable is the economic significance of the process represented.

Criteria 1–4, the ones generally used to judge the efficacy of leading indicators, will be examined in some detail in Section 16.3. Criteria 8 and 9 are not of immediate concern here, because our analysis is restricted to the postwar period. For practical purposes this is also what the NBER does; its list of series and data presently available cover the period 1947 to the present. Statement 10 can be met by adding additional series; 11 refers to the fact that the underlying causes of the fluctuations should remain unchanged. Criteria 5–7, statistical in nature, are considered in Section 16.2.

The idea of choosing various economic series to determine and predict business cycle peaks and troughs without any apparent theoretical structure was severely criticized by Koopmans in a well-known article entitled "Measurement Without Theory"[7] which was a criticism of Burns and Mitchell's *Measuring Business Cycles*. Koopmans states: "The tool kit of the theoretical economist is deliberately spurned. Not a single demand or supply schedule or other equation expressing the behavior of men or the technical laws of production is employed explicitly in the book."[8] His first argument is that economic theory is helpful and necessary for choosing those series which will be most useful in predicting business cycle turning points. His second argument is that without resort to theory, the findings and results cannot be used for policy decisions or other useful tasks because the observed patterns are of unknown reliability. Thus they cannot be qualified by additional information because the underlying structural relationships are unknown. A third argument advanced by Koopmans, which serves to detract somewhat from the issue of primary importance, is that better estimates could be obtained by using more rigorous statistical techniques.

This criticism could hardly be expected to go unanswered, and the reply was undertaken by Vining.[9] His argument is essentially that until several methods have been tried and tested, it is an unnecessary restriction on economic research to insist on one method instead of another. Acceptance of the best method must hinge on results. As for the usefulness of this method for policy decisions, Vining points out (and Koopmans agrees in his reply)

---

[7] T. C. Koopmans, "Measurement Without Theory," *Review of Economics and Statistics*, Vol. 29, No. 3 (August, 1947), pp. 161–172.

[8] *Ibid.*, p. 163.

[9] R. Vining, "Koopmans on the Choice of Variables to Be Studied and of Methods of Measurement," *Review of Economics and Statistics*, Vol. 31, No. 2 (May, 1949), pp. 77–94.

that it is not possible to assign values of social utility to research projects which have not yet been completed.

In our view the rebuttal by Vining is well taken. If a group of economists, or any scientists for that matter, wish to develop a method for prediction without the use of theory, the main issue in such a case should be whether in fact this method is successful on a true *ex ante* basis. If such a method has a better record than another method based on theory, then for strictly predictive purposes the former method is to be preferred. However, such a choice makes it all the more important to examine the predictive record of the NBER leading indicators in some detail. Before turning to this problem, though, it is necessary to explain the methods of data adjustment and combination which are used to generate the series used for prediction. The reader who is not interested in these statistical problems is advised to turn to Section 16.3 at this point.

16.2   STATISTICAL TECHNIQUES OF DATA ADJUSTMENT

The economic time-series data analyzed by the NBER often contain many erratic fluctuations which make it very difficult to ascertain turning points. Several methods of adjustment are used to smooth the data and separate cyclical movements from seasonal and erratic fluctuations; the most important method is seasonal adjustment. Not all time series need to be seasonally adjusted; movements in stock prices and interest rates, for example, contain no seasonal component. However, components of aggregate demand, particularly retail sales, have large seasonal fluctuations. Employment (and unemployment) also have definite seasonal patterns. Typical patterns for these series are shown in Figure 16.1.[10]

The most common method of seasonal adjustment is known as the ratio to moving average method. A moving average of the data is first calculated, and then the ratio of each individual observation to the corresponding moving average figure is obtained. These ratios are then averaged separately for each month; the resulting averages are the monthly adjustment factors. Each observation is then divided by its respective monthly adjustment factor to obtain a seasonally adjusted figure.

A slight variant of this process is to assume that the seasonal adjustment factor is of constant size instead of a constant proportion of each observation. In this case, the actual difference between the yearly average and the *i*th month is calculated. These differences are then averaged separately for each month and the respective monthly average is added to each observation. In regression analysis this is done through the inclusion of seasonal dummy

---

[10] 1963 figures are used because unemployment remained almost steady and retail sales rose steadily during that year. Thus almost all the variation shown in these graphs is due to the seasonal component.

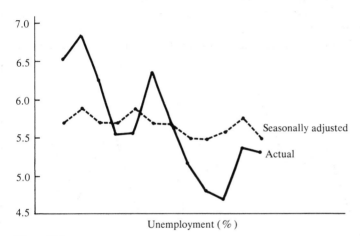

Figure 16.1

variables in the regression equation. Although this method may be useful for ratios or other trendless variables, it will give very poor results if applied to series with strong trends. The retail sales series, for example, has just about the same percentage increase in December as it did 20 years ago. However, the volume of retail sales is about three times as large as it was then, so the absolute size of the seasonal adjustment is also about three times as large. A seasonal adjustment factor that remains at a constant absolute size is worthless in this case, a case that applies to most of the NBER series and in fact to most of the time series used in aggregate econometric analysis.

A third method, the one used extensively by the NBER, is to calculate seasonal adjustment factors, which can change over the sample period. The method of calculation is quite complex and is not considered here in detail.[11]

---

[11] For a detailed explanation, see *The X-11 Variant of the Census Method II Seasonal Adjustment Program*, Census Bureau Technical Paper 15 (Washington: Government Printing Office, 1965).

In brief, recent observations in the sample period are given greater weight in determining the seasonal adjustment factors than observations in the more distant past. Thus if the percentage of yearly sales in a given month has recently increased, the seasonal adjustment factor will incorporate this information and adjust to a new value. As an example of how flexible seasonal adjustment factors might be useful, we consider manufacturing sales and profits for the period 1947–1949 and the period 1963–1965. Three-year averages for these time periods are shown in Figure 16.2.

If seasonal adjustment factors were used that retained the same value for each year in the sample period in spite of changing seasonal patterns, they might average to zero over the sample period. Then the observed unadjusted data would also masquerade as seasonally adjusted data. This would be a most unsatisfactory resolution of the problem.

This variable-weight method of seasonal adjustment has been criticized by some econometricians because it removes more than strictly seasonal components and may distort the true underlying pattern of cyclical fluctuations

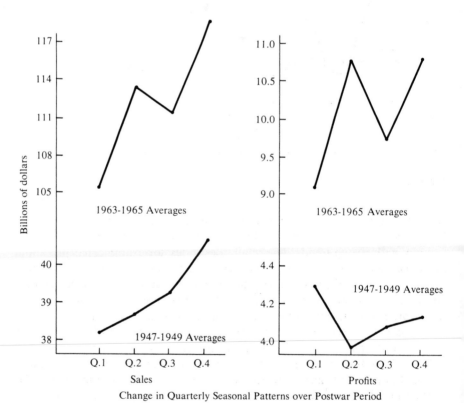

Change in Quarterly Seasonal Patterns over Postwar Period

Source: Quarterly Financial Report for Manufacturing Corporations

Figure 16.2

in the economy.[12] However, the alternative method often proposed—of constant-value seasonal adjustment factors (for example, through dummy variables)—sometimes fails to remove any of the seasonal component. This is hardly a more satisfactory result. For example, the use of constant seasonal weights based on 1947–1965 data would not have removed the downturn in manufacturing sales and profits that occurred in the third quarters of 1963, 1964, and 1965. This would have given the totally erroneous impression that recessions were beginning in the summers of each of these three years. Because the NBER moving seasonal adjustment program eliminates problems of this sort, it is an important tool in analyzing current trends in economic time series.

Even when seasonal fluctuations are eliminated from the data, some series still contain erratic month-to-month fluctuations that obscure their true cyclical behavior. To minimize this problem, moving averages of the seasonally adjusted series are taken. The length of moving average is equal to the number of months for cyclical dominance, which is computed as follows. First, a smoothed moving average is calculated from the seasonally adjusted data which eliminates virtually all erratic fluctuations. This is the *cyclical component*. Then the absolute value of the average monthly percentage change is calculated for both the seasonally adjusted data and the smoothed moving average. The ratio R of these two averages,

$$R = \frac{\text{average percentage change of seasonally adjusted series}}{\text{average percentage change of moving average}}$$

is known as the *irregular component*. The irregular and cyclical components are then computed for one-month, two-month, and up to five-month spans. The length of the moving average is equal to the first time span for which the average change of the cyclical component is larger than the average change of the irregular component, provided this relationship continues to hold for all longer spans. If changes in the irregular component are still larger than in the cyclical component for five-month spans, the length of the moving average is arbitrarily set at six months. A moving average of the data, where the length of the average is equal to the months necessary for dominance by the cyclical factor, is used to analyze those indicators with large erratic monthly fluctuations.

There are some drawbacks to this method which are more serious than those connected with the seasonal adjustment process. First, the results are sensitive to the way in which the moving average of the seasonally adjusted data is constructed. Different interpretations of the length of the original moving average may lead to different measures of months for cyclical dominance, which itself affects the turning points. Second, since moving

---

[12] See especially M. Nerlove. "Spectral Analysis of Seasonal Adjustment Procedures," *Econometrica*, Vol. 32, No. 3 (July, 1964), pp. 241–285, especially p. 270.

averages are involved, two or three additional months are lost before a trend in the data may be ascertained. This may be quite important when trying to predict turning points. However, some further refinement of the data is necessary if one is going to use series that do have large erratic fluctuations; this can be seen in such diverse series as housing starts and inventory investment, shown in Figure 16.3.

One might conceivably argue that such widely fluctuating series ought not to be included in a list of leading indicators. However, if it can be shown that moving averages of these series are themselves reliable indicators that signal downturns and upturns far enough ahead to compensate for the additional lost two or three months, then they can reasonably be considered as useful indicators.

Besides smoothing the data for individual series, different indicators are combined by the NBER into a single composite series known as a *diffusion index*. A diffusion index simply records the percentage of components of the composite series which has risen over a given time span, which usually varies from one to nine months. The range of each diffusion index is thus defined to extend from 0 percent (all components turning down) to 100 percent

Housing Starts 1964-1965

Inventory Investment 1964-1965

Figure 16.3

(all components turning up). One could conceivably construct a diffusion index for all leading indicators, or various subsets of the leading indicators, but so far this has not been done. Instead, the indices are based on firm or industry components of a certain economic indicator, for example, new orders for 36 durable goods industries, stock prices of 80 industries, or profits of 700 companies. Most diffusion indices are leading indicators, although some are also calculated for coincident and lagging indicators. They are used for predicting turning points, much as the individual leading indicators are used, and the patterns of the two are rather similar. One drawback is that most of the diffusion indices are based on a nine-month span, which adds an additional four-month delay before the results are available.

An interesting idea that has recently been suggested but is still in the experimental stage is the amplitude-adjusted composite index. On a preliminary basis, composites have been made of 8, 12, and 20 leading indicators, 6 coincident indicators, and 3 lagging indicators. The absolute value of the average percentage change per month (or per n-month span) is calculated for each indicator. Then the (current percentage change/average percentage change) ratio is calculated for each indicator and these normalized changes combined into a composite index. Such an index might prove quite useful, because it would show present changes in all the leading indicators weighted in a meaningful way. However, since these indices are not yet published on a regular basis by the NBER or Department of Commerce, one can only speculate on how helpful they might be.

16.3   PREDICTIVE POWER OF THE LEADING INDICATORS

The real test of the usefulness of the NBER approach to business cycle analysis is the predictive accuracy of the leading indicators. Recall from Section 16.1 that the four principal criteria were (1) average lead time, (2) uniformity of lead time, (3) one-to-one correspondence with reference cycles, and (4) clearly defined specific cycles. These criteria are now examined for each of the 30 leading indicators over the postwar period. Conditions (1) and (2) can be measured simply as the mean lead time and its standard deviation. For (3) and (4) the main problem has been extra cycles indicated by the leading indicators. In only 2 of 117 cases did a leading indicator miss a turning point indicated by a reference cycle. The number of extra cycles (if any) are determined for each leading indicator and the average percentage change of the indicator during these false cycle(s) is compared to the change during true reference cycles. If the change during the false cycle(s) is very small, its existence is not very serious, but if this change is large enough to be confused with a true downturn, the usefulness of the indicator is seriously impaired. Although the leading indicators could conceivably indicate either false downturns or false upturns, none of the latter has occurred, partially because the postwar recessions have all been quite short and mild.

All the data used to calculate these tests are taken from *Business Cycle Developments*. However, the actual peaks and troughs of each series were chosen by us, since exact turning points are not given for most of the leading indicators at reference cycle peaks and troughs and are not given for any of the indicators at false turning points. The actual seasonal adjusted data were used to determine peaks and troughs in most cases; occasionally moving averages were used where there were large erratic fluctuations. As mentioned earlier, a peak or trough was established for monthly series if the series declined or rose respectively in each of at least the next three months. Sometimes this rule was breached when there was a very small decline from a peak or rise from a trough, but this hardly ever occurred. For quarterly series, the same method was followed, with peaks and troughs being defined if they were followed by at least two consecutive quarters of decrease or increase, respectively. The results for average lead time and uniformity of lead time are given in Table 16.2.

In assessing the usefulness of various indicators, we can first disregard any series with a mean value of four months or less, since peaks and troughs have been defined to occur only when changes in the following three months of a suspected turning point are all in the same direction; an additional month is necessary to collect and publish the data. This eliminates 6 series at the peaks and 24 series (both out of 30) at the troughs. Next, those series can be disregarded where the mean is less than 1.5 times the standard error; this removes from consideration those series that have a very erratic lead time and are likely to turn down two or more years before a reference cycle peak is reached. This eliminates 19 of the remaining 24 series at the peaks and 3 of the remaining 6 series at the troughs. Only 2 of the series are useful for predicting both peaks and troughs: accession rate and the change in unfilled orders. This is not a very impressive record.

We now examine the question of "false cycles" for the leading indicators. As indicated, no false signals of recovery have occurred in the postwar period, so that only false signals of recession are examined. In this typical situation, shown in Figure 16.4, the decrease in the series from D to E represents a decline associated with a reference cycle peak, whereas the decline from B to C represents a false indication of a downturn. In Table 16.3 the average percentage decrease of each leading indicator during the four postwar recessions is compared to the decline in that indicator during the "false cycles," which occurred in 1952, 1956, 1959, and 1962 (see p. 459).

Only four of the leading indicators signaled no false downturns; only three more had downturns that were all less than half the average downturn in actual recessions. Although the 1952 "false recession" was the most extensively documented, almost half of the indicators also turned down in 1962. The indication of a recession at that time was given added credibility

TABLE 16.2 LEAD TIMES OF LEADING INDICATORS

Series Name[a]	At Peaks		At Troughs		Where Significant
	Mean	Standard Deviation	Mean	Standard Deviation	
Average workweek	10.5[b]	7.2	2.0	3.2	
Accession rate	7.8[b]	4.9[b]	4.5[b]	2.4[b]	Both
Nonagricultural placements	0.5	0.5	−1.5	1.4	
[c]V Layoff rate	2.5	1.4	2.0	3.0	
V Temporary layoffs	8.3[b]	6.1	2.0	3.3	
V Unemployment claims	5.3[b]	5.3	1.2	2.4	
New orders, durable goods	6.3[b]	5.0	3.5	4.0	
New orders, machinery and equipment	10.7[b]	12.5	−1.5	2.4	
Construction contracts	3.3	8.5	1.0	3.2	
Contracts and orders	13.0[b]	18.4	1.8	3.1	
Capital appropriations	7.3[b]	9.1	0.5	2.1	
Housing starts	13.2[b]	10.6	4.8[b]	5.1	
New building permits	12.8[b]	9.8	5.5[b]	5.7	
Net business formation	9.7[b]	10.3	2.3	2.2	
New business incorporations	3.3	3.3	1.3	2.1	
V Liability of business failures	11.3[b]	8.2	2.8	2.6	
V Large business failures	11.2[b]	12.8	3.8	3.3	
Profits after taxes	10.0[b]	7.8	2.5	4.4	
Price/unit labor costs	12.8[b]	11.4	0.0	2.2	
Profits/sales	7.0[b]	4.4[b]	2.5	4.4	Peaks
Profits/income originating	11.0[b]	6.6[b]	4.0	3.9	Peaks
Stock prices	3.5	2.4	5.2[b]	4.0	
Change in business inventories	6.8[b]	8.8	2.5	4.4	
Change in manufacturing and trade inventories	6.0[b]	6.7	1.0	3.2	
Change in manufacturing inventories of materials and supplies	4.0	2.6	2.5	3.5	
Percentage reporting higher inventories, purchased materials	10.0[b]	11.1	1.0	1.7	
Buying policy, percentage reporting commitments 60 days and up	7.0[b]	4.6[b]	0.5	2.1	Peaks
Vendor performance, percentage reporting slower delivery	10.2[b]	8.5	6.7[b]	3.5[b]	Troughs
Change in unfilled orders	11.7[b]	6.7[b]	7.5[b]	4.0[b]	Both
Industrial materials prices	12.8[b]	9.8	5.5[b]	5.7	

[a] Series are listed in the order in which they appear in *Business Cycle Developments*.
[b] In means column, mean value greater than 4.0 months; in standard deviations column, mean greater than 1.5 times standard deviation (significantly different from zero at the 10 percent level).
[c] V represents an inverted series.

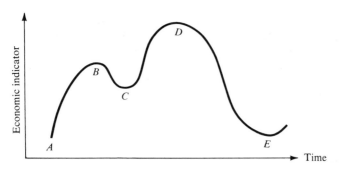

Figure 16.4

by the fact that the stock market had its biggest percentage decrease in the entire postwar period. Although it might at first appear that only a few indicators predicted a downturn in 1956, 11 other indicators turned down in 1955 and did not turn up again until the 1958 trough.

One might think that the diffusion indices would work better than the individual leading indicators, since they smooth out erratic fluctuations. However, a look at these indices shows that these false downturns were not erratic but were spread throughout much of the economy. If anything, the false recessions of 1952, 1956, 1959, and 1962 are more apparent in the diffusion indices than they are in the individual series. Of the seven diffusion indices calculated for leading indicators, five of five (two were not available then) turned down in 1952, and all seven turned down in 1955 and 1959. In 1962, the indices for profits and capital appropriations did not turn down (although actual constant-dollar investment did) but all the remaining five registered a downturn.

What conclusions can be drawn from this poor performance? Clearly the set of 30 leading indicators considered together cannot be used to forecast turning points, because the lead time is either too short or too erratic, and too many false recessions are signaled. However, it is possible that certain of the indicators might be more useful than others and could be singled out as reliable leading indicators. The indicators with substantial and reliable lead times, however, all have at least two extra cycles. This suggests that, like other series, they turned down with varying lead times, but then, unlike the others, turned up again when the recession did not materialize. But this is not very useful when trying to decide whether a turning point has in fact been reached.

In spite of this, some valuable information can be gathered from these indicators. First, the economy has never turned down without ample warning from these indicators. Thus the loose talk that suggested downturns in the latter part of 1964 and 1965 was not based on any analytical or statistical knowledge and can hardly be explained on any rational grounds. Second,

TABLE 16.3 FALSE SIGNALS OF RECESSION BY LEADING INDICATORS

Series Name	Percent Downturn in:				Av. Reference Cycles	Number False Cycles
	1952	1956	1959	1962		
Average workweek	2.7				4.9	1
Accession rate	23.4	17.0			35.5	2
Nonagricultural placements	9.2				19.4	1
Layoff rate	67.7	38.1	44.8	29.2	56.1	4
Temporary layoffs	45.6			20.1	47.7	2
Unemployment claims	34.6				46.2	1
New orders, durable goods	28.3			5.5	27.0	2
New orders, machinery and equipment					26.0	0
Construction contracts	41.8				26.1	1
Contracts and orders					22.4	0
Capital appropriations					33.1	0
Housing starts	33.7				20.6	1
New building permits	50.3				28.7	1
Net business formation	3.5		3.2		16.7	2
New business incorporations	19.5				11.0	1
Liability of business failures	24.2	40.0			43.3	1
Large business failures					42.5	1
Profits after taxes	37.9				24.3	1
Price/unit labor costs					8.4	0
Profits/sales	28.8	14.8		5.8	28.9	3
Profits/income originating	43.4			3.6	24.5	2
Stock prices		10.9		20.9	13.4	2
Change in business inventories	17.5			2.2	11.2[a]	2
Change in manufacturing and trade inventories	23.3		8.5	2.7	13.2[a]	3
Change in manufacturing inventories of materials and supplies	8.8	1.9	4.5	3.4	3.9[a]	4
Percentage reporting higher inventories, purchased materials	52.4			27.6	46.8	2
Buying policy, percentage reporting commitments 60 days and up	40.5			13.1	38.1	2
Vendor performance, percentage reporting slower delivery	81.3			25.0	62.9	2
Change in unfilled orders	3.6			0.9	2.7[a]	2
Industrial materials prices				8.6	26.0	1
Number of series turning down	23	6	4	14		
Number turning down with decrease greater than half of reference cycle average	21	4	3	4		

[a] Absolute change, not percentage change.

the widespread downturn of the indicators in latter 1955 might have been a warning signal to the then current administration that there were fundamental weaknesses in the economy, and that a policy of tight money, when it finally became effective, would make the ensuing recession just that much more severe.

We have considered the NBER approach from a forecasting point of view, which is its most vulnerable flank. It should be pointed out that their approach does give a general picture of the forces that cause the cumulation of prosperity, and some of these, such as the profit squeeze, form an integral part of our business cycle theory. Their painstaking collection and verification of hundreds of series is also extremely valuable for documenting cycles; their reference cycle dates are virtually undisputed. The series serves as a valuable historical record and sheds light on the causes of past depressions. But as a practical method of forecasting, the leading indicators cannot be used very effectively or accurately.

CHAPTER 17

FORECASTING WITH
ANTICIPATORY DATA

17.1   CONSUMER ATTITUDES AND BUYING PLANS

It is often thought that the course of aggregate economic activity is largely determined by exogenous shifts in anticipations and expectations about the future. From a forecasting viewpoint, predictive ability may be improved by using indices incorporating these exogenous factors if they cannot be closely approximated by the endogenous variables of the system. Such indices are not intended to explain the structure of the economy or the theory of a given component of aggregate demand; rather, their usefulness depends on how well they predict. The nature of the various indices is sometimes questioned, with suggestions that they might predict better if certain changes were made. Although this method of approach presents an interesting area for consideration in its own right, it is not considered here. Instead the presently available indicators are analyzed for their predictive content.

The type of indicators used to predict purchases of consumer durables, especially automobiles, is considered first. The survey most widely used for this purpose has been developed by the Survey Research Center (SRC) at the University of Michigan. The information gathered for predictive purposes at the center is basically of two types: attitudinal data (what the consumer thinks about the general state of the economy) and buying plans. The questions that are used to form indicies of attitudes and buying plans are the following:

Attitudes:
1. We are interested in how people are getting along financially these days. Would you say that you and your family are better off or worse off financially than you were a year ago?

2. Now, looking ahead—do you think that a year from now you people will be better off financially, or worse off, or just about the same as now?

3. Now turning to business conditions in the country as a whole—do you think that during the next twelve months we'll have good times financially, or bad times, or what?

4. Looking ahead, which would you say is more likely—that in the country as a whole we'll have continuous good times during the next five years or so, or that we will have periods of widespread unemployment or depression, or what?

5. About the things people buy for their house—I mean furniture, house furnishings, refrigerator, stove, television, and things like that. In general, do you think now is a good or a bad time to buy such large household items?

6. Now, speaking of prices in general, I mean the prices of the things you buy—do you think they will go up in the next year or so, or go down, or stay where they are now?

Buying Plans:

1. Do you expect to buy or build a house for your own year-around use during the next twelve months?

2. Do you people expect to buy a car during the next twelve months or so?[1]

Participants in the survey are also asked additional questions, but these are the ones that are used to obtain the indices which are used for prediction. The answers given to each question are scaled (2 = positive or optimistic, 1 = neutral, and 0 = negative or pessimistic). The total point score obtained for each family unit surveyed is then averaged for all participants and converted to some index figure. One index consists of only the first six questions; this is commonly known as the attitude index or six-point index. A separate index is available for the buying plans, and a third index, called the eight-point index, combines both attitudes and buying plans. Note that in all indices each included question is weighted equally.

These data can be analyzed either on a cross-section or time-series basis. In the early years of the survey, insufficient observations were available for time-series analysis. Early cross-section analysis suggested (through reinterviews) that the buying plans were useful for predicting purchases of consumer durables but that the attitudes were not.[2] However, as more observations have become available and several time-series studies were made, this view has been decidedly reversed. In a review of the 10-year forecasting record of the attitudes and buying plans, Eva Mueller, one of the coworkers at the SRC, found after a thorough study that "throughout, the contributions of car buying intentions is negligible when attitudes also appear in the equation."[3] A very similar result

---

[1] These are taken from George Katona *et al., 1963 Survey of Consumer Finances,* Monograph 34, Survey Research Center (Ann Arbor: University of Michigan, 1964), and F. G. Adams, "Consumer Attitudes, Buying Plans, and Purchases of Durable Goods: A Principal Components, Time Series Approach," *Review of Economics and Statistics,* Vol. 46, No. 4 (November, 1964), p. 348.

[2] See for instance, J. Tobin, "On the Predictive Value of Consumer Intentions and Attitudes," *Review of Economics and Statistics,* Vol. 41, No. 1 (February, 1959), pp. 1–11.

[3] Eva Mueller, "Ten Years of Consumer Attitude Surveys: Their Forecasting Record," *Journal of the American Statistical Association,* Vol. 58, No. 4 (December, 1963), p. 913.

was also found by Adams.[4] On the basis of these studies, we conclude that the six-point (attitude) index is the relevant one for prediction on a time-series basis, and restrict further discussion to this series. Further work has also suggested that the attitudes are most useful in predicting purchases of automobiles rather than other durables. Thus the following analysis refers to auto purchases unless otherwise stated.

The question of lag structure must also be examined. The SRC attitude index, like all other anticipatory data, is useful only if it can be used to predict purchases in the future. In most of the studies undertaken, this index was used to predict car sales either one or two quarters ahead. A monthly comparison by Friend and Adams[5] showed that maximum predictive power is obtained with a four- or five-month lag, which agree with the quarterly studies. Thus the attitudes index should be lagged one or two quarters if used in a regression explaining purchases of automobiles.

The reasons for using attitudes in forecasting have been explained by Mueller. We quote extensively from her explanation to make clear what we are criticizing later.

> If consumer sentiment were fully determined by income level or recent income change, the collection of attitudinal data would be superfluous. It is more plausible to assume that consumer confidence and expectations are affected by a wide variety of changes in the environment—some financial, others nonfinancial. Data on consumer attitudes are needed for three reasons. First, a considerable number of financial developments may affect consumer sentiment such as income level, income changes, price level and price change, debt, amount of liquid reserves, recent additions to savings, possibly capital gains and capital losses (even if unrealized). These factors may have to be combined in complicated patterns to approximate their joint impact on consumer sentiment. Measuring attitudes directly may be easier and more reliable than attempting to derive attitudes indirectly from all financial sources which may be relevant. Secondly, similar financial developments may be perceived differently under different circumstances (for example, the same stimulus may be seen differently when it occurs a second time) and therefore may provoke different emotions and reactions. Expectations are not merely a projection of recent trends but are influenced by current perceptions and news received. Thirdly, attitudes may be influenced by political and economic events which are nonquantitative in nature.[6]

The most questionable part of this argument is the insistence that factors other than income that affect durable purchases be lumped together in the "exogenous" category and left unexplained. As shown in Chapter 6, it is quite reasonable to expect previous stocks, relative prices, credit conditions and supply shortages to be important determinants of the purchases of consumer durables. If these variables can be readily determined and easily quantified, there would appear to be no reason why they should not be included in such a function.

[4] Adams, *op. cit.*, especially p. 358.

[5] I. Friend and F. G. Adams, "The Predictive Ability of Consumer Attitudes, Stock Prices, and Non-Attitudinal Variables," *Journal of the American Statistical Association*, Vol. 59, No. 4 (December, 1964), p. 1002.

[6] Mueller, *op. cit.*, pp. 901–902.

Another questionable point is the view that consumer attitudes consist of many diverse economic and noneconomic phenomena which are reflected in the compiled index. Most of the questions deal with how individuals feel about the future state of the economy. Since the average individual is probably not a very good forecaster, the future state of the economy in his mind probably is closely related to the present state.[7] Thus a large percentage of the variance of the attitude index might well be explained by some cyclically sensitive indicator. Several such variables were tried by Adams and Green, including the unemployment rate, length of the work week, net accession minus layoffs rate, and an index of capacity utilization, as well as per capita disposable income. They found that 85 percent of the variance of the attitudes index could be explained by a regression of the attitudes on per capita disposable income, length of the work week, and net accession minus layoff rate.[8] Thus one or more of these easily available variables could be used in the automobile equation in place of the attitudes index. As reported in Chapter 6, this was tried in a related study by Friend and Adams, who found that length of the work week worked best. They found that "between 1957 and 1962 the non-attitudinal work week variable does distinctly better than the attitudes. The addition of the S.R.C. attitudes ... does not improve the $\bar{R}^2$ and it appears that their effect is entirely taken care of by the objective variables." They also find that "the relatively good performance of the S.R.C. attitudes ... in 1955 may indicate that they record more effectively the strength of underlying economic forces in some boom periods than do our other variables. However, this inference is based on a single period during which numerous special circumstances apply and we would hesitate to generalize it."[9]

The 1955 situation, which has been discussed in some detail in Chapter 6, deserves more consideration, because the attitudes did predict a rise in auto purchases of approximately the magnitude that occurred. This would agree with Mueller's claim that the same general economic setting may result in different purchasing plans at different times. However, the 1954–1955 period was distinctly marked by a very great easing of credit conditions, partially due to the discontinuation of Regulation W and partially due to the extension of length of contract and percentage of loan to dealer cost beyond previous limits. Inclusion of these credit terms accounts for a large amount, but not all, of the increase in car sales in 1955. Furthermore, the greater availability of cars compared to the Korean War period may also have had some effect on 1955 sales.

George Katona has argued that there were at least three times in the postwar period when consumer purchases of automobiles (and consumer attitudes)

---

[7] For example, less than two months before the passage of the 1964 tax cut, two thirds of the people surveyed by the SRC thought there would not be a tax cut.

[8] F. G. Adams and E. W. Green, "Explaining and Predicting Aggregative Consumer Attitudes," *International Economic Review*, Vol. 6, No. 3 (September, 1965), p. 281.

[9] Friend and Adams, *op. cit.*, pp. 999–1001.

diverged from prevailing movements in income. In 1949, "consumers maintained their optimistic attitudes" in spite of the recession of that year; in 1951 there was "consumer resentment against price increases and their uncertainty or anxiety about the cold war"; and in 1954 "consumers were impressed by the small damage done by the widely advertised recession of 1953, by price stability, and by the availability of 'good buys.' "[10] However, there may be alternative explanations for these occurrences. In 1949 consumers were able to purchase cars without waiting for the first time in the postwar period, as automobile manufacturers finally completed their conversion to peacetime uses and expanded their plants to meet the postwar demand. Furthermore, the stringent regulations of Regulation W were eased and then ended in early 1949, making it much easier for individuals to purchase automobiles on credit. In 1951, Regulation W was reimposed, and fewer cars were available as production was again partially diverted to military needs. Many individuals had rushed out to buy cars at the beginning of the Korean War and thus did not purchase new cars in 1951. Finally, the "resentment against price increases" can be interpreted as the normal downward-sloping demand curve, because, as shown earlier, the demand for cars is highly price-elastic. In 1954 (and 1955) ease of credit restrictions and increases in supply again were important in increasing the number of cars purchased. Finally, given the lack of knowledge of the state of the economy by the average consumer, it is most unlikely that many individuals bought cars because they were impressed by the fact that unemployment went up to 6 percent instead of 8 or 10 percent. Thus it is our view that most of the fluctuations in the attitude index can be explained either by a general cyclical variable or by changes in credit or supply conditions. Empirical evidence for this was presented in Chapter 6, where it was shown that the addition of the consumer attitude index did not improve the explanation of purchases either of autos or other durables.

Mueller's third contention, that car purchases (and attitudes) reflect nonquantitative variables (such as changes in the stock market, war or threat of war, and so on) does not seem to be borne out by the facts. As one major example, the slump in the stock market in 1962, which was the largest percentage decrease to date in the postwar period, did not affect car sales noticeably. The various stages of escalation of the conflict in Vietnam through 1963–1965 had no appreciable effect on car sales, which increased steadily (except for a GM strike) throughout this period. When car sales slumped somewhat in spring 1966, however, all bases were touched in an effort to determine what caused the decrease in sales. Prominently mentioned were the war in Vietnam (which until then had had no effect), the slump in the stock market (milder than 1962 or 1964), the safety campaign, the bad weather, and so on. Somehow

---

[10] G. Katona, "Change in Consumer Expectations and Their Origin," in *The Quality and Economic Significance of Anticipations Data*, Universities—National Bureau Conference, Vol. 10 (Princeton, N.J.: Princeton University Press for NBER, 1960), p. 79.

lost in the confusion was the fact that the economy had been growing at an exceptionally rapid rate during the last quarter of 1965 and the first quarter of 1966. When this rate of growth (in other sectors than the automobile industry) slackened somewhat, cyclically sensitive indicators such as unemployment and length of work week were affected, which in turn affected car sales. Furthermore, inflation and increased social security taxes had decreased real per capita disposable income to the extent that 1966 levels were below corresponding 1965 levels.

We have suggested that success of the attitudes in the early postwar period was due to changing credit and supply conditions: when these variables are included in a regression explaining car purchases, the attitudes make no additional net contribution. We have quoted from other studies to show that the attitudes did not add to predictive power in the 1957–1962 period. In the 1963–1965 period their performance was no better. As discussed in Chapter 6, the attitudes predicted a decrease in car sales in mid-1963 that did not occur, and they have also had several other minor fluctuations that cannot easily be related to movements in car purchases. Furthermore, they have underestimated the growth in car purchases that occurred during the latter period. In the period 1952–1962 a 1 percent increase in the attitudes index was associated with a 1.8 percent increase in car purchases.[11] However, in the period 1963–1965, the attitudes index increased less than 9 percent, while actual car purchases increased almost 30 percent. Thus their predictive record does not appear to have improved in the recent past.

17.2   INVESTMENT ANTICIPATIONS

The next anticipatory data considered is the expectational series used to predict fixed business investment. Although many different series are issued by various public and private organizations, our analysis will concentrate on the best-known and most widely used data, that issued jointly by the Office of Business Economics and the Securities and Exchange Commission. These anticipatory data, referred to here as the OBE-SEC data, are issued both on a yearly basis (in March of the current year) and on a quarterly basis. The usefulness of both of these series is examined below. We also briefly consider one other well-known series, the McGraw-Hill survey of capital expenditures, which is issued annually in November of the previous year.

The OBE-SEC data are fundamentally different from the consumer attitudes series generated by the Survey Research Center. At definite intervals, firms are asked to state both their investment during the previous time period and their investment plans during the following time period. In this way, the coverage on anticipated and realized investment is identical, so that the two

---

[11] Friend and Adams, *op. cit.*, p. 992.

series may be compared directly without any intervening transformation. No regression equation is necessary to establish the relationship between the two series, although it may be instructive to calculate such a relationship for other purposes. The surveys are restricted to each individual firm's own invest-ment plans. Participants are not asked to supply their views on the economy in general, the cold war, the President's health, creeping socialism, and other related matters.

Because of the identical coverage of planned and actual investment, it is possible to test the efficacy of these anticipations somewhat more rigorously than was the case for the consumer attitude series. The first comparison designed to test the usefulness of anticipatory data is often made with so-called *naive models*. Naive models can be defined in this context as mechanical projections of previously known data without the use of any judgment. Typical naive models used here include the following:

1. This period will be the same as last period.
2. The change during this period will be the same as the change during the last period.
3. The change during this period will be equal to the average change over the sample period.

If an average of these naive models predicts better than a given anticipatory series, it is safe to say that this series will be of little help in forecasting. Both the quarterly and yearly OBE-SEC series far outperform these naive models over the postwar period, however, so that it is reasonable to consider further tests of their predictive ability.

If the anticipations outperform the naive models, it is still possible that a function containing only endogenous variables might predict better than the anticipations. If this were the case, one would expect to find that the percentage of the variance of investment which was explained would be higher for the endog-enous function, and that the expectations, when added, would not be significant and would not improve the fit of the equation. The best way to assess the rela-tive predictive efficacy of these two methods is to compare predictions made from the expectations with predictions made from the endogenous function *outside* the sample period. However, the test described here (which is usually the one performed) is the comparison of the two sets of predictions within the sample period. This biases the results in favor of the endogenous functions, particularly if there are a few extreme values. An estimate of this bias for yearly data is given below, suggesting that it is not a serious problem. If the anticipa-tions term is clearly not significant when added to an endogenous function, it is most unlikely that this is due entirely to the sample period bias. There-fore the next logical test to consider is a comparison of the anticipations with an endogenous explanation of investment. Arthur Okun states the case strongly for preferring the former: "The investment anticipations reported in the Commerce-SEC survey have an impressive record of predictive accuracy.

... I know of no naive model and no "causal" explanation resting on pre-determined variables which rivals the anticipations data in accuracy."[12]

A more stringent test has been proposed, following the approach developed by Modigliani[13] and extended by Jorgenson and Eisner[14] of dividing the investment function into an anticipations function and a realizations function. It has been argued that if the anticipations represent all the relevant information at the time of the investment decision, then the only variables that should be significant in an investment function containing the anticipations are those variables which are part of the realizations function. As has been stressed in Chapter 4, this would include only a short-lagged sales variable. This viewpoint has been stated most forcefully by Modigliani:

> If investment plans are meaningful—a proposition which, of course, cannot be assumed *a priori*, but is by now supported by a number of empirical investigations—then they embody all the information pertaining to the appropriate level of investment in the current period, as seen at the time the plan is made. This information includes, in particular, all relevant initial conditions and anticipations of future variables. ... Actual investment should be expected to deviate from plans only in so far as the actual course of the anticipated variables differs from the anticipations.[15]

This statement, and the previous one by Okun, represent clear testable hypotheses which are now examined.

The yearly anticipations are considered first. These are made available in March on the basis of firms' knowledge through the end of January. Since they do not appear at the beginning of the year, they do not forecast investment a full year ahead; however, they do appear before the first quarter figures are available. The series have appeared since 1947; however, our comparisons begin with 1948. The 1947 predictions were very far off, partially because the survey was just beginning and partially because widespread inflation increased expenditures much more than was expected. The variance of the error from that year alone is almost as large as the variance of the errors of all other years together, and it does not seem reasonable to distort the results because of this one year. Furthermore, 1947 is not included in any of the estimated endogenous investment functions, because the lag structure would require values from 1945, which are heavily influenced by the war.

Actual year-to-year percentage changes are regressed on anticipated yearly percentage changes. These results, which are given below, are compared with a function of endogenous variables in which yearly percentage changes in investment are a function of changes in capacity utilization, last year's changes in

---

[12] A. Okun, "The Predictive Value of Surveys of Business Intensions," *American Economic Review Papers and Proceedings*, Vol. 52, No. 2 (May, 1962), p. 221.

[13] See the references quoted with respect to this point in Chapter 4, p. 97.

[14] D. W. Jorgenson and R. Eisner, in J. S. Duesenberry, G. Fromm, L. R. Klein, and E. Kuh, eds., *The Brookings Quarterly Econometric Model of the United States* (Chicago: Rand McNally, 1965), chaps. 2 and 3.

[15] F. Modigliani, "Comment" on L. R. Klein, "A Postwar Quarterly Model: Descriptions and Applications," in *Models of Income Determination*, Studies in Income and Wealth, Vol. 28 (Princeton, N.J.: Princeton University Press for NBER, 1964), p. 46.

retained earnings, and last year's level of capacity utilization (a proxy variable for lagged sales and the reciprocal of capital stock).

$$(17.1) \quad \frac{I_p - I_{p-1}}{I_{p-1}} = 1.91 + 0.849[(ANP^y - I_{p-1})/I_{p-1}]$$
$$(0.103)$$

$$\bar{R}^2 = 0.806, \ S_e = 4.6 \text{ percent}$$

$$(17.2) \quad \frac{I_p - I_{p-1}}{I_{p-1}} = -110.34 + 2.097\Delta Cp + 2.013\Delta RE_{-1}$$
$$(0.271) \qquad (0.372)$$

$$+ 1.317 Cp_{-1} \qquad \bar{R}^2 = 0.839, \ S_e = 4.2 \text{ percent}$$
$$(0.324)$$

where I_p = plant and equipment expenditures as measured by the OBE-SEC
ANP^y = yearly anticipations of investment as measured by the OBE-SEC
Cp = index of capacity utilization
RE = corporate retained earnings

All lags are in years. All variables are in billions of current dollars except for the index of capacity utilization.

Unless the sample period bias is severe, it would appear that the endogenous function outperforms the anticipations, despite the generally good record of the latter.

To test this bias we estimated the above endogenous equation separately for every year in the sample period, *in each case omitting the year that was to be predicted*. Thus in every case, the prediction was made outside the sample period for which the regression was estimated, so that this source of bias was eliminated. This method would be partially vitiated if the series were highly autocorrelated, for then the missing observation would be highly correlated with the observation in the next time period. However, this problem did not arise, because first differences and annual data were used. The overall results obtained in this manner are very similar, indicating that the sample bias is very small under these conditions. The endogenous function is still better than the anticipations, although it is neither better nor worse than a regression equation between the anticipations and actual investment.

One valid objection to this comparison is that the endogenous function used contains current capacity utilization, which is clearly not known at the time of release of the anticipations. Although this year's rate of capacity utilization can be estimated from last year's data, this will give poorer results than the correct figures. To adjust for this we estimate an additional equation where some sales expectations constructed by us were used instead of capacity utilization; these were of the form[16]

$$\frac{\Delta S_m}{S_m} = (1.03) \times \frac{\text{January sales in year } t}{\text{average sales in year } t - 1}$$

---

[16] The rationale of this term is discussed in Section 17.3.

January sales were used because these are the latest sales figures available at the time of the March release of the investment anticipations. The 1.03 factor represent 1 + the average rate of growth of manufacturing sales during the postwar period. The results are not quite as good as those from the regression equation relating anticipations and investment but are as good as the anticipations themselves.

Such results raise the question of whether the anticipations are at all useful in forecasting yearly investment. This can be determined by calculating a regression containing both endogenous variables and the anticipations; this equation is

$$(17.3) \quad \frac{I_p - I_{p-1}}{I_{p-1}} = -61.14 + \underset{(0.237)}{1.258\Delta Cp} + \underset{(0.380)}{0.516\Delta RE_{-1}}$$

$$+ \underset{(0.229)}{0.735 Cp_{-1}} + \underset{(0.114)}{0.556[(ANP^y - I_{p-1})/I_{p-1}]}$$

$$\bar{R}^2 = 0.941, \ S_e = 2.5 \text{ percent}$$

The anticipations term is clearly significant, and over two thirds of the unexplained variance of the endogenous function is explained by the addition of the anticipations. Note however that the ΔCp and Cp_{-1} variables are still significant; only the RE variable has slipped slightly below the margin of significance. Thus the most stringent test, that only the anticipations are significant except for variables in the realization function, is clearly not met.

The results of all these various experiments are given in Table 17.1 for further examination, because they are contrary to findings by several other economists, including those quoted above.

The McGraw-Hill investment anticipations, which are made available in the first November issue of *Business Week*, are also included in this comparison, but it is clear that they do not measure up to the high standards of the OBE-SEC anticipations. They are available well before the other anticipations, but the advantage of the additional lead time is overcome by the disadvantage of their poor record. A naive model which states that the increase in investment next year would be equal to the average increase over the postwar period (of 7 percent) does somewhat better than the McGraw-Hill figures. Similarly, a naive projection of sales known at the time of the release of the anticipation (calculated as third quarter sales/first quarter sales) regressed on actual percentage changes in investment also gives better predictions than the McGraw-Hill survey; relevant statistics are given in Table 17.1. These figures suggest that businessmen cannot forecast their investment expenditures very accurately in October of the previous year.

The failure of the McGraw-Hill anticipations to predict investment of the following year very accurately is not confined to early years in the sample. The recent predictions for 1964 and 1965 have also been poor. In releasing the

TABLE 17.1 PERFORMANCE OF VARIOUS INVESTMENT RELATIONSHIPS *(all figures are percentage changes)*

Year	Act^a	ANP^b	e_1^c	ANP_r^d	e_2	$Endg_1^e$	e_3	$Endg_2^f$	e_4	$Endg_3^g$	e_5	$Comb^h$	e_6	MGH^i	e_7	Nms^j	e_8
1948	19	15	4	15	4	18	1	17	2	13	6	16	3	-8	27	12	7
1949	-6	-5	-1	-2	-4	-8	2	-8	2	0	-6	-8	2	-5	-1	10	-16
1950	2	-13	15	-9	11	4	-2	5	-3	-4	6	-1	3	-13	15	0	2
1951	24	29	-5	27	-3	21	3	20	4	29	-5	26	-2	45	-21	27	-3
1952	3	4	-1	5	-2	2	1	1	2	0	3	5	-2	13	-10	1	2
1953	7	2	5	4	3	10	-3	12	-5	10	3	9	-2	6	1	6	1
1954	-5	-4	-1	-1	-4	-4	-1	-4	-1	-2	-3	-5	0	-4	-1	4	-9
1955	7	1	6	3	4	15	-8	17	-10	11	-4	10	-3	6	1	2	5
1956	22	22	0	21	1	21	1	21	1	13	9	21	1	30	-8	9	13
1957	5	6	-1	7	-2	4	1	4	1	5	0	6	-1	11	-6	3	2
1958	-17	-13	-4	-9	-8	-15	-2	-14	-3	-14	-3	-15	-2	-7	-10	3	-20
1959	7	4	3	5	2	2	5	-1	6	4	3	6	1	1	6	7	0
1960	10	14	-4	14	-4	11	-1	11	-1	7	3	11	-1	10	0	5	5
1961	-4	-3	-1	-1	-3	1	-5	3	-7	-1	-3	-2	-2	-3	-1	1	-5
1962	9	8	1	9	0	3	6	3	6	10	-1	7	2	4	5	10	-1
1963	5	5	0	6	-1	9	-4	9	-4	9	-4	7	-2	3	2	4	1
1964	14	10	4	10	4	8	6	8	6	12	2	10	4	4	10	7	7
1965	16	12	4	12	4	19	-3	19	-3	11	5	16	0	5	11	7	9
D.F.^{k}			17		16		14		17		14		13		17		16
S.E.^{l}			4.9		4.6		4.0		4.7		4.9		2.5		10.9		8.6

[a] Act, actual annual percentage change in fixed business investment included in the OBE-SEC survey.

[b] ANP, yearly OBE-SEC anticipations available in March.

[c] e_i, errors for each of the categories.

[d] ANP_r, investment predicted from a regression of investment on anticipations [Eq. (17.1)].

[e] $Endg_1$, endogenous function explaining investment [Eq. (17.2)].

[f] $Endg_2$, same equation as in $Endg_1$, but with the year being predicted removed from the sample period in each case.

[g] $Endg_3$, same equation as $Endg_1$ with sales expectations substituted for capacity utilization.

[h] $Comb$, function with both endogenous and anticipatory variables [Equation (17.3)].

[i] MGH, McGraw-Hill survey of investment anticipations, as published in *Business Week* in November of the previous year.

[j] Nms, naive model using only sales figures available through September regressed on actual investment.

[k] D.F., degrees of freedom, used for calculating the standard error of estimate.

[l] S.E., standard error estimate of residual, adjusted for degrees of freedom. A figure of 4.9, for example, means that the standard error estimate of investment in this particular function was 4.9 percent.

1966 figures, *Business Week* noted that the anticipations indicated an 8 percent increase in investment, but admitted that this figure would probably be revised upward.[17]

We have shown so far in this section that an investment function of endogenous variables predicts investment just about as well as the anticipations, even when sample period bias is taken into account and sales expectations are substituted for current capacity utilization. This result should not be interpreted as denigrating the accuracy of the anticipations but rather as indicating that investment may not be as hard to predict as is sometimes assumed. The standard error of an investment function which used only last year's variables and sales expectations based on January sales was only 5 percent compared to an average absolute error of over 10 percent. This is partially due to the fact that investment is primarily a function of lagged variables, as stressed elsewhere in this text.

An intensive special survey conducted by OBE and SEC based on 1955 investment plans and realizations of firms has been used to help determine what kinds of firms had the greatest errors in their anticipations and what were the primary causes for the differences between anticipated and actual investment.[18] The three main reasons were found to be (1) changes in sales and earnings, (2) incorrect or incomplete anticipations, and (3) delays in construction and deliveries. With respect to the first reason, Eisner has shown that although firms may think that earnings affect their change in investment plans, they actually have no independent influence.[19] It is the change in sales and not the (usually) concomitant change in earnings that influences investment realizations. This agrees with the often-stated viewpoint in this text that the realization function depends only on sales, which are included with a short lag to reflect this effect.

The second and third reasons are not included in the realization function, so the anticipations of those industries for which these reasons are most important would probably have the poorest predictive record. Additional information on the second point was added by answers to other questions in this survey. They showed that large firms and/or large investments for a given firm relative to its capital assets were planned accurately, whereas anticipations of small purchases of small or medium-sized firms were apt to be incomplete or grossly in error. Thus the anticipations are less likely to be accurate in those industries

---

[17] "Biggest Year Ever Coming Up," *Business Week*, November 6, 1965, p. 70.

[18] Reports of this survey appear in M. Foss and V. Natrella, "Investment Plans and Realization—Reasons for Differences in Individual Cases," *Survey of Current Business*, Vol. 37, No. 6 (June, 1957), and their "The Structure and Realization of Business Investment Anticipations," in *The Quality and Economic Significance of Anticipations Data, op. cit.*, pp. 387–403.

[19] R. Eisner, "A Permanent Income Theory for Investment: Some Empirical Explorations," *American Economic Review*, Vol. 52, No. 3 (June, 1967), pp. 363–390. He finds that "the relations between past profits and what businesses *say* they will invest the following year is a better one than the relationship between past profits and what they actually do invest. Their actual investment, even merely the timing of it, is more influenced by past sales changes ..." (p. 377).

where small firms account for a relatively large share of investment. This occurs primarily in the commercial and other sector and only negligibly in manufacturing and regulated sectors. Although there are certainly many small firms in manufacturing, they account for a very small percentage of manufacturing investment. Many of these firms buy used plant or equipment, which is not included in the investment figures.

The third point mentioned above would seem to apply more to construction than equipment purchases, and more in turn to equipment purchases with long lead times than with short lead times. The percentage of construction to total plant and equipment is much higher for regulated and commercial investment than for manufacturing investment. The problem of long lead times for equipment is one occurring primarily in the regulated sector. Thus even though almost all the investment in the regulated sector is done by large firms that presumably make complete anticipations, the uncertainties in construction and deliveries are large enough to dilute the efficacy of the anticipations for this sector.

Separate analysis of various sectors shows that this pattern does exist. Anticipations in the manufacturing sector clearly improved any endogenous function that was tried and made a significant contribution to the predictive ability of any manufacturing equation. The anticipations were not as useful for predicting other types of investment. The general quality of anticipations for different sectors is shown in Table 17.2. The anticipations for the manufacturing sector clearly have a better record than those for other sectors. Although the anticipations and endogenous functions do equally well for total investment, the anticipations alone do outperform an endogenous function for the manufacturing sector. A combination function explains 95 percent of

TABLE 17.2   COMPARISON OF INVESTMENT ANTICIPATIONS
FOR DIFFERENT SECTORS

	Manufac-turing	Public Utilities	Transpor-tation	Communica-tions and Commercial	Total Invest-ment
Standard deviation of yearly percentage changes in investment	17.1	12.1	17.8	10.6	12.4
Root-mean-square error of anticipations	6.7	7.2	12.6	6.2	4.9
Percentage of variance explained by regression of investment on antici-pations (estimated in yearly percentage differences)	92	62	58	77	81

the variance of yearly percentage changes in manufacturing investment, a rather high percentage of such a cyclically volatile component of aggregate demand.

The quarterly anticipations are considered next. There are actually two types of quarterly anticipations: those available *before* the current quarter begins (known as first anticipations) and those available midway through the current quarter (known as second anticipations). The discussion here is limited to the first anticipations. Predictions for the first, second, third, and fourth quarters appear in the December, March, June, and September issues of the *Survey of Current Business*, respectively. The second anticipations for the fourth quarter (for example) would also appear in the December issue, but final figures for the fourth quarter are not available until the following March. Thus the first anticipations are available six months before the actual data are released, although they do not predict investment six months ahead of the date when they appear.

The quarterly results are somewhat different from those for the yearly anticipations. The main reason for this is that the *yearly* anticipations, which are available in March, can predict investment 10 months ahead with a smaller standard error than the *quarterly* anticipations, which only predict investment four months ahead. This somewhat surprising result holds for both the entire sample period and for the 1953–1965 subperiod (the anticipations were modified and improved in 1952.3); it holds for total investment and for the broad subgroups listed above. On the other hand, the quarterly endogenous functions are substantially improved by the specification of a more detailed lag structure. The net result of this is that the quarterly anticipations are not as useful as their yearly counterparts for short-term economic forecasting.

There are two principal reasons for the relative deterioration of the quarterly anticipations. One is that the problem of delays and uncertainties of construction and deliveries becomes a much more serious problem for quarterly data than for yearly data, particularly when supply shortages develop and backlogs lengthen. Consider, for example, the situation in 1956 and early 1957 when these developments occurred. Although the changes predicted by the yearly anticipations in 1956 for both manufacturing and other investment were within $\frac{1}{2}$ percent of the actual changes, the quarterly anticipations were high in both categories for five quarters in a row, as noted in Table 17.3. Presumably firms wanted to invest more during the year than they had originally planned at the beginning of the year but could not get delivery as fast as desired. Similar results are found in other periods of short supply.

The second reason for the poorer performance of the quarterly anticipations is their failure to predict turning points very well. This problem is apparent in both manufacturing and other investment. For both categories there is virtually no correlation between changes in actual investment and changes in anticipations for the quarters during which turning points occurred. There is, however, in most cases a highly significant correlation between changes in

TABLE 17.3   PERFORMANCE OF
ANTICIPATIONS IN PERIODS
OF SHORT SUPPLY

(*all figures are in billions of 1958 dollars*)

	Manufacturing		Other	
	Actual	ANP[a]	Actual	ANP
1956.1	14.9	15.1	21.5	20.0
1956.2	15.9	17.0	21.5	21.6
1956.3	16.9	17.5	21.5	22.2
1956.4	16.5	18.0	21.6	22.2
1957.1	16.6	17.2	21.5	22.2
1957.2	16.6	17.5	21.2	21.6

[a] ANP, quarterly first anticipations.

investment during the quarters of the turning point and changes in anticipations during the *following* quarter (that is, after the turning point has already occurred). This tendency is especially marked in the manufacturing sector, as shown in Table 17.4. The correlation coefficient between changes in investment and anticipations of the same quarter is $r = 0.24$, definitely not significant, whereas between investment and lagged anticipations it is $r = 0.91$.[20] A similar

TABLE 17.4   PERFORMANCE OF MANUFACTURING
ANTICIPATIONS AT TURNING POINTS

Date of Turning Point	Actual ΔInv	ΔANP	ΔANP_{-1}
1950.1	0.6	1.2	0.9
1952.2	−0.1	0.5	0.2
1952.4	0.6	0.8	0.2
1953.2	−0.3	−0.7	−0.3
1955.2	0.6	−0.2	0.5
1956.4	−0.4	0.5	−0.8
1957.1	0.1	−0.8	0.3
1957.4	−1.2	−0.3	−1.3
1959.1	0.5	−0.8	1.0
1960.3	−0.1	0.4	−0.3
1961.3	0.1	0.5	0.1
1963.1	−0.1	0.1	0.2
1963.2	0.4	0.2	0.5

[20] The relevant levels of significance are $r = 0.53$ (at the 5 percent level) and $r = 0.66$ (at the 1 percent level).

relationship holds for nonmanufacturing investment. Such results give substantial credence to the claim that businessmen forecast as if "tomorrow will be like today."

The main reason that the yearly anticipations do not exhibit similar tendencies is that in almost all cases a turning point signaling recession or recovery had already occurred by January of the year for which the anticipations were prepared. This also explains why the investment function with a naive sales expectations variable based on January sales performed almost as well as a function that used the current rate of capacity utilization. However, the quarterly results show that the anticipations data are more reliable at identifying a turning point after it has occurred than predicting it in advance.

Because of the larger predictive errors of the quarterly anticipations, it should not be surprising to find that they are not as useful when added to endogenous functions. The principle difference is the finding that the anticipations are not significant and do not improve the fit of the endogenous equation for *total* fixed business investment. To test this a "combination" investment function was constructed that used relevant endogenous variables from each of the sector functions. As can be seen, the manufacturing-sector variables dominate. The results are

$$(17.4) \quad Ip^* = 8.48 + 0.756 ANP \qquad \bar{R}^2 = 0.842, \ S_e = 1.58$$
$$ (0.040)$$

$$(17.5) \quad Ip^* = -29.86 + 43.88 Cp_{-1} + 0.0234[(Z_{-1} + Z_{-2})/2] + 0.1283$$
$$ (3.91) \qquad\quad (0.0151) \qquad\qquad\qquad (0.0227)$$

$$\times \sum_{i=0}^{7} A_i X_{m_{i-2}} + 0.3873 \sum_{i=0}^{7} A_i L_{m_{i-2}} - 0.1651 \sum_{i=0}^{7} A_i(i_L)_{i-3}$$
$$\phantom{\times \sum_{i=0}^{7} A_i X_{m_{i-2}} + } (0.0947) \qquad\qquad (0.0637)$$
$$\bar{R}^2 = 0.948, \ S_e = 0.91$$

$$(17.6) \quad Ip^* = -27.28 + 40.22 Cp_{-1} + 0.0238[(Z_{-1} + Z_{-2})/2] + 0.1016$$
$$ (4.79) \qquad\quad (0.0151) \qquad\qquad\qquad (0.0271)$$

$$\times \sum_{i=0}^{7} A_i X_{m_{i-2}} + 0.3642 \sum_{i=0}^{7} A_i L_{m_{i-2}} - 0.1392 \sum_{i=0}^{7} A_i(i_L)_{i-3}$$
$$\phantom{\times \sum_{i=0}^{7} A_i X_{m_{i-2}} + } (0.0958) \qquad\qquad (0.0664)$$

$$+ 0.1007 ANP \qquad \bar{R}^2 = 0.948, \ S_e = 0.91$$
$$(0.0771)$$

where Ip^* = fixed business investment reported by the OBE–SEC surveys (this differs somewhat from the national income accounting concept)

Cp = Wharton School index of capacity utilization, fraction

Z = final sales originating in the private sector

X_m = output originating in the manufacturing sector

L_m = corporate cash flow in the manufacturing sector

i_L = average yield on corporate bonds, percent

ANP = first quarterly anticipations of OBE-SEC survey

A_i = Almon weights (as given in Chapter 15, p. 439)

All relevant variables are seasonally adjusted at annual rates in billions of 1958 dollars.

In the manufacturing sector, anticipations still contribute to predictive accuracy, but this is not true for the other sectors. Since different endogenous functions exist for the regulated and commercial and other sectors, it would seem reasonable to compare endogenous and anticipatory data for this breakdown of investment. However, the communications anticipations are always included with the commercial and other anticipations, so these optimal comparisons cannot always be calculated. In such cases several alternative results have been provided. The summary statistics for the various sectors are given in Table 17.5.

Except for the manufacturing sector, the results are inconsistent. The anticipations for total nonmanufacturing are not significant when included in the nonmanufacturing investment equation; they are significantly positive in the regulated investment function and are negative in the commercial investment function. This might suggest that there is a definite correlation between investment and anticipations in the regulated sector which is diluted by lack of any

TABLE 17.5 COMPARISON OF ANTICIPATIONS AND ENDOGENOUS VARIABLES

	Anticipations Only		Endogenous Only		Combination Equation		t = ratio of
	$\bar{R}^2$	S_e	$\bar{R}^2$	S_e	$\bar{R}^2$	S_e	ANP
Manufacturing	0.809	0.92	0.889	0.70	0.948	0.48	9.1
Total non-manufacturing	0.782	0.97	0.920	0.59	0.921	0.58	1.2
Regulated	0.431	0.95[a]	0.810	0.55	0.827	0.52	2.7[b]
Commercial and other	0.696	0.57[c]	0.811	0.45	0.820	0.44	2.0[d]

[a] $\bar{R}^2$ between regulated investment with communications and anticipations without communications. The $\bar{R}^2$ between I_{pr} and ANP_r both without communications was even lower (0.427)

[b] The ANP here are *total* nonmanufacturing. The regulated-sector anticipations were non-significantly negative.

[c] $\bar{R}^2$ between commercial investment and commercial anticipations plus communications. The $\bar{R}^2$ between commercial plus communications investment and the corresponding anticipations is substantially higher (0.853).

[d] The ANP here are commercial plus communications.

relationship in the commercial sector. However, when the sector equations are examined, just the opposite result occurs. The regulated sector anticipations are *negatively* correlated with investment in that sector, whereas there is a significant positive relationship between commercial investment and the corresponding anticipations. Although occasional significant correlations do occur between investment and anticipations in these sectors, the results are too irregular to be very useful. On the other hand, the manufacturing sector anticipations are highly significant; yet even in this sector a function of endogenous variables performs better over the sample period than the anticipations alone.

The regulated anticipations perform surprisingly poorly. This is undoubtedly due to the great volatility of investment, even on a quarterly basis, of the transportation industry. As can be seen, it makes virtually no difference whether communications anticipations are included in this group or not.

The method of constructing the anticipations was improved starting in the third quarter of 1952, so it might be argued that most of their poor performance is due to values early in the sample period. This hypothesis was tested in some earlier work by this author,[21] and the results are very similar. For this "improved" period, the $\bar{R}^2$ of the regressions between investment and anticipations were somewhat higher (0.854 for manufacturing and 0.730 for nonmanufacturing), but again the anticipations were helpful only in the manufacturing sector. This is the general pattern for both yearly and quarterly data, and for both the complete and truncated sample period.

A function explaining the difference between the anticipations and actual investment has been formulated by Eisner.[22] His function can be written

$$(17.7) \qquad \left(\frac{Ip - ANP}{ANP}\right)_t = a_0 + a_1 \dot{S}_{t-1} + a_2 \dot{\pi}_{t-1}$$

$$+ \sum_{i=0}^{\infty} \left[\gamma^i \left(a_3 \dot{S}_{t-i} + a_4 \dot{\pi}_{t-i} + a_5 \dot{U}_{t-i} \right. \right.$$

$$\left. \left. + a_6 \frac{Ip_{t-i-1} - ANP_{t-i}}{Ip_{t-i-1}} \right) \right]$$

where $\dot{S}$, $\dot{\pi}$, and $\dot{U}$ are percentage changes in sales, profits, and unfilled orders of machinery. Readers will note the similarity between this function and Eisner's regular investment functions, discussed in Chapter 5. This function is transformed by the usual Koyck distributed lag, so that $[(Ip - ANP)/ANP]_{t-1}$ is also an independent variable.

[21] M. K. Evans and E. W. Green, "The Relative Efficacy of Investment Anticipations," *Journal of the American Statistical Association*, Vol. 61, No. 1 (March, 1966), pp. 104–116.

[22] R. Eisner, "Realization of Investment Anticipations," in *The Brookings Model ...*, op. cit., chap. 3.

This function was tested in a variety of forms (by omitting various combinations of variables) for durable manufacturing, nondurable manufacturing, public utilities, and commercial investment. However, the results cannot be said to have worked very well. Only 6 of the 26 change in sales terms were significant and only 3 of the 22 change in profits terms were significant. The change in unfilled orders variable fared somewhat better, 4 of 9 terms being significant. However, the interpretation of this term is somewhat ambiguous. Its positive sign throughout (except public utilities) indicates that it represents demand factors rather than supply factors. However, as pointed out in Chapter 5, unfilled orders are significant only in those industries where sales represent primarily transitory components of demand. With Eisner's emphasis on the permanent income hypothesis for investment in his other work, it is somewhat surprising that he does not mention this possibility here. At any rate, the sales and profits terms add very little to the explanation.

Without these intermediate terms, the equation becomes

$$(17.8) \qquad \frac{Ip - ANP}{ANP} = b_0 + b_1 \frac{Ip_{-1} - ANP}{Ip_{-1}} + b_2 \left(\frac{Ip - ANP}{ANP} \right)_{-1}$$

To simplify this somewhat, cancel like numerators and denominators; then

$$(17.9) \qquad \frac{Ip}{ANP} = b_0' - b_1 \frac{ANP}{Ip_{-1}} + b_2 \left(\frac{Ip}{ANP} \right)_{-1}$$

or, almost the same thing,

$$(17.10) \qquad \frac{Ip}{ANP} = c_0 + c_1 \frac{Ip_{-1}}{ANP} + c_2 \left(\frac{Ip}{ANP} \right)_{-1}$$

The coefficients c_1 and c_2 are highly significant.

Thus Eisner has shown that the ratio of actual expenditures to anticipations is a function of combinations of lagged values of these variables. There is substantial serial correlation in the errors of the anticipations; however, it was suggested above that this was due to supply phenomena rather than demand phenomena. Eisner does not explicitly test this hypothesis. In either case, the hypothesis that anticipations reflect all previous responses on investment and that the difference between them and actual expenditures can be explained by the change in sales is again rejected.

How, then, should the anticipations be regarded? For the manufacturing sector, they clearly do add to predictive ability, a result that has been verified by every test tried by us. This suggests that more refinement of the other sector series might yield better results. With the series now available, endogenous variables do give a better explanation than the anticipations for nonmanufacturing investment. However, in the absence of a good forecasting equation for investment, one might be well advised to use the anticipations, particularly if forecasting less than a year ahead. They do not predict downturns when none occur, and they are substantially better than naive models. They do tend to miss turning points, but this is an easily observable phenomenon of consensus forecasts. The value of consensus forecasts, especially to timid forecasters, should not be underestimated, for the blame for incorrect predictions can then be spread much more easily. Although endogenous equations tend to give somewhat better predictions on the average, the investment anticipations should continue to be useful to many forecasters.

17.3   INVENTORY AND SALES ANTICIPATIONS

Besides fixed business investment anticipations, the OBE-SEC also issues anticipations for sales and for manufacturing inventories. We consider only manufacturing sales, because other sales (mainly retail) will certainly follow their pattern. The sales anticipations have been issued on a yearly basis since 1948, appearing each March at the same time as the yearly investment anticipations. Since mid-1959, quarterly sales and inventory anticipations have been made available on a regular basis. Most economists agree that the sales anticipations are of very little value. They are the only such series issued by OBE-SEC which give poorer predictions than a naive model. At the time when the yearly sales anticipations are made available, actual January sales figures are also released. As pointed out by Okun,[22] the January sales data contain more relevant information about the course of sales during the year than do the anticipatory data. In other words, the ratio of January sales to the average sales of the previous year, adjusted for a 3 percent growth rate (approximately the average increase in manufacturing sales during the postwar period) gives a better estimate of the change in current year sales than do the March anticipations.[23] This is shown in Table 17.6.

The record for the quarterly sales anticipations is quite similar; their predictive record is no better than a similarly constructed naive model. To compare the anticipations with the correct naive model it is necessary to consider the timing of the release of the quarterly anticipations. Although they predict only one quarter ahead, the figures for the present quarter are not known at the time of their release. Thus the performance of the anticipations must be related to actual figures two quarters ago. Predicted values of this quarter minus actual values of two quarters ago are compared with the actual change over the past half year. These errors of prediction are then compared with the errors of prediction of a naive model. In this case the naive model for predicting $S_{m_t} - S_{m_{t-2(\text{quarters})}}$ is

$$1.01 \times \left[\frac{S_{m_{t-4\text{ months}}}}{S_{m_{t-2\text{ quarters}}}} \right]$$

---

[22] Okun, *op. cit.*, p. 219.

[23] This naive model is similar to one used in B. P. Pashigian, "The Relevance of Sales Anticipatory Data in Explaining Inventory Investment," *International Economic Review*, Vol. 6, No. 1 (January, 1965), p. 79.

TABLE 17.6 PERFORMANCE OF YEARLY SALES
EXPECTATIONS

Year	Actual Change, %	Anticipated Change, %	Error	Projected Change,[a] %	Error
1948	12	5	7	11	1
1949	7	−1	−6	3	−10
1950	16	2	14	1	15
1951	17	9	8	21	−4
1952	4	5	−1	3	1
1953	10	7	3	13	−3
1954	6	−3	−3	−2	−4
1955	13	4	9	10	3
1956	5	6	−1	6	−1
1957	4	8	−4	9	−5
1958	−5	−2	−3	−3	−2
1959	11	9	2	10	1
1960	2	8	−6	8	−6
1961	0	3	−3	−2	2
1962	8	7	1	10	−2
1963	4	4	0	4	0
1964	7	6	1	8	−1
1965	8	6	2	8	0
Average Absolute error			4.0		3.4
RMS error			5.4		5.0

[a] Projected from the naive model

$$\frac{\Delta S_m}{S_{m-1}} = \frac{1.03(S_m \text{ this January})}{S_m \text{ in previous year}}$$

(S_m are manufacturing sales).

For example, the naive projections for forecasting sales for the second quarter
would be

$$\frac{1.01 \times \text{January sales this year}}{\text{average fourth-quarter sales previous year}}$$

The growth rate of 1 percent is used because sales are being projected ahead
an average of one third year.

For the anticipations, the absolute average error is $2.0 billion and the
root mean square error is $2.7 billion; for the naive model, the corresponding
figures are $2.2 billion and $2.7 billion. This would seem to suggest that the
anticipations are marginally better. However, the results are somewhat clouded
by the steel strike in 1959 and the auto strike of 1964. The naive model predicts

that sales in the next quarter will continue to fall at the same rate as they did in the quarter of the strike. This is obviously not a very realistic assumption and does account for the biggest errors in the naive predictions. The strikes might also not be accounted for in the sales expectations, so that large errors would be predicted by the expectations in the strike quarters (compared to the quarters after the strikes for the naive projections). To test this the relevant two observations from each series were deleted and the test statistics were recalculated. The $2.0 and $2.7 billion figures for the anticipations were unchanged, but the figures for the naive model were reduced to $2.0 and $2.5 billion, respectively, suggesting that without the strike quarters the naive model does at least as well as the anticipations, if not better. The conclusion to be drawn from the quarterly sales anticipations is that a naive model predicts just about as well as the anticipations themselves.

Because of their relatively poor performance, the OBE-SEC sales anticipations have not often been used for predictive purposes. The few cases where they have been used are in fixed business investment realization functions or in inventory investment functions. The use of the yearly sales anticipations compared with several naive projections in the latter type of function has been extensively tested by Pashigian. He develops a model of the form

$$(17.11) \qquad (I_i)_t = a_0 + a_1 S^E + a_2 S_t + a_3 (I_i)_{Jan}$$

where I_{i_t} = manufacturing inventory stocks at the *end* of the tth quarter

S^E = the *yearly* sales anticipations for manufacturing (available in March) *or* some naive models based on January sales

S_t = manufacturing sales in the *last month* of the tth quarter

$I_{i_{Jan}}$ = manufacturing inventory stocks at the end of January (since, like sales, this is the most recent figure known when the yearly anticipations are released)

As would be expected, the present sales term is usually not significant, for reasons explained in Chapter 8. The test is essentially whether the sales anticipations can predict inventory investment better than naive projections of sales based on January and previous sales. Although it has been shown that the naive projections actually predict sales better, it is possible that there may be some information contained in the sales anticipations about what businessmen think is going to happen which will help explain how they act in their inventory policy. This is actually the hypothesis being tested.

The most direct test of this hypothesis would include both the anticipations and the naive projections in the same function and would see which one(s) remain significant. Pashigian does not do this, but instead tests separate functions and compares the fits (measured here as $\bar{R}^2$). This is done both for the function given above and for the same function in ratio form. Inventories are estimated for March, June, and September. The results are given in Table 17.7. If one wants to predict inventory stocks at the end of March with figures

**TABLE 17.7   RELATIVE PERFORMANCE OF SALES
ANTICIPATIONS AND PROJECTIONS IN
AN INVENTORY INVESTMENT FUNCTION**

Function Used to Predict I_i in:	$\bar{R}^2$ for Anticipations	Naive Model Projections
	Levels	
March	0.999	0.998
June	0.989	0.992
September	0.972	0.987
	Ratios	
March	0.793	0.756
June	0.755	0.850
September	0.697	0.858

released in mid-March, the anticipations are slightly better. However, for June and September, the naive projections are decidedly superior. Pashigian draws the conclusion that "the differences in results between the use of the anticipations and the use of a simple proxy do not seem large."[24] We would disagree. For the September figures, the amount of residual variance left unexplained is more than twice as great (in both forms of the function) using the anticipations than using the projections. This does not seem like a negligible difference.

The anticipations for manufacturing inventories are considered next. Unlike the other OBE-SEC anticipatory series, these have never been available on a yearly basis, and were first issued on a regular quarterly basis in mid-1959. Any conclusions based on these few years of information must necessarily be tentative, and in fact very few studies have been undertaken so far on these anticipations because of the lack of data. Earlier inventory anticipations released by other organizations were found to have little forecasting value.

The actual inventory anticipations taken from the surveys conducted by OBE-SEC were also of little value. Participants were also asked whether they felt that their inventory stocks were "high," "about right," or "low." It was clear from the answers that this information was also poorly correlated with actual inventory investment; in *each* of the 26 quarters from 1959.3 to 1965.4, more participants answered that their stocks were "high" rather than "low," but inventory investment nevertheless increased in all but 3 of the 26 quarters. By itself this would not seem to be a very useful piece of information. However, it was observed that there was a very definite correlation between the *error* in the inventory anticipations and the percentage of firms reporting "high" inventories minus the percentage reporting "low" inventories (referred to as

---

[24] *Ibid.,* p. 87.

the "net high" percentage).[25] When the net high percentage was close to zero (that is, almost as many firms thought stocks were low as thought they were high) there was a comparatively large understatement of inventory investment by the anticipations. When the "net high" percentage itself was large, inventory anticipations did not understate actual inventory investment. Thus the inventory anticipations modified by the "net high" percentage (using a regression between the two computed by Foss) have turned out to be a rather helpful set of anticipations for the brief time during which they have been available. Not only do the anticipations outperform the naive models, but (together with lagged inventory stock) they also outperform a function of only endogenous variables. This can be seen from the following regression equations:

$$(17.12) \quad I_{im} - I_{im-2} = 0.03 + 0.846(I_{im}^e - I_{im-2}) \qquad \bar{R}^2 = 0.615$$
$$(0.132)$$

$$(17.13) \quad I_{im} - I_{im-2} = -0.01 + 0.825(I_{im}^e - I_{im-2})$$
$$(0.118)$$

$$-0.735 I_{im-2} \qquad \bar{R}^2 = 0.694$$
$$(0.347)$$

$$(17.14) \quad I_{im} - I_{im-2} = 0.58 + 0.238 S_{m-1} - 0.053(U_{-1} - U_{-2})$$
$$(0.076) \qquad (0.109)$$

$$+ 0.070(U_{-2} - U_{-4}) - 0.505 I_{im-2} \qquad \bar{R}^2 = 0.635$$
$$(0.088) \qquad (0.180)$$

$$(17.15) \quad I_{im} - I_{im-2} = -0.10 + 0.088 S_{m-1} - 0.064(U_{-1} - U_{-2})$$
$$(0.092) \qquad (0.098)$$

$$+ 0.066(U_{-2} - U_{-4}) - 0.128 I_{im-2}$$
$$(0.079) \qquad (0.223)$$

$$+ 0.526(I_{im}^e - I_{im-2}) \qquad \bar{R}^2 = 0.706$$
$$(0.214)$$

where I_{im} = inventory stocks

S_m = sales

U = unfilled orders

I_{im}^e = OBE-SEC first anticipations

All figures are for the manufacturing sectors and are in billions of current dollars. All regressions are estimated for the period 1959.3–1965.4.

A few comments are in order about these functions. First, they are presented in current-dollar values rather than constant-dollar values, which were used for inventory investment functions estimated elsewhere in this book. This was

---

[25] M. Foss, "Manufacturers' Inventory and Sales Expectations," *Survey of Current Business*, Vol. 41, No. 8 (August, 1961), pp. 25–31.

done primarily because the anticipations are made in current dollars. However, the wholesale price level remained virtually unchanged for the sample period (1959–1965), so that this should make almost no difference. When all the equations were reestimated in constant dollars, the conclusions above were unchanged without exception, and the levels of significance of the variables were almost identical. Because of this, the constant-dollar results are not presented separately.

The change in the unfilled orders variable, which is so important in determining manufacturing inventory investment for the total postwar period, is not significant in any of these regressions and sometimes enters with the wrong sign. This is not too surprising, because the 1959–1965 period (except for perhaps the last quarters of 1965) was noted for its excess capacity. Since there were almost no shortages of crucial parts and materials, there was no need to increase stocks beyond present needs. This suggests that perhaps the entire relationship for this period represents an unusual case and that the performance of the inventory anticipations cannot be generalized to a period nearer full employment. In this respect it might be mentioned that the anticipations were much poorer for 1965 than for any other previous year.

Our previous discussion of inventories in Chapter 8 stated that inventory decisions were made on the basis of previous sales and that production plans within one quarter were quite flexible. However, both of these statements would suggest that inventory anticipations would be less useful rather than more so. If businessmen do not take future changes in sales into account (except for projecting current trends), one could argue that the expectations would be unlikely to be very accurate. If firms are able to adjust quickly to unexpected changes in sales, inventories may be brought to desired levels within one quarter, but they will not be very close to the anticipated figures. Perhaps these positive results of inventory anticipations suggest a slight modification in the explanation of inventory investment, as follows.

When sales change, businessmen adjust their production schedules to replace unexpectedly depleted inventories and keep their inventory stocks at the anticipated level. They do not, however, immediately view this change in sales as permanent. Therefore, they do not further adjust their inventory stocks to this changed demand until one or more quarters has elapsed and there has been a better chance to decide whether the change in sales is of a permanent or temporary nature. If this is the case, the anticipations could provide useful information about whether businessmen feel that given sales changes are temporary or permanent.

It would be foolish to try to develop a modified theory of inventory investment decisions based on a few years' data which has been characterized by substantial excess capacity. It would even be somewhat foolhardy to declare that the inventory anticipations are of substantial benefit in forecasting. Because of the paucity of observations, this series has not yet been incorporated into a model used for true *ex ante* forecasting, so it is not possible to say how well they will actually predict. Yet the available evidence does suggest that they may well be useful, and their performance in the near future should be of considerable interest to short-term forecasters.

17.4   SHORT-TERM FORECASTING MODELS WITH ANTICIPATORY DATA

We have shown in Sections 17.1–17.3 that the only widely used anticipatory series which adds to predictive accuracy is the OBE-SEC fixed business investment anticipations for the manufacturing sector, with a decision not yet reached on the inventory anticipations. Many economists use these anticipations to predict investment and then use an *ad hoc* procedure to predict other components of GNP. The total of these components is often inconsistent with the total GNP predictions made by other methods.[25] If one believes that good forecasts can be generated from the investment anticipations, it would seem almost mandatory to combine this information with estimates of other exogenous forces in the economy (such as fiscal policy), derive an overall multiplier, and calculate internally consistent estimates of GNP. The size of a model necessary to accomplish this will depend on the number of components of GNP one wishes to predict separately but may be quite small. Such models have been developed by Friend and others.[26] Friend finds that semiannual models give somewhat better predictions than quarterly models, presumably because of the averaging out of erratic short-term changes in the data. The model discussed here is actually calculated for overlapping half-years, for example,

$$\frac{1963.4 + 1963.3}{2} - \frac{1963.2 + 1963.1}{2}$$

The next observations would be one quarter later,

$$\frac{1964.1 + 1963.4}{2} - \frac{1963.3 + 1963.2}{2}$$

The model that has been used most extensively for actual forecasting is the Friend–Taubman model:

$$\Delta C = 2.18 + 0.37\Delta X^* + 0.10\Delta C_{-1}$$
$$\quad\quad\quad (0.05) \quad\quad (0.10)$$

---

[25] For example, at the National Industrial Conference Board Economic Forum in November, 1963, the consensus forecast of total GNP was $615 billion, whereas the consensus forecast obtained by summing sectoral predictions was $622 billion.

[26] I. Friend and R. Jones, "Short-Run Forecasting Models Incorporating Anticipatory Data," in *Models of Income Determination*, Studies in Income and Wealth, Vol. 28 (Princeton, N.J.: Princeton University Press for NBER, 1964), and I. Friend and P. Taubman, "A Short-Term Forecasting Model," *Review of Economics and Statistics*, Vol. 46, No. 3 (August, 1964), pp. 229–236.

$$\Delta I_h = 0.35 + 0.06(\Delta X^* - \Delta X_{-1}) + 0.58\Delta HS_{-1/2} - 0.16\Delta ANP$$
$$\quad\quad\;(0.01)\quad\quad\quad\quad\quad\quad\quad(0.09)\quad\quad\quad\;(0.07)$$

$$\Delta I_p = -0.82 + 0.08(\Delta X^* + \Delta X_{-1}) + 0.63\Delta ANP$$
$$\quad\quad\;(0.02)\quad\quad\quad\quad\quad\quad\quad(0.14)$$

$$\Delta(\Delta I_i) = 1.51 + 0.025\Delta S^e - 1.15\Delta I_{i-1} + 1.70\Delta ANP$$
$$\quad\quad\quad(0.005)\quad\quad(0.19)\quad\quad\;(0.61)$$

$$\Delta C + \Delta I_h + \Delta I_p + \Delta(\Delta I_i) + \Delta(G + F) = \Delta X$$

All variables are in billions of 1954 dollars, seasonally adjusted at annual rates, and

C = total consumption expenditures

I_h = residential construction

I_p = fixed business investment

ΔI_i = inventory investment except farm sector (which is assumed to be zero)

$G + F$ = government purchases of goods and services plus net foreign balance

X = GNP

X^* = computed value of GNP estimated from a reduced form (to eliminate least-squares bias)

HS = housing starts

ANP = average of *second* anticipations of first quarter of the half-year and *first* anticipations of the second quarter of the half-year, OBE-SEC series ($\Delta ANP = ANP - I_{p-1}$)

S^e = synthetic sales expectations constructed by Friend and Taubman:

$$S^e = S_{-1}\frac{ANP}{I_{p-1}}\quad\quad (S = \text{total business sales})$$

The subscript -1 ($t - 1$) represents the previous *half-year* (not the previous quarter)

The uses for which this type of model is intended are sometimes misunderstood. First, it clearly cannot be used for forecasting a year ahead or more, because the anticipations are not available that far in advance. Second, since few policy variables are included, its use for examining alternative policy decisions is very limited. Third, it is designed only to forecast aggregate demand and thus cannot predict prices, unemployment, income distribution, capacity utilization, and so on. Fourth, the parameters are in general not intended to be structural parameters; that is, they are not intended to reflect underlying theoretical relationships in the economy.[27] For example, the "long-run *mpc*"

---

[27] It should be pointed out that this same comment can be made about some of the equations in large-scale models. For example, if the consumer durables or fixed investment functions contain anticipation indices, none of the parameters in those equations are structural.

out of GNP is estimated to be 0.4, which corresponds to a "long-run *mpc*" out of disposable income of 0.6, far from the usually accepted value of around 0.9. However, no claim is made that this value represents an estimate of the value of the actual long-run mpc. The consumption relationship used here is instead a useful empirical relationship for short-term forecasting.

Since this model does not forecast a year in advance, it is somewhat difficult to compare its forecasting record with most other forecasts, which are often based on annual models and are usually presented shortly before the end of the previous year. However, two comparisons are calculated and the results are tabulated in Tables 17.8 and 17.9. The first comparison is with a naive model which states that the change in this half-year is the same as the change in the previous half-year; the second is with forecasts made from the Wharton EFU model. The comparison with the naive model is considered first.

The *ex ante* forecasting record of the Friend–Taubman model is just as good as the *ex post* record, a commendable balance. However, the naive model improves remarkably in the *ex ante* period. This is, of course, a coincidence, but it does suggest that this particular period might have been easier to forecast than one containing cyclical fluctuations. Although the naive model gives better predictions than the forecasting model, it is hard to imagine any model that would do better than predict GNP four months ahead with an average absolute error of only $1.1 billion for almost a three-year period. By comparison, revisions in the official national income accounts of the *quarterly changes* in GNP have averaged over $3 billion for the last few years.

Naive models are often a hazardous standard of comparison. A naive model that predicted continuing rapid rates of growth in GNP throughout the 1963–1966 period would have worked well, but few economists thought that this was likely to happen. Whenever possible it is preferable to compare model forecasts with other true *ex ante* publicly released predictions made at the same time. In this case we can compare forecasts of the Friend–Taubman model with those made using the Wharton EFU model.[28] Since the forecasts from the Wharton EFU model are made quarterly and in current dollars (they are also made in constant dollars, but the entire solution is influenced by the price levels because it is solved simultaneously), it is necessary to transform them somewhat to correspond to the Friend–Taubman predictions. This is done in two steps. First, the quarterly forecasts are averaged and first differences are taken to correspond to the overlapping half-year format. The Friend–Taubman predictions are then converted to current dollars. Since no price predictions are made in that model, a "naive" prediction is used— $\Delta p = \Delta p_{-1}$. An additional

---

[28] The equations given in Section 15.3 were all estimated using national income data revised in July, 1965. Earlier versions of the Wharton EFU model have existed since 1963; obviously these earlier versions were used to make pre-1965 forecasts. Although we have referred to all versions estimated by this author and L. R. Klein as "the" Wharton EFU model, the basic structure has been reestimated from time to time. Further details are given in the references cited in footnotes 2 and 3 of Chapter 15 (Section 15.3).

TABLE 17.8 COMPARISON OF FRIEND–TAUBMAN MODEL WITH NAIVE MODEL[a]
(all figures are in billions of 1954 dollars)

Half-Year Ending in	Actual Change	Predicted Change	Error	Naive Prediction[b]	Error
		Ex post forecasts			
1961.1	−5.6	1.0	6.6	−2.3	3.3
1961.2	0.0	3.2	3.2	−5.6	−5.6
1961.3	11.3	11.3	0.0	0.0	−11.3
1961.4	18.1	19.7	1.6	11.3	−6.8
1962.1	18.6	20.6	2.0	18.1	−0.5
1962.2	14.1	16.9	2.8	18.6	4.5
1962.3	9.3	6.2	−3.1	14.1	4.8
		Ex ante forecasts			
1962.4	7.6	5.6	−2.0	9.3	1.7
1963.1	8.6	7.1	−1.5	7.6	−1.0
1963.2	8.8	9.1	0.3	8.6	−0.2
1963.3	8.9	9.4	0.5	8.8	−0.1
1963.4	11.0	18.7	7.7	8.9	−2.1
1964.1	11.8	14.0	2.2	11.0	−0.8
1964.2	12.4	14.0	1.6	11.8	−0.6
1964.3	11.6	14.6	3.0	12.4	−0.8
1964.4	10.4	16.5	6.1	11.6	−1.2
1965.1	10.9	15.4	4.5	10.4	−0.5
1965.2	13.3	13.6	0.3	10.9	−2.4
Av. absolute error			2.8		2.7
RMS error			3.5		3.9
Ex post period only:					
Av. absolute error			2.8		5.3
RMS error			3.3		6.1
Ex ante period only:					
Av. absolute error			2.8		1.1
RMS error			3.6		1.3

[a] The author is indebted to Professor Friend for his cooperation in supplying these forecasts.

[b] $\Delta GNP = \Delta GNP_{-1}$.

set of calculations is made with the correct price levels, to determine whether the naive prediction of prices worsened the overall forecasts. As it turns out, the forecasts with the projected price levels are slightly better than those with the actual price levels.

The Wharton EFU forecasts were not available until 1963.2, and the Friend–Taubman forecasts were not issued for several quarters after the fundamental revision of the national income accounts in 1965.3. Thus nine quarters of *ex ante* forecasts are compared in Table 17.9.

Sometimes forecasts are adjusted by inserting the correct values of the exogenous variables used in the model. Although this might decrease the absolute error in both cases here, it should not alter the relative performances. Both sets of forecasts were regularly calculated and released at the same times of the year (early March, June, September, and December), so the same information about fiscal and monetary policy was known to both sets of predictors. Although both models were high in 1964.4 because of the auto strike, the degree of information known to both parties was the same, so that again conditions under which the forecasts were made are comparable in virtually all respects.

The record here is not clear-cut, although the Wharton EFU model does have a moderately better forecasting record. To draw any definite conclusions would be hazardous, because the prediction period is too short and contains no downturns. However, the evidence would suggest that large equation systems can certainly predict at least as well as small systems, plus the obvious advantage that large-scale models predict further into the future (at least one full year ahead) and can forecast a wider range of variables.

TABLE 17.9 COMPARISON OF FRIEND–TAUBMAN MODEL WITH WHARTON EFU MODEL

(*all data are in billions of current dollars and are based on the pre-1965-revised national income accounts*)

Half-Year Ending	Actual GNP	Wharton EFU Model Predictions	Error	F–T Predictions Assumed Prices	Error	F–T Predictions Actual Prices	Error
1963.2	574.6	578.2	3.6	577.0	2.4	578.0	3.4
1963.3	582.3	586.3	4.0	584.4	2.1	584.9	2.6
1963.4	593.1	587.6	−5.5	601.3	8.2	601.3	8.2
1964.1	603.9	601.7	−2.2	604.0	0.1	603.4	−0.5
1964.2	613.7	616.2	2.5	614.9	1.2	615.4	1.7
1964.3	623.5	626.4	2.9	626.1	2.6	627.2	3.7
1964.4	631.5	635.7	4.2	639.5	8.0	639.0	7.5
1965.1	641.7	642.4	0.7	647.9	6.2	646.8	5.1
1965.2	653.4	656.6	2.8	653.4	0.0	653.4	0.0
Av. absolute error			3.1		3.4		3.6
RMS error			3.4		4.6		4.5

In both papers on the subject, Friend has drawn the conclusion that "a simple small-scale model is likely to do at least as well in the present or foreseeable future as the more complex, multi-equational and multivariate models."[29] This is too general a statement; although it may apply to some large-scale models, it certainly does not apply to the Wharton EFU model. Friend and Jones, in a discussion of other quarterly models, discuss (1) the Klein quarterly model[30] and (2) the Duesenberry–Eckstein–Fromm (DEF) model.[31] The Klein–Goldberger annual model is mentioned briefly as "not having done well"; this is a debatable assumption discussed in Chapter 18, but in any case this model predicts a full year ahead and is not comparable with the short-run Friend models. The results for the DEF model are not presented because of a fundamental data revision after the model had been completed. However, this model was designed only for recession periods and thus could not have been used to predict the period 1963–1965. The few forecasts of the Klein quarterly model that have been analyzed do indicate that this particular model did not predict as accurately as the small-scale models.

The short-term forecasting models of Friend and Jones and of Friend and Taubman have a very respectable record for the period of both *ex post* and *ex ante* forecasts. Although direct comparisons with yearly forecasts are not possible, the available evidence (where quarterly breakdowns are given) would seem to indicate that this model does forecast much better than the average *ad hoc* forecast. The combining of investment anticipations and other exogenous variables into a consistent framework is a method that many forecasters could well emulate. But there is no evidence seen by the author to indicate that these small models predict any better than reliable large-scale models.

If one is primarily interested in predicting the level of GNP, there is no particular reason a five-equation model should represent the optimal size. For simplicity and ease of computation, it could be argued that the reduced form of such a model, presented as a compact one-equation annual model, might be even better. We have estimated just such a one-equation model, which has as its independent variables many of the lagged and exogenous variables taken from larger-scale models. This model is

$$(17.16) \quad \Delta X = 41.58 + 0.640\Delta G - 2.916\Delta I_{i-1} - 33.43(\Delta i_{L-1})$$
$$ (0.303) \quad\quad (0.822) \quad\quad\quad (6.69)$$

$$+ 0.583\Delta U_{-1} + 1.656\Delta C_{ns-1} - 1.454\text{STXR} \quad \bar{R}^2 = 0.806$$
$$ (0.254) \quad\quad\quad (0.644) \quad\quad\quad (1.072)$$

[29] Friend and Taubman, *op. cit.*, p. 229.

[30] L. R. Klein, "A Postwar Quarterly Model: Description and Applications," *op. cit.*

[31] J. S. Duesenberry, O. Eckstein, and G. Fromm, "A Simulation of the United States Economy in Recession," *Econometrica*, Vol. 28, No. 4 (October, 1960), pp. 749–810.

where X = GNP, billions of 1958 dollars

$\quad$ G = government purchases of goods and services, billions of 1958 dollars

$\quad$ ΔI_i = inventory investment excluding farm inventories, billions of 1958 dollars

$\quad$ i_L = long-term bond yield (Moody's), percent

$\quad$ U = unfilled orders, end of year, billions of 1958 dollars

$\quad$ C_{ns} = consumption of nondurables and services, billions of 1958 dollars

$STXR$ = starting (first bracket) tax rate for personal income taxes, percent

All lags in this model are in *years*.

All the independent variables in this model are lagged except for government purchases of goods and services and the starting tax rate. Thus with these two assumptions about fiscal policy it is possible to predict GNP without knowing any values for endogenous variables of the present year. Although the model does contain variables representing monetary and fiscal policy, it should not be used for policy simulations, because the coefficients do not represent structural parameters. The relationships here represent only useful empirical approximations. This model has performed very well over the sample period, correctly matching all the recessions and clearly outperforming various naive models, as shown in Table 17.10.

To test this model outside the sample period *ex post* forecasts were calculated for 1965 and 1966. Comparisons are made in constant dollars, since this model contains no price equations. The average predictive error for 1965 and 1966 is substantially smaller than the standard error during the sample period. Unfortunately, true *ex ante* predictions have not been made with this model. However, the *ex post* forecasts involved no change in any of the parameters. One would expect them to be superior to *ex ante* forecasts only to the extent that government expenditures were correctly known. For 1966 this would have made a difference of $2.2 billion, assuming the same error in forecasting government spending as was made in the Wharton EFU model. However, this test is not conclusive. A very poor *ex post* forecast might have resulted in a respecification of the model.

It seems to us that the conclusion to be drawn from these results is that if one is interested *only in predicting GNP*, the size of the model is largely independent of the accuracy of the predictions. (This, of course, implies neither a positive nor a negative correlation.) Rather, it depends primarily on how accurate the individual equations are. On the other hand, if one is interested in using the model for more than predicting GNP (and a few components of aggregate demand), a large-scale model is almost certainly a prior requirement. For the 1966–1968 period, the two most important variables to be forecasted were undoubtedly the price level and the rate of unemployment rather than the actual level of GNP. Although these quantities are certainly interrelated,

TABLE 17.10 PERFORMANCE OF ONE-EQUATION ANNUAL MODEL

Year	Actual Change in GNP	Predicted Change	Error	Naive Model[a] II Error	Naive Model[b] III Error
1948	13.8	9.7	4.1	16.5	−1.6
1949	0.4	6.5	−6.1	−13.4	−15.0
1950	31.2	31.4	−0.2	30.8	15.8
1951	28.1	30.7	−2.6	−3.1	12.7
1952	11.7	7.9	3.8	−16.4	−3.7
1953	17.7	20.4	−2.7	6.0	2.3
1954	−5.8	−3.7	−2.1	−23.5	−21.2
1955	31.0	27.2	3.8	36.8	15.6
1956	8.1	16.6	−8.5	−22.9	−7.3
1957	6.4	8.3	−1.9	−1.7	−9.0
1958	−5.2	−5.5	0.3	−11.6	−20.6
1959	23.4	27.8	−4.4	28.6	8.0
1960	11.9	4.6	7.3	−11.5	−3.5
1961	9.5	11.8	−2.3	−2.4	−5.9
1962	32.7	27.6	5.1	23.2	17.3
1963	21.2	17.1	4.1	−11.5	5.8
1964	30.1	25.2	4.9	8.9	14.7
1965[c]	35.6	29.2	6.4	5.5	20.2
1966[c]	35.9	33.7	2.2	0.3	20.5
Av. absolute error[d]			3.8	15.8	10.6
RMS error[d]			5.7[e]	18.8	12.7

[a] $\Delta X_t = \Delta X_{t-1}$.
[b] $\Delta X_t = \overline{\Delta X_t}$.
[c] *Ex post* forecast.
[d] Calculated for sample period (1948–1964).
[e] Standard error adjusted for degrees of freedom.

a small model does not include the necessary conversion equations nor does it allow for possible feedback. The effects of government defense and non-defense spending, personal income tax, corporate income tax, and excise tax rate changes, increased transfer payments, and monetary variables are just a few of the policy problems that should be of interest to a wide variety of economists. Although these additional predictions are necessarily based on a good forecast of GNP with some control assumptions, a single estimate of GNP, unsupported by other detail or structural parameters, is not acceptable to most economists today. Since these are the broad problems with which this book is concerned, we now turn to the type of large-scale models that are based on the analysis developed in previous chapters.

FORECASTING WITH
ECONOMETRIC MODELS

18.1 A REVISED KLEIN–GOLDBERGER MODEL

In Chapters 16 and 17 we have considered two alternative methods of forecasting: the use of leading indicators and the use of anticipatory data. It was found that in general both these methods have an unsatisfactory forecasting record. To make a meaningful comparison, the predictive record of econometric models should be tabulated and compared with these alternative methods of prediction. There is, of course, a more basic reason for examining econometric models in some detail. The structure of the economy and the underlying parameters, such as the various marginal propensities to spend, are of great importance for policy applications. This structure has been developed in this book, first by examining the underlying theory of each individual equation and then by considering the interaction of these forces to determine a theory of income determination and of the business cycle. Now that this theory has been developed, the usefulness of an econometric model based on this analysis can be assessed by investigating its ability to forecast accurately. Both the theoretical and empirical strands have been synthesized to produce a model that is useful both for prediction and for general structural analysis.

Recall from Chapter 13 the basic outline of the Keynesian system; that outline was

$$C = C(X)$$

$$I = I(X, i)$$

$$C + I + G = X$$

$$X = X(N, K, t) \quad \text{or} \quad N = (X, K, t)$$

$$\frac{\partial X}{\partial N} = \frac{w}{p} \quad \text{or} \quad p = \frac{w}{\partial X / \partial N}$$

$$w = w_0 \quad \text{or} \quad \Delta w = w(\Delta p, Un)$$

$$\overline{M_s} = M_d = kpX - \lambda pi$$

$$Un = L - N$$

This simple model, if estimated, would not be useful for forecasting or analysis, both because of absence of any lag structure and because of the paucity of variables. The relevant lag structure has been explained earlier; in this section we show how additional equations can be added to this Keynesian outline to develop a workable econometric model.

First, the components of aggregate demand should be expanded somewhat. Consumption of durables is a cyclically volatile component of GNP, with a short-run income elasticity substantially in excess of unity. Consumption of nondurables and services has a short-run income elasticity much less than unity and is heavily influenced by past patterns of consumer spending. Investment should be disaggregated into plant and equipment, residential construction, and inventory investment, for these have widely differing patterns over the business cycle. Inventory investment is quite volatile and has accounted for over half of total fluctuations in GNP during postwar recessions. Plant and equipment investment is influenced primarily by lagged variables, so it tends to lag the cycle. Residential construction is counter-cyclical because it receives residual factors of production from other sectors of the economy. The net foreign balance is completely exogenous in the simplest Keynesian model, but at least imports certainly ought to be endogenous. Thus at least four equations of aggregate demand should be added.

The second type of addition to the basic Keynesian model is the necessary distinction between GNP, national income, and personal disposable income, since consumption depends on the latter, whereas plant and equipment and inventory investment depend on total output or some close variant. To do this it is necessary to explain the intermediate variables in the identities linking these terms. Separate functions are needed for depreciation, taxes and transfers, and corporate savings. Taxes and transfers should be separated into functions for personal income taxes, corporate income taxes, indirect business taxes, and transfers. Corporate savings depend on after-tax corporate profits, which can be estimated either directly or as a residual. If the latter is done, it is then necessary to estimate equations for other factor shares: wages, unincorporated business income, and rentier income.

Two more minor additions are also needed. The labor input variable in the production function is man-hours, so a separate function is needed to explain hours worked to calculate employment and unemployment. Fixed business investment depends on the long-term interest rate, but money-market activity determines the short-term rate, so an additional equation is needed to explain the term structure of interest rates.

A model thus expanded from the basic Keynesian structure by expanding aggregate demand components and separating personal, corporate, and national income forms the basis of a long series of econometric models developed by Klein, starting in 1946[1] and including the famous Klein–Goldberger (K–G) model, estimated in 1953.[2] Little would be gained by discussing the original version of that model here. It has been repeatedly and thoroughly analyzed;[3] furthermore, there have been three major revisions of the national income accounts since that time, so the original model could not now be used for prediction or policy purposes even if the underlying theory were found to hold. Of more interest are the descendants of this model. Three distinct branches can be distinguished on the family tree of Klein econometric models, which are the following:

1. The K–G model has been considerably expanded and reestimated in first differences, while remaining an annual model. In this form it has been and is currently being used by the Research Center in Quantitative Economics at the University of Michigan to generate annual forecasts. The forecasting record of this model is examined in Section 18.3.

2. The underlying economic structure of the K–G model has been respecified to include greater sectoral disaggregation and has been refor-mulated on a quarterly basis. The most recent example of this is the Wharton EFU model.[4]

3. The K–G model itself has been updated and reestimated with revised data. The latest version, estimated for the sample period 1929–1964 (omitting 1942–1945) is presented later in this section.

---

[1] The first outline of an econometric model by Klein to appear in the literature was abstracted in *Econometrica*, Vol. 14, No. 2 (April, 1946). pp. 159–162.

[2] L. R. Klein and A. S. Goldberger, *An Econometric Model of the United States, 1929–1952* (Amsterdam: North-Holland, 1955).

[3] Some of the more well-known studies published are listed here; the list is not meant to be exhaustive. C. F. Christ, "Aggregate Econometric Models," *American Economic Review*, Vol. 46, No. 2 (June, 1956), pp. 385–408. K. Fox, "Econometric Models of the United States," *Journal of Political Economy*, Vol. 44, No. 2 (April, 1956), pp. 128–142. I. Adelman and F. L. Adelman, "The Dynamic Properties of the Klein–Goldberger Model," *Econometrica*, Vol. 27, No. 4 (October, 1959), pp. 596–625. A. S. Goldberger, *Impact Multipliers and Dynamic Properties of the Klein–Goldberger Model* (Amsterdam: North-Holland, 1959).

[4] An earlier model in this branch is L. R. Klein, "A Postwar Quarterly Model: Description and Application," in *Models of Income Determination*, Conference on Income and Wealth, Vol. 28 (Princeton, N.J.: Princeton University Press for NBER, 1964). This model was subsequently bequeathed to the Office of Business Economics, where it was estimated with revised data and some structural changes were made. This revision is found in M. Liebenberg, A. Hirsch, and J. Popkin, "A Quarterly Econometric Model of the United States: A Progress Report," *Survey of Current Business*, Vol. 46, No. 5 (May, 1966), pp. 13–39.

The latest version of the K–G model has been used for forecasting, but its principal uses are for experimentation with simulations and alternative methods of parameter estimation. The model is a particularly useful tool for these studies because its dynamic properties are well known. Thus problems of divergence, instability, or multiple equilibria, which have often plagued solution patterns of other models, are absent. Another advantage to the model is that it can serve as a useful pedagogical device. It represents the minimum size of model useful for both forecasting and policy analysis. Although some relevant information is necessarily sacrificed, the much simpler lag structure and the absence of sectoral disaggregation makes it much easier to comprehend.

A list of the equations of the model follows, after which a list of the variables used in the model is given. The symbols correspond to those used in the Wharton EFU model and elsewhere in this text except that constant-dollar magnitudes are in 1954 dollars instead of 1958 dollars (see pp. 498–499).

Although most of this model is based on familiar principles, a few comments are necessary. It is quite a bit smaller than the Wharton EFU model, so that many terms, particularly relative prices and ratios, are eliminated. Some of the equations are in slightly different form from that suggested by the analysis developed previously and merit an additional word of explanation.

Equations (18.1), (18.3), and (18.9) are written in a somewhat unusual way: the dependent variable is of the form $X - \lambda X_{-1}$. This is, however, an ingenious transformation of the usual form of the equation which eliminates the need to include three extra capital stock variables. For example, consider the consumer durables function. The standard form of the equation is (without relative prices)

$$C_d = a_0 + a_1 Y + a_2 K_{d-1} \qquad a_2 < 0$$

where

$$K_d = \sum_{i=0}^{\infty} \lambda^i C_{d-i}$$

Substituting this expression explicitly in the durables function gives

$$C_d = a_0 + a_1 Y + a_2 \sum_{i=0}^{\infty} \lambda^i C_{d-i-1}$$

Applying the familiar Koyck transformation gives

$$\lambda C_{d-1} = \lambda a_0 + a_1 \lambda Y_{-1} + a_2 \sum_{i=0}^{\infty} \lambda^{i+1} C_{d-i-2}$$

and thus

$$C_d - \lambda C_{d-1} = a_0(1 - \lambda) + a_1(Y - \lambda Y_{-1}) + a_2 C_{d-1}$$

This is the form of the equation that is estimated.

EQUATIONS of the Revised Klein–Goldberger Model

^{d}(18.1) $\quad C_d - 0.7C_{d-1} = 0.230(Y - 0.7Y_{-1}) - 0.105C_{d-1} - 4.51$
$\qquad\qquad\qquad\quad (0.047) \qquad\qquad\qquad (0.096)$

*(18.2) $\quad C_{ns} = 0.228Y + 0.752C_{ns-1} - 1.468$
$\qquad\qquad\quad (0.050) \quad\; (0.065)$

^{d}(18.3) $\quad I_h = 0.0517Y - 0.0402i_{s-1} + 0.335I_{h-1} - 1.853$
$\qquad\qquad\quad (0.0088) \quad\; (0.0213) \qquad (0.112)$

^{d}(18.4) $\quad I_i = 0.137(X - \Delta I_i) + 0.396I_{i-1} - 24.702$
$\qquad\qquad\quad (0.021) \qquad\qquad\quad (0.100)$

^{d}(18.5) $\quad F_i = 0.0284X - 10.14(p_i - p) + 0.463F_{i-1} - 0.942$
$\qquad\qquad\quad (0.0068) \qquad (4.06) \qquad\quad (0.149)$

*(18.6) $\quad [X - (W_g/p)] - 0.95[X - (W_g/p)]_{-1} = 0.364(I_p + I_h) + 3.532[(N_w - N_g + N_s)$
$\qquad\qquad\qquad\qquad\qquad\qquad\qquad\qquad\qquad (0.065) \qquad\qquad (1.086)$

$\qquad\qquad\qquad\qquad\qquad\qquad\qquad\qquad\qquad\qquad\qquad - 0.95(N_w - N_g + N_s)_{-1}]$

$\qquad\qquad\qquad\qquad\qquad\qquad\qquad\qquad\qquad\qquad\qquad + 1.335(h - 0.95h_{-1}) - 6.483$
$\qquad\qquad\qquad\qquad\qquad\qquad\qquad\qquad\qquad\qquad\qquad\quad (0.614)$

^{o}(18.7) $\quad h = -0.450\Delta w - 1.996(N_L - N_w - N_s) + 1.157$
$\qquad\qquad\qquad (0.103) \qquad\quad (0.272)$

*(18.8 $\quad [(W - W_g)/p)] = 0.413[X - (W_g/p)] + 0.282[(W - W_g)/p]_{-1} - 10.607$
$\qquad\qquad\qquad\qquad\qquad (0.026) \qquad\qquad\qquad (0.048)$

*(18.9) $\quad \Delta w = -1.697(N_L - N_w - N_s) + 1.116(\Delta p)_{-1} + 0.184$
$\qquad\qquad\qquad (0.471) \qquad\qquad\qquad\qquad (0.520)$

^{o}(18.10) $\quad i_L = 0.157i_s + 0.835(i_L)_{-1} + 0.335$
$\qquad\qquad\qquad (0.051) \quad\; (0.066)$

^{s}(18.11) $\quad RE = 0.788(P_{cb} - T_c) - 0.667(P_{cb} - T_c - RE)_{-1} - 0.148$
$\qquad\qquad\qquad (0.052) \qquad\qquad\quad (0.100)$

^{s}(18.12) $\quad PB = 0.0107pX + 0.898(PB)_{-1} + 0.674$
$\qquad\qquad\qquad (0.0074) \qquad (0.082)$

^{s}(18.13) $\quad RI = 0.0623p(I_p + I_h) - 0.0230\Delta i_L + 0.938(RI)_{-1} + 0.394$
$\qquad\qquad\qquad (0.0095) \qquad\qquad (0.0337) \qquad (0.025)$

*(18.14) $\quad I_p - 0.95I_{p-1} = 0.0656(X - W_g)_{-1} - 2.11(i_L)_{-1} - 0.590I_{p-1} + 9.329$
$\qquad\qquad\qquad\qquad\qquad (0.0158) \qquad\qquad (0.56) \qquad (0.150)$

^{s}(18.15) $\quad D = 0.0492 \sum_{i=1}^{20} p_{-i}(I_p + I_h)_{-i} + 0.0856Du + 1.411$
$\qquad\qquad\qquad (0.0016) \qquad\qquad\qquad\qquad\qquad (0.0063)$

*(18.16) $\quad i_s = 1.145i_d - 0.815RR_{-1} + 0.533Du - 0.511$
$\qquad\qquad\qquad (0.082) \quad\; (0.335) \qquad\quad (0.186)$

*(18.17) $\quad X = C_d + C_{ns} + I_p + I_h + \Delta I_i + G + F_e - F_i$

^{s}(18.18) $\quad pY = pX - D - T_i - RE - T_c - T$

EQUATIONS of the Revised Klein–Goldberger Model (*Continued*)

[s](18.19) $P_{cb} = pX - D - T_i - W - RI - PB$

[s](18.20) $W = whN_w$

   [*] The seven basic equations in the outline of the Keynesian system presented at the beginning of the chapter.
   [d] The additional aggregate demand equations.
   [s] The additional factor share equations.
   [o] Other equations (hours and interest rates).

DEFINITIONS OF VARIABLES

C_d	consumption of durables, billions of 1954 dollars
C_{ns}	consumption of nondurables and services, billions of 1954 dollars
D	capital consumption allowances (depreciation), billions of 1954 dollars
*Du	dummy variable: 0 for 1929–1946; 1 for 1947–1962
*F_e	exports, billions of 1954 dollars
F_i	imports, billions of 1954 dollars
*G	government purchases of goods and services, billions of 1954 dollars
h	index of hours worked per week, 1954 = 1.00
*i_d	average discount rate at all Federal Reserve Banks, percent
I_h	residential construction, billions of 1954 dollars
I_i	stock of inventories, billions of 1954 dollars
i_L	average yield on corporate bonds (Moody's), percent
I_p	investment in plant and equipment, billions of 1954 dollars
i_s	yield on prime commercial paper, four to six months, percent
*N_g	government employees, millions
*N_L	total labor force, millions
*N_s	self-employed workers, millions
N_w	wage and salary workers, millions
p	implicit GNP deflator, 1954 = 1.00
PB	proprietors' income, billions of current dollars
P_{cb}	corporate profits including inventory valuation adjustment, billions of current dollars
*p_i	implicit price deflator for imports, 1954 = 1.00
RE	retained earnings including inventory valuation adjustment, billions of current dollars
RI	rental and net interest income, billions of current dollars
*RR	year-end ratio of member banks' excess to required reserves
†T	personal taxes + contributions for social insurance − government and business transfer payments − interest on government debt, billions of current dollars
†T_c	corporate profits taxes, billions of current dollars
*T_i	reconciling item between net national product and national income, billions of current dollars
W	wages and salaries and supplements, billions of current dollars
w	annual wage rate of all employees, thousands of dollars per year
*W_g	wage bill of government employees, billions of current dollars
X	GNP, billions of 1954 dollars
Y	personal disposable income, billions of 1954 dollars

   [*] Exogenous variables.
   †Functions are not given for these variables because of frequent changes in the tax laws.

The transformation of the fixed business investment function is very similar to the consumer durables function. The original form is

$$I_p = b_0 + b_1 \sum_{i=0}^{\infty} \mu^i(X - W_g)_{-i-1} + b_2 \sum_{i=0}^{\infty} \mu^i(i_L)_{-i-1} + b_3 K_{p-1}$$

where

$$K_p = \sum_{i=0}^{\infty} \mu^i Ip_{-i}$$

Similar transformations to those used above give the estimated form of the equation. One interesting feature of this investment function is that *all* the independent variables are lagged. Although we have repeatedly stressed the importance of lagged variables in the investment function, this equation may overstate the case. Similarly, the production function may be transformed from its original state,

$$X - Wg = c_0 + c_1(Nw - Ng - Ne) + c_2 \cdot h + c_3(Kp + Kh)$$

to its estimated form. The labor input, man-hours, is separated into employment and hours, but this is done only to make the system linear.

It should be stressed that this form of the production function measures *actual* output, not full capacity or full employment output. Although this function can be used to determine maximum output, as is done in larger models, this concept is not used here. Since actual output has already been obtained by summing the components of aggregate demand, this function actually determines the *demand for labor*. A separate function is provided for hours worked, so employment is determined by this function.

Since the production function estimates the demand for labor, the marginal productivity equation, $MPP_L = \partial X / \partial L = w/p$ no longer serves this purpose. Instead, it becomes a *price mark-up* equation determining the overall price level. For a Cobb–Douglas function, as explained in Chapter 10,

$$\frac{\partial X}{\partial L} = \alpha \left(\frac{X}{L} \right)$$

so that

$$p = \frac{1}{\alpha} \frac{wL}{X} = \frac{1}{\alpha} \frac{W}{X}$$

for perfect competition and profit-maximizing behavior. In the Klein–Goldberger model, this function occurs in slightly disguised form as the wage-bill equation [Eq. (18.8)]. However, money wages are defined as the product of the wage rate, hours worked, and employment, all of which are determined by other functions in the model. Thus the equation for the wage bill in constant dollars really serves to define the price level, and is in fact easily transformed to the price-markup equation. Neglecting lags, the wage-bill equation is of the form $W/p = aX$ or $p = (1/a)(W/X)$. Thus a should equal α, which is approximately $\frac{2}{3}$: the estimated value is 0.57, which is fairly close.

The remaining two equations in the basic Keynesian system, the wage rate and the liquidity-preference function, are substantially changed. The idea that workers have money illusions has been found to be false. Also, wage bargains are determined partially by the tightness of the labor market, being negatively related to unemployment $(N_L - N_w - N_e)$. The wage-rate function becomes

$$w = w_0 + d_0 + d_1(N_L - N_w - N_e) + d_2(\Delta p)_{-1} \qquad d_1 < 0$$

and since w_0 (the "floor" for wage rates) is usually closely related to the previous year's wage rate, this function can be written

$$\Delta w \cong d_0 + d_1(N_L - N_w - N_e) + d_2(\Delta p)_{-1}$$

where $w_0 \cong w_{-1}$. Note that in this form the equation is a disequilibrium function, as explained earlier.

The emphasis of the liquidity preference function has been altered substantially, and it has also been changed to a disequilibrium function. In equilibrium,

$$\overline{M}_s = M_D = kpX - \lambda pi$$

However, suppose $\overline{M}_s \neq M_D$, ex ante. Then the *market* rate (i_s) is likely to be different from the exogenous rate fixed by the authorities (i_d), so

$$\overline{M}_s - M_D = kp(X - \overline{X}) - \lambda p(i_d - i_s)$$

If it is assumed that the second term of the equation (the speculative motive) is more important than the first term (the transactions motive) in determining interest rates, the equation can be approximately reduced to

$$\overline{M}_s - M_D \cong \lambda p(i_d - i_s)$$

If $\overline{M}_s - M_D$ is approximated by excess reserves in the commercial banking system,

$$i_d - i_s \cong \frac{1}{\lambda p}(RR) \qquad \text{and} \qquad i_s = i_d - \frac{1}{\lambda p}(RR)$$

Although this is a very crude approximation because changes in prices and output are ignored, it does relate movements in the short-term interest rate to the demand (and supply) of money.

The other equations are formulated along lines explained elsewhere in the book and requires little explanation here. Consumption of nondurables and services is a function of present and past income. Residential construction depends on present and past income and short-term interest rates, which represent general credit conditions. Inventory investment is positively related to sales and negatively related to past inventory stocks (the equation is actually written in the stock form). Imports are related to present and past output and relative prices (linearized). This is the only place relative prices are used in the model, because there is only one endogenous price level; import prices are, however, exogenous. In all these equations the Koyck distributed lag is used.

The system is closed with equations for the long-term interest rate, which is an average of present and past short-term rates; for an index of hours worked, which is negatively related to unemployment and changes in the wage rate; and factor-share equations. Corporate saving depends on after-tax corporate profits, rentier income depends on investment and changes in the long-term interest rate, and income of unincorporated businesses follows movements in GNP. Again, all these functions use a Koyck distributed lag. Note that while the aggregate demand functions are estimated in constant dollars, the factor share equations are estimated in current dollars. Changes in the price level have substantial redistributive effects on income shares. Finally, the depreciation (function of capital stock) and tax equations complete the model. The tax equations are not listed here, because they change every time the tax rates change. However, for actual solutions and simulations, tax equations for personal income tax, corporate income tax, excise taxes, and transfer payments are included.

As interesting and instructive as the revised Klein–Goldberger model is, there are several places where it needs to be enlarged. First, the restriction of only one endogenous price level raises several difficulties. The identity stating that aggregate demand equals the sum of its components can hold either in constant dollars or current dollars, but not in both as long as there is only one price level in the system. Relative price terms are also missing from several of the aggregate demand equations. Second, the failure to separate the cyclically volatile manufacturing sector from the rest of the economy makes it much harder to estimate such critical variables as the rate of capacity utilization and rate of unemployment. Furthermore, an annual model cannot be used to predict the pattern of GNP during the year. The claims of Suits and others that meaningful quarterly consumption functions cannot be estimated (discussed in the next section) does not obscure the fact that the quarterly movements of the economy are often at least as important as the yearly average. For example, real GNP was higher in 1960 than in 1959, but the quarterly figures clearly show that a recession started in mid-1960 and continued into 1961. In 1957, real GNP was substantially higher than in 1956, but the important question was whether a downturn would occur in the latter half of the year. Similar examples can be cited for almost every year in which there was a turning point. Thus the obvious paths of progress in econometric model-building after the Klein–Goldberger model have been refinement to a quarterly model, inclusion of a more realistic price sector, and disaggregation to at least a two-sector model.

We have already discussed the Wharton EFU model as an example of a model incorporating many of these refinements. Yet more disaggregation and expansion is certainly feasible within the framework of an econometric model. We next consider the largest econometric model project that has yet been undertaken for the U.S. economy.

18.2   THE BROOKINGS MODEL PROJECT[9]

During 1959 a group of economists headed by Lawrence R. Klein and James S. Duesenberry started planning the construction of a large-scale quarterly model of the U.S. economy which would contain 150 to 200 equations and which might ultimately be expanded to over 400 equations. Since this job seemed much too large for any one individual to undertake, more than 20 well-known economists, each an expert in his field, were asked to contribute equations for the model in their fields of specialization. This research project was originally funded by the Social Science Research Council but now resides at the Brookings Institution and is officially entitled the Brookings Quarterly Econometric Model of the United States. We have added the word "project" to the heading of this section to indicate clearly that, as of 1969, work on the model is still progressing, and that the volume published in 1965 represents more of a progress report than a finalized version of the model. Several satellite volumes have been or will be released describing some of the modifications and extensions of the model that have taken place: various multipliers of the model have been estimated, and plans are underway to expand the model by including additional industrial classifications. Furthermore, if the model is to be useful in the future it will have to be reestimated periodically using the revised data of the national income accounts as they become available.

One question often asked about the model is whether it has to be so big. Although the model is much larger than any other currently in existence, an argument can be made that it is not that much larger than the Wharton EFU model. The expansion has proceeded in two main directions. First, the Brookings model was expanded from two sectors (manufacturing and nonmanufacturing) to seven sectors. These are durable manufacturing, nondurable manufacturing, trade, regulated, construction, farming, and residual industries (mining; finance, insurance, and real estate; and services). Although the farm sector is separated from the rest of the Wharton EFU model, it is exogenous. A first step toward separating the regulated sector from other nonmanufacturing was taken in the Wharton EFU model fixed business investment equations when it became apparent that regulated investment was dependent on a substantially different lag structure and different financial

[9] J. S. Duesenberry, G. Fromm, L. R. Klein, and E. Kuh, eds., *The Brookings Quarterly Econometric Model of the United States Economy* (Chicago: Rand McNally, 1965).

variables than other fixed business investment. The separation of the highly cyclical capital-goods durable manufacturing sector from the nondurable manufacturing sector should be beneficial in the same way that the separation of the manufacturing sector from the total economy was advantageous in a two-sector model. The highly volatile production and demand components which are the main determinants of the business cycle can then be analyzed more closely. Thus a good a priori case can be made for disaggregation to the seven-sector model. Whether such a move proves in practice to provide substantial additional information is an empirical question to be answered by the actual results of the model, but work on the Wharton EFU model does indicate several areas where disaggregation should be promising.

The other principal expansion undertaken was to increase the number of equations in certain sectors which were virtually neglected by the Wharton model: the government, agriculture, financial, and labor force sectors. The financial sector was much too condensed in the Wharton model and some expansion in this area is certainly called for. The inclusion of the enlarged and useful financial sector is a definite improvement in the Brookings model. Not as much can be said for the other three sectors. Although the number of equations in each sector was considerable, the increase in informational content was often low. Many of the equations were of the form of pure auto-regressions, or autoregressions plus time and dummy variables. Although such equations may fit well in the sample period and may even predict well (although this is less likely), they are quite unlikely to explain the structure of the economy. Most of the equations from these three sectors were deleted in the actual version of the model used for solution.

Another question often asked about the model is whether it can be used to predict accurately. As pointed out in Chapter 17, we feel that the predictive ability of any econometric model is largely independent of its size, and its overall predictive performance will depend on the structure of a few key equations. In spite of the advances made in the Brookings model on the supply side (especially prices and wages) to be discussed later, the U.S. economy is still a mature economy with recurring excess capacity and cyclical fluctuations, so that certain strategic aggregate demand equations still hold the key to the short-term forecasting ability of any model. It might be noted that most of the expansion of the model occurred on the supply side and in the special sectors mentioned above: the demand side actually increased very little. Although no comment about the quality of either model is implied by counting equations, it may be of interest to compare in Table 18.1 the number of stochastic equations in each sector of aggregate demand for the Wharton EFU model and the Brookings model.

It should be stressed at this point that each individual contributor (including any coauthors) submitted a chapter on his specialty which included the estimated regression equations. The entire model was then reestimated by consistent methods of estimation, and the latter version has been solved for

TABLE 18.1 COMPARISON OF EQUATIONS IN AGGREGATE DEMAND SECTORS

	Wharton EFU Model	Brookings Model
Consumption	3	5
Fixed business investment	3	5
Residential construction	1	3[a]
Inventories and orders	3	6
Foreign sector	4	3

[a] Excluding some price equations also included in this sector (all other price equations are explained outside the aggregate demand sectors).

policy simulations. In some cases, no changes were made in the equations originally submitted except for the consistent estimates. In other cases the general nature of the equations was retained, but the specification of some of them was changed. In still other cases, almost the whole sector was changed. It can reasonably be inferred that those sections which were substantially changed were found to be unsatisfactory by the editors of the model for one reason or another.

Considering the aggregate demand equations first, we think that in general the original equations were quite unsatisfactory. Substantial experience with forecasting has indicated time and again that the key equations to an accurate forecast are consumption of durables, investment in plant and equipment, and inventory investment. Although it is certainly possible to make a bad forecast by other misspecifications in the model, it is most difficult to compile an accurate forecasting record if these strategic equations predict poorly.

The consumption sector has several questionable features. This is partially due to the belief by the authors, D. B. Suits and G. R. Sparks, that quarterly functions are somewhat illusory and that "the only 'quarterly' aspect of these equations is the slight shift in timing of the lag terms ... the reader will do well to remember that the title of this chapter (consumption regressions with quarterly data) was deliberately chosen."[10]

In particular, Suits and Sparks are wary about including lagged consumption as an independent variable in a quarterly function. They state that "there are serious statistical problems associated with the use of the lagged dependent variable, especially when levels, rather than first differences, are used in the regressions ... that may yield not only spuriously high correlation but serious bias in the estimates of the other coefficients."[11] Some experimentation with

---

[10] *The Brookings Model ... , op. cit.*, p. 218.

[11] *The Brookings Model ... , op. cit.*, p. 206. The reader may recall that just this problem was discussed in Chapter 3 and the ratio form of the consumption function was suggested to meet these difficulties.

a weighted average of lagged income leads them to the conclusion that lagged consumption is important in the consumer services function but not in the functions for food or other nondurables. In the consumption of food equation, lagged consumption becomes insignificant when population is added.

These results are not unreasonable by themselves. However, the resulting values of the long-run *mpc*'s do not appear to be at all reasonable. The problem is confounded by the use of the consumer attitude index in the consumption of autos equation. Besides being of dubious forecasting value, it substantially reduces the parameter estimate of income and leads to erroneous results in policy simulations. This latter problem is also pointed out by Suits and Sparks.

The reestimation of the consumption functions by the editors of the Brookings model is hardly more satisfactory. The lagged consumption terms are reinstated in the food and other nondurables equations, where they are both significant. However, their other modifications do not work as well. Relative prices are included in all the consumption functions but are significant only in the other nondurables equation. This reverses the finding of Suits and Sparks that relative prices are highly significant in the food and services equation. Neither group finds a significant price term in the car equation, which contrasts significantly with the results presented in Chapter 6. The stock-adjustment term in the car equation is replaced by a nonsignificant relative price term, further clouding the interpretation of short- and long-run effects. The population term is shifted from the food equation to the services equation with the result that income is now insignificant in the latter function. Finally, a liquid-assets term used by Suits and Sparks in all the consumption functions except food and autos is retained only in the services equation. In any case the liquid-assets variable is of questionable validity, because the substantial increase in the liquid assets/income ratio since 1958 has not been matched by movements in any of the broad consumption/income ratios considered here.

The short- and long-run *mpc*'s for both sets of consumption functions are given in Table 18.2. Although the short-run (quarterly) values are well in line with other estimates, the long-run values in both cases are significantly less than the apc and far below any of the values calculated for the variety of consumption functions estimated in Chapter 3. This finding alone would tend to cast doubt on the accuracy of long-run policy simulations calculated with the Brookings model.

The deletion of the stock term from the car equation may lead to unrealistic results even in the short run, because there is no longer a stock-adjustment effect in this equation. When the attitude index is included, this reduces the income elasticity in the revised equation to a value below unity. This seems inconsistent both with other empirical estimates and with the short-run income elasticity of other durables, which is estimated to be over 3. The problems caused by omitting the stock-adjustment term were spotlighted

TABLE 18.2 VALUES OF THE *mpc* IN THE BROOKINGS MODEL
CONSUMPTION FUNCTIONS

Category of Consumption	Original Suits–Sparks Estimation		Revisions by Editors of the Brookings Model	
	Short-Run (Quarterly) *mpc*	Long-Run *mpc*	Short-Run (Quarterly) *mpc*	Long-Run *mpc*
Autos	0.079	0.040	0.050	0.050
Other durables	0.161	0.077	0.242	0.166
Food	0.066	0.066	0.087	0.149
Other nondurables	0.169	0.169	0.146	0.200
Services	0.051	0.292	0.019	0.064
	0.531	0.644	0.544	0.629

by a simulation of the Brookings model which was used to analyze the effect of the 1965 excise tax cut.[12] Since cars were the commodity most affected by this tax cut, the effect of the reduction of the excise tax depends largely on the form of the automobile equation. The simulation results showed that the effect of the excise tax was small at first but increased over time. If a more usual stock-adjustment function had been used, the simulation results would have been reversed, with the effect being largest at first and then declining.

The fixed business investment functions (both anticipations and realizations) originally estimated for the model have been discussed in earlier chapters, so there is no need to elaborate here. However, these functions were not used in the solution of the model. There was, understandably, some doubt whether the anticipations functions, which depend almost entirely on lagged values of investment, would predict ahead accurately for an eight-quarter period. Instead, some other investment functions were used, which have been described as "very ordinary" and "garden variety" by the editors. These investment functions happen to be just the ones described in Chapter 4, except for the misplaced short-lag interest rate, which has already been discussed in detail. Thus we shall not comment further on these functions. It might be pointed out, however, that similar functions have worked quite well in predicting investment for the period 1963–1965, so they are likely to work well in the Brookings model simulations, provided the predictions of output and interest rates are accurate.

The inventory and orders functions also have performed poorly. The reason for this is somewhat more puzzling. The functions for the manufacturing

---

[12] P. Taubman, "An Analysis of the 1965 Excise Tax Cut," paper delivered at the Rome meetings of the Econometric Society, September, 1965.

sector reported by Michael Lovell were quite reasonable, with the usual sales, lagged stock, and unfilled orders variables all significant with the correct sign (except for a nonsignificant negative sign for the change in unfilled orders variable in nondurable manufacturing). However, when these functions were reestimated the signs became nonsignificant. One problem may have been the fact that Lovell used actual sales, while the reestimated equations, to conform to the rest of the model, used a "sales-originating" variable equal to output originating minus inventory investment in that sector. After the first Brookings volume had gone to press, poor results with the inventory functions led to the respecification of the lag on the unfilled orders variable. This gave somewhat better results, but they were still not entirely satisfactory.

It appears as though work on the other inventory investment functions was never quite completed. The trade inventory equation that was estimated excludes auto inventories. No function for them is included in the model, thus leaving a quite volatile component of aggregate demand unexplained. Although auto inventories may be hard to explain in the short run, this is not a particularly good reason for completely neglecting them. The residual sector inventory investment function was also quite unsatisfactory, with sales originating actually having a nonsignificant negative sign.

The orders equations seem to be reasonable, with the change in sales, level of sales, change in the wholesale price index, and change in national defense expenditures all significant with the correct signs. However, in actual simulation, the nondurables orders equation predicted negative unfilled orders, a physical impossibility. This problem was solved by setting the orders at zero for the rest of the period. It should be pointed out that nondurable unfilled orders are a very small magnitude (about $2.5 billion) compared to durable unfilled orders (about $70 billion), so even if much larger errors were made in the durables equation, they would not have shown up as negative numbers. However, this section of the model could also be improved.

The remaining sectors of aggregate demand were changed very little by the editors. The residential housing equation sector was carefully done by Maisel. It includes an estimation of housing starts and then the use of a Department of Commerce identity to phase housing starts into actual construction. Maisel also constructed series on vacancies, removals, and completions used in his system. Alterations and modernizations were separated from new construction, and an additional equation was added to explain private construction by religious, educational, and social groups; however, this last equation is an autoregression. Maisel's treatment represents a real advancement compared to work previously available in the econometric literature.

The foreign sector is also well done, although somewhat brief. The forms of the equations are very similar to the ones used in the Wharton EFU model, since we borrowed many of the ideas, and thus require little additional comment.

We now turn to the supply side of the model, which undoubtedly represents the most interesting new work done in the model. One very useful study is the determination of wages and prices by Schultze and Tryon. The other is an interesting aggregation of prices and outputs into a consistent format. More than anywhere else in the model, this aggregation represents the collaboration of several of the authors of the Brookings model rather than a case of isolated study.

The price and wage equations have been discussed before in Chapter 10, so it is not necessary to review them again in detail. Prices in the version of the model used for simulation are a function of normal and actual unit labor costs and the change in the inventory-output originating ratio. The sign of the latter term is negative, because when inventories are too high, firms will reduce their prices in hopes of selling excess merchandise. However, when inventories are increasing, this may put pressure on demand (if the economy is nearing full employment) so that prices may rise. The 1965–1966 price increase was associated with an increase, not a decrease, in the inventory-sales ratio. These functions also fail to take account of the fact that firms are more likely to raise their prices when business is good and the elasticity of demand is lower. In the Wharton EFU model this relationship is represented by a capacity utilization term, but some other measure of output relative to a trend output could also have been used. These particular functions would be unlikely to predict the observed increase in manufacturing prices for the 1964–1965 period, because unit labor costs remained steady or even fell slightly then.

The wage equations are of the disequilibrium type discussed earlier. The percentage change in wage rates is positively related to percentage change in the consumer price index, the profit rate, and the reciprocal of unemployment, and negatively related to last year's percentage wage changes. All these variables are significant and with the correct sign except the profit rate, which is significantly positive in only two of the six sectors (the farm sector is omitted here). As mentioned earlier, the wage functions in the Wharton EFU model follow these equations closely except for the use of the profit variable, which in our calculations always entered with a negative sign. One slight improvement might be made by substituting the unemployment rate for key demographic groups, in place of the overall unemployment rate. It will be interesting to see if such an approach does improve these functions, as it has in the Wharton EFU model. Meanwhile, these wage functions represent an improvement in an area that has been noted for its casual empiricism.

It was necessary to convert the prices for the *sectors* into prices for the components of aggregate demand, for these were not estimated independently in the model, nor could they be if both the current dollar and constant dollar identities are to hold. This conversion is accomplished in two main steps. First, components of final demand in each sector must be estimated. They can be calculated from the relationship $\mathbf{F} = (\mathbf{I} - \mathbf{A})\mathbf{X}$, where $\mathbf{F}$ is the vector of final demand, $I - A$ is a 7 by 7 input-output matrix, and X is the vector of gross output. Both F and X are in constant dollars. The seven-sector input-output matrix was aggregated from the detailed 1947 BLS input-output table. The numbers for the X vector are simply output originating in each sector. Computed sector final demands were then calculated for the period 1947–1960 from this vector equation. The input-output matrix was assumed to remain constant throughout the sample period.

Once the series for final demand were estimated, they were regressed on the components of GNP. These standard regression equations can be represented as

$$F_j = w_{jk}GNP_k \qquad j = 1, \ldots, 7$$

where the w_{jk} are the regression coefficients. These coefficients are then used to calculate the price regressions. The value of total final demand must be equal to GNP, so that

$$\sum_{j=1}^{7} p_j F_j = \sum_k p_k GNP_k$$

But the F_j have just been estimated as equal to $w_{jk}GNP_k$, so

$$\sum_j p_j w_{jk}GNP_k = \sum_k p_k GNP_k \qquad \text{or} \qquad \sum_j p_j w_{jk} = \sum_k p_k$$

The p_k, prices for the components of aggregate demand, are thus functions of the p_j, prices of final sector demand. The regression constants are equal to the estimated relations between the sectors of final demand and the sectors of gross national product.

Some approximations were made in this process. A constant input-output matrix was used for the entire sample period, and the equations estimating the F_j did not fit exactly. Thus the actual deflators for the components of GNP diverged somewhat from the predicted values. To improve these relationships, some autoregressive correction factors were tried of the form

$$p_k = a_0 + a_1 p_k^* + a_2(p_k - p_k^*)_{-1}$$

where the p_k^* are the values calculated from final demand weights and the p_k are the actual price deflators for the demand components of GNP.

To close the supply side equations are needed to explain factor shares: these were estimated by Edwin Kuh. They are primarily production functions, inverted to become labor requirements functions; that is,

$$X = f(L, K, t)$$

is rewritten as

$$L = g(X, K, t)$$

Other equations are also needed for unincorporated business income, rent and interest income, dividends, and inventory valuation adjustment. All these are supplied except the equations for rent income and unincorporated business income. The latter is not included because "simple ratio estimates appear adequate to portray unincorporated business income."[13]

The labor requirements functions are somewhat unusual in several respects. First, the dependent variable is employment, rather than man-hours, which is the correct labor input variable in the production function. Presumably this could be the result of dividing man-hours into employment and hours worked. However, one would then expect employment and hours to be negatively correlated, while a strong positive correlation between them is reported. The function is of the form

$$N = aX - bK + ch$$

which implies that for X and K constant, an increase in hours will raise employment. This is not a reasonable result. What is actually happening is that the hours variable is measuring the general cyclical behavior of the change in labor's share. A similar problem occurred with the capacity utilization variable in our estimates of production functions in this inverted form. The sign of the variable was consistently positive instead of negative as it should have been.

It was shown in Chapter 10 how the Cobb–Douglas production functions gave substantially different results from the linear production functions (as estimated here). Yet Kuh does not estimate any log-linear functions. He does state that "it is always possible to reinterpret the elasticities associated with the function as if they were the parameters of a log-linear Cobb–Douglas relation."[14] However, the problem is that the estimated elasticities of the two forms of the function are quite different from each other. For one example, the estimated long-run elasticity of employment with respect to output for total manufacturing is 8.6, far different from the usual estimate of about 1.0.

Kuh disaggregates production and overhead workers in the manufacturing sector. As expected, he finds that overhead workers are less subject to cyclical influences. He also posits a negative relationship between production workers and capital stock and a positive relationship between overhead workers and capital stock. However, for nondurable manufacturing, this latter relationship is significantly negative. This is attributed to "an aggregation fluke."

The equations explaining hours worked (for the manufacturing and construction sectors) have hours as a function of percentage changes in output and lagged hours. While the use of the lagged dependent variable is one way of separating the short-run and long-run effects of the other independent variable(s), the results are the reverse of what might normally be expected.

---

[13] *Ibid.*, p. 277.
[14] *Ibid.*, p. 241.

Since hours serve as a buffer, one would expect that changes in output would affect hours more in the short run, when they are more likely to be regarded as temporary, than in the long run, when employment is more likely to be adjusted. However, with the positive lagged hours term, just the opposite effect occurs. This does not seem to be a sensible finding. These functions would undoubtedly be improved by the use of some general cyclical variable and a restructuring of the equations to take account of the buffer nature of hours.

We now consider the separate submodels built for the monetary, agricultural, government, and labor force sectors. Expansion of the monetary sector beyond the usual perfunctory treatment usually given these equations in econometric models was clearly necessary, and deLeeuw supplies a detailed treatment of seven financial markets in his chapter in the Brookings model volume. This model was condensed into five equations by deLeeuw for the final version of the model. Both versions of his model introduce the interest rate(s) as the rate(s) clearing the market instead of as some linear function of policy variables.

The required reserves of commercial banks are defined as being equal to the required reserve ratio on demand deposits times the amount of demand deposits, plus the required reserve ratio on time deposits times the amount of time deposits. The amount of demand deposits and time deposits are then explained as functions of various interest rates and several aggregate variables, such as recent values of GNP, personal disposable income, and corporate cash flow. This determines required reserves within the model.

To determine interest rates, deLeeuw makes use of the identity that required reserves plus free reserves must be equal to unborrowed reserves. This last term is exogenous. Since required reserves are already determined in the submodel, this identity determines free reserves. A function is also included which explains free reserves: they depend on excess reserves, the short-term treasury bill rate, and the discount rate. However, since free reserves have already been determined by the identity, this function actually determines the short-term interest rate. The greater the pressure to borrow from the Fed (which is determined by required reserves, excess reserves, banks' portfolios, and the discount rate), the more the short-term rate will rise in order to clear the market.

Once the treasury bill rate is determined in this manner, other equations explaining the term structure of interest rates are used to explain the long-term rate and the rate of time deposits. These type of equations were discussed in Chapter 11, so the explanation is not repeated here.

The other three submodels will be discussed only briefly, because most of the equations originally estimated are not used in the working version of the model. The price and quantity equations for the agricultural sector are calculated from a 24 by 24 consumer demand matrix of different categories of food. This was aggregated into the three categories of food livestock, food crops, and nonfoods: nonfoods are not estimated in this sector. The consumption of livestock and the price of crops are then taken to be exogenous. Although this may be appropriate for any given quarter, it is not a satisfactory procedure if these equations are to be used for prediction or policy purposes more than one or two quarters ahead. These agricultural figures are adjusted to correspond to prices and quantities that are consistent with the rest of the model. Other equations for fixed business investment, inventory investment, employment, gross income, and depreciation in the farm sector are primarily or entirely functions of exogenous variables or lagged dependent variables. Some of these (such as the fixed business investment functions) were dropped: others were retained.

In the model of the government subsector, both receipts and expenditures are estimated in considerable detail. The receipts equations represent disaggregation of the standard functions: personal income taxes, corporate income taxes, excise taxes, and contributions for social insurance. The expenditures equations, except for transfer payments, represent the first attempt to estimate government spending within the framework of a quarterly econometric model.

Receipts are estimated separately for federal and state and local governments. Some of the income tax equations are based on tax rates, while others are based on actual income. The excise taxes are disaggregated into nine functions: taxes are a function of the tax rate and the taxable income in each. Log-linear functions are used, so that the estimated elasticity of taxation remains constant throughout the sample period. Most of these elasticities seem quite reasonable, and in general this section seems well done. However, the disaggregated excise tax functions were dropped from the final version of the model. Contributions for social insurance were also disaggregated into four equations, some of which were later retained. Functions are also included for corporate and personal income taxes both at the federal and state and local levels.

On the expenditure side of this sector model, retirement and disability payments are generally a function of the relevant subsector of the population and the maximum monthly benefit payment. Again the equations are estimated in log-linear form and most of the elasticities seem reasonable. The equations for purchases of goods and services, however, are a bit more dubious. They depend mainly on estimates made in the President's budget of the current year and on autoregressive variables. Average annual earnings of government employees are simply related to the same figure in the total economy. State and local construction is subdivided into construction expenditures for education, hospitals, administrative and service facilities, highways, sewer and water systems, and all other purchases. An attempt is made to build stock-adjustment models for each of these categories. In some cases the attempt is successful, but in other cases population and the lagged dependent variable are the main variables.

The government sector model carries disaggregation further than do any of the other sectors. This is primarily responsible for the reduction of its size in the final version, although some of the autoregressive equations were dropped because they were not found to be very useful. The treatment of the tax and transfer equations—the use of tax rates and the tax base—is a useful one which could well be followed in other econometric models. Although additional work is necessary for the equations explaining purchases of goods and services, these equations represent an interesting start toward reducing the degree of exogeneity of econometric models.

The last sector to be considered is the endogenous explanation of the labor force and the marriage rate. Most of these functions estimated are in the form of participations rates, which are related to general cyclical factors such as the unemployment rate and hours worked per week. The size of the armed forces is also an important variable in several equations. The marriage rate is a function of similar variables. The selection of the equations for the complete model is reduced to four participation rate equations (male and female, 14–19 and 20 and over) and the one marriage rate equation. Even these equations were found "somewhat disappointing" by the editors, and in the actual version used for solution none of the equations from this sector was used.

One of the principal stated aims of the Brookings model was to use it for short-term forecasting. Judged from this viewpoint it is hard to see how it can be considered a successful project. Almost ten years after its inception, it has yet to be used to generate a single *ex ante* forecast. The time lag from the earliest planning stages of the project in 1959 to a consistent set of estimates in mid-1963 was not unreasonable considering the pioneering nature of building such a large-scale model and the inevitable problems of coordination among a sizable group of widely separated research workers. If the model had been used to generate *ex ante* forecasts starting in 1964 or even 1965 on a continuing basis, this would have been a considerable accomplishment.

Instead, it was found necessary to respecify and reestimate most of the model. This can be seen in the version used by Fromm and Taubman for more recent work.[15] Besides the use of the alternative investment functions, the critical consumer durables equations and inventory investment equations were reestimated. Fromm developed a completely new agricultural sector, the labor-force equations were dropped, and the monetary sector was corrected (in the previous version, the subsector had six endogenous variables but only five equations). Since then other changes have been made; in particular, Fromm has reestimated the price and wage functions, because he found that "this sector is one of the larger contributors of error in the aggregate results."[16]

---

[15] G. Fromm and P. Taubman, *Policy Simulation with an Econometric Model* (Washington: The Brookings Institution, 1968).

[16] *Ibid.*, p. 9.

Much of this work has yielded instructive results. The model has been programmed for solution and eight-quarter *ex post* forecasts have been obtained for 1961–1962 and 1963–1964. Several simulation studies and multiplier calculations have been prepared for these periods; some of the results are reported in Section 20.3. Ten-year simulation studies have also been prepared, and additional experiments are in progress.

However, what was novel and pioneering in 1959 has become commonplace ten years later. Several other models whose size approaches the Brookings model are currently not only fully operative but have been reestimated, if necessary, with the latest set of national income accounts. This has not been done for the Brookings model, although it must be done periodically for any model that is to be used for generating *ex ante* forecasts. As an example of the faster pace of more recent model building, the Federal Reserve Board–Massachusetts Institute of Technology (FRB–MIT) model of over 125 equations was planned, estimated, simulated, and used to generate forecasts by a small group of experts in a period of less than two years.[17] The current version of the Wharton EFU model, listed in Section 15.3, was constructed and programmed for solution and forecasting in less than a year and was completely reestimated and reprogrammed on the basis of the 1965 data revision in three months.

Some of the problems connected with the Brookings model undoubtedly arise from the fact that in spite of the seminars in which all the participants exchanged ideas, the model is essentially a number of independent studies that were combined at a later date. Thus some of the independent variables used in the individual equations were not included in the overall model, and the equations had to be changed. The outstanding example of this is in the inventory investment sector, where sales variables (used in the original equations) worked well but output originating (used in the final equations) gave much poorer results. In other cases, the factors fitted well during the sample period but were of little forecasting value. This was usually the case in those equations where time trends and lagged dependent variables were used almost exclusively as independent variables.

Naturally the Brookings model has its supporters. Duesenberry and Klein claim that "it is certain that no single individual or small team could have uncovered so many interesting and revealing relationships in a single model in a time span of three years."[18] However, the real problem in the "model by committee" approach is not the original estimation but the future—to make the model operational and keep it up to date. Progress continues to be made on the Brookings model; many of the equations are being improved,

---

[17] For an overall view of this model, see R. H. Rasche and H. Shapiro, "The FRB–MIT Econometric Model: Its Special Features and Implications for Stabilization Policies," *American Economic Review*, Vol. 48, No. 2 (May, 1968).

[18] *The Brookings Model . . . , op. cit.*, p. 22.

and the entire model is to be reestimated with the most recent data. When this has been accomplished, it is reasonable to suppose that the model will predict well and be a useful test for analysis. Nevertheless, recent experience indicates that models of comparable size and performance can be built in much less time by small research teams, who will retain greater capability to keep them operational.

18.3   THE PREDICTIVE RECORD OF ECONOMETRIC MODELS AND OTHER FORECASTS

Earlier we discussed alternative methods of forecasting. It is now time to compare the actual record—true *ex ante* forecasts—of these various methods of prediction. This is the acid test that must be used to judge all serious methods of prediction. With today's modern technology, good sample period fits and good *ex post* forecasts are limited only by the amount of available computer time, the number of research assistants, and one's own

TABLE 18.3   COMPARISON OF *EX ANTE* FORECASTS OF GNP MADE BY SEVERAL DIFFERENT METHODS
(all figures are in billions of current dollars)

Year	Actual Old Data[a]	Actual New Data[b]	Federal Reserve Compilation[c]					Error (Rel. to Av.)	Mich-igan[d,h]	Error	CEA[g]
			Av.	Median	Mode	High	Low				
1959	483	484	470	470	470	480	463	−13	464	−19	
1960	503	504	507	507	500	516	493	4	493	−10	
1961	519	520	512	512	513	523	507	−7	521	2	
1962	556	560	560	560	565	566	551	4	560	4	570
1963	584	591	573	573	567	582	565	−11	578	−6	578
1964[f]	623	632	616	616	615	630	607	−7	619	−4	619
1965	666	685	656	656	660	662	647	−10	652	−14	660
1966[m]	732	748	725	725	722	735	710	−7	725	−7	722
1967	781	790	785	785	790	795	755	4	794	13	787
Av. absolute error 1959–1967								7.4		8.8	
Av. absolute error 1963–1967								7.8		8.8	

[a] Based on most recent figures available *at the time of prediction.*
[b] Revised GNP figures taken from the July, 1968, national income accounts.
[c] Compiled from public statements and releases made in the fourth quarter of the preceding year.
[d] Forecasts made the last week in October. Data are taken from D. B. Suits, "Forecasting and Analysis with an Econometric Model," *American Economic Review*, Vol. 52, No. 1 (March, 1962), pp. 121–123, through 1961, and from the *Federal Reserve Bulletin* tabulations thereafter.
[e] Forecasts made early in January. Data are taken from various issues of the *Economic Report of the President.*
[f] Forecasts are made in the fourth quarter. Data are taken from various mimeographed releases.
[g] Forecasts made in mid-March. Data are taken from various mimeographed releases supplied by Professor Friend.

patience. On the other hand, predictions publicly released ahead of the period being forecast are unlikely to be merely a product of data manipulation, particularly if they continue to predict well year after year.

Most of the analysis in this section will deal with the forecasting record of various econometric models. However, it may also be instructive to examine the average record of general forecasts as well as those of some particular models. Approximately 50 yearly forecasts of GNP and other variables made in the fourth quarter of the previous year are gathered and tabulated annually by the Federal Reserve Bank of Philadelphia. The average figures together with some other statistics are listed here. We compare the average of these predictions with forecasts made by the University of Michigan's Research Seminar in Quantitative Economics, the Council of Economic Advisors, the Friend–Taubman model, and the Wharton EFU model. The comparison of all these forecasts with each other, the actual data, and "predictions" of various naive models is given in Table 18.3. Although the record of the Michigan model has been available since 1953, the figures given here begin in 1959, the first year for which the Federal Reserve Bank of Philadelphia tabulations are available.

TABLE 18.3 (*Continued*)

ror	Wharton EFU^f	Error	Friend–Taub-man^{g,h}	Error	Naive Model II^i	Error	Naive Model III^j	Error	Naive Model IV^k	Error
					447	−36	472	−11	464	−19
					521	−18	502	−1	503	0
					522	3	511	−8	523	4
4					535	−1	559	3	539	−17
6	585	1	588	4	594	10	582	−2	575	−9
4	625	2	628	5	612	−11	614	−9	606	−17
6	662	−4	663	−3	661	−5	663	−3	646	−20
0	728	−4	n.a.		724	−8	721	−11	708	−24
6	784	3	n.a.		791	10	788	7	768	−13
	—		—		11.3		6.1		13.7	
6.4	2.8		4.0		8.8		6.4		16.6	

^{h} Forecasts are actually made in constant dollars. Correct price levels were used to convert figures to current dollars.
^{i} $\Delta GNP_t = \Delta GNP_{t-1}$.
^{j} $GNP_t = 1.75(\underline{GNP}_{t-2\,quarters} - GNP_{t-4\,quarters}) + GNP_{t-2\,quarters}$; see the text.
^{k} $\Delta GNP_t = \overline{\Delta GNP}$(average over the sample period).
^{l} Based only on forecasts assuming tax cut.
^{m} Forecasts made during January, 1966. Owing to widespread escalation of the 1966 forecasts, coinciding with similar movements in military expenditures, a special survey was conducted at the end of January by the Federal Reserve Bank. The average forecast was \$12 billion higher than the result obtained in their regular fourth-quarter survey, so \$12 billion was added to their figures and the Michigan forecast. The Wharton forecast is an actual one made at the end of January, 1966.

The forecasts made by the Council of Economic Advisors (excluding the 1962 forecast), the Wharton EFU model, and the Friend–Taubman model predict better than the consensus forecasts or the naive models, although unfortunately the *ex ante* record is only available for five years. The Friend–Taubman forecasts are made in mid-March, long after the other forecasts have been placed on record, so that their record is not really comparable. The Wharton EFU forecasts appear to have the best record of any of the models tested, at least for this five-year period. It is shown below that the overall record is not as glossy as the surface picture; some of the components are poorly predicted, and some of the quarter to quarter movements should have been forecasted better. Even so, we feel that this record stands as a direct refutation to those who would argue that some combination of sophisticated judgment and simple arithmetic will generate a series of forecasts superior to those from any econometric model.

Somewhat surprisingly, the Michigan model performs somewhat more poorly than the average noneconometric forecast for the 1959–1967 period and the 1963–1967 period. Both the Federal Reserve Board average forecast and the Michigan predictions perform more poorly than naive model III, which is an extrapolation of the change between the first quarter and third quarter GNP through the following year. This naive model is calculated as follows: Let GNP for the first quarter of year $t - 1$ equal x_1; let GNP for the third quarter of year $t - 1$ equal x_2. Then using simple extrapolation and projecting the same trend,

$$\text{GNP}_{t,\,1\text{st quarter}} = x_2 + 1.0(x_2 - x_1)$$
$$\text{GNP}_{t,\,2\text{nd quarter}} = x_2 + 1.5(x_2 - x_1)$$
$$\text{GNP}_{t,\,3\text{rd quarter}} = x_2 + 2.0(x_2 - x_1)$$
$$\text{GNP}_{t,\,4\text{th quarter}} = x_2 + 2.5(x_2 - x_1)$$

so that for the yearly average,

$$\text{GNP} = x_2 + 1.75(x_2 - x_1)$$

as given in Table 18.3.

It should be pointed out that GNP grew rather smoothly over the period 1962–1967 so that this naive model undoubtedly worked better for this period than it would over a more representative period. Yet the 1960 recession was also well gauged by this method. It should also be mentioned that the two other naive models, used in Chapter 17 as well as here—that the change in GNP this year equals the change in GNP last year, and the change in GNP this year equals the average change in GNP over the sample period to date —give far inferior results. Naive model I, which states that $\text{GNP}_t = \text{GNP}_{t-1}$, was not even tabulated here because of its inferior performance. While all the actual forecasts tabulated give much better predictions than the average of these naive models, some of the forecasting records can be bested by an extrapolation of recent changes in GNP.

The main problem with the comparisons tabulated in Table 18.3 is that in many cases they cover only five years. This is probably too short a time to make any definite statements about the relative efficacy of various methods of forecasting. Furthermore, the Wharton EFU model has not had to predict a year in which a recession has occurred. This is generally believed to be a more stringent test than the prediction of continued prosperity. However, we might examine the evidence on this point.

The forecasting record of the Michigan model is available back to 1953. From that time through 1967 there have been recessions in 1954, 1958, and 1960. The error of prediction in each of these three years was $0, 3, and −10 billion, respectively. In the case of 1960 the forecast of GNP was understated even though it turned out to be a recession year. This average absolute error of $4.3 billion compares to average absolute errors of $8.4 billion for the remaining years in the 1953–1967 period and $7.8 billion for the 1959–1967 period. Clearly this model has been more successful at predicting recessions than forecasting upturns and continued prosperity. Corroborative evidence is offered by the average of the Federal Reserve Board forecasts. The error of prediction of $4 billion in 1960 was *smaller than any other error* for those forecasts in the 1959–1967 period. Although these findings cannot be applied unequivocally to the Wharton EFU model, they do suggest that predicting recessions has not been the major problem of economic forecasters in the postwar period.

To obtain a more complete picture of the forecasting record of the Wharton EFU model, we present a quarter by quarter compilation of the actual *ex ante* forecasts made one and two quarters ahead. The most meaningful comparison of these forecasts would be with predictions from other models or alternative methods of forecasting. However, such disaggregated information is not available on a quarterly basis for other predictions. The forecasting record of the components of the Wharton EFU model is compared exclusively with actual values and various naive models.

The results of Table 18.3 suggest that it is not feasible to compare predicted values directly with revised actual values, since the latter are subject to extensive revision. Instead, we compare predicted changes with actual changes. These are defined as follows:

Predicted changes: predicted values at time $t + j$ minus the latest actual values available *at the time of prediction*

Actual changes 1963.2–1965.2: values taken from the July, 1965, *Survey of Current Business*, which are prerevised data

Actual changes 1965.3–1966.4: values taken from the July, 1967, *Survey of Current Business*

It should be pointed out that we usually make several alternative forecasts each quarter to assess the effects of different monetary and fiscal policies. For purposes of the predictive record, however, the *control solution*, which incorporates our own best estimates of exogenous variables, has been used as a basis for comparison in all cases.

A word of explanation might be added about the timing of these forecasts. In general, preliminary data for a given quarter are made available about a month after the quarter ends. There is on the average a two-week lag while we process the data and make the predictions. This means that predictions for quarter *t* first appear midway through the quarter they are predicting. However, no data for that quarter are yet available, so the result is a true *ex ante* forecast. The predictions listed in Table 18.3, which are made midway in the fourth quarter of the previous year, actually predict five quarters ahead, since the fourth quarter is not yet known.

The first forecasts from the Wharton EFU model were made in early 1963 for a period of four quarters; this period was later extended to eight quarters. This pattern has been continued except for a break in the predictions following the massive data revision in mid-1965. The complete model had to be reestimated at that time because the nature and definition of many of the series had changed. This was not completed until the end of the year, so that two quarters of predictions are missing. Some interim forecasts based on a hastily adjusted version of the model proved unreliable and are not included here. With this exception, detailed comparisons of predicted and actual changes for all major components of GNP one and two quarters ahead for the period 1963–1966 are presented in Tables 18.4 and 18.5. Summary statistics are given in Table 18.8 (see pp. 522–528).

A comparison of the summary statistics in Table 18.8 reveals that the error of prediction two quarters ahead is not much larger than one quarter ahead for most components of GNP. This suggests that erratic quarter to quarter fluctuations in the data tend to cancel when predictions are averaged over more than one quarter. To test this hypothesis further we compare predictions of GNP one, two, three, and four quarters ahead with a four-quarter average of GNP forecasts. These results are given in Table 18.6. There it is shown that the absolute error of the four-quarter average forecasts ($3.6 billion) is much smaller than the average forecast error of each quarter taken separately ($5.3 billion) and is even considerably smaller than the forecast error for two quarters ahead ($4.3 billion).

As a final check on the predictive accuracy of the Wharton EFU model, we present the annual end-of-the-year forecasts in greater detail in Table 18.7. These forecasts are probably more important than the others because of the preponderance of calendar year planning both by business and government. They are usually more accurate than forecasts made at other times of the year because more is generally known about monetary and fiscal policies during the next four quarters at the end of the year than in midyear (although this was not the case with defense expenditures in late 1965).[19]

A brief word on the interpretation of the results in Tables 18.4 to 18.8 is in order here. Unfortunately no completely objective measure is available for assessing the relative performance of the sector predictions. The best method of comparison, as has been stressed, is to relate our results to other publicly released forecasts available at the same time. Although this was done with the annual forecasts for GNP, such detail is not available for quarterly sectoral forecasts. Comparisons are thus tabulated for actual changes and some of the naive models.

The only sector forecast for which exact comparisons are available is fixed business investment. Both the McGraw-Hill annual anticipations and the OBE-SEC quarterly intentions can be used for comparison. The Wharton EFU model forecast better than either series in the 1963–1966 period. For the annual forecasts made in the fourth quarter, the predictive error of fixed business investment was only 1.8 percent compared to an average absolute error of 6.3 percent for the McGraw-Hill anticipations. For forecasts made two quarters ahead, the average absolute error of prediction was 2.0 percent compared to an error of 2.2 percent for the OBE–SEC intentions survey.[20] In this respect it can be said that the plant and equipment investment forecasts were quite accurate. There is also additional evidence that these forecasts were useful, or would have been if they were used. In mid-1966, a well-known business forecaster stated that "a prediction in 1962 or even early 1963 that business capital investment was about to break out of the pattern of general stagnation which had characterized the previous five years would have been exceedingly useful not only to capital goods producers but also to investors."[21]

The overall GNP forecasts seem to have small errors relative to actual changes, other forecast errors of alternative predictions, and various naive models. One surprising finding is that the forecast of GNP two quarters ahead is poorer than the "predictions" given by naive model II. Subsequent calculations given in Table 18.8 reveal that GNP forecasts of one, three, four, and an average of the last four quarters are all substantially better than "predictions" from the same naive model. On balance it would seem clear that the naive model is inferior; this is also confirmed by the annual (year-end) forecasts.

Evaluations of the other sectors must necessarily be more subjective. In general it would seem that the prediction of consumption of nondurables

---

[19] In a few cases, predictions three and four quarters ahead which were originally based on the old data were compared with an extrapolation of those data instead of the new data. This was necessitated because the revisions in certain components of GNP (consumer durables, fixed business investment, and inventory investment) differed from the old data by an amount that steadily increased over time. The adjustments used were $0.5, $1.0, and $0.5 billion per quarter, respectively. These exceptions are explicitly noted in Tables 18.6 and 18.7.

[20] More detail on these predictions is given in Section 17.2.

[21] W. F. Butler, "Public Policy and Business Forecasting," in L. V. Conway and T. C. Gaines, eds. *Forecasting Business and Economic Activity* (Chicago: American Statistical Association, 1967), p. 136. (It might be mentioned that Mr. Butler did receive the Wharton EFU forecasts.)

TABLE 18.4 PREDICTIVE RECORD OF THE WHARTON EFU MODEL ONE QUARTER AHEAD (*all figures are in billions of current dollars*)

Variable[a]	1963.2 Actual Change	Predicted Change	Error	1963.3 A	P	E	1963.4 A	P	E
C_{ns}	2.4	3.7	1.3	4.7	2.8	−1.9	2.5	3.0	0.5
C_d	0.4	0.3	−0.1	0.7	−2.4	−3.1	1.4	−1.9	−3.3
I_p	1.5	3.9	2.4	1.8	2.2	0.4	1.2	2.2	1.0
I_h	0.8	−0.8	−1.6	0.3	−0.2	−0.5	0.8	0.2	−0.6
ΔI_i	0.0	3.8	3.8	0.6	2.6	2.0	2.2	1.6	−0.6
F	0.9	−0.1	−1.0	−0.1	−0.9	−0.8	1.6	0.4	−1.2
G	−0.5	0.8	1.3	1.9	5.1	3.2	2.0	5.2	3.2
GNP	5.6	11.6	6.0	9.8	9.2	−0.6	11.8	10.8	−1.0

Variable[a]	1964.4 Actual Change	Predicted Change	Error	1965.1 A	P	E	1965.2 A	P	E
C_{ns}	4.4	4.8	0.4	5.7	5.3	−0.4	6.4	4.8	−1.6
C_d	−2.4	−2.1	0.3	5.7	4.0	−1.7	−1.4	−0.4	1.0
I_p	0.8	2.3	1.5	2.0	1.6	−0.4	0.7	3.0	2.3
I_h	−0.6	0.2	0.8	1.1	1.5	0.4	0.1	−1.1	−1.2
ΔI_i	2.9	1.7	−1.2	1.1	0.9	−0.2	−1.1	1.4	2.5
F	0.7	−0.3	−1.0	−2.7	−1.3	1.4	2.1	2.0	−0.1
G	0.5	1.6	1.1	1.0	2.0	1.0	2.6	2.8	0.2
GNP	6.2	8.2	2.0	14.0	14.1	0.1	9.4	12.4	3.0

Variable[a]	1966.4 Actual Change	Predicted Change	Error
C_{ns}	3.9	6.6	2.7
C_d	−0.3	−1.2	−0.9
I_p	1.6	2.3	0.7
I_h	−2.8	0.9	3.7
ΔI_i	7.1	−0.5	−7.6
F	−0.3	−0.9	−0.6
G	4.0	5.6	1.6
GNP	13.2	12.8	−0.4

[a] C_{ns}, consumption of nondurables and services; C_d, consumption of durables; I_p, investment in fixed plant and equipment; I_h, investment in residential construction; ΔI_i, inventory investment; F, net foreign balance; G, government purchases of goods and services; GNP, gross national product.

TABLE 18.4 (*Continued*)

Variable[a]	1964.1 Actual Change	Predicted Change	Error	1964.2 A	P	E	1964.3 A	P	E
C_{ns}	6.3	3.9	−2.4	5.1	2.9	−2.2	6.8	5.6	−1.2
C_d	2.3	0.7	−1.6	1.1	0.1	−1.0	1.7	1.5	−0.2
I_p	2.0	2.3	0.3	0.8	2.3	1.5	1.5	2.8	1.3
I_h	0.7	−0.3	−1.0	−0.7	−1.0	−0.3	−0.5	−0.4	0.1
ΔI_i	−3.9	−0.3	3.6	1.2	4.6	3.4	−0.9	1.5	2.4
F	1.9	−1.1	−3.0	−2.0	−3.0	−1.0	1.3	−0.2	−1.5
G	0.4	5.2	4.8	4.4	5.8	1.4	−0.1	1.8	1.9
GNP	9.8	10.4	0.6	9.8	11.6	1.8	9.8	12.6	2.8

Variable[a]	1966.1 Actual Change	Predicted Change	Error	1966.2 A	P	E	1966.3 A	P	E
C_{ns}	7.5	5.6	−1.9	6.7	7.7	1.0	5.9	9.3	3.4
C_d	3.0	−0.3	−3.3	−3.4	−1.1	2.3	2.7	2.6	−0.1
I_p	2.6	1.6	−1.0	0.4	1.7	1.3	2.5	2.3	−0.2
I_h	0.3	−0.6	−0.9	−1.2	−0.7	0.5	−1.9	0.1	2.0
ΔI_i	0.0	2.2	2.2	4.1	2.1	−2.0	−2.6	−2.9	−0.3
F	0.0	1.5	1.5	−0.7	0.4	1.1	−0.8	0.4	1.2
G	4.2	3.5	−0.7	4.7	3.4	−1.3	6.5	4.9	−1.6
GNP	17.6	13.5	−4.1	10.6	13.4	2.8	12.3	16.7	4.4

TABLE 18.5 PREDICTIVE RECORD OF THE WHARTON EFU MODEL
TWO QUARTERS AHEAD (*all figures are in billions of current dollars*)

| Variable | 1963.3 | | | 1963.4 | | | 1964.1 | | |
	Actual Change	Predic- ted Change	Error	A	P	E	A	P	E
C_{ns}	7.1	7.8	0.7	7.2	5.1	−2.1	8.8	8.6	−0.2
C_d	1.1	0.7	−0.4	2.1	−2.9	−5.0	3.7	−1.6	−5.3
I_p	3.2	4.9	1.7	3.0	2.7	−0.3	3.2	4.0	0.8
I_h	1.1	−1.0	−2.1	1.1	−0.6	−1.7	1.5	−1.1	−2.6
ΔI_i	0.6	2.8	2.2	2.8	0.5	−2.3	−1.7	0.9	2.6
F	0.8	−0.1	−0.9	1.5	−1.1	−2.6	3.5	0.1	−3.4
G	1.4	2.8	1.4	3.9	7.1	3.2	2.4	7.2	4.8
GNP	15.4	17.9	2.5	21.6	10.8	−10.8	21.6	18.2	−3.4

| Variable | 1965.1 | | | 1965.2 | | | 1965.3 | | |
	Actual Change	Predic- ted Change	Error	A	P	E	A	P	E
C_{ns}	10.1	11.0	0.9	12.1	11.0	−1.1	12.3	10.7	−1.6
C_d	3.3	1.0	−2.3	4.3	5.8	1.5	0.9	−0.3	−1.2
I_p	2.8	1.8	−1.0	2.7	5.1	2.4	2.9	4.0	1.1
I_h	0.5	0.8	0.3	1.2	1.5	0.3	−0.1	−0.9	−0.8
ΔI_i	4.0	3.9	−0.1	0.0	3.2	3.2	0.0	−2.0	−2.0
F	−2.0	−0.6	1.4	−0.6	−0.7	−0.1	1.0	1.5	0.5
G	1.5	3.0	1.5	3.6	3.8	0.2	6.0	4.3	−1.7
GNP	20.2	20.9	0.7	23.4	29.8	6.4	23.0	17.3	−5.7

TABLE 18.5 (*Continued*)

	1964.2			1964.3			1964.4		
Variable	Actual Change	Predic-ted Change	Error	A	P	E	A	P	E
C_{ns}	11.4	11.9	0.5	11.9	9.4	−2.5	11.2	11.0	−0.2
C_d	3.4	2.2	−1.2	2.8	2.7	−0.1	−0.7	2.2	2.9
I_p	2.8	3.8	1.0	2.3	3.6	1.3	2.3	4.2	1.9
I_h	0.0	−0.2	−0.2	−1.2	−1.0	0.2	−1.1	−0.1	1.0
ΔI_i	−2.7	0.2	2.9	0.3	5.1	4.8	2.0	0.6	−1.4
F	−0.1	−1.1	−1.0	−0.7	−3.0	−2.3	2.0	−0.2	−2.2
G	4.8	7.2	2.4	4.3	6.8	2.5	0.4	3.6	3.2
GNP	19.6	24.0	4.4	19.6	23.5	3.9	16.0	21.3	5.3

	1966.2			1966.3			1966.4		
Variable	Actual Change	Predic-ted Change	Error	A	P	E	A	P	E
C_{ns}	14.2	12.4	−1.8	12.6	14.8	2.2	9.8	15.9	6.1
C_d	−0.4	0.7	1.1	−0.7	0.1	0.8	2.4	3.1	0.7
I_p	3.0	5.0	2.0	2.9	3.8	0.9	4.1	5.6	1.5
I_h	−0.9	−1.0	−0.1	−3.1	0.4	3.5	−4.7	−0.1	4.6
ΔI_i	4.1	1.4	−2.7	1.5	0.3	−1.2	4.5	−3.2	−7.7
F	−0.7	1.4	2.1	−1.5	0.0	1.5	−1.1	0.2	1.3
G	8.9	7.0	−1.9	11.2	6.9	−4.3	10.5	8.7	−1.8
GNP	28.2	26.8	−1.4	22.9	25.5	2.6	25.5	30.2	4.7

TABLE 18.6 PREDICTIVE RECORD OF THE WHARTON EFU MODEL: TOTAL GNP ONE, TWO, THREE, AND FOUR QUARTERS AHEAD

(all figures are in billions of current dollars)

Year	One Quarter Ahead			Two Quarters Ahead			Three Quarters Ahead			Four Quarters Ahead			Fourth Quarter Average Ending in Given Quarter		
	Actual Change	Predicted Change	Error	Actual Change	Predicted Change	Error	Actual Change	Predicted Change	Error	Actual Change	Predicted Change	Error	Actual Change	Predicted Change	Error
1963.2	5.6	11.6	6.0												
1963.3	9.8	9.2	-0.6	15.4	17.9	2.5									
1963.4	11.8	10.8	-1.0	21.6	10.8	-10.8	27.2	21.8	-5.4						
1964.1	9.8	10.4	0.6	21.6	18.2	-3.4	31.4	16.5	-14.9	41.2	22.9	-18.3	26.0	14.9	-11.1
1964.2	9.8	11.6	1.8	19.6	24.0	4.4	31.4	33.5	2.1	41.2	46.0	4.8	26.5	27.1	0.6
1964.3	9.8	12.6	2.8	19.6	23.5	3.9	29.4	37.5	8.1	35.6	48.9	13.3	23.6	30.2	6.6
1964.4	6.2	8.2	2.0	16.0	21.3	5.3	25.8	32.9	7.1						
1965.1	14.0	14.1	0.1	20.2	20.9	0.7	30.0	26.0	-4.0	39.8	42.7	2.9	23.8	27.7	3.9
1965.2	9.4	12.4	3.0	23.4	29.8	6.4	29.6	31.5	1.9	39.4	35.9	-3.5	23.9	24.0	0.1
1965.3	14.6	n.p.[b]		23.0	17.3	-5.7	34.9*	29.0	-5.6	41.3*	36.2	-5.1	24.3*	24.0	-0.3
1965.4	18.4	n.p.		33.0	n.p.		36.9*	27.6	-9.3	50.9*	35.5	-15.4	30.3*	27.1	-3.2
1966.1	17.6	13.5	-4.1	36.0	n.p.		50.6	n.p.		51.6*	34.6	-17.0	29.1*	23.0	-6.1
1966.2	10.6	13.4	2.8	28.2	26.8	-1.4	46.6	n.p.		61.2	n.p.		38.8	n.p.	
1966.3	12.3	16.7	4.4	22.9	25.5	2.6	40.5	40.5	0.0	58.9	n.p.		39.2	n.p.	
1966.4	13.2	12.8	-0.4	25.5	30.1	4.6	36.1	39.5	-3.4	53.7	53.1	-0.6	33.5	33.4	-0.1
Av. absolute error		2.3			4.3			5.6			9.0			3.6	

[a] All actual changes through 1965.2 are based on the old data; 1965.3 and later are based on the new data except where an asterisk indicates that an extrapolation of the old data has been used (see the text).

[b] n.p., no prediction made.

TABLE 18.7 PREDICTIVE RECORD OF THE WHARTON EFU MODEL: ANNUAL FORECASTS MADE DURING THE FOURTH QUARTER OF THE PREVIOUS YEAR

(all figures are in billions of current dollars)

Variable	1963[a]			1964			1965			1966[c]		
	Actual Change	Predicted Change	Error	Actual Change	Predicted Change	Error	Actual[b] Change	Predicted Change	Error	Actual Change	Predicted Change	Error
C_{ns}	13.6	14.1	0.5	19.6	19.2	-0.4	23.7	22.9	-0.8	28.5	26.7	-1.8
C_d	4.6	2.6	-2.0	4.9	0.9	-4.0	5.1	3.9	-1.2	4.3	2.6	-1.7
I_p	3.2	4.9	1.7	5.6	7.7	2.1	5.4	5.9	0.5	9.1	10.6	1.5
I_h	1.0	-0.8	-1.8	0.8	0.3	-0.5	0.1	0.7	0.6	-2.6	-1.2	1.4
ΔI_i	1.2	1.9	0.7	-0.7	2.9	3.6	2.9	0.0	-2.9	4.0	-1.8	-2.2
F	0.0	-1.1	-1.1	2.6	-0.5	-3.1	-1.3	-0.2	1.1	-1.9	1.1	3.0
G	6.4	9.4	3.0	5.9	10.4	4.5	7.0	5.8	-1.2	17.9	13.8	-4.1
GNP	30.0	31.0	1.0	38.7	40.9	2.2	42.9	39.0	-3.9	59.3	55.4	-3.9

[a] Forecast actually made in March 1963, as model was not available before then.
[b] Actual data based on extrapolation of old data—see the text.
[c] Forecast made at the end of January, 1966. See note e, Table 18.3.

527

TABLE 18.8 SUMMARY STATISTICS FOR THE WHARTON EFU MODEL PREDICTIONS

(all figures are in billions of current dollars)

	One Quarter Ahead			Two Quarters Ahead			Annual (Fourth Quarter) Forecasts			
Variable[a]	Av. Absolute Change	Av. Absolute Error of Prediction	Av. Absolute Error of Naive Model II[b]	Av. Absolute Change	Av. Absolute Error of Prediction	Av. Absolute Error of Naive Model II	Av. Absolute Change	Av. Absolute Error of Prediction	Av. Absolute Error of Naive Model II	Av. Absolute Error of Naive Model III[c]
C_{ns}	5.3	1.6	1.8	10.7	1.6	1.3	21.4	0.9	2.6	1.9
C_d	2.0	1.5	3.0	2.3	1.9	2.1	4.7	2.2	1.2	2.2
I_p	1.5	1.1	1.2	2.9	1.3	0.9	5.8	1.4	1.3	1.3
I_h	0.9	1.0	0.7	1.3	1.4	1.0	1.1	1.1	1.2	2.2
ΔI_i	2.1	2.4	3.5	2.1	3.0	2.4	2.2	2.4	2.5	3.3
F	1.2	1.2	1.8	1.3	1.6	2.0	1.5	2.1	1.7	2.1
G	2.5	1.8	1.8	4.9	2.4	2.0	9.3	3.2	3.2	3.4
GNP	10.8	2.3	2.7	21.4	4.3	2.9	42.7	2.7	8.1	4.5

[a] Symbols as defined in Table 18.4.
[b] Naive model II: $(X_t) - (X_{t-1}) = (X_{t-1}) - (X_{t-2})$.
[c] Naive model III: Same as Table 18.3.

Addendum

	Av. Absolute Change	Av. Absolute Error of Prediction	Av. Absolute Error of Naive Model II
GNP			
Three quarters ahead	32.1	5.6	7.0
Four quarters ahead	43.9	9.0	11.3
Av. of four quarters ahead	26.8	3.6	6.2

528

and services was quite satisfactory. The predicted values tracked the actual values closely in almost all quarters, including the period of the large personal income tax cut. In all cases except the 1966.1 forecast, large errors of prediction in this sector can be traced to errors in predicting personal disposable income elsewhere in the model. In 1966.1 almost the whole error was due to a sudden and sharp rise in farm prices. Although our constant-dollar figures were reliable, the current-dollar estimates were considerably underestimated.

The most poorly performing sector is undoubtedly inventory investment, although it is interesting to note that the average error of prediction of the annual forecast is not much larger than for one quarter ahead. This is the only sector for which the forecasts are generally inferior to naive model "predictions." Part of the error has been caused by erratic fluctuations due to stockpiling for expected steel strikes and then decreasing of stocks when strikes did not occur. We tried to adjust for this in our forecasts but without noticeable success.

The forecasts for consumer durables and housing present a mixed record. Early forecasts of consumer durable purchases were very poor and were responsible for the poor 1963.4 (two quarters ahead) forecast. Since that time, the equations have been reformulated and have given considerably better predictions. The forecasts from the residential construction equation were neither noticeably good or bad until the late 1966 forecasts, when an almost unprecedented tightening of credit led to a near-collapse of the new housing market. Although the housing equation does contain a term representing tightness of credit, it is only a proxy variable and evidently unable to handle situations of this severity. Further work is necessary to obtain a true structural relationship for this equation.

Predictions of net foreign balance and government purchases of goods and services are largely exogenous and do not require extended comment at this point. Although the Wharton EFU model does contain endogenous equations for imports and exports, the latter depend largely on exogenous estimates of world trade and prices. Furthermore, an endogenous export equation was not actually used for prediction during much of the period.

We have not discussed the predictive accuracy of the equations explaining wages, prices, interest rates, unemployment, income distribution, or other supply phenomena. Early versions of the Wharton EFU model and its predecessors were relatively skimpy in these areas. Although substantial expansion of the model has recently been made, a complete set of forecasts for these variables is not available for the 1963–1966 period.

The forecasting record of the Wharton EFU model for the period 1963–1966 is not as good as we would have liked it to be. In particular, the forecast showing very slow growth in consumer durables in early 1964, and the bad forecast made in late 1963 should have been better. The inventory investment functions clearly require more work in the future. But we feel that this record

CHAPTER 19

METHODS OF STABILIZATION
AND MULTIPLIER ANALYSIS

19.1   THE NATURE AND IMPORTANCE
          OF AUTOMATIC STABILIZERS

In the preceding chapters of this text we have developed a theory
of the business cycle, empirically estimated this theory, and examined its
predictive record, which was found to be quite accurate over the short time
that *ex ante* forecasts have been available. This model has also been used for
determining the effects of different alternative fiscal and monetary policies
on various components of aggregate economic activity. In Chapter 20, we shall
consider some of the actual multiplier calculations of the Wharton EFU
model and other econometric models. However, we first discuss the methods
available for controlling cyclical fluctuations and achieving other economic
goals. The possible incompatibilities of these goals are considered next. Some
examples of multiplier calculations for simple models are analyzed before
realistic calculations based on more complex models are presented.

When discussing stabilization policies, one should always remember that a
major reason for the relatively small cyclical fluctuations of the postwar
U.S. economy has been the existence of *automatic stabilizers*. These are usually
defined as relationships that reduce the amplitude of cyclical fluctuations in the
economy without any direct action by government, businesses, or individuals.
These stabilizers may be countercyclical or they may be independent of cyclical
fluctuations. Most of these automatic stabilizers are of recent vintage, having
been noticeably absent in the massive 1929–1933 contraction.

Government purchases of goods and services are closely related to automatic stabilizers, although they are not technically included in this category.

In general, these purchases do not follow a cyclical pattern, although large decreases in defense spending have occasionally caused mild recessions, such as in 1954. It is possible that government purchases could follow a definite countercyclical pattern, but this has not been the case to date. State and local government expenditures have shown no cyclical pattern at all during the postwar period. Federal government expenditures have fluctuated because of defense requirements, but except for 1954 these fluctuations do not correspond to cycles in GNP. A case can be made that the curtailment of defense spending in 1957 was one of the causes of the 1958 recession. However, this cutback was undertaken in response to inflationary pressures that occurred during 1956; thus this action should properly be classified as countercyclical fiscal policy. When the 1958 recession did occur, no additional attempt was made to decrease federal government expenditures. It is natural that movements in government spending will to some degree be reflected in movements of GNP, because there is a definite multiplier effect. However, by classifying government expenditures as being similar to automatic stabilizers, we mean that no attempt is made to reduce public expenditures when GNP decreases, unlike spending in the private sector. This was not always the case historically. During the 1929–1933 contraction, an attempt was made to balance the federal budget in the face of declining revenues, and Roosevelt campaigned on a pledge to balance the budget. Although many people today are still in favor of balancing the budget over the cycle and of having some surplus at full employment, it is now generally recognized that government deficits are preferable in recession years.

Another reason that government spending acts as an important stabilizing influence on the economy compared to the prewar and interwar periods is its large increase as a proportion of GNP. In 1929 total government purchases of goods and services were less than 10 percent of GNP; today they are 20 percent. The rise in federal spending is even greater, increasing from less than 2 to approximately 10 percent. This figure includes only purchases of goods and services, not government transfer payments, which have risen from less than $1 billion to over $60 billion annually; these are discussed later.

The second most important automatic stabilizer (including government expenditures in this category) is the progressive income tax structure for both personal and corporate federal income taxes, which account for almost two thirds of total federal government receipts. Although there is no tendency for government purchases to decline in recessions, tax receipts decline proportionately more than GNP. In the 1957–1958 recession, for example, the federal budget went from a surplus of $2.6 billion to a deficit of $12.4 billion; total GNP, by comparison, fell only $12 billion from peak to trough. Thus there is clearly a very sharp element of progressivity in existing tax collections.

There are two somewhat different reasons for this observed behavior. One reason is the progressive nature of the tax schedule for personal income taxes. As an individual's income decreases, his remaining income is taxed at a lower rate. The existence of substantial deductions also increases this progressivity.

Even an individual who remains in the same tax bracket will find that his effective tax rate decreases when his income declines because of deductions.

The tax schedules for corporate income taxes actually contain very little progressivity, since the rate is fixed at a constant level for all profits over $25,000. Yet corporate tax receipts do fluctuate a great deal over the cycle and thus act as a major automatic stabilizer, because corporate profits themselves are much more volatile than other components of aggregate income. If taxes are approximately half of profits, both will fluctuate substantially over the cycle. Thus tax receipts can serve as automatic stabilizers if either the tax schedule is progressive or the taxes are levied on a cyclically volatile component of aggregate income.

The third most important automatic stabilizer is the heterogeneous component known as transfer payments; we restrict ourselves here to government transfer payments. They include payments that are both countercyclical and independent of cyclical influence. The best known and most important category of the former type is unemployment compensation insurance, which covers a majority (but by no means all) of the employees in the labor force. These funds are administered and paid by the states, although some of the money is contributed by the federal government. Since the compensation rates are set by the states, they vary greatly, depending on location, type of job, and numerous other specific considerations. In general, however, weekly payments are of the order of half of the weekly wage the unemployed worker was formerly earning. Thus there is still a considerable drop in income to the workers. However, spendable income does not drop by the full amount of the difference between the wage and the unemployment payment. The worker may actually retain 60 to 70 percent of his former spendable income, because the unemployment insurance payments are taxed at a lower rate or not at all, and any expenses connected with working (such as transportation, uniforms, and so on) are absent.

It should be pointed out that although these payments initially go into effect automatically, they are limited in most cases to 26 weeks per year. Thus in the 1958 recession, which was the most severe of the postwar recessions, additional legislation had to be passed authorizing the payment of supplemental unemployment benefits for 13 additional weeks to those who were still unemployed. Although it is comforting to see such legislation speedily passed, it does point out that there is nothing automatic about these extra payments, because direct action by Congress was needed.

The other major type of government transfer payment to civilians is often lumped under the heading "social security payments." The best known of these payments are retirement payments; some payments for survivors and the disabled are also included in this category. These payments are quite independent of the business cycle, and they are set at rates that are periodically raised by Congress. Since payments for social insurance by employees, employers, and self-employed are directly proportional to earned income up to a certain upper limit, which is also periodically raised, a drop in personal income below this limit will also cause a reduction in payments for social insurance. A certain amount of additional stability is thus included in disposable income. The stability originating from this source should not be overrated, however, as there is some regressivity in social security taxes. The social insurance contributions of an employee whose income drops from (for example) $12,000 to $10,000 will remain the same.

Similar in nature to these types of transfers are military payments, which also are determined by fixed rate schedules and are invariant to changes in economic activity. Veterans' bonuses and disability payments are major examples of these payments. Certain types of military transfer payments can on occasion be destabilizing, however. One such instance occurred in early 1950, when refunds from national life insurance dividends of over $2.5 billion ($10 billion at annual rates) were made to World War II veterans. This injected extra spendable income into the economy just before the time when the Korean War began. The cumulative effect was to contribute to panic buying of consumer durables and a price increase of over 25 percent at annual rates. These life insurance dividends have continued, but they are now distributed in much smaller amounts on a regular basis, usually January of each year. These dividends, although clearly transfer payments, are usually excluded when the stabilizing nature of such payments is discussed.

Another type of transfer payment is the interest on government debt, which now amounts to over $10 billion per year. However, at least part of these payments should also be excluded from the conventional grouping of automatic stabilizers. Much of the government debt is marketed in short-term securities that are held primarily by large corporations and financial institutions. Most government debt held by individuals is in the form of Series E savings bonds, which do not pay out interest until they are cashed. This type of interest payment cannot be considered a continuing source of income independent of the cycle. However, these last exceptions should not negate the basic premise that most transfer payments either are paid at the same rate or increase during recessions, and do serve the function of an important automatic stabilizer.

The other two automatic stabilizers, government payments to farmers and stability of dividends, do not affect the economy as much as do the stabilizers previously mentioned. The first of these stabilizers usually takes the form of guaranteed minimum prices on major crops in the form of a loan-purchase agreement. The farmer "loans" the crop to the government and receives a set minimum price. If the market price exceeds this fixed price, the farmer is free to "buy back" the crop and sell it on the open market; if not, he "defaults" on the loan and the government keeps the crop. There are of course many complex sides to the farm problem, and it is not our purpose to discuss them here. We merely wish to point out that guaranteeing farm income is another way of stabilizing the economy in terms of recession. Since both the short-run demand and supply curves for agricultural products are very inelastic, even a slight downward shift of the demand curve would send farm income plummeting without support prices. It might be added that the question of whether prices are set so high that they are above equilibrium levels in good years and bad was suddenly resolved in 1966; wheat surpluses disappeared and acreage allotments had to be increased considerably.

The last automatic stabilizer to be considered is the constancy of dividend payments relative to after-tax profits. Although after-tax profits fluctuate only half as much as before-tax profits in absolute terms, the relative fluctuations are very similar. However, dividend payments have fluctuated much less than profits both in relative and absolute terms in all postwar recessions. Again referring to the 1958 recession, before-tax profits dropped $11 billion, after-tax profits dropped $5 billion, and dividends only fell $0.7 billion. This performance has been typical of the postwar recessions. This relationship probably would disintegrate in the face of a prolonged depression such as 1929, but it has held up very well in the postwar period.

It should be pointed out that farm income is now a much smaller percentage of personal income than it was in the 1920s, when the collapse of farm prices and income was an important cause of the later depression. However, inasmuch as these stabilizers are operative, they do help to mitigate recessions, although not on the order of other automatic stabilizers.

As important as these automatic stabilizers are, they have been insufficient to prevent four recessions in the postwar period. Although these recessions have unquestionably been much milder than they would have been in the absence of these stabilizers, there are times in the course of the business cycle when discretionary policy moves are needed. There are several courses of action open to the federal authorities, which are considered in turn. The ways in which these discretionary policies affect the economy will not be considered in detail at this point but will be examined in conjunction with the multiplier analysis developed later.

19.2   DISCRETIONARY STABILIZERS AND SELECTIVE CREDIT CONTROLS

Fiscal policy can take either the form of a discretionary change in the amount of government expenditures or a change in the tax rates for personal income taxes, corporate income taxes, excise taxes, or transfer payments; in the last case, both the rate of tax and the rate of benefits may be changed. As will be shown in Chapter 20, the most powerful short-term policy weapon the government has is the ability to change its purchases of goods and services. These may take the form of defense spending, purchases of goods and services from the private sector of the economy (such as construction of roads), or additions to government employment. The government may also increase its outlays by increasing transfer payments, which may be made directly to individuals or to state and local governments. In the latter case these payments are likely to add to increased government expenditure at the state and local levels.

During 1964 and 1965, fiscal policy used to increase the rate of growth of GNP took the form of decreases in tax rates. Personal income taxes, corporate income taxes, and excise taxes were all reduced during these years. Transfer payments were increased in 1966 through the introduction of Medicare, but the rates for social security contributions were raised to cover part of this added expense. A further measure, which was undertaken somewhat earlier than the tax cuts, was the liberalization of depreciation schedules and the institution of an investment tax credit which allowed firms to deduct 7 percent of the cost of new investment from their tax liabilities. The net decrease in corporate taxes resulting from these new policies when they were introduced in 1962 was estimated to be about $2.0 billion. Since fixed business investment has increased more than 50 percent since then, the benefits have also increased substantially.

Of all these recent tax cuts, the personal income tax cut that took place in 1964 (a second stage occurred in 1965) had the greatest effect on the economy, as it was by far the largest. The excise tax cut of 1965 was partially rescinded in 1966 and later years but appeared to be of major importance in stimulating sales of consumer durables, particularly automobiles. The effects of the corporate income tax cut and the investment tax credit, which act on the economy in a similar way, are somewhat harder to assess. They have clearly increased after-tax profits; investment has risen very rapidly, but this could be explained by the very rapid rise in sales. The effects of all these changes in the tax rates are examined in detail in later sections.

There are three tools of monetary policy which the Federal Reserve Bank can use: changing the discount rate, open market operations, and changing required reserve ratios of commercial banks. Traditionally, the discount rate is supposed to follow short-term interest rates already set in the market. If this were the case, its primary function would be to regulate commercial bank borrowing at the Federal Reserve Bank discount window. Presumably when the discount rate is raised, this type of borrowing is decreased, commercial banks must obtain the required reserves from other sources, and this reduces the money stock by some multiple of the original withdrawal.

However, it is quite possible that the discount rate actually helps to determine the short-term market interest rate instead of merely following it. If this were the case, changing the discount rate would be of additional importance, for it would change the short-term and long-term interest rates, which would alter the amount of fixed investment.

No clear-cut statement can be made about the direction of causality between changes in the discount rate and changes in the treasury bill rate (taken here as indicative of short-term rates), because they change almost simultaneously virtually all the time.[1] Thus if the discount rate follows the market, it does so with surprising alacrity. On the other hand, if the bill rate changes after the discount rate has been set, it does so almost instantaneously.

Open market operations are the monetary policy tool most often used. When the Federal Reserve system buys bonds from commercial banks, they have more money available with which to buy other interest-earning assets or make loans. This process, once started, will converge with the money stock increased by some multiple of the original open-market transaction. This multiple is sometimes thought to be the reciprocal of the required reserve ratio, which is currently about one sixth. However, owing to leakages in the system in the form of excess reserves, loss to hand to hand circulation, and other causes, the ratio is actually about 3. The same pattern exists in reverse if the Federal Reserve System sells bonds to commercial banks.

A second consequence of open market operations is the effect on the interest rate. If the Federal Reserve System buys bonds, this will increase the demand for bonds relative to the supply, thus raising the price and lowering the interest rate. The 3:1 expansionary result on the money stock will also lower interest rates somewhat. In the Wharton EFU model, the effect of open-market operations shows up entirely through this second effect on interest rates. Although it is clear that this is an oversimplification, this secondary result should not be overlooked.

During the postwar period, open-market operations have been somewhat hampered by some of the rules set by the Treasury. In the period immediately following World War II, the Fed was pledged to redeem all Treasury bonds at par. Since many of these were issued at very low interest rates, this meant that the Fed had to buy bonds continually in order to keep the price up and the interest rate down. The result was a substantial net addition to the forces of inflation that were already much in evidence in the early postwar years. In 1951 the Treasury and the Fed reached an accord which stated that the Fed would no longer have to support bond prices, thus giving them a chance to use restrictive monetary policies if they felt they were necessary. For much of the rest of the 1950s, however, the Fed was somewhat hampered by the "bills only" policy. According to this policy, changes in short-term interest rates would diffuse throughout the entire bond market and would influence long-term rates as well. Thus all desired changes in the long-term bond yield could be obtained through open-market operations conducted entirely in short-term government bills. This sometimes led to a thin market and irregular movements in the long-term interest rate, which is the important rate to control to influence fixed business investment. In the 1960s, this thinking was entirely reversed with the introduction of "operation twist," which claimed that the short-term and long-term securities markets could be separated and that interest rate changes in one would not affect rates in the others. The reason for

---

[1] This point is discussed in greater detail in Section 11.3.

such wishful thinking was that the government wanted to keep the short-term rate high to attract more "hot money" and to keep the long-term rate low to attract more domestic fixed investment. This plan turned out to be a flop, as long-term rates rose to their highest levels since the 1920s. Although the theory behind "bills only" was not without its defects, it was closer to the truth than the thinking behind "operation twist."

The third tool of monetary policy, changing the reserve requirements of commercial banks, is used less frequently than the other two policies but acts in a similar way. If banks must hold less reserves per dollar of deposits, they can make more loans, which will expand the money stock and lower the interest rate. Whenever changes in the required reserve ratio have been made, they have never been larger than 0.5 percent after offsetting open-market operations (that is, a rise would result in banks selling some of their government securities to the Fed), a small percentage of the current ratio of approximately 16 percent. Since the results from this course of action are very similar to those resulting from open-market operations, the former has generally been preferred by the Fed, since they are much more flexible and easily reversible.

We now consider selective credit controls. There are a number of these which have been used in the past, but at the present selective credit controls have very little effect on the economy. The main control currently in operation regulates the amount of margin that can be used for buying stocks. This regulation is intended to damp speculative buying on the stock market; however, it has very little effect. When money is easy and loans for buying stock are easy to obtain, the margin requirement is often circumvented by suggesting that the loan might be for some other purpose. On the other hand, when money is tight, loans only for the legitimate margin are often not available, and the Fed frowns on banks that make such loans; it may even deny them discount window privileges. Thus the amount of stock that can be bought on margin is more a function of general tightness in the money market rather than the stated margin requirement.

During the 1940s and the early 1950s, Regulation W was in effect on several occasions. It regulated the amount of down payment and the number of months for installment contracts for most consumer durables. The actual requirements in practice related mostly to automobiles, as discussed in Chapter 6. The very fact that the regulation was so successful led to its demise, as consumers felt they were unduly hampered by its restrictive assumptions, and it was allowed to lapse in 1953. Although there is occasionally talk of reviving it, this seems very doubtful.

During the 1958 recessions, during which car sales fell some 20 percent, Senator Paul Douglas proposed that the excise tax on automobiles be temporarily reduced 1 percent for every additional 1 percent that the automobile companies would reduce prices. Since the excise tax on autos was 10 percent at that time, this would have meant up to a 20 percent price reduction in the price of new cars. The idea was allowed to languish, and several years later the auto companies were able to get the excise tax reduced with no additional decrease in price, so this idea can no longer be used. However, this would have unquestionably provided a powerful stimulus to car sales at a time when they were severely depressed. The plan also could have been used to inhibit inflationary pressures on the economy by reinstating the tax (and, presumably, the price increases) during boom periods.

The other sector of the economy that has been subjected to specific credit controls is the housing industry. In 1950, plans for Regulation X were drafted, which was similar to Regulation W in that the amount of down payment and the length of mortgages were to be regulated. When the regulation finally did go into effect in 1951, it was accompanied by a substantial decrease in residential construction. However, unlike the case of autos, where credit lines are very elastic and relatively unaffected by tight money elsewhere in the economy, the lines of causation are very blurred here. It can be argued that housing would have turned down anyhow because of the booming economy and the accompanying tight money and high relative costs of construction. Furthermore, the proposal took a long time to draft, and, as all construction started before it took effect was exempt, the main result of this regulation was to shift construction that would have ordinarily occurred in 1951 into 1950. It is doubtful whether this regulation had much of an effect on residential construction activity.

Regulation X to the contrary, most of the credit manipulations in the housing market have been intended to increase the supply of funds to mortgages, not decrease it. Early steps in this direction were the availability of federally insured loans under the Federal Housing Administration (FHA) and the Veterans Administration (VA). These loans are made by private lending institutions but are insured by the federal government. They carry very small down payments which can be as low as 3 percent for FHA and 0 percent for VA and vary depending on location and other factors. Ceiling rates that were set on the loans kept their rates well below the market rates in periods of tight money, so during such periods these mortgages would be granted only if they were sold below par, which resulted in the lender in effect paying more stringent terms than stipulated in the contract. These ceiling rates have been periodically raised but are still below market levels.

Another agency designed to ensure the flow of mortgage money to banks is the Federal National Mortgage Association (FNMA), universally known as "Fannie Mae." The purpose of this agency is to release mortgage money into the market when funds are tight, and withdraw it when excess funds are available. When funds are tight, banks sell federally-insured mortgages to FNMA; this provides banks with additional funds for conventional mortgages. When excess funds are available, FNMA sells these federally insured mortgages back to the banks, which provides them with an outlet for otherwise idle funds. Since periods of tight and easy money have historically alternated with each other, it was thought that this process could continue with a relatively small amount of capital. However, in mid-1966, amid the continued pressue of tight money, FNMA almost went broke, and it was necessary for Congress to appropriate an additional $4.76 billion so that these secondary market operations could continue and FHA- and VA-insured mortgages could be offered at all.

19.3   ALTERNATIVE ECONOMIC GOALS

In the historic Employment Act of 1946, the President was empowered to take the necessary steps to keep the economy at full employment. With the memory of the Great Depression still vivid and prominent forecasts implying eight million unemployed after World War II, this goal seemed of primary importance. However, during the postwar period other goals have come to the attention of the American public and their elected representatives, and some of these other goals have seemed at times to overshadow the goal of full employment.

The first alternative goal to come to the forefront was the control of inflation, after prices rose by 50 percent from 1945 to 1948 and another 15 percent in the six months following the outbreak of the Korean War. Direct price controls were reinstituted in 1951, but they were rescinded when the war ended amid general feeling that prices should be regulated by tools of fiscal and monetary policy if at all, rather than by direct controls.

The feeling that the economy could not operate at full employment with price stability is bolstered by the findings of the Phillips curve, discussed in Chapter 10. Since this curve is nonlinear, price increases accelerate as full employment is reached. Gloomy reports have been issued showing that historically the United States needed an unemployment rate over 6 percent for a stable price level. Thus there was much talk of a "tradeoff" between full employment and stable prices, and for the period 1959–1963 unemployment averaged 5.8 percent, wholesale prices were completely stable, and consumer prices rose at slightly more than 1 percent per year.

The Kennedy administration as well as most of the economy felt that 6 percent unemployment was too high for an equilibrium value, so it set about to use fiscal and monetary policy to reduce this figure. However, still wary about the possibilities of inflation, the administration instituted wage–price guidelines. According to those in charge of administering the guidelines, the average annual rate of productivity increase during the past five years had been 3.2 percent, so that if wages rose by 3.2 percent annually, unit labor costs would remain stable and therefore prices would remain stable. In certain industries where productivity gains were less than 3.2 percent, prices could rise; in industries where productivity gains were greater than 3.2 percent, prices should fall. The guidelines were largely ignored and gradually collapsed in mid-1966, when many labor leaders made it a point to tell their constituencies and the public that the latest settlement had violated the guidelines.

In retrospect there appear to have been two main problems with the guide-lines. Implicit in the proposition that unit labor costs and prices remain constant was the assumption that labor's share would also remain constant and wages and profits would rise at the same rate. However, profits rose at an annual rate of 11 percent for the period 1961–1965, whereas the wage bill rose at 5 percent. There were two reasons for this:

1. The guidelines were incorrectly set too low. Productivity in the manu-facturing sector grew at approximately 4 percent per year, which would have been all right except that almost no industries lowered their prices. Thus unit labor costs fell but prices did not, and profit margins increased.

2. In 1965, the wholesale price level (excluding farm products) rose 1.3 percent, not a large rise but clearly inconsistent with the guidelines, since unit labor costs in that sector were still falling. Thus the spread between price and unit labor costs widened still further.

To make a bad situation even worse, in 1966 food prices rose almost 10 percent, and social security taxes rose as both the rate and taxable income base were increased. In mid-1966, the average laborer found that not only was his *relative* share decreasing, but his *absolute* take-home pay in constant dollars was less than it had been a year ago. At this point, labor leaders decided to ask for 3.2 percent plus the increase in consumer prices, or about 6 percent, in forthcoming negotiations. Anticipating this cost increase, many industries raised their prices further, and the guidelines were officially dead. In their wake they left much bitterness among laborers, who felt that they restrained their wage demand for four years while inflation was not noticeably impeded.

Because the guidelines were consistently flouted and because they decreased labor's share of output, they are unlikely to be accepted again at an early date unless they are made mandatory and a wage–price freeze becomes law. This is a possible but unlikely event in peacetime, at least in the United States. Thus one solution that at first seemed plausible for controlling inflation has died an unnatural death, and replacements are unlikely to be forthcoming soon. This leaves only the solution of greater unemployment as an antidote to more inflation, a solution most people find unacceptable.

Another alternative goal that became popular shortly after the launching of the first Sputnik is maximizing the rate of growth of the economy. This can be accomplished both by increasing investment and by raising productivity. In general, this goal is compatible both with full employment and stable prices; however, the relationship with prices is more tenuous than the one with employment. Increased capacity and improved technology should result in lower unit costs and thus lower prices. However, if bottlenecks are encountered as the economy nears full employment, prices may rise in spite of improved technology. If one is committed to a full-employment policy, a higher growth rate is to be preferred to a lower growth rate on all counts. This means choosing fiscal and monetary policies that favor more rapid growth in investment than consumption without engendering too much inflation.

The fourth goal, which has attained prominence quite recently, is to stem the gold flow and eliminate the balance of payments deficit. This problem was discussed in some detail in Chapter 9, so not too much more will be said here. In reference to the other goals mentioned, price stability will also help our balance of payments problems, since relative prices are important determinants of exports and imports. A high rate of growth may help the net foreign balance if it increases capacity and thereby lowers prices, but an increase in income will increase imports, which may negate this advantage. If greater imports here result in higher exports and higher national incomes in countries already operating at full capacity, this may result in more inflation abroad and thus raise our exports. However, in most cases a faster rate of growth of income in this country will decrease our net foreign balance somewhat.

The effect of various policy alternatives on all these goals and many other economic variables can be assessed with the aid of an econometric model by calculating price and output multipliers for each policy change. In Sections 19.4 and 19.5 the theory of multipliers will be discussed for some simple models, and in Chapter 20 actual calculations from the Wharton EFU model and other models will be presented and analyzed.

19.4   BASIC MULTIPLIER ANALYSIS

As shown earlier, a large number of monetary and fiscal policy alternatives is available to the federal government. However, unless the effect of each of these policies on various variables can be assessed accurately, the usefulness of these moves is sharply reduced. If fiscal and monetary policy is to function effectively, there must be a clear idea of the multipliers and the timing of the effects of the available measures. One of the primary purposes of this book is to estimate these multipliers and to assess the relative efficacy of various policy moves. The estimates are taken from functions developed earlier in the text, and from the combinations of these functions which are molded into an overall theory of the business cycle.

Before presenting and analyzing these multiplier estimates, it is useful to review some of the fundamentals of multiplier theory. Although some of the properties of multipliers have been used elsewhere in this book, the results are grouped here for convenience.

The very simplest model is

Case I.

$$C = a + bY$$

$$I = \bar{I}$$

$$C + I + G = Y$$

$$a + bY + I + G = Y$$

$$Y = \frac{I + G + a}{1 - b}$$

Only a multiplier for government expenditures can be calculated in this simplest case, because there are no taxes in the model. If G changes,

$$\Delta Y = \Delta G \frac{1}{1 - b} \qquad \text{where } b = mpc$$

Case II. The results are basically unchanged if investment is made endogenous. Then

$$C = a + bY$$

$$I = c + dY$$

$$C + I + G = Y$$

$$a + bY + c + dY + G = Y$$

$$Y = \frac{G + a + c}{1 - b - d}$$

$$\Delta Y = \Delta G \frac{1}{1 - b - d}$$

The term d is easily identified as the marginal propensity to invest.

Case III. Taxes are usually introduced into the model by making consumption a function of disposable income, that is, total income minus taxes. Taxes can be made either autonomous or dependent on the level of income; we take the simpler case first. Then

$$C = a + b(Y - T)$$

$$I = \bar{I}$$

$$G = \bar{G}$$

$$T = \bar{T}$$

$$a + b(Y - T) + I + G = Y$$

$$Y = \frac{I + G + a - bT}{1 - b}$$

$$\frac{\Delta Y}{\Delta G} = \frac{1}{1 - b}$$

$$\frac{\Delta Y}{\Delta T} = -\frac{b}{1 - b}$$

The relationship between these two multipliers has given rise to the so-called "balanced-budget theorem." This states that a change of any given amount in both government expenditure and taxes will change GNP by this same amount. Thus an increase in government spending will be expansionary, even if fully financed by taxes, and vice versa for a decrease in government spending. This can easily be shown to be the case for the above simple model, since

$$\frac{\Delta Y}{\Delta G} + \frac{\Delta Y}{\Delta T} = \frac{1}{1-b} - \frac{b}{1-b} = \frac{1-b}{1-b} = 1$$

for all values of b between 0 and 1. However, as soon as the model is changed at all, this theorem no longer holds exactly.

Consider

$$C = a + b(Y - T)$$

$$I = c + dY$$

$$G = \bar{G}$$

$$T = \bar{T}$$

$$C + I + G = Y$$

$$a + b(Y - T) + c + dY = G = Y$$

$$Y = \frac{G + a + c - bT}{1 - b - d}$$

$$\frac{\Delta Y}{\Delta G} = \frac{1}{1 - b - d}$$

$$\frac{\Delta Y}{\Delta T} = -\frac{b}{1 - b - d}$$

$$\frac{\Delta Y}{\Delta G} + \frac{\Delta Y}{\Delta T} = \frac{1 - b}{1 - b - d} \neq 1 \qquad \text{for } d \neq 0$$

Case IV. We now consider a more realistic tax function in which taxes depend on the level of income. Then

$$C = a + b(Y - T)$$

$$T = v + \tau Y$$

$$I = \bar{I}$$

$$G = \bar{G}$$

$$a + b(Y - v - \tau Y) + I + G = Y$$

$$Y = \frac{a + I + G - bv}{1 - b(1 - \tau)}$$

$$\frac{\Delta Y}{\Delta G} = \frac{1}{1 - b(1 - \tau)}$$

There are two possible ways in which taxes can be changed. Either the constant can be changed (such as a change in the amount of the personal exemption) or the slope can be changed. In the first case,

$$\frac{\Delta Y}{\Delta v} = \frac{-b}{1 - b(1 - \tau)}$$

which is similar to the above cases except that the value of the overall multiplier is reduced, owing to the leakage of a positive marginal tax rate. For a change in the tax rate, which is the more usual case, the algebra is slightly more complex. For ease of exposition we write:

$$Y[1 - b(1 - \tau)] = a + I + G - bv$$

Therefore,

$$Y[b\Delta\tau] + [1 - b(1 - \tau)]\Delta Y = 0$$

and

$$\Delta Y = \frac{-bY\Delta\tau}{1 - b(1 - \tau)}$$

If we choose $Y\Delta\tau = \Delta v$, then the result is identical to the one above. However, as the value of Y changes over time, these two expressions will differ. The "balanced budget multiplier" now becomes

$$\frac{\Delta Y}{\Delta G} + \frac{\Delta Y}{Y\Delta\tau} = \frac{1}{1 - b(1 - \tau)} - \frac{b}{1 - b(1 - \tau)} = \frac{1 - b}{1 - b(1 - \tau)}$$

which will always be less than 1 for $0 < b, \tau < 1$. The reason for this is that the extra addition to disposable income will not be subject to the tax leakage, because the adjustment is made *after* taxes.

With induced investment,

$$C = a + b(Y - T)$$

$$T = v + \tau Y$$

$$I = c + dY$$

$$G = \bar{G}$$

$$C + I + G = Y$$

$$a + b[Y(1 - \tau) - v] + C + dY + G = Y$$

$$Y = \frac{a + c + G - by}{1 - b(1 - \tau) - d}$$

$$\frac{\Delta Y}{\Delta G} = \frac{1}{1 - b(1 - \tau) - d}$$

$$\frac{\Delta Y}{\Delta v} = \frac{\Delta Y}{Y \Delta \tau} = \frac{-b}{1 - b(1 - \tau) - d}$$

$$\frac{\Delta Y}{\Delta G} + \frac{\Delta Y}{Y \Delta \tau} = \frac{1 - b}{1 - b(1 - \tau) - d}$$

which may be greater or less than unity.

Case V. We now introduce an import function into the model, in which imports depend on income. This is similar to the consumption and investment functions, except that an increase in imports clearly decreases GNP. Exports are usually considered to depend on exogenous variables, except for domestic prices, even in large scale models. The model is

$$C = a + b(Y - T)$$

$$T = v + \tau Y$$

$$I = c + dY$$

$$M = f + gY$$

$$G = \bar{G}$$

$$E = \bar{E}$$

$$C + I + G + E - M = Y$$

$$a + b[Y(1 - \tau) - v] + c + dY - f - gY + G + E = Y$$

$$Y = \frac{a - bv + c - f + G + E}{1 - b(1 - \tau) - d + g}$$

$$\frac{\Delta Y}{\Delta G} = \frac{1}{1 - b(1 - \tau) - d + g}$$

$$\frac{\Delta Y}{\Delta v} = \frac{\Delta Y}{Y \Delta \tau} = \frac{-b}{1 - b(1 - \tau) - d + g}$$

Case VI. Even in simple multiplier examples, one should distinguish between personal and corporate income. One simple way to approach this problem is to subtract corporate savings (S_c) from personal income and include it as a separate determinant of investment. Then we have

$$C = a + b(Y - T - S_c)$$

$$I = C + dY + e(S_c)$$

$$M = f + gY$$

$$G = \bar{G}$$

$$E = \bar{E}$$

$$C + I + G + E - M = Y$$

$$T = t + \tau Y$$

$$S_c = j + kY$$

Then

$$a + b[Y(1 - \tau - k) - t - j] + c + dY + ej + ekY - f - gY + G + E = Y$$

$$Y = \frac{a - bt - bj + c + ej - f + G + E}{1 - b(1 - \tau - k) - d - ek + g}$$

$$\frac{\Delta Y}{\Delta G} = \frac{1}{1 - b(1 - \tau - k) - d - ek + g}$$

$$\frac{\Delta Y}{Y\Delta\tau} = \frac{-b}{1 - b(1 - \tau - k) - d - ek + g}$$

Whether a rise in corporate savings will raise or lower GNP depends on the relative sizes of b and e. In general $b > e$, so a redistribution of income away from dividends toward corporate savings would tend to lower GNP, holding everything else constant. However, corporate savings are likely to rise faster than dividends at the same time when GNP is growing very rapidly. This acts as a stabilizing influence on the economy unless the *mpc* out of dividend income is also very low.

19.5   EXTENSIONS OF MULTIPLIER ANALYSIS FOR NONLINEAR AND DYNAMIC SYSTEMS

It would be possible to continue to make the model more realistic by adding more equations to the structure already developed. However, such an exercise would yield sharply diminishing returns for pedagogical value. Furthermore, there are two important reasons why this method cannot be used regardless of the number of equations in the system. When nonlinear terms are used, the values of the multiplier are slightly different for each time period. When dynamic (lag) structure is introduced into the model, the values of the multiplier may change considerably from one period to the next. These problems are considered now.

We return briefly to a very simple model; however, this time a distinction is made between current and constant dollars. Consider the model

$$C = a + bY$$

$$I = c + dY$$

$$G = \bar{G}$$

$$C + I + G = Y$$

$$p_c C + p_k I + p_g G = p Y$$

$$p_c = e + f \cdot p$$

$$p_k = g + h \cdot p$$

$$p_g = \overline{p_g}$$

where p_c = price index of consumer purchases

p_k = price index of capital goods

p_g = price index of government expenditures

p = price index of total GNP

The current-dollar identity defines p, so no additional equation is needed to explain it.

This model could be solved for GNP either in constant or current dollars. The solution is the same as given previously in constant dollars, but it is somewhat different in current dollars. Then we have

$$pY = (e + fp)(a + bY) + (g + hp)(c + dY) + p_g G$$

or

$$pY = (bf + dh)pY + (af + ch)p + (eb + gd)Y + (ea + gc) + p_g G$$

$$\Delta(pY) = (bf + dh)\Delta(pY) + (af + ch)\Delta p + (eb + gd)\Delta Y + \Delta(p_g G)$$

We now need to derive expressions for Δp and ΔY in terms of $\Delta(pY)$, $\Delta(p_g G)$, and levels of the other terms. First,

$$Y = \frac{G + a + c}{1 - b - d} = \frac{p_g(G + a + c)}{p_g(1 - b - d)}$$

Therefore,

$$\Delta Y = \frac{\Delta(p_g G)}{p_g(1 - b - d)}$$

Since

$$\Delta(pY) = p\Delta Y + Y\Delta p,$$

$$\Delta p = \frac{\Delta(pY)}{Y} - \frac{p}{Y} \frac{\Delta(p_g G)}{p_g(1 - b - d)}$$

Substituting this in the expression for $\Delta(pY)$ gives

$$\Delta(pY) = (bf + dh)\Delta(pY) + \frac{af + ch}{Y}\Delta(pY) - \frac{(af + ch)p}{p_g Y(1 - b - d)}\Delta(p_g G) +$$

$$\frac{eb + gd}{p_g(1 - b - d)}\Delta(p_g G) + \Delta(p_g G)$$

Therefore,

$$\frac{\Delta(pY)}{\Delta(p_g G)} = \frac{1 - \dfrac{(af + ch)p}{p_g Y(1 - b - d)} + \dfrac{eb + gd}{p_g(1 - b - d)}}{1 - (bf + dh) - [(af + ch)/Y]}$$

It can be seen that the value of the multiplier depends on the levels of p, p_g, G, and Y as well as the parameters of the model, so unique multipliers cannot be computed.

If $p_c = p_k = p_g = p = 1$, then $e = g = 0$ and $f = h = 1$, and after a little manipulation it can be seen that this reduces to

$$\frac{\Delta(pY)}{\Delta(p_g G)} = \frac{1}{1 - b - d}$$

If a relative price term is introduced into one of the aggregate demand equations, the same type of problem appears even for the constant-dollar solution. For example, suppose we write

$$C = a + bY + j\frac{p_c}{p}$$

and all the other equations from the previous case are unchanged. Then

$$a + bY + j\left(\frac{e}{p} + f\right) + c + dY + G = Y$$

where p is given implicitly by the equation

$$(e + fp)(a + bY) + (g + hp)(c + dY) + p_g G = pY$$

Therefore,

$$p[Y(1 - bf - dh) - af - ch] = p_g G + e(a + bY) + g(c + dY)$$

and

$$p = \frac{p_g G + e(a + bY) + g(c + dY)}{Y(1 - bf - dh) - af - ch}$$

Therefore,

$$\frac{\Delta p}{\Delta G} = \frac{\begin{array}{c}[Y(1 - bf - dh) - af - ch][p_g + (eb + dg)(\Delta Y/\Delta G)] \\ - [p_g G + e(a + bY) + g(c + dY)](1 - bf - dh)(\Delta Y/\Delta G)\end{array}}{[Y(1 - bf - dh) - af - ch]^2}$$

From the above equation for Y,

$$Y(1 - b - d) = a + c + G + jf + (1/p)(je)$$

$$\Delta Y(1 - b - d) = \Delta G - \frac{je\Delta p}{p^2}$$

Therefore,

$$\frac{\Delta Y}{\Delta G} = \frac{1 - (je/p^2)(\Delta p/\Delta G)}{1 - b - d}$$

Substituting the expression for $\Delta p/\Delta G$ and solving, it can be seen that the government multiplier depends on p_g, G, Y, and Y^2 as well as the parameters of the model.

Many more nonlinearities arise in realistic, more complex models. Several relative price terms and other ratios are used. Logarithmic functions are sometimes used for production functions. In the Wharton EFU model, the wage bill is defined as the product of the wage rate, number of workers, and hours worked. The methods usually used in solving these nonlinear systems involve various iterative procedures.

All the multiplier calculations performed thus far in this chapter have used a time period of unspecified length, and no attempt has been made to specify lags in the system. Yet this is one of the most important aspects of multiplier analysis, and a large part of this text has been devoted to the determination of these lags. Thus it is important to show how these lags influence the value of the multipliers at time $t, t + 1, \ldots, t + j$ after the original disturbance.

In general, two main types of lag distributions are of primary importance. Other types of lag distributions used in the Wharton EFU model, with the exception of the Almon lag weights, can be considered here as more sophisticated combinations of these two basic types. Both types of distributions are based on the Koyck transformation, but with opposite effects. In one case, the Koyck transformation is applied to levels of purchases; in the other case it is applied to stocks, and it appears as a stock-adjustment function when transformed to flows.

For the first case, take

$$C_t = a + b \sum_{i=0}^{\infty} \lambda^i Y_{t-i}$$

which is transformed to

$$C_t = a(1 - \lambda) + bY_t + \lambda C_{t-1}$$

If Y_t changes one unit at time t, C_t will change by the following amounts over time:

Period	$\Delta C/\Delta Y$
t	b
$t + 1$	$b + \lambda(b) = b(1 + \lambda)$
$t + 2$	$b + \lambda b(1 + \lambda) = b(1 + \lambda + \lambda^2)$
$\vdots$	$\vdots$
$t + j$	$b(1 + \lambda + \cdots + \lambda^j)$

As $j \to \infty$,

$$(1 + \lambda + \cdots + \lambda^j) \to \frac{1}{1 - \lambda}$$

so that in the long run,

$$\frac{\Delta C}{\Delta Y} = \frac{b}{1 - \lambda}$$

This can also be seen in another way. The long-run equilibrium value will occur when the original change in Y no longer has an effect on C. Then $C_t = C_{t-1}$ and

$$\Delta C_t = b\Delta Y_t + \lambda\Delta C_{t-1}$$

Therefore,

$$\Delta C(1 - \lambda) = b\Delta Y$$

$$\frac{\Delta C}{\Delta Y} = \frac{b}{1 - \lambda}$$

As shown in Chapter 3, this formula needs to be modified if consumption and income are growing steadily; then

$$C_t = (1 + \rho)C_{t-1}$$

and

$$\frac{\Delta C}{\Delta Y} = \frac{b}{1 - [\lambda(1 + \rho)]}$$

For the second case, take

$$K_t = c + d \sum_{i=0}^{\infty} \gamma^i Y_{t-i}$$

which is transformed to

$$I_t = c(1 - \lambda) + dY_t - (1 - \gamma)K_{t-1}$$

where

$$K_t \equiv \sum_{i=0}^{\infty} \mu^i I_{t-1}$$

and $\gamma \neq \mu$, in general, although they might be the same. If Y_t changes by one unit at time t, I_t will change by the following amount:

Period	$\Delta I / \Delta Y$
t	d
$t + 1$	$d - d(1 - \gamma) = \gamma d$
$t + 2$	$d - d(1 - \gamma)(\mu + \gamma)$
$t + 3$	$d - d(1 - \gamma)[1 - (1 - \gamma)(\mu + \gamma) + \mu\gamma + \mu^2]$

The $(t + j)$th term is not straightforward, so we proceed directly to the long-run solution. In that case

$$I_t = I_{t-1} = \cdots = I_{t-j} = I$$

so

$$K_t \equiv \sum_{i=0}^{\infty} \mu^i I_{t-i} = \frac{I}{1 - \mu}$$

Then

$$I = c(1 - \lambda) dY - \frac{1 - \gamma}{1 - \mu} I$$

Therefore,

$$\frac{\Delta I}{\Delta Y} = \frac{d}{1 + [(1 - \gamma)/(1 - \mu)]}$$

Note that if $\mu = 1$ (that is, no depreciation) $\Delta I / \Delta Y = 0$. This would be the case for inventory investment.

To show how the introduction of these lags influences the values of various multipliers over time, consider the time path of GNP for this simplified model:

$$C_t = a + bY_t + \lambda C_{t-1}$$

$$I_t = c + dY_t - (1 - \gamma)K_{t-1}$$

$$C_t + I_t + G_t = Y_t$$

$$K_t \equiv \sum_{i=0}^{\infty} \mu^i I_{t-i}$$

Combining and collecting terms,

$$a + bY_t + \lambda C_{t-1} + c + dY_t - (1 - \gamma)K_{t-1} + G = Y$$

$$Y_t(1 - b - d) = a + \lambda C_{t-1} + c - (1 - \gamma)K_{t-1} + G$$

$$\left(\frac{\Delta Y}{\Delta G}\right)_t = \frac{1}{1 - b - d} \qquad \text{at time } t$$

$$\left(\frac{\Delta C}{\Delta G}\right)_t = \left(\frac{\Delta C}{\Delta Y}\right)_t\left(\frac{\Delta Y}{\Delta G}\right)_t = b\left(\frac{\Delta Y}{\Delta G}\right)_t$$

$$\left(\frac{\Delta K}{\Delta G}\right)_t = \left(\frac{\Delta I}{\Delta Y}\right)_t\left(\frac{\Delta K}{\Delta I}\right)_t\left(\frac{\Delta Y}{\Delta G}\right)_t = d\left(\frac{\Delta Y}{\Delta G}\right)_t \qquad \text{since}\left(\frac{\Delta K}{\Delta I}\right)_t = 1$$

At time $t + 1$,

$$\left(\frac{\Delta Y}{\Delta G}\right)_{t+1} = \frac{1 + \lambda b(\Delta Y/\Delta G)_t - (1 - \gamma)d(\Delta Y/\Delta G)_t}{1 - b - d}$$

$$\left(\frac{\Delta C}{\Delta G}\right)_{t+1} = b\left(\frac{\Delta Y}{\Delta G}\right)_{t+1} + \lambda b\left(\frac{\Delta Y}{\Delta G}\right)_t$$

$$\left(\frac{\Delta K}{\Delta G}\right)_{t+1} = d\left(\frac{\Delta Y}{\Delta G}\right)_{t+1} + d(\mu + \gamma)\left(\frac{\Delta Y}{\Delta G}\right)_t$$

At time $t + 2$,

$$\left(\frac{\Delta Y}{\Delta G}\right)_{t+2}$$

$$= \frac{1 + \lambda\left[b\left(\frac{\Delta Y}{\Delta G}\right)_{t+1} + \lambda b\left(\frac{\Delta Y}{\Delta G}\right)_t\right] - (1 - \gamma)d\left\{\left(\frac{\Delta Y}{\Delta G}\right)_{t+1} + (\mu + \gamma)\left(\frac{\Delta Y}{\Delta G}\right)_t\right\}}{1 - b - d}$$

$$= \frac{1 + [\lambda b - d(1 - \gamma)]\left(\frac{\Delta Y}{\Delta G}\right)_{t+1} + \{\lambda^2 b - d(1 - \gamma)(\mu + \gamma)\}\left(\frac{\Delta Y}{\Delta G}\right)_t}{1 - b - d}$$

where $(\Delta Y/\Delta G)_{t+1}$ and $(\Delta Y/\Delta G)_t$ are as given above.

The long-run government expenditure multiplier for this simple case is

$$\left(\frac{\Delta Y}{\Delta G}\right)_{\substack{t+j \\ j \to \infty}} = \frac{1}{1 - \dfrac{b}{1 - \lambda} - \dfrac{d}{1 + [(1 - \gamma)/(1 - \mu)]}}$$

It is often thought that this multiplier is larger than the first-quarter (impact) multiplier. However, this need not be the case. For approximate values $\gamma = 0.9$,

$\mu = 0.95$, $\lambda = 0.3$, $b = 0.3$, and $d = 0.2$, the long-run multiplier will be some-what smaller than the impact multiplier.

These calculations can be represented much more easily in matrix form. The inverse of the matrix can be used to find any desired impact multiplier and the effects of a change in any exogenous variable on each of the endogenous variables. Again consider the following simple model:

$$C = aY + b + eC_{-1}$$

$$I = cY + d - fK_{-1}$$

$$G = \bar{G}$$

$$C + I + G = Y$$

We could write

$$Y = (a + c)Y + (b + d) + G + eC_{-1} - fK_{-1}$$

and

$$Y = \frac{b + d + G + eC_{-1} - fK_{-1}}{1 - a - c}$$

However, suppose the equations were transformed to the form

$$C \quad - aY = b + eC_{-1}$$

$$I - cY = d + fK_{-1}$$

$$-C - I + \quad Y = G$$

or, in matrix notation,

$$\begin{bmatrix} 1 & 0 & -a \\ 0 & 1 & -c \\ -1 & -1 & 1 \end{bmatrix} \begin{bmatrix} C \\ I \\ Y \end{bmatrix} = \begin{bmatrix} b + eC_{-1} \\ d - fK_{-1} \\ G \end{bmatrix}$$

Then

$$\begin{bmatrix} C \\ I \\ Y \end{bmatrix} = \frac{1}{1 - a - c} \begin{bmatrix} 1 - c & a & a \\ c & 1 - a & c \\ 1 & 1 & 1 \end{bmatrix} \begin{bmatrix} b + eC_{-1} \\ d - fK_{-1} \\ G \end{bmatrix}$$

This expresses all the endogenous variables of the system in terms of only the exogenous and lagged variables. In general these equations can be written

$$\mathbf{AY} - \mathbf{BZ} = 0$$

$$\mathbf{Y} = (\mathbf{A}^{-1}\mathbf{B})\mathbf{Z}$$

$$\mathbf{A} = \|a_{ij}\| \qquad \mathbf{B} = \|b_{ij}\|$$

$$\mathbf{A}^{-1}\mathbf{B} = \|\alpha^{ij}\|$$

and the elements of $(A^{-1}B)$ provide the multipliers. Writing this out,

$$C = \frac{1-c}{1-a-c}b + \frac{a}{1-a-c}d + \frac{a}{1-a-c}G + \frac{(1-c)eC_{-1}}{1-a-c} - \frac{afK_{-1}}{1-a-c}$$

$$I = \frac{c}{1-a-c}b + \frac{1-a}{1-a-c}d + \frac{c}{1-a-c}G - \frac{(1-a)fK_{-1}}{1-a-c} + \frac{ceC_{-1}}{1-a-c}$$

$$Y = \frac{1}{1-a-c}b + \frac{1}{1-a-c}d + \frac{1}{1-a-c}G + \frac{eC_{-1} - fK_{-1}}{1-a-c}$$

$\Delta Y/\Delta G$ can easily be calculated as $1(1-a-c)$. Furthermore, $\Delta C/\Delta G$, $\Delta I/\Delta G$, and all other such combinations can be calculated just as easily. Also,

$$\frac{\Delta C}{\Delta Y} = \frac{\Delta C}{\Delta G} \bigg/ \frac{\Delta Y}{\Delta G} = \frac{a/(1-a-c)}{1/(1-a-c)} = a$$

and other similar terms can be obtained. Thus the elements α^{ij} in the inverse matrix can be immediately identified as the multiplier for a change in the ith endogenous variable relative to a unit change in the jth exogenous or lagged variable.

There is probably no advantage to using matrix algebra for a simple three-equation model. But it has just been shown how quickly the algebra becomes cumbersome as equations are added. The advantage of using matrix algebra is that the inverse need only to be found once.[2] This inverse can then be used to calculate multipliers for single exogenous variables or any combination of variables. The limitations of this method are that this matrix holds exactly only for a strictly linear system and gives only the value of the impact multipliers.

Most empirical systems of equations will not be entirely linear. Terms of the sort p_i/p_j, P_iQ_i, and $W = wNh$ (wage bill = wage rate times employment times hours) are typical of those nonlinearities met in the Wharton EFU model.[3] One way to solve these problems is to divide the model into a "price" block and a "quantity" block. The solution of the model is then obtained through an iterative process. The quantity block is solved first, with all variables in the price block treated as exogenous and hence known at time t. Reasonable guesses ("starting values") are used for the prices, and an initial solution of the quantity variables is obtained. These values are then used as exogenous inputs in the price block, and a first set of prices are obtained. These price estimates are used again as exogenous variables in the quantity block, and a second iterative solution is obtained. This process of shifting between blocks is continued until the values of the jth and $(j+1)$st iteration agree for all variables within

---

[2] Actual numerical estimates are used for the elements of the A matrix, and it is only a matter of a few seconds to invert a 40 by 40 matrix on a large-scale computer.

[3] For a detailed treatment of the solution of the Wharton EFU model, see M. K. Evans and L. R. Klein, *The Wharton Econometric Forecasting Model* (Philadelphia: University of Pennsylvania, 1967).

a specified degree of tolerance. The inverse matrix of the last iteration is usually the one used to derive impact multipliers. Note that this matrix contains various price terms; thus the inverse will change any time the price levels (or other terms in the price block) change. Although the changes are not large, a slightly different inverse matrix (and thus slightly different multipliers) exist at each period of time.

This system can be expanded to include as many blocks as needed. In the Wharton model, only two simultaneous blocks are necessary. A third block is added which is entirely recursive. All variables in that block depend either on lagged or exogenous variables or on variables previously solved for in the same block. Thus investment depends entirely on lagged variables; capital stock, estimated later in the same block, depends on investment. Since wage rates depend entirely on lagged values, they are estimated in the recursive block; employment is then estimated in the quantity block and hours in the price block.[4]

There is no straightforward way to calculate dynamic multipliers of a non-linear system, because the inverse matrix changes every period. One method of solution is simply to fix the prices at their initial values, compute an initial inverse matrix, and obtain the impact multipliers. The values taken from the inverse matrix can then be applied to each future period in turn, as was done in our simple example. Besides being very tedious, this method is only approximate and the values obtained may depart substantially from the exact multipliers for long time periods if relative price terms are important. An exact method is to calculate a "control" solution for as many quarters as desired, and then to calculate a "disturbed" solution with one or more of the exogenous variables changed. The value of any given variable for the disturbed solution can be subtracted from the corresponding value for the control solution, and the value of the multiplier can be obtained by dividing this change by the change in the particular exogenous variable. This is the method used to calculate the multipliers presented in Chapter 20.

---

[4] Another method used is to solve for each equation separately, using values for the independent variables taken from the previous iteration. This method is described in L. R. Klein and M. K. Evans, *Econometric Gaming* (New York: Macmillan, 1968).

CHAPTER 20

MULTIPLIER VALUES AND
POLICY SIMULATIONS

20.1 GOVERNMENT EXPENDITURE AND TAX CUT
MULTIPLIERS OF THE WHARTON EFU MODEL

The multipliers presented in Chapter 19 are useful only for methodological purposes, as they are based on very oversimplified models. In this section impact and dynamic multipliers are presented and analyzed for several alternative fiscal and monetary policies. The effects of these policies on different economic goals are then compared.

One can think of the generalized multiplier formulas:

$$(20.1) \qquad \frac{\Delta X}{\Delta G} = \frac{1}{1 - mpc(\Delta Y/\Delta X) - mpI + mpf}$$

$$(20.2) \qquad \frac{\Delta X}{\Delta T} = \frac{mpc}{1 - mpc(\Delta Y/\Delta X) - mpI + mpf}$$

where Y = personal disposable income

X = GNP

G = government expenditures

T = personal income taxes

mpc = marginal propensity to consume

mpI = marginal propensity to invest

mpf = marginal propensity to spend out of net foreign balance (equal to the marginal propensity to import minus the marginal propensity to export) as a useful designation for the multiterm expressions that actually exist, keeping in mind that each symbol represents several separate terms. In particular, all the marginal propensities include price effects as well as income effects, and the *mpI* also includes the effect of corporate cash flow as well as output, disposable income, and sales on the various types of investment. It is instructive to consider the multipliers in this way to get an overall picture of the relative importance of the various marginal propensities to spend when government expenditures or personal income tax rates change.

Since the model is nonlinear, the exact size of the multipliers will depend on the levels of many of the variables during the solution period and also on the cyclical position of the economy, since wages and prices will rise faster near peaks than near troughs. All multiplier calculations in this chapter have been made for a 40-quarter period starting in 1966.1. The values of government expenditures and other exogenous variables were chosen to be those which resulted in unemployment remaining close to 4 percent throughout the simulation period. This in turn implies a yearly growth rate of 4 percent in constant dollars and an annual price increase of 2 percent. The solution generated by this set of assumptions is known as the *control solution*. Several subsequent solutions were calculated in which different exogenous variables were adjusted; these are known as *disturbed solutions*. We can then easily compute the difference between the disturbed and control solutions for the endogenous variables per unit change in each particular exogenous variable.

All changes in the exogenous variables were in the direction that raised GNP, a convention followed throughout this chapter unless specifically noted otherwise. For small changes in the system around the same starting value, equal increases or decreases in a given exogenous variable should produce almost symmetrical results.[1] This by no means implies that the same policies should necessarily be used to reverse recessions and booms. A particular policy which changes unemployment substantially but has little effect on prices will be quite useful for ending recessions but of little value for stopping inflation. Rather, the symmetry of these changes implies that both small increases and decreases of any given exogenous variable will have almost the same absolute effect on each endogenous variable.

We first consider multiplier calculations for a $1 billion increase in constant dollars in nondefense government spending and a change in the personal income tax rate which reduces personal income taxes by $1 billion in constant dollars in the base period. As income grows over time, a fixed change in the tax rates multiplied by an increasing level of personal income will result in *ex ante* decreases of personal income taxes of more than $1 billion. The effects of these two changes on different components of consumption, investment,

---

[1] This need not be the case for larger disturbances from equilibrium. For example, simulations of the Brookings model have shown that a larger excise tax cut has a *proportionately* greater effect than a smaller one. See G. Fromm and P. Taubman, *Policy Simulations with an Econometric Model* (Washington: The Brookings Institution, 1968).

and disposable income are shown in Tables 20.1 and 20.2. Multipliers are calculated for each of the first 12 quarters, the twentieth quarter, and the fortieth quarter; the latter may be considered a close approximation to the long-run multipliers determined by the model.

A slight methodological digression may be in order here to clarify the interpretation of the following multiplier results. It has been suggested that these results tell us more about the properties of the model than the real world. If the two were far apart and bore scant resemblance, there would be little excuse for presenting simulation results. However, we have argued in Chapter 18 that the Wharton EFU model has forecast changes in the economy well during a period when there were substantial changes in personal income, corporate income, and excise tax rates as well as large shifts in monetary policy and government spending.

One of the main reasons for analyzing these predictions in detail was to show that the model is reliable enough to be used to assess the effects of various policy changes. The fact that the model was in most cases able to forecast the effect of these changes accurately suggests that hypothetical multiplier calculations should also present realistic approximations to what would happen in actual situations. It is in this spirit that the following results should be evaluated.

This argument applies more for short-run periods, since longer-range forecasts of the Wharton EFU model are not analyzed. In this case, we have argued that the constancy of the consumption/income and capital/output ratios which arise from the long-run solutions of the consumption and investment functions agree with observed phenomena. This point is discussed below in greater detail.

The government expenditure multiplier is considered first. Somewhat surprisingly, there is very little difference between the impact (first quarter) and long-run multipliers. The increase of the *mpc* for nondurables and services over time is offset by the accelerator (or stock-adjustment reaction) in the consumer durables, fixed business investment, and inventory investment sectors. Furthermore, changes in the net foreign balance are negatively related to changes in GNP in the long run, *cet. par.* (that is, no offsetting changes in foreign markets). The quantity of residential construction is negatively related to the price of housing, which in turn is positively related to the amount of fixed investment; as the latter rises, the price of housing increases and the quantity of residential construction declines. This relationship is just one example of the importance of including the relative price terms in the multiplier calculations. The negative effect of the net foreign balance, although not unexpected, is due to both income and price effects. The latter are often disregarded and the effect of income on imports is usually known as the "marginal propensity to import." However, price effects also need to be considered. Since imports and exports both depend on relative prices, an increase in U.S. prices relative to foreign prices will result in a lower net foreign balance. In these

TABLE 20.1 DETAILED MULTIPLIER VALUES FOR INCREASE IN NONDEFENSE GOVERNMENT EXPENDITURES[a]

Variable	1	2	3	4	5	6	7	8	9	10	11	12	20	40
C_{ns}	0.32	0.40	0.41	0.45	0.48	0.50	0.54	0.58	0.61	0.64	0.67	0.69	0.83	0.91
C_{na}	0.16	0.18	0.15	0.14	0.12	0.11	0.11	0.12	0.12	0.11	0.11	0.11	0.11	0.09
C_a	0.29	0.28	0.23	0.20	0.18	0.16	0.15	0.15	0.15	0.14	0.15	0.14	0.13	0.10
C	0.77	0.86	0.79	0.79	0.78	0.77	0.80	0.85	0.88	0.89	0.93	0.94	1.07	1.10
I_p	0.00	0.21	0.25	0.24	0.25	0.27	0.28	0.31	0.33	0.33	0.32	0.32	0.29	0.21
I_h	0.03	0.03	0.03	0.01	-0.01	-0.03	-0.03	-0.03	-0.03	-0.03	-0.03	-0.03	-0.04	-0.05
ΔI_i	0.25	0.37	0.19	0.13	0.06	0.05	0.04	0.06	0.06	0.04	0.04	0.04	0.03	-0.01
I	0.28	0.61	0.47	0.38	0.30	0.29	0.30	0.34	0.36	0.34	0.33	0.33	0.28	0.15
F	-0.07	-0.12	-0.13	-0.14	-0.14	-0.15	-0.15	-0.16	-0.18	-0.17	-0.19	-0.20	-0.22	-0.32
G	1.00	1.00	1.00	1.00	1.00	1.00	1.00	1.00	1.00	1.00	1.00	1.00	1.00	1.00
X	1.98	2.35	2.13	2.03	1.94	1.91	1.95	2.03	2.06	2.06	2.07	2.07	2.13	1.93
W_m	0.44	0.57	0.51	0.45	0.38	0.35	0.37	0.39	0.41	0.41	0.43	0.45	0.57	0.64
W_n	0.48	0.60	0.56	0.55	0.53	0.51	0.52	0.55	0.57	0.57	0.58	0.59	0.66	0.66
W_g	0.60	0.60	0.60	0.60	0.60	0.60	0.60	0.60	0.60	0.60	0.60	0.60	0.60	0.60
$PB + Dv$	0.18	0.22	0.21	0.22	0.23	0.22	0.23	0.25	0.25	0.26	0.26	0.27	0.30	0.33
Tr	-0.30	-0.34	-0.30	-0.27	-0.26	-0.26	-0.26	-0.27	-0.27	-0.27	-0.27	-0.27	-0.30	-0.22
$-Tp$	0.26	0.30	0.29	0.28	0.27	0.26	0.26	0.27	0.28	0.28	0.28	0.29	0.32	0.34
DI, current \$	1.14	1.35	1.29	1.27	1.21	1.16	1.20	1.25	1.28	1.29	1.32	1.35	1.54	1.67
DI, constant \$	1.04	1.16	1.07	1.04	0.97	0.92	0.94	0.99	1.01	1.00	1.03	1.05	1.14	1.08

[a] All demand variables are in 1958 dollars and all income variables in current dollars unless otherwise specified. For assumptions about change in the exogenous variables, see Table 20.3.

TABLE 20.2 DETAILED MULTIPLIER VALUES FOR DECREASE IN PERSONAL INCOME TAX RATES[a]

Variable	1	2	3	4	5	6	7	8	9	10	11	12	20	40
C_{ns}	0.48	0.57	0.60	0.67	0.73	0.78	0.85	0.91	0.96	1.01	1.05	1.10	1.41	1.98
C_{na}	0.24	0.24	0.22	0.20	0.19	0.18	0.18	0.19	0.19	0.18	0.18	0.18	0.20	0.24
C_a	0.25	0.25	0.20	0.19	0.17	0.16	0.15	0.16	0.16	0.15	0.15	0.15	0.15	0.20
C	0.97	1.06	1.02	1.06	1.09	1.12	1.18	1.26	1.31	1.34	1.38	1.43	1.76	2.42
I_p	0.00	0.25	0.30	0.29	0.32	0.35	0.38	0.41	0.43	0.45	0.45	0.46	0.47	0.52
I_h	0.03	0.04	0.04	0.03	0.01	-0.01	-0.01	-0.02	-0.02	-0.02	-0.02	-0.03	-0.04	-0.02
ΔI_i	0.29	0.38	0.16	0.13	0.08	0.06	0.06	0.08	0.07	0.05	0.05	0.05	0.06	0.03
I	0.32	0.67	0.50	0.45	0.41	0.40	0.43	0.47	0.48	0.48	0.48	0.50	0.53	0.53
F	-0.10	-0.15	-0.16	-0.16	-0.18	-0.20	-0.21	-0.22	-0.23	-0.23	-0.23	-0.24	-0.28	-0.34
X	1.19	1.58	1.36	1.35	1.32	1.32	1.40	1.51	1.56	1.59	1.63	1.67	2.01	2.61
W_m	0.51	0.62	0.55	0.52	0.49	0.47	0.49	0.51	0.51	0.51	0.51	0.53	0.58	0.69
W_n	0.16	0.28	0.24	0.24	0.24	0.22	0.24	0.27	0.28	0.28	0.30	0.31	0.40	0.55
$PB + Dv$	0.12	0.16	0.16	0.17	0.18	0.19	0.20	0.22	0.24	0.25	0.26	0.27	0.35	0.53
Tr	-0.08	-0.13	-0.11	-0.09	-0.09	-0.09	-0.09	-0.10	-0.10	-0.10	-0.10	-0.11	-0.11	-0.11
$-T_p$	-0.98	-0.96	-0.98	-1.01	-1.02	-1.04	-1.05	-1.06	-1.07	-1.08	-1.10	-1.12	-1.24	-1.60
DI, current \$	1.69	1.89	1.82	1.85	1.84	1.83	1.89	1.96	2.00	2.02	2.07	2.12	2.46	3.26
DI, constant \$	1.54	1.63	1.54	1.54	1.52	1.49	1.54	1.59	1.63	1.63	1.68	1.72	1.99	2.58
$PI \Delta\tau_p$, constant \$[b]	1.05	1.05	1.07	1.08	1.09	1.10	1.11	1.13	1.14	1.15	1.17	1.18	1.30	1.61

[a] All demand variables are in 1958 dollars and all income variables in current dollars unless otherwise specified. For assumptions about changes in the tax rate, see Table 20.6.
[b] This is the decrease in taxes ex ante, that is, before the inclusion of the increase in taxes induced by increased personal income. These values should be used for normalizing changes in other variables for comparison with the government expenditure multiplier.

simulations the price effects account for a larger change in the net foreign balance than the income effects.

There are some small cyclical fluctuations in the value of the multiplier; it does not asymptotically approach its long-run value. These small cycles are quite heavily damped and are of sufficiently short duration that they are properly identified as inventory subcycles rather than fluctuations dominated by fixed business investment. These calculations do not assume changes in monetary policy, changes which in practice have amplified cyclical fluctuations.

The long-run multiplier estimates can be compared with those values that would be obtained under the assumption of balanced growth in all sectors of the domestic economy. This would occur if the long-run elasticities of consumption with respect to income, capital stock with respect to output, and disposable income with respect to GNP were all unity, and if all prices grew at the same rate. It is still possible that the ratio of imports and exports to GNP might change because of differential movements in the price and quantity of foreign trade. Under these conditions, the long-run *mpc* would equal the *apc*; the long-run change of net investment with respect to private output would be zero and of gross investment would be equal to the change in depreciation. Using the generalized multiplier adjusted for the fact that investment is a function of private output.

$$(20.3) \qquad \frac{\Delta X}{\Delta G} = \frac{1 - mpI}{1 - mpc(\Delta Y/\Delta X) - mpI + mpf}$$

and substituting the following approximate long-run values,

$$mpc = apc = 0.93$$

$$\frac{\Delta Y}{\Delta X} = \frac{Y}{X} = 0.70$$

$$mpI = \frac{D}{Y} = 0.07 \text{ (not including } D_h)$$

$$mpf = mpm - mpe = 0.06 - (-0.10)\text{(including price effects)}$$

gives

$$(20.4) \qquad \frac{\Delta X}{\Delta G} = \frac{1 - 0.07}{1 - 0.93(0.70) - 0.08 + 0.16} = \frac{0.93}{1 - 0.57} = 2.16$$

This value is slightly higher than the figure of 1.93 obtained in the detailed calculations; the slight discrepancy occurs because the calculated value of $\Delta Y/\Delta X$ is not as large as the actual average value of Y/X. This is undoubtedly due to the effects of income redistribution through inflation, which is part of the simulation solution. Near full employment, wage earners bargain for greater increases in money wages than at low levels of employment. This might be expected to raise disposable income relative to GNP during booms, but this is not what occurs. As long as economic activity is high, any increases in unit labor costs will be fully passed along by businesses. Since prices rise by the full amount of the increase in unit labor costs, the relative position of workers has not improved. Although laborers may bargain for higher money wages because of higher prices, any increased costs will again be fully passed on and laborers will again be unable to better their relative position. In the real world these increases are not permitted to continue indefinitely. Restrictive fiscal and monetary policy are used and a recession is likely to ensue. However, such countercyclical movements are not considered in this multiplier calculation.

Even if the ratio of labor income to GNP remains constant, the relative share of disposable income is likely to decrease. Since tax schedules are based on money income instead of real income, any rise in the price level will increase the percentage of income going to taxes, *cet. par.* Furthermore, rent and interest payments and transfer payments are based on fixed contracts and schedules, so real income from these sources will decline. In actuality, social security schedules are continually revised upward, usually by more than the amount of the intervening price increase; but these adjustments also are not considered in this simulation. Thus it should be no surprise that the calculated long-run $\Delta Y/\Delta X$ ratio is somewhat lower than the historically observed average ratio. This finding does suggest that with continued mild inflation the relative share of disposable income is likely to decline in the absence of further tax cuts and upward renegotiation of payment schedules for social security and other transfer payments.[2]

It should be mentioned that this multiplier value of 1.93 is strongly influenced by the relative price terms in the import and export equations. If the effect of these terms was omitted by assuming that domestic and world prices were to change at the same rate, the *mpf* would be reduced to 0.05, and

$$(20.5) \qquad \frac{\Delta X}{\Delta G} = \frac{0.93}{1 - 0.67} = 2.8$$

If it were assumed, in addition, that domestic income and the quantity of world trade grew at the same rate, the *mpf* would be zero and the multiplier would be

$$(20.6) \qquad \frac{\Delta X}{\Delta G} = \frac{0.93}{1 - 0.72} = 3.3$$

Further multiplier calculations will be performed with both the price and income effects of foreign trade included. One should keep in mind, however,

---

[2] This could happen even if labor's share of output remained constant, because that is calculated before taxes and transfers.

that substantially different multiplier values do result from alternative assumptions about changes in foreign prices and the quantity of world trade.[3]

The multipliers for a change in the personal income tax rate are now considered. It can be seen that the values of the tax multiplier are much smaller than the government expenditure multiplier during the first year. They gradually increase over time until they appear to be larger, but this is somewhat of an illusion. Since income is increasing, the actual change in taxes also increases over time for a fixed change in the tax rates. For a more accurate comparison of the two multipliers, one should divide the increase in constant-dollar GNP by the actual decrease in constant-dollar taxes. After 40 quarters, the change in GNP divided by the change in personal income taxes is equal to 1.62, slightly smaller than the long-run value of the government multiplier. There are, however, greater sectoral differences in the effects of these two multipliers. It is assumed that there is no additional increase in government expenditures when taxes are cut; thus if the difference between the two multipliers is less than unity, other components of aggregate demand must increase more than they do when government spending rises. Since consumption depends primarily on personal disposable income, a decrease in personal income taxes will clearly result in a greater increase in that sector. After 40 quarters, consumption of nondurables and services accounts for 77 percent of the increase in aggregate demand when taxes are cut, compared to 48 percent when government expenditures are increased. There is also a larger proportionate increase in the fixed business investment sector because investment is a function of private output rather than total output. An increase in government expenditures does not initially raise fixed business investment, which grows only after purchases in the private sector of the economy have increased. Although the decrease in personal income taxes does not directly affect fixed business investment, the rise in private output per dollar of change is much higher, and thus plant and equipment expenditures rise much more.

There is little difference in the long-run values of the government expenditure and tax-change multipliers. This might suggest that in the long run the so-called "balanced-budget multiplier" is close to zero. But this simple concept is not really applicable to complex, realistic models. It is one thing to state that equal increases in government expenditures and personal income taxes will have approximately offsetting effects on GNP. But it does not follow that such moves will result in a balanced budget once induced changes in tax receipts are considered.

It is of considerable importance to stress that in the first year or two, a $1 billion increase in government expenditure will raise real output more than will a $1 billion decrease in personal income taxes. If rapid changes are desired

---

[3] In the control solution it is assumed that foreign incomes and prices grow at approximately the same rate as their domestic counterparts. However, when an extra $1 billion is added to government expenditures or subtracted from taxes, no additional adjustments were made for foreign sector variables.

(such as to end a recession) government expenditures are clearly preferred to tax cuts. But if the primary aim of fiscal policy moves is to continue to keep the economy near full employment when it is presently expanding, then on economic grounds there is much to recommend a tax cut. In the long run, there will be almost an equal increase in GNP both per dollar of tax cut and per dollar of additional government spending. Since private investment depends on private output, investment is stimulated more with a tax cut and thus capital stock and total capacity grow faster. This reduces upward pressure on prices and retards their rate of increase. Since prices do not rise as rapidly, the net foreign balance does not decline as much. With respect to the economic goals discussed in Chapter 19, the tax cut is to be preferred over government spending in the long run. The advantage of an increase in government spending, which may be considerable at certain times, is its more rapid effectiveness.

20.2   COMPARISON OF ALTERNATIVE FISCAL AND MONETARY POLICIES

Although the multipliers for an increase in government spending and a decrease in personal income tax rates are probably the most familiar, there are many other multipliers that can be calculated. Many other fiscal and monetary policy tools are currently used, and the effect of exogenous changes on private sector variables could also be examined. From a wide list of possible alternatives we have chosen six other multipliers to be examined. The two cases that have already been analyzed are also included here in the same format for ease of comparison. The eight cases are:

1. Increase of $1 billion in nondefense government spending.
2. Increase of $1 billion in defense government spending.
3. Increase of $1 billion in exports (for example, due to a change in the price or quantity of world trade).
4. Decrease of $1 billion in personal income tax rates.
5. Decrease of $1 billion in corporate income tax rates.
6. Decrease of $1 billion in excise tax rates.
7. Decrease of 1 percent in the discount rate.
8. Decrease in reserve requirements so that free reserves/required reserves ratio rises by 10 percent.

Changes 1–6 are in constant dollars.

For the tax-cut multipliers, the rates were adjusted so that the change in the tax rate multiplied by the level of taxable income in the previous period was equal to $1 billion in constant dollars. The change in the reserve ratio at current rates is approximately equal to $2 billion; this result is scaled down to $1 billion for easier comparison in the final summary table.

It should be mentioned that these calculations merely scratch the surface of possible policy simulations that have been tried. Well over 100 different simulations have been undertaken and analyzed in connection with the forecasts of the Wharton EFU model. In many of these experiments, several alternative policy moves were combined to examine their joint effect. The multipliers have also been calculated at different levels of unemployment and capacity utilization to examine the effects of the nonlinearities in the system. Furthermore, many other exogenous variables have been changed. The effects of exogenous wage increases, increased transfer payments, increased social security taxes, the introduction of Medicare, changes in farm price support policy, reimposition of selective credit controls, removal of the investment tax credit, steel strikes, auto strikes, and changes in productivity are only a few of the many changes that have been calculated and compared with "control solutions" or forecasts. Although it is not feasible to discuss all these alternative simulations in this text, the wide range of applicability of a medium- or large-scale model should be kept in mind. For it is here, rather than in the forecasting of GNP, that the advantages of a larger model relative to a smaller one become most apparent.

In all the following calculations, the effects of a given change in selected exogenous variables are shown for constant- and current-dollar GNP, the implicit GNP deflator, disposable income, corporate profits, and the rate of unemployment. In most cases changes in particular additional relevant variables are also shown. As in the previous tabulations, multipliers are shown for the first 12 quarters, the twentieth quarter, and the fortieth quarter. Since all changes are made in constant dollars, the actual multipliers can be found in the first column, which is the change in GNP in constant dollars. As mentioned previously, care must be taken in the case of the tax multipliers to compare the increase in GNP to the actual decrease in taxes, (that is, rate change times current base) not the original $1 billion. In the notes below Tables 20.3–20.10, the 40-quarter multiplier is calculated per $1 billion decrease in taxes; this figure is obtained by dividing the amount of increase in GNP by the amount of the actual decrease in tax revenues, where both figures are in constant dollars. Because of the lag structure, this method cannot be used accurately to calculate normalized tax multipliers for the earlier quarters. The increase in GNP at time t depends on changes in taxes both in this quarter and previous quarters. Since the time path of GNP is still fluctuating in the earlier quarters, all the lagged values of taxes would have to be included with the appropriate weights to obtain the exact multiplier. Failure to do this would tend to bias the multiplier calculations downward slightly if the values are increasing. In these particular calculations, the errors would not be large because the multiplier values do not change very much from one quarter to the next. By the 40th quarter, the system is assumed to have settled into equilibrium, and thus the approximation is almost exact.

The multipliers for the eight policy alternatives mentioned are given below in Tables 20.3 through 20.10.

TABLE 20.3 MULTIPLIERS FOR INCREASE IN NONDEFENSE GOVERNMENT EXPENDITURES

Quarter	X^a	GNP^b	p^c	DI^b	$P_{cb}{}^b$	Un^d	$I_p{}^a$	Govt.^{a} Surplus
1	1.98	2.33	0.02	1.14	0.50	−0.25	0.00	−0.08
2	2.35	2.85	0.03	1.35	0.71	−0.29	0.21	0.03
3	2.13	2.69	0.04	1.29	0.67	−0.25	0.25	−0.07
4	2.03	2.63	0.05	1.27	0.67	−0.23	0.24	−0.12
5	1.94	2.56	0.05	1.21	0.70	−0.21	0.25	−0.15
6	1.91	2.55	0.05	1.16	0.73	−0.21	0.27	−0.15
7	1.95	2.62	0.05	1.20	0.75	−0.22	0.28	−0.14
8	2.03	2.73	0.05	1.25	0.79	−0.22	0.31	−0.10
9	2.06	2.81	0.05	1.28	0.81	−0.22	0.33	−0.09
10	2.06	2.84	0.06	1.29	0.81	−0.22	0.33	−0.10
11	2.07	2.87	0.06	1.32	0.81	−0.21	0.32	−0.09
12	2.07	2.92	0.06	1.32	0.82	−0.21	0.32	−0.09
20	2.13	3.25	0.09	1.54	0.88	−0.20	0.29	−0.08
40	1.93	3.72	0.13	1.67	1.13	−0.15	0.21	−0.13

^{a} Billions of 1958 dollars.

^{b} Billions of current dollars.

^{c} Index, 1958 = 100.0.

^{d} Per cent.

Variables changed: government purchases, + $1.0 billion, 1958 dollars; government wage bill, + $0.6 billion, current dollars; government output originating, + $0.5 billion, 1958 dollars; government employment, + 0.1 million.

TABLE 20.4 MULTIPLIERS FOR INCREASE IN GOVERNMENT DEFENSE EXPENDITURES

Quarter	X^a	GNP^b	p^c	DI^b	$P_{cb}{}^b$	Un^d	$I_p{}^a$	Govt.^{a} Surplus
1	2.19	2.60	0.02	1.29	0.63	−0.23	0.00	0.03
2	2.96	3.63	0.05	1.70	1.02	−0.31	0.28	0.30
3	2.21	2.94	0.06	1.36	0.85	−0.23	0.36	−0.04
4	2.10	2.85	0.07	1.35	0.83	−0.20	0.30	−0.09
5	1.71	2.48	0.07	1.12	0.79	−0.16	0.33	−0.22
6	1.69	2.46	0.08	1.07	0.85	−0.16	0.31	−0.22
7	1.78	2.58	0.08	1.11	0.89	−0.16	0.35	−0.20
8	1.88	2.71	0.08	1.17	0.93	−0.17	0.38	−0.15
9	1.90	2.78	0.08	1.18	0.96	−0.17	0.39	−0.14
10	1.89	2.79	0.08	1.18	0.98	−0.17	0.39	−0.16
11	1.90	2.82	0.08	1.21	0.98	−0.17	0.37	−0.15
12	1.91	2.86	0.08	1.24	0.98	−0.16	0.36	−0.15
20	2.05	3.21	0.09	1.38	1.11	−0.15	0.33	−0.12
40	2.02	3.90	0.13	1.57	1.56	−0.12	0.27	−0.12

[a] Billions of 1958 dollars.
[b] Billions of current dollars.
[c] Index, 1958 = 100.0.
[d] Percent.

Variables changed: government purchases, +$1.0 billion, 1958 dollars; government defense purchases, +$1.0 billion, 1958 dollars; government wage bill, +$0.6 billion, current dollars; government output originating, +$0.5 billion, 1958 dollars; government employment, +0.1 million.

TABLE 20.5 MULTIPLIERS FOR INCREASE IN DEMAND FOR EXPORTS

Quarter	X^a	GNP^b	p^c	DI^b	$P_{cb}{}^b$	Un^d	$I_p{}^a$	$F_e{}^a$	Govt.^{a} Surplus
1	1.75	1.87	0.00	0.87	0.47	-0.20	0.00	1.00	0.75
2	2.34	2.60	0.00	1.19	0.72	-0.25	0.17	1.09	0.97
3	2.46	2.80	0.00	1.29	0.77	-0.26	0.24	1.20	0.99
4	2.69	3.09	0.00	1.44	0.86	-0.27	0.27	1.35	1.10
5	2.93	3.40	0.00	1.57	0.97	-0.28	0.31	1.50	1.22
6	3.03	3.55	0.01	1.61	1.05	-0.29	0.37	1.55	1.25
7	3.17	3.72	0.01	1.69	1.11	-0.30	0.42	1.60	1.30
8	3.32	3.92	0.01	1.78	1.16	-0.31	0.47	1.64	1.34
9	3.42	4.07	0.01	1.86	1.21	-0.31	0.52	1.67	1.39
10	3.48	4.17	0.01	1.88	1.24	-0.31	0.55	1.69	1.41
11	3.54	4.25	0.01	1.95	1.25	-0.31	0.57	1.70	1.42
12	3.58	4.34	0.01	2.00	1.27	-0.30	0.58	1.72	1.43
20	3.70	4.66	0.02	2.19	1.30	-0.28	0.42	1.73	1.41
40	3.51	4.92	0.04	2.36	1.33	-0.20	0.47	1.65	1.36

^{a} Billions of 1958 dollars.
^{b} Billions of current dollars.
^{c} Index, 1958 = 100.0.
^{d} Percent.
Variables changed: shift in export function, $+\$1.0$ billion, 1958 dollars; long-run multiplier per dollar of exports, $3.51/1.65 = 2.13$.

TABLE 20.6 MULTIPLIERS FOR DECREASE IN PERSONAL INCOME TAX RATES

Quarter	X^a	GNP^b	p^c	DI^b	$P_{cb}{}^b$	Un^d	$I_p{}^a$	$T_p{}^{a,e}$	Govt.^{a} Surplus
1	1.19	1.33	0.00	1.69	0.49	−0.06	0.00	−1.05	−0.37
2	1.58	1.88	0.02	1.89	0.73	−0.11	0.25	−1.05	−0.33
3	1.36	1.72	0.02	1.82	0.70	−0.09	0.30	−1.07	−0.44
4	1.35	1.75	0.03	1.85	0.73	−0.08	0.29	−1.08	−0.44
5	1.32	1.77	0.04	1.84	0.78	−0.07	0.32	−1.09	−0.46
6	1.32	1.80	0.04	1.83	0.84	−0.07	0.35	−1.10	−0.46
7	1.40	1.91	0.04	1.89	0.88	−0.07	0.38	−1.11	−0.43
8	1.51	2.06	0.04	1.96	0.95	−0.08	0.42	−1.13	−0.41
9	1.56	2.16	0.04	2.00	1.00	−0.08	0.44	−1.14	−0.39
10	1.59	2.22	0.05	2.02	1.04	−0.08	0.46	−1.15	−0.40
11	1.63	2.28	0.05	2.07	1.06	−0.08	0.45	−1.17	−0.39
12	1.67	2.36	0.05	2.12	1.09	−0.08	0.46	−1.18	−0.39
20	2.01	2.92	0.06	2.46	1.33	−0.08	0.47	−1.30	−0.38
40	2.61	4.23	0.09	3.26	1.91	−0.07	0.52	−1.61	−0.48

^{a} Billions of 1958 dollars.

^{b} Billions of current dollars.

^{c} Index, 1958 = 100.0.

^{d} Percent.

^{e} Calculated as $PI \, \Delta\tau_p$, that is, excluding the increase in taxes induced by increased personal income.

Variables changed: decrease in slope of personal income tax rate of 0.00207, corresponding to a decrease in personal income taxes of $1.0 billion in constant dollars at 1965.4 levels of income. Long-run multiplier per dollar of tax cut = 2.61/1.61 = 1.62.

TABLE 20.7 MULTIPLIERS FOR DECREASE IN CORPORATE INCOME TAX RATES

Quarter	X^a	GNP^b	p^c	DI^b	$P_{cb}{}^b$	Un^d	$I_p{}^a$	$T_c^{a,e}$	Dv^b	Govt.^{a} Surplus
1	0.11	0.14	0.00	0.16	0.05	−0.01	0.00	−1.00	0.14	−0.97
2	0.15	0.20	0.00	0.21	0.08	−0.01	0.02	−1.01	0.15	−0.94
3	0.19	0.24	0.00	0.24	0.09	−0.01	0.04	−1.03	0.17	−0.93
4	0.23	0.30	0.01	0.28	0.12	−0.02	0.06	−1.05	0.21	−0.93
5	0.30	0.38	0.01	0.34	0.15	−0.02	0.09	−1.10	0.24	−0.94
6	0.34	0.43	0.01	0.37	0.18	−0.02	0.12	−1.12	0.25	−0.94
7	0.38	0.50	0.01	0.40	0.21	−0.02	0.14	−1.13	0.28	−0.94
8	0.43	0.56	0.01	0.43	0.24	−0.02	0.17	−1.14	0.29	−0.93
9	0.45	0.60	0.01	0.45	0.26	−0.03	0.19	−1.17	0.31	−0.92
10	0.47	0.62	0.01	0.47	0.28	−0.03	0.20	−1.19	0.32	−0.94
11	0.49	0.64	0.01	0.48	0.29	−0.03	0.20	−1.21	0.34	−0.96
12	0.50	0.67	0.01	0.50	0.30	−0.03	0.21	−1.23	0.36	−0.96
20	0.70	0.92	0.01	0.63	0.39	−0.03	0.24	−1.41	0.44	−1.08
40	1.11	1.57	0.02	0.97	0.62	−0.03	0.29	−1.85	0.69	−1.39

^{a} Billions of 1958 dollars.
^{b} Billions of current dollars.
^{c} Index, 1958 = 100.0.
^{d} Percent.
^{e} Calculated as $P_{cb} \Delta\tau_c$, excluding induced changes.
Variables changed: decrease in slope of corporate income tax rate of 0.01474, corresponding to a decrease in corporate income taxes of $1.0 billion in constant dollars at 1965.4 levels of profits. Long-run multiplier per dollar of tax cut = 1.11/1.85 = 0.60.

TABLE 20.8 MULTIPLIERS FOR DECREASE IN EXCISE TAX RATES

Quarter	X^a	GNP^b	p^c	DI^b	$P_{cb}{}^b$	Un^d	$I_p{}^a$	$T_b{}^{a,e}$	$C_d{}^a$	Govt.^{a} Surplus
1	1.80	1.17	−0.13	0.91	1.01	−0.10	0.00	−1.00	0.91	0.08
2	1.99	1.57	−0.11	0.74	1.56	−0.14	0.39	−1.00	0.76	0.16
3	1.46	1.00	−0.10	0.51	1.38	−0.08	0.38	−1.01	0.64	−0.04
4	1.59	1.16	−0.10	0.58	1.47	−0.09	0.35	−1.03	0.62	0.00
5	1.75	1.42	−0.10	0.91	1.33	−0.10	0.40	−1.04	0.66	0.05
6	1.54	1.24	−0.09	0.60	1.56	−0.08	0.49	−1.05	0.52	−0.01
7	1.52	1.18	−0.08	0.63	1.50	−0.06	0.48	−1.05	0.53	−0.04
8	1.65	1.34	−0.08	0.68	1.59	−0.07	0.51	−1.07	0.52	−0.01
9	1.81	1.57	−0.08	0.90	1.54	−0.08	0.53	−1.08	0.56	0.05
10	1.57	1.31	−0.07	0.54	1.78	−0.07	0.56	−1.09	0.43	−0.08
11	1.55	1.23	−0.08	0.58	1.66	−0.05	0.50	−1.10	0.34	−0.06
12	1.64	1.33	−0.09	0.61	1.75	−0.05	0.05	−1.12	0.34	−0.01
20	1.91	1.60	−0.10	0.72	2.00	−0.06	0.48	−1.22	0.33	0.00
40	2.34	2.42	−0.06	1.00	2.91	−0.05	0.52	−1.52	0.32	0.03

^{a} Billions of 1958 dollars.
^{b} Billions of current dollars.
^{c} Index, 1958 = 100.0.
^{d} Percent.
^{e} Calculated as $NI\,\Delta\tau_h$, excluding induced effects.
Variables changed: decrease in slope of excise tax rate of 0.00192, corresponding to a decrease in excise taxes of $1.0 billion in constant dollars at 1965.4 levels of national income. Price of consumer durables decreased by 1 percent. Long-run multiplier per dollar of tax cut = 2.34/1.52 = 1.54.

TABLE 20.9 MULTIPLIERS FOR DECREASE IN THE DISCOUNT RATE

Quarter	X^a	GNP^b	p^c	DI^b	P_{cb}^b	Un^d	I_p^a	I_h^a	Govt.^{a} Surplus
1	0.00	0.00	0.00	0.00	0.00	0.00	0.00	0.00	0.00
2	0.00	0.00	0.00	0.00	0.00	0.00	0.00	0.00	0.00
3	0.36	0.42	0.00	0.19	0.14	−0.02	0.18	0.00	0.16
4	3.32	3.97	0.02	1.71	1.29	−0.32	0.55	1.34	1.51
5	4.35	5.46	0.06	2.25	1.94	−0.39	1.25	1.24	1.95
6	4.65	6.08	0.10	2.43	2.30	−0.37	1.81	1.13	2.06
7	4.77	6.47	0.13	2.50	2.63	−0.32	2.28	0.92	2.12
8	4.66	6.61	0.17	2.39	2.92	−0.27	2.67	0.69	2.11
9	4.52	6.70	0.20	2.22	3.22	−0.22	2.91	0.54	2.08
10	4.33	6.70	0.24	2.05	3.43	−0.17	3.04	0.41	2.03
11	4.06	6.56	0.25	1.84	3.59	−0.12	3.06	0.31	1.92
12	3.84	6.46	0.26	1.66	3.73	−0.07	3.05	0.23	1.86
20	3.23	6.32	0.30	0.75	4.67	+0.12	2.67	−0.02	1.69
40	4.27	9.73	0.43	0.64	7.79	+0.15	2.70	−0.10	2.57

^{a} Billions of 1958 dollars.
^{b} Billions of current dollars.
^{c} Index, 1958 = 100.0.
^{d} Percent.
Variables changed: decrease in the discount rate by 1 percent.

TABLE 20.10 MULTIPLIERS FOR INCREASE IN THE FREE RESERVE RATIO

Quarter	X^a	GNP^b	p^c	DI^b	$P_{ch}{}^b$	Un^d	$I_p{}^a$	$I_h{}^a$	Govt.^{a} Surplus
1	0.00	0.00	0.00	0.00	0.00	0.00	0.00	0.00	0.00
2	0.00	0.00	0.00	0.00	0.00	0.00	0.00	0.00	0.00
3	0.32	0.37	0.00	0.17	0.13	−0.02	0.16	0.00	0.14
4	2.99	3.58	0.02	1.54	1.16	−0.30	0.49	1.20	1.36
5	3.92	4.91	0.05	2.02	1.74	−0.35	1.12	1.12	1.76
6	4.18	5.47	0.09	2.19	2.07	−0.33	1.63	1.02	1.86
7	4.30	5.83	0.12	2.25	2.36	−0.29	2.05	0.83	1.91
8	4.20	5.96	0.16	2.16	2.62	−0.25	2.40	0.62	1.89
9	4.07	6.04	0.18	2.01	2.89	−0.20	2.62	0.49	1.87
10	3.90	6.03	0.21	1.85	3.09	−0.16	2.74	0.37	1.83
11	3.66	5.91	0.23	1.67	3.23	−0.11	2.76	0.28	1.73
12	3.46	5.82	0.24	1.50	3.25	−0.06	2.75	0.21	1.68
20	2.91	5.69	0.27	0.68	4.20	+0.10	2.41	−0.01	1.52
40	3.84	8.75	0.39	0.58	7.01	+0.14	2.43	−0.09	2.31

[a] Billions of 1958 dollars.
[b] Billions of current dollars.
[c] Index, 1958 = 100.0.
[d] Percent.
Variables changed: increase in the ratio of free reserves to required reserves of 10 percent.

The principal difference between the multipliers for defense and non-defense spending occurs in the early quarters. The main differential effect of these two types of expenditures is that changes in defense spending cause additional changes in unfilled orders and thus in inventory investment. One would expect this effect to be operative primarily in the first year because of the short lag in the inventory investment function; this is what does occur. The multipliers for defense spending fall below those for nondefense spending during the second and third years because inventory investment decreases to a greater extent and there is a slightly greater cyclical effect. The price rise, although not particularly large, occurs mainly in the first year; by the end of the year a $1 billion increase in defense spending is associated with a 0.07 percent increase in the price level.

Changes in defense spending cause greater changes in both output and prices during the first year per dollar of expenditure than any other type of fiscal or monetary policy examined here. Thus a change in defense spending of a given amount requires a much larger dollar outlay of countermeasures in the short run to offset its effects. A decrease in defense spending coupled with an equal rise in nondefense spending would lead to a slight decline in output and prices during the first year; the opposite conclusion would hold if the pattern were reversed. After three or four years, however, these differences will disappear as short-run fluctuations in inventory investment become negligible.

The multipliers for a change in exogenous private spending, taken here to be an increase in exports, at first appear to be much larger than the government spending multipliers. However, as in the case of the tax change multipliers, this is not really the case. A $1 billion initial increase in exports will lead to a further increase in exports over time, because present exports depend on lagged exports. Thus the actual export multiplier, $\Delta X/\Delta F_e$, is only slightly larger than the government and tax multipliers. We would expect the export multiplier to be somewhat larger than the government spending multiplier because an increase in exports, being part of private output, affects investment directly, whereas an increase in government spending raises investment only after private spending has already been stimulated. The export multiplier should be greater than the tax-change multiplier because the entire initial increase represents additional aggregate demand, not just the part that is consumed. The long-run multiplier estimates obtained are fully consistent with these conditions.

Besides having a larger long-run multiplier than other policies, an increase in exports is also beneficial in other ways. Besides the obvious increase in the net foreign balance, prices rise less than in any other of the policy simulations. This occurs because the supply curve of exports is very elastic, and almost no increase in prices will occur in that sector. There will be moderate price increases in other sectors, but much less than those occurring when investment or government spending are directly influenced by policy actions.

The effects of a personal income tax cut and an excise tax cut on GNP are similar, but the effects on the price level are quite different. A decrease in excise taxes will initially result in lower prices if any part of the tax cut is passed along to the consumer. Unlike a change in personal income taxes, which has a straightforward effect on personal disposable income, a change in excise taxes will directly affect several components of GNP. Usually excise tax reductions are partially passed on to the consumer and partially retained by businesses. Assume that this is the general case. The consumer will then pay a lower unit price for those items on which the tax has been reduced. This will increase his real disposable income, and will also result in greater purchases of these items if they have any negative price elasticity. The price effect may be negligible; in general those items for which excise taxes are the largest percentage of the price, such as tobacco and gasoline, have price elasticities that are very close to zero at present prices. The part of the tax cut not passed along will raise after-tax profits. This will raise dividends, which will increase personal disposable income. It will also raise corporate cash flow, which will stimulate fixed business investment. Thus many components of aggregate demand will be directly affected by a change in excise tax rates.

There are actually a great many excise tax cut multipliers that can be calculated, depending on which items are selected for tax removal and the percentage passed on to the consumer. In the calculations shown in Table 20.8 it has been assumed that the excise tax reductions affected only consumer durables, and that 70 percent of the price decrease was passed on to the consumer.[4] It can be seen that under these assumptions the price level initially decreases about 0.13 percent per each $1 billion decrease in excise taxes. In later quarters prices rise slightly, but not enough to offset the initial decrease; there is a net long-run decline in prices. The multipliers for changes in GNP are rather high in the first few quarters, fluctuate somewhat, and then gradually decrease below the original value (when correctly normalized for the amount of the tax decrease). The high initial response is due to the high impact price elasticity of cars. Because of the stock-adjustment relationship in the car equation, the number of additional automobiles purchased due to the price cut will gradually decline. Thus although the long-run GNP multipliers for the personal income tax and the excise tax are about the same, the latter has a greater initial impact and results in a long-run price decrease.

The pattern of income distribution is also quite different for the two tax cuts. When personal income taxes are reduced, most of the extra income goes to disposable income; when excise taxes are reduced, most of it goes to profits. This occurs for several reasons. First, the 30 percent of the tax cut retained by corporations increases profits substantially. Second, when excise taxes are

---

[4] This figure is slightly generous in terms of the actual 1965 excise tax cut. In general, 70 percent of the tax was passed along if it had previously been levied at the manufacturer's level, 50 percent if it had been levied at the retail level on goods, and 0 percent if it had been levied on services, such as club dues and entertainment. In the case of taxes levied at the manufacturer's level, assume that an item originally wholesaled for $110 including 10 percent tax; with the standard 40 percent markup, it retailed for $154. After the tax was removed, it would wholesale for $100 and retail for $144 if the entire $10 was passed along to the consumer. Even so, the price reduction would be $10/154$, or about $6\frac{1}{2}$ percent, not the full 10 percent.

removed primarily from consumer durables, much of the increase in sales will occur in high-profit industries, particularly autos. Third, since the consumer price index has gone down slightly, wages will not rise quite as much as otherwise and unit labor costs will decline. This additional decrease in costs is quite unlikely to be passed along to the consumer in the form of lower prices at a time when capacity utilization is rising, so profits will also increase for this reason.

Since the marginal propensity to spend out of disposable income is much higher than out of corporate profits, multipliers for these different tax cuts can be the same only if the excise taxes are fully passed on or are removed from those items that are highly price-elastic, in this case automobiles. This would suggest that other excise tax cuts on items such as tobacco, gasoline, and liquor would have much less effect in increasing GNP. Furthermore, since the excise tax cut of 1965, there are relatively few additional items on which the federal excise tax could be removed. There is much less room for maneuverability here than in the case of the personal income tax, which can still be decreased by substantial amounts. Although total excise tax collections are approximately the same magnitude as total personal income tax collections, most of the excise taxes are collected by state and local governments. Many of these taxes are property taxes, which are very unlikely to be cut at all. The reimposition of excise taxes could be effectively used to slow down booms, the main disadvantage being that this move would raise prices at a time when inflation is likely to be a problem.

Unlike the personal income and excise tax cuts, the corporate income tax cut has very little effect on any variables except corporate taxes, profits, and dividends. The long-run GNP multiplier is far less than unity, and the effect on prices and unemployment is correspondingly small. One might expect changes in corporate taxes to have a substantial effect on fixed business investment, but this does not occur either. Corporate cash flow is an important determinant of investment only in the manufacturing sector, and even there has a low marginal coefficient. The only substantial effect of the corporate income tax cut is to increase dividends, which raises personal disposable income and thus increases consumption. However, in terms of dollar expenditures, it is a very inefficient tool for influencing economic activity. The multipliers for the first few quarters are only about 10 percent of those for the other tax cuts, and even in the long run are below 40 percent. It is also clear from these results that fixed business investment will increase more in response to a personal income tax cut or excise tax cut of the same size than a corporate income tax cut. On the other hand, for those who think that increased government spending should be financed by increased taxes, an increase in corporate profits taxes will accomplish this with very little effect on aggregate economic activity. It would thus seem that the corporate income tax rate should be decided more on equity grounds or as a means of balancing the budget than as a method of regulating GNP.

Both monetary policy multipliers act on the short-term interest rate in the same way in this model, so the results of changing the discount rate and changing the required reserve ratio given here are identical except in degree. At first the multipliers may seem very large, but it should be recalled that a 10 percent increase in the free reserve ratio amounts to approximately a $2 billion decrease in required reserves. Thus for direct comparability, these multiplier figures should be divided by 2, which gives a multiplier of about 2. Thus a $1 billion injection of spendable funds into the economy, whether through increased government expenditures, decreased personal income or excise taxes, or monetary policy, all result in almost a $2 billion increase in constant-dollar GNP in the long run. Thus the choice between these alternative monetary and fiscal policies must be based on some factor other than the long-run increase in GNP.

Several other important objectives should be considered. First, the problem of timing is important for short-run purposes. Monetary policy has only a slight effect in the first year, because it acts only with a lag. This was stressed in some detail both in the chapters on fixed business investment and residential construction.[5] Because of this, economists and others who often become disillusioned after waiting almost a year and seeing little effect of monetary policy conclude that it cannot regulate booms or recessions. These are often the same people who blame monetary policy for causing the 1958 and 1961 recessions. Monetary policy is relatively inflexible; its largest effect is not felt until a year after the policy changes are made. Furthermore, a $1 billion change in required reserves represents a rather large change relative to past policy, but a $1 billion increase in government spending or decrease in taxes is rather small relative to recent experience. A rise of 5 percent in the required reserve ratio (for example, from 0.160 to 0.168) coupled with a 2 percent increase in the discount rate would bring about a recession similar to the ones actually observed in the postwar period. Such actions could occur but monetary policy moves are unlikely to be of this magnitude. Even if they were used, over a year would ensue before the main effect would be felt.

The behavior of prices and unemployment for a change in monetary policy are also quite different from those for other policies examined. It is seen that prices rise much faster than they do for increases in government spending or tax cuts. This may seem a little surprising, because monetary policy acts primarily on investment, and we have said earlier than an increase in investment leads to more capacity and thus less pressure on prices. However, other aspects of the situation must be considered. The supply schedules for fixed business investment and residential construction are more inelastic in the short run than in the long run, so a sharp increase in expenditures in these sectors will

---

[5] It might be noted that the tightening of credit that began in late 1965 affected the housing market in mid-1966, approximately three quarters later; it had no appreciable effect on fixed business investment throughout 1966.

cause a substantial rise in prices. In the other policy simulations, fixed investment increases gradually, since it is stimulated by a gradual rise in output that originated in other sectors. In this case, a shift to monetary ease will raise investment, particularly construction, very rapidly. This will cause prices and profits to increase very rapidly also. Unemployment decreases but real disposable income does not rise very fast.

Unlike the other policy simulations, for which economic activity stops fluctuating and approaches an equilibrium value after two or three years, perverse effects of monetary policy begin to appear after several years. As pointed out above, a decrease in the discount rate or the required reserve ratio acts primarily on investment and raises the price of capital goods. This increase in investment eventually leads to overcapacity, which reduces GNP and investment somewhat. The main long-run effect of substitution of capital for labor is a slight rise in the unemployment rate. Meanwhile, profits are continuing to grow and prices are continuing to rise, but laborers do not get a full share of these increased profits. Their bargaining position is weakened by increasing unemployment. Such are the long-run effects of *easy* monetary policies.

For tight money, just the opposite would occur. After the initial lag, investment, profits, and prices would drop substantially. Approximately three to five years later, the lack of new productive facilities would result in a slight increase in employment and disposable income. Businesses, saddled by the use of obsolete equipment, would continue to find profit margins slipping even though GNP was rising slightly.[6]

Because monetary policy acts directly on the principal determinant of the cost of capital, it changes the optimal capital/labor ratio. This move has many more long-lasting and complex effects than any of the other policies examined here. This evidence would argue in favor of those who crusade for an autonomous monetary policy in which the money supply grows at a constant rate.

Before considering other economic goals, it may be useful to look at the government surplus or deficit resulting from each of these policy simulations. It is clear that an increase in exports or an easing of monetary conditions with no offsetting fiscal policy will lead to a government budget surplus.[7] Of greater interest is the net surplus or deficit that occurs after changes in government expenditures or tax rates take place. It is seen from the preceding tables that an increase in government expenditures induces almost enough extra taxes to leave the budget in balance. In the first two quarters, an increase in defense expenditures generates a slight surplus, after which a slightly greater deficit occurs; in the long run the relatively small deficits for defense and nondefense spending are almost identical. The deficit due to a cut in personal income tax rates fluctuates between 30 and 40 percent of the decrease in taxes; on the

---

[6] As an example of this, consider the profit squeeze of the early 1960s which followed the tight money policies of the middle and late 1950s.

[7] It is of course the marginal effect that is relevant here. In the following discussion, it is assumed that the government budget was previously balanced.

average, the size of the *ex post* deficit is only one third of the size of the tax cut. An excise tax cut similar to the one used here for simulation (for example, primarily affecting purchases of consumer durables) induces enough extra taxes to eradicate the *ex post* deficit completely. Only the corporate income tax cut fails to generate very much additional revenue, a finding consistent with the result that changes in corporate income taxes have little effect on aggregate economic activity.

Many of these conclusions can be compared with the actual postwar experience. Changes in corporate income and excise tax rates in the postwar period have either been small or have occurred at a time when they have been overshadowed by even larger changes in fiscal policy. However, some calculations can be made for changes in defense expenditures and personal income tax rates. During the 12 quarters of the Korean War, the average government budget surplus was $3.0 billion, even though purchases of goods and services by the federal government rose from $17.1 to $57.8 billion (all figures are based on the July 1967 national income accounting tables). The surplus was largest in the early quarters of the war, reaching an annual rate of $18 billion in the first quarter of 1951. Since the Korean War was financed partially by increased taxes, these comparisons are not altogether convincing. Hence it is of interest to note that a decrease in government spending at the end of the Korean War led to a $3 billion increase in the deficit. No changes in tax revenues occurred until 1954, so this would seem to be a clear case of the induced decrease in economic activity yielding a greater reduction in tax receipts than the original decline in defense expenditures.

The 1964–1965 experience may also be instructive. The 1964 personal income tax cut was widely hailed as a $9 billion tax cut, meaning that tax revenues would drop by this much if income remained unchanged. However, the net increase in the deficit over 1963 was only $3.7 billion, slightly more than one third. This result agrees closely with the simulation calculations. It might also be noted that the second stage of the personal income tax cut, an excise tax cut, a corporate income tax cut, and increased defense expenditures in Vietnam had the combined effect of changing a 1964 deficit of $3.0 billion into a 1965 surplus of $1.4 billion and a first-half 1966 surplus of $2.7 billion. Although government purchases of goods and services rose by $9 billion and total federal government expenditures rose $19 billion in the eight-quarter period 1964.3–1966.2, tax receipts rose $26 billion in the same period, even though several varied tax cuts occurred. These examples should make it clear that not only do changes in fiscal policy have a significant effect on economic activity, but each policy (except changes in corporate income taxes) leaves the budget almost in balance instead of creating almost an equal surplus or deficit.

We now briefly consider the relative efficacy of these alternative policies on other goals of economic policy: full employment, maximum growth (measured here by the increase in investment), price stability, and improvement of the balance of payments. Only the long-run multipliers are considered here, because most of these goals are longer range targets than the short-run adjustments in GNP which are often the object of fiscal and monetary policy.

An increase in government spending causes the greatest long-run rise in employment but only because fixed business investment increases the least. It is thus seen that in the long run labor and capital are substitutes, as would be expected. A policy that encourages high capital formation will lead to less of an increase in employment for a given increase in output. Thus in the long run the two goals of full employment and maximum growth are not fully compatible. An easier monetary policy, which increases investment by the greatest amount, actually causes a slight rise in unemployment in the long run. This would suggest that increased government expenditures need to accompany an easy money policy for optimal long-run results.

A decrease in excise taxes lowers the overall price level because prices are initially decreased on certain goods and the rise in prices resulting from the expansion is less than the initial drop. Except for this one policy alternative, prices always change in the same direction as does output. However, this change is much less for an increase in exports than for any other exogenous change considered here. The price increases are somewhat greater for the personal income and excise tax cuts and government expenditures and much greater for an easy monetary policy.

The net foreign balance decreases somewhat in all cases except for the obvious case of the increase in exports. The amount of decrease is governed mainly by the price level of exported goods, because income changes are approximately the same. The deterioration of the net foreign balance of goods and services is found to be about the same for the income and excise tax cuts, because the lower prices due to excise tax reductions will not affect the price of exported goods. It is somewhat worse for the increase in government spending, and much worse for an ease in monetary policy. In addition, easy money will result in the flow of hot money to foreign countries, so that the total gold outflow will be worse than the deficit indicated for the net balance of goods and services.

A change in monetary policy that stimulates the economy has only rapid growth to recommend it; there is a perverse long-run effect on unemployment, a rapid price increase, and the largest decrease in the balance of payments. A change in the corporate income tax rate has very little effect on any of these economic variables and is not recommended as a policy variable at all except to balance the budget. Income and excise tax cuts are to be preferred slightly to government spending increases, because they result in greater investment, a smaller increase in prices, and a somewhat better balance of payments situation.

In this respect it would seem eminently reasonable to suggest that the amount of government spending should be determined by international and domestic needs determined by the President and Congress, and that tax rates should then be adjusted to bring the economy to the desired level of employment and price stability. If a balanced budget is also desired, it can be achieved by adjusting the corporate income tax rate. This point is discussed at greater length in Chapter 21.

20.3   MULTIPLIER COMPARISONS WITH OTHER MODELS

Although frequent references were made to alternative empirical studies in Part I, there has been scant reference to other econometric models in Part III. The Suits (Michigan) model and the Friend–Taubman model[8] were the only models whose forecasting records were compared, because these are the only models for which *ex ante* forecasts have been made available. However, it is useful to calculate and discuss multipliers for any model in which the parameters are supposed to represent estimates of structural coefficients instead of simply serving as useful empirical approximations.

The most famous econometric model of the U.S. economy is the Klein–Goldberger model; the multipliers for this model were later calculated separately by Goldberger.[9] A revised and updated version of this model was presented in Chapter 19; the multipliers are similar but slightly lower than the earlier versions. The quarterly model by Klein and its subsequent refinement by the Office of Business Economics[10] are not suitable for multiplier analysis, because these models both contain several exogenous anticipations terms in the aggregate demand equations. These reduce the coefficients of the income and output terms and thus bias the multiplier estimates downward.

Another yearly model was estimated by Morishima and Saito[11] for the U.S. economy from 1902 to 1952. This model concentrates on long-run supply phenomena as well as short-term cyclical fluctuations. Yearly multipliers for the first nine years have been calculated by the authors.

Other quarterly models that have been estimated include those by Duesenberry, Eckstein, and Fromm (DEF),[12] and T. C. Liu.[13] The DEF model was designed only to simulate recessions; it is not a closed system, and fixed investment functions and several income-determining functions are omitted. The Liu model represents a complete system, but it is doubtful whether the parameters represent estimates of true structural coefficients. All his stochastic equations are of the form $X_t = f(X_{t-1}, X_{t-2},$ and other variables), and in general X_{t-1}

---

[8] See Section 18.3 for complete citations.

[9] A. S. Goldberger, *Impact Multipliers and Dynamic Properties of the Klein–Goldberger Model* (Amsterdam: North-Holland, 1959).

[10] See Section 15.3 for complete citations.

[11] M. Morishima and M. Saito, "A Dynamic Analysis of the American Economy," *International Economic Review*, Vol. 5, No. 2 (May, 1964), pp. 125–164.

[12] J. Duesenberry, O. Eckstein, and G. Fromm, "A Simulation of the United States Economy in Recession," *Econometrica*, Vol. 28, No. 4 (October, 1960), pp. 749–810.

[13] T. C. Liu, "An Exploratory Quarterly Econometric Model of Effective Demand in the Postwar United States Economy," *Econometrica*, Vol. 31, No. 3 (July, 1963), pp. 301–348.

and X_{t-2} are highly significant, while the other variables are often not significant. Although such a model may be good for forecasting (except at turning points), it is not very useful for multiplier analysis.

The multipliers for a $1 billion change in government expenditures for the annual models mentioned above are tabulated in Table 20.11.[14] The Wharton EFU model multipliers are added for comparison. Also included in this comparison are the multipliers from an earlier model by this author which did not include a foreign sector. Two sets of multipliers for the Evans model have been shown; one for the original model and the other with the foreign sector of the Wharton EFU model grafted on. The main point of this last comparison is to show the effect of the foreign sector on these multipliers.

As can be seen, the difference in the multiplier values between the two versions of the Evans model are quite large, again demonstrating the importance of alternative assumptions about the foreign sector. The somewhat higher values of the Evans model with the foreign sector included are due to the fact that in this model the $\Delta Y / \Delta X$ term does reach the average value of Y/X instead of being somewhat lower. This is primarily due to a different formulation of the equations explaining income distribution and prices: wages, rather than profits, are explained as a residual. The differences in the time pattern of the multiplier values are due to different treatment of the lag structures in the consumer durables and fixed business investment equations.

Except for the initial year values, the multipliers of the Klein–Goldberger, Morishima–Saito, and Wharton EFU models are very similar. The low first-year values for the Klein-Goldberger and Suits models occur because fixed

TABLE 20.11 COMPARISON OF MULTIPLIER VALUES OF VARIOUS MODELS

Model Name	Year					Long Run
	1	2	3	4	5	
Klein–Goldberger	1.23	1.95	2.21	2.27	2.26	2.11
Suits	1.30	1.62	1.58	1.55	1.34	1.10
Morishima–Saito	1.86	1.96	2.14	2.09	2.13	2.37[a]
Wharton EFU	2.12	1.96	2.07	2.10	2.13	1.93[b]
Evans	2.36	2.71	3.54	3.90	3.92	4.00
Evans + Wharton EFU[c] foreign sector	2.06	2.21	2.63	2.78	2.72	2.32

[a] Nine-year multiplier.
[b] 40-quarter multiplier.
[c] *mpf* added from Wharton EFU model and multiplier recalculated.

[14] A more detailed analysis of these multipliers can be found in M. K. Evans, "Multiplier Analysis of a Postwar Quarterly U.S. Model and a Comparison with Several Other Models," *Review of Economic Studies*, Vol. 33, No. 4 (October, 1966), pp. 337–360.

business investment is determined only by lagged variables. Although the lag between changes in economic variables and actual investment is well documented, these functions seem to be an extreme form of this hypothesis. They do not allow for any adjustments or cancellations in investment orders that have already been placed. In the Klein–Goldberger model, inventory investment is included in the same function with fixed business investment. This means that even changes in inventories are assumed to respond to changes in output with a full year lag. The first-year multipliers of these models are too low for a second reason. The first year change in disposable income relative to GNP is less than 0.4 in both models; a more realistic estimate would be about 0.7. Thus even if the marginal propensity to consume were of the correct magnitude, the change in consumption relative to GNP would still be much too low. These two errors reduce the magnitude of the first-year multipliers appreciably.

In the second and following years, the multipliers of the Klein–Goldberger model increase considerably as the effect of the investment function is included and the ratio of disposable income to GNP rises. However, the multipliers from the Suits model remain unrealistically low. There are several reasons for this:

1. The long-run *mpc* of nondurables and services is severely understated. Instead of a value close to the average propensity to consume of 0.8, a value of 0.48 is obtained.

2. Stock-adjustment equations are used in the model but no allowance is made for depreciation of the capital stock terms. Although this model contains an overall depreciation function, this is used only to close the relationship between GNP and national income and is unrelated to capital stock. Thus the rate of gross investment in the long run is equal to zero, instead of being equal to the depreciation rate.

3. The long-run ratio of the change in disposable income to the change in GNP is too low for two reasons. The long-run wage rate and employment relationships are almost the same as the short run, which were already too low. Furthermore, the relationship between total property income and corporate profits states that 90 percent of the former goes to the latter. This figure is much too high, because the average ratio is about 40 percent in the long run.

The government spending multiplier for the Suits model almost returns to unity in the long run; the corresponding personal income tax multiplier is 0.5. These figures are clearly too low for the model to be useful for policy simulations.

It is of interest to note that except for the multipliers from the Morishima–Saito model, which keep growing indefinitely by an amount approximately equal to the growth rate, all the government spending multipliers are lower in the long run than after five years. This is because the *mpc* for nondurables and services has attained virtually its maximum value by that time, while the stock-adjustment terms in the investment and consumer durables functions take longer to reach their full effect. These results do show that there is no tendency for the multipliers to keep increasing indefinitely over time.

It might be tempting to argue that the fairly close agreement of the long-run multiplier estimates (except for the Suits model) help to establish a rather narrow range for the value of the government multiplier. However, closer inspection reveals that this clustering of values is at least partially due to offsetting influences. If the components of the long-run multipliers are individually examined, it becomes apparent that the differences are stronger than the similarities. These results are shown in Table 20.12.

TABLE 20.12 COMPONENTS OF LONG-RUN GOVERNMENT
EXPENDITURE MULTIPLIER VALUES

Model Name	mpc	$\Delta Y/\Delta X$	$\Delta C/\Delta X$	mpI	mpf	Long-run multiplier[a]
Klein–Goldberger	0.724	0.490	0.355	0.218	0.017	2.11
Suits	0.476	0.320	0.152	0.0	0.060	1.10
Morishima–Saito	—[b]	—[b]	0.570	0.0	−0.010[c]	2.37
Wharton EFU	0.970[d]	0.587	0.570	0.078[e]	0.166	1.93
Evans[f]	0.888	0.718	0.638	0.097[e]	0.166	2.32
Postwar average	0.93	0.685	0.637	—	—	

[a] Taken from Table 20.11.
[b] Consumption estimated directly as a function of GNP.
[c] The negative sign means an increase in GNP raises the net foreign balance.
[d] High value includes effects of relative prices on consumer durables.
[e] Adjusted for the fact that investment is a function of private output.
[f] Including the foreign sector of the Wharton EFU model.

In particular, note that the $\Delta C/\Delta X$ ratio is below the average value in all models except the Evans model; sometimes this occurs because the mpc is too low, but in other cases the cause is too low an estimate of the $\Delta Y/\Delta X$ ratio. The long-run multiplier for the Evans model (adjusted) is only slightly larger than those for other models because of the much larger value of the mpf. This in turn is due to the fact that none of the other models contains any relative price terms; relative price effects are quite important in the foreign sector, particularly for the export function. Since it seems probable that marginal growth in domestic prices and incomes will be at least partially matched by increases in foreign prices and incomes, the mpf is probably overstated and thus the multiplier is understated. For this reason, the long-run value of the government multiplier is likely to be at least 2.5. If half of the rise in domestic prices and income were matched by increases abroad, the multipliers of the Wharton EFU and Evans models would increase to 2.35 and 2.87, respectively.

Although these multiplier calculations do serve as a useful check on the value of the multipliers obtained for the Wharton model, they are not fully comparable.

First, except for the Evans model, the other multipliers compared are all taken from yearly models. Second, these multipliers deal only with changes in government expenditures. Multipliers for various kinds of tax rate changes and monetary policies are also needed. Third, all the other calculations (except for the foreign sector grafted on the Evans model) are made for no change in prices. Relative price effects, which may be of considerable importance, are thus excluded. Furthermore, no estimates are available for the amount of change in the overall price level that will result from the use of different policy tools.

Quarterly impact and dynamic multipliers for a wide range of policy variables have been calculated for the Brookings model by Fromm and Taubman.[5] These multipliers have been tabulated and analyzed for ten quarters; although simulations for longer periods have been undertaken, it is claimed that after ten quarters the multipliers of the Brookings model are nearly at their equilibrium values. In almost all cases these multiplier values are directly comparable with those calculated from the Wharton EFU model. The comparisons are shown for certain selected variables in the following tables. In all cases the multipliers are based on a $1 billion change in constant dollars in the particular policy variable. In the case of the tax change multipliers, this means that the actual changes have been normalized by the tax change in the current period. As explained on p. 566, this will bias the multipliers down slightly. However, the tax multipliers grow slowly over time, so this bias is minimized. In any case both the Brookings and Wharton EFU model multipliers are adjusted by the same bias.

A few words of explanation may be necessary about the minor incompatibilities of these multiplier calculations. The Brookings model multiplier values are calculated for the period 1960.3–1962.4, the Wharton EFU model values for the period 1966.1–1968.4. Since the former period was one of recession and excess capacity and the latter was assumed to be one near full employment, it might be expected that output would rise slightly more and prices slightly less per unit change in the Brookings model than in the Wharton EFU model.

There are also a few minor inconsistencies in the individual simulations. In the government expenditure calculations, a more detailed disaggregation of government purchases was followed in the Brookings model than in the Wharton EFU model. Although the calculations for the latter model show the effect of a change in an average of all nondefense expenditures, a distinction was made in the former model among government expenditures for durables, nondurables, employment, and construction. The nondurable expenditure multipliers were chosen as being the most directly comparable. In the original personal income tax cut calculations of the Brookings model, interest rates increased substantially because of greater holdings of money by consumers;

[15] Fromm and Taubman, *op. cit.*

this reduced investment and thus lowered the value of the tax-cut multiplier. To adjust for this phenomenon an additional tax cut simulation was added in which interest rates were kept at their previous level. This calculation is more directly comparable with the tax cut multiplier for the Wharton EFU model. The excise tax cut multiplier for the Brookings model was estimated for both a $1.6 billion and a $2.7 billion tax cut. The results *per dollar of tax decrease* are substantially different, leading to the conclusion of Fromm and Taubman that there are increasing returns to scale for excise-tax reduction.[16] This would suggest that the smaller of the two tax cuts is more directly comparable with the Wharton EFU tax-cut multiplier, which assumed a decrease of $1.0 billion in excise taxes. The reductions in reserve requirements calculations are directly comparable, although the figures given for the Brookings model are not the ones used for final comparisons by Fromm and Taubman. Instead they use the change in GNP per initial dollar change in aggregate demand, omitting the link between changes in reserves and initial changes in expenditures; these figures are not at all comparable with the Wharton EFU model results. The calculations for both the Brookings and Wharton EFU models for a reduction in reserve requirements show the change in selected variables relative to a $1 billion decrease in required reserves, not relative to a $1 billion change in consumption plus investment. Some comparisons are given in Tables 20.13 through 20.17.

At first glance these multipliers look quite different from one another, and certainly far different from the multipliers obtained from other yearly models. By far the greatest difference occurs in the multiplier calculations for a reduction in required reserves. This change acts on investment in a process that requires several steps, and any one of the intermediate relationships could provide the difference between the two estimates. We can write

(20.7)
$$\frac{\partial X}{\partial R} = \frac{\partial X}{\partial I} \frac{\partial I}{\partial i_l} \frac{\partial i_l}{\partial i_s} \frac{\partial i_s}{\partial R}$$

where R = required reserves
i_s = short-term interest rate
i_l = long-term interest rate
I = fixed investment
X = GNP

Since the investment functions in the Brookings model are somewhat similar to those in the Wharton EFU model, it is reassuring to find that the term $\partial I/\partial i_l$ is almost identical for both models. The term $\partial X/\partial I$ which is similar to the government spending multiplier, is somewhat larger in the Brookings model but not enough to make a fivefold difference. Thus the differences must be found in the equations for the money market, which is not too surprising,

---

[16] *Ibid.*, p. 66.

TABLE 20.13 CHANGES IN CONSTANT-DOLLAR GNP
FOR VARIOUS POLICIES

	Quarter									
	1	2	3	4	5	6	7	8	9	10
Government spending										
Brookings	1.4	2.0	2.3	2.4	2.5	2.4	2.8	2.9	2.9	2.9
Wharton EFU	2.0	2.4	2.1	2.0	1.9	1.9	1.9	2.0	2.1	2.1
Personal income tax										
Brookings[a]	0.8	1.0	1.2	1.1	1.2	1.2	1.2	1.2	1.2	1.2
Brookings[b]	0.7	1.0	1.2	1.3	1.4	1.4	1.6	1.6	1.6	1.7
Wharton EFU	1.1	1.5	1.3	1.3	1.2	1.2	1.3	1.3	1.4	1.4
Excise tax										
Brookings[c]	1.1	1.2	1.4	1.2	1.2	1.5	1.5	1.5	1.4	1.3
Brookings[d]	0.9	1.1	1.4	1.4	1.6	1.8	2.0	2.2	2.2	2.2
Wharton EFU	1.8	2.0	1.4	1.5	1.7	1.5	1.4	1.5	1.7	1.4
Reduction in required reserves										
Brookings	−1.5	2.7	2.6	4.5	5.1	11.6	8.9	8.9	7.9	8.6
Wharton EFU	0.0	0.0	0.2	1.5	2.0	2.1	2.1	2.1	2.0	2.0

[a] No offsetting change in monetary policy.
[b] Accommodating change in monetary policy (see the text).
[c] $1.6 billion excise tax cut, 80 percent passed along.
[d] $2.7 billion excise tax cut, 80 percent passed along.

TABLE 20.14 CHANGES IN THE IMPLICIT GNP DEFLATOR
   (1958 = 100.0)*

	Quarter									
	1	2	3	4	5	6	7	8	9	10
Government spending										
Brookings	−0.15	−0.22	−0.25	−0.28	−0.28	−0.22	−0.19	−0.12	−0.06	−0.03
Wharton EFU	0.02	0.03	0.04	0.05	0.05	0.05	0.05	0.05	0.05	0.06
Personal income tax										
Brookings[a]	−0.09	−0.12	−0.15	−0.15	−0.14	−0.14	−0.11	−0.08	−0.05	−0.05
Brookings[b]	−0.09	−0.12	−0.15	−0.18	−0.17	−0.16	−0.15	−0.12	−0.10	−0.10
Wharton EFU	0.00	0.02	0.02	0.03	0.04	0.04	0.04	0.04	0.04	0.04
Excise tax										
Brookings[c]	−0.38	−0.38	−0.38	−0.38	−0.29	−0.21	−0.13	0.00	0.00	0.06
Brookings[d]	−0.36	−0.41	−0.50	−0.57	−0.57	−0.54	−0.48	−0.44	−0.40	−0.36
Wharton EFU	−0.13	−0.11	−0.10	−0.10	−0.10	−0.09	−0.07	−0.07	−0.07	−0.06
Reduction in required reserves										
Brookings	0.20	−0.40	−0.30	−0.50	−0.60	−1.20	−0.70	−0.70	−0.60	−0.50
Wharton EFU	0.00	0.00	0.00	0.01	0.03	0.05	0.06	0.08	0.09	0.10

* Brookings model in 1954 = 100.0 prices. Footnotes as in Table 20.13.

TABLE 20.15 CHANGES IN THE UNEMPLOYMENT RATE* (*in percent*)

	Quarter									
	1	2	3	4	5	6	7	8	9	10
Government spending										
Brookings	−0.03	−0.06	−0.09	−0.12	−0.16	−0.16	−0.12	−0.16	−0.16	−0.16
Wharton EFU	−0.25	−0.29	−0.25	−0.23	−0.21	−0.21	−0.22	−0.22	−0.22	−0.22
Personal income tax										
Brookings[a]	0.00	−0.03	−0.06	−0.06	−0.06	−0.06	−0.06	−0.06	−0.06	−0.06
Brookings[b]	0.00	−0.03	−0.06	−0.08	−0.08	−0.08	−0.08	−0.08	−0.10	−0.10
Wharton EFU	−0.06	−0.10	−0.08	−0.07	−0.06	−0.06	−0.06	−0.07	−0.07	−0.07
Excise tax										
Brookings[c]	0.00	−0.07	−0.07	−0.07	−0.07	−0.07	−0.07	−0.07	−0.07	−0.07
Brookings[d]	0.00	−0.05	−0.05	−0.09	−0.09	−0.08	−0.08	−0.12	−0.12	−0.12
Wharton EFU	−0.10	−0.14	−0.08	−0.09	−0.10	−0.08	−0.06	−0.07	−0.07	−0.06
Reduction in required reserves										
Brookings	0.00	0.00	−0.10	−0.20	−0.20	−0.40	−0.50	−0.50	−0.50	−0.50
Wharton EFU	0.00	0.00	−0.01	−0.15	−0.18	−0.16	−0.15	−0.13	−0.10	−0.08

* Footnotes as in Table 20.13.

TABLE 20.16 CHANGES IN FIXED BUSINESS INVESTMENT*

	Quarter									
	1	2	3	4	5	6	7	8	9	10
Government spending										
Brookings	0.00	0.16	0.22	0.25	0.25	0.44	0.53	0.59	0.59	0.59
Wharton EFU	0.00	0.21	0.25	0.24	0.25	0.27	0.28	0.31	0.33	0.33
Personal income tax										
Brookings[a]	0.00	0.06	0.09	0.12	0.11	0.11	0.13	0.13	0.13	0.13
Brookings[b]	0.00	0.06	0.12	0.12	0.11	0.18	0.23	0.24	0.24	0.26
Wharton EFU	0.00	0.24	0.28	0.27	0.29	0.32	0.34	0.37	0.38	0.40
Excise tax										
Brookings[c,e]	0.00	0.08	0.15	0.15	0.23	0.29	0.33	0.33	0.27	0.27
Brookings[d,e]	0.00	0.09	0.14	0.17	0.22	0.29	0.36	0.44	0.44	0.44
Wharton EFU	0.00	0.39	0.38	0.34	0.38	0.47	0.46	0.48	0.49	0.51
Reduction in required reserves										
Brookings	0.00	0.50	0.30	0.40	0.60	3.3	2.1	2.2	2.4	2.5
Wharton EFU	0.00	0.00	0.08	0.25	0.56	0.8	1.0	1.2	1.3	1.4

* Footnotes as in Table 20.13 ; note e : including residential construction, not available separately.

TABLE 20.17 CHANGES IN REAL DISPOSABLE INCOME*

	Quarter									
	1	2	3	4	5	6	7	8	9	10
Government spending										
Brookings	0.8	1.1	1.2	1.3	1.4	1.3	1.5	1.5	1.4	1.4
Wharton EFU	1.0	1.2	1.1	1.0	1.0	0.9	0.9	1.0	1.0	1.0
Personal income tax										
Brookings[a]	1.5	1.6	1.7	1.7	1.7	1.7	1.6	1.7	1.7	1.6
Brookings[b]	1.4	1.6	1.7	1.7	1.7	1.8	1.8	1.8	1.8	1.8
Wharton EFU	1.5	1.6	1.4	1.4	1.4	1.4	1.4	1.4	1.4	1.4
Excise tax										
Brookings[c]	1.5	1.5	1.6	1.5	1.4	1.4	1.4	1.3	1.3	1.3
Brookings[d]	1.4	1.6	1.7	1.7	1.8	1.9	2.0	2.1	2.1	2.1
Wharton EFU	1.5	1.3	1.1	1.1	1.4	1.1	1.2	1.2	1.5	1.1
Reduction in required reserves										
Brookings	−1.0	1.5	1.3	2.4	2.8	6.3	4.9	4.8	4.2	4.5
Wharton EFU	0.0	0.0	0.1	0.7	0.9	0.9	0.9	0.8	0.8	0.7

* Footnotes as in Table 20.13.

because the monetary equations estimated for the two models are quite different in structure.

Recall that in the Wharton EFU model a change of 1 percent in the discount rate or a comparable change in required reserves of \$2.2 billion resulted in a 1 percent change in the short-term interest rate in the same quarter with no further change. This movement in the short-term rate affected the long-term rate rather sluggishly; it took about eight quarters until the long-term rate had changed by the full 1 percent. The monetary equations in the Brookings model behave in an entirely different manner. The short-term rate is not determined directly by the discount rate and reserve position but is determined indirectly as the rate that clears the market. In equilibrium, a \$2.2 billion change in required reserves does lead to a 1 percent change in the short-term rate, almost an identical finding to the Wharton EFU model. However, in the short run the results are quite different. In the first quarter, a change in required reserves causes the short-term rate to overshoot its new equilibrium value and change by 3 percent. This type of behavior just does not actually occur in the money market. Furthermore, most of this instability is reflected in changes in the long-term interest rate in the same quarter. Thus the vastly overinflated monetary policy multiplier is due to the fact that interest rate estimation in the model is much more unstable than in the real world. In the Wharton EFU model, long-term interest rates eventually rise by the full amount of the change in the short-term rate, but this process is asymptotic and not cyclical. Furthermore, by the time the long-term interest rate has reached its new equilibrium value, the stock-adjustment terms tend to reduce the amount of investment.

The second irreconcilable difference between the two models is the unusual pattern of price changes when real GNP increases. Ordinarily, increases in GNP and industrial production are associated with rising prices, decreases with steady or falling prices. This does not seem to be the case in the Brookings model. There are two reasons for this perverse behavior of prices. First, they depend primarily on unit labor costs, which decline slightly in the first few quarters of these simulations. Since wages depend primarily on lagged variables and employment depends mainly on lagged employment in the Brookings model, increases in output are at first accompanied by less than proportionate increases in labor costs. Although this may not be an entirely unrealistic relationship, these decreases in unit labor costs are reflected in lower prices much too quickly. Second, changes in prices are inversely related to the inventory/sales ratio. As pointed out earlier, this relationship arises only because of a few observations at the beginning of the Korean War and is not significant for other time periods. In the initial quarters of these simulations, inventories rise faster than sales, which has a further negative effect on prices. No capacity variables of any sort are included to portray the fact that firms are more likely to raise their prices when business is good than when it is bad. These price equations are thus of little reliability for policy simulations.

The third principal difference, although not as crucial as the first two problems discussed, is the structure of the equation estimating consumption of automobiles. Although stock-adjustment equations are used for consumption of other durables, all fixed business investment equations, and all inventory investment equations, this form was not used for the car equation. It seems difficult to justify this choice on rational grounds, particularly when alternative estimates prepared by this author and others showed a capital stock term to be highly significantly negative in the car equation. As a result, car purchases grow steadily over time instead of gradually declining, as is the case with all the other components of aggregate demand estimated with stock-adjustment equations. This results in making the early quarter multipliers too low and the later quarter multipliers too high. This affects all the policy simulations, particularly the multipliers for the excise tax cut, because its effect is realized primarily through the purchases of additional new cars. It would appear from the Brookings calculations that the initial impact of the excise tax cut is quite small for the first year but that it grows steadily over time. Actually the opposite effect is more likely to occur.

There are of course many other minor differences between the multipliers of these two models. One would expect no less in complicated structures containing 75 and 170 equations. However, there are certain defects in the Brookings model which it would seem could be easily remedied. Alternative equations have already been prepared for the consumption of cars and for price formation, and currently work is under way to develop further equations for the money market. Since the principal value of the Brookings model lies in policy simulations, it is hoped that the poorly performing equations will continue to be weeded out. Except for the car equation, the aggregate demand equations used to calculate these multipliers in mid-1966 are in general substantially improved over the equations appearing in the original volume of the Brookings model. If this process of selective improvement continues, there is no reason why the Brookings model cannot become a very powerful tool for policy analysis.

CHAPTER 21

CONCLUSION

21.1   THE RECORD OF PERFORMANCE OF THE POSTWAR ECONOMY

The performance of the U.S. economy during the postwar period has indeed been mixed. On the one hand, deep depressions have been eliminated. This is primarily due to institutional shifts in the economy—the emergence of a much larger federal government sector, much more powerful automatic stabilizers, and the Employment Act of 1946, which at a minimum commits the government to keep recessions from becoming too serious. On the other hand, with the large backlog of consumer and business demand after the war and the ready availability of countercyclical monetary and fiscal policy, a record of four recessions in 15 years is not a commendable one. The loss in both economic and social terms has been formidable.

To determine the loss to the economy that occurred during recessions and other underemployment years, it has become standard practice to connect the peak years by trend lines and calculate the rate of growth from these lines, extrapolating the most recent segment of the line from the last peak to the present if necessary. The gap between trend and actual GNP is then taken to be the potential GNP lost to the economy. The postwar record of the economy is diagrammed in Figure 21.1. Using this method we find that the total loss to the economy in the 20-year postwar period is $295 billion, which is equal to $90 per capita per year.

As substantial as this amount is, it must certainly understate the true net loss to the economy, for the maximum attainable rate of growth is greater than the amount determined in this manner. The size of the cyclical peaks

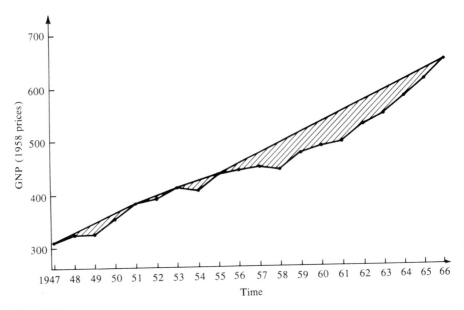

Figure 21.1

are in large part determined by the available capital stock, which depends on previous investment. Thus the lower were past levels of investment, the lower is the subsequent ceiling rate of output. If the economy had grown at an annual rate of 4 percent in real terms, the loss in GNP calculated as above would have been $175 per capita per year. For a 5 percent rate of growth the *annual* per capita loss would rise to a staggering $490 (all figures in billions of 1958 dollars).

One can easily calculate the maximum growth rate of the economy which can reasonably be expected and the minimum rate necessary to absorb all entrants into the labor force. For long-run behavior the Cobb–Douglas production function provides a close approximation. If

(21.1) $X = aL^{\alpha}K^{\beta}e^{\gamma t}$

then

(21.2) $\dot{X} = \alpha\dot{L} + \beta\dot{X} + \gamma$

where the dots represent percentage changes.

Over the past hundred years, the historical growth rate of the U.S. economy has been observed to be close to 3 percent.[1] This is often explained by stating

_____

[1] These and the following long-run average statistics are taken from Department of Commerce, *Historical Statistics of the United States* (Washington: Government Printing Office, 1961), chap. F.

that each of the three terms in the above production function has accounted for approximately 1 percent of this growth. Thus $\alpha \dot{L} = 0.01$, $\beta \dot{K} = 0.01$, and $\gamma = 0.01$. Since $\alpha \cong \frac{2}{3}$ and $\beta \cong \frac{1}{3}$, this implies that the labor force grew at about $1\frac{1}{2}$ percent, capital stock grew at about 3 percent, and productivity grew at about 1 percent annually.

To determine the full-employment equilibrium rate of growth for capital stock, rewrite $\dot{K}$ as

$$(21.3) \qquad \dot{K} = \frac{\Delta K}{K} = \frac{I}{K} = \frac{I}{X}\frac{X}{K} = \frac{S_p + S_c}{X}\frac{X}{K}$$

where S_p is personal saving and S_c is net corporate saving. Using long-run average figures, personal disposable income is about $\frac{2}{3}$ of GNP and net profits before direct taxes are about $\frac{1}{10}$ of GNP. The average personal savings rate is about 7 percent and the average corporate savings rate is about 25 percent, so

$$(21.4) \qquad \frac{S_p + S_c}{X} = \frac{2}{3}(0.07) + \frac{1}{10}(0.25) = 0.072$$

Since the capital/output ratio is approximately 2, $\dot{K} = 0.036$. This figure is somewhat higher than the 3 percent figure mentioned above, but this is to be expected. The economy has not always been at full employment; during recessions and depressions, net saving and investment rates were lower than 7.2 percent. According to this calculation, full employment throughout the last hundred years would have raised the growth rate to at least 3.2 percent annually.

These growth-rate calculations are not very appropriate for the postwar period, however. The labor force has been growing at approximately 2 percent per year and technological progress has also increased at about 2 percent annually. If net capital stock continues to grow at 3.6 percent per year at full employment, then the equilibrium growth rate can be calculated as

$$(21.5) \qquad \dot{X} = \frac{2}{3}(0.02) + \frac{1}{3}(0.036) + 0.02 = 0.045$$

In other words, the economy must grow at $4\frac{1}{2}$ percent per year merely to absorb all entrants into the labor force. If the unemployment rate is to decrease, the rate of growth must be higher. At an annual growth rate of 5 percent, it would take 6 years to reduce the unemployment rate 2 percentage points; at 6 percent, only 2 years.[2]

Mention of such a high growth rate relative to historical standards invariably raises the question of the effects of such a policy on price stability

---

[2] The growth rate of 5.8 percent during the three-year period 1964–1966 reduced the unemployment rate by 1.7 percent. This indicates that the labor force itself grows more rapidly near full employment. Our simplified calculations do not take this into account

and equilibrium of the net foreign balance. It is often argued that if substantial inflation and deterioration of the net foreign balance persist it will be necessary to initiate stringent monetary and fiscal policies. These will retard the growth rate and thus the goal of "superheated" expansion will eventually be self-defeating.

It should first be established that growth per se does not lead to inflation. If the economy remains at a high level of unemployment and a low level of capacity utilization, wages will rise slowly and firms will not often attempt to widen their profit margins by raising prices. This follows from our analysis of wage and price equations in Chapters 10 and 11 and is easily observable in the postwar period. For example, in the 1961–1964 period GNP in constant prices grew at an average rate of 5.4 percent, substantially in excess of the estimated 4.5 percent needed to maintain a given unemployment rate. Yet the economy was far away from maximum output, as shown both by substantial unemployment and considerable excess capacity. The wholesale price index increased by only 0.1 percent per year and the GNP deflator by only 1.3 percent annually. However, when the economy approached full employment in 1966, price increases approached 3 percent. This agrees with our earlier analysis of Phillips curves, which suggested that an unemployment rate of 4 percent would lead to inflation of between 3 and 4 percent per year.

Since we have been using the Wharton EFU model for policy analysis, it may be of interest to see how well the model reflects these long-run patterns of growth. This has been done by simulating the model for the 48-quarter period 1952.3–1964.2 without intervening adjustments. In these simulations actual values of exogenous variables are used but all values of lagged endogenous variables are internally generated by the 48-quarter solution. The time path of GNP, consumption, investment, and the GNP deflator are shown in Figures 21.2–21.5. Although there are occasional areas of divergence between actual and predicted values, the model simulation ends up very close to the actual values in 1964. There is a definite tendency for the simulation to contain cyclical fluctuations that correspond with actual turning points; however, these are not always identical. These discrepancies disappear if we consider the eight-quarter simulations of the model. For these shorter simulation exercises the timing of the actual and predicted turning points agree in all cases, although there is some error in the actual magnitudes. This comparison is shown in Figure 21.6.

What are the chances of reducing the rate of inflation near full employment? One possibility is suggested by Table 21.1, where it is shown that the periods of most rapid inflation have often been accompanied by *slower* than average growth rates. Some simple calculations confirm that there is no significant correlation between changes in either price level and changes in GNP,[3]

---

[3] The correlation coefficients between the change in either price and changes in GNP were both nonsignificantly negative.

TABLE 21.1   RELATIONSHIP OF PRICES, OUTPUT, AND
GROWTH IN THE POSTWAR PERIOD

Year	$\frac{\Delta p}{p}$	$\frac{\Delta p_w}{p_w}$	$\frac{\Delta X}{X}$	Un	Cp
1947	11.8	22.0	−0.9	3.9	96.4
1948	6.7	8.5	4.5	3.8	93.1
1949	−0.6	−2.1	0.1	5.9	81.8
1950	1.4	3.6	9.6	5.3	89.4
1951	6.7	10.4	7.9	3.3	90.5
1952	2.2	−2.3	3.1	3.1	89.1
1953	0.9	0.8	4.5	2.9	93.3
1954	1.5	0.3	−1.4	5.6	84.2
1955	1.5	2.2	7.6	4.4	92.2
1956	3.4	4.4	1.8	4.2	92.2
1957	3.7	2.8	1.4	4.3	89.5
1958	2.6	0.3	−1.1	6.8	79.2
1959	1.6	1.8	6.4	5.5	86.9
1960	1.7	0.0	2.5	5.6	85.4
1961	1.3	−0.5	1.9	6.7	82.0
1962	1.1	0.0	6.6	5.6	85.2
1963	1.4	−0.1	4.0	5.5	84.0
1964	1.5	0.5	5.5	5.0	86.1
1965	1.9	1.3	6.1	4.5	90.0
1966	2.7	2.1	5.8	3.8	94.0

[a] p, implicit GNP deflator, 1958 = 1.00; p_w, wholesale price index, 1958 = 1.00; X, GNP, billions of 1958 dollars; Un, rate of unemployment, percent; Cp, Wharton School index of capacity utilization for the manufacturing sector, percent. See L. R. Klein and R. Summers, *The Wharton School Index of Capacity Utilization* (Philadelphia: University of Pennsylvania, 1967), table 19 (and later mimeographed releases).

although there are high correlations between changes in prices and either capacity utilization or unemployment. This suggests that in 1947 and 1956, bottlenecks in capital equipment were a major deterrent to increased output and contributed substantially to the price increases that did occur. Higher investment in previous years would undoubtedly have led to less inflation. Continued increases in the capital stock at least equal to the average growth of GNP would be one way of eliminating many bottlenecks and this cause of inflation.

Another possible method is the wage–price guidelines. However, they have been consistently disregarded and unless they are made mandatory are unlikely to be of much help, particularly in times of full employment and full capacity utilization. The guidelines may have been of some help in the

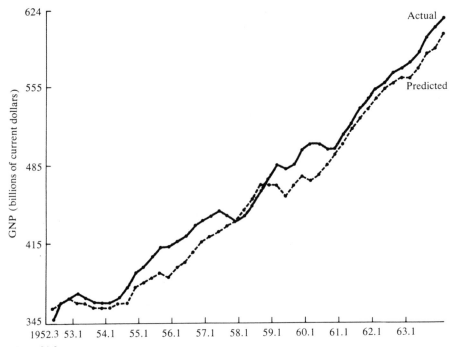

Figure 21.2

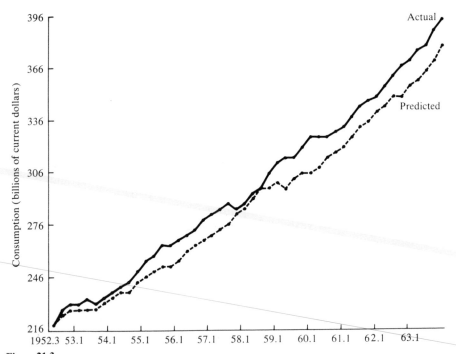

Figure 21.3

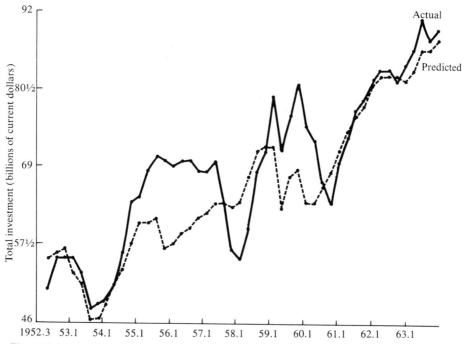

Figure 21.4

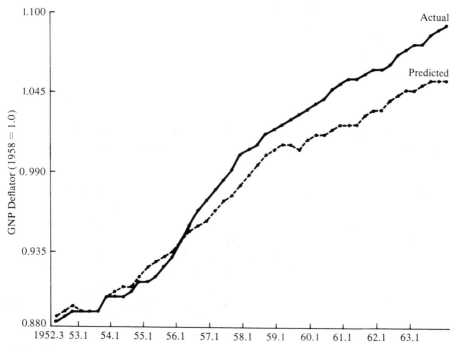

Figure 21.5

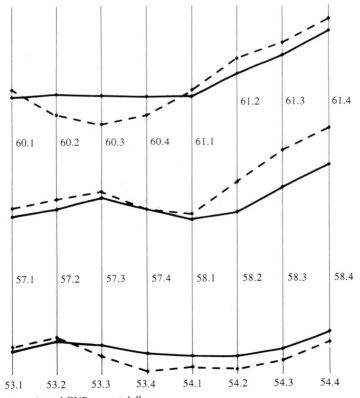

——— Actual GNP current dollars

- -→ Predicted GNP current dollars

Figure 21.6

1962–1964 period when they prevented price increases in key industries, notably steel. However, in 1966 prices and wages rose rapidly in areas such as food and services which are not easily covered by voluntary guidelines.

As was shown in Chapter 9, a rapid rate of growth need not cause a decrease in the balance of payments situation if countries with which we trade are at full employment and if domestic prices do not rise. The problem is then seen to be once again one of controlling prices at full employment. Again citing the experience of recent years, exports of goods and services increased from $5.1 billion in 1961 (a recession year) to $8.3 billion in 1964, but then declined to $4.4 billion in 1966 as prices began to rise more rapidly in the United States.

Even if the unemployment rate stays at low levels, it should be stressed that the Negro unemployment rate has remained very high; indeed, the Negro *teen-age* unemployment rate has been growing almost steadily, showing very few of the gains that have recently been recorded by the rest of the economy. As shown in Table 21.2, recent Negro teen-age unemployment rates are higher than they were in the 1949, 1954, or 1958 recessions and are at almost the same level they reached during the 1961 recession. The decrease of one third in national unemployment rates since 1961 has not benefited the Negro teen-age situation at all. In fact, their 1965 unemployment rate of 25.3 percent is higher than the overall unemployment rate in *any* year of the Great Depression.

The social and economic loss represented by these high unemployment rates can in many cases be traced directly to the relatively low growth rates of the 1950s, which caused steadily increasing unemployment rates. The lack of jobs for Negroes then contributed heavily to disintegrating family situations, which in turn led to a lack of education and motivation for many of today's Negro teen-agers. The slow rate of economic growth during the 1950s resulted not only in too small a demand for labor in the aggregate but a special class of unemployed engendered by a second generation suffering lack of opportunity. As has become painfully obvious in the light of recent events, this pattern cannot be reversed in a matter of a few years.

TABLE 21.2 UNEMPLOYMENT RATES FOR DIFFERENT GROUPS IN THE POSTWAR PERIOD
(*All figures are given in percentages*)

Year	National	White	Negro	Negro 14–24 Years
1948	3.8	3.6	5.9	9.7
1949	5.9	5.6	8.9	14.9
1950	5.3	4.9	9.1	14.4
1951	3.3	3.1	5.3	9.4
1952	3.1	2.8	5.4	9.5
1953	2.9	2.7	4.5	7.9
1954	5.6	5.0	9.8	14.7
1955	4.4	3.9	8.7	14.8
1956	4.2	3.7	8.4	17.4
1957	4.3	3.9	8.0	18.0
1958	6.8	6.1	12.6	25.0
1959	5.5	4.9	10.7	23.5
1960	5.6	5.0	10.2	22.1
1961	6.7	6.0	12.5	25.4
1962	5.6	4.9	11.0	23.7
1963	5.5	5.1	10.9	28.4
1964	5.0	4.6	9.8	26.2
1965	4.5	4.1	8.3	25.3

21.2   FUTURE CONTROL OF THE CYCLE

More than 20 years ago, Abba Lerner presented the idea of "Functional Finance,"[4] which stated that government revenues should never be collected for the purposes of obtaining money (which could be done much more easily by printing it) or balancing the budget, but should be used to regulate the level of aggregate economic activity. This idea has gained acceptance slowly, but did receive a noticeable boost from the highly successful 1964 personal tax cut.

In his original work, Lerner spoke of the average citizen and politician making the totally invalid comparison between accumulation of private and public debt. He felt that opposition to government deficits arose primarily from this source, and some popularizers have followed this approach. However, today's arguments against budget deficits are more realistic and are based mainly on the views that deficits cause inflation and a misallocation of resources in the private sector, or the desire to see the government sector reduced in scope.

The multiplier calculations in Chapter 20 should have indicated that changes in aggregate demand and change in the government surplus or deficit need not be in the same direction. Consider, for example, a $10 billion increase in corporate taxes and a $5 billion increase in government spending. After the third year (using the calculations presented in Tables 20.3 through 20.10) the corporate tax increase will cause a surplus of $9.6 billion and reduce GNP by $5.0 billion while the government spending increase will cause a deficit of $0.9 billion and raise GNP by $20.7 billion. The net effect will clearly be to raise GNP by $15.7 billion while causing a surplus of $8.7 billion.

Even in the more usual case where the change in the deficit and aggregate economic activity do move together, the view that deficits cause inflation needs to be rephrased to state that an increase in the government deficit, if accompanied by an increase in aggregate demand, will result in higher prices *than would otherwise be the case*. The opposite conclusion of course holds for a decrease in the deficit. However, such changes are often superimposed on opposing movements of much greater magnitude. For example, a surplus of $13 billion in 1947 was not enough to keep wholesale prices from rising 22 percent, and a deficit of $10 billion in 1958 was insufficient to keep GNP from declining and the unemployment rate from rising to 6.8 percent. These surpluses and deficits, as large as they were, clearly were insufficient to reverse the underlying patterns of inflation and recession that did occur. It is indeed fortunate that attempts were not made to balance the budget in these years.

A government deficit occurring when the economy is already at full employment will usually be accompanied by inflation, although even this is

---

[4] Abba Lerner, *The Economics of Control* (New York: Macmillan, 1944), chap. 24.

not always true. In fiscal 1953 the government budget deficit was $7 billion and the unemployment rate was only 2.9 percent, yet wholesale prices rose only 0.8 percent. However, this is an exception; the more usual pattern is that on the margin government deficits during periods of economic slack raise output while those during periods of full employment raise prices. This has led to the suggestion that the budget be balanced over the cycle, which would presumably stimulate the economy during recessions and retard inflationary pressures during booms. This idea is usually well received in the abstract but breaks down under the attempt to define full employment. Even so, it does suggest that deficits have a detrimental effect only when inflation is a serious problem.

The desire to see the government sector reduced in scope has in reality very little to do with the size of the deficit for the simple reason that deficits can be generated either by increasing government expenditures or by reducing taxes. This symmetry is often overlooked by proponents of a smaller government sector. It should be obvious that a balanced budget could be changed into a deficit by cutting government expenditures if taxes were cut even more. It is sometimes argued that such a move would have a deflationary effect on the economy. According to the multiplier calculations presented in Chapter 20, this is not the case after the first year or two. Such confused thinking is caused partially by the belief that the balanced budget multiplier, which can be shown to work for a simple two-equation system, has some relevance when applied to the complexities of the actual economy. An early demise of this "theorem" would help to reformulate discussions of the advantages of large or small government expenditures on a more realistic level.

At less than full employment situations, a government deficit need cause no complaints whether one favors increasing or decreasing the scope of the government sector. This suggests the following rule, which can be followed by proponents of either a larger or smaller government sector: Choose the rate of unemployment that corresponds to full employment, remembering that there is likely to be more inflation the lower the unemployment rate. Then choose the level of government expenditures that is most desirable. Finally, adjust personal income tax rates to achieve the degree of output and employment desired. This may or may not lead to a balanced budget; in general, it will not. If a balanced budget is still of importance for political reasons, the corporate profits tax rate can then be adjusted, since this will have a very small effect on the economy.

This is really just a restatement of Lerner's rule, but does stress that the same economic level may be accomplished either by raising government expenditures or lowering taxes. Full employment may be accomplished either at high or low levels of government spending. Contrary to the balanced budget theorem, the performance of the economy will be independent of the level of government purchases (after short-run adjustments). It need not even depend on the surplus or deficit of the budget if corporate taxes are adjusted to keep the budget in balance.

It seems that this represents a reasonable framework for intelligent discussion of future economic policy. In political terms, those who continue to defend the hypothesis that the rate of unemployment is determined exclusively by the private sector and is not the province of government are likely to disappear from public life. They will be replaced by both liberals and conservatives who agree that a primary responsibility of government is to keep the economy at full employment but who differ about the size and scope of the government sector. Renewed deterioration of the rate of unemployment is likely to lead to an economy with much more government control and a greatly expanded government sector.

In such a general framework, conservatives would show how at full employment the economy can grow more rapidly and more efficiently with a smaller public sector. They would argue that increased incentives offered by the private sector would lead to greater productivity. Many projects currently undertaken by the public sector are done at a far greater cost than would be the case if the private sector did the same job. Liberals, on the other hand, would argue that the vicious circle of poverty has not and cannot be eradicated by the private sector. Individuals with lack of education will receive low wages or will be unemployed, so they will be unable to improve their position or the educational standards of their children. In these and other areas, they would show that the private sector finds it uneconomical to solve these problems and that only the government can rectify the existing deficiencies.

21.3   A FINAL SUMMARY

The record peacetime expansion that began in 1961 has given support to the view by a few economists that recessions are a thing of the past and that in the future the economy should continue to grow continuously. In fact, the opposite view more nearly represents what has actually happened. In spite of massive doses of expansionary monetary and fiscal policy, there were several times during the most recent upswing when slight pauses looked suspiciously like the beginning of downturns. In mid-1966, in spite of near-record growth rates and substantial inflationary pressures, indices of consumer and business sentiment such as the stock market and various measures of attitudes and buying intentions indicated that a majority of the nation expected an end to the current expansion within a year. These indices are of course not infallible; they were also wrong in 1962, 1963, 1964, and 1965. They do, however, reflect the generally accepted viewpoint that the problems of the business cycle are still with us. It has taken considerable policy guidance to keep the expansion that began in 1961 going for a record time.

For it should be recalled that the current boom has had several dissimilar features from the other postwar expansions:

1. It started much further away from full employment, so that bottlenecks developed much more slowly and industrial prices remained steady for several years.

2. Because of steady prices, the net exports of goods and services continued to improve instead of acting in countercyclical fashion.

3. Easy monetary policy prevailed for the first several years.

4. Expansionary fiscal policy occurred throughout the period.

5. Several tax cuts went into effect, headed by the large personal income tax cut of 1964 and 1965 but also including decreases in corporate profits and excise taxes and liberalization of depreciation allowances.

6. Defense expenditures were increased substantially starting in 1965.

All these represent different patterns of behavior from other postwar expansions. Even with the favorable conditions that existed during 1961–1963, some simulations estimated with the Wharton EFU model show that without the 1964 tax cut, the economy would have had another recession similar to that of 1960–1961. Other simulations show that without the increased defense expenditures starting in 1965, the economy would have turned down more than it did in early 1967. The business cycle is potentially still very much a part of aggregate economic activity, but definite steps have finally been taken to counteract it.

Thirteen years after the trough of the Great Depression was reached, the Employment Act of 1946 was passed, ensuring that no such situation would occur again. Now that we know much more about the use of monetary and fiscal policy tools, it is time to extend this act to make it an effective weapon against less severe recessions. The theory of how monetary and fiscal tools can be applied and the numerical calculations showing their approximate effects, which are presented in this text and elsewhere, suggest that if the cycle cannot be completely eliminated, it can at least be mitigated to such an extent that the economy will remain near full employment at all times.

INDEXES

INDEX
OF NAMES

INDEX
OF SUBJECTS

Money stock (*Continued*)
easy throughout cycle, 428
increases in recessions, 426–427
IS-LM diagram, effect on, 356–357
not proportional to money output, 352
tightened when inflation occurs, 425, 428
See also Credit, curtailment at upper turning point; Quantity theory; Velocity
Monopoly power, degree of, 287, 293
Morishima-Saito model, comparison of multipliers, 583–586
continue to grow over time, 584
as long-run model, 582
Moving average of data, 453–454, 456
Multicollinearity, 51–52
between cash flow and output, 123
between cash flow and stock prices, 111
between income and population, 224
Multiplier, analysis of, 542–556
balanced budget multiplier, 543–545, 604
dynamic extensions, 551–554
for policy simulations, 542
generalized multiplier formulas, 557
nonlinear models, 547–550, 555–556
for change in government expenditures, 558, 559
comparison for several econometric models, 583–586
comparison with personal income tax multipliers, 564, 581
foreign trade, effect of assumptions about, 563–564
government budget surplus, effect on, 579
long-run effect on growth and employment, 581
long-run equilibrium value, 562–563
Wharton EFU model estimates, 560, 561, 568
value understated in Wharton EFU model, 562–563
for change in personal income taxes, 558
alternative economic goals, effect on, 565
comparison with government expenditure multipliers, 564–565, 581
government budget surplus, effect on, 564, 579
normalized over time, 566, 586

Wharton EFU model estimates, 561, 570
IS-LM diagram, 354, 355–357, 361
missing from classical system, 327, 338, 340
values, empirical estimation, 560–561, 567–573, 583, 585
depend on starting values for non-linear models, 558
long-run simulation properties, 558
meaning of long-run results, 559
methodological interpretation, 559
scale factor effect of disturbances from starting values, 558
See also Brookings model multipliers; Wharton EFU model multiplier values

Naive models, 467, 480–483
compared to econometric models, 516–518
Friend-Taubman model, 489
one-equation annual model, 493
method of calculation, 518
National Bureau of Economic Research, 4, 445–460
National Industrial Conference Board, 486
National life insurance dividends, 33, 534
Natural rate of interest, 331, 335, 340
Negro unemployment rate, 602–603
Negro-white savings differentials, 29–30
Net accession rate, as general cyclical indicator, 464
Netherlands, government expenditure multiplier, 235
"Net high" percent of inventory anticipations, 483–484
New orders, 340, 344, 423
Nonlinear constraints on growth, in Harrod-Domar, 398
in Hicks, 404–405
Nonlinear equation systems, 547–556
effects on multiplier analysis, 547–550
method of solution, 555–556
Nonmonetary demand theories of the cycle, 327, 333–335

OBE econometric model, 496, 582
OBE-SEC investment anticipations, 466–480
behavior at turning points, 475
compared to endogenous function, 467–471
described, 466–467
in Friend-Taubman model, 487
quarterly series, 474–478
reasons for errors, 472–473

Real rate of interest, 331–332
Recessions, four in 15 years, 595
  loss during, 595–596
  in 1920-1921, 427
  in 1937-1938, 446
  in 1949, end of Regulation W, 465
    optimistic consumer attitudes, 465
  in 1954, optimistic consumer attitudes, 465
  in 1958, 502
    deficit of $12 billion, 532, 604
    possibly caused by decreased defense expenditures, 532
    stability of dividends, 535
  in 1960, 502
Reference cycles, asymmetrical, 448
  average length, 448
  determined, 447
  explained, 446
  false turning points, 455–456
  list since 1854, 447
Regulation W, 174, 181–183, 194, 464, 465, 538–539
Regulation X, 193–194, 539
Relative income hypothesis, 17–19, 344, 408
Remittances and pensions, 236, 237–238
Required reserve ratio, 315–317
Replacement theory, 154–155
Research Center in Quantitative Economics, 496, 517
Reserve assets, 237, 239
Reserve requirements, 329
Residential construction, 184–200
  collapse in 1966, 198–199
  compared to fixed business investment/GNP ratio, 198–200
  cost of construction, 194–195
  countercyclical pattern, 184, 188–194, 198–200, 421
  credit availability, see Credit availability to homebuilders
  determinants, long-run, 185–187
    credit conditions, 186–187
    family formation rate, 186
    households, number of, 186
    income, 186
    interest rate, 187
    mortgage yield, 187
    population, 186
    price of housing, 186–187
  fixed-rate theory, 192–193
  income, as short-run determinant, 197
  lag structure, 196–197
    in countercyclical pattern, 199–200
    modification term, 197
  price of housing, in short run, 194–196
    relative to rental prices, 195–196

supply of housing in national income accounts, 184–185
Rental income, 283
  fluctuation over cycle, 289

Sales anticipations, OBE-SEC, 480–483
  compared to naive model, 480–481
  in inventory investment function, 482–483
  synthetic series constructed for Friend-Taubman model, 487
"Samuelson Cross," 352–353
Savings, deflationary effect of, 336, 338–339
  nonlinear function, 387–390
  See also Consumption function
Savings bonds, Series E, 534
Say's Law, defined, 322
  in classical theory, 322–324
Seasonal adjustment methods, 450–453
  dummy variables, 450–451
  ratio-to-moving average, 450
  variable-weight pattern, 451–453
Self-employed, 260–261
Serial correlation bias, see Distributed lag bias
Shortage of capital, 332, 333, 339
Simulations of econometric models, Klein-Goldberger, 4–5, 420
  Wharton EFU model, 429
Simultaneity bias, see Least squares bias
Sine curve, cycle as represented by, 4, 417
Social science research council, 503
Social security payments, 165, 534
Social security taxes, 466, 541
  See also Fiscal policy as discretionary stabilizer
Spectral analysis, 453
Speculative motive, for inventories, 203, 205, 207, 211–212
  for money demand, 309, 349, 354
Sputnik, 541
Stability condition, Keynesian system, 351
Stabilizers, see Automatic stabilizers; Fiscal policy as discretionary stabilizer; Monetary policy as discretionary stabilizer
Statistical discrepancy, 274–275
Steel industry, profits, 278
  strikes, 219, 223, 447, 481, 529, 566
Stock-adjustment model, for fixed business investment, 82, 85, 334, 383, 389, 421, 550
  for inventory investment, complete adjustment, 204
    partial adjustment, 205–206, 266